Perspectives on the
EUROPEAN PAST
Conversations with Historians

NORMAN F. CANTOR
Distinguished Professor of History
State University of New York at Binghamton

The Macmillan Company, New York

COLLIER-MACMILLAN LIMITED, LONDON

Printed in the United States of America

The Macmillan Company
866 Third Avenue, New York, New York 10022

Collier-Macmillan Canada, Ltd., Toronto, Ontario

Library of Congress catalog card number: 72–134516

First Printing

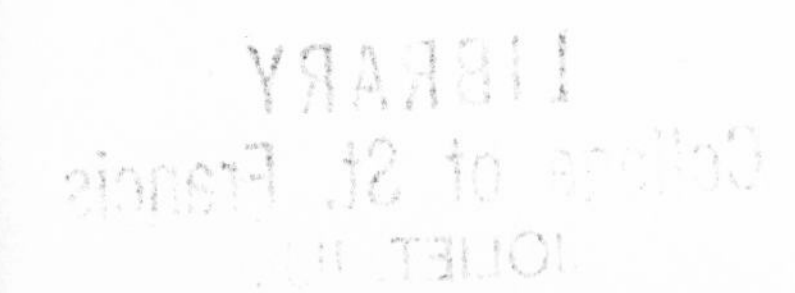

1972

Perspectives on the European Past

CONVERSATIONS WITH HISTORIANS

To Mindy

Acknowledgments

I wish to acknowledge the assistance of Mrs. Nancy Melia, Mrs. Clarissa Atkinson, Mr. Paul Shiffer, and my wife in preparing this book for publication. I am also grateful to Professor Leonard W. Levy, Mr. Robert J. Patterson, and Mr. James J. Carroll, Jr., for advice and assistance.

N. F. C.

Contents

Introduction

Modern historiography has gone through three phases, and because the emergence of one phase has not canceled out or entirely superseded a previous phase, there can be said to be at the present time three approaches to historiography, three schools of historical thought.

The first of these is humanist historiography, derived from the classical historians and philosophers and re-invigorated by the Renaissance humanists and by the *philosophes* of the Enlightenment. Characteristic of humanist historiography is first of all an emphasis upon politics—upon men's struggles for power, men's struggles to control the state, the authority exercised by the state and political leaders in society, and the relationships between states. Humanist historiography gives a great emphasis to political action, to international relations, and to war. A second characteristic of humanist historiography is its emphasis upon great personalities. Although in its classical form humanist historiography had a cyclical, determinist quality to it, this was gradually softened by the impact of the linear doctrines of the Judaeo-Christian tradition, and the determinism largely evaporated. The emphasis in humanist historiography is upon great personalities as the bearers of historical change. Thus humanist historiography is very much inclined to the writing of biography and (in expository historical writing) to concentration upon great leaders, particularly great political leaders who have supposedly or apparently altered the course or destiny of whole peoples. A third characteristic of humanist historiography is its tendency toward narrative history, toward the telling of a progression of events related to one another. And this proclivity to narrative history is tied in with a prime aim of humanist historiography, which is to communicate to a large group of people. Humanist historiography aims to address the whole educated public, either for entertainment or (more usually) with the more serious purpose of instructing educated people in what has happened in the past so that they may act in the future with knowledge of the collective experience of mankind.

The second phase and second school of modern historiography came with the Romantic movement of the early nineteenth century, and the contribution of the great Romantics to historiography is incalculable. It is not entirely accidental that the leading center of historical study and scholarship in the nineteenth century was in Germany, because the German universities were so much influenced by the Romantic Idealist philosophy. The first contribution of Romantic historiography was its emphasis upon a nation or a people as a unit, taking primacy away from the great individual and giving it to a social group, particularly the group of the nation. In Romantic historiography the nation became the whole focus of historical development; it became a personality, and its continuity over a long period, the rise and the triumphs as well as the anguish and the failure of the nation, became the purpose of the historian's exposition. The second contribution of Romantic historiography was a broadening out from political history to include all manifestations of the functioning of a people: social life, economic life, life-style, and also literature, art, and popular culture. In order to portray the nation as a living organism developing through time, political action was not sufficient. The activity of the nation had to be demonstrated in the round.

Romantic historiography somewhat narrowed the vision of the historian in that it led to concentration of the historian upon the national group rather than upon humanity in general. Although in actual fact humanist historians—in spite of their professed universalism and cosmopolitanism—often tended to write about the history of one particular people, there was in humanist historiography a philosophical universalism, which was somewhat narrowed by the Romantic emphasis on the history of a nation. This often led to a kind of obliviousness, even blindness, to similar or parallel or even identical manifestations of political, social, economic, and cultural activity among various nations in Europe and other societies. The nation was treated as a distinctive organism, and the similar phenomena occurring in other nations were often ignored. Like the humanists, the great Romantic historians of the early nineteenth century aimed to address as wide an audience as possible. Indeed, they often saw themselves as educators of the masses in the national destiny and used the history of the nation to give as many people as possible a consciousness of their identity in the nation, of their common historic past and future.

In the late nineteenth and early twentieth centuries both the humanist and the Romantic approaches to historiography were affected by the academization of history, by its absorption into the university, and by the almost inevitable tendency to try to make history into a science. This led to what has been called positivist history. Positivism was not really a school of history having a program with a set of aims and ideals and attitudes—it was merely a method. The positivist method was to accumulate as much data as possible, to be very cautious in the accumulation of data and the reaching of conclusions, and to limit the historian's assertions to what was obviously verifiable. The consequence of this was a great narrowing of vision on the part of the historian, a progressive erosion of the historian's former aim to address as wide a group of people as possible, in as inspirational and exciting a way as possible. The historian's writings became narrow and dry research reports, and by the early twentieth century (at least by the 1920's), when positivism or scientism in historical writing had reached its fullest development, the tendency of historians was indeed to fulfill Tolstoy's famous definition of an historian as somebody who answers questions that nobody asks.

The revivification of history as an instrument of education, as an instrument of inspiration, and generally its intellectual revitalization, came with the emergence of a third school of historical thought, the comparative school. The fundamental purpose of the comparative school (which began in the 1930's and 1940's, particularly in the work of French historians, and has now come to flourish in the United States and to some degree in Britain and Germany as well) was to identify common phenomena in various societies and to examine the past for recurring patterns of social and political change. The comparative historians were not determinists; they did not claim that these patterns emerged in different societies with absolute, identical repetition, but they did seek recurrent patterns such as industrialization, bureaucracy, revolution, and urbanization, and they sought to identify these patterns and to work out general modes of social, political, and economic behavior in the past. Although this work has been again inspired by scientism and has not yet really found a very wide audience (or has not usually been addressed to a very wide audience), nevertheless it has made history a much more intellectually vital subject. The comparative historians have drawn upon many of the concepts of the social sciences, particularly of sociology and to a lesser degree psychology and anthropology, and they have given to history a new seriousness and a new purpose and brought history within the framework of the social sciences.

There are, however, three different kinds of comparative history. First, there is impressionistic comparative history, in which the historian communicates his impression of the recurrence of similar patterns of phenomena. He studies not one country but two, three, or four, and he notes parallel institutional or cultural development. This kind of comparative history builds largely upon Romantic historiography, but the historian's vision goes beyond a particular nation to western Europe, or perhaps when he is particularly bold, to comparing phenomena in several different civilizations —e.g., the Russian, French, and Chinese peasantry, or revolutions in Asia and the Middle East with those in western Europe and Latin and North America. This kind of comparative history can be said to be not a radical departure from but a progression beyond humanist and Romantic historiography. It follows up the Romantic emphasis upon group action but within the humanist principle of universality, or at least common humanity.

The second kind of comparative history follows in the course of late nineteenth- and early twentieth-century positivism and scientism. It gathers statistical data, quantitative data, and actually establishes quantitative generalizations, mathematically expounded. This of course is easiest for economic history, for such subjects as economic growth and demographic development. This kind of comparative history has been very successful where it has been done; it is limited, of course, to those areas of history which are quantifiable. Determining just what areas of history are or are not quantifiable is a very difficult matter. Recently, quantifying comparative historians have been able to expand their purview beyond economic and demographic phenomena to certain kinds of political phenomena, as in statistical, quantifiable studies of voting records in relation to social and group backgrounds. However, the quantified comparative history that has been published up to now leaves out a great deal of what is interesting in history. It leaves out human feelings, personalities, and moral judgments that individuals and groups have had to make. It seems to take the humanity out of history and to lead to a kind of very abstract and atrophied, or at least limited, history.

The third kind of comparative history takes its departure from the sociologists, particularly from the sociology of Max Weber, although it owes a great deal to Karl Marx (as Weber himself owed a great deal to Marx). This variety of history involves model building: the historian builds a model of a certain kind of society or social situation, a model which may not have precisely existed but is the abstract model to which societies are related, as actual states are related to Plato's ideal republic. Thus the historian builds a model of the stages of individual revolution and then he examines the French, Russian, American, Chinese, and British experience in the perspective of this model of industrial revolution. Similarly the historian may build a model of an agrarian society and then study medieval English, nineteenth-century Russian, and nineteenth- and twentieth-century Chinese peasantry. This approach has aroused much greater controversy than either the impressionistic or quantifiable comparative history, but it is of immediate obvious value. It actually allows the historian a new kind of approach because it gives him a criterion by which to examine the history of a particular country and compare it with that of other countries. It is likely that model building will become more central to all historical interpretation. The model-building comparative historian seems to be much more interested than the quantifying historian (although let it be said that sometimes model building is combined with quantifying, as in the case of certain kinds of economic history) in addressing a large public, because he feels that he has something to communicate to educated men—a way of understanding their society and the problems of other contemporary societies by looking at them under the aspects of general models. It can be said that in recent years the historian has gotten away from the pompous, self-satisfied, and elitist proclamations of academic scientism, and while not abandoning his commitment to empirical research and to rigorous analysis, the historian has again become eager to address a large public and to educate society.

The historians whose views are presented in this book reflect this pattern of historiographical development in the last one hundred and fifty years. It could be said that perhaps none of them can be identified as absolutely humanist, absolutely a Romantic nationalist, or entirely a comparative historian, but it will become evident from reading their opinions that most of them do indeed fall into one or the other schools if we had to engage in identifying them and pigeonholing them in this way. It will become evident from reading their opinions that they are very conscious of the stresses which the historical profession has come under in recent years from the emergence of the social sciences, and that most of them are eager to acknowledge the value of behavioral-science concepts and methods without surrendering the autonomy of the historical discipline as a distinct form of human knowledge.

This book is based upon tape-recorded interviews I conducted with thirty-two historians in the United States, Britain, Canada and Australia between 1968 and 1970. I chose scholars whom I admired for having written important books and for being vigorous and challenging in their ideas and often controversial in their interpretations. The scholars range in age from forty to seventy-six. They all hold senior professorships, or their equivalents, at important universities. What I wanted was to have the opportunity to get the opinions of prominent members of the peer group of the historical profession at the end of the 1960's on the important problems in their fields and the important problems facing historical interpretation in the contemporary world. Ideally I would have liked to go and talk with them and then have them write an essay along the lines of the problems I posed to them. However, to do this would have taken several years, given the fact that eminent historians are very busy and that many of them would have found it very hard to write the essay that I requested of them, if they were willing to do it at all. I used the tape recorder as a way of getting their opinions as rapidly as possible and also of guiding them to answer what I considered to be questions of critical importance on their fields and on historical method and interpretation.

The method in which this book was prepared is as follows: I visited the historian and we talked into a tape recorder for three to five hours. In some cases the historians requested a list of questions beforehand, and I gave them such a list if they preferred, but at no time did I feel compelled to stick to the questions. Rather, I pursued problems and issues arising in the course of our conversation that seemed to me of special significance, and I pursued those questions that seemed most central to the particular historian's interests. The tape was then transcribed and edited to remove all the hesitancies and confusions that are common in oral discourse. In some cases a transcript was abbreviated—that is, certain blind alleys and irrelevancies were removed. In some interviews I prodded the historian with a variety of very brief questions, and then the historian's answers to these questions were conflated into a longer statement and most of the original questions were removed from the edited text.

The edited text was then sent to the historian, and he approved it before publication, making any additions or emendations that he wished. In each case I feel that the result has been worth the time and effort involved, and what we have here is a very important cross section of opinion among leading scholars not only on the problems in their fields but on the whole problem of the historian's craft in the contemporary world—what the historian is about, what he should aim at, and how he should achieve his aims. The audience to which this book is addressed is not only the professional scholar who will find this a very intriguing collection of views but also the layman and the beginning student who should have no difficulty in understanding the historians' comments and opinions. The student and layman will find this book a highly readable and authoritative introduction to the main problems in the interpretation of European history.

What kind of profile of historians as people and as minds seems to come out of this enterprise? Just to speak of what strikes me as the most obvious and significant: First, historians are not intellectually dead, by any means. They are quite aware of contemporary problems; they are not hiding behind their library walls from the contemporary world but are very much engaged in considering its problems. They are very conscious of the contributions of the social sciences. Nevertheless, at the same time it must be said that there is a remarkable kind of middle-of-the-road quality and reasonableness and absence of extremism in these historians' opinions. I think that I obtained a considerably good cross section of historians of the English-speaking world, but in no case do any of these people strike me as extremists either of the political left or of the right. Most of them seem to me to be of the moderate (or liberal) left, which is the tradition among English-speaking academic historians that has prevailed at least since World War I.

Furthermore, these historians are not extremists intellectually, and this is perhaps to a degree a surprise and a disappointment. That is, the concepts of sociology, psychology, and anthropology are frequently shown to have given the historian food for thought and perhaps directed his thinking, but I found no historian who was a Freudian, no historian who was committed to the theories of Marshall McLuhan or Claude Levi-Strauss, just as I found no historian who was dedicated to the doctrines of Karl Marx, Mao Tse-tung, or Spiro Agnew. They seem to be middle-of-the-road intellectually as they are politically, and perhaps here is an absence of something that could be of value. Even the younger historians here, although they are extremely eager to reconsider traditional historical interpretations, are not prone to any kind of extreme intellectual position. This is not a call for intellectual extremism on my part, but rather the expression of a wish that we had more intellectual gadflies in our profession who took revolutionary, provocative positions.

As people, this group of men are by and large what might be called even-tempered, easy to get along with, highly professional—again, reasonable men. They strike me as being middle to upper-middle class in their tastes. None of them struck me as suffering from poverty, and quite a few are obviously highly affluent, either as a result of inherited means (hardly any), success in writing best sellers, or attaining eminent positions in the academic world. Historians do not seem to live lavishly or even up to their possible means, but on the other hand they do not live humbly. They do seem to offer to their families a very comfortable and pleasant existence. Most of them seem to be good family men, very conscious of the welfare of their wives and children.

I had personal conversations over lunch or dinner with many of the scholars I interviewed, and by and large I did not find their conversation overly full of references to contemporary art, literature, music, etc. This may be due to a certain reticence on their part or to my failure to elicit this kind of response in private discussion. It may also be a reflection of a certain kind of Philistinism on the part of historians.

An unsurprising theme that ran through my discussions with many of these historians was their increasing dismay at the developing crisis in the university, particularly in the United States, their feeling that the university is disappearing as a center of learning, and a certain disappointment with their own students. These historians are the products of teachers who were themselves largely in the somewhat rigid and demanding positivist attitude. I would say that these men as teachers are much more permissive and generous than their own teachers, yet many of them express disappointment that their students do not seem to be able to take advantage of this permissiveness and generosity.

At times one feels in talking with these men, particularly those in their forties and fifties, that they may see themselves as the last generation of historians. Several of the scholars I interviewed expressed the view that because of the turmoil in the academic world, the increasingly anti-intellectual tone of the undergraduate population, and the attractiveness of the social and behavioral sciences to the better minds of the emerging university generation, the historical profession had entered its last golden twilight. There would be very few in the new generation of academics to perpetuate the great humanistic and Romantic historiographical traditions. This may indeed happen, but it will be caused not only by the factors and forces enumerated above, but also by the intellectual revolution that is taking place in historical thinking and to which the scholars represented here have made very significant contributions—the departure from humanistic and Romantic-national historiography toward comparative and sociological understanding of the past. This is not likely to be the last great generation of historians; it may very well be the last generation that bridges the older and newer historiography and is able to combine the most valuable aspects of both kinds of interpretation.

Anyone who reads these interviews right through will find here not only a compendium but also a serious analysis and critique of the dominant ideas that are now prevalent in the academic historical world. This book will serve as a guidebook to the recent work in the field and should inspire the reader to go on and read the important works of these thirty-two historians (or as many of them as he is interested in) and beyond that the other important literature. There is no doubt that in the last twenty years the historical profession has achieved more than it has at any time since the late nineteenth century, and the articulateness, breadth of view, humanity, and wisdom that are reflected in these interviews and thus serve to illuminate the European past, are the consequences of the intellectual advance of the historical profession since World War II.

Perspectives on the European Past

CONVERSATIONS WITH HISTORIANS

Part I

FROM

Prehistory

TO

The Scientific Revolution

1

Prehistory

ROBERT BRAIDWOOD

THE HISTORIOGRAPHICAL CONTEXT

The main concern of prehistory, at least for the historian of European civilization, is the transition from prehistoric to historic society. That is, the major purpose of the study of prehistory is to determine by what steps and for what reasons human society advanced from a pastoral hunting, fishing, and food-gathering society to one of food production, urbanization, metallurgy, writing, and organized bureaucracy. There would seem to be three possible general answers to the question of the causes of this transition. The first approach is that of environmental and technological determinism. It is claimed that some change in environment and technology, some alteration of the material circumstances of human life on an important scale, precipitated the transition. The second approach would take just the opposite tack and argue from the ideational or psychological base rather than from a material one. It would claim that somehow the ideas of civilization are fundamental to the human mind and that in a certain time in development they direct human society toward civilized life. A third approach posits some subtle interaction between man and his environment, between human nature and the material circumstances of human life. This may be called the functional approach. This interpretation posits neither environmental upheaval nor psychic pattern as the immediate cause of the transition from prehistory to historic society, nor does it simply believe in the extrapolation of civilization from the characteristics of the human mind. Rather it sees a functioning relationship between the human organism and its environment.

The last approach is the most reasonable one and also the most difficult to define in a detailed and circumstantial way. Robert Braidwood of the University of Chicago's Oriental Institute has been the preeminent spokesman for this interpretation. It is his thesis on the relationship between man and his environment—i.e., of a functional relationship occurring in certain parts of the hills and slopes of the Tigris-Euphrates Valley in the fourth millennium B.C.—which has won the widest support as an explanation for the origins of civilization in that part of the world. And the beginnings of civilization in the ancient Near East mark the opening chapter in the history of western civilization.

Braidwood, born in 1907, is a native midwesterner, and he has retained many of the stereotyped characteristics of the midwesterner. Although trained at the Oriental Institute, he is largely self-taught, having begun as an architect and then moved on to cultivate his interest in archaeology. He is a great field worker, who analyzes the materials of archaeological finds with both a midwesterner's caution and a kind of humanity and reasonableness that avoids dogma, ideological fantasies, and overly rash and facile generalizations. He is a kind of homespun humanist, with a wonderful sense of humor, willing to listen to the opinions of other scholars but constantly going back to test very carefully and empirically the archaeological materials and artifacts that have turned up as a result of his own and others' work.

Whereas it had been traditional to divide prehistory into schematic divisions such as paleolithic, mesolithic, and neolithic, Braidwood has discovered that these traditional divisions do not have a great deal of meaning when related to actual archaeological materials and that they have been more an encumbrance than a help in understanding the actual functioning of prehistoric societies. He has proposed a simple but meaningful division of prehistoric society into food-gathering and food-producing societies. Some years ago Braidwood wrote a book called *Prehistoric Men,* intended originally for high school students, which has become a classic in the field and has had influence immensely out of proportion to its original modest aim. In this little book Braidwood draws upon years of research, his shrewdness and caution, and his firm mastery of the actual materials to communicate to the layman the way in which prehistoric societies functioned. In the hands of many people who have written on prehistory, the prehistoric world becomes an infinitely mysterious and complicated one. Braidwood does not take away from its complexity and mystery, but he does make the people of prehistory human beings, recognizably our kinsmen, dealing with problems of living and social organization in recognizably human terms.

Chronological Outline

The creation of the earth over three billion years ago.

600–225 million years ago: Paleozoic era. First traces of plant and animal life on land.

225–65 million years ago: Mesozoic era. The period of the great reptiles.

65–3 million years ago: Tertiary period. The era of mammals.

3,000,000–10,000 years ago: The Pleistocene or ice age, the last great geological period. Large masses of the earth were covered with ice on three or four separate occasions. Mankind originated about one million years ago, in the Old World.

over one million years ago: The australopithecine-habiline stage, which may or may not be directly linked to the evolution of modern man. Crude stone tools have been found with at least some of the beings.

500,000–40,000 years ago: The early human food-gathering stage, starting with Java Man and Peking Man, the premodern remains of Steinheim and Swanscombe, and extending through the classic Neanderthalers and their contemporaries.

50,000–10,000 years ago: The first traces of fully modern men appear in Europe at the beginning of this period. About 24,000 years ago Cro-Magnon man appears, emerging as the predominant evolutionary type of modern man. Extensive cave paintings dating late in this period have been found in southern France and northwestern Spain.

c. 10,000 years ago: The beginnings of effective food production in the Near East—the era of incipient cultivation and animal domestication.

c. 9,000 years ago: The era of primary village-farming communities in the Near East, which soon begins to spread into southeastern Europe. By 5,000–4,000 B.C. farming also occurs in northwestern Europe.

3500 B.C.: The beginnings of civilization in southern Mesopotamia. The beginnings of writing mark the advent of "history." Primitive irrigation and governing systems.

3100 B.C.: The beginning of the First Dynasty in Egypt (preceded only slightly by the beginning of writing). The Stone Age comes to an end as the use of metal (bronze) becomes widespread.

Norman F. Cantor

Particularly to the historian who works with literary sources, the career of a prehistorian is fascinating. Did you begin as a scholar and archaeologist? How did you come into this field? Who were your teachers? How were you trained?

Robert Braidwood

I am a Depression-forced drop-out from architecture. After two years at the University of Michigan in the college of architecture, I spent a year in office practice when I found that I didn't have the gift of design or the anticipation of a rich wife (one or the other is necessary for being a successful architect). When I went back to school, it was the autumn of 1929; things were falling completely apart in the building game. In addition, integral calculus and what they called "French for engineers" threw me for a loop, and I found myself on probation. I decided to pursue an old dream to be an archaeologist or paleontologist—I can't remember which because I wasn't very clear on the distinction between them at the time. Professor Carl Guthe, at the University of Michigan's Museum of Anthropology, devised a program for me in which I studied archaeology but remained momentarily in the architecture department until I had worked off my probation. I took a course in Biblical archaeology with an old professor named Waterman, who was really a cuneiform scholar. Within six months I was on my way to Iraq to do drafting with Waterman's University of Michigan excavations at a site south of Baghdad which eventually turned out to be Seleucia on the Tigris, a site very late in the historic range of Mesopotamia.

This was the field season of 1930–31. Then I came back to the University of Michigan, shifted out of the architectural college completely, and finished my B.A. in 1932 and my M.A. in anthropology and ancient history under Carl Guthe and Arthur Boak in 1933. For work in the more prehistoric aspects of the Old World there was nothing offered at the University of Michigan at that time, and so I came over to the University of Chicago. But because the Oriental Institute there stressed language study—which I knew was not my bag—I held off starting work on my Ph.D. I managed to get a job with the Institute's Syrian expedition, in the Syro-Cilician corner (now politically Turkey). The sites of this expedition yielded material mostly in the so-called Syro-Hittite period, the earlier part of the first millennium B.C. It was customary at that time to send the youngest kid on the expedition down to the bottom of the mound to see what the earliest material was, and so my real introduction to prehistoric archaeology was kind of self-taught on a site called Judaidah in what is now the Hatay province in Turkey.

From 1933 to 1938 I had five field seasons in that area. Then, because war seemed near, scholars were returning from the field, and Henri Frankfort (who had been the director of an Oriental Institute expedition in Iraq) came to Chicago to teach. Since his interests were not so specifically in the ancient Oriental languages, we devised a program leading to a Ph.D. under him. (I still had to take two quarters of Hebrew—and within two weeks after I had finished I couldn't have read "kosher" on a store window. This is not a reflection on the level of teaching but rather on my mental capacities!) My program was a major in Near Eastern archaeology and two minors in ancient history and anthropology. Within a year I was offered a teaching assistantship in Old World prehistory in the Department of Anthropology at Chicago. I was involved in a meteorological training program during the war but was able to continue teaching a course at the University, and in 1947 I had my first directorship of a field expedition.

Would you comment on the changes in methods and techniques during the last twenty years in archaeological work, particularly in dating?

During the war large numbers of people were brought to the University of Chicago for the Manhattan Project. One of these was the scientist Willard Libby, who devised a method for the dating of organic material (charcoal, bone, skin, and so on) by measuring the radioactive carbon still remaining in it. Simply put, every living thing ingests a certain amount of radioactive carbon (carbon 14) while it is alive; immediately upon death the radioactivity begins to disappear, but does so slowly over a long range of time. To get an indication of the number of years that have gone by since death took place, one must simply measure the amount of radiocarbon remaining.

At first, most of us in archaeology

thought that radiocarbon dating would solve everything. It has not been that simple, of course. Just this last year, at a symposium in Uppsala arranged by the Nobel Foundation, the implications of certain fluctuations in the radioactivity that the earth receives from outer space through time became more clear. Using radiocarbon dating one determines, then, what are called radioactive carbon years, but these are not absolutely guaranteed to be the exact equivalent of calendrical years. For example, determinations that run on the order of forty-five hundred to five thousand years ago affect the beginnings of literate urban societies in Egypt and Mesopotamia very importantly. But these radioactive carbon determinations may be four or five hundred years short of calendrical years. This disparity has caused a lot of argument, of course. Primarily through the work of Professor Hans Seus, who is at La Jolla, it is becoming possible to correct for carbon-14 variations through time. Measuring the radioactive content of rings in bristle-cone pines—the yearly ring of a tree absorbs radiocarbon of that year but not of subsequent years—Seus (and Ferguson at Arizona) has set up a dendrochronology that reveals variations in radiocarbon levels to seven thousand years ago.

The refinement in archaeological techniques has been in a fairly large way a response to a changing milieu of archaeological financing. Until the period following World War II, one financed a field expedition by attracting the attention and interest of some individual millionaire. The expedition concentrated on bringing things home, and in some cases the donor got a cut. The increasing influence of "big science" and the creation of the National Science Foundation have largely eliminated the role of the individual patron. Now one must convince colleagues who sit on foundation boards of the worth of an expedition. The large amounts of money coming from the NSF have tended to benefit those working in prehistoric or maybe protohistoric ranges of time rather than those in the more conventional historic time range. Money has probably come more to archaeologists operating within the anthropological tradition than to those of the humanistic tradition.

When the NSF was first set up, there was no program allowing for work in the social and behavioral sciences, but some of the people in the Foundation were interested in expanding its activities. A few of us were approached by people in the Foundation who offered us for the first time professional, fully qualified colleagues in zoology, botany, and geology to examine at first hand the paleo-environmental conditions of our sites. Up to that time, if an archaeologist wished to identify the animal bones or plant impressions found in his excavation, or wondered what the general landscape in which the site sat had looked like in the past, he had to bring bits of evidence home. And once back in the United States it was usually difficult to find colleagues in the natural sciences who would undertake identifications and interpretations. Anyway, I jumped at the opportunity to have natural science colleagues in the field. An official of the Foundation even helped me devise a proposal which was submitted under the program called "biology and medicine." (The proposal had a wonderful title, something like "Environmental and Demographic Study of the Appearance of Food Production in Southwestern Asia.")

A great variety of other new techniques for the study of archaeological materials have also appeared since World War II. Even more important are the questions which the archaeologists ask themselves even before choosing a site for excavation. For example, we would no longer choose a site for excavation because it was suspected of being Troy or

Babylon and might therefore yield rich treasures. Our choice would depend, rather, on what the site might be expected to yield in knowledge concerning some problem or several problems in general culture history.

Is it possible to say where and when modern man, or HOMO SAPIENS, *appeared?*

The question is well removed from my competence as a culture historian, but I think that this is still an open question. There are, of course, a fair number of fossil men—bits and pieces of skeletons—that do not appear before late Pleistocene times, but the physical anthropologist who wants to describe a population on statistical grounds would want a hundred and fifty to four hundred skeletons (preferably mature individuals of one sex) for almost every individual fossil that we can name. There are opinions, for example, that the Steinheim fossil of Germany and Swanscombe in England (going back well over a hundred thousand years) were already anatomically modern or very close to anatomically modern. In that they appear before the classic Neanderthal fossil types, there was an anatomically modern strain earlier than the classic Neanderthals of western Europe. The weight of authority, however, tends to think that fully anatomically modern man had developed by fifty thousand to forty thousand years ago in Europe. These fossil types are not to be confused with the far earlier ones of Europe, Asia, and Africa, such as some of Louis Leakey's African finds, which are well over a million years old but not yet anatomically modern. The Palestinian material of Skuhl Qafseh may show some type of curious cross between a Neanderthal type (less extreme than those of Europe) and anatomically modern man. This would be slightly earlier than the anatomically modern types in Europe. I repeat, however, that such matters are beyond the specific competence of culture historians and need the authority of a proper human paleontologist.

Is the concept of race of any value or meaning to a prehistorian?

I wouldn't say that race doesn't have validity. A poodle with American Kennel Club registration is a breed, variety, or race of dog, and if this strain breeds true, then it can be race with a capital *R*. Human beings are not so controlled in their breeding, however. Most respectable physical anthropologists would insist on talking about races in bulk, a notion that deals with populations. A race is a biologically perpetuating population, which varies much more greatly around the edges of its regional distribution than it does in its center. To get *the* word on race, and on biological anthropology in general, you need a physical anthropologist, not a prehistorian. To date, we are lacking the significant skeletal population for the range of fifteen thousand to five thousand years ago, which would allow us to establish a racial notion of population.

Is it possible to distinguish distinct stages in the development of tool making?

Yes, it is, and we can go beyond that to establish levels of technological and economic achievement through time. The farther back our evidence goes, the more the protohuman species would seem to have been restricted to warmer (perhaps semisavanna) types of environment. But one begins to see evidence, as time proceeded, from regions that are a little more rigorous in terms of environment, and the inventories of tools become somewhat more complex. As they acquired more and more culture, men seem to have accustomed themselves to an increasingly variable range of environments. By the time anatomically modern man appeared, fifty thousand to forty thousand years ago, most but not all of the inhabitable world was beginning to be occupied. By fifteen thousand years ago man was probably occupying all the possibly inhabitable environments. The shift from food gathering to food production occurred during this time.

I think that one can look at tools—at the things that human beings produced to help them cope with their environments—as extracorporeal means of evolution, of adjusting to the situations in which they lived. One must be careful here to avoid the Victorian notion of the goodness of progress. Tools do not always get better and better. For instance, there are much sharper cutting edges on long, parallel-sided flint blades—and sometimes obsidian blades—made about eight thousand to seven thousand years ago in certain parts of the Zagros and Tauros than on blades made three to four thousand years later. Also, by the latter period there had been a shift to bronze, which would not take quite so sharp a cutting edge. It may be that the people were willing to put up with a more pesky cutting edge because bronze could be used to greater advantage in a variety of other ways. Or perhaps they no longer needed such a sharp cutting edge—because the archaeological record is so incomplete, we do not know if they still used materials that needed a sharp cutting edge.

What is known about the culture of earliest prehistoric men, Peking man and Java man who lived perhaps half a million years ago?

Not a great deal. We know that they are on the way to standardization of tool types. Earlier than the *Pithecanthropus* range—the Peking man and Java man range—there probably are not even very standardized tool types. The appearance of standardization can suggest some interesting notions for us. First, it indicates the beginnings of a persistent tradition in tool making, the passing of skills of know-how from father to son to grandson, both in the way individual tools are made and in the ways tools for different jobs are made. Do we know the size of family groups or the circumstances in which people lived if they didn't have caves handy, or how a hunt was organized? I would have to say No.

As early as a hundred thousand years ago, when the Neanderthaloids, more or less extreme cases of the Neanderthal physical types, appeared, the variety of standardized tool types increased, along with the variety of tool types within the inventories. Within the time range of pre-anatomically modern men, there was found not too long ago, in a cave on the French Riviera, traces of a kind of lean-to shelter, evidently built for a nuclear family, probably to protect them from the cold. Purposeful burial begins at about this time. A colleague of mine at Chicago, Leslie Freeman, recently made a brilliant clearance of the burial of a Neanderthal who had been buried with hunks of meat (in all likelihood for the journey into the next world). In addition to a vague notion of an afterlife, this suggests the individual seen as having been of some value to other individuals.

Viewing the evidence of forty thousand years ago, we can see how the variety of inventories—i.e., the whole kit of tools, decorative objects, and living circumstances—was increased, while individual regional and subregional inventories had become more elaborate. More and more open-air sites, outdoor settlements with huts, are being found (finally dispelling the idea of the latter part of the last century that prehistoric human beings always lived all the time in caves). Excavations are now done with such care that tools of different types are isolated in the ground in circumstances that suggest certain activities being performed in certain spots, perhaps by persons who are more or less specially trained to do a particular thing. In archaeology such spots are called activity clusters, or activity specific areas. For instance, if our own modern houses went into ruins and some archaeologist two thousand years hence cleared them with any attention, he could identify one room as the kitchen, another the bathroom, and so on.

I think one could make a pretty clear case for settlements of groups of families that might involve six to twelve huts in some of these newly discovered sites. Doubtless the families participated together in the hunting or food collecting that was done. The Russians claim to have some sites yielding traces of numbers of campfires within a single long hut structure. They are, of course, pleased to read these are evidence of communal living, something like an Iroquois long house. I do not know how carefully controlled these earlier excavations may have been, and since newer information from Russia does not emphasize this so much, there may have been a little leaning over backwards to interpret things to follow a political line.

Where, when, and why did art begin?

There is probably very little that might be considered decorative "art" which comes before the range of anatomically modern man. But following his appearance which in western Europe at least is fixed about forty thousand years ago, there is increasing evidence of both *art mobilier* (the decoration of artifacts that can be moved around), and engraving and painting of the walls of caves. About fifteen thousand years ago, cave painting began to culminate in what is called the Magdalenian assemblage (or inventory), particularly in southern France and northern Spain (the so-called Franco-Cantabrian area).

Usually the subject of these cave paintings is an animal. Because one picture is frequently painted on top of another, prehistorians have concluded that the importance was in the act of painting itself. Perhaps the act of painting or engraving a certain animal was expected to give the artist some sort of power over it during his next hunt. Or perhaps it was intended to placate an animal which the artist had just killed. A French colleague associates women with one group of animal types and men with another. There are numerous theories about what this art meant. One can say with certainty only that there was much more in the doing of this art than there would be in today's creative art.

In your book Prehistoric Men *you do not use the traditional divisions of prehistory —paleolithic, mesolithic, neolithic. Why do you think that these divisions are no longer useful?*

I should perhaps recall that *Prehistoric Men* was originally written at a high school level for popular museum audiences. But, also, I have always felt that these words imply a kind of intellectual snobbery (maybe not using them is an inverse intellectual snobbery!). Certainly much imprecision in meaning has been hidden by using these fancy words. Authors have often used them, within a single piece of writing, to mean (1) periods of time, (2) technologico-typological complexity, and (3) general sociocultural level. Obviously, these are three separate and distinct phenomena, and should be clearly set forth as such.

But there are further difficulties with these terms. The inventories of the peoples normally referred to as neolithic do not yet have metal, but they do have ground stone. The people who lived in what is normally called the paleolithic used chipped stone—so ran one of the earliest definitions. Then other traits began to be added to these definitions. Gordon Childe argued that since ground stone appeared in a series of intermediate inventories which followed the ice age but came before food producers' inventories, and which were called mesolithic, that the word *neolithic* should be reserved for inventories which included food production. One of the most respected of our Russian colleagues, however, a man named Oklodnikov, still wants ground stone, the bow and arrow, and pottery to be the basis for the definition of the neolithic. These appeared long before food production in the parts of Siberia in which he is working, but this discrepancy does not worry him at all. Clearly there is difficulty with a word which may imply time (chronology) or technological type or culture-historical interpretation or a hash of all three.

It seemed to me that in a book like *Prehistoric Men,* when I was speaking of a level of time I might just as well go ahead and make an informed guess at the time. A prehistorian's guess of time is probably as good as anyone else's. If I am speaking of a way of life that depended on hunting and collecting, I say that. For convenience I find myself in *Prehistoric Men* not boggling too much on a term like *paleolithic,* by which I mean ways of life that depended on the gathering, collecting, and hunting of food during the Pleistocene ice-age times (i.e., until the end of the last effective glaciation). *Mesolithic* has a kind of precision of meaning if restricted to northern Europe and those artifactual traces which show cultural re-adaptation to the succession of post-glacial forest environments. But since these are mainly lacking in southwestern Asia, the term *mesolithic* means very little to me there.

Where does the transition from food gathering to food producing occur first? Does it matter where it occurs first?

I certainly do not think that it matters where it occurs first, in that we are not trying to establish a priority for any particular modern country or people. I tend to see it as the consequence of the trend towards intensified adaptation to an increasingly varied series of environmental pockets or niches. I see no reason to doubt—going back even twenty or twenty-five thousand years—that modest degrees of manipulation of certain plants and animals went on in one or another environmental situation. If somebody lived in southeast Asia and his group adjusted ever more completely to one of its tropical rain forest environments, with its own peculiar, potentially domesticable foods, it is not unlikely that low levels of manipulation of these plants or animals went on.

Just about a year ago, reports began coming of a site in Thailand which yielded some plant materials that have been recognized by a botanist at the University of Hawaii as domesticates—certain kinds of beans, what we call the Chinese water chestnut, and so on. Questions have been raised as to whether this was a natural assemblage (the plants recognized don't quite sound as though they belonged within the same environmental niche). Nevertheless, the case overall suggests—with radiocarbon determinations of about eleven thousand years ago—that manipulation of these plants was sufficient to change their botanical morphology so that they might be recognized as domesticates. If this evidence gains general authoritative acceptance, then it is about the earliest instance of domestication that we currently have.

While there has been no discovery of plant material in southwestern Asia contemporary with the above, interesting animal remains have been uncovered at a site in southwestern Asia which ought to be about the same age. There a colleague, Ralph Solecki of Columbia, recovered a number of animal bones from a cave and an open site in Iraqi-Kurdistan. The Shanidar cave goes back to the Neanderthal range. It is possible to establish the kinds of animals hunted during various periods through inventories of Mousterian (normally associated with Neanderthal), Baradostian, and Zarzian tools (ending about twelve to eleven thousand years ago), and then an inventory containing ground stone which corresponds very closely to a site we had worked earlier called Karim Shahir. In this last level, Solecki found an abrupt jump in the number of sheep bones and also in the number of young sheep which could be recognized. None of these bones can be specifically said to be of morphologically domesticated sheep, but Dexter Perkins, who assessed this material, reasons that unless there had been some kind of human control of a herd itself, this composition of bone finds would be extremely unlikely.

The earliest suggestions for domesticated plant material in the New World date probably not much earlier than 7000 B.C.; few animals were ever domesticated in the New World, and the pace of domestication seems to have been a little slower than in the Old World. Two years ago I would have said that domestication happened very late in southeast Asia; now we are told that it *may* have been as early as any place we know. If you asked me to guarantee that there was nothing as early or even earlier in sub-Saharan Africa, I could not do it, because we do not know sub-Saharan Africa that well. Something could turn up down there or in the Amazon Basin, or in a variety of archaeologically poorly known parts of the world.

Why did the domestication of plants and animals occur independently in various locations sometime after 11,000 B.C.*?*

We do not yet know enough to say that any specific kind of ecological situation or ecological balance or imbalance kicked the thing off. I am not an environmental or geographical determinist. But one important generality over prehistoric time is that men continued to increase their ability to adjust to and to "live into" a growing variety of environmental situations. If an environmental situation happened to have potential domesticates or particularly favorable sources of plant or animal food that man could depend upon, we know the result in certain instances so far examined archaeologically.

Despite a lack of evidence, the beginning of plant and animal domestication used to be explained almost always as a direct result of a climate change toward warmth and desiccation at the end of the ice age. My own earlier thinking certainly went a bit too far in the other direction. However, Professor H. E. Wright, one of my colleagues, has studied pollen cores from a lake in the Zagros, which show a cold artemesia steppe land from earlier than fourteen thousand years ago down to about eleven thousand years ago followed by a trend toward a woodland situation (evidenced by oak and pistachio pollen), in which present conditions were reached by about fifty-five hundred years ago. His evidence tends to show that there were indeed degrees of environmental change in the higher Zagros. It is not yet totally clear if this extended over the entire area. Wright thinks that it did; on the other hand, there are other sites like Solecki's Shanidar in the Zagros that seem to have been in continuous occupation and have animals which are by no means characteristic only of cold artemesia steppes.

I used to say, "Don't look to environmental change to find an impetus to food production, look rather to cultural change." And being an anthropologist I am still inclined to favor such a consideration. But I cannot quantify it any better than I ever could, and I cannot eliminate considering the probability of degrees of environmental change over the last fifteen thousand years as I once used to think that I could.

Turning to Europe, when did food producing appear there? Did it spread from village farming in the Near East, or was it an independent development?

The answer has to be both. The general idea and certain elements of food production moved up from southwestern Asia into Europe, probably through the Aegean, across the Bosporus or the Dardanelles, into Thrace, thence up to the Danube and toward the west, with pauses for re-adaptation on the way. The same thing happened in the central and western Mediterranean, where movement doubtless depended on boats of some sort. On the other hand, Dr. Sandor Bökönyi, a Hungarian zoological colleague interested in the domestication of animals, has quite good evidence for the domestication of cattle in Europe in several instances. Wild cattle were native both to southwest Asia and to Europe.

We do not know exactly how many people moved how far, from exactly which points along the way, or how they influenced the people they met at the next point. The opening of the frontier in North America is not a very good model: the pioneers were much more superior (technologically) to the Indians than would have been the case in late prehistoric transition to food production in Europe.

We can date the changeover to food production in Europe to a degree. There are radiocarbon determinations in Greece that go back to the seventh millennium B.C. Not too long afterward, food production moved up into Yugoslavia, probably in the main over the Vardar-Morava Divide. Following the theory of a Dutch colleague that there were pulses in the movement, by the end of the sixth millennium B.C. people were adjusting themselves to a farming way of life in the Hungarian plain; when a new potential built up, they moved on again. By not much later than 4500 B.C., there were food producers in modest-sized villages in Holland and northwestern Atlantic Europe. Up to now, there are more gaps in the evidence for the western Mediterranean than for the Danubian case, but I am prepared to see food production spreading in much the same way in the western end of the Mediterranean as well.

Was the impetus to change that was felt in southwestern Europe also present along the African coast? Following 6000 B.C. there are inventories of ground stone and pottery (which most people would call neolithic) along the African coast, but up to now the archaeology done there has not specifically identified either plant or animal domesticates. I would be very surprised if they are not there.

This raises another issue. Evidence of domestication depends upon identification of a morphologically domesticated animal or plant by zoologists or botanists. For Dexter Perkins' work at Zawi Chemi Shanidar there is some reservation to complete agreement, because the total number of animal bones still remains relatively small. If it were possible to go back to Zawi Chemi Shanidar in Iraq—which lies in a politically unsettled part of the country—probably one could get a larger group of bones and reach definite conclusions on a statistical level. Childe spoke of the appearance of domestication as the "neolithic revolution," intimating that it happened quite quickly, but in my view a low level of domestication of plants and animals may have begun a very long time ago. In either case, how long would it take a wild wheat kernel to look like a domesticated one or a wild sheep, whether he is herded or not, to look like a domesticated sheep? None of our botanical or zoological experts will dare tell us yet.

The secondary evidence of domestication—mainly tools of chipped or ground stone—leaves us very much with the same problem. For example, are the standard tools called celts to be seen as axes, as adzes, or as hoes? If these tools are hoes and were used to cultivate the ground into which you put seeds, then you were well on the way to food production. But we cannot yet really distinguish to which uses the celts were put. The same is true of so-called milling stones or querns. We have found a lot of milling stones from ten to twelve thousand years ago, particularly along the east Mediterranean littoral. But when these things show traces of anything we've yet recognized, it tends to be of ochre, as though the stones had been used for grinding some kind of paint. Actually, we do not even know if people first bothered to grind wheat into what we would call flour. They probably first consumed wheat as a kind of gruel, made with the whole kernel and water (or at best they might have cracked it). If some of this lay about and fermented, they would have had beer. And so beer may have preceded bread. The point is that there will always be this range of incipience that we will not be able to nail down really tightly.

We know that by about 7000 B.C. they were over the hump in southwestern Asia. At Jarmo, a site we began to work in 1948, this is clear. But at the more exciting sites—Karim Shahir, Solecki's Zawi Chemi Shanidar, Jean Perrot's Mallaha—where the people built simple round houses and where there are animal bones, there probably is a level of food production in the icipient range, even if it cannot yet be decisively demonstrated. The site of Mureybat on the middle Euphrates was definitely a village, but the legumes, wheat, and animal bones have all been assessed as wild. Childe used to tell us that until food was produced it would have been impossible for people to settle down perennially in a village; now we are not so sure of this. Primary evidence in the form of morphologically demonstrable plant or animal domesticates is lacking in some of these sites. On the other hand, people may have already been manipulating plants and animals whose forms cannot be identified as domesticates in any way we now know.

By 4000 B.C. there were village farmers already established in Germany and in France as well as in the Netherlands. Food production spread through the Danube-Rhine channel, and the great likelihood is that it had spread into southern France along the Rhone. So far the carbon-14 age determinations for England are later, and the earliest now available determinations for produced food in the British Isles are in Ireland rather than England. (It may have come up by boat from the Bay of Biscay.) Food production must also have traveled by boat in the Mediterranean, for there are no known traces of paleolithic occupation in either Crete or Cyprus, and certainly there was no land bridge to get food producers out there during that time. Nevertheless, by 6000 B.C. food producers appear in Crete and a little later in Cyprus.

Would it be true to say that after around 7000 B.C. western Europe might be called a colonial area, receiving most of its impetus to development from the outside?

Yes, I suppose one could make such a case. In this connection, H. T. Waterbolk, a Dutch colleague, cites evidence for a depopulation of central Europe at the end of the ice age. He thinks that there were portions of southeastern Europe into which food producers could have moved without much resistance on the part of already established people.

Certainly, however, I cannot visualize food production being brought to Europe by mass hordes migrating from the Near East; the single traveling salesman doesn't quite ring a bell, either. In northwestern Europe there is considerable interest in what they call the neolithicization process—i.e., how the "mesolithic" inhabitants became "neolithicized." How did food production impinge upon a variety of societies that not too much earlier had had to adjust themselves to a series of postglacial environments that were different from what they had been during the paleolithic range? Gordon Childe, in the preface to the first edition of *The Dawn of European Civilization*—and he kept saying this in one way or another until he died—argued that the people of Europe "were not slavish imitators: they adapted the gifts from the East . . . into a new and organic whole capable of developing on its own original lines." That is probably true. Of the elements of food production, however, the probability is that only cattle and the pig, and perhaps einkorn (the lesser of the two wild wheats, which has a distribution into southeastern Europe) were native to Europe. The emmer-type wheat, and the sheep and goat, without question had to be introduced. On the other hand, my wife and I have had many chances to compare the harvesting process in both southwestern Asia and Austria. No Turk, no Kurd, no Arab, could cope with what has to be done to get the harvest in in Austria. The plants themselves are obviously the same, but the ways in which they have to be manipulated are completely different.

Is anything known about the culture, social organization, family structure, or political organization of these farming communities in southwestern Asia in about 5000–4000 B.C.

Not too long ago I attempted to assess how many sites we have for the first level of effective village-farming communities, sites like Jarmo and the so-called pre-pottery neolithic B of Jericho, of about 7000–6000 B.C. We actually have less than two dozen sites, and on the average less than 5 percent of each individual site has been exposed. Whatever we say about architectural exposures, let alone a village plan—I could not guarantee you a whole village plan for any site in southwestern Asia for this time—is still largely stabbing in the dark. We do know that the sites of this range contain pretty well all rectilinear house plans. Each house has several small rooms (four or five at most), suggesting that they sheltered individual families.

In the range of incipience immediately preceding this period, we know far less. But the sites we do know contain not very large round houses—what I would think were individual family units. How many in a given site is pure guesswork.

Let me give an example of how roughly we calculate the population size of a site. At Jarmo, making allowances for a third of the site having been eroded away by gully-cutting since it was occupied, we made a map of the terrain. Similarly, we made plan drawings to scale of the one or two house plans which were, we thought, completely excavated. We placed our drawings of the house plans at the same scale over the map of the site, then supplied more cardboard cutouts at house-size scale on the site map, spacing them as far apart as similar houses lie in the villages of our own workmen. This gave us a total of only eight to ten houses on the site. Reckoning something on the order of seven people to a house, we arrived at the figure of seventy-five to a hundred, perhaps a hundred and fifty people, as having lived at Jarmo. Not a very large village.

Our calculations become even more flimsy if we try to calculate how many villages there might be in a given valley plain or how large was the population of a valley plain, surrounded by mountains (upon which agriculture would probably be impossible). From what we know of this range of time, there is no way to approach a population size reliably.

The valley in which Jarmo lies is about ten to fifteen miles wide and maybe thirty miles long. We know of at least three more sites there with a surface yield (they have not been excavated yet) suggesting the same inventory as Jarmo. We cannot tell whether they were occupied at the same moment in time or within the same hundred to two hundred years, but the probability is that there were more sites than Jarmo alone in this valley plain at the same time. It would be very difficult for us to say what association or cooperation or political unity (or lack of it) or warfare there was between these villages. I would expect that within the valley there was probably fairly ready interchange (e.g., interchange of wives), and if one could speak of these people as being on a tribal level, this was probably one tribe.

It is interesting that the natural volcanic glass obsidian is very scarce in sites of the range of Zawi Chemi Shanidar, Karim Shahir, and so on, which date to 9000–7250 B.C. In the Jarmo range immediately following that, however, about 40 percent of the count of chipped stone tools are made of obsidian. Obsidian comes from restricted natural sources: as far as southwestern Asia is concerned (unless one goes off to the island of Melos in the Aegean), there are three well-known and about three or four areas of suspected flow, all up in Turkey. In other words, at Jarmo there is the first hint of a kind of a bulk-carrying trade in southwestern Asia (and in the world for this range of time). What this suggests about the more extended sociopolitical unity of things (or lack of it) at the time of Jarmo is interesting. Using what we know of the penetration in from the sea of shells in northeastern Australia, we can make an analogy. We know that a lot of this went on simply on a level of exchange from tribe to tribe. There is no complete, overriding tribal unity within which such a distribution goes. The distribution occurs beyond the tribal level.

Because I enjoy the field so much, it always gives me great consolation to say that the really important questions still have not been answered, and so we are in no danger of being out of a job yet because we still have a great deal of work to do.

2

Egypt and the Ancient Near East

JOHN A. WILSON

THE HISTORIOGRAPHICAL CONTEXT

European history can be said to begin with the Egyptian and Mesopotamian societies of the third millennium B.C. This is so for several reasons. In the first place, these were the first civilized societies with organized government (in the form of bureaucracy making use of written materials), with centralization, with a well-defined class structure, with organization by the state of the economic resources of society, and with a religious hierarchy and the use of religious ideals to effect social control. Also in these societies one finds literacy and literate expression of ideals and of the day-to-day affairs of government and business.

The study of the ancient Near East began when Napoleon Bonaparte invaded Egypt and expanded during the nineteenth century roughly parallel to the European powers' imperial penetration of the Near East. The most important work was done by English, French, and somewhat later, but with great skill, by German scholars. Some of the work was accomplished with the support of governments; much of it was done by individual scholars (sometimes rather eccentric ones): and during much of the nineteenth century, the field was dominated by men who were as much interested in the collection and sale of antiquities as in historical research, perhaps more so. Because much of the archaeological work done in the nineteenth century was scarcely above the level of grave robbing, much valuable data was lost either due to improper archaeological work or to the dissemination of materials from one place to various libraries, museums, and private collections. Since then, improved methods have resulted in great advances in historical knowledge of the field. During the late nineteenth and early twentieth centuries, British and German archaeologists working in Egypt and Mesopotamia developed systematic and scientific ways of archaeological investigation which greatly elevated the kind of work done on sites. More specifically, the discovery of the Egyptian papyri, and their recognition as unparalleled sources on economic and social life was a tremendous achievement.

In the twentieth century, particularly since about 1920, the greatest center for the study of the ancient Near East has been consistently the Oriental Institute of the University of Chicago, which was founded with Rockefeller money and established under the leadership of a great self-taught American scholar, J. H. Breasted. Breasted's most illustrious disciple is John Wilson, a native American, born in New York in 1899, who received his Ph.D. from Chicago in 1926 and another Ph.D. from the University of Berlin in 1928. Wilson was therefore the product of the two leading centers of Egyptology of the earlier twentieth century. For two decades Wilson was the Director of the Oriental Institute, guiding it through the difficult times of the Great Depression and World War II. Wilson is an expert at archaeological field work and a master philologist, but he is also very much an historian and belongs to the great tradition of early twentieth-century humanist historiography. He draws upon archaeology and philology to illustrate and understand the human condition in Egyptian society. His summary of his lifelong research and enquiry, published originally in 1951 as *The Burden of Egypt* and in revised form as *The Culture of Ancient Egypt,* is one of the monumental works of twentieth-century scholarship, a book which is as fascinating for the layman as it is constantly instructive and illuminating for the scholar. Wilson is a self-conscious kind of historian, very much aware of shifts in historiographical method and attitude, and in fact he has written a fascinating book on the development of Egyptology down to the early twentieth century. In this book he examines the great Egyptologists as people and shows the same kind of penetration into human personality as he does when examining the personalities of the ancient Egyptians as far as they can be established. Wilson is very much an American: he is free from arrogance, determined to support and advance scholarship, and willing to help younger scholars. Also, he is American in his extraordinary administrative capacity which he demonstrated as Director of the Oriental Institute. As he talks, his face shines with his enthusiasm for the discovery, revivification, and re-creation of a whole civilization that has long ago past but whose impact on the subsequent development of western civilization was profound and persistent.

Chronological Outline

c. 3100 B.C.: The two kingdoms of Egypt (Upper and Lower) are united. The first three dynasties are largely involved with the search for security and the consolidation of the city-kingdoms into a system of central leadership. Invention of the 365-day calendar takes place sometime during these initial dynasties.

c. 2980–c. 2500 B.C.: The Old Kingdom of Egypt—Dynasties III–VI. The era of the great pyramid builders, Snefru and Cheops of the Third and Fourth dynasties.

c. 2500–c. 2150 B.C.: Dynasties VII–X in Egypt. Dissolution of the power of the Pharaohs. Development of a strong aristocracy, especially in the north, divides Egypt into many semi-independent kingdoms.

c. 2480 B.C.: The First Dynasty of Ur in Mesopotamia.

c. 2340–c. 2223 B.C.: Sargon and Naram-Sin found the Akkadian Empire, adopting and modifying the indigenous Sumerian culture of Mesopotamia.

c. 2250 B.C.: The reign of Gudea—the classical period of Sumerian sculpture and literature and a thriving commercial era.

c. 2150–c. 1700 B.C.: The Middle Kingdom is established by Theban nobles in Egypt after the First Intermediate Period. Dynasties XI–XIII. About the year 1674 B.C. Asian invaders (Hyksos) conquer the kingdom.

c. 2030–c. 1900 B.C.: Decline of the Empire of Ur and the Sumerians.

c. 1900–c. 1600 B.C.: The First Dynasty of Babylon. Hammurabi, its sixth king (fl. c. 1775), conquers all Mesopotamia and establishes an excellent system of public works, a vibrant administration, and a law code.

c. 1850 B.C.: The Hebrews, a group of Semites, exist as a separate people after the patriarch Abraham leads his family from Ur to Canaan in southern Syria and Palestine.

c. 1600–c. 625 B.C.: Invasion of Babylonia by several tribes. Assyrians conquer the empire in 729 B.C. and rule it until 625 B.C., when it regains its independence.

c. 1570–c. 1090 B.C.: The New Kingdom of Egypt—Dynasties XVIII–XX. The Hyksos are expelled, and Egypt expands into western Asia (Palestine and Syria) and the south. Growing power of the priesthood of Amon. The Pharaoh Akhenaton (c. 1375–c. 1358 B.C.) moves the capital from Thebes and worships the solar disk Aton. His successors, however, return to worshiping Amon. After Ramses II (c. 1292–c.1225 B.C.) the power of the Egyptian Pharaohs and the state itself declines.

c. 1225–c. 1215 B.C.: Moses leads the Israelites out of Egypt. They gradually reconquer Canaan at the end of the second millennium B.C.

c. 1090–c. 718 B.C.: Dynasties XXI–XXIII. Fragmentation of Egypt into smaller states loosely connected by trade relationships and ruled by kings of Libyan and Nubian origin.

c. 1000–c. 900 B.C.: Israel flourishes under Kings David and Solomon.

c. 1000–c. 612 B.C.: The Assyrian Empire controls Mesopotamia.

c. 750–c. 550 B.C.: Era of the great Prophets—Amos, Hosea, Isaiah, Micah, Jeremiah, Ezekiel.

c. 700–663 B.C.: The Assyrian Empire controls Egypt.

663–525 B.C.: Egypt regains its independence, and there occurs a renaissance consolidating the cultural and aesthetic achievements of the Old and Middle kingdoms.

605–562 B.C.: Reign of Nebuchadnezzar, who erects the hanging gardens of Babylon and in 586 B.C. destroys Jerusalem and deports thousands of Hebrews to Babylonia.

550–529 B.C.: Cyrus the Great leads the Persian armies to conquer Babylonia. His son rules Egypt.

405 B.C.: Egypt regains its independence but is no longer powerful.

332 B.C.: Alexander the Great conquers Egypt and Babylonia.

Norman F. Cantor

Would you discuss your career as an Egyptologist? How did you come to enter the field? With whom did you study? In what expeditions have you participated?

John A. Wilson

I was always interested in history. Then I became interested in ancient languages, and after something like six years of Latin and Greek in high school and college, I thought that my field might be classical history. But when I finished college in 1920, I was unable to finance graduate study, and so I took a position teaching at the American University of Beirut in Lebanon. In the next three years my interest changed from classical history to ancient Near Eastern history. A teacher there, who had his Ph.D. in Egyptology from Professor James H. Breasted at the University of Chicago, encouraged me to think of Egyptology as a career. By an extraordinary accident of timing, Breasted was then developing the Oriental Institute and wanted young American students. From the Institute I received a magnificent fellowship of eight hundred dollars, which was ample for eleven months of study.

My graduate work at Chicago was pushed through at the alarming rate of only three years of study, including my doctorate. I would not now sanction a candidacy which had only language and history, with no art or archaeology or something in the generality of the culture of the ancient world. But in those days it was believed that mastering the languages meant that you could master the history, which was all that was necessary.

From Chicago I went into field work in Egypt. I spent five years there, not excavating but copying in a temple at Thebes (Luxor), and then came back to Chicago in 1931 to spend a year as a visiting teacher. It has stretched into thirty-seven years of teaching. When Breasted died in 1935, I succeeded to the directorship of the Oriental Institute. This was something of a liability, because it was the depths of the Depression, and the sources of support for the Institute had largely disappeared. My obligation became to reduce the Oriental Institute to something between 30 and 40 percent of what it had been. Field expeditions were brought down from nine to three, and the work being done at home was reduced drastically. Fortunately, the good staff understood the financial necessities, so that we weathered the crisis and for the most part got the field work published, which was the main obligation of those lean years.

To a certain degree the field work resumed after World War II. Two factors were responsible for that. First, nearly everybody had gone away during the war for various kinds of service, and so we had a rather fine saving in the budget. We were able to use that backlog for field work. Second, John D. Rockefeller, Jr., who had created the Institute, felt a responsibility to what he called the "Breasted backlog" of things that Breasted had wanted to do, and agreed to finance such things as publication and public presentation, which took some of the load off the budget. Every year we were able to send into the field one copying expedition and one excavation, and about every third year a second excavation. We have continued in the field regularly, as long as politics would permit.

You have written a fascinating book on the development of Egyptology down to the 1940's. In the last quarter century, what have been the main trends of research, and what changes have there been?

The big trend in the field has been toward prehistory—how did we get to historic time when there was writing? To put it in cartoon terms, what happened to make man come out of the caves and live in villages and begin writing? This has become a very highly skilled profession, of interest not only to westerners but to the local services of antiquities in places like Turkey and Egypt, Iraq and Israel.

The great men who opened up the field were largely philologists, who read ancient Egyptian or cuneiform or Hebrew, and it was assumed that they could go out with their students and excavate. Excavation has become a profession now, having its own particular skills which have nothing to do with philology. For work in prehistory, an expedition now may be staffed with as many as seven westerners but may not have a single language man at all. If the texts are expected to be limited, they may just call in an expert for the problems that they have. In such circumstances I would not be a fully welcome member of an expedition. If they had no hieroglyphic inscriptions and were working on prehistoric problems, there would be no specialized job for me. Back in 1927 when I went to Megiddo in Palestine to learn digging, it turned out that all four members of the expedition had malaria or were otherwise involved, and for two weeks I in my ignorance ran an excavation. The government services would not permit such ignorance today; they have tightened their standards of control just as the archaeologists have.

Another trend, which may be enforced by finances, is cooperation—between two or more western institutions or between a western institution and the local service of antiquities. Often one agency cannot afford the whole job. The trend is also enforced by the fact that specialities are recognized as specialities. One institution may offer one expertness and another may supplement it with something quite different. This is a very healthy trend, going against that of the 1920's. Then we jealously held our jobs to ourselves, not simply against people from other countries but against our own compatriots. We paid social calls on each other, but never let out any of our secrets.

The big trend, though, is to find out what we formerly were not even interested in. There is a British dental surgeon trying to find out how the Egyptians ground their bread. We have always taken for granted that the basic staple food for the Egyptians was bread, supplemented with vegetables and perhaps eggs, and rarely with meat, fish, or fowl. Until Dr. Leek started on it, no one was interested in examining the composition of ancient bread. He discovered that the composition was the same as today, but the grinding must have been different. There is an analogy that I heard last week: the potato came from the New World to the Old World but no one has ever written a treatise on the importance of the potato in the diet of Europe. Another problem of no interest in the past was how they achieved a glaze on pottery. What amount of heat was needed to make a good, uniform glaze on the outside of pottery? This kind of question represents a turn from political to social history.

The scholars you described in your book on Egyptology were very colorful people. Would you say that the Egyptologist today is liable to be less of an individualist, more of a certain kind of academic person?

As a general rule the Egyptologist today fits more into pattern. Compared to Egyptologists forty years ago, there is far less individualism, far less arbitrary action. It used to be that the word of a leader of an expedition was law; today the director of an expedition is still in charge and responsible, but he relies so much on the specialities of other people that he cannot afford to be arbitrary. I don't think that we prize and admire eccentricity in academic circles as much as we did a few generations back. The eccentric who puts on a high performance in class is becoming rare; he has to pass the hurdle of departmental appointment instead of having an arbitrary appointment from the chairman of a department. Not simply in universities but also in museums, the tendency is to be safe and get a sound and noneccentric man. Flinders Petrie, the founder of scientific method in excavation, could not at the age of thirty or thirty-five have found a university or museum job these days. He was far too angular, too arbitrary, too eccentric to pass the approval of a group of judges.

I think that there is a decided loss in this. As we become safe, we become repetitive and lose our adventurous experimentation. When we try something new, it now is usually introduced from outside the field. For instance, in excavation they have now accepted a person called a geomorphologist, a man who knows how soils are made. He can say, "This was once agricultural soil," while to us it is just gravel or sand. The excavators have accepted this but would probably not have thought of it themselves, preferring to play it safe rather than go off into the unknown.

It is hard to think of anyone who affected the whole of excavation as much as Petrie did by rejecting former method, in particular by saying, "You have been after gold and silver; I am after pottery, broken pottery," and using broken pottery as the key to historical development. Now obvious to us, at the time this was a stroke of genius.

Breasted achieved an enormous reputation and influence as a teacher and popularizer. How would you evaluate him as a scholar?

At the age of thirty-four, Breasted was accepted as a foreign collaborator for the great hieroglyphic dictionary being composed at Berlin. This was the center of controlled work on the ancient Egyptian language, and ever since, it has been the standard dictionary of ancient Egyptian. For a young foreigner to be accepted was a high mark of distinction. At the age of forty, he published a translation of all the historical texts of ancient Egypt then known—five volumes of ancient records. Subsequently he became a very busy administrator, and it was then felt that he had left scholarship. But in 1930 he brought out the translation of an Egyptian medical papyrus, which a review called "impeccable." He had not lost his gift for handling the Egyptian language. Opposed to the detailed attention he gave to texts, he was a visionary about ancient Egypt as a source of human culture. This came out in his great history of Egypt of 1906, and perhaps pre-eminently in a book called *The Dawn of Conscience,* which appeared toward the end of his life.

There he argued that social conscience—man's feeling of responsibility for other men—started in Egypt about four thousand years ago. This was a product of the late nineteenth century's optimism and expectation for human betterment, and Breasted wanted to build a single clear line from ancient Egypt down to our day and, by implication, beyond that.

It became very difficult for anyone else to follow this beautiful vision, after the Depression and World War II and our present problems. First, it seemed to imply that man finds good and never loses it: to the good from Egypt, the Greeks added good, the Renaissance added good, and modern democracy has added good—all on top of each other without any loss. Second, it was unilinear from Egypt, to the Greeks, to Europe, to the United States. We now view things as far more complicated. There is a complex of forces which build into the culture of any people, and to think that the single central thing in that culture is derived from only one other place is too simple. Breasted's vision is one of the greatest enthusiasm, but in our day hardly anyone is able to take it at the value he gave to it.

Within the Egyptian language Breasted was a great scholar. In the vision he had—not simply of Egyptology but of other fields—he was brilliant. In his ability to make things simple and clear to other people, he was unchallenged, but the word *naive* has been applied to him by some critics. While I tend to resent that because I admired him very much, I would accept the term *visionary*.

Has the German school of Egyptology recovered from the Nazi era and the effects of World War II?

No. In Germany there was a very great loss; some of their best people were Jewish by Nazi definition and had to come to this country. Then the whole purport of Nazi scholarship was an attempt to force people into a single pattern of thought, which was highly repugnant to what was called the Berlin school (it was not merely Berlin but included Leipzig and Munich, and so on). They lost their elders around the time of Hitler and World War II, and the younger people they have are good but not outstanding. Curiously, France, which in the 1920's was held in low esteem for its controlled work—Maspero's brilliance was really justified, for he had had a feeling for the ancient cultures, but when other people tried to make a pronouncement without evidence, they did not succeed—now has produced some of the most brilliant younger people. France probably now stands at the top of the European field. I will not compare it to America, for I may be prejudiced if I try to do that. The good men in Germany are trying a little too hard to re-establish *German* scholarship rather than scholarship. Breasted, of course, studied in Berlin, and so he encouraged me to have some summer semesters first at Berlin and then at Munich after I had finished my work at Chicago. For study abroad now, the direction would probably be to Paris.

What happened to the attempt of the 1920's to develop a native Egyptian school of Egyptology?

In the middle 1920's, there was a brilliant Russian, Vladimir Golenischev, teaching at Cairo, who was a philologist of great accomplishment. There were also courses at the National University at Cairo in archaeology under the influence of a Britisher, Newberry, and an Austrian, Junker. And there was a very able group of a dozen young Egyptians who were planning to be not simply Egyptologists but scholars.

Egyptology is still taught in the national universities of Egypt at Cairo, Ain Shems, and Alexandria, but it prepares government officials, not scholars. More inspectors are needed than ever before because the antiquities service now places one on every single expedition. When the Egyptians do a job of excavation, they publish a preliminary report but are not given any opportunity to pursue it. They will write it up in ten pages, which can be done in a week's time, but never have the six months to develop it into a scholarly proposition. Instead, they are taken off it and put onto something else. The system is "do the desk job, and don't pretend to be a scholar." The youngsters growing up in this are stifled, obviously. I know of only two Egyptians—both coming out of that school of the middle 1920's —who are productive in publishing, and they are both near the ends of their careers. The system makes even the professors in the universities take on one single publication job which they work at for most of their careers. It is tragic, because they are good. I saw three of them at Luxor this past winter who wanted to publish, but they could see no real opportunity for it because they were kept busy. Not only were they kept busy developing new excavation, but whenever there were distinguished visitors, they had to spend two or three days taking them around.

What is the status of the problem concerning the transition from food gathering to food production in Mesopotamia?

The transition has been best charted on the fringes of the Fertile Crescent around Mesopotamia, where various beginnings on high land (say fifteen hundred feet above sea level) have been seen. There was a fringe there which was about the lowest level of wild wheat and wild barley; it also was, generally speaking, the lower range of the wild sheep, cattle, goats, and so on. Within this environment man arrested his roving and started to settle down in the company of the wild things which ultimately would become the domestic things. In this highland on the rim of the Fertile Crescent, there were settlements with constructed houses and a form of wheat which was not yet domestic (the animals are harder to classify). We assume that man settled down up where the wild things were before he, over long centuries, brought them down into the alluvial plain. When he brought them down into the alluvial plain, they had to change species, and there was a process of trial and error which ultimately produced modern types of grain and modern types of animals.

In the last five years this theory has been complicated by the observation of settlements where there is no agriculture. In northwestern Mesopotamia along the Euphrates, there are at least two settlements showing the structure of houses, but their refuse heaps show no wheat or barley, and the animal bones are pretty much assumed to be wild. It would seem, then, that there is an intermediate stage, when men did not settle down with plants and animals. In this stage they built their crude huts, but still ranged out for their food gathering. One does not know whether the less mobile members of the community—women, small children, and old people—stayed put and tickled the wild things into domestication while the men were away gathering food.

One great puzzle is that we do not have an analogous situation for the Nile Valley. On the flanks of the Nile Valley, geological conditions suggest that there was not, at times when man might be so active, an area where there would be wild wheat and barley and a great number of wild animals that could be domesticated. You have to go up to the sources of the Nile in Ethiopia before you find those wild forms; and to bring them north along the Nile, say fifteen hundred miles to Egypt, would be pretty difficult. The suggested implication is that Egypt borrowed domestication from Mesopotamia.

Egyptologists do not favor this view, but at the present time we must admit that Egypt is lacking the logical sequence which Mesopotamia shows.

How does one account for the transition from these domesticated villages to organized government, irrigation, and so on?

We can only theorize on the transition, and the theory quite commonly brings in the factor of irrigation. There was a simple little village in which it is conceivable that everybody belonged to the same family or tribe. The villagers had a certain amount of mobility: the men might seasonally go away hunting, while the women were doing the agriculture. The village was a simple organism, and self-sufficient, too. The villagers made their own tools and clothes; they made their own weapons and built their own houses. There must have been always, however, some who were more skilled at making certain things than others. But still, from a simple standpoint, a community was self-sufficient.

When eventually they wanted greater production from their own area, they had to bring water from a distance for irrigation. In turn, they had to establish relations with other villages if they were to bring water across the areas of other villages. As the village became complex in its relationships, its organization became bigger. It was now necessary to have a single governing word to cover a dozen villages: if they were to share the water without fighting over it, they had to agree to some arbitrator who said, "This is the way you are to share it." Thus a nonrelated ruler, ultimately a king, evolved because of the quarreling about water. There was also a greater factor of trade. One village may have been closer to the source of good flint for making tools and weapons; another may have been closer to a source of some valuable stone (like garnet or amethyst) and therefore had beads of magical quality; one may have been off toward a pastoral area so that it produced more leather than another that was more thoroughly agricultural. Trade enters the picture, and gradually specialists develop. There is the ruler, with his messengers and his army; there is the potter and the sandal maker and the flint-tool maker.

Then the villages enter Gordon Childe's urban revolution of a group of communities held together by interdependence and specialization of function. When Childe uses the word *urban,* it is not modern urban. It is an enlarged village which is dependent on other enlarged villages. When he says *revolution,* he is probably talking about something which developed over a few millennia, perhaps as many as three thousand years. This explanation is 80 percent theory. We think that it had to occur that way, but as we discover small elements in the picture, we see that it is not necessarily a single line of development leading along from one stage to another.

The urban revolution ended up with what probably could be called cities. Places like Ur and Warka in Mesopotamia and Memphis in Egypt were organisms of much higher complexity. They went into a kind of revolution, the revolution marking the beginning of civilization when writing appears, about 3000 B.C. Kings appeared with an impersonality of rule: they were unrelated to the people they ruled, and the people might never see their king, only his agents. This is a factor, I think, of the end of Childe's urban revolution or the beginning of civilization. No longer did the king hear about trouble on the frontier of his little state, go out with his army to check on it, and return to his capital by nightfall. That is a city-state, which can be controlled from a single nucleus by relatively personal relations. Babylonia had city-states until 2300 B.C., when Sargon built an empire. In Egypt the nation ruled by the agents of the king started as early as 3000 B.C., and things became very different with these factors of impersonal rule and writing.

I sometimes think of it as the "chair revolution" because in both Babylonia and Egypt that stiff, uncomfortable machine on four legs appeared. The four legs were animal legs. The "law giver" or "law decider" had to be stiff and erect at a higher level (although less comfortable) than those whom he was judging, visibly showing that he was more important; it was as though he were riding on the back of a beast at a higher level than they were. I know of no other reason for the appearance of this mechanism. It is interesting that we still continue with this machine, although we are now trying to break up the form and give ourselves chairs that are quite different from that four-legged animal of five thousand years ago.

In the historic era of Egypt—the Old Kingdom and the Middle Kingdom—was Egypt largely a self-contained civilization?

If you ask one scholar and then another scholar this question, you will get quite different answers. Toward the end of his career, Petrie wrote a book called *The Making of Egypt,* and for him every new period was created or influenced by outside. The so-called Libyan period of the Twenty-second Dynasty (900 B.C.) was to him not Libyan but Elamite, because the name Sheshonk suggested to him Susa over in Elam. At the other extreme, people (and I am one of them) would admit there were outside influences but would say that they were not creative but catalytic. Egypt reached a point where change was probable or necessary, and the outside influence might only be that drop which was the catalyst to make the change.

Henri Frankfort argued that there was Mesopotamian influence at the beginning of the First Dynasty, and I agree with him in that. Perhaps a good half of my Egyptological colleagues disagree, arguing that the architecture which we see as Mesopotamian is really Egyptian, not in mud brick but in wood. While I have accepted Frankfort's Mesopotamian stimulation of Egypt at the beginning of the dynasties, I rejected (perhaps inconsistently) Asiatic influence between the Old and Middle kingdoms. I argue that there was essentially a breakdown of the heavy and complicated structure of the Old Kingdom as it became economically a burden on the state (maintaining all those pyramids and tombs) and that the Egyptians had to come out of the breakdown of their own volition and with their own effort. The Middle Kingdom was a time of far less absolutism. But all of this was natively Egyptian. In the time between the Middle and New Kingdoms, I go back, again inconsistently, to outside influence. The Asiatic Hyksos conquered Egypt, and the New Kingdom arose as a reaction against that humiliation. I probably can talk out of both sides of my mouth by saying that the essentials must be internal. No one is persuaded in his own judgment to do anything by an outsider; he must convince himself of the necessity of change. If that is true, he denies the outside influence and insists that he did it himself, and very often this may be true.

Was there any degree of social mobility in ancient Egyptian society?

There was quite a respectable factor of social mobility, and there were two reasons within it. First, the nobility which governed started out a certain size. When their job became more complicated, they had to call upon other persons to apply themselves to do the job. Also, as time went on the nobility became more noble and did the more traditional jobs but wanted someone else to do the more active work out in the field. As a result, they summoned other people to do important jobs, and craftsmen and high stewards became what might be called cabinet officers. We have one Old Kingdom biography in which a man says that he started out carrying the stick for an architect (i.e., carrying the chain for a surveyor), then became a builder, deputy architect of the state, and finally commissioner of public works for all of Egypt. He also says that he came from obscure origins.

Clearly there were people who were born in relative obscurity who became decision makers in the state. Since Egypt also had its periods of collapse, it is quite clear that in an intermediate period some of the old nobility would go down into obscurity, and when Egypt came out of the dark period there would be other active and aggressive forces who became powerful. This is even true of the dynasties. The king of Egypt was by definition a god, always the same god, and when one king died his successor would then become the Horus (the god of rule). He would be the son of the god Ra (the sun god) and thus belong within the hierarchy which was divine. This provided a mechanism to discover that someone relatively obscure had been procreated by the sun god, and if this was recognized by the appropriate priests he might become a king. There is even an Egyptian folk tale about the builder of the Great Pyramid Khufu: he was told by a prophet that after his son and his grandson, rule would be taken over by the children of the wife of a relatively obscure priest in the Delta.

Coming down to the New Kingdom, when foreign captives were kept as slaves, we find these slaves became critical factors within the palace. Being slaves, they could by definition be trusted to do what their masters wanted them to do. Ultimately they exercised this function so well that they became people of decision. When there was a conspiracy in the royal harem in the Twentieth Dynasty, several of the judges to try the conspirators had foreign names, suggesting that they or their fathers or grandfathers started out as slaves, and that they functioned so well within the palace that they were given important judging power.

There was no caste system in Egypt. Within the culture it was possible to rise from low estate into the artisan class and from there to gain the esteem of kings and nobles and ultimately become kings and nobles. The household functionary who was ultimately so good at it that he took over power from his lord and became a ruler himself was far from unknown. There are even texts which support this. The sun god said, "I made every man like everybody else, and if men have failed to recognize this it is not my responsibility but theirs." The system in its top definition was very arbitrary: the king was a god and was not like other men. But within that system, over the centuries, there was quite a bit of mobility.

One difficulty is that most of our material is from carving in stone. The vast majority of our texts are in temples and tombs; they represent a longstanding tradition, that what religion said was right. There is an emphasis on status, an emphasis on continuing the tradition as religion has established it from the creation onward and of not tolerating social revolution. These inscriptions tell us that there is no forward movement; at best there is a going back to the good times. Even papyri, such more temporary texts as we get, tend to confirm that what was set down was unchanging tradition.

Within that picture we can still see a fairly respectable degree of change. Certainly difference is visible in such physical things as architecture and art, where it is usually possible to date something with moderate precision because of the changing mode. Specialists in art can say, "This is the very end of the fifth century B.C. because of the treatment of the eyebrows and ears," or "This is middle Eighteenth Dynasty rather than late Eighteenth or Nineteenth." In architecture we can say that peripheral temples were built until the time of Amenhotep III (1400 B.C.) and then changed to temples with the columns inside. From the physical we can see constant change; if we see it less in social or economic evidence, we can still argue that it must have been there too. Economic change is visible because there are documents which tell the cost of a unit of grain or of a donkey or slave: in the middle twelfth century B.C. there was an extraordinary inflation, when the cost of a unit of wheat rose 200 percent. There seems to have been great distress in the land, and the government closed its eyes to mining the treasure in the royal and noble tombs at Thebes. The same man was commissioner of police in western Thebes for seventeen years while the tombs were being robbed. The only conclusion one can reach is that the government considered the robbery economically useful.

Jaroslav Černý will publish a book very soon about the workers' community in western Thebes. Out of scraps of pottery and a few pieces of papyrus, it will show the social setup of a single small and relatively isolated community for about four generations. For Egypt over a very brief time we will have things that are comparable to the cuneiform documents of Mesopotamia, which have given an understanding of how a household was organized, what it had to pay for the things that it needed, and so on.

Within our embarrassment that most of our documents are religious, there are here and there bits of evidence about how life went on comparable to what the Metropolitan Museum found in the 1920's. The half-dozen letters then discovered were written by a small farmer at Thebes who, while absent caring for other fields in the Delta, wrote fussy letters home saying, "Buy me more land but don't pay too much for it," and "Don't overwater our land." Here in just a few letters is a brilliant invasion of the darkness that surrounds most of Egyptian agriculture. The letters also reveal the inside of a household: the farmer's love for his smallest son whom he pampered unmercifully, his direction that his concubine must be treated with more respect by his sons, and so on.

How would you compare the condition of the peasant of ancient Egypt with that of the Arab fellaheen in modern times?

The conditions of life of the peasant of ancient Egypt continued to exist until about seventy years ago—forced labor was legally abolished only in the 1890's, and even after that time it was still undertaken here and there in situations of desperation when a job had to be done. Of course, the Suez Canal was in the first instance built by such forced labor, and it was an international scandal that the people who were rounded up to build this canal, which was to be an international rather than local canal, were given no housing and no food at first and were just forced to scoop out that canal.

The ancient Egyptian culture could have done whatever it did without any slaves at all. There is the popular statement that the pyramids were built by slaves cringing under the lash of the overseer. The lash of the overseer was probably there; but the people who built the pyramids were Egyptians forced to do that under the system of forced labor. We know of at least one case near a pyramid where the government had a village constructed for these people; in another case we know that there had to be a ration of food and clothing. They might even have been better off than those who were requisitioned for the Suez Canal. But still it was a system in which the peasant had no recourse. They probably did their big construction jobs in a nonagricultural time of the year, after the Nile had gone down to a point where production of grain or flax was not indicated. In the inundation season quarrying could be undertaken, and the quarried blocks could be floated across the Nile to where the pyramids were being built.

When the Egyptians had slaves from foreign conquests, they used them in addition to, not replacing, Egyptian peasants. Certain documents suggest to us that when they got slaves, those slaves were put into the household. There is a papyrus in Brooklyn which lists the Asiatic slaves in a certain household, and they were cooks, weavers, gardeners, doorkeepers, and so on. They had positions of greater privilege than the Egyptians who labored in the field. They were closer to the food production and food consumption than the peasants themselves. It is conceivable that it was a situation similar to ours in the American South under slavery, that the household slave was physically better off and more privileged than those working in the fields. One might have thought that it would have been a cause for rebellion among the peasants, but there is no indication that such rebellion ever occurred.

The modern Egyptian fellah is in some respects better off than the fellah of three generations ago. He now is told that he is the voice of the government, that he can elect the people who have the control, that his children must go to school. In terms of his ability to make the most important decisions, in terms of his responsiveness to the demands of the state, and in terms perhaps of his intake of calories, he probably is no better off. The population increase in Egypt means that there is competition for every mouthful of food, and so the Egyptian peasant is still in a situation of some desperation. For about five thousand years the peasant in Egypt has been in about the same situation.

It is characteristic of traditional agricultural societies that the population will at certain times expand very rapidly; then a period of famine and plague will cause the population to decline. Is there evidence that this happened in ancient Egypt?

Little is known about the volume of population in ancient Egypt. A classical author estimated the population of ancient Egypt at 7 million; at the time of Napoleon's incursion into Egypt the estimate was 2.25 million; three generations later it was 5 million; and now it is more than 30 million. This analogy of the last 170 years may or may not apply to ancient Egypt. We read of famines, of successive years of low Nile when people starved and died; we read of plagues, of the gods who bring plagues and the goddess who takes away plague. The big difficulty is, again, that most of the texts come from temples and tombs which in essence denied disease and death, stressing immortality for the good. A scene showing people starving carved in the causeway of a Fifth Dynasty king at Sakkarah is extraordinary and exceptional. Texts from a physician claim that he cured and kept alive; they do not admit that he had a desperate time when there was plague. It is fully within the cards that there were times in ancient Egypt when the population was down toward that 2.25 million estimated in 1800 A.D. and other times (when distress was more under control) when it was up toward the 7 million estimated in Roman times. It is a matter of theory. In times when the kingship did not control the land well, the use of the annual inundation broke down so that the control of the water toward agricultural production was fitful or nonexistent. Then there would be famine and distress. When the central power was restored, government agents down south at the second cataract predicted what the flow of the Nile was going to be so that there might be controlled use of that water. At the times of central control, the irrigation canals and catch basins for water were kept in repair, and the water was used over a longer period of time for a greater agricultural production. During the First Intermediate Period of one hundred years and the Second Intermediate Period of close to two hundred years, there probably were distress and famine, and the population probably dropped. Then in the New Kingdom, when consistent control lasted for about four hundred years, the population should have risen. Again it has to be theory. We do have constant texts about famine showing that it was a threat hanging over Egypt at all times; we have less information about plagues, but the analogy up to very recent time suggests that plagues must have been almost endemic in the land.

What was the social background of the Egyptian priesthood? What is known about the organization and functioning of the priesthood?

In its top echelons the priesthood belonged to the nobility, and there was a very considerable overlap. High nobles served apparently a quarter of the time as priests in the temple. Whether this was a sort of lay readership or whether it was the effective priesthood we do not know. But in the Old Kingdom there may have been no difference between nobility and priesthood. Not until temples became far more complex were there full time professional priests. The temple service in the Old Kingdom seems to have required only a thin top layer of those who spent most of their time on it, and most of the rest came out of the working nobility.

Around 1500 B.C. the Egyptian gods, through the use of the oracle, began to direct the ruler. On advice from the oracle, the kings moved out into the south to Nubia and the Sudan, or out into the north to Libya or Asia. When tremendous victories were won, the god was rewarded with tremendous loot from the victories and tremendous income from the economy of Egypt. The temples then became large and complex: the example given is always that of Amon at Karnak at Thebes. A professional, continuing, working priesthood was the governing bureaucracy of a single temple. We have a papyrus from around 1200 B.C. which tells us of the tremendous holdings of the Egyptian temples. The estimates of the proportion of agricultural land in Egypt belonging to the temples are immense. Scholars do not agree on whether these were additions to the holdings of the temples or were the total holdings of the temples, but they were in the range of 12 percent of all the agricultural land of Egypt. We know from another papyrus that temple holdings were taxed, but their economic position was still solid. Indeed, the temples came to rival the palace as the great power in Egypt. At some times they may have been even more important than the palace: the high priest of Amon at Thebes was a controlling factor in the state through the importance of the oracle of the god and the economic holdings of the temple. Within this time there was a family overlap of priest and high lay official. The vizier, the prime minister for Upper Egypt, may have had one son who was the chief tax collector for Upper Egypt and another son who was the high priest of Amon. This was quite common, and in fact one or two individuals held both the office of prime minister and that of high priest before the thing became more complicated and each one became a full-time job.

We moderns probably have some skepticism about the responses of the oracle. The texts say that the king consulted the god and the god gave a Yes or No answer. The priest of the god was responsible for the answer. Is it conceivable that he did it cynically and knowingly to his own advantage and the advantage of the god? It is my feeling that the system could not have continued for the fifteen hundred years from the Eighteenth Dynasty into Roman times if it were based clearly and specifically on cynicism. They must have been in a psychological setting where the priest was receptive to the voice of the god as it came to him in his heart, and must have responded, "The god says Yes," or "The god says No," not trying to deceive the king or the populace. If it had been based on deception, the system would have been revoked by the king who was being directed or by the nobles who were being left out of it. Within that setting the priesthood really became controlling. Writing in Roman times, Diodorus says that the king of Egypt was the luckiest of individuals because he simply followed the directions of those who knew better. This absolute monarch in the dogma of earlier times has become a palace captive for whom the hours at which he rises, has his meals, gives judgment, or even goes to bed with his wife are laid down by other persons on the basis of religion.

While the priesthood became extraordinarily important, of course there were different kinds of priests. For the little people of Egypt there were probably little priests who may not have had a full temple. The goddess of the west at Thebes, which was the Gurnah mountain overlooking the tombs at Thebes, may have had no specific temple, but people worshiped her because she was right there, and some workman may have been closer to her than others and served as her priest. Just as there were high nobles, little nobles, and small farmers, so there probably was a hierarchy of the priesthood from the most powerful to those who were unsure about their power.

What is considered to be the position and influence of Akhenaton in Egyptian history?

Professor Breasted said that Akhenaton was the first idealist and the first individual in human history. This, like all absolute claims, is subject to criticism from others. At the other extreme, a social anthropologist said that the course of Egyptian history would have been the same if Akhenaton had been a sack of sawdust, that he was merely a tool of social forces. I would say that the truth has to be found somewhere between these extremes.

There were forces for change in Egypt before Akhenaton became king. By his time Egypt had experienced a full century of internationalism. It was recognized that the country was not limited to the banks of the Nile but extended as far as could be trod by Egyptians, to the Euphrates in Asia and the fourth cataract in the Sudan. Within this extension of horizon, there was an internationalism of art, and we can see that factors were borrowed from outside. Frankfort saw the flying gallop of the Egyptian horses and chariot as something borrowed from Crete, and whether or not that is specifically and narrowly true, there undoubtedly were forces coming in and apprising Egyptians of the accomplishments of other people. Pottery and metalwork were brought back from the conquests abroad and kept as treasures in Egyptian households; household slaves who had different ways of doing things were accepted from outside. For a full century before Akhenaton, there had been a sense of "otherness" in the air.

Akhenaton hacked out the name of Amon from inscriptions, in some places hacked out the word *gods* in the plural, attacked the names of other gods, and worshiped one single force, the life-giving power of the sun. This then was a working monotheism, which was quite new. On the other hand, unifying texts had been written which tended to merge the gods into a single life-giving and life-sustaining force, even before Akhenaton identified that force as the Aton, the disk of the sun. Before his time there are visible changes in art from the two-dimensional angularity which was set down in the Fourth Dynasty. Its solidity was permanence, and art wanted to express undying permanence. This firm, strong line was being softened into a roundness, a softness which is impermanent. Art even had begun to represent events happening within an artist's lifetime, not simply within a stretch of eternity.

Before his time, then, there are antecedents to what he did. I would still insist that he did it, however. He almost did it within a single year. In certain monuments—for instance the tomb of Ramose at Thebes—the art suddenly explodes from one wall to another. There is a traditional art on one wall; the next wall in the same tomb has the exaggerated, excited, new art of great emotional quality in which everybody has the same scrawny neck and potbelly as the king and is in highly exhausting movement. This also appears in some monuments at Karnak, where Akhenaton started a temple to the sun god in the old art (perhaps in his first years of reign) and then suddenly changed to a temple in the new art. I find it difficult to say that social process alone moved with that speed. I think there was a man in it who said, "We have reached the point where we are going to give free expression. The young people in our land are demanding this new expression and we are going to have it. We are going to have it in art, religion, in telling the story of what happened today rather than what happened in eternity." I think that this person had a great individual impact on what happened. It is possible to go Freudian on Akhenaton and say that he was a physical weakling, much attached to his aggressive little mother Queen Ti, reacting against his father, who was a great hunter and outdoor person. Akhenaton in his physical weakness turned against what had been the pattern for the king and became a patron of the arts and intellectual things. It was a *reaction.* He went back to the rule of the sun god which had been established in the Old Kingdom; he went back to the centrality of the pharaohs (which had been the pattern in the Old Kingdom), disregarding the oracle of the god. But in its formal expression it was an explosion of the new, and I think that he personally had great influence in releasing certain forces which were already present. Within those terms he was a great individual.

Was he the first monotheist in ancient history? You would have to define monotheism, because there was god the father and god the son in the new religion. There was god the Aton, the life-giving force up in the sky; but also worshiped was his son Akhenaton, who accepted the slavish adoration of his people. In the pictures at Tell el Amarna, the people are reaching up to him in their adoration, while he and his wife Nefertiti reach up to the disk of the sun. Certain Egyptologists said that this was monotheism, that the two gods were one, and a trinitarian who accepts God the Father, God the Son, and God the Holy Spirit is perhaps at some obligation to say that divinity may express itself in different forms and still be unitary. In any case, monotheism had to be rediscovered later because Egypt reacted against it after Akhenaton.

How do we account for fluctuations or breaks in the rule of the central government?

The texts tend to insist that there is no change and that the first king of the Nineteenth Dynasty is in proper succession to the last king of the Eighteenth Dynasty, that they are all products of the sun god, and that the sun god is therefore continuing to procreate the kings of Egypt without break. We do see occasional things that can be called revolution, as between the Fourth and Fifth dynasties. In the Fourth Dynasty there were tremendous symbols of centralized power, the pyramids. In the Fifth Dynasty the pyramids were modest in relation to the symbols of the sun god, and the sun temple stood beside the pyramid of a fifth-century king sharing bigness and control. At the same time in the Fifth Dynasty, the king became the son of Ra, the sun god, and his name from that time was compounded with the name of Ra. We say that there was a revolution of the priesthood of Ra, or one using the priesthood of Ra to control the absolute power of the king.

Between the Eighteenth and Nineteenth dynasties there was another change. The Eighteenth Dynasty ended with Akhenaton and his successors, who had broken with the old establishment, the group of ruling nobles and priests who had controlled things. Even the restoration after the deaths of Akhenaton and his son-in-law Tutankhamen was only one of police action, trying to get things in proper order so that taxes could be collected. There was a period of incomplete restoration until, with the Nineteenth Dynasty, the army moved in. Ramses I and Seti I came out of the Egyptian army and became the Pharaohs of Egypt, the god who ruled over the land. Clearly Egyptian society was ready for a complete restoration effected by the one element in the government which could immediately and completely exert control—the army. The nobility had their households and the priesthood had their temple servants, but if there were to be a full change of government, the nobility or priesthood had to call on that wing of themselves which was the army. During the Twenty-sixth Dynasty the Assyrians conquered Egypt, and when they retired they enthroned princes of the Egyptian Delta who would be in such control of the country that Assyria would not have to worry about it. Thus there were changes of dynasty in which we can see reason; but there were other changes in which we see no apparent social, economic, or political reason.

During the First Intermediate Period after the Sixth Dynasty, one force went on trying to rule at Memphis but seems to have been ineffective. Why its rule was not accepted by the rest of Egypt is unknown. The state then broke up into north and south, and small rulers competed with each other before there was a restoration and the Middle Kingdom came in to reconquer all of Egypt and set up a single rule. One curious element is that rule arose out of the south of Egypt. Menes of the First Dynasty came from Upper Egypt; Mentuhotep of the Eleventh Dynasty came from Upper Egypt; Ahmose of the Eighteenth Dynasty came from Upper Egypt. The Persians and Romans discovered that if there were going to be revolutions in Egypt they would start somewhere in the general vicinity of Thebes, Upper Egypt. Why there was a relative calmness of the north and a relative resistance from the south, both in pharaonic Egypt and when outsiders controlled the country, is unknown. It is possible to make glib answers that the north was a mercantile area and wanted trade to go on no matter who was ruling, whereas the south insisted that they were not benefiting by the outside rule and wanted to re-establish the ancient glory. But I would not accept this as a full explanation.

How do you account for the general decline of Egypt after Ramses II?

Here again there is speculation. One can start with the fact that the iron age came in (generally speaking) about the time of Ramses II. In the preceding copper and bronze age Egypt had an advantage in that it controlled ample sources of copper to make fighting weapons or tools. When the iron age came, Egypt had no usable iron and had to purchase it from outsiders—for instance, the Hittites in Anatolia. From that time on, Egypt became secondary to other forces. I tend to distrust any explanation which is a single one and particularly a physical factor. It clearly must have been much more complicated than that.

Another possible factor arose during the New Kingdom (the Eighteenth, Nineteenth, and Twentieth Dynasties). In the Egyptian conquest of Asia and Africa around 1500 B.C., the texts give credit to "our army" for the glorious conquest. As they went on and conquered the world, they came to rely much more on foreign mercenaries, and the army of Ramses II had a considerable mercenary contingent of Nubians, Libyans, and Asiatics, who were the scouts and shock troops. In a similar way at home, as they became wealthy, the Egyptians relied much more on factors to run their temples and estates. Formal voluntary activity on the part of Egyptians themselves was dying out. This is even shown in the texts: in the Eighteenth Dynasty there are statements like "I was a man who served the government so vigorously that the king was graciously pleased to reward me"; in the late Nineteenth and Twentieth Dynasties there are statements like "Be silent," "The good man is the silent man," and so on. Voluntary activity was discouraged, not encouraged, and people were induced to quietness and patience. Spirit had run out, they did not see how to surmount their difficulties, and they were encouraged to be patient in difficulty. But certainly it is more complicated than that. There must be other factors which we do not see.

Perhaps one was the weight of a religion which was disproportionate to the economy of the state. The papyrus which tells about the tremendous holdings of the Egyptian temples suggests that they were a kind of dead hand on the economy, that a significant portion of the economy was taken out of the fullest production to present offerings in the temple and in the tombs of the nobles for some three hundred years. The service for dead Egyptians and the service for gods was disproportionate to the economy of the land.

From the time of Ramses III there was a lack of vigorous and continuing force. The merchant kings and the priest kings divided Egypt in the Twenty-first Dynasty; the Libyans governed the country in the Twenty-second Dynasty; there were attacks by Assyrians, Persians, and ultimately Alexander the Great. There were also attempts to assert the older Egypt, the most successful of which was the Twenty-sixth Dynasty (the so-called renaissance) which was maintained on the throne by foreign mercenaries. Psammetichus I, who started the Twenty-sixth Dynasty, introduced Greek-speaking peoples from the Greek mainland or the Aegean islands or Asia Minor as his police force, gave them cities in the Delta as a reward, and was maintained on the throne by foreign mercenaries. The old vigorous Egyptian spirit could not find ways of asserting itself or else was moribund, and there was a kind of fossilization of Egypt for the last thousand years. This is a long time for an organism to go on in a relatively stagnant state, and I have no answer that satisfies me as to what happened to the Egyptian spirit, why it ran out, and if it ran out how a social, economic, and religious system went on for a final thousand years before disappearing.

In the nineteenth century the prime motive for investigating Egypt was the hope that it would provide an historical context for the Hebrew Bible. Did anything significant turn up relating to the Hebrews historically?

The straightforward answer to that is No. We have all sorts of single factors: one stele was discovered by Petrie in the

1890's which gives the word Israel; in the Egyptian text a term is used which is the same ultimate term as Hebrew but in the original sense was not a single clan or group; a certain section of the Book of Proverbs is also a papyrus wisdom book in Egypt; Egyptians appeared on Palestinian soil from the fourteenth into the twelfth century B.C.; and single limited concepts were shared here and there. But in terms of the sojourn in Egypt, the oppression, and the exodus, in terms of Joseph's service in Egypt, we have not a single word which is fully confirming. Joseph's interpretation of Pharaoh's dream about seven lean years has a curious parallel in an Egyptian text which talks about seven years of famine, but it has no relation to the specific time of Joseph, and the seven may be in each case a traditional term, which is not the same seven lean years.

The Egypt Exploration Society was founded to confirm or test the Bible story. In its last fifty years it has been relatively unconcerned with that search, however, and has concentrated on discovering the Egyptian story. That story is part of the same period of time as the Bible story and thus in a broad and vague sense has a relation to the Bible. In the sense that history is not unilinear, that the Hebrews were part of a culture which had contact with Egypt in one direction and with the Phoenicians in another, all of this is good material for the broader understanding of the Bible. But nothing specific has been discovered about Joseph, Jacob, Abraham, Moses, and so on.

Would it be true to say that the Mesopotamian societies were more urban than Egyptian society?

Yes. We had a symposium here a dozen years ago in which we addressed ourselves to the problem of urbanization in the ancient Near East. I took the role of devil's advocate and exaggerated by saying that ancient Egypt until Ptolemaic times really had no cities in the urban sense. There was no central organism that was so inevitable that it had to continue through time, no eternal city like Rome or even Alexandria. The capital of Egypt was where the king was, and there were certain inevitable mercantile areas (the apex of the Delta was a crossing place from one side of the Nile to the other and had economic importance throughout history), but there was no organism sprawling over great numbers of acres. As one contrasts this with Nippur or Babylon in Mesopotamia, one sees in Mesopotamia an organism of much greater size, complexity, and inevitability, while Egypt lacked the urban organism which had its own river port and a tremendous body of trade which it continued to have after kingship shifted elsewhere. In Egypt the capital moved from Memphis to Thebes to Tanis, and so on, to wherever the king was and established himself. This did not happen with the same force in Babylonia (although it may be true in Assyria to some degree), but even Nineveh seems to have had a larger size and continuing life than some of the areas in Egypt. My colleague Charles Nims estimates that the working capital at Thebes had only a limited number of acres—compared to the three hundred acres in Nippur or Babylon it was perhaps only a sixth of that size. How could the Egyptian state go on without a nucleus which remained the eternal city? It did so go on, and to the best of my knowledge went on successfully until Alexander founded Alexandria, which for some centuries became a focal point for Egypt.

How do you compare the institution and concept of kingship in Egypt and Mesopotamia?

There is a dogmatic difference. From as early as we can see, the king of Egypt was a god—the god of rule (Horus) or the god who was the son of the sun god (Ra). Therefore he did not belong to any one part of Egypt but to the realm of the gods and could be accepted all over the land. In Mesopotamia the *lugal* was the deputy of the gods, their representative on earth. In those terms Mesopotamia had a harder time establishing a nation and moving from the city-state to the nation where a king from the south had acceptance in the north. It had to be the genius and force of Sargon and Naram-sin and that group of Akkadian kings which welded Mesopotamia into a nation by force of arms. The idea of divine kingship never took good root outside of Egypt. Among the Hebrews the King was the anointed, the appointed one of God; the Persians played with the idea but really didn't accept it; Alexander the Great was a military genius and so his claim that he was a god had a very considerable measure of acceptance, but his successors the Ptolemies had less luck in establishing that. This dogmatic difference in terms of its effectiveness over a few centuries may be immaterial; but in terms of facilitating the re-establishment of rule in each period of Egypt, it was simpler to control a nation there than elsewhere.

How do you compare Mesopotamian societies with Egypt in regard to their mathematics, natural sciences, and technology?

Egyptian architecture in stone was of such precision that it involved a comparable quality of mathematics and geometry. The Great Pyramid has an accuracy which is of the greatest fidelity, suggesting that their geometry was far better than that in any of the papyri that have come to us. Mesopotamia had to bring its stone for the most part from a long distance, did less precise building, and so developed less precise geometry. On the other hand, the continuing precision of observation which goes into astronomy in Babylonia is not visible in Egypt. When the Greeks took over astronomy—which perhaps we should call astrology—from the Babylonians, they had a continuous series of observations which led Thales of Miletus (if he was the first one) to carry that precision of record on toward prediction in the future. Classical physicians learned from the Egyptians' superior knowledge of the human body. The necessarily precise knowledge of what was possible to preserve for mummification and the specialization of Egyptian physicians—there were physicians for the brain, heart, stomach, descending colon, and so on—seem to have carried down into the classical period. Egypt did one job from which the science of classical times could benefit, and Babylonia did a different job. Babylonia may have had more impact on the classical world, but there was definitely an Egyptian contribution.

How do the two cultures compare in their devotion to tradition?

There is a greater written emphasis on tradition in Egypt than in Mesopotamia because of the mortuary religion, which said, "Keep on, things are going to go on in their best throughout eternity." Their emphasis on the good old days and the continuing of the good old days and immortality and eternity is dogmatically very, very visible in the Egyptian texts. In Mesopotamia continuing life was not that important. There were exceptions like the so-called royal tombs of Ur, where there was an elaborate preparation for the next world, but generally the continuance of the individual Mesopotamian didn't have that investment of time, effort, and goods that it had in Egypt.

Do you find it encouraging that courses in ancient Near Eastern history are becoming more and more popular?

Yes, but I find it a little puzzling. My beginning class in ancient Egypt used to be one to three students; in the last five years it has increased to six to eight. In terms of numbers this is no tremendous thing, but in terms of the clearly visible openings in the field it is extraordinary. There are only a very, very few possible new jobs, and yet there is this extraordinary interest. I don't find it necessarily an escape from the problems of today, because these youngsters are positive. They are not trying to hide away from the present time; they are vigorously interested in what happened in other cultures at other times. It is partly due to our American awareness of "other." Just as classes in Russian and Chinese and Swahili and Russian history and African history have increased, so cultures in other times have seemed to youngsters to be of valid interest. And I think that this is good. In terms of the population of the United States, it is such a small fraction that it is not going to have tremendous impact, but there should be an assertion that other times and other places had really vigorous importance.

Do you think that a student in this field today benefits from the sociological, anthropological, and social-psychological theories that have developed?

Yes, I found while I was a teacher that Redfield's course on the theory of the primitive society as contrasted with modern urban society was of tremendous value. This concept of transition between two points was extremely important, and the anthropologists are doing things in social anthropology which our students definitely must know about for their analytical framework. When you come to social-psychological theories, I am not quite sure whether I understand what is being done. The psychology that I hear of has its very modern specific, and I am not convinced that this very modern specific can be easily transferred to a framework which was myth-making and centered on the activity of the gods. Sociology and anthropology, yes; psychology, possibly.

3

Judaism, the Ancient Near East, and the Origins of Christianity

WILLIAM F. ALBRIGHT

THE HISTORIOGRAPHICAL CONTEXT

There can be no more important subject in the history of Western civilization than the emergence and development of ancient Judaism and the origins of the Christian faith and Church. Because the whole outlook of Western man has been fundamentally shaped by the theological and moral and historical conceptions of the Bible, the historicity of the Old and New Testaments remains a subject of crucial importance to students of European culture.

The critical historical analysis—the so-called higher criticism of the Bible—was inaugurated in German universities in the middle decades of the nineteenth century. The work of several great scholars on the Old Testament was brought to fruition by Julius Wellhausen in the 1870's and 1880's. Using the techniques of philological analysis and literary criticism, Wellhausen and the German school concluded that the Hebrew patriarchs and Moses were semimythical figures and cast grave doubts on the historical value of the Hebrew Bible, particularly the Pentateuch. Both the literary-philological techniques and the conclusions of nineteenth-century biblical criticism have been challenged by twentieth-century scholarship. Extensive archaeological work in Israel and Jordan since the 1920's has greatly increased the historical authenticity of the Old Testament accounts of early Hebrew history.

The scholar who has played a pre-eminent role in this very difficult archaeological investigation and historical analysis has been the American William F. Albright. From 1929 to 1958 he was W. W. Spence Professor of Semitic Languages at Johns Hopkins University; since 1958 he has been

Professor Emeritus of Semitic Languages there. He has spent many years in archaeological field work in Palestine and has often lectured at the Hebrew University in Jerusalem. Albright's *From the Stone Age to Christianity* is the classic summary of twentieth-century scholarship on the history of ancient Judaism. This beautifully written book has succeeded in communicating to the widest possible audience the results of several decades of intensive research.

Albright is a soft-spoken and generous person, passionately devoted to biblical scholarship and to Johns Hopkins University. Advancing years and failing health have in no way diminished his enthusiastic pursuit of the truth nor dimmed his extraordinary capacity to place minute archaeological discoveries within a long-range historical perspective.

Chronological Outline

1300 B.C.: A group of Semites, the Hebrews, come out of the Arabian desert and settle between Egypt and Mesopotamia in modern Palestine. The term *Hebrews* includes the nations tracing their ancestry back to Abraham (2100 B.C.) and his brother Harran.

1225–1200 B.C.: Moses leads the Jews out of Egypt. Yahweh is declared the God of Israel.

1028–1013 B.C.: The Israelites under the leadership of King Saul at first defeat the Philistines; Saul is later slain in battle with the Philistines.

1013–973 B.C.: David gains the kingship, unifies Israel, and makes Jerusalem his capital.

973–933 B.C.: The administration of Solomon. Massive public building and growth of trade. The Kingdom of Israel lasts until the conquests of the Assyrians in 722 B.C.

c. 750 B.C.: Amos declares that Yahweh is an international god of justice, and this leads into Isaiah's assertion (c. 550 B.C.) that Yahweh is the only god in existence.

750–550 B.C.: Era of the great prophets—Amos, Ezekiel, Hosea, Isaiah, Micah, Jeremiah.

586–168 B.C.: The Jews under the rule of Babylonia (586–538 B.C.), Persia (538–332 B.C.), the Ptolemies 320–198 B.C.) and the Seleucids (198–168 B.C.).

168–63 B.C.: First rising of the Maccabees led by Judas Maccabaeus.

63 B.C.: Beginning of Roman rule in Judea.

4 B.C.: Birth of Jesus.

33 A.D.: The Crucifixion. The conversion of Paul.

64 AD.: Persecution of Christian sects by Nero. Death of Peter and Paul.

40–80 A.D.: The Four Gospels.

Norman F. Cantor

How do you view the development of historical criticism of the Old Testament, and what are the leading schools of interpretation?

William F. Albright

The so-called higher criticism of the Old Testament may be said to have begun in the late eighteenth century, largely as a result of the impression made on scholars by Wolf's *Prolegomena to Homer.* In the early nineteenth century, schools of historical criticism began to form. They were at first quite naïve, but because they were not very elaborate in structure they proved to be more correct than their successors. In the second quarter of the nineteenth century, H. G. A. Ewald recognized the great importance of early Hebrew poetry, largely on the basis of his profound knowledge of early Arabic literature. In Ewald's day, scholars tended to attribute the so-called priestly document to the earliest time and to call it the *Grundschrift* ($G = P$).

Hegelian categories were introduced into biblical studies through the influence of Vatke and other scholars such as Graf, Kuenen, and Wellhausen. Vatke himself, a disciple of Hegel, was the most important precursor of Julius Wellhausen. Wellhausen was basically not interested in philosophy, but he adopted Hegelian modes of thought although he did not formally state them in his critical analyses of the Old Testament. He utilized the Hegelian concepts of thesis, antithesis, and synthesis, and his scholarly reconstruction spread throughout Germany and all over the world.

Like those of his predecessors and immediate followers, Wellhausen's scholarly analyses were developed almost totally without benefit of any knowledge of the ancient Near East. Wellhausen himself refused to accept the decipherment of cuneiform, and he was very dubious about the decipherment of Egyptian. He never even mentioned such important documents as the Amarna tablets, written mostly in Palestine and southern Syria in the fourteenth century B.C., which shed such a great deal of light on life in Canaan before the Israelite conquest. Wellhausen's point of view was thus altogether too schematic; it lacked an empirical basis and was doomed to be discarded after the recovery of the archaeological past.

About the end of the nineteenth century, H. Gunkel developed the theory of literary forms which is now known as form criticism. He was well aware of the importance of oral tradition, and he realized that a substratum of actual events must underlie Israelite written sources. Gunkel is now best remembered for his work on the Psalms, which he distributed among a series of literary categories.

A number of noteworthy scholars followed Gunkel in the first few decades of the nineteenth century. R. Kittel, J. Pedersen, and other investigators continued to emphasize the importance of early oral tradition, which had first been transmitted by word of mouth and fixed in poetic form. The oral tradition was consolidated on paper, as it were, keeping its poetic meter and stylistic form. It was even more firmly fixed in songs and epic poems which were chanted to the accompaniment of instruments. Virtually all of ancient oral poetry went through this process, and part of it survives in this form today. All over the ancient world, wherever we find evidence of literature, we find that poetry of a region must be treated very seriously by historians. For instance, we are now learning to recognize the great value of the Homeric tradition; it antedated the Greek alphabet and yet was remarkably tenacious in historical detail. Of course there was a great deal of refraction, chronological transposition, and a tendency to snowball descriptions of striking events and charismatic figures. The same mixture of myth and history is characteristic of *Beowulf,* of Islamic folk poetry, and of the early historical traditions of many countries throughout the world. No real exception has been found to the rule that poetry preceded prose in the literatures of Hittites, Phoenicians, Egyptians, Arabs, and other peoples of the Near East.

The early poetry of the Bible provides us with an opportunity to cross-check parallel prose accounts derived from various oral sources. We learn from Canaanite (Ugaritic) epic poetry, which was composed several centuries before it was written down in the fourteenth century B.C., that both long and short poems were transmitted in this manner. For example, the closest of all early biblical poetry to Ugaritic in poetic structure and grammatical features is the "Song of Miriam" in Exodus 15. On this basis we can determine that this poem, which contains a number of passages identical in wording with some that occur in earlier Canaanite literature, is an invaluable historical source which cannot be appreciably later than the time of the Exodus (thirteenth century B.C.). The "Song of Deborah" (Judges 5) is also very archaic and historically valuable. We can, then, correlate the poetic traditions and their prose forms with other known data to reconstruct probable historical backgrounds.

Another rich source of information comes from archaeological sources. Here the information is contained in literally over a million inscriptions of every possible length from long papyrus rolls to short graffiti. Clay tablets and fragments have been found in all parts of the ancient Near East, some from as early as the late fourth millennium B.C. Such archaeological discoveries have proved conclusively that Wellhausen's hypothesis of retrojection—that is to say, his assumption that events and modes of life characteristic of the first millennium had been attributed by late Israelite scribes to the second millennium also—did not occur to any great extent in the transmission of the Hebrew tradition. For instance, names, traditional history, and legal material contained in the early patriarchal narratives have, in general, been shown by archaeology to be reliable. The whole Wellhausen structure has collapsed. Meticulous research among surviving documents and archaeological remains is imperative in order to determine authenticity and date. There is no clear evidence anywhere that later institutions were projected back into the Hebraic past by the later editors of Pentateuchal traditions, as Wellhausen thought.

Knowledge gained from archaeological discoveries during the past few decades has thus overshadowed all previous research on the sources of the Old Testament and the history of the ancient Near East. Scientific archaeology has recast our understanding of archaic times. It demands an empirical approach and types of scientific analysis that were never possible before in biblical studies. Even if no written documents had survived, current archaeological method could fix the character and succession of ancient culture by typological and stratigraphical means. Typology deals with the classification and interpretation of similar objects, wherever found, and stratigraphy, with the study of the successive strata deposited in a mound (or any other site of human occupation) in different ages. Very often strata are separated from one another in a manner which indicates an ancient conflagration or other form of destruction, and this helps us to date the strata by correlating the evidence with other archaeological and literary data. Pottery remains encased in each stratum are often markedly different, again indicating a serious disruption or gap in the history of occupation.

But for direct light on the Bible, the scholar must naturally rely chiefly on the discovery of documents in many scripts and languages. Interpretation of them began in the eighteenth century, and the decipherment of cuneiform scripts in the first half of the nineteenth century gave this work its main impetus. The Egyptian scripts were deciphered about the same time, and since then many more scripts and languages have been decoded. Among them are especially Hittite and other languages of ancient Asia Minor (Anatolia), in different scripts, Hurrian, Urartian, Elamite, Ugaritic, and many other Semitic scripts and dialects, as well as Linear B. In 1966 I published a decipherment of the proto-Sinaitic script, which is the oldest known example of our own ancestral Semitic and Greco-Roman alphabet, although many more inscriptions must be found before we can be sure of all details. Written documents enable us to reconstruct the higher culture and the socio-economic life of ancient civilizations like those of the Akkadians of Mesopotamia, the Canaanites (later Phoenicians), and the Egyptians.

The study of these cultures is extremely important because the biblical tradition stresses the Mesopotamian background of the Patriarchs, who are said to have maintained relations with the region of the Two Rivers for generations. Recent discoveries have confirmed this tradition over and over again. There is now direct evidence that the early Hebrews borrowed extensively from Mesopotamian culture, and that Hebrew tribes from Mesopotamia were the ancestors of the people of Israel. For example, it has recently been demonstrated by the discovery of many new religious texts from Babylonia by S. N. Kramer and W. G. Lambert that most of the cosmogonic traditions of Genesis, chapters 1–11, were derived from Mesopotamian sources. The differences between the accounts of Creation and the Flood are minor and may be explained by the long oral tradition and by the different religious backgrounds of the two cultures. In Israel all of this cosmogonic material was demythologized. All the polytheistic divinities of the earlier account were erased, leaving only one Creator, and all strictly mythological allusions were deleted. In the Hebrew version of Genesis, no reference remains to the battle between the gods and the primordial monsters of chaos. As far as the Hebrews were concerned, Yahweh had always existed; before Him, there was no existence at all—much less any philosophical notion of "pure being."

Another example of borrowing from Mesopotamia is the tradition of customary law that developed among the mixed Hurrian and Semitic settlers of northern Mesopotamia. Both of the Patriarchal cities of Genesis, which existed in northern Mesopotamia at this time—Haran and Nahor—were occupied by mixed populations, according to the testimony of contemporary cuneiform tablets. It has been demonstrated by E. A. Speiser and others that many of the customary practices of the Patriarchs as described in Genesis do not appear either in later Israelite tradition or in the law codes of Babylonia. This customary law was apparently handed down orally through generations of mixed Hurrian and Hebrew communities. Excavations at Nuzi in northern Mesopotamia have brought to light thousands of cuneiform documents from the fifteenth century B.C. which describe traditional Hurrian family law in some detail. Oral transmission of legal traditions has long been the subject of investigation on the part of comparative historians of law; here its control by early Hebrew and cuneiform sources has been exceedingly instructive.

A comparison of the earlier strata of Mosaic law and the Babylonian cuneiform law codes of the eighteenth and seventeenth centuries B.C., especially that of Hammurabi, betrays marked similarity. For example, the *lex talionis*—the principle of an eye for an eye—occurs in both the Babylonian and Mosaic codes. This principle is never stated specifically in the Hammurabi code. It may be noted that these Babylonian codes were all derived from case situations, and the growth of generalized law codes was deferred until the Greek philosophical revolution. The *lex talionis* stands as an early move toward the establishment of more general legal statements. For the first time, equal justice supersedes the practice of the vendetta and the time-honored resort to a scale of different penalties for different social classes.

Would you expand upon the relationship between the religion of the Patriarchs and its Near Eastern background?

It is quite certain, as stated above, that the Babylonians exerted great influence upon the ancient Hebrews. The parallels between the ancient law codes, the family traditions, and the cosmogonic myths and narratives are striking indeed. This influence over Israel was renewed in and after the eighth century B.C., though in less fundamental ways.

Egyptian influence was also important, especially in the age of Moses. During the Middle Empire (2000–1700 B.C.) the Pharaohs extended their imperial control over Palestine and Phoenicia, especially under strong rulers; Egyptian remains are found everywhere. Egyptian domination continued, with relatively short interruptions, until after Israel had occupied Canaan. Egyptian influence is particularly evident in the narratives of Joseph and Moses.

Phoenician culture, basically maritime and commercial, exerted much more significant influence on the Hebrews. Sidon and Tyre, capitals of southern Phoenicia, were only a few hours from the Israelite borders, and the language of northern Israel was virtually identical with the Phoenician tongue. It stands to reason that the culturally rich Phoenicians should have exerted as much influence on the Israelites in the first millennium as had their Canaanite precursors in the second. It is, however, often very hard to tell whether given influences came from the earlier Canaanites or the later Phoenicians.

Several other cultures had direct influence upon certain aspects of Israelite life. The Hittites and Hurrians are two examples. To illustrate, the principle of the covenant between the God of Israel and His people would not be understood today if it were not for the surviving Hittite treaties between a state and its vassal state. Upon analysis by G. E. Mendenhall, these suzerainty treaties were shown to have the same structure as the covenant made between God and Israel in the time of Joshua, about the thirteenth century B.C. Moses, then, appears in a very different light, for we now know that the principle in question was a very ancient Hebrew tradition. The covenant with Abraham has been shown by Speiser to be very archaic. So far we find no trace of the term *berith* (covenant) among non-Israelites except in the form of labor contracts, but it was indispensable to Israelite religious thought.

The early Hebrews began as a trading people. C. H. Gordon has long held the opinion that Abraham was a traveling Hittite merchant. Recent scholarship, however, has established the identity of Ur, Abraham's traditional home, with the Babylonian Ur, so in this respect Gordon is mistaken. Passages in Genesis (20:1; 13:1–3; 15) certainly strongly suggest, on the other hand, that Abraham engaged in caravan trade and became very successful. The trade routes between Egypt and the Negev have been reconstructed from remains of stone structures and pottery fragments of a type common in Palestine between 2000 and 1800 B.C. In those days the camel had not yet been domesticated; the donkey was in wide use throughout the Middle East as a beast of burden between 2300 and 1200 B.C.

(cf. the tradition in Numbers 31). In the late twelfth or early eleventh century B.C., according to Judges 6, the camel came into military use and soon became the chief caravan animal. Before then, against many hundreds of specific references to donkey caravans in Anatolia, Mesopotamia, Syria, Palestine, Arabia, Sinai, Egypt and Nubia, there is not one mention of camel caravans!

As caravan leaders and traders, the Hebrews made contacts and contracts of all possible kinds. Most of their contracts were oral in nature, although sometimes stones were set up to mark the agreement just as we read in Genesis. They contracted with suppliers for donkeys and provisions for the caravan. They had to deal with the chieftains of the territories through which they passed. In short, the covenant type of contract was by far the most important element in their social and economic life. Soon, it was to assume equal importance in their religious life.

It cannot be emphasized too strongly that there is no evidence of a religious revolution after the time of Moses. Any notion that the post-Mosaic religion of Israel departed in any vital way from the Mosaic traditions must be discarded. Y. Kaufmann, the famous Israeli historian, has demonstrated this point in overwhelming fashion. To say that Moses represented the genius of Israel as Plato represented the genius of Greece is probably an overstatement, and yet it would be unthinkable for a figure like Moses to arise from the background of any country other than Israel at that time.

Kaufmann, influenced by the romanticism of his early days, asserted that Moses was a child of the desert, and there I must differ sharply from him. The idea that there is some mysterious connection between the desert and monotheism is sheer nonsense. The pre-Islamic Arabs were anything but monotheistic; the inscriptions of South and North Arabia teem with the names of gods of all kinds, male and female. On the contrary, monotheism must have arisen in a highly developed culture of Egyptian or Mesopotamian type. It is probably no accident that Moses bears an Egyptian name, as did others of his close relatives. In the generation preceding Moses, the Amarna heresy, a sort of monotheism, held sway in Egypt for some twenty years. This was not true monotheism in the later Jewish sense, but it did assert that the only god was the solar disk (Aton). The fact that this god was the solar disk and not the sungod Ra indicates an attempt at abstraction. To be sure, the solar disk did appear in three manifestations, and this concept has been rather anachronistically compared with the Trinity. The solar disk was said to be incarnated in the person of King Amenophis (Akhenaton). Moses appeared just after the decease of this nascent monotheism, and perhaps unintentionally introduced the religious reforms that led into the formation of so much of the Jewish tradition. Perhaps it is the mark of the truly great religious innovator that he never intends to create a new religion, but only to reform an existing one.

There is much reason to believe that Yahweh had spiritual antecedents in Hebrew tradition, especially since He was expressly identified with El-shaddai, the Mountain god, and was also called *Zur*, "the Mountain." The covenant tradition itself was derived from Hebrew experience of the past, and was further developed after Moses by the religious leaders of the community. Moses and his followers were the primary agents in transforming this cultural heritage into theological terms. The inequalities of the old Babylonian law codes of Hammurabi and Eshnunna were eliminated in this refining process. The new codes were strikingly more humane in their treatment of slaves and women, for example. In short, the Mosaic code was remarkably modern in its humanity while it remained faithful to the traditional heritage of Mesopotamian law and family custom. Occasional barbarities of ancient practice survived for a time, but there was an increasing tendency from the time of the Patriarchs to weed them out. Abraham is said to have been willing to sacrifice his son Isaac, but God rescinded the order. We now know that the practice of sacrificing human beings at the death of a king was normal in Ur in the twenty-first century B.C., but it was no longer in vogue in Babylonia in the sixteenth century B.C.

The Yahwism of Israel emerged from the ancient Near East, and its development must be evaluated against this background. One has to consider the general evolution of morality and religion there and view Yahwism as the outstanding facet of this development. The primary elements that the Hebrews distilled from it were the principle of monotheism and the concept of a close reciprocal relationship between a god and his chosen people. The idea of a covenant with the divine, which emerged from quite mundane sources, was translated into the realm of the spiritual and pervades the entire law of Moses and the religion of later Israel. Along with these concepts came empirical rules of sanitation and hygiene, including a dietary ban on animals dangerous to human health and the laws of purity that complemented the spiritual aspects of Hebraic law and still characterize Orthodox Judaism. In modern times, of course, with the enormous advance in medical science, it is no longer necessary for health to carry out some of these provisions in the manner originally intended. They remain, however, part of the covenant between Yahweh and His people. These rules, incidentally, have not been found among any of the other Near Eastern peoples, though many individual regulations can be paralleled either among Egyptians or Babylonians. All the Mosaic laws were directed toward the moral and the spiritual health of the people, and their survival demonstrates the tremendous importance of the work of Moses, which stands as a unique historical achievement.

How do you view the period between Moses and the prophetic age?

In my opinion the probable date for the Exodus is the first decade of the thirteenth century B.C. The conquest of Palestine took place in stages, and we can clearly determine from the traditions that Transjordan was occupied first. For this information it is wiser to consult the older poetic traditions than the prose accounts which were gleaned from them. It must have taken a generation for the Hebrews to consolidate control of Transjordan and move on to western Palestine.

A series of recent archaeological discoveries makes it fairly certain that the critical phase of the conquest of western Palestine came in the third quarter of the thirteenth century, about 1234 B.C. In order to understand what happened, we must remember that according to the later tradition of Israel—particularly the book of Chronicles from the early fourth century B.C. and Jubilees from the early second century B.C.—only a small part of Israel went down to Egypt with Jacob. Both early and late traditions inform us that parts of Palestine were already conquered in the patriarchal age (by which I mean here anywhere before 1400 B.C.). In other words, the Hebrews had already occupied parts of Palestine between the eighteenth and thirteenth centuries B.C. At first, they probably lived in the forested hill country of Palestine and Syria, and they gradually moved into the plains. Most of the Hebrews who migrated to Egypt settled in the extreme northeastern Delta, the Egyptian terminus of the caravan routes of the late Bronze Age between the sixteenth and thirteenth centuries B.C. Since there were close ties of kinship between these Hebrews and those who went on to Egypt, there is reason to believe that the two groups were in cultural contact throughout the period. (We recall that Egypt and Palestine formed a single empire during most of the time between 2000 and 1200 B.C.)

As I have pointed out, all the caravans recorded by the hundreds before about 1200 B.C. in southwestern Asia and northeastern Africa were composed mainly of donkeys. After horses came into general military use in the eighteenth century B.C., horses and especially mules gained rapidly in popularity for many purposes. The chief caravan routes across Sinai were rerouted north of the desert, and roads were built across the sand for chariots and carts. Donkey caravans had lost part of their importance even before the camel became the chief caravan animal.

The main period of the Israelite conquest came after treaties had been made between the newcomers and the established Hebrews in Palestine, as referred to in the book of Joshua. Here there was a new confederation of tribes, all of which accepted the worship of Yahweh and the construction of a central sanctuary. This confederation has been compared to the amphictyonic leagues of ancient Greece and Italy; the analogy is well taken. Of course, this does not mean that we may reconstruct what we do not know about the early Israelite confederation from an analysis of Greek parallels.

The period of the Judges was characterized by attacks from all sides. The editor of Deuteronomy-Second Kings attributed these harrowing experiences to the wrath of Yahweh aroused by Israelite violation of the covenant. There was undoubtedly some backsliding from Mosaic monotheism, and pagan customs were reasserting themselves through the still-thin veneer of monotheistic dogma. The Mosaic system, rather abstract and difficult to understand at the time, was also undeniably drab and demanding. Many Israelites remained attached to ancient pagan customs and beliefs as well as to those of the surrounding Canaanites. We still do not know to what extent Baal, the chief god of the Canaanites, was identified with Yahweh, for the folklore of the Hebrews and the Canaanites was very similar. We do know that many of Baal's attributes were subsequently transferred to Yahweh in the Hebrew Bible itself, not to mention later "backsliding" Israelites. Eventually the very name of Baal was given up by the Israelites, and the change to Yahweh was complete. Evidence for this shift is found in Hebrew personal names and other sources. The documents containing Baal names were contemporary with successive phases of biblical history, whereas the biblical narrative is often difficult to date and pinpoint regionally; it must be critically examined with an eye to possible editorial changes for theological consistency.

Constant harassment from all sides served to consolidate Israel as a single state, much as a single nation is being forged out of the seventy language groups of modern Israel under Arab pressure. During the period of the Judges, the Philistines overran parts of Israel and established trade routes, which they were determined to maintain at all costs. Together with their allies, other Sea Peoples who settled along the coast of Palestine in the late thirteenth and twelfth centuries, they were apparently not interested in absorbing the Israelites but tried to keep them as vassals. To prevent competition they made it as difficult as possible for the Israelites to develop the new art of forging and manufacturing iron implements, thus protecting their own monopoly on iron production.

In the twelfth to eleventh century B.C., the state of Ammon was founded on the fringe of the desert, and the same period saw the expansion of Moab and Edom. At the same time camel caravans were first introduced, and the Phoenicians (who called themselves Canaanites) were admirably equipped to take advantage of the innovation, extending their trade both by land and by sea.

The most remarkable event of the period of the Judges was the appearance of Samuel in the latter part of the eleventh century. The capture of the Ark of the Covenant, together with the slaughter of the priests (which is mentioned specifically in Psalm 78), marked the end of the confederation and the ascendancy of one-man rule in Israel. The traditions concerning the rise of Samuel often conflict, and they must be carefully examined to put the whole movement in perspective. At this point I should like to remark that the use of historical analogy is an extremely delicate and dangerous process. Rather than drawing analogies between isolated circumstances in different periods, ideally we should draw meaningful comparisons between whole eras and processes. Before we can draw any analogies, of course, we must be sure of the chronology of each period. As I have pointed out, one of the key sources for the dating of events in the ancient Near East is analysis of the relation of oral tradition to its written form. An examination of the form and style of the traditions, both poetic and prose, often enables us to date the periods from which they come. We may then examine their content and interpret them historically.

Samuel instituted kingship in Israel, and by founding the prophetic movement he brought into existence the balance of influence between priests and prophets which set Judaism on its historical course. There is an inherent capacity for reform in the Judeo-Christian view of religion that asserts itself periodically. Under Samuel, political and religious reform went hand in hand. This built-in capacity for reform has good analogies for its manifestations throughout the history of Israel and subsequent Judaism as well as its daughter, Christianity. But Samuel does not seem to have planned the course of political and religious transformation which actually took place during the following century or two. The first kings were anointed as *nagid,* "leader," not as *melekh,* "king." The charismatic prophets of Samuel's time became custodians of the civil obligations of covenant law, and had little to do with cultic practice. The tension between priests and prophets was never fully reconciled. Saul, of course, gave the support of the new national state to the reformed, hierarchic priesthood, campaigning against the excesses of the early prophets, who were outside the religious structure of the "Establishment." He rebuilt the Tabernacle and set it up only a few miles from his own home in Gibeah. David brought the Tabernacle to Jerusalem, and his son Solomon built the First Temple.

Dr. C. S. Mann has pointed out that the later prophets can be best understood as representatives of the people who often prosecuted or defended in civil courts. In my opinion, this view is substantially correct. Samuel was said to have "judged" Israel by setting up circuit courts throughout the nation. In fact, he appointed his two sons as judges in these courts. This explains both how the later prophets lived, and why they so often put moral questions in the form of legal cases. For example, in a famous parable Nathan the prophet rebukes David for sending the husband of Bathsheba into the forefront of a battle so that he would be killed. In the Gospels and early rabbinic literature, moral questions were often put into the form of case laws, almost universal in ancient Oriental and early Greek law. All through the Prophets we find a remarkable interest in civil, international, and moral law in general. Yahweh was envisioned as sitting in judgment in the heavenly court upon Israelite infringements of the covenant. In the works of the writing prophets, there are literally scores of descriptions of or allusions to these hypothetical court cases in heaven.

This explains why the prophets from Elijah to Jeremiah took such a great interest in matters of social morality—especially oppression of the poor.

The position of the prophets is comparable in some important respects to the position of the Sophists in classical Athens. According to Athenian law, no man was allowed to hire an attorney to represent him in court—he had to plead his own case. That meant that he needed legal and forensic training, and that is where the Sophists came in. They coached citizens in the principles of law and effective public speaking so that they could defend themselves successfully in court. The Sophists themselves were not allowed to represent their clients. In a somewhat similar way, the evolution of written and common law in Israel necessitated the development of legal abilities among the citizen body. In Second Chronicles we are told that a sweeping reform of the court system took place during the ninth century. This tradition is historically correct, for Ezra—the probable editor of the Chronicles—was himself an accomplished lawyer.

In Egypt also there were two successive reforms of the judiciary system under King Harmais (Haremhab) at the end of the Eighteenth Dynasty in the fourteenth century B.C., and under Ramses II in the thirteenth century B.C. Priests and laymen served together. The addition of priests to the panels of judges was evidently supposed to lend an air of religious authority to the proceedings, and to discourage judicial corruption. Judges had all too often ruled in favor of the side that proffered the larger bribe. It was hoped that the priests would prove to be more honest than the laymen; in Israel, as in Egypt, priests were guardians of the moral and ethical standards of the land.

Someone had to represent the accused before the courts of Israel, and who was better suited to this role than the prophets? This became one of the most important functions of the prophet—explaining the superb poetical and rhetorical qualities of extant prophetic literature. At the same time many prophets continued to be diviners, as their pagan precursors had been, long before Samuel. As the moral reputation and the ethical standing of the prophets rose, a distinction was increasingly made between "true" and "false" prophets. In legal terms, the difference would be that between an honest lawyer and a shyster.

It is hard to see any real evolution of monotheistic ideas in the writing prophets of the Old Testament. The first of these was Amos, who flourished about 750 B.C.; the last was Malachi, whom I should date in the late sixth century B.C. After the sixth century the prophets rapidly disappeared, to be replaced by scribes and learned men (*hakhamim*). Within the period of the prophets, however, we do find a development of political ideas. Under the monarchy of Judah, the house of David was specially sacred; it continued without interruption from David himself until the Babylonian Exile in 587/6 B.C. Saul, David, and Solomon were each anointed *nagid*, or military leader of the kingdom. The term *melekh* or king was not given to them formally. The charismatic *nagid* was supposed to hold office for his lifetime. Inevitably the dynastic principle came into operation, and the Davidic dynasty lasted over four centuries.

After the fall of Samaria in the first months of 721 B.C., the city of Jerusalem became a symbol; since the conquest of David, it had never been destroyed by an invading conqueror. The northern provinces of Palestine never achieved the sense of political continuity of the southern portion, ruled by the Davidic dynasty. This changed after the Exile as Ezekiel tried to re-establish common ground between Israel and Judah. From recently discovered documents it has been ascertained that the movement toward religious reunification of the south and north of Israel—even in exile—increased in strength after the time of Ezekiel.

There was a sharp difference between the attitudes of Isaiah and Jeremiah toward the surrender of the sacrosanct city of Jerusalem. To Isaiah, Jerusalem would remain inviolate. Jeremiah violently rebuked the men of Jerusalem for their idolatry and advised them to surrender to the Babylonians. He thought they had forfeited any right to national independence by their wicked behavior. Perhaps this attitude explains why the prophet Jeremiah was unpopular for centuries after his time, while Isaiah became immensely popular. I have not mentioned Elijah in this connection because we do not have his original oracles and cannot determine just what his views were. For instance, we do not know whether he tolerated the cult of the Israelite temples at Bethel and Dan, or whether he was chiefly interested in eradicating the pagan cult of Baal. There is no doubt about Amos' views, however, since he and the northern prophet Hosea attacked the cult at Bethel very strongly. The motivations in Elijah's time are simply not as clear to us, and in addition the lines of demarcation between pagan heresies and orthodox Yahwism were not so clearly drawn. The young bull (golden calf), for example, traditionally carried Baal standing on his back. After some time the bull was represented alone, and came to have symbolic significance and was reproduced on an Israelite seal of the early ninth century. Yahweh was no longer a visible figure, and the young bull was a symbolic substitute. Such symbols were sometimes borrowed directly from pagan cult and were therefore repudiated by the prophets.

What were the principal teachings of the prophets?

The great interest of the prophets in the world around Israel was governed in part by their interest in law, particularly in civil law and international relations. The striking affinity between the curses invoked on violators of covenants in the prophetic literature and those corresponding sections of certain ancient Near Eastern treaties again illustrates the strong influence of formal covenants between God, Israel, and foreign countries on the prophets. By the very nature of covenant law, the prophets became involved in both foreign relations and civil rights.

An overwhelming interest in legal affairs is evident in the writings of Amos, who put Judah and Israel on the same level as the surrounding countries, since Yahweh ruled over them all. This remarkably broad-minded attitude with regard to international relations and morality is unique in ancient literature. Only in Deutero-Isaiah during the Exile can we find a world view even more universal than that of Amos. This was put forward by the so-called Second Isaiah, who wrote the poems which are included in chapters 40–66 of the collected anthology which circulated under the name of Isaiah.

In Second Isaiah, composed around 540 B.C., the concept of a universal God is stressed more than ever before. Judah had disappeared from existence, the Jewish people were scattered over the world, and the fate of Israel and the nations was inextricably bound together. The Persian king Cyrus appears as the savior of Israel as well as the herald of a new age. This would have been unthinkable to the earlier prophets. There is no evidence anywhere, however, of a new theology or new morality. During the Diaspora, the Jews paid increasing attention to the situation in the countries where they lived, as well as to the possibility of restoring their own nation once more.

To what extent did Hellenistic thought influence the Exilic and post-Exilic development of Judaism?

As a result of my studies during the past decades, I have recently changed my view on this matter. A few scholars have long suggested that skepticism was somewhat earlier than the usual dating. In my opinion, the evidence is now almost conclusive to this effect. To illustrate, the Book of Job is a classical case of the theodicy debate, bearing on divine justice and the inscrutable distance between the moral levels of God and man. This philosophical dilemma does not correspond to any specific philosophical development of later times. Job was certainly not written during the Hellenistic period, as often thought. There is no trace of the sectarian movements of the last pre-Christian centuries in Judaism, nor is there any trace of Greek philosophical influence. Yet the resemblance between the general background of Job and the work of Theognis in the sixth century B.C. has been noted by a number of scholars. It is now clear that Job reflects the higher culture of Phoenicia—its cosmology, astronomy, and esoteric lore. The known Phoenician hierophant or expounder of sacred mysteries was actually in some cases a former divinity himself, as in the case of Taauth (Thoth), who also appears in Job. Others bear names of human type which appear in Ugaritic and other documentary archives of the late Bronze Age. Many of the old gods had been turned into natural forces by the sixth century B.C., both in Phoenicia and in Greece.

In any event, the god Taauth of the Egypto-Phoenician cosmogony is called by the Phoenician skeptic Sanchuniathon the "wisest man who ever was under the sun"—the same expression that is used over and over again in Ecclesiastes, which I date in the fifth century B.C., with reference to Taauth who is spoken of in Job as a person in whom God has placed special wisdom. It may be added that the same expression "under the sun" appears in the same type of context in Phoenician inscriptions from the reigns of Eshmunazor and Tabnit in the early fifth century B.C. Furthermore, it occurs in Euripides (late fifth century B.C.). No really similar expressions are found in later writings. I think we can now prove from classical accounts that Sanchuniathon wrote in the second or third quarter of the sixth century B.C., and that he shares both the skepticism and the quasi-philosophical approach of the Greek thinkers of the sixth century, especially Thales and Anaximander. There are some striking parallels between Job and Phoenician literature on the one hand and the early Ionian philosophers on the other. The common features seem to have been familiar to both Greeks and Phoenicians; with Otto Eissfeldt I consider that the Phoenicians were, in general, the donors. On the other hand, there is no reason to credit the Phoenicians with philosophical originality as such; Thales remains the probable originator of abstract philosophical thought. The author of Job, probably a North Israelite, was profoundly influenced by Phoenician culture and literature. But his religion was thoroughly monotheistic, though scarcely orthodox in the later Jewish sense.

In my opinion, Job was written sometime in the seventh century B.C. or possibly in the early sixth. Ecclesiastes was probably written in the late fifth century. There are no Persian words in Job, but there are several in the later Ecclesiastes. There are no Greek words in either book, no quotation from Greek sources, and no clear reference to any Greek philosophy. On the other hand, we do have the same vaguely metaphysical skepticism in early Greek literature and in Sanchuniathon. So much for the supposed Hellenic influence on Job and Ecclesiastes. I do not mean to suggest for a moment that Job and Ecclesiastes themselves influenced Greek thought. I am merely pointing out that the Phoenicians, the richest maritime people in the world at that time, were an important source of the skeptical point of view which was a necessary prelude to the philosophical thinking of Thales and

Anaximander. There are, of course, other sources of their thought into which we need not enter here.

We know next to nothing about Jewish sectarian life in the sixth and fifth centuries B.C. What we do know suggests that there was much more variety in this society than was commonly thought by most scholars. A recent discovery of papyri from this period in Egypt has demonstrated that the Jewish colony founded at Elephantine was, to say the least, not orthodox. They had several divinities with the rather improbable names of Anat-Bethel and Eshem-Bethel, who received monetary contributions paid into the temple of *Yahu* (the usual shortened form of *Yahweh*). The mixed religion of the Jewish colonists in Egypt thus had pagan elements combined with pre-Exilic Hebrew religious tradition.

Since Job contains no scriptural quotations, it was probably written before the canonical form of the early books of the Old Testament was first systematically edited in the seventh century B.C. (Ecclesiastes also shows no use of Scripture), yet the God of Job is unmistakably the God of Israel. The morality of Job is the covenant morality of Israel. Job might question divine justice, but he accepted it in the end. The God of Ecclesiastes, while a much vaguer figure, is also the God of Israel, though Ecclesiastes takes a much more skeptical view of God's role in the world than does Job. While Ecclesiastes recognized that he was dealing with the God of Israel and the creator of the world, to whom he was accountable, he still doubted the operation of God's justice in the world. Such doubt would have been all but impossible in earlier Hebraic times. The men of Samaria and the people of Gilead also seem to have had highly heretical views at this time, but unfortunately we know very little about them. We do know that they had their own temples. This heresy disappeared without a trace in the forced conversion of Samaria to Sadducee Judaism about 130 B.C., and the sect of Samaritans with which we are familiar in later times was much less extreme.

I believe that no part of the Hebrew Bible can be dated with any confidence later than the fourth century B.C., except for Daniel, which almost certainly dates from the early second century B.C. Since we have no other documents from the fourth and very few from the early third century (aside from a few books of the Apocrypha), there is not enough evidence to outline the development of the later sects in detail. We can say only that before the end of the third century B.C., the Wisdom of Ben Sira shows an orthodox Judaism of the same type as that of the later books of the Hebrew Bible, which later developed into the Sadducee teaching. Ben Sira does not mention the resurrection or angels and has little to say about other matters which became part of the Pharisee point of view. It is true that Ben Sira is more predestinarian than the Sadducees are said to have been, but since no known Sadducee literature is extant, it is very difficult to determine their exact theological positions. The Pharisees are said to have been strongly predestinarian, and we know that they arose as a distinct sect in the early or middle decades of the second century B.C. It is probable that the Sadducees appeared as a distinct sect about the same time, though the origin of both sects must be traced back into early post-Exilic times. The discovery of the Dead Sea Scrolls has enormously extended our understanding of the development of Jewish sects; we can at last reconstruct the history of the Essenes in considerable detail, now that we have a substantial part of their literature as well as many books and fragments of books which they considered with favor.

Archaeology, numismatics, and paleography have definitely dated the scrolls and fixed their place and date of origin. Paleographic research has, of course, played a key role in the dating of the scrolls. The discoveries of Wadi Daliya have produced a quantity of fragments dating between the 380's and the 330's B.C. The latest forms of script shown on these papyri and sealings, found in the Jordan Valley north of Jericho, are almost identical with the script of the earliest fragments from Qumran. We know now that these fragments must date no later than the first half of the third century B.C. The script is also very close to that of some of the Edfu papyri from Egypt, which date from the reign of Ptolemy Philadelphus (285–246 B.C.). The latest date of the Qumran material, as fixed partly by numismatics and partly by Josephus, is A.D. 68, when the Romans devastated the land of Judaea before laying siege to Jerusalem. The manuscripts from Qumran thus span almost 350 years, with most of the written material dating to the first century B.C.

The Essene sect appears to have developed out of the "early pietists (Hasidim)" after about 160 B.C. The Essenes were closely related to the Pharisees, and indeed formed a kind of radical wing. The War Scroll has been attributed to the Zealots and not to the Essenes, but this view will not hold because of the clear evidence, both geographical and descriptive, of Josephus and other ancient writers. On the other hand, it is quite true that the War Scroll does lean toward attitudes similar to those of the Zealots. In the War Scroll we find references to angels (e.g., the angel Michael) which are quite different from anything else in Essene literature. Yet it is clear that the author of the War Scroll (probably in the second half of the first century B.C.) had Essene interests in mind. Apparently, we must infer that many Essenes became Zealots and that splinter-groups of the Essenes were of Zealot origin. It is well known that the Zealots' career began about A.D. 8, and ended with the destruction of the fortress of Masada by the Romans in A.D. 73. Essenes also played a role in the First Revolt of the Jews against the Romans in A.D. 66–70.

Perhaps the most important aspect of the Qumran discoveries is the light they shed upon the dating of the so-called inter-Testamental books—that is, the books of the Apocrypha and Pseudepigrapha which have often been dated quite erroneously. Tobit probably dates from the Persian period, apparently about the fifth or fourth century B.C. instead of two or three centuries later. The reason for such an early dating is not only its content, but also the fact that some of the Qumran fragments are in good Imperial Aramaic. This, the normal language of the Persian Empire, rapidly changed after the fall of the empire. Judith also seems to date from the Persian period. Even clearer is the evidence of Qumran for the dating of the different parts of Enoch, which can now be assigned with certainty to Hebrew and Aramaic originals of the second century B.C. and a little later. Other books are still later in origin, such as Wisdom, written originally in Hebrew and Greek; the latter shows strong Hellenistic influence. Surprisingly enough, Greek thinking influenced the Apocrypha only to a very minor extent, which again indicates its relatively early age. In this connection, it must be remembered that the Essene literature known from Qumran, which dates chiefly from the period 160–40 B.C., seems to have borrowed surprisingly little from Greek sources. For example, there do not appear to be any Greek loanwords in the manuscripts from Qumran (though Greek proper names do occur sparingly). Yet, even here, Greek influence has penetrated, for we do have, for the first time in Jewish literature, part of a theological creed presented in the "Manual of Discipline" written almost certainly before 100 B.C. In the Old Testament, there indeed are what are sometimes called kerygmatic passages, which give a brief summary of the acts of God on behalf of Israel. There is not, however, anything that may be called a creed in the Greek sense of the term. Thus, the presence of even a portion of a creed in the "Manual of Discipline" suggests that some time had elapsed since the superficial Hellenizing of the Eastern world by Alexander the Great and the publication of the "Manual."

It is probable that the theological differences between the Sadducees and the Pharisees were due partly to indirect Greek influence. The Old Testament contains passages which are quite deterministic, passages that express attitudes of free will, and passages that question the immutability of the will of God. Nowhere, however, can one find any sort of systematic presentation of either determinism or free will. The Pharisees and Essenes, on the other hand, show a thoroughly predestinarian attitude. This almost certainly means that Greek philosophical approaches had begun to influence religious thought in Jewish circles about this time. Thinking men were prodded into greater consistency; they brought systematic reasoning into theology after the Greek manner. Previously, logic had been empirical; it now began to develop along formal Greek lines.

If more were known about the culture of Hellenistic Jews, our inferences would be on much firmer ground. Unfortunately, no significant new material on the religion of Hellenistic Jewry has turned up in recent years. Much more is known about the social and political milieu of the Jews living in Egypt under the Lagide dynasty founded by Ptolemy I in 323 B.C., in the other Greek states, and in the early Roman Empire.

How do you perceive the development of historical criticism of the New Testament?

New Testament criticism began about the same time as that of the Old Testament, but it was not clearly formulated until well into the second quarter of the nineteenth century with the rise of the Tübingen school. This school, founded by F. C. Baur, was avowedly Hegelian in its approach, and the classic thesis, antithesis, and synthesis formed the logical categories of its structure. The thesis was Petrine Christianity, the antithesis was Pauline Christianity, and the synthesis was the post-apostolic Church.

After this school came a period of confusion, during which leading Dutch scholars dated most of the New Testament as late as the second century A.D. This period of transition was ended by the emergence of the *Religionsgeschichtliche Schule,* the school of the History of Religions. This school's basic premise was the influence of the "mystery" religions, especially the Eleusinian and Mithraic, but also the mysteries of Isis, and so on. It was believed by many that the mysteries were all pre-Christian, and that Christianity evolved directly from them.

In 1919, criticism of the New Testament based on literary forms appeared in independent publications by Martin Dibelius and Rudolf Bultmann. Though based largely on the older work of H. Gunkel (Old Testament) and E. Norden (*Kunstprosa*), it soon changed its character. Bultmann later transferred the emphasis from form to interpretation. In this way, he altered the entire concept of form criticism as foreshadowed by Gunkel after he moved to Marburg, where he came under the strong influence of Martin Heidegger, the founder of recent existentialism. According to Bultmann, not only was the earliest Christianity Gnostic in type, it was also greatly influenced by the mystery religions. All had to be reinterpreted on the basis of existentialism. This was the philosophy fathered by Kierkegaard in the second quarter of the nineteenth century. Kierkegaard was a refugee from Hegelianism as well as from established Danish Lutheranism. He was more of a poet than an historical thinker, and his own ideas were tinged with more than a little Gnosticism. When his point of view was adopted by the so-called phenomenological school of E. Husserl, it was changed into a systematic ontology. Heidegger began as a pupil of Husserl but eventually became so distinct that his position was labeled as *existentialism,* a term which he often tried to repudiate—but without success.

Bultmann became an ardent disciple of Heidegger. He decided that the whole of the New Testament should be demythologized, which in his terminology meant that it should be interpreted in existential terms. The concepts of the New Testament were to be classified in existential categories: the place of man in the universe and his relation to the basic facts of his existence. The outcome was very strange, for Bultmann produced an analysis which had practically nothing to do with the history of ideas or philological analysis of meaning. His approach to the New Testament was characterized by a totally unhistorical treatment of its Jewish background. Furthermore, Bultmann actually tried to interpret Greek philosophers existentially, with results which astounded A. D. Nock, the great historian of Hellenistic and Roman religion. Bultmann's premise was that existential philosophy could be applied to any history, and although a small school of existentialist historians has now come into existence at Heidelberg, there is as yet no concrete evidence that any addition to our understanding of history can be made by the translation of facts of experience into the abstract language of ad hoc existential structures. In my opinion, while existential points of view may be useful in calling attention to philosophical or theological problems, they cannot be used effectively in any historical research except in appraising the intellectual and cultural life of our own time.

Within the past quarter century two archaeological discoveries have completely revolutionized our approach to New Testament problems. The first was the discovery of scrolls and fragments at Qumran, Masada, and Murabba'at. The second was the discovery of early Gnostic and Hermetic codices (bound volumes) at Chenoboskion in Upper Egypt about the same time as the discovery of the Dead Sea Scrolls. Both the Dead Sea Scrolls and the Chenoboskion codices are now in process of publication. While the greater part remains to be published, we already know a great deal about the unpublished material. These discoveries have so completely transformed our whole approach as to antiquate all past critical schools. It must be remembered that the same thing has happened in Old Testament studies, where the school of Wellhausen, for example, was founded before the basic archaeological discoveries were even planned. Here also, the dominant Wellhausen school was largely demolished by scientific analysis.

If anything is clear today, it is that the New Testament stands historically between Qumran and Chenoboskion—by this I mean between the formative period of Jewish sectarianism and that of Gnosticism. The finds at Chenoboskion have corroborated the Church Fathers to a wholly unexpected extent. Most of the Church Fathers apparently wrote with extreme care and tried to follow the best sources. Their late Roman age was one in which original scholarship had largely been replaced by compilation and synthesis. A scholar was judged by his accuracy. Karl Mras, editor of the critical edition of Eusebius for the Austrian Academy of Sciences, demonstrated in a recent series of studies that Eusebius was extremely accurate in quotations and citations. It is often possible to correct and confirm passages in our editions of ancient Greek authors by comparing quotations from them in Eusebius. These quotations almost invariably turn out to be correct, if not altered by the errors of later copyists.

In any event, the rehabilitation of the Church Fathers means that we can no longer assume that their statements can be discarded at will. The Church Fathers all agreed in naming Simon Magus as the founder of Gnosticism. They also traced the origin of the only Gnostic sect mentioned by name in the New Testament—the Nicolaitans—to Nicholas of Antioch, who is mentioned as a deacon in the book of Acts. Gnosticism, therefore, originated in about the late thirties or forties of the first century A.D., and not sometime toward the end of the first century and into the second. Almost all modern writers agree that the so-called mythological Gnostics—namely, the Simonians, Nicolaitans, and related groups—preceded the philosophical Gnostics founded by Valentinus in the second quarter of the second century A.D. Among the Coptic volumes of the Chenoboskion hoard are a number of treatises of the mythological Gnostics. According to the discoverer of the nature of the hoard of manuscripts, Jean Doresse, some of these Gnostic writings may be traced to the immediate disciples of Simon and perhaps to Simon himself. However this may be, we must note that there is no influence from any of these Gnostic systems on New Testament writers and even less, if possible, in the Dead Sea Scrolls. The latter do have a form of theological dualism, but there is nothing Gnostic about it.

In Gnostic systems, the Jewish God of the Old Testament was identified with Satan. He was contrasted with the God of the New Testament who was incorporated into a kind of Gnostic pantheon headed by the highest God, who was pure light and could not be reached by ordinary human beings. Gnosticism was a relatively late import, chiefly from Iranian sources with a strong Greek infusion on a foundation of sectarian Judaism and ancient oriental paganism. Nothing could be more remote from Gnosticism as we now understand it than the Dead Sea Scrolls. Much the same is true of the New Testament, although the latter is closer to the beginnings of Gnosticism, whose founder was a former Samaritan diviner briefly converted to Christianity. Some of the problems that troubled the Gnostics also disturbed the authors of the New Testament. They were conscious, however, of the dangers of Gnostic thought, which are mentioned in several places.

The approach to New Testament problems now has new tools. For example, the terminology of the Gospel of John, which is in part so different from that of the Synoptic Gospels, is now recognized as derived from the words and phrases of Essene literature. The theological differences, though very much greater than the similarities, do not cancel them out. Recent attempts to compare John to the Hermetic writings are just as impossible as previous attempts to connect John with imaginary Gnostic sources. There is nothing Hermetic in John. It must be observed that Hermetic literature may now be dated more accurately, thanks to Coptic translations of Hermetic treatises found in the hoard of Chenoboskion. These treatises are definitely older in content than the extant medieval corpus of Hermetic writings. More archaic Egyptian mythology is preserved in the Hermetic writings from Chenoboskion than in the works preserved by the medieval alchemists. Yet the total of Egyptian mythology even in the Chenoboskion codices is relatively small. Moreover, the early alchemists, with whom the Heretic writings are connected by a rich later tradition, cannot have flourished in the second or third centuries, as was supposed by students of the past generation, but lived in the fourth or fifth century A.D. These alchemists cultivated the Hermetic literature. All the Gnostic materials found at Chenoboskion were certainly copied no later than the fourth century A.D.; it goes a long way toward proving that the composition of the Hermetic writings found with them can be dated somewhere between the second and fourth centuries A.D., when Egyptian religion was falling to pieces. Hermetic literature was then much too late to influence John. However, an influence in the opposite direction is quite likely, because there can be no doubt that John was a popular Gospel among the Gnostics, who interpreted it along Gnostic lines. Since Hermeticism was itself a kind of pagan gnosis, we can draw this line of development without hesitation.

Among new tools of research is our greatly improved knowledge of the linguistic background of the New Testament. We now know that the everyday Greek of the New Testament, *Koine* (nonliterary Greek), is in part an adaptation of Hebrew and Aramaic to the popular language of the Greek-speaking world. This does not mean, as thought by some scholars, that the New Testament books were actually translated from original Hebrew and Aramaic writings, but rather that the men who wrote them were Jews who were familiar with Hebrew and Aramaic. (We shall discuss the case of St. Paul later.)

In the case of the Gospels, we now recognize the Essene background of the phraseology of John. We can also see that many of the sayings of Jesus and the narratives in the Synoptic Gospels were translated into Greek from Hebrew or Aramaic oral tradition. It is now often possible to change the usual translation to adapt it to obvious Hebrew or Aramaic oral tradition. Recently it has become clear what an almost complete break occurred in the continuity of Jewish and Christian life in Palestine as a result of the First Jewish Revolt (A.D. 66–70), with the destruction of Jerusalem and the leveling of all known Jewish places of worship in other parts of Palestine. Not a single synagogue of Galilee survived the war, and most were not rebuilt until the late second century.

The situation was even worse for the Christians, because they were regarded as Jews by the pagans (including the Roman legions) and as traitors by the Jews. Therefore, they were massacred by the pagans and ostracized by the remaining Jews. We are told by Eusebius that the Christians who fled from Jerusalem before the siege found refuge at Pella in the northern Jordan Valley. This, of course, does not mean that they settled there, because it was simply an oasis in the Jordan Valley surrounded by their enemies. It could only have been a base for further migration to Syria and Mesopotamia. These Christians carried their oral tradition with them, and this underlies the Syriac translation of the Gospels. Strangely enough, this has been overlooked in recent times, but virtually all the place and personal names of Aramaic origin in the Gospels are correctly spelled in Syriac. This would not have been possible if the translation had been made from the later Greek text. In the Syriac recensions of the second or third century A.D., we have clear evidence of the persistence of the original oral tradition in the case of proper names. The natural corollary of this is that these names were part of an oral tradition that included many if not most of the extant Gospel narratives and sayings of Jesus. This does not mean that we may simply transcribe the Syriac back into the original Aramaic, but it does mean that key words and often key phrases have been preserved in substantially their original form. We have found this principle extremely useful in our work on the Gospel of Matthew. No longer can we say that either Hebrew or Aramaic was the major source of the Semitic influence, because while nearly all Palestinian Jews could read and many could speak Hebrew, they all spoke Aramaic. Therefore, we must depend on the context and character of the material to form an opinion about the specific language. Thanks to the Dead Sea scroll finds, we now have rich material for both the literary and spoken Hebrew of the time, as well as for the written Aramaic, which was then close to the spoken tongue.

The Gospel of John seems to translate Hebrew, though it is often hard to tell whether the original was in Hebrew or Aramaic. The Apocalypse (Revelation), which probably drew on Hebrew sources, is difficult to pinpoint for similar reasons. After all, Hebrew and Aramaic were then closer than Spanish and Catalan, or French and Provençal.

One of the most unexpected discoveries at Qumran was that commentaries on biblical books were already being written in the first century B.C. by Essene scholars. It had previously been supposed that no Jewish commentaries were written before the Middle Ages. Just as the Egyptians and Babylonians wrote commentaries on their ancient books, so the pre-Christian Jews did. (An esoteric commentary on Homer in the fourth century B.C. Greek script has recently turned up in mainland Greece.) There is a remarkable difference, however, between the Qumran commentaries and the kind of exegesis of the Old Testament which we find in the Pauline Epistles. On the other hand, while we do find a certain amount of what may be called early allegorical exegesis (*haggada*) in the Pauline Epistles, the interpretation of Scripture is generally literal, like rabbinical *peshat*. That is, it is based on the logical norms of hermeneutics and a relatively literal understanding of the text. This is very different from the Essene method and even from the Hellenizing metaphysics of Philo of Alexandria (which often reminds one of the existential exegesis of Bultmann).

St. Paul was a member of the school of Hillel the Elder, because he was, as stated in Acts, a student of Hillel's grandson, Gamaliel the Elder. Thanks to the work of Saul Liebermann and David Daube, it is clear that the rabbinic tradition according to which the exegetical norms (the *middot*) were introduced by Hillel is correct. These *middot* are strictly logical in character and follow the principles of Alexandrian hermeneutics. It is hard to imagine a greater difference than that between the exegesis of Qumran and that of the school of Hillel. Naturally, it took some time for the exegetical methods of the Alexandrian school—adopted by most Pharisees—to prevail over the older methods. Unfortunately, we do not know to what extent Shammai agreed with Hillel on the *middot*. By the time of Paul, however, the schools had pretty well merged so far as hermeneutic methods were concerned, even though they may have disagreed over details of the resulting interpretation.

The Dutch scholar van Unnik has elegantly demonstrated that Paul came to Jerusalem when he was very young and enrolled in the school of Hillel, the head of the Pharisee teachers. This puts an end to the long debate as to whether or not Paul received a good Greek education in Tarsus. There is not a trace anywhere in Pauline writing of any real knowledge of classic Greek literature. The true Greek scholar was supposed to know Homer and the Greek dramatists by heart, and there is not a trace of this in Paul's writings. He was thoroughly acquainted with Pharisee and Essene ideas as well as with the teachings of the infant Church. He must have known Greek perfectly well for ordinary purposes; he quoted proverbial sayings and was eloquent in *Koine*. At every step, however, he betrays his lack of a formal Greek education. There is no evidence that he himself read Scripture in the Septuagint version; he must have known by heart the books then regarded by the Pharisees as canonical, and his editors often must have inserted the standard reading of the Greek Bible (the Septuagint).

Since most of the Epistles of Paul were certainly published before any of the extant Gospels, it is best to deal with his theology first. We have already spoken of Paul's background, and now we should stress some of his doctrinal views. Of all his views, the best known is undoubtedly his strong revulsion against written and oral law. By written law, I mean the particular legislation found in the Hebrew Bible and possibly a few early books that may have circulated among the Pharisees, like the recently recovered but still unpublished Temple Scroll. The oral law was a body of law and custom still transmitted by word of mouth; it was probably not written down until after their codification in the second to fourth century A.D. Paul's revulsion against the law was rather extreme—it certainly went far beyond the dislike Jesus felt for some of the oral case law of his time. From the standpoint of his mission to the Gentiles, it won many converts, but it undoubtedly resulted in the decay of personal hygiene, safety from infection and contagion, and so on, until the rise of nineteenth-century pathology.

Paul was much disturbed by the emphasis placed upon good works, and he began to emphasize faith. The Pauline use of the term *faith* is partly Hebrew and partly Greek. In part, he means *emunah* —loyalty to the covenant; in part, he means *pistis*—a confidence in God and His ways which should take precedence over any emphasis upon works. Some of the apostles objected strenuously to Paul's interpretation, as we know from the controversy between Peter and Paul in Acts and from the Epistle of James, in which works are strongly emphasized: "Faith without works is dead." Paul's concept of faith, which was a blend of Jewish and Greek ideas, is a vital element in Christianity, and his point of view has been followed by Augustinians, Lutherans, and Calvinists, together with many other Catholic and Protestant bodies.

Another important doctrine of St. Paul was his extension of the Essene concept of the perpetual war between good and evil. In the Gospels, this point of view is reflected in certain rather concrete instances, but we do not find the general tone that is so evident in the Pauline material. This aspect of Paul's teachings has only become clear since the publication of some of the Dead Sea Scrolls; it has been emphasized by K. G. Kuhn and K. Stendahl in recent years. Not only was there conflict on earth between good and evil, but it extended to the entire cosmos. This cosmic war was carried on between divine and satanic forces of vague character. Paul uses terms originating among astrologists and commonplaces of cosmology at that time; they were later picked up by the Gnostics, who developed them along non-Pauline lines. At times we do not know just what Paul means by them, and one must always be wary of the context in which they are used. The forces of evil and good in the cosmos are not clearly defined, and there is no hint of a belief in astrology on the part of St. Paul. It remains a moot question as to whether or not belief in such superhuman powers was accepted by orthodox Pharisees at that time.

It must again be emphasized that there is absolutely nothing specifically Gnostic in Pauline teaching, nor is there anything which indicates any interest in mystery religions. The use of the term *mysterion* in the sense of "divine decree" or "divine secret" has nothing to do with the term *mysteria,* which the Greeks applied to the "mystery" cults springing up around them. This was vigorously pointed out by A. D. Nock before the publication of the first Dead Sea Scrolls, and his suggestion that the term might be of Jewish origin has proved to be correct. It has been demonstrated by R. E. Brown that the terminology of *mysterion* is continuous; the term began in early Hebrew as *sôd,* "decision," which then came to mean "secret," Iranian *raz;* in this sense the word passed into Greek as *mysterion.* Greek plural *mysteria,* used of secret cults, never appears in the New Testament, whereas the use of *sôd* and *raz* is the same in the Dead Sea Scrolls and the Pauline Epistles. Nock's point of view has been completely corroborated, and there can no longer be any possibility that Paul borrowed from mystery religions. This does not mean that there may not be a common source for certain *mythologoumena* in the mystery religions and *theologoumena* in the New Testament, but simply that possible common origins had been buried deep in antiquity, and that it is so far impossible to establish anything but vague analogies. That there were ties connecting some ancient myths of the Near East to later Judaism and Christianity is certain. But these connections were very long-range and they were deeply embedded in the very nature of visions and apocalyptic imagery from the most remote antiquity. A distinguished Catholic New Testament scholar has coined the term *des mythes baptisés*. We might equally well use the term *des mythes circoncis*. I might be misunderstood, but the fact stands that demythologized elements are found in both Judaism and Christianity, and that both religious groupings are the richer for their presence.

What differences do you find among the Four Gospels?

The words and acts of Jesus were handed down by oral tradition and put into their present form between A.D. 60 and 70—even according to the view of the late Erwin Goodenough, who was in some respects very radical. The usual idea—that all of them, with the possible exception of Mark, must be dated after the destruction of the Second Temple (A.D. 70)—is fallacious, and the discovery of papyrus manuscripts of the Gospels has directly disproved a second-century dating. We do not know nearly enough about the life of Jesus on the basis of Gospel tradition to write a biography, but the evidence of the Greek and Syriac Gospels has given us enough information to cross-check our sources. There is no basis whatsoever for the idea that the early Christian Church invented or rewrote any part of the extant sayings of Jesus as recorded in the Gospels to satisfy ecclesiastical or dogmatic needs. It is clear that the Gospel tradition was preserved because of its value for the young Church. In other words, sayings which were not particularly significant or striking were probably not retained and were soon forgotten. By preserving the cream, so to speak, the quality of all surviving tradition is greatly enhanced. There are several forms of discourse: parables, miracle narratives, and so on. These special literary forms and other similar types are present in all biblical tradition as a matter of course, and it is generally impossible to fix the date of the traditions themselves on the basis of mere literary form.

Thanks to recent archaeological discoveries, we can not only place the teaching of Jesus squarely between the formative period of Essenism and that of Gnosticism, we can also establish its Jewish origin. Many features of Jewish messianic belief can be documented from the finds at Qumran, as well as on the apocryphal or pseudepigraphic literature which has survived and which can be dated much more accurately in the light of Qumran. The messianic interpretation of the Old Testament in the Gospel of Matthew shows that its author was very learned in Scripture. He included passages of the Old Testament that have not generally been associated with the messianic faith of the earliest Christians. It is also clear that Jesus was influenced by what may be called the orthodox Jewish tradition as represented by the Pharisees, as well as by the unorthodox Jewish sect of the Essenes, reflected (with drastic changes) by John the Baptist.

John the Baptist began as an Essene

and ended as the founder of a new sect distinct from both Christians and Essenes. Unfortunately we know comparatively little about his teachings, though we do know that the scattered traditions about him in the Gospels are well supported by what we know of Essene beliefs and practices. John came from a Zadokite family of priests and was educated in the desert by Zadokites (Essenes); he reacted against certain ideas and practices of the Essenes, and he kept others. For instance, for him baptism became a sacramental indication of salvation, not just a rite of purification. It is also clear that he expected the end of the age to come at any moment, and that some of his followers identified him with Elijah *redivivus*. John's execution by Herod Antipas seems to have triggered the series of events which ended with the Crucifixion.

There is no evidence that Jesus rejected any of the written law, nor is there any proof that he was opposed to all oral law. He does object to certain aspects of the oral law which in his opinion were of a pettifogging (casuistic) nature. In our commentary on Matthew, C. S. Mann and I try to show that the parables are actually generalized case laws. In other words, they are examples of the case-law form employed for pedagogical purposes —to clarify and drive home various teachings of Jesus. The term *hypocrites* applied to the Pharisees does not mean what it means today, for it comes from the Greek *hypokrino,* "to make sharp distinctions," to use clever exegesis in order to interpret the law to the satisfaction of a few. As is well known, in later Talmudic jurisprudence many earlier laws were revised and amended to make them applicable to the contemporary needs. It is noteworthy that most of Jesus' objections to the legal casuistry of the Pharisees had to do with the cultic law of the Second Temple, the way in which dues were collected, and the costs of ceremonial acts. We have substituted the term *casuist* or *pettifogger* for the quite erroneous *hypocrite*. Jesus was not opposed to the law per se, but rather to its misapplication. We must remember that little of this kind of cultic detail is preserved in the second-century Mishnah, edited a century or more after the destruction of the Temple. It is quite possible that Jesus and his followers disliked the new hermeneutics of Hillel because of the casuistry it encouraged; on the other hand, it has been repeatedly shown that there is a marked similarity between the liberal, humanitarian approach of Hillel and that of Jesus. So we may assume that the teachings of Hillel and Jesus were much closer than the relations between Jesus and the Pharisees half a century later. To repeat, there is no proof that Jesus rejected the written law or that he rejected all of the oral law. The background of Jesus was much broader and more diversified than usually thought. He knew Jewish law well, and in Matthew we have a narrator who was particularly interested in this aspect of Jesus' teaching. He was equally familiar with the teachings of John the Baptist and probably with those of the Essenes. In John the apostle we have a narrator who came almost certainly from among the disciples of John the Baptist and was specially interested in this aspect of the teaching of Jesus. Mark almost certainly preserved Petrine tradition in the main, and Luke, drawing largely on his own investigations, followed the same oral source (*Q*) as Matthew, to which he added traditions which he collected himself.

To recapitulate briefly, all the authors of the New Testament were Jews. The only possible exception is Luke, but he shows special interest in the background of John the Baptist, good knowledge of Jewish beliefs and practices, and records a wide range of Jewish reactions. Luke is a typical Latin freedman's name, one adopted by the free son of a formerly enslaved father. The traditional view of the Eastern Orthodox Church was always that Luke was a Jew; it is only in the West that he was believed to have sprung from non-Jewish origins.

I accept the view of Goodenough that there is no clear evidence for an evolution of doctrine within the books of the New Testament. What we have are the reactions of different early Christians to the traditions surrounding the life and teaching of Jesus. In Goodenough's opinion, all the books of the New Testament were written within half a century and more probably within thirty to forty years, say between A.D. 40/50 and 80.

What were the sources of the later character of the Church?

This question requires a complex answer. There can be no doubt that Christianity did develop very early into a sacramental, sacerdotal, hierarchic organization, but this was not out of keeping with the previous history of Israel and early Judaism. The entire sacrificial system of Israel was essentially sacramental. That is to say, sacral offerings were made in which there was an undefinable but real relationship between the offerer, the offering, the divinity, and the purpose/effect of a rite. The old sacrifice became symbolic, but the sacramental element was there from the beginning through the fall of the Second Temple in A.D. 70. We do not know exactly how the Last Supper developed, but it seems to have been a combination of the celebration of Passover and that of the communal meal after the establishment of the Messianic age, which was foreshadowed by a communal meal before this event. It was a long tradition, that culminated in the Eucharist.

The sacerdotal element was also present in Judaism from the time of the Judges, if not from that of Moses, when there was a chief priest who presumably corresponded to the high priest of Ugarit and other nearly contemporary centers of the ancient Near Eastern world. After the Exile, the priests became much more important than they had been between the time of Samuel and the fall of the First Temple in 587/6 B.C. The High Priest, as representative of the Persian king, reigned over the vassal state of Judah. This continued through much of the fourth and even of the third century B.C. under the Ptolemies. The priesthood of the early Christian Church developed from the institution of elders, which was important among both Essenes and Pharisees. The term *sacerdotal* is drawn from pagan Roman terminology.

The hierarchic organization was also of pre-Christian origin. Among the Essenes, overseers (*mebaqqerim*) were appointed to manage the affairs of the community. These *mebaqqerim* included both laymen and priests. Although the context is somewhat ambiguous, it seems that there were twelve laymen and three priests on the ruling council. The term *bishop* goes back to the Greek *episkopos* (overseer), which renders Hebrew *mebaqqer*. There is now no reason to deny the Pastoral Epistles to St. Paul because bishops are mentioned, because the Essenes had developed this simple hierarchic organization at least a century and a half before. It must be confessed, however, that the institution of bishop as described in the Pastoral Epistles of Paul and the Essene "Damascus Covenant" is quite different from the form it took in the Christian Church of the late second and third centuries A.D. However, the institution may safely be traced back through the Essenes, in view of other far-reaching parallels between early Christian and Essene organization. The overseer became a bishop, aided by his committee of elders and by various deacons (ministers). Nowhere do we find any abrupt break in the underlying Christian continuity, but it cannot be denied that there was a great break in A.D. 66–70 between the early Christians and the general body of Judaism. From then on the Christians were not just another splinter-sect of Judaism but a new world religion which was destined to spread over most of the world, but never to lose its unique relation to the older faith from which it sprang.

4

Greek Civilization

H. D. KITTO

THE HISTORIOGRAPHICAL CONTEXT

In the past hundred years no aspect of European history has been more intensively studied by an unsurpassed array of great scholars than Greece from the middle of the second millennium to the fourth century B.C. And this is only as it should be, for in ancient Greece, and particularly in Athens, lies the fount of Western civilization. After all the effort devoted to explaining the rise of Greek civilization, we still stand in awe and wonder at what these people achieved in literature, philosophy, and art, in political theory and the arts of government, in their perception of human nature, and in their formulation of human values.

The analysis of the roots of Greek civilization has greatly benefited from the archaeological work that has contributed a persuasive knowledge of the Mycenean civilization of the mid-second millennium B.C. Modern interpretation has also been distinguished by the subtle relating of political and social change with intellectual and cultural trends.

Among the many brilliant efforts by English-speaking scholars to explain Greek civilization to the student and lay reader of today, H. D. Kitto's *The Greeks* (1962) is pre-eminent by virtue of its felicitous style, and at the same time its simplicity and eloquence, by the clarity of its exposition, and by the restrained but convincing passion of the author's love for the Greek way of life. Born in England, Kitto was for many years Professor of Greek literature and history at the University of Bristol. Since his retirement from this chair, he has spent several semesters teaching in American universities and conducting study tours of the Greek islands. A happy, enthusiastic man, Kitto avoids historiographical clichés and dogmatisms. He brings to his analysis of ancient Greek civilization the learning, subtlety, and enthusiasm of the true humanist. With his mastery of Greek literature and philosophy, he convinces his audience that he understands the Greek mind from the inside, as it were, propounding Athenian values as they were formulated by Socrates, Sophocles, and their contemporaries.

Chronological Outline

c. 2000–c. 1900 B.C.: The emergence of an urban culture on Crete (the Minoan civilization), thought to have centered at Knossos. Until the fifteenth century B.C. Crete is the leading commercial power in the Mediterranean.

c. 1400–1150 B.C.: Mycenaean civilization dominates the Mediterranean. In the twelfth century B.C. Mycenaean forces sack Troy.

c. 1200–800 B.C.: Mycenaean civilization is destroyed after an invasion from the north by the Dorians, who introduce the Iron Age. Some Greek peoples migrate to the coast of Asia Minor. During the "Dark Ages" of Greece, the epic poems the *Iliad* and the *Odyssey* are composed orally (and written down in the eighth century B.C.).

c. 800 B.C.: Beginnings of the formation of the Greek city-states.

776 B.C.: The first Olympiad.

594 B.C.: Solon's economic and judicial reforms in Athens. All citizens are allowed some voice in the government.

561–527 B.C.: Pisistratus seizes power in Athens. Though a tyrant, he attempts to rule within the law and Athens becomes an important commercial city.

c. 508 B.C.: Cleisthenes overthrows the tyranny and initiates a democratic reform of the constitution. Attica is divided into three sections—Athens, the coast, and the interior. Creation of the *demes,* or townships.

c. 506 B.C.: Cleomenes of Sparta invades Attica in an attempt to overthrow Cleisthenes and restore the aristocracy but is repelled by the Athenians.

500–449 B.C.: Continuing warfare between the Persian empire and the Greek city-states. In 490 B.C. the Athenians repel a large Persian force at Marathon. In 480 B.C. the Panhellenic League headed by Sparta faces the Persian forces: a Spartan force led by Leonidas is massacred at Thermopylae and Athens is razed, but the Greek fleet defeats the Persians at the Battle of Salamis. The Spartans defeat the remnants of the Persian army at Platea in 479 B.C. Athens forms the Delian League the next year and pushes the Persians back until a truce is concluded in 449 B.C.

443–429 B.C.: Under Pericles Athens becomes the cultural center of the world. The Parthenon is built. The Delian League is transformed into an Athenian empire.

431–404 B.C.: The Great Peloponnesian War. The Great Plague of 430–429 B.C. and factional strife seriously weaken Athens. Athens is decisively defeated by Sparta, supported by the Persians. Demoralization and decay lead to chaotic factional disputes and prosecutions of various intellectuals and artists, among them Socrates (in 399 B.C.).

359 B.C.: Philip II becomes regent of Macedon. Demosthenes unsuccessfully tries to warn Greece of the Macedonian menace in his orations of 351–341 B.C.

338 B.C.: The Battle of Chaeronea. Philip annihilates the allied citizen armies of Greece and forms the Hellenic League.

336 B.C.: Assassination of Philip and the rise of Alexander the Great, who rules until his death in 323 B.C.

Pythagoras: c. 582–c. 507 B.C.
Aeschylus: 525–456 B.C.
Pindar: 518?–c. 438 B.C.
Sophocles: c. 496–c. 406 B.C.
Euripides: c. 485–406 B.C.
Herodotus: 484?–425? B.C.
Socrates: c. 469–399 B.C.
Hippocrates: c. 460–c. 370 B.C.
Thucydides: c. 460–c. 400 B.C.
Aristophanes: c. 448–c. 380 B.C.
Plato: 427?–347? B.C.
Aristotle: c. 384–322 B.C.
Euclid: c. 330–275 B.C.
Archimedes: c. 287–212 B.C.

Norman F. Cantor
What is known about the government, economy, and society of Minoan Crete?

H. D. Kitto

I would like to amend the question: For "what is known" read "what can be inferred," for this reason. The evidence we have is all archaeological: lots of pottery, plain or decorated, ruins of half a dozen palaces, foundations of homes, some pieces of fresco calcined by the fires that destroyed the palaces, cult objects found either in the palaces or in sacred caves high up in the mountains, and some clay tablets baked hard in the fires, inscribed with a syllabic script that we can't decipher, written in a language that we don't know. Not much else, except that pottery and other artifacts of Minoan make are found anywhere from Egypt and Syria to Sicily—and Egyptian artifacts, in Crete. There is also the fact that the place-name Minoa survived into historical times in various parts of the eastern Mediterranean, always on a coast. It is rather like looking into a large room through a plate-glass window: we can see parts of pictures on the wall, and shadows of some of the people in it, but cannot hear a word of what they are saying.

Evidently, in the first half of the second millennium, Crete dominated most of the eastern Mediterranean commercially; perhaps, in part, politically as well: one recalls the legend of Theseus and the annual tribute of youths and maidens that Athens had to send to King Minos.

As for government and economy (for the evidence almost compels us to take them together), it seems clear that each was highly centralized—in the palaces. These are large, elegant, complex—and unfortified—buildings, with courtyards, state rooms, private quarters for the royalty, bathrooms with proper drains, and a maze of storage-chambers, some of which still contain the man-size earthenware jars that must have held grain, oil, perhaps wine. Add to this the clay tablets accidentally preserved—presumably, like those of later date found on the mainland, inventories and the like—which imply a staff of clerks: what emerges is a picture of a highly organized economic system controlled from, and in, the palaces. It is a system known to have been common in the Near East, and it reappears later on the Greek mainland, notably at Pylos (southwestern Peloponnesus) in the late Mycenaean period.

Perhaps I should say a little more about these tablets. They were found, in Knossos, by Evans, the first excavator. On inspection, they proved to be in two related but distinct scripts. The earlier one Evans called Linear A ("linear" because it used straight lines), the later, Linear B. In 1939, Carl Blegen discovered several hundreds of such tablets at Pylos, also in Linear B; these too had been baked in the fire that had destroyed the palace, Nestor's Palace. Then, in 1953, Michael Ventris, to his own surprise, discovered that the language of Linear B is Greek. (Linear A is still undeciphered; certainly not Greek.) Here then was proof of what had already been surmised from the analysis of objects of art in Knossos; that in the middle of the fifteenth century Knossos had passed into the power of Greeks from the mainland. They must have taken over the art of writing from the Cretans and adapted Linear A (more or less) to their own language.

Society? We can't say much; at least, *I* can't. As a guide, we have what remains of Cretan art and the foundations of a few ordinary dwellings; not much more. One gains the impression of a society that was elegant, vivid, gay. A favorite sport—to watch—seems to have been bull-jumping. In the paintings, the athlete was always gracefully successful; one suspects that in reality the bull often might have won. The result would not have been pretty—but apparently high society in Knossos didn't mind *that.*

Who were the Mycenaeans? Do you know anything about where they came from, what kind of life they had, whether their government and society were very different from that of Crete?

The first Greek speaker entered the peninsula, whether from the north or from the northeast, round about 2000 or 1900 B.C. That is fairly certain. They pushed in, often destructively, sometimes not. In some ways the civilization that they found was higher than what they brought with them. We must always allow for the possibility of a gradual fusion of the two. A fair proportion of "Greek" place-names and names of plants and the like are demonstrably non-Hellenic: Athena, Corinth, Parnassos, hyacinth, absinth. . . .

By the sixteenth century, powerful dynasties had arisen in various parts of central and southern Greece: how, our evidence cannot tell us. The richest and most powerful built the fortress-palace of Mycenae, from which fact the period, and the culture, have been labeled Mycenaean. Here it was that Schliemann found a grave-circle that contained an incredible number of gold objects, including the death-mask which he called Agamemnon's. That was a mistake: there may well have been an Agamemnon ruling in Mycenae, but two or three hundred years later—near the end of the thirteenth century B.C.

To judge from their art, these people —presumably those whom Homer was to call Achaeans—were at first very much under the influence of Crete. We would like to know how they got their wealth; a likely answer is piracy. They were obviously warlike; very different from the elegant Minoans. By the mid-fifteenth century, they were overhauling Crete both in commerce and political power. As I said just now, some king or prince must have overthrown the Minoan lord of Knossos. It must have been there that Linear A was adapted to the Greek tongue and brought back to Greece. Its use there must have enabled what look like the fortresses of robber barons to become also the centers of an elaborate palace-economy like the one that we now recognized at Pylos.

Social conditions? We can guess. With so much power and wealth concentrated in the castles—unproductive wealth too, when it was buried gold—we can guess that social conditions were pretty poor outside the ruling circles. But we don't *know*—at least, *I* don't.

What became of Mycenaean civilization and society?

It fell to bits. Pylos went up in flames at about 1200 B.C.—at about the traditional date for the Trojan War, which is awkward; but then, Homer was a better poet than some have realized and a much worse historian.

It was a disastrous century all round. The Hittite empire disappeared in fragments; Egypt had to repel seaborne attacks; lines of communication were cut; commerce dwindled. To judge from the Pylos tablets, government and the economy may have become dangerously rigid and brittle. Hard times may have stimulated internal wars, reflected perhaps in legend: two Argive attacks on Thebes. Social revolt is a possibility. Until fairly recently the ancient Greek tradition was accepted: a Dorian invasion from the northwest. Certainly, rude people who spoke Doric Greek moved in, but the idea of a massive invasion has been given up: as detective-story writers are apt to say, "It looks like an inside job." The evidence is that in decorated ware, the previous "international style" is succeeded by village styles, but if an ignoramus may blurt out an opinion, some of late Mycenaean vase painting was pretty poor stuff.

It was the beginning of a Dark Age, which lasted for some three centuries, though vase painting, in a severely "geometric" style, begins to be impressive again in the tenth century B.C. in Athens.

Do the Iliad *and the* Odyssey *reflect the Mycenaean period, or do they reflect this later period after the invasion?*

Both, but what is more important is that each poem reflects the mind of a great poet.

The Greeks of the Mycenaean age would have been strange people if they did not have commemorative songs. When they migrated across the Aegean—those who could—it would have been just as strange if they promptly forgot these songs, their only "literature." We have to postulate two or three centuries of oral tradition before Homer—or perhaps two Homers—arrived on the scene; and we might not be wrong if we assumed that the singers, or the best of them, were more intent on producing attractive songs than in piously handing down to posterity the details of a Trojan War. Homer himself says, "A new song is always the best."

It was exciting when Schliemann went to Hissarlik and proved that Troy was not the creation of fancy but had been a real city, in fact a long succession of cities. One of them had been sacked and burned at (say) 1260 B.C.; its successor, at some date close to 1200. The later one must be Homer's Troy. Unfortunately, Homer indicates—I carefully do *not* use the word *describes,* for in the *Iliad* the city is never described—a city of some magnificence: the earlier of these two cities *was* splendid; the later one wasn't. But why should we be surprised? The Troy of the singers' tradition and of the *Iliad had* to be a splendid city; what Troy was *actually* like at about 1200 B.C. was of no concern to those who were listening to the songs—one reason why Homer never describes it, except in general terms, like "Troy of the wide streets," which would apply to any fine city. Compare Tennyson's "many-towered Camelot." A certain "willing suspension of belief" seems not out of place.

Certainly, the tradition remembered (as we say) many precise details of the Mycenaean age. A notable instance is the Catalogue of the Ships: that gives a political map, so to speak, of Greece which we now know to be true, in general, of the Mycenaean age and utterly unlike Greece of Homer's time. Obviously, the Catalogue is a venerable poem which Homer included in his *Iliad* because he saw no reason to exclude it. But equally, he saw no reason for harmonizing it, in detail, with the rest of his poem. In a similar way, he always gives Ajax a big shield, protecting the whole body "like a tower," which had long passed out of use by the time of Agamemnon, yet no character in the *Iliad* ever asks Ajax from which museum he had got it. For all we know, the detail may have come down from a sixteenth-century song: no singer would have altered it, because no singer ever saw reason why he should; a picturesque detail would have been lost, and nothing would have been gained.

When the Pylos tablets were deciphered, some surprise was expressed at first that the poetic tradition remembered nothing of the elaborate bureaucracy which the tablets prove. Of course not: we ourselves have remarkably little poetry about the Civil Service. In short, the singers were not doing their best to transmit to later generations a picture of the heroic age: we should use our judgment, as best we can.

The same applies to Homer's own age. Of course that is reflected in the poems; how could it be otherwise? The fact is more obvious in the more relaxed *Odyssey,* in its pictures of traders, of pirates, of a kingdom in disorder, in much else—but we must not be naïve. For example, in the *Iliad,* a poem very far from being relaxed, we can be quite sure that we have glimpses of contemporary life in the frequent similes—of the shepherd on the mountain hating the storm, of the woodman who fells a tall poplar by a stream and leaves it to season until he turns it into wheels for a chariot; also in such a passage as the scenes described on the shield of Achilles; passages which are, so to speak, marginal illustrations, "free." Elsewhere, a certain degree of caution may not be out of place. From the descriptions of the fighting, we might suppose that the heroes alone fought; that the common soldiers did little more than throw stones—though Homer is inconsistent even in this. But, similarly, one might suppose from Henry James's novels that he inhabited a world in which no one had actually to work for his living. We should at least consider that to describe anonymous death was not to Homer's purpose.

And what was that? Here we have to consider a remarkable fact. Toward the end of the oral tradition, a singer of quite exceptional stature composed, very likely over a period of years, a poem of quite exceptional length, the *Iliad,* followed by another such poem (whether by the same or by a second poet), the *Odyssey.* Mr. G. S. Kirk aptly compares the event to the equally sudden appearance of the "monumental" vases of the Dipylon type. Why should the poet of the *Iliad* have done it? I think that the explanation offered by Kirk is the only possible one: he had, as it were, something to say that could not be said except on this scale. (Bach's monumental *Mass in B minor* would be something of parallel.) Homer would be a singer supremely well trained in the oral tradition, loving and respecting it, but entirely transcending it. How?

Aristotle pointed out that Homer did what the other epic poets would not do: he gave a real unity to his poems; he did not compose a mere narrative poem about the Trojan War. That is obvious enough. We sometimes call the *Iliad* the tragedy of Achilles. A tragic poem indeed. The shade of Aeschylus will forgive anyone who should call the poet of the *Iliad* the greatest of Greek tragic poets: Aeschylus more or less said so himself, according to report. But "tragedy of Achilles" won't really do; it is bigger than that. For one thing, why doesn't it end with the death of Achilles? Homer himself says that his subject is Anger: the quarrel that sent so many brave men to their death; and what begins the quarrel is Agamemnon's inhuman treatment of the old priest, Chryses.

It is not a poem about the Trojan War; still, at the beginning of Book III, Homer creates the impression that we are at the beginning of the war—I mean, in the scene on the wall, when Helen identifies, for Priam, the chief of the Achaean leaders; and then a little later, when Paris, the wrongdoer, challenges Menelaus to settle the whole affair, without involving the two armies, by single combat. Wise men have pointed out that these two scenes, coming so late as the ninth year of the war, are out of place. Wiser men smile. The solemn truce and compact are treacherously broken, and grave words are spoken by Agamemnon, that now Troy is doomed, by this breach of faith sworn to by all the gods. They are echoed later, in Book VII, by the Trojan Antenor: "We cannot win, since we have turned our solemn oaths into lies." Paris, then, is willing to give back all of Helen's wealth, but not Helen herself. It reminds one of Claudius: "Can we be pardoned, and retain the offence."

It's a tragic poem and the doom of Troy is no small part of the tragedy—a doom not arbitrary, but born of Paris' crime and confirmed by broken faith. There are brave men dying in vain, because of Achilles' anger—and of course there is Achilles himself. He puts himself more and more in the wrong; at last makes his fatal half-recantation: "It seems that it was not possible to keep up my anger forever." Then with Patroclus dead, his anger against Agamemnon is swept away with a still more appalling anger against Hector and all the Trojans. He becomes inhuman—and from time to time we see fury and hatred made incarnate in Hera and Athena: as Zeus says to Hera, "I believe you would eat the Trojans raw!" And so we could continue: Hector with Andromache, he knowing Troy must fall and his wife and child be carried off as slaves, yet while he lives he must fight; Priam, speaking so simply to Achilles about such simple things, and the tears of both men that wash away hatred, anger, inhumanity; and as the poem is so much ampler than a tragedy of Achilles, inevitably it does not end with the death of Achilles. We have done with Achilles and Agamemnon and hatred and ferocity: the poem ends with the last scene of all—a burial and mourning.

Such was the poem into which this greatest of all poets grew, year by year—so I imagine; and that is the reason why it had to be a long poem: more than the tragedy of Achilles; more like the tragedy of man himself.

How is the development of the Greek language related to the classical poems and plays?

I don't know how to answer this one, except in vague terms. Attic Greek, the dialect that we think of as "classical

Greek," is different from Homeric Greek, though I could hardly describe the differences except in highly technical terms; and later developments affected prose, but not poetry—or not much.

Then there is another point. Take the two contemporary tragic poets, Sophocles and Euripides: their "language" is quite different, but this is a matter of personal style, not of a development in "the Greek language."

More than any other language known to me, Greek could form compound words very freely—a great poetic resource. For example, Homer—in an English translation—will say "Sparta of-beautiful-women": my hyphenated epithet is clumsy, but I am translating a compound adjective which, in the Greek, is natural and delightful. German, of course, can make compounds: "the art of slicing sausage" would be (I suppose) *die Wurstschneiderkunst;* clear enough, in moderation, but it suggests effort; the German compound is rarely an unstudied, graceful gesture, like the Greek.

Early Greek was deficient in abstract terms—a nuisance for the (later) philosophers, who had to invent them, but a blessing for the poets, since it meant that they had to use concrete terms—though perhaps I am putting the cart before the horse: abstract terms hardly existed, since the poets preferred to be concrete and therefore direct and simple. You don't catch them talking about Beauty: they use the neuter form of the simple adjective: *ta kala,* for which we have to say "(all) those things that are beautiful." Again, Greek relies on verbs rather than nouns—like decent English. As it were, instead of saying: "In the event of the implementation of these proposals"—sixteen syllables, three abstract nouns—it will say: "If this is done."

What was the influence of the physical environment, and was Greece as arid in the classical period as it is today?

The second part of the question admits of an answer that can be positive and perhaps even correct: No. A character in Plato's *Critias* remarks that in a certain temple there are timbers which were cut from a forest on Mt. Hymettus "which today can support nothing but bees," and that Attica is like a skeleton land, since in the absence of the earlier forests the rain has swilled the soil into the sea. The goat has always been a problem: by eating the young shoots it prevents a forest from regenerating itself.

The first part is not so easy. Obviously, physical environment has a profound influence, but analyzing it is another matter.

Let me start with a point that seems quite clear. Greece is not, like Spain, a solid, square mass, with a pretty wild ocean on two sides. In Greece, land and sea are always mixed up, and although the Aegean is no millpond its behavior is fairly predictable, and in good weather you can cross it, almost, without losing sight of land. Contact with the older cultures of Asia and Egypt was relatively easy.

Then, Greece itself is very much cut up not only by intrusions of the sea but also by mountain ranges, some of them formidable; large plains are few. Hence, small communities were the rule, and since each would usually possess land at very different altitudes, the country being at least hilly, each could have a diversity of agriculture and be reasonably self-sufficient, at least in unsophisticated conditions. These physical facts favored the development of the innumerable small city-states—though it is well to remember that there were parts of Greece which were the same but city-states absent, and other parts where the facts were different but city-states flourished.

Environment and religion: at the remote temple of Apollo at Bassae I was once asked by an intelligent youngster: "But why did they build a temple *here,* so far from any town or village?" I was inspired to answer—no doubt by Apollo himself: "We build our churches where the people are; the Greeks built their temples where the gods are." The Greek landscape is impressive, and not oppressive. The Greek had every reason to believe in the gods, and to be modest. It (or Zeus) rains in torrents on the mountain, and next day the farmer below sees his fields littered with boulders, his crop ruined. The only thing to do is to cart away the stones and begin again. The gods can be kind or they can be cruel; God knows why. We moderns have put the gods in their place. An expanding economy we take for granted; anything is possible—and we *do* anything. Now we are frightened of pollution; the gods are getting back at us. We have learned to live on capital: coal, oil, that we did not make; the Greek knew he had to live on income—and a limited income, since the gods in Greece are grudging. He could expand his economy only by working harder and a bit more intelligently. A Greek philosopher declared: "The limited is good; the unlimited, bad." For us, the limited is no good at all; the unlimited is just around the corner. In a simpler world, it was easier to understand its rules.—Next question, please.

How do you explain the burst of creativity that marked every aspect of Athenian life in the fifth century B.C.?

I wouldn't presume to "explain" either this or the comparable outburst in Elizabethan England; what one can do is to note some favoring circumstances. During the sixth century, thanks to a sage reformer (Solon), to an intelligent dictator (Peisistratus), and to her own sensible moderation, Athens had solved, more or less, various economic and political problems which condemned certain other Greek states to continuing internal strife. By the end of the century she was becoming, for the first time, one of the leading Greek states—politically, economically, artistically. The foundations of her democracy were firmly laid, and the old aristocratic families, far from sulking and holding aloof, supplied most of the leaders of that democracy during most of the fifth century. There was no hostile class of helots, no landless peasantry. It was a fairly homogeneous and "open" society.

In 490 B.C., Athens, standing alone, repelled a Persian primitive invasion at Marathon. In 480, having doubled or trebled her navy, she contributed more than any other Greek state to the defeat of a much more serious Persian attack; she was now unquestionably on a par with the traditional number one, Sparta. For defense against the Persians a (very incomplete) Hellenic League had been rigged up, naturally under Sparta. When it became a matter of clearing the Persians out of the Aegean and liberating the Greek cities of Asia Minor from Persian control, Sparta lost interest. The League offered the leadership to Athens, by far the most powerful of its members. She accepted it, naturally, and gradually assumed more and more control. "Contributions" to the League became, within a generation, "tribute" paid to Athens—in return, one must say, for services rendered. Her ships were everywhere, from the Black Sea to the coasts of Syria and Egypt; she did her share, more than her share, of the fighting; she even sent two squadrons up the Nile—and lost both. Money flowed in to Athens: energy, and blood, flowed out. Nothing like it had been seen before. One is not compelled to admire the Athenian empire, though some aspects of it were admirable—yet one can hardly disagree with Pericles' remark: "At least they cannot complain that they are being ruled by a city unworthy of ruling." And the great point is that this was the work not of an "imperialist clique" but by a town meeting, willing indeed to accept the rewards but also to accept, personally, the labor and the dangers.

There is something else—something that I cannot explain, perhaps even hardly express. Among Greeks, the sharp division was that between Dorians and Ionians. The Dorians, in the main, were of the Peloponnesus; the Ionians, of the Aegean islands and fringe of Asia Minor. Generalizing rather grandly, one may say that the Dorians were in most respects solid, serious, traditional; the Ionians, enterprising, individualistic, brilliant. The Ionians had the sea at their front door, and were in contact with the older and richer civilizations of Asia; the Dorians lived among their unchanging mountains. Dorian art was severe; the Ionian, elegant. The characteristic type of Dorian poetry was the choral lyric, a hymn-with-dance composed for public performance; not necessarily solemn, but still, communal. The Ionians too had such a choral lyric, but when we think of Ionian song, we think first, and naturally, of the highly personal lyrics of such as Archilochus, Anacreon, Minnermas: songs of love or hatred or wine or melancholy, some of them irresponsible in a way that must have displeased many a Dorian Greek. Plato, legislating for his ideal Republic, would admit Dorian music modes and rhythms but exclude the Ionian as enervating or lascivious. Inevitably, it was among the Ionians that philosophy and photoscience arose; the Dorians, on the whole, were incurious.

Now, the point of this short and oversimplified disquisition is this. Attica stood, as it were, at the crossroads. The Athenians claimed that they were the mother city of the Ionians, but like the Dorians they were mainlanders, and until, say, the mid-sixth century B.C. they were almost entirely an agricultural state and still subsisted very largely on what their fields produced. Whatever this explanation of mine may be worth, the fact is that in their art, and to some extent in their political behavior, they represent a blend of Dorian and Ionian.

The art peculiar to Athens was tragic drama, and it is patent that new art form was in the beginning an exceptionally creative fusion of the choral lyric (which I have asserted to be a characteristically Dorian form) with the solo actor, the individual. This may seem fanciful; but it is commonplace that the glory of Doric architecture in Athens is that it combined the strength and dignity of Doric with the grace of Ionic.

Just a word on intellectual creativity. I know that some of my classical colleagues will courteously disagree when I assert, as I do, that the two tragic poets Aeschylus and Sophocles are, as thinkers, peers of the Ionian philosophers. (I omit Euripides only because everybody admits that he was a very devil for thinking.) The difference is characteristic. Ionian thinking, as it were, took off into space—and it is certainly breathtaking; the two Athenians—and the Ionians in their way were hardly more bold than was Aeschylus in his—did their thinking within the ambit of the city, of human society, of the human condition; and one might truly say that this pattern was continued by that well-known Athenian stonemason Socrates, for he had (as we know) studied the Ionians, and then said, in effect: "Fascinating; but, you know, it is getting us nowhere. The first question is: How are we to order our lives?"

I am not sure if this answers your question about the outburst of creativeness in fifth-century Athens, but it may go some way towards explaining the character which that creativeness assumed. Perhaps one cannot really say much more than this, that they were, even among Greeks, exceptionally intelligent and energetic; perhaps indeed, since the soil of Attica is not rich, they had to be creative in order to survive; and certainly (to use a phrase from Pericles' funeral speech) they were "in love with Athens."

Was Greek religion of the fifth and fourth centuries significantly different from the religion of the Homeric age?

Just to be provocative, I reply that the real break in religious thought occurred not between Homer and the fifth century, but between the fifth century and the fourth.

Some important aspects of Greek "religion" we can easily get entirely wrong, partly because of the difficulties of translation. Our word *religion* is Latin by origin, and the surprising fact is that Greek had no corresponding word at all —only a periphrasis like "what pertains to the gods." And there is another difficulty: the word *god* is Teutonic by origin, and the Greek word *theos* is, or can be, very different. In many ways the two words overlap; in others they do not—and this is where we get caught.

Greek poetry and plastic art alike present *theoi* in vivid human shape—often, as we say, "all too human." Therefore we think that they, for the Greeks, were sharply defined divine persons; as perhaps they were, for the Greek was (and still is) highly imaginative. But the point is that he was well able to think of his *theoi* at one moment on this mythological level and the next on quite a different one. I don't know of any other people who could both laugh heartily at their "gods," as Homer sometimes does, and the later comic poets, and treat them with deep reverence—and invent new gods at the drop of a hat, as Homer does when he turns Strife and Panic and Terror into *theoi*. And what do we make of a passage in Herodotus in which Poverty is a *theos,* who has taken up permanent residence in a certain island? In the plays of Aeschylus and Sophocles, there are passages that speak of Zeus in tones of the deepest reverence, and we think: "Greek religious thought is getting on. This is very nearly Christian." Then, to our well-deserved confusion, Aeschylus writes one play, the *Prometheus,* in which Zeus is a new and cruel tyrant; and another, the *Agamemnon,* in which he first "sends" Agamemnon to fight a bloody war of vengeance (a war that he was going to fight in any case), and then has him punished because he has shed blood. Sophocles sets a similar problem in his *Electra*—as I will show in a moment.

We all know about the beautiful and not excessively "religious" Aphrodite, goddess of love, who gets wounded by Diomedes in the *Iliad.* Aeschylus makes her say that she is the power that moves in all Nature, the power that makes the Earth bring forth fruit when she is impregnated by the Sky and its rain. Some thirty years later Euripides, in his *Hippolytus,* represents Aphrodite as a jealous, vindictive "goddess" who will destroy Phaedra *en passant* in order to vent her rage on Hippolytus, a one-sided young man who is so pure that he loathes Aphrodite and all her works. Now, it would be not far from childish to say that Aeschylus "believes" in Aphrodite, and Euripides is denouncing any belief in so ungodly a "goddess." In this case, in every such case, the *theos* prefigures some permanent reality in human experience, be it comfortable or uncomfortable. Aeschylus and Euripides were not expressing theological beliefs about a certain goddess: they were talking about certain realities that penetrate our existence. Poverty was a permanent condition in the island of Andros—therefore would be made a *theos,* like Strife, Panic, Fear, in the *Iliad.*

I want to say a word about the *Electra* because it brings up, very acutely, a situation that is quite regular in Greek tragedy, and fairly common in Homer too: men do something, and *theoi* too have designed it, or are operating in it. As I said just now, Zeus "sent" Agamemnon to fight the war, but, evidently, he was going to do it anyhow—and when he returns, the chorus leader tells him straight that when he began that war, for a wanton like Helen, he had thought it a disastrous mistake. (Queer religion, isn't it, when a plan made by the Supreme God is dismissed by a man as insane?)

The *Electra* deals with the vengeance taken by Orestes and Electra on their mother and her paramour, who had murdered their father. Among much else, the play contains a magnificent character study of Electra, the daughter who had dedicated her whole life to the avenging of her father. Our difficulty is twofold at least. One is that the play ends with the double murder, without any hint of unpleasant consequences. Apparently we are expected to regard matricide as quite O.K. Many critics have been perturbed by this; somehow, it doesn't seem quite right. The other difficulty is that "gods" are involved in the action, notably Apollo. Obviously (we think), if a god is concerned, he must be the commanding officer: he is omnipotent, and the human actors are his instruments, even puppets. But one has only to read the text to see that this is not true. Orestes is not "god-commanded": he made his decision—for reasons that Sophocles pointed out—and asked Apollo only for practical advice, which Apollo gave to him. In spite of that, and of the completely convincing presentation of Electra's, and Orestes', characters and circumstances, the play makes it clear that half a dozen gods are with them in what they are doing, even though the gods do not lift a finger to help, even though the end is matricide, even though Sophocles is known to have been a deeply "religious" man. How do we get out of this mess? By realizing that Greek "religion" is not what we would expect and sometimes—to our confusion—take for granted. The *theos* may or may not typify something that is good: he always typifies something that is real and permanent. The point of the *Electra* is that the murder of the King, the usurpation, confiscation, adultery, so work upon Electra and Orestes that inevitably they live for nothing but vengeance and restitution. Without the *theoi* the play would be no more than an exciting revenge tragedy; with them it becomes a statement of a universal fact: crimes like those generate a grim recoil like this.

I know that there are other aspects of Greek religion: the many cults, the mystery religions, and so on. Those we can understand. What I am saying here is that the "religion" and the *theoi* of Greek poetry, down to the fifth century B.C., have to do with the way in which our human universe seems to operate. The break came when the philosophers began to ask a totally different question: not "How does our universe work?" but "What is the nature of the Divine?"—a metaphysical question. Plato was willing to identify the highest form of pure Being with the *theos*—as indeed Euripides had been, more or less, in his occasional and often incongruous metaphysical moments. Naturally, to this question nobody could give the answer that the *theos* was, or could be, cruel, or vindictive; hence Plato's rejection of the *theoi* of the poets—and of poetry itself. This does not mean that Plato had a "higher conception of religion"; only that he and the tragic poets were answering entirely different questions.

What view of human nature, or the human condition, is set forth in the tragedies?

I am tempted to say that the tragic poets had no interest in depicting human nature. If they had, they, like Shakespeare, would have populated their plays with men of all sorts and conditions instead of using as few characters as possible. The human *condition,* yes indeed: the constitution of our universe is such-and-such; the *theoi* are what they are. It is for us to take note of the fact—if we can. There is a sharp difference here, I think, between Euripides and the other two poets. They, on the whole, see a universe that is orderly; it has its own laws. Euripides does not. He sees tensions and conflicts and wreckage; *theoi* like Aphrodite and Artemis, or Dionysus—facts in our lives with which we have to cope, to reconcile—if we can; but so often, we cannot; and of course they show no mercy.

What does Sophocles say about the human condition in the Oedipus?

It is impossible to give a credible answer to this question without first saying something about the play. There are a dozen or more interpretations floating about. I suggest that none is worth listening to unless it gives a reasonable answer to a lot of quite formal questions about the play, and I would not call it a reasonable answer to say that Sophocles didn't know how to design a play intelligently. I give only a sample, or your tape will run out.

Aeschylus made a version of the Oedipus myth, a trilogy of which only the last play, the *Seven Against Thebes,* survives. We know that he made Laius wantonly defy a divine injunction, given three times, not to beget a son: we can be pretty certain that Aeschylus had preceded this with the story of Laius' abominable treatment of the lad Chrysippus. That is to say, his myth had the normal tragic sequence: sin and punishment. Sophocles abolished it. Why? In his myth there is no sign of justice. To save time, take the case of Jocasta. In Sophocles' version, there is not the slightest reason why she, the widowed Queen, should not have accepted marriage with the new King—no unusual arrangement. But what she did in complete innocence destroys her.

Then, first Laius and then Oedipus receive a prediction from Delphi which Sophocles leaves quite unexplained. There is no Divine Plan—or, if there is, Sophocles does not profess to understand what it is. Nor does he give the impression that the god is pulling strings off stage. On the contrary, each is told that a particular thing is going to happen, each does what he thinks reasonable and sufficient to avoid it; each is frustrated by chance circumstances that could not possibly be foreseen. Now, this is doubly odd. First, because elsewhere in Greek tragedy, and Shakespearian too, the dramatic function of prophecy is to link the coming catastrophe with some intelligible universal law. In this play, nothing of the kind is discernible. Second, because all our evidence is that the Delphic oracle did not prophesy if it could help it, and then only in ambiguous terms. The Greeks normally went to Delphi for advice, information, or moral support, not for prophecy. As for belief in Delphic utterances, my own impression is that if Sophocles had told his friends that he firmly believed in their infallibility, they would have been as much flabbergasted as Shakespeare's friends in the Mermaid would have been if he told them that he firmly believed in magicians who could raise storms at will.

The idea that the play is about inexorable Fate is nonsense. One writer, believing this, concludes—logically—that in Greek tragedy there is no connection between guilt and suffering. Nothing sillier could be said about the other plays we know; about this one play it seems plausible. Why?

If we are correct in supposing that Sophocles was a sensible and responsible man there must be quite a simple answer to such questions; also to similar ones about the play itself, if we are to believe that he was a reasonably competent playwright. For example, to some modern directors the end of the play seems so feeble that they replace it with something much more tragic, spectacular and, in a way, logical: the blinded King gropes his way out of the theater into hopeless exile.

How did Sophocles come to miss it? He didn't miss it; he rejected it. He makes Oedipus demand precisely that several times, and makes Creon say No. Again, we are sometimes told that Oedipus is the heroic King who sacrifices himself to save his city from the plague. How odd, then, that in the last eight or nine hundred verses there is not the slightest allusion to the plague.

Even more startling: near the middle of the play, Oedipus is terribly frightened and is led off by Jocasta. The chorus begins an ode with a solemn prayer for purity and holiness and the observance of the eternal Unwritten Laws. But on the evidence carefully presented by Sophocles, it would not have made the slightest difference to Oedipus or Jocasta if they had scrupulously obeyed all those laws—nor are we told that they haven't done so. And, by the way, if Sophocles were preaching inexorable Fate, he would have been very silly to insert this prayer for holiness.

I could go on like this for some time, but I will now try to answer your question instead. Perhaps I have said enough to show that before one can answer it at all correctly, certain homemade stumbling blocks have to be removed.

For a reason at which we can guess —presently—in this one play Sophocles is contemplating, even to the point of exaggeration, one aspect of our human universe which we know to be real: it can be, and sometimes is, baffling, unjust, cruel. It often seems to be governed by mere chance. Toward the end of the fifth century, a pseudophilosophic immoralism was current in Athens which argued that life *is* random, therefore the traditional "laws" of morality were only make-believe; the wise man should take no notice of them, but act at any moment according to his own best judgment.

Sophocles was not impressed. He so modifies his myth as to present this incomprehensible aspect of life in an extreme form. The (unusual) oracles in the play are not Sophocles' confession that he, among Athenians, is intellectually retarded; their dramatic function is to contradict the doctrine of a random universe: we accept Divine Omniscience, if only as a dramatic convention, as Aristotle remarks in the *Poetics*, and obviously, what Omniscience can foresee cannot be a random event. Sophocles is careful—as I said just now—*not* to suggest that what happens here is just or even intelligible—at least, to *our* intelligence.

He opens with the plague, and the picture of Oedipus the ideal King. The plague serves two or three dramatic ends; one of them is to suggest, at once, that there is an underlying Order in events, even though it may often be uncomfortable to us. As at the beginning of *Hamlet:* "Foul deeds will rise, though all the earth o'erwhelm them to men's eyes." And Sophocles had enough of the "scientific" spirit in him to know that in this region, innocence and ignorance do not avert consequences.

The dominant image of the play is Blindness. In the scenes that immediately follow, Oedipus is faced with an accusation which he, being ignorant of the controlling fact, must find incredible. Being intelligent, he leaps to a conclusion which is not, itself, unreasonable, though unlikely. His hybris, the only hybris of which he is guilty in the play, is that he will listen to nothing but his own intelligent, though blind, judgment: not to Creon's oath, his reasonable argument, his challenge to go to Delphi and find out, nor to one or two cautious warnings from the chorus.

The third ode is so remote from the immediate dramatic situation that it is a challenge. It has parallels in other plays: for example, the second ode in the *Antigone*. In such cases, the dramatist is bringing to the surface the underlying theme. Here it is the way of hybris, the defiance of law and moral restraints, and the way of religion. It is true that Oedipus and Jocasta are not about to suffer because they have been wicked, but we all know that strictly moral behavior is not an insurance policy. In this play Sophocles is facing some grim facts of life. But throwing overboard moral restraints does ensure violence and ruin.

Then comes the surprising stanza about the validity of these predictions and the validity of religion itself. But we have only to wait. Soon the tragic Iocasta learns that a second prediction has failed. She draws the logical conclusion: life is random, therefore live at random.

There is a further point in the predictions. Quite exceptionally, first Laius and then Oedipus are specifically warned of a coming disaster. Each does what he judges sufficient to ward it off. Each is frustrated by unforeseeable circumstances. We *know* that this kind of thing does happen; it is essentially true to life. The last verse of the play is: Do not hope to have control everywhere. And as for the current pseudohumanistic doctrine of acting exclusively on your own intelligent calculations, how intelligent are they likely to be, when at any moment you may be ignorant of the one fact that matters? Life can be hard indeed, as we all know, but it is sheer folly to abandon the teaching of experience, to abandon restraint. That can only make it worse.

It has been said that one of the main themes of the Antigone *is that of the clash between the dictates of conscience and the demands of the social order. Do you agree with this interpretation?*

There is no conflict between "conscience" and the social order. Conscience is a word that comes easily to us but is quite misleading, and the whole point of the play is that Creon's behaviour is of the kind that destroys the social order. He talks to Haemon about discipline, obedience; these preserve a city or an army or a family. But the outcome of his policy is that the city is imperiled and his own family wiped out; and the last words of the play are about the supreme value of understanding.

We say that Antigone is performing a religious duty—and so she is, but in a Greek context the word *religious* can be misleading. Sophocles makes it very plain that she is in total, passionate, instinctive revolt against Creon's decree, that her brother's body shall be eaten by animals. Creon, she says, is defying the laws of the *theoi,* but the difference between the laws of the *theoi* and the instinctive sanctities of our own humanity is one that we cannot make. (Sophocles makes the same point towards the end of the *Ajax.*) The common people of Thebes, so Haemon reports, are all on Antigone's side, because she tried to save her brother's body from being eaten by animals. It is an inhuman horror.

But besides the personal conflict of Antigone with Creon, there is the conflict of Haemon with Creon—and in fact it is on this one that the tragedy turns. In this one, too, Creon is defying a *theos*—to his cost. To Creon, the fact that his son is in love with Antigone is irrelevant; he can marry any girl he likes, except this one. When Haemon had rushed out in despair, Sophocles writes for his chorus a short ode on the invincible power of Aphrodite. Why? The ode exists on two levels. This is not the only time in the play that Sophocles makes the sage, politically-minded chorus say the right thing but about the wrong person. Here, they are thinking of Haemon's regrettable behavior to his father: he is misled by love. But when we hear later how Haemon blindly ran at his father with his sword drawn we shall reflect (if we are fifth-century Athenians) that here is the power of invincible Aphrodite made manifest—yet another *theos* whom Creon thought he could set aside.

It is not a conflict between private conscience and State law. Sophocles' point is that a statecraft is doomed if it thinks it can override the ultimate human sanctities.

How do you relate the dramatists' attitudes to the historical work of Herodotus and Thucydides? How would you compare Herodotus and Thucydides as historians?

Sophocles borrowed a story from Herodotus in his *Antigone* (vv.904–920) unless the passage is an interpolation, as many scholars have believed. Apart from this, I don't think one can find any particular contacts either way, so far as Herodotus is concerned. As for Thucydides, he must have known Athenian tragedy well, until he was banished from Athens in 424 B.C. He would then have been about forty. When he was allowed to return, after 404, both Euripides and Sophocles were dead, and I don't think there is any reason to suppose that they knew anything of his work—which anyhow he left unfinished.

The tragic poets must have influenced him—or any other intelligent young Athenian. Some scholars have even thought that he took tragedy as a literary model—his *History of the Peloponnesian War* is the earliest work in Attic prose—and that he derived many of his moral ideas from Herodotus; in ideas, because so often he seems to echo Aeschylean ideas about hybris, atê (Infatuation), and the like; in spirit, because he is certainly the most tragic of the historians. Maybe, but there is also the fact that his was one of the most powerful minds that we know of, in literature. It may be that what chiefly influenced Thucydides was, after all, the mind of Thucydides.

Herodotus came from Halicarnassus, on the southwest corner of Asia Minor. The fact may be significant: he was not Athenian. He seems to belong to a different age; in fact, he was only about thirty years older than Thucydides. He wrote a history of the Persian invasion (of 490 B.C. and 480–479); but the Greek word *historia* means "enquiry," "researches"—whether historical, geographical, anthropological, economic—anything. Herodotus does not arrive at his "historical" subject until more than halfway through his *Historia,* because he had first to enquire into the history, customs, beliefs, habitat, of the various peoples who became involved in the wars. He traveled widely, enquired acutely, observed accurately—and loved a good story. One of his chapters begins with these arresting words: "The following is the nature of the Camel"; one of his declared principles, as historian, is: "I am bound to relate what I was told; I am not bound to believe it." He seems to have been interested in, and to have set down, everything that came into his net. He—apparently—swallowed many a tall story, but modern specialists speak highly of him as an observer. The result is a most humane and genial book.

Thucydides the Athenian is utterly different: austere—at first very puzzling. His subject too was a war, the long war, 431–404 B.C., between the Athenian empire and the Spartan alliance, but instead of bringing in everything relevant he leaves out much that we think essential. He gives a close, accurate, impartial account of the military operations, but tells us very little about their economic, financial, logistic, diplomatic aspects; he neglects the internal politics of the chief cities concerned and he gives no description of the empire—which, more or less, is what the war was about. The reason is not that he was a bookish recluse: his family owned gold mines, so that he had probably heard about business and money; and one year he was elected to the Board of Generals, so that he certainly knew something about the way in which wars are run. Yet he says so little about it.

Again, some students of his work have wondered why he did so unusual a thing—unusual in a historian—as to undertake the history of an event in progress; and it used to be said that he showed poor historical judgment in calling his war a bigger event than the Persian War: the Persian War decided the course of European history for centuries to come, while this was only a local struggle. Thucydides himself answers both those problems: all we have to do is to read what he says, and to conceive it possible that ours may not be the only possible way of being intelligent about history. He foresaw, he says, that the coming clash between the two alliances would be the biggest in known history; and at the end of his prefatory chapters he says that never before, in a comparable length of time, had so many cities been destroyed and left desolate, or been repopulated with strangers, so many men killed or driven into exile. In other words, he is considering the war not as a complex political event but as the greatest human catastrophe ever known.

In that, he shows the same cast of mind as the tragic poets, and his mode of composition is similar: "dramatic" not in that he goes much in for vivid description (though he can describe more vividly than most, when he chooses), but in a more fundamental way. At critical points in his narrative he will insert a speech, real or invented, or two opposing speeches, in which future policy is debated, plans, hopes, fears expressed; then, in accurate and mostly unadorned narrative, he will tell us what happened. He himself, usually, will make no comment; he leaves it to us to compare prospects with results, to ask what went wrong, and why. In a sense, he has already made his own comment, silently in the juxtaposition of speech and narrative. He said himself: "I have not written a Book of the Month but one to last for ever," and as we reread it and reread it again, we feel ourselves in the presence of a mind which has investigated that catastrophe most patiently and has distilled from it much of what is permanent in human nature, human political actions, and the human condition.

How do you account for the emergence of Greek philosophy?

It is often said that Greek philosophy began in the sixth century B.C. among the Ionian Greeks, with Thales of Miletus. It was he and his successors who began to enquire systematically into the nature, constitution, laws, of the universe. It began in Ionia, not in European Greece, because Ionia was more in touch with the older cultures of Asia and Egypt; Thales had traveled a lot, and had picked up bits of knowledge about mathematics, astronomy, and the like which set him thinking—and that started it.

This is true enough, but to my mind it doesn't explain enough. Why hadn't philosophy already got going among those older cultures?

Another point. With all proper respect for Hittite sculpture, Hebraic poetry, Egyptian architecture, and so on, I suppose everyone would admit that among the Mediterranean peoples the Greeks were far and away the most artistic. Isn't it then a bit of a paradox—at least at first sight—that they were also the only ones who can be called the "scientists" of antiquity? Criticize their "science" as you like: the fact remains that in mathematics, astronomy, medicine, biology, they did more than any other people until relatively modern times. Strange, perhaps, for a race of artists?

What I am coming to is this: the Milesians were the first Greeks to engage in systematic philosophical thinking, but the philosophic *temper* was there from the beginning. The imaginative vitality and the profusion of Greek myth, the apparent irresponsibility of their "religion," the unending delight they took in particular details—for instance, Homer will usually tell us exactly where the spear point went into the body of an unlucky hero, and often where it came out again—all this tends to obscure from us the poet's underlying concern with general and permanent truth. The *Odyssey* has its wildly romantic and delightfully irrational details, all over the place, but there is also Athena, and she shows that the poet's mind is also engaged on a deeper level: order as against disorder. The same with the tragic poets: their "religion" is often unintelligible until we realize that their *theoi* are not necessarily edifying moral conceptions, but do, always, relate to some aspect of a permanent order—comfortable or uncomfortable. I think that it is this instinctive assumption of a universal Order that lies behind particular events and phenomena that is the link between Greek art and Greek philosophy. Surely it would not be unreasonable to find, in this assumption, the forerunner both of Thales' indeterminate substrate, which he called "the Moist," or Water, and of Plato's metaphysical world of Forms ("Ideas").

As for Socrates, I will—in prudence—say only one thing, but that perhaps one of the most important. He was familiar (if we are to believe Plato) with the "scientific" speculations of the Ionian philosophers and had come to two conclusions: that they were not getting anywhere, and that in any case there was a question of prior importance—as there still is, namely: How are we to live? The truth about the stars would be fascinating, if we could find it, but the truth about Man and the proper ordering of our conduct is more important. This of course had been a major concern of the Attic tragedians, but Socrates (according to Plato) rejected them because they could not *prove* that what they were saying was true. The age of great poetry was ending; the age of great prose was beginning.

What are the differences between the great philosophers and the playwrights in their view of the human condition?

What immediately comes to mind is something that Aristotle says on tragedy, that it would be intolerable, in a play, to see a man of high character falling "from happiness into unhappiness"; there must be some justifying, or partly justifying, error or fault. The tragic poets (as it were) knew better: the major point of the *Oedipus Tyrannus,* for example, is that Oedipus, Jocasta, and (prospectively) the two daughters have their lives ruined although they have done nothing whatever to deserve it.

Again, there is the Socratic doctrine that nobody does wrong except out of ignorance; we do not willingly choose the "bad," or "what is bad for us," instead of the good. That is philosophically true, but it has little relation to "the human condition," in which we do not as a rule have this perfect knowledge. It has often been suggested that Euripides' *Medea* was, in some sort, the poet's reply to Socrates: he makes Medea say "My passions overcome my judgment."

Could one say this? that the poets view the human condition as it is, and the philosophers as it isn't, but might be, if . . . The poets, naturally, accept as a fact human mortality; Plato does all kinds of intellectual gymnastics to prove, or make plausible, Immortality.

You have developed the theme that there was a central tradition of Greek thought—responsibility, order, justice, restraint. Was this continued in Plato and Aristotle?

Certainly. These are among the virtues that any mature society must value, and the ethical philosophy of both Plato and Aristotle was firmly rooted in the idea of the Greek *polis* as the natural form of civilized society.

The *Antigone* ends with the reflection that "The greatest part of well-being is Understanding"; meaning, as I said just now, that statecraft—what Plato was to call "the political art"—must comprise an understanding of the laws, moral and otherwise, which govern human existence; without this it is not a "craft," only an ignorance that will end in disaster. Doesn't Plato say the same in the *Republic*—of course much more elaborately and intellectually? His Governors are to be vigorously trained in the art of knowing; those who rule must *understand;* the rest must perform their appropriate functions under their direction.

Plato's "Justice," Aristotle's theory of the Mean—that the Good is the Mean between two extremes, both bad—seem to me to continue the Greek tradition.

5

The Hellenistic World

MORTIMER CHAMBERS

THE HISTORIOGRAPHICAL CONTEXT

The Hellenistic empires, the successor states to Alexander the Great's world conquests, are among the great losers of history. Drawing upon Greek culture, the heritage of the old civilization of the ancient Near East, enjoying the comforts and benefits of large urban centers and the prosperity of vibrant international commerce, these Mediterranean societies of the last three centuries A.D. yet fell all too easily before the Roman onslaught. Historians have too often tended to follow the human proclivity to favor the victor and denigrate the vanquished, and the Hellenistic world has never received the lavish attention given to Athens and Rome. Yet we know how important was the contribution of the Hellenistic societies to the making of Western civilization—the ideal of universal citizenship and the proliferation of sacramental religions being only the most obvious aspects of the Hellenistic heritage. Recent scholarship has abandoned the old image of the Hellenistic societies as effete and decadent, and the complicated history of these highly creative cultures is beginning to receive its due attention.

To understand in broad perspective the development of the Mediterranean world over three centuries requires not only great learning but an unusual breadth of historical insight and imagination. In this kind of invaluable work of generalization and comparative analysis, the younger generation of American historians studying the European and Mediterranean past have shown themselves particularly adept. Perhaps it is the heterogeneous makeup of their own society, certainly their standpoint outside of Europe and its national traditions, which has contributed to this facility. Hence Mortimer Chambers, born in 1927, Professor of Ancient History at the University of California at Los Angeles, who has made several significant contributions to Greek and Roman history, is well suited to deal with the long- and far-ranging Hellenistic world. (Chambers is typical of American scholars of his generation in his combination of a mastery of academic scholarship with a straightforward, down-to-earth articulateness, and a skill in high-level conceptualization and generalizing.)

Chronological Outline

359 B.C.: Philip II becomes regent of Macedon.

336 B.C.: Alexander the Great becomes king of Macedon at the age of twenty.

336–323 B.C.: The spread of Greek culture by the conquests of Alexander as far as the Indus Valley, and the creation of Greek cities throughout Asia. Foundation of Alexandria in 331 B.C. and the death of Alexander in Babylon in 323 B.C.

334 B.C.: Aristotle opens the Lyceum in Athens. Death of Aristotle in 323 B.C.

c. 323–c. 275 B.C.: Alexander's empire is divided among his commanders. Ptolemy I rules in Egypt and founds the great library and museum at Alexandria. Alexandria becomes the intellectual and cultural capital of the world. Seleucus rules the largest of the Hellenistic kingdoms, the Seleucid empire in Asia and Asia Minor. Antigonus founds a dynasty in Macedon which exercises an overlordship of Greece. The Aetolian League of western Greek cities and the Achaean League of towns in the northern Peloponnesus emerge; in the future they will sometimes support, sometimes oppose the Macedonian kingdom.

315 B.C.: Birth of Theocritus of Syracuse, the originator of pastoral idyllic literature.

c. 300 B.C.: Euclid invents his system of geometry. Zeno of Cyprus and Epicurus father their respective doctrines of inner discipline—Stoicism and Epicureanism. The rival Peripatetic school concentrates on science and history.

292 B.C.: Death of Menander, the great model for later Roman writers of comedy.

287 B.C.: Birth of Archimedes.

c. 250–c. 100 B.C.: The Hebrew Bible is translated into Alexandrian Greek (the Septuagint).

230 B.C.: Pergamum becomes an independent kingdom.

202? B.C.: Birth of Polybius, Roman historian.

c. 185–182 B.C.: The Seleucid empire is defeated by Roman armies.

171–167 B.C.: After almost fifty years of intermittent warfare, the Macedonian kingdom and its Greek allies are defeated decisively by the Romans. The Greek cities are forbidden to form leagues and Macedonia is divided into four separate republics under Roman control.

146 B.C.: After putting down an attempt to revive a Macedonian kingdom, Rome annexes Macedon.

64 B.C.: The Seleucid empire is made a Roman protectorate.

31 B.C.: The forces of the last Hellenistic kingdom, Ptolemaic Egypt, are defeated by Rome at the Battle of Actium. The following year it is annexed to Rome.

Norman F. Cantor
What are the major sources for our knowledge of the Hellenistic Age?

Mortimer Chambers
Perhaps we should begin by defining the Hellenistic Age. I consider that it began with the death of Alexander the Great in 323 B.C. and lasted until Cleopatra, the last Macedonian monarch, ceased to reign in 30 B.C. Hers was the last Mediterranean kingdom founded on Greek and Macedonian ancestral privileges.

Hellenistic historians inherited from the classic ancient historians a marvelous historiographic machine. Herodotus and Thucydides set the writing of history on a sound basis by simply inquiring into the facts they observed. Neither of them was completely objective, of course; Herodotus in particular wished to exemplify certain ethical maxims such as "Know thyself" and "Nothing too much." These Delphic utterances (never explicitly mentioned) underlie his description of the attempts of the magnificent Persian empire to overcome the Greeks. In some instances Herodotus resorted to the Fates for causation, and occasionally he invoked divine machinery. He even explained the destruction of part of the Persian fleet as the gods' will. Apparently, as he thought, they did not want one fleet to have a great advantage over the other!

Mythological explanations are less frequent in the work of Thucydides, whose tone is one of objectivity and restraint. He was not completely aloof, however; he stated that he was writing for the man who wanted to understand the future, for the future would resemble the past. I imagine that the Greek medical writers, with their interest in prediction or *prognosis,* influenced Thucydides' enquiry into causality.

In the fourth century a strong interest in rhetoric and literary style (even at the expense of accuracy) was suddenly infused into the classic historiographic system. The man most responsible for the change was Isocrates, who converted history into a branch of persuasion or even journalism. His pupils, Theopompus and Ephorus, followed Isocrates and lost the accuracy and clinical objectivity sought by Herodotus and Thucydides.

Scholars have recently argued that Hellenistic historians consciously attempted to infuse poetic and tragic qualities into the writing of history. A new kind of dramatic portraiture appeared. Biographical writing, which scarcely existed in the classical period, flourished in the fourth century. It was influenced by the new trends, and particularly by Aristotle. In his *Ethics* he searches for analyses and classifications of various kinds of man—the brave man, the magnanimous man, the self-disciplined man, and so on. Theophrastus, Aristotle's pupil, wrote a series of sketches called the *Characters,* in which he defined the superstitious man, the cowardly man, and others, and gave examples of their behavior. The book was typically Greek in one way, for Greek philosophers always delighted in defining the precise use of words. The compulsion to clarify and classify was a strong theme in Greek thought.

The Hellenistic interest in biography influenced the work of an Alexandrian scholar named Hermippus, who wrote lives of Greek authors and historical characters. He occasionally wrote in violent deaths in order to wind up the careers of his subjects dramatically. Hermippus also invented a purely fictitious economic background for Solon, the Athenian reformer, to explain this statesman's liberal positions. Thus arbitrary motivations were introduced into historical writing in the fourth century.

The new interest in character and lives made it possible for historians to illustrate human character by weaving it into a historical context. This movement reached its climax in the work of Plutarch, a Greek writer of about A.D. 100. He wrote an extremely popular series of biographies. Plutarch's portraits were often based on the writings of the later Greek historians, and his tone is that of a judge of the behavior of historical figures. In his life of Alexander, Plutarch stated that he was not writing history, but lives. Therefore he might overlook anything that did not contribute to a knowledge of character. Just as a portrait painter concentrates on the most revealing lines and expressions of a face, Plutarch concentrated on the actions that most clearly revealed the characteristics of his subject.

Any examination of ancient Greek civilization must rely on materials selected by Byzantine librarians and scholars after the fall of the Roman Empire. There was a great deal of material that the Byzantines did not choose to pass on. Aeschylus, for instance, is said to have written more than ninety tragedies; we have the texts of only seven. Apparently the plays we do have are those considered by Byzantine scholars to be most exemplary of each man's work. There are many surviving manuscripts of Sophocles' play *Ajax*, for example, and it may have been selected because of its connection with the poems of Homer.

This process of selection has maimed our knowledge of the Hellenistic historians, who were numerous but are almost all lost to us. Apparently the Byzantines concluded that none of them was of the stature of Herodotus or Thucydides, for they ignored the later historians and preserved the classical works. The Hellenistic historians that we do know survive mainly in fragments—not so much in scraps of papyrus as in citations in the writings of other men. These fragments have been reassembled in the twentieth century in a monumental set of volumes by the great German scholar Felix Jacoby. His work is titled *Die Fragmente der griechischen Historiker* (*The Fragments of the Greek Historians*). It comprises seventeen volumes and was still unfinished at Jacoby's death.

The Hellenistic historian that we know best is Polybius, a careful and accurate writer. Polybius' father was a prominent official of the Achaean League during the period when Rome was beginning to dominate the Greek states. Polybius himself was deported to Rome and was forced to remain there for several years. He was not totally restricted in his movements and managed to meet many well-educated Romans. There is a parallel, incidentally, in the career of Thucydides, who was exiled from Athens for twenty years, visited the Spartan side, and gained valuable information for his work. The same thing happened to Polybius. In the circle of Scipio Aemilianus he learned much about Roman mores, law, and society that he could not have discovered in any other way. This experience also suggested to him a particular view of history. Polybius believed that the Mediterranean world would inevitably fall to Rome. By his writings he hoped to save the Greeks from throwing away their lives in vain resistance and to ready them for their position within the Roman Empire.

Whether or not we like the concept of inevitable history—and most modern scholars do not—Polybius' predictions were quite correct. In forty volumes he documented the spread of Roman supremacy throughout the Mediterranean basin. Of these volumes, five have survived complete and many others in sections. Perhaps the Byzantines selected the first five books because they set the stage for all that followed.

Polybius wanted to take a world-historical approach to his task. Time and again he attacked those Hellenistic historians who tried to write history in monographs. A favorite target was Timaeus, who wrote a history of his native island, Sicily. Polybius believed that a man could no more learn history from monographs any more than he could master the workings of the human body by examining its parts in isolation. Only when the parts are united in an organic relationship can one truly understand the whole. He did not specifically name Herodotus as his model, but we moderns can see a similarity between his notion of universal history and the broad scope of the chronicler of the Persian Wars.

Polybius' theory of causation is characteristic of his period. During the Hellenistic Age there was an enormous disruption of everyday life. The explosion of Greek life to the East, the rise and fall of kingdoms and dynasties, immersed the Mediterranean world in an atmosphere of insecurity. No one could be sure how long his king would remain on the throne or his country at peace. Hellenistic Greeks turned to various intellectual frameworks to give meaning and direction to their lives. Polybius relied on the working force that he called Fortune, or *Tyche*. Fortune was personified as a goddess, and Polybius believed that her vagaries had much to do with the way things happened. He stated that one of Fortune's most spectacular creations could be studied in the rise of the Roman Empire, implying that the rise of Rome was supernaturally controlled.

There is an important contradiction in this view of Fortune. In his clear demonstration of how the Romans came to dominate the Mediterranean, Polybius had no need to adopt supernatural explanations. He analyzed the economic, political, and social factors that went into the forging of the Roman Empire. Thus two notions of causation ran parallel in Polybius' work. One—readily acceptable to any modern historian (or to Thucydides)—demonstrated that diplomatic and military skill carved out the Roman Empire. The other notion is highly characteristic of the Hellenistic Age. Everything was in turmoil, and the currents of upheaval were so strong and so whimsical that they could be explained only as the activities of the goddess Fortune. The contradiction between the two views is striking, and it provides some insight into the mind of Polybius. He was the product of his environment, but he was able to transcend it to some extent.

How must we rate Polybius as a follower of Herodotus and Thucydides? On the whole he did rather well. He was not yet alive during some of the events that he recorded, and for these he turned to a careful examination of the sources. He did his best to evaluate the work of earlier historians, and while he sometimes was hypercritical, this is only an excess of a virtue. He did not accept anything on faith. At considerable risk to himself, he traveled to the sites of many of the events he described. Polybius was a pioneer in documentary research; he found on an Italian promontory an inscription of Hannibal's that recorded data concerning the Carthaginian military forces. This was far indeed from those Hellenistic historians who were content to pick and choose from earlier writings.

Polybius was chiefly interested in political and diplomatic history, and he coined the phrase "pragmatic history" to describe it. The word *pragmatic* did not necessarily mean history of practical use to a statesman, but rather history concerned with serious events. The Greek word *pragmata* denotes events of some importance. Polybius concentrated on the actions of great men, dwelling on social and economic history only to a limited degree.

His portraits of great men are among his finest pages. For example, there is Flamininus, the Roman general who skillfully managed a military and diplomatic war against Philip V of Macedonia. Or again, an unusually gentle and sensitive episode describes the friendly relations between Polybius himself and the young Scipio Aemilianus who became his companion at Rome. Most unforgettable of all is the towering figure of Hannibal, the brilliant Carthaginian general who invaded Italy in 218–217 B.C. The exploits of Hannibal, in Book Three, are told with concentrated narrative and profound sympathy.

The portion of Polybius' sixth book that deals with the Roman constitution has received a great deal of attention. He analyzed the history of the constitution largely in terms of political philosophy, a method of analysis that was initiated by Plato and continued by Aristotle. Polybius described the Roman system as an example of a mixed constitution, a blend of the three forms of government: monarchy, aristocracy, and democracy. This was a form much esteemed by Aristotle. The monarchic element in Rome was represented by the consuls and other magistrates; the aristocratic by the Senate, the advisory body to the magistrates; the democratic by the popular assemblies. Polybius had a good sense of their relative functions, and he revealed the system of checks and balances built into the Roman constitution.

Polybius also raised the question of how constitutions may be transformed. Here again he drew on earlier political theory and was influenced, no doubt, by the fall of numerous kingdoms in his own time. He demonstrated to his own satisfaction that there exists a kind of constitutional cycle in which a state with a stable political form suffers a progressive decline and eventually deteriorates into mob rule. At that point, autocratic rule must be imposed again in order to regain a stable administration, and the cycle resumes. The cyclic theory seems to imply that all constitutions must go through a spiral of decline, but Polybius apparently made an exception for Rome. He believed that the judicious mixture of elements in the Roman constitution would somehow preserve the stability of the state. Here again there is an interesting contradiction between Polybius' philosophic models and his depiction of actual events. He failed to harmonize the contradictions because he was not a skillful philosopher.

Despite his philosophical flaws, Polybius is far and away the best representative of the Hellenistic historians, and he may well have been the best. (This, of course, is a risky assertion because so many of the others have been lost.) His work is especially valuable for Western readers because it documents the mixture of the Greek and Roman worlds.

Polybius, unlike most modern historians, did not have a true sense of Hellenistic civilization. He did not imply that a new civilization was growing in the cultural melting pot of the Mediterranean, but he did recognize (with Herodotus) the essential unity of ancient Mediterranean history with that of his own period. Although he did not see history from our perspective, he was one of the few historians of his time with any sense of evolution. Polybius saw that the Mediterranean Sea did not divide Europe, North Africa, Egypt, and Palestine but rather connected them in a common political and cultural destiny. Today we are much closer to this civilization than to that of the Hittites, Babylonians, or Sumerians.

Polybius was sometimes pedantic and humorless when he congratulated himself on uniting the various histories of the Mediterranean; still, his perception deserves praise even if his performance sometimes fell short of his vision. The great German historian Mommsen said of Polybius, "His books are like the sun in the field of Roman history." For much of ancient history we have to grope through legend and myth, but with Polybius the clouds part over the men and events of Roman times.

What picture do our sources give us of the important kingdom of Macedonia and of the reign of Alexander the Great?

We must divide history into periods in order to handle it conveniently. As I have said, the Hellenistic Age begins with the death of Alexander the Great; but it is worthwhile to go back and examine the civilization that produced the last great king of pre-Roman times.

In the classical period of Greek history, the fifth century B.C., Macedonia was only a kind of appendage atop the Grecian peninsula. The Peloponnesian War brought Macedonia into the picture for a while, but only as a potential ally for one side or the other. In the fourth century it suddenly assumed massive importance in Greek affairs, and this was primarily because of the constant internecine warfare of the Greek city-states. The Peloponnesian War lasted for twenty-seven years; it shed the lifeblood of the Greek democracies and splintered any possible resistance to the Macedonian onslaught. The breakdown of morale in the city-states made it difficult to raise armies, as is evident in the Philippic orations (speeches delivered against Philip) by Demosthenes. Philip II of Macedonia brought his state into Greek politics by a series of intrigues, and he captured the heartland of the Greek peninsula at the decisive battle of Chaeronea in 338 B.C.

What was Macedonia, and who was its king? Unlike most of the classical city-states, Macedonia was a kingdom. In fact we can almost see in the Macedonian state the survival of ancient Homeric ideas of kingship. We have virtually no Macedonian source material, but it is possible to gain some insight into Macedonian ideas by examining the Homeric traditions. Macedonian kings were hereditary monarchs, but they ruled only as long as they could command the allegiance of their armies. Modern scholars are in the habit of saying that the Macedonian army elected the ruler, but this was not exactly the case. I would say instead that the army had to approve or confirm the accession of a king. As long as the king conceded certain traditional rights to the army—such as the right to try important men—and as long as the monarch was able and vigorous, the army followed him. Macedonia had no constitution, and forms of government were not so well developed as those of classical Greece.

There were centers of population in Macedonia, but little of the creative urbanization of classical Greece. Each Greek city had its gymnasium, its place of meeting, and its market, all of which contributed to public life. Macedonia, by contrast, was an agricultural and hunting kingdom. In a country void of intellectual recreation, the two prime off-duty activities were hunting and drinking. Macedonians drank wine without mixing it with water as the Greeks did, and they indulged in savage and primitive drinking bouts. Many of Alexander's most despicable acts were committed under the influence of wine.

Literature and philosophy were nonexistent, although attempts were made to import some of the cultural achievements of the Greeks. Aristotle tutored Alexander, and Antigonus—a third-century monarch—was considered a philosopher-king. But as far as native Macedonian thought is concerned, this was not an intellectual society.

Philip II, the great king who conquered Greece, was cunning and treacherous, but the skill of his diplomatic accomplishments cannot be denied. Both Philip and Alexander admired the civic achievements of the Greek states. After the Battle of Chaeronea, when Philip had Athens at his mercy, he did not allow his troops to pillage the city. He acted not out of mercy but mature political consideration, hoping that Athens would act as the balance wheel in the political structure that he intended to establish in Greece. Philip organized the city-states into the League of Corinth, which was not an association of equals but a Macedonian hegemony. He hoped that the

League would give him formal moral status in the Greek world.

Philip planned to do just what many Greek generals had envisioned: to attack and pillage the Persian empire. The Greeks had kept the Persians at arm's length, but their attacks on Persian coastal cities had almost no effect on the monolithic empire. Philip was assassinated, however, just as he was about to set out on this voyage of conquest. The assassin was a disaffected Macedonian noble, and the best efforts of scholars have failed to unravel his motives. Some assert that Alexander, as the chief gainer, must have organized the murder, but the matter has not been settled. In any event, history has rarely offered such opportunities to any young prince.

To understand Alexander the Great we first have to look at the problem of the sources that can inform us about his life. This is a further study in Hellenistic historiography, a subject that we discussed a little earlier. We have no ancient narrative of Alexander's life that is even remotely contemporary with him. In fact, the oldest surviving one is in the universal history of Diodorus of Sicily, a late Hellenistic historian writing toward the end of the first century B.C.—already three hundred years later than Alexander. The question at once arises: What sources did Diodorus use? Unfortunately he does not say, and scholars have not yet sorted them out. The situation is a little clearer with our best source, Arrian, whose life of Alexander was written in the second century A.D.

Arrian states that he follows two sources above all: Aristobulus and Ptolemy. The former of these participated in Alexander's expedition and should have been fairly well informed. As for Ptolemy, he was of course one of Alexander's marshals and also the founder of the Ptolemaic dynasty that ruled Egypt for nearly three centuries. His narrative about Alexander is usually thought to have been fairly reliable. That, at least, is how Arrian considered it, but he gave a naïve reason for his trust in Ptolemy: since Ptolemy was a king, it would be more disgraceful for him to lie than for a private citizen. Whaever we think of this strange reasoning, Arrian did follow Ptolemy most of the time, and the result is a generally well-balanced and acceptable biography.

There are serious differences among modern historians about the character of Alexander. We might start with the first German historian of Greece, Johann Gustav Droysen (1808–1884). He wrote three volumes on Alexander and his successors down to 221 B.C. His conception of Alexander was very favorable—he saw in him the fulfillment of Greek historical destiny—and has not been wholly overcome to this day. Less fortunate was the clear influence of the philosopher-historian Hegel on Droysen. Much of his work embodies the assumptions of determinism: for example, he called Alexander the "tool of history." This overlooks the high probability that events happen mainly through choices made by people.

A modern restatement of the heroic view of Alexander was made by Sir William Tarn. In 1933 and several times afterward, Tarn asserted that Alexander intended to blend East and West—that the king conceived himself as fulfilling an ideological mission for the benefit of mankind. Perhaps we can understand Tarn's beliefs if we examine his background. Sir Frank Adcock, in an obituary of Tarn published by the British Academy, said that Tarn was a man of a naturally aristocratic state of mind. He wanted Alexander, and all world leaders, to be noble and generous. In fact, however, few if any historians accept Tarn's theory that Alexander was working for the "brotherhood of man." It basically rests on a flight of rhetoric by Plutarch, in his "On the Fortunes of Alexander."

And it has been attacked several times, most decisively by another British-trained historian, Professor Badian. After a critical and withering analysis of Tarn's evidence, Badian draws the conclusion, which I endorse, that we have no proof that Alexander was working toward international brotherhood. The famous banquet, where Alexander poured a libation to the spirit of Harmony took place at a critical time for his rule, and the king was probably pleading for stability in his forces.

If we eliminate the philosophical ideals that Tarn attributed to Alexander, we can interpret his actions in a more convincing way. In studies published during the last ten years, Badian has demonstrated that Alexander was often repressively suspicious of his generals. He condemned several of them to death on questionable charges, a fact suggesting the political purges in Europe during the 1930's rather than the actions of an idealistic young prince. The lack of contemporary documentation prevents any final resolution of this debatable subject, so Alexander will continue to inspire biographical study.

Given the difficulty of judging Alexander as a man, how are we to characterize his achievements as statesman and conqueror? His father, Philip, initiated the conquest of Persia, and Alexander followed directly in his father's path. In a series of brilliant battles, he beat the Persians decisively. Their king became a fugitive who was eventually murdered by one of his own subordinates. Alexander had accomplished his objectives up to that point. He had captured the Persian treasuries and amassed a fortune of 180,000 talents in uncoined money, a sum beyond description. But instead of consolidating his victories, he plunged on to Pakistan and crossed the Indus, traveling to the very fringes of the known world.

Why did Alexander go on to further conquest? He certainly could not have hoped to gain booty comparable to that of Persia. It may be that Alexander simply could not return to Macedonia to contemplate his achievements. He preferred adventure, violence, and conquest. He had fantastic endurance, and his men followed him mostly with devotion. Rarely has a military leader inspired such loyalty. This is the heroic side of Alexander. On the other side is the wasteful expenditure of human and economic resources for no apparent gain. Alexander finally went as far as humanly possible. He began to make his way back to the west, and during this final journey Tarn's banquet took place at Opis. Alexander never got home, for he died near Babylon of a fever aggravated by an all-night drinking bout. Suddenly, this meteoric figure disappeared from the stage of world history.

In Tarn's phrase, Alexander "lifted the civilized world out of one groove and set it in another." He was largely responsible for the explosion of Greek culture into the eastern world, into Egypt, Asia Minor, and to some extent even Iran and India. Today we analyze history in terms of impersonal social and economic forces, but here one man's personality left a decisive imprint on the world.

With all his achievements, Alexander did not consolidate an empire that could survive him. Soon after the king's death, his generals parceled out his territories, and there followed the complex events known as the Wars of the Successors, in which the empire was dismembered. The process lasted for four or five decades. At the end of this period, the empire was divided into three blocs that corresponded to natural divisions. The first was Macedonia, on the Greek mainland, ruled by the descendants of Antigonus—the Antigonids. The second great section was the Near East, as we might call it, corresponding roughly to the old Persian empire, and this was ruled by the Seleucids. The third unit was the Egyptian state taken over by

Alexander's general Ptolemy, whose dynasty endured until the suicide of Cleopatra in 30 B.C. These three great kingdoms were the inheritors of Alexander's empire.

To these three sections we must add a fourth: the kingdom of Pergamum in Asia Minor, which seized its independence in the third century. It was not so strong or extensive as the other three; but, ironically, this fourth partner was one of the agents that involved the Romans permanently in the affairs of the Greek world.

When Alexander's empire was broken up into separate Hellenistic kingdoms, what kinds of states emerged? Specifically, what was the administrative structure of the Ptolemaic and Seleucid monarchies?

The Hellenistic kingdoms about which we know most are the Ptolemaic kingdom of Egypt and the Seleucid kingdom based on the region of Syria. For Egypt, our main sources are hundreds of papyrus documents preserved in the arid sands of the desert. Egypt was the only kingdom to use papyrus to a large extent, and many documents survive that are still undeciphered. It will take several generations for all this material to be processed. Sources for the Seleucid kingdom are much less copious; the most revealing are inscriptions—chiefly documents on stone. We also have several narratives, including that of Polybius—who did not, however, treat problems of administration.

In the Ptolemaic kingdom, one society imposed itself upon another in an effort to achieve order and rationalization. The young kingdom of the Macedonians imposed its administrative structure upon the immemorial society of the Nile, one of the oldest of all civilizations. The Ptolemies governed the Egyptians by right of naked conquest, without any pretense of lawful accession to the throne. The basic element in their rule was always the Macedonian army. With the help of a significant number of imported Greeks, this foreign force kept the Egyptians under control. From the beginning, then, the government was militaristic and bureaucratic. It maintained a great many employees to collect taxes and to control all its subjects up and down the Nile.

To what degree was this oppressive system new, and to what degree did it proceed from the Egyptian past? Egypt had had a rigid system ever since the unification of the Upper and Lower kingdoms. When Ptolemy I took over Egypt after Alexander's death, he was not doing anything new. Some scholars assert that he adopted many of the administrative practices that he found, and introduced others only to deal with special problems. The Macedonians found a going concern and kept it going. They did, however, improve the bureaucratic system, and the correspondence of one Zenon, who lived in the third century B.C., testifies to the pedantic care with which the Macedonians managed the Egyptian economy.

Egypt's lack of urbanization—in other words, the concentration of people in villages along the Nile—helped the Ptolemies to control the country. There were few important cities, and of these the most impressive was the Hellenistic city Alexandria, which was in no way typical of an Egyptian farming village. Large urban centers tend to foster revolution and civic dissatisfaction more readily than isolated farming communities, where people are exclusively concerned with their struggles with the land. This is, of course, by no means a hard and fast historical rule, but it seems to hold true for Egypt. The Ptolemies did not want cities, and they kept the country in its rural state.

The most Hellenized region of Egypt was the Delta, the mouth of the Nile just south of Alexandria. Here Greek cultural influence was strongly felt, and that influence declined as one traveled up the Nile in a southerly direction. Some Macedonians and Greeks were given allotments of land to hold as absentee landlords who were free to concentrate upon military affairs. This system, practiced in other Macedonian kingdoms as well, was derived from ancient Sparta.

Eventually the Macedonians in Egypt were not numerous enough to man the increasingly complicated bureaucracy, and they had to employ more Egyptians. At the same time, uprisings occurred more and more often and it became necessary to supplement the Macedonian army with Egyptian contingents. Toward the end of the third century, increasing numbers of Egyptians were taken into the armed forces. It was no longer possible for the Macedonians to maintain themselves as an exclusive elite in control of Egyptian society.

The Macedonian kings of Egypt owned the entire land, and government monopolies of various products ensured their control of the economy. The entire supply of oil, for instance, was owned by the king, who sold it at a fixed price and outlawed any private sale, thus guaranteeing his own revenue. This would not have been possible in a Greek state; it points toward the state economies of the Roman Empire. In this as in other ways, the Hellenistic Age served as a bridge between the classical Greek and Roman worlds.

It would not be fair to imply that the Ptolemies exploited the kingdom without making any economic improvements. One thing they did for the Egyptians—out of self-interest—was to introduce various agricultural products such as the vine, which grew all over Greece on land too poor to support grain. The Macedonians introduced the vine and the olive to Egypt largely for the sake of the Greek population, which required wine to supplement the native beer. Here as elsewhere it is difficult to dissociate economic motivations from humane promptings. The Ptolemies often freed prisoners at harvest time, for example, but this again was a practical economic move rather than a kindness.

The most important economic innovation of the Ptolemies was the extensive use of money. Lynn White has said that coinage is the only technological invention found in the Greek world that was not present in the old eastern kingdoms. All the other technology—the plow and pottery making, for example—was native to the ancient Near East. The expansion of coinage in the Macedonian kingdoms stimulated commercial activity during the Hellenistic Age.

Another aspect of Greek culture imported by the Ptolemies was the gymnasium, the meeting place and social nucleus of the classical Greek communities. Gymnasia and similar centers fostered the civic intensity and political concern of classical Greece. Like the vine, the gymnasium probably was introduced to the Egyptian world to satisfy the ruling Greeks and Macedonians.

The kingdom of the Ptolemies long outlasted the Macedonian Greek and Seleucid domains. The Egyptian kingdom was administered in a paternalistic manner, but all operations of government were established and organized to guarantee the welfare of the rulers. Some observers speculate that the kings won the affection of the people, and this is certainly possible.

Some Egyptians fought on the side of the Macedonians even during the uprisings already mentioned, and it would be fallacious to characterize these conflicts as a clear split between oppressed native masses and an overbearing ruling class. I doubt, however, that any spirit of affection preserved the kingdom as much as the political efficiency with which it was managed.

The cult of rulers may have played some part in the stability of the Ptolemaic kingdom. Alexander the Great had exploited the Greek tradition of hero worship (even in the fifth century, certain Greek heroes were revered as demigods); one of his subordinates apparently suggested that the Greek states should offer him divine homage. Alexander died before the new institution could be fully tested, but ruler cult was taken up by the Oriental kingdoms, in which the distinction between god and man had always been unclear. The cult was especially successful in Egypt, because the pharaohs had been considered divine from the very beginning of Egyptian civilization. The Ptolemies represented themselves as the latest pharaohs.

The first Ptolemy tried to introduce an official state deity, Serapis, into Egypt. Serapis, though an old Egyptian god, was introduced in Hellenic form; he was a Zeus-figure, a lord and creator of the world. The purpose behind the cult, I imagine, was to give the old Egyptian religion a form compatible with that of the Ptolemies. Apparently the cult did not succeed and died out. The second Ptolemy sought to introduce a similar reform when he established Dionysiac festivals. However, none of the Ptolemies could overturn the religious traditions of ancient Egypt, and they were shrewd enough to recognize their failures and cut their losses.

It is illuminating to compare the administration of the Ptolemies with that of the Seleucids. The Seleucid kingdom had a much more complex mixture of people than that of Egypt, where natural isolation enforced genetic uniformity. Persians, Hittites, Jews, and Babylonians were only a few of the many peoples within the Seleucid kingdom. The Seleucids had to rule with the army; they could not rely on the natives of the Near East to maintain stability. As we have seen, the Ptolemies distributed land up and down the Nile to soldiers in the hope that they would protect their vested interests and keep the peace. The Seleucids, with a much greater area to control, could not use this method alone. In addition to it they urbanized the kingdom, founding as many cities as possible to serve as nuclei of Hellenic civilization. Some of these urban areas—notably Antioch—became important world capitals. The new cities had to administer an enormous expanse of territory. Egyptian administration may be characterized by the swarms of bureaucrats and dozens of taxes spread up and down the Nile, while the Seleucid administration was based on a close core of royal advisers who held sway in administrative units throughout the kingdom.

Like the Ptolemies, the Seleucids attempted to build a new state within a functioning system. The administrative structure they inherited went back to the Persian and Assyrian tradition of the satrapy. The satrapies were the traditional divisions of the realm, and about twenty-five were in existence when the Seleucids took over.

The Seleucid attempt to impose one society on another had interesting implications for the Jewish community in the Hellenistic world. For reasons that no historian can explain, the Jews managed to maintain their cultural identity if not their political integrity, mainly through religious devotion. In the middle of the second century B.C., the Seleucids made an attempt to Hellenize the Jews. They placed a statue of Zeus in the Temple of Jerusalem—a serious and tragic affront to Judaism that inspired a rebellion led by the Maccabees, who succeeded in cleansing the Temple of the image. The Jews could not be Hellenized, not by the Seleucids and not by Roman conquerors later on. The Romans did not at first seek to profane the Jewish religion, but they fell heir to the rancor aroused by the Seleucid rulers.

The Seleucids did not survive as long as the Ptolemies, probably in large part because their territory was harder to administer than the valley of the Nile. They could not prevent local areas from declaring independence, as in the example of Pergamum already mentioned. The people of Pergamum were always afraid of falling under Seleucid domination once more, which explains their alliances with the Romans. The Pergamene kings hoped that Rome would maintain the balance of power and guarantee the freedom of their rebel state.

These monarchies included many Greek cities; how did the Hellenistic city differ from the Greek city of classical times?

The new cities of the Egyptian and Seleucid kingdoms were given the formal independence of the old Greek state, or *polis*. Even though the *polis* was outmoded as an independent state by the advent of more powerful military and political confederations, it endured in some form well past the end of the Hellenistic era. New cities were granted the traditional rights of the *polis*, but of course they were not nearly so uncontrolled. Kings dominated Hellenistic cities, and their actual freedom of action varied with the strength or weakness of the central power. They had to pay tribute to the king, even though they retained such symbols of liberty as their own local officers and administration.

One obvious difference between new and old cities was that the new ones could be planned more deliberately, because they were often completely new foundations. Town planning certainly was known in classical Greece; one of the more important names in this field is Hippodamus, who designed several Greek cities in the fifth century. The rectangular gridiron pattern that he and others used persisted into the Hellenistic era. The prototype of Hellenistic cities was Alexandria, which was designed by architects under the personal supervision of the king himself. Here the two main streets were nearly a hundred feet wide. Some other cities, such as Pergamum in Asia Minor, discarded the traditional grid pattern and showed a creative approach to the natural terrain. Hellenistic town planning is thus a development of techniques known in classical Greece; but the opportunities to exploit urban architecture were more frequent.

How did the population of these cities support itself, and what were their economic bases?

In the Hellenistic Age, as in all human history until the nineteenth century, economic activity was mostly agricultural. Of course, agriculture was not practiced in Greek or Hellenistic cities: the population depended on the agricultural land surrounding the city, called the *chora*. In this respect there was little difference between the classical and Hellenistic periods. The economic life of the Hellenistic era was thus a continuation of classical patterns rather than a revolutionary new system.

The great Russian historian Rostovtzeff wrote two monumental books on the social and economic history of the Hellenistic world and of the Roman Empire. He appreciated the dynamism of an economic interpretation of history, and consequently he gave a prominent place to commerce and industry in his analysis of Hellenistic economics. All would admit, I think, that agriculture came first; the cities could not have supported themselves through trade alone, without the agricultural foundation of the outlying *chora.* (An exception would have to be made for Alexandria, which was built away from the shore of Egypt and could not have had a large farming area around it.) The question is what part commerce played.

That is not to say that there were no advances in economic practices. Banking flourished under the Hellenistic kings. A particular function of finance was to convert goods of all kinds into money. The kings would not want to store up oil, wheat, animals, and the like; so it was up to financial machinery in the city to turn such collections into cash. But not even in the Hellenistic world did people install a system of token or fiduciary currency: coin was always precious metal.

What were the Hellenistic contributions to education, literature, and philosophy?

Hellenistic scholars developed even further the Greek methods of education and passed its valuable heritage on to the Romans. Greek thought and literature was the foundation of the Roman educational system. Roman orators and men of letters often studied in Greece, and in the third century B.C. Athens became a sort of university town. In Rome itself, Greek slaves acted as tutors. The first book ever written in Latin was by a Greek slave, Livius Andronicus, who was freed by his masters and subsequently produced the first Latin translation of Homer's *Odyssey* as a teaching text for the Romans. He followed the Greek word order as closely as possible, thus introducing into Latin the tiresome separation of noun from adjective that makes learning the language so arduous.

The first Roman to attempt a history of his own state wrote around 200 B.C.—using Greek, because Greek was still more widely read than Latin. Greek was also the acknowledged language of historiography—Herodotus, Thucydides, and all the Hellenistic historians had written in Greek. For a long time, Greek remained the language of the cultured world.

It has been said that the Hellenistic world produced the first European humanism. It might be more appropriate to say that Hellenistic scholars, looking back upon the classical world, were aware of the need to create a solid educational system. The first two Ptolemies founded and maintained a magnificent library in Alexandria, one of the wonders of the ancient world. At one time it probably contained over five hundred thousand rolls of papyrus and maintained a sort of research center for scholars from all over the Hellenistic world. Aristophanes of Byzantium was one of the directors of the library, and it is significant that a scholar from Byzantium actually traveled all the way to Alexandria. The library must have enjoyed enormous prestige all through the ancient world. Alexandrian scholars recognized the need to edit texts of the classical authors, whose works down to that time had been preserved in a rather haphazard manner. Homer was one of the authors studied in this way. By comparison of manuscripts and a more accurate knowledge of the ancient Greek language, Alexandrian scholars edited a version of Homer that remains our basic text today.

This initiative in education and academic scholarship extended to science and literature as well. Hellenistic scientists gave the world some amazing achievements. Archimedes, for one, made important mathematical discoveries, and he has been credited—though this has been disputed—with the discovery of the waterscrew for irrigation. Archimedes invented several mechanical devices, but he regarded them as trivial compared to his discoveries in pure mathematics. To the Greeks, pure knowledge was more precious than its technical application because it was closer to philosophy. The Greeks worshiped ideas, and Archimedes even had one of his mathematical theorems inscribed on his tombstone.

Euclid, the father of geometry, was another prominent Hellenistic scientist. Neatly and eloquently, he summarized the geometric knowledge of antiquity and organized the known geometric proofs. The idea of proof is distinctly Hellenic—the concept that the truth of a fact must be proved is the very basis of the Socratic teachings. If a man's life could not be logically explained and his motivations scrutinized, then his life lacked meaning and direction. At the highest level, Greek science and philosophy were joined.

Alexandria became a literary center during the Hellenistic Age. The entire library was catalogued, and the catalogue included biographical notes about various authors and an index of their works. It became a valuable reference tool. The man responsible for the massive job was Callimachus, whose poetry also reflects his concern with erudition. His work has not been completely preserved, but fragments reveal the close association of scholarship and literature. Depending on one's taste, this may or may not have been a salutary influence. In Callimachus' poem "Causes," for example, he did not use a simple phrase when a convoluted one could replace it. The poem itself is a rather pedantic work describing the causes of various phenomena.

The poet Theocritus was not a librarian, but he was quite as self-consciously learned as Callimachus. He did reveal a freer strain of emotion, and he wrote bucolic poetry that has lasted longer than anything of Callimachus. His influence on the Latin poet Vergil helped to establish the genre of pastoral poetry that eventually influenced Edmund Spenser as well. Apollonius of Rhodes, a Hellenistic poet, wrote an epic about Jason and the Argonauts. However, it turned out to be only a fraction as long as the Homeric poems: Hellenistic writers found it very difficult to compete with the timeless accomplishments of antiquity.

Literary forms changed significantly during the Hellenistic period. Less tragedy was written, or at least not much of it has been preserved. Hellenistic poetry was composed in erudite, complex patterns with various metrical systems; it was highly personal in content and technique. Individualism became a concern of the writer in a new way. The classical Greeks were strikingly individual in their thoughts, but their individuality went only so far; the Greek could not reject the framework of his community without being regarded as eccentric, if not dangerous. The Hellenistic city did not exert this kind of influence; its residents were merely part of a much larger kingdom. The hugeness of the new social structure made the development of individuality possible—in fact, almost inevitable. The impersonal turmoil of kingdoms caused a retreat into the personal world and a refinement of individual personality. It is not surprising that Hellenistic philosophy concerned itself with the achievement of individual happiness.

There were two main schools of Hellenistic philosophy: the Stoic and the Epicurean. The prophet of Stoicism was Zeno of Cyprus, who taught that individuals could discover a pattern to events in the world. Once a man found his place in the pattern, he could live happily in the knowledge that he was fulfilling his cosmic duty. In a chaotic age, this philosophy was very attractive. Western readers can approach an understanding of late Stoicism by studying the *Meditations* of the Roman emperor Marcus Aurelius. As espoused by the emperor, Stoicism was a philosophy of endurance in which the individual was advised to do his duty passively and not to worry about the overall scheme of the universe. If a man could fit into the scheme, happiness was his reward. With its emphasis upon duty and inner discipline, Stoicism appealed strongly to the Roman upper classes.

Epicureanism was devised by Epicurus of Athens around 300 B.C. He taught that the world was composed of atoms—one of those brilliant analytic flashes of insight that the Greeks did not have the time or ability to follow up. If man was made of atoms, a time would come when these would no longer cohere and the man would disappear. This emphasis on the transience of existence implied that human actions were unimportant, as no "judgment" followed personal dissolution. Epicurus also tried to provide a philosophy of comfort, but he did not insist upon adherence to duty. He recommended man to avoid the extreme of pain and pleasure, commitment and involvement. Epicureanism made its way to Rome; of the two most important assassins of Caesar, Brutus was a Stoic and Cassius an Epicurean. Lucretius' poem "On the Nature of the Universe" is an excellent source for Epicurean thought in the Roman world. Epicureanism had less influence upon the ruling Roman elite than Stoicism because it was considered self-indulgent. For Hellenistic Greeks, however, in a world ripped by political instability, any philosophy of comfort was assured of a following.

Both these philosophies are fundamentally different from the teachings of Plato and Aristotle, which emphasized knowledge of the world and understanding of human experience. I think also that there was a lessening of the creative impulse which characterized Greek philosophy. Instead of charting new seas for philosophy or even recharting the old ones, the Hellenistic schools deliberately turned their backs on tradition and concentrated on human survival amidst the unstable conditions of the world.

Apart from its influence on the Greco-Roman world, did Hellenistic thought influence Christian theology?

Christianity emerged from Judaism, but it incorporated important elements of Hellenistic thought. Jesus and the first Christians both rebelled against and confirmed Judaism. They denied many Jewish dogmas, but they believed that Jesus was the Messiah foretold in Hebraic Scriptures. Christians thus defined themselves against the Jews; Jewish theology was the mirror in which Christianity was reflected. But if Christianity had remained within the Jewish framework, it could not have expanded to become a world religion. Not until it merged with the world of Hellenic paganism could Christianity spread to those nations of the West with whom its fortunes would rise or fall.

The supreme example of this movement can be found in the person and philosophy of Saint Paul, a Hellenized Jew. Paul was present in Jerusalem to witness the martyrdom of Saint Stephen, and on the way back to Damascus he was ordered by God to undertake the propagation of the Christian faith. Paul was able to communicate with Greeks and Greek-speaking people in various parts of the Roman Empire. His Epistles were the first great organizing documents in the history of Christianity. Paul's success depended on his ability to make the Christian faith compatible with the attitudes and traditions of prospective converts.

Paul and other early Christians clothed their theology in an air of philosophical consideration that linked it with speculations of the ancient Greeks. In the Gospel of John, for example, Jesus is equated with the *Logos,* or the spoken Word of God. *Logos* was a common term in Greek philosophy, and John appears to have made a conscious attempt to restate the ethos of Christianity in the language of Greek thought. Almost three centuries later, the Arian controversy over the divine nature of Jesus was conducted largely within the terms of Greek philosophical discourse.

Christians adopted the ancient pagan tradition of common sacrificial meals. In the Dionysiac rites of Greece, the body of a deity was consumed as a sacramental action; the worshipers hoped to imbibe some of the physical and spiritual powers of the god. Immersion in sacred liquids, such as the blood of a sacrificed bull, was believed to wash away the worshiper's sins, and this suggests the Christian ritual of baptism. Many pagan practices are directly analogous to Christian sacraments and ceremonies. This is not to suggest that Christianity arose out of paganism, but in the early phase its similarity to various pagan antecedents may have won converts.

Early Christians were confronted with the polytheism of Greek religion, and there they followed the influence of the Jews instead of the Hellenes. Zeus had never been worshiped ahead of other deities except by individual choice; a Greek paid homage to whatever deity he wished. The Greeks never developed a set of sacred beliefs or laws analogous to the Jewish Scriptures, and here too Christianity departed from paganism.

Similarly, Hellenistic thought included no concrete or favorable depiction of the afterlife. The Egyptians, by contrast, had a clear and calm view of the afterlife which may have reflected the permanence of Egyptian society. Their tombs testify to their optimistic outlook. In the Greek world—and in the Old Testament—there was little emphasis on the afterlife and no concept of a spiritual catharsis in the bosom of God. Christians may have picked up this concept from the East, notably from Persia, with its dualistic religious system. The Persians believed in a good god and a bad god, and a man had to choose which one to follow during his life on earth. Then, in a Last Judgment reminiscent of Christianity, each man discovered whether he had chosen wisely. This dualism survived in the West; Saint Augustine struggled against dualistic Manichees, and the Albigensians of southern France maintained their dualistic creed even in the twelfth century.

How does Hellenistic art reflect the various cultural trends of the Hellenistic Age?

Many well-preserved examples of Hellenistic art exist, chiefly in the forms of sculpture and architecture. Not so many paintings survive, and most of those that have endured come from the Italian towns of Pompeii and Herculaneum. These paintings were executed in the first century A.D., but they are essentially Hellenistic. They are realistic and attractive, and their approach to perspective is at times strikingly modern.

The development of sculpture is recorded more thoroughly by surviving examples than that of painting. Classical sculpture embodied physical and philosophical ideals. The models were usually attractive young men and women, often athletes, who were perfectly proportioned and indeed handsome. Even sculptors in the time of Pericles made few attempts at realistic portraiture; the features of the man were masked by the features of the ideal. As far as I know, the first series of realistic portraits were those of Socrates. His remarkable personality emerged from the obscurity of the ideal, initiating a freer and more realistic tone in sculpture after 400 B.C.

Hellenistic sculptors were increasingly interested not only in realism, but in deformity. One example is the famous study of a drunken old woman holding an empty pitcher; another is the statue of a boxer with a mutilated ear. Statues of children appeared for the first time in the

Hellenistic period. Perhaps this concentration upon imperfection reflected the artists' attitude toward their equally imperfect and hazardous world. By contrast, the atmosphere of the ancient *polis* inculcated artistic and philosophical expressions of the ideal.

The dynamism of Hellenistic art is evident in the statue of Laocoön and his sons fighting off the great serpent. It has a pathos, a melodramatic quality that would not have been tolerated in the classical period. In the statue of the Dying Gaul from Pergamum, we see the struggle with death playing across the subject's face and contorting his body. Earlier Greek portraits had a quality of meditation and acceptance best exemplified by the statue of Athena leaning quietly upon her spear.

Hellenistic architecture is notable for the sheer magnificence and grandiosity of its buildings. The great altar at Pergamum (now reconstructed in Berlin) is surrounded by a long frieze of reliefs that seem to leap out of the wall at the observer. The sense of dramatic action, of gesture and explosiveness, was new in Hellenistic art. It paralleled the dynamic and ever-changing social conditions of the period.

This dynamic spirit in the visual arts resembles that of Hellenistic literature. Hellenistic writers explored the emotions on an individual and personal level. Obscene literature from this period attests to freedom of expression, and the great variety of forms and richness of mythological allusion produced a dramatic mixture of thought and emotion. This surging kaleidoscope of creative expression reflects the pace of life in Hellenistic times.

In time, the Hellenistic world met the rising power of Rome; what was the process by which Rome conquered the Hellenistic states?

The Roman conquest was a process of cultural mixing or absorption analogous to the Hellenistic inroads into Egypt and the old Persian empire. The process was under way while Polybius was writing, and he anticipated its consequences.

To a student of history, it is remarkable that the two worlds of Greece and Rome did not encounter and clash sooner than they did. Both these societies entered western Europe at about the same time —roughly 2000 B.C., during the Indo-European dispersal. For more than a thousand years they developed independently, perhaps partly because of the great mountain ranges in western Greece and eastern Italy that cause the two lands to face away from each other. Greece faces the Aegean and down to Persia and Egypt, while Rome—on the western shore of Italy—faces Spain and North Africa. The early wars of these two societies did not overlap, but there is some evidence that the Romans knew of the Delphic Oracle and had some desultory contact with the Greeks.

Greece and Rome finally collided during the Hellenistic Age, when the great period of Greek warfare and diplomacy had ended. Their first contact on the Greek side of the Adriatic occurred in the 230's B.C., when the Romans intervened on the western shore of modern Yugoslavia to police the seas from a group of pirates. This action committed a Roman force to the area, but they had no plans for conquest and permanent settlement there. Rome was drawn more intimately into the Hellenistic world through a series of involvements too complicated to outline here.

The main reason for Roman participation in Greek affairs was the aggressive policies of the Macedonian kingdom. The Macedonians made a series of unfortunate aggressive moves toward the Roman state in the late third century B.C. From a mixture of motives, the Romans answered the call of the Aetolian League and of the kingdoms of Rhodes and Pergamum against Macedonia around 200. The subsequent conflicts embroiled them in Greek affairs. The Romans made several attempts to withdraw their legions but were lured back by a continuing state of unrest in Greece. The decisive moment arrived in 133 B.C., when the king of Pergamum willed his kingdom to Rome—his way of cooperating with the inevitable and forestalling conquest by the Seleucids. Once the Romans had possessions in Asia Minor they had to protect them, and the history of the Hellenistic kingdoms became part of the history of Rome.

Some historians charge the Greeks with cultural failure because they did not maintain their national integrity and succumbed to a more militant and less cultured society. But if there was any failure it was primarily military and not cultural, for as Edward Gibbon said, the Romans were sometimes vanquished in battle but always victorious in war. One may ask how this was managed, for the Greek military tradition, stretching back to Alexander and beyond, was skillful and crafty. However, the Greek kingdoms had weakened themselves in internecine and frontier warfare. Even without the Greek wars, the Romans would have had an excellent chance to subdue the Greeks with their superior manpower. Polybius tells us that the Romans could draw up eight hundred thousand men, and even though not all these soldiers could be armed at one time, the Romans could take the field again after a disastrous defeat.

The Roman form of government, even within the Republic, was especially suited to the formation of a conquering state. Not even in theory was there any idea that all citizens had an equal hand in the ruling of the state. There was no *democratia,* as in Athens. Voting was manipulated in Rome to keep the ruling aristocracy in power. The principle of oligarchy was built into the constitution more strongly than that of democracy. A small circle of families in the Republic maintained their leadership, and this stability fostered that parallel stability and rigidness in military and diplomatic organization that led to conquest.

The Hellenistic kingdoms, like many others, used mercenary troops, and this may have been a factor in the Roman conquest. It is a truism that mercenaries do not fight as well as citizens committed to the defense of their own soil. "Rome does not negotiate with her enemies when they are on Roman soil" is a statement attributed to a Roman senator when Pyrrhus invaded southern Italy in the third century B.C. It indicates the military fervor of the Roman ethos.

At least in the political sphere the Hellenistic Age had ended by the year 30 B.C., for no independent Macedonian monarchies remained. This is not to say that the cultural traditions of the Hellenistic Age were exhausted, and Rome was now able to absorb more of Hellenic culture. Roman literature and education were greatly influenced by Greek examples, and Hellenistic philosophies found numerous disciples in the Roman world.

The Romans also inherited the administrative structures of the conquered kingdoms. They more or less maintained the Seleucid system of satrapies, altering it only to conform to the Roman unit of the province. In Egypt, the Romans preserved and extended the military rule initiated by the Macedonians. There was no more token conciliation of the Egyptians, but rather open exploitation. However, it is by no means certain that the Hellenistic kingdoms—if left to themselves—would have attained a standard of living for their subjects any higher than that ultimately achieved by the Romans. This is particularly true for the Seleucid monarchy, which was rapidly disintegrating at the time of the Roman conquest. Even the Ptolemaic kingdom of Cleopatra was on the decline. The Roman conquest, brutal as it often was, may have had quite salutary consequences for the conquered territories in the long run.

A remarkable consequence of the Roman onslaught was the conquest of Rome itself by Christianity. As we have seen, Christianity was a Judaic religion strongly influenced by Hellenistic culture disseminated through the West by the vehicle of the Greek language. The acceptance of Christianity—originally the religion of conquered peoples—may be regarded as one of the chief legacies of the Hellenistic world. After the fall of the Roman Empire of the West, the Christian faith provided the bulwark which supported the Empire of the East for another thousand years. In the Eastern Empire, the preservation of Hellenic thought by a process of capricious selection continued. Not until the High Middle Ages, when the West could learn more of the cultural traditions of Greece, was the mainstream of western culture able to flow free of obstruction again.

We must not overstress uniformity of the Hellenistic period, for the era was full of contrasts. Conditions in the Ptolemaic kingdom were quite unlike those in the Seleucid domain. And yet a Greek at home in Alexandria would not have felt lost in Antioch or Seleucia on the Tigris, or in the Greek cities recently unearthed in Afghanistan. Greek traditions were altered or recast by the mixture of Hellenic and Oriental civilizations, but they survived with remarkable freshness and vigor to take their places as nuclei of western culture after the Roman conquest.

We began by discussing some of the ancient sources for the Hellenistic period; who are some of the leading modern historians of this field, and what new methods have they used?

The Hellenistic Age was first defined as a separate field of historical study by Johann Gustav Droysen, who "discovered" and named the period and wrote up its history in the early and middle nineteenth century. Droysen (as I said earlier) believed that history displayed a series of inevitable patterns—a prominent theme in German historical thinking in the nineteenth century, and represented in our century by Oswald Spengler.

Not until fairly recently has the Hellenistic Age become a recognized field of study in the undergraduate curricula of western universities. Tarn himself held no major university post while he was composing his works on the Hellenistic period. America's first prominent Hellenistic historian was a Canadian who migrated to our country—William Scott Ferguson, most of whose career was spent at Harvard; his *Hellenistic Athens* (1911) was a pioneering work in its day. The great Rostovtzeff wrote his study of the Hellenistic world in America; as a professor at Yale, he was the teacher of some of the leading historians of today. The edition of the lost Greek historians by Felix Jacoby, which I have mentioned, has made possible an understanding of the later development of Greek historical thought, as well as studies of individual Hellenistic historians.

The study of Greek religion contributes basically to our knowledge of this period, especially since the Greeks now met and came to terms with various eastern religions. Arthur Darby Nock, an English scholar who worked for more than thirty years at Harvard, and Martin P. Nilsson of Lund have been among the leading researchers in this field. Only during our century have the papyri of the Ptolemaic kingdom been analyzed; here I would mention Ulrich Wilcken, who also wrote a life of Alexander that has been translated into English. Numismatics is another growing field of investigation, and discoveries in this area will deepen our knowledge of the economic life of the period.

It is premature to try to estimate the work of the many excellent scholars whose careers are not yet concluded; so at this point we might draw our discussion to a close.

6

The Roman Republic and Early Empire

SIR RONALD SYME

THE HISTORIOGRAPHICAL CONTEXT

The Roman impact on Western civilization has never been denied; the problem for historians has been to achieve a realistic appraisal of this complicated, originally obscure people from the Tiber, who combined idealism with a ruthless yearning for mastery, self-restraint with unbounded greed, humanity with bellicosity and cruelty. Until about forty years ago, the rise of the Romans to the status of world conquerors that they enjoyed in the first two centuries A.D. was interpreted largely through the artfully developed political myths and idealized stereotypes that the Latin historians and political propagandists themselves formulated. A more realistic appraisal of the Roman aristocracy and the complexities of Roman politics was inaugurated by the German scholar M. Gelzer, and this revisionist interpretation was brought to fruition in the work of the Oxford historian Ronald Syme, whose *The Roman Revolution* (1939) is one of the truly seminal works of twentieth-century historiography. Syme's method—which was being applied at about the same time by Lewis Namier to the eighteenth-century neo-Romans, the English aristocracy—was to analyze Roman politics in terms of the struggles for dominance among aristocratic families and factions. He succeeded in depicting the Roman imperial masters not as they wanted to appear to the world, but as the politicians and power brokers that they were.

Sir Ronald Syme (born in 1903) is in every respect an elegant man—elegant in his fastidious dress, in the quiet opulence of his beautiful rooms at Brasenose College, elegant above all in the clarity and coherence of his historical insight into a very complicated historical theme. He does not need the authority of the distinguished chair of Ancient History at Oxford that he holds. The vastness of his learning, the vigor of his exposition, the forcefulness of his argument, impart the conviction always disseminated by a master historical mind.

Chronological Outline

753 B.C.: Traditional date of the foundation of Rome by Romulus.

c. 500 B.C.: The founding of the Roman republic. Overthrow of Etruscan supremacy at Rome. First consuls appointed.

c. 500–c. 300 B.C.: The plebeian class gradually gains a larger role in the patrician-dominated government.

280 B.C.: Rome conquers the Greek cities of southern Italy, defeating an army led by Pyrrhus of Epirus.

264–241 B.C.: The first Punic War—Rome defeats Carthage and gains Sicily and Sardinia.

218–201 B.C.: The second Punic War—Rome defeats Carthage once again, despite Hannibal's daring march across the Alps.

149–146 B.C.: The third Punic War—Roman forces invade northern Africa and destroy the city of Carthage.

146 B.C.: Macedonia and Greece become Roman provinces.

133 and 121 B.C.: The murders of Tiberius and Gaius Gracchus, advocates of agrarian reform in Rome.

90–88 B.C.: The Social War. Rome puts down a revolt of non-Roman Italy.

82–79 B.C.: Dictatorship of Sulla.

60 B.C.: The first triumvirate—Julius Caesar, Crassus, and Pompey. Caesar conquers Gaul (58–51 B.C.) and invades Britain.

48–46 B.C.: Caesar defeats Pompey and emerges as sole ruler of Rome.

44 B.C.: Assassination of Caesar on the Ides of March. The second triumvirate of Antony, Lepidus, and Octavian is established in 43 B.C. Cicero is executed by Antony's agents. Antony defeats Cassius and Brutus at Philippi in 42 B.C.

43 B.C.–A.D. 17: Life of Ovid, author of the *Metamorphoses.*

31 B.C.: Defeat of Antony and Cleopatra at Actium. The birth of the Roman Empire under Augustus, who reigns until A.D. 14.

A.D. 4–33: Life of Jesus.

A.D. 17: Death of Livy, author of the *History of Rome.*

A.D. 19: Death of Vergil, author of the *Aeneid.*

A.D. 54–68: Reign of Nero. The Great Fire in Rome in A.D. 64.

c. A.D. 55–117: Life of Tacitus, historian who is severely critical of Rome of his time.

A.D. 66–70: Repression of the Jewish revolt in Judea. Destruction of the Temple.

A.D. 79: Eruption of Mt. Vesuvius buries Pompeii and Herculaneum.

A.D. 117–138: Reign of Hadrian, successor to the emperor Trajan. Suppression of the revolt of the Jews—Jerusalem is closed to the Jews. Under barbarian pressure Rome concentrates on defending, rather than extending its boundaries.

A.D. 161–180: Reign of Marcus Aurelius and the triumph of Stoicism in public life. Near economic unification of the empire, but Italy is already yielding its economic and political supremacy to the prospering provinces.

A.D. 212: The Edict of Caracalla extends Roman citizenship to virtually all free inhabitants of the empire.

Norman F. Cantor

Would you discuss how you became interested in your approach to Roman history, and how you came to develop your interpretations?

Sir Ronald Syme

In my school days I was much drawn to the Latin language, and notably to Tacitus. When I embarked on Roman history at the University I did not study the period of the republic, mainly because so many people had written about it that it seemed not very exciting or remunerative. I studied the empire, particularly the time of Tacitus, who was born about A.D. 57 and may have lived until 120.

It was my special curiosity to find out what was *not* in Tacitus, what was *not* in the literary sources; and as an undergraduate I became familiar with Latin inscriptions. The contemporary inscriptions set forth the administrative and the military structure beautifully, and they provide information about a number of important people who just do not appear in the literary record. For instance, we know a great deal about an important military man of the time of Trajan—a man who came from the modern city of Turin—from inscriptions in his honor, but Pliny the Younger (who also came from northern Italy and lived about the same time) does not mention him at all in his many letters about high society. Sixty or seventy years ago, a Greek inscription was discovered at Pergamum in Asia Minor of a man who had twice been consul at Rome and had governed the important province of Syria in the early period of the reign of Trajan (from about A.D. 101 to 104). The significance of this is obvious: after the establishment of the empire, in the fourth generation after the Battle of Actium, men from the Greek east were entering the Roman Senate and rising to the highest positions. That sort of discovery appealed to me enormously.

Secondly, Tacitus (as his second small work in the year 98) wrote an ethnographical treatise on the Germans, the *Germania*. This also interested me very much, and I wrote a short dissertation on it. After taking my degree I went to Germany to study the German frontiers —not only the Rhine, about which a great deal is known, but also the Danubian lands in the Balkans, about which less is known.

Not long after returning to Oxford in 1929, I was invited by the editors of the *Cambridge Ancient History* to produce a chapter on the northern frontiers in the time of Augustus. That is, the conquest by the Romans of the Alpine regions, of the Danube lands and of Thrace, and the failed attempt to conquer both Germany and Bohemia. From studying the war of this period I became interested in the higher command (the provincial governors and the generals), and I developed a notion of the continued existence of an oligarchy. This was not composed entirely of soldiers; in the early empire, as in the late republic, the high administrator or commander of an army was an educated person, not only a military man. I could see the parallel to what I had studied as an undergraduate—the important people (contemporaries of Tacitus) of the time of Domitian and Trajan.

Continuing to investigate the personnel of government, I noticed that a number of men who had risen through the wars of the Revolution were coming to the fore during the time of Augustus, when careers were open to talented "new men." In the same period, however, men of ancient families and good birth were still commanding armies. As the century went on, under the successors of Augustus, birth and nobility came under suspicion and very few aristocrats continued to command armies. Their places were taken by small-town Italians, and after a time by persons from outside Italy, from the western provinces. I thought of writing a book on the invasion of Rome by the élite deriving from Spain and the south of France. One aspect is the accession of Trajan (a man of an old Italian family settled in Spain) in A.D. 98.

While I studied the rise of people from the towns of Spain and southern France, I did not neglect their predecessors, who came from Italian towns. That made me think about the late republic, about certain things that have been said about Caesar. It seemed to me that there were some permanent results of his brief autocracy, namely the admission to the Senate of large numbers of men from the back country of Italy—army officers, contractors, businessmen, and representatives of good old local families.

It seemed logical to tie the whole thing together by studying the whole period from the late republic on, bringing in my previous interests. I had become extremely skeptical of the study of the Roman constitution, and I disliked the habit of interpreting either a republic or an empire in terms of the life and habits of a single person. After all, the ruler does not do it all by himself: he may be a puppet in the hands of a group, or he may be half off his head, and the government will still go on. I wanted to see what happened to Caesar's adherents after his assassination. What was Mark Antony up to? What about Octavian (later Augustus), who at nineteen raised an army to emerge as Antony's rival?

I wished to study the wars for supremacy and the establishment of the power of Augustus. What happened to the admirals and generals in the years of peace? What did Augustus, triumphant, do with Rome, Italy, and the world? Naturally, a return to normal government was published—"the restoration of the republic." But if one holds that the constitution was really a facade or a convenience under the republic, so it must have been under the supremacy of Caesar Augustus. I wanted to look at the chief adherents of the emperor: how was Augustus going to run the government, how would he secure a regular stream of promotions into the government, and what would his relations be with what was left of the old aristocracy? Quite a lot of it was left. As often happens in civil wars, people of high birth tended to survive through protection or connivance. Naturally, I saw that one man could not control the whole world. A syndicate of two, three, or four people might have been necessary: that had been tried when the Caesarian party came together, a year and a half after the assassination of Caesar. That is, the triumvirate of Antony, Lepidus, and Octavian. Augustus outshone everyone in Rome through the prestige of his achievements; the dictator Caesar had been deified, and therefore Augustus was *divi filius*. He gave large powers to a man called Agrippa, and in the years between 27 and 13 B.C., these two men were seldom in the same place. From 17 to 13 B.C., Agrippa was running the whole of the Roman world east of the Adriatic. He was an organizer, engineer, and soldier. Augustus needed a diplomat, too, to manage public opinion—his old friend the subtle Maecenas, who knew all the literary people.

I was further interested in how this huge area—the Roman Empire—managed to hold together. It nearly split into pieces about the year 260; when it was tidied up, it became evident that one emperor could not manage the thing, and so there developed the system of Diocletian, with two senior emperors and two juniors—four rulers of the world. Hence, as I looked at Augustus in the early empire, I wanted to find out who did all the work.

My book, *The Roman Revolution,* published in the first week of the Second World War, marked a departure from earlier interpretations. The emphasis was not on Caesar, Cicero, and Augustus, but on the history of oligarchy, which is the connecting link between the republic and the empire. I would be tempted to say that Rome was always ruled by an oligarchy. For the late republic I did not look at everything through the eyes of Cicero, and for the civil wars and the period of Augustus I preferred not to look at things through the eyes of Augustus. His modern admirers and idolaters, completely forgetting his early career and the proscriptions, regarded him as a kind of prince of peace, or (in the typical English view) a "good headmaster" who did not need to bully the staff because he always got his way and ultimately could have them removed. In the preface, I admitted to being a bit too favorable to Julius Caesar and to Antony.

Considering Roman government and society in its early formative period before the Punic Wars, what do you think of the idealized views presented by Livy and other Roman writers?

I find it difficult to believe in history composed two or three hundred years after the event, when there had been no contemporary writing of history. One can generally get something out of contemporary authors even though they may be ignorant or mendacious (for example, if it comes to that, some of the fathers of the Church). Unfortunately, the first Roman historian—a certain Fabius Pictor—wrote about 215–205 B.C., and in Greek at that. Whatever inscriptions and records of the early republic might have been extant, Fabius Pictor—being an educated man—followed the influence of Greek historical writing. At first this conjures up something good (Herodotus, Thucydides), but it was other aspects of Greek historiography (the origins of nations and peoples, the retelling of the Homeric story, and all sorts of fiction) that influenced Fabius Pictor. For example, he gave the exact total of the Roman armed strength in the reign of Romulus and the cost in Greek talents of the Temple of Capitoline Jupiter, built by Tarquin. All this is in the historical category of things that might be true but are not authentic.

Cato, a very respectable writer of the second century, was also influenced by Greek models. And in the first half of the first century B.C., certain annalists wrote at enormous length about the early republic; earlier annalists had written about the kings of Rome, following an established legend, but next to nothing about the fifth century B.C. These people filled up their histories with all sorts of corroborative detail and vivid pictures, a number of them based on contemporary political issues, and they include quite a lot of fictional history. We can see the contrast in the case of Polybius. Beginning with the first Punic War, he drew on

Fabius Pictor as well as good Greek sources, for he knew that these would be biased and he hoped for balance. For the later history, being in exile at Rome he had wonderful opportunities to get in touch with people in high places. He wrote the kind of history which is credible, and also useful to the statesman; he had a high notion of the utility of history.

If, in your opinion, the Roman republic was always dominated by an oligarchy, why did Livy hold an idealized and unrealistic view of the history of the republic?

As Livy portrays it, he simply followed what had already been written, did a better job, and drove previous works from the market. He does let us see the importance of noble families, including the exploits (good or bad) of people with names like Valerius and Claudius. Like his predecessors, however, he was dominated by the improving view that these men were struggling not for ambition, power, and wealth, but for the good of the commonwealth. This view was held also by his predecessors in the late republic—it was conventional journalistic history.

This idea of the "commonwealth" was ideology. At the end of the republic, politicians protested that they were acting only for the good of the commonwealth. However, this pretense ought not to blind us to the moral grandeur (as well as the tenacity) of the Roman aristocracy of earlier ages. It is symbolized by the story of an ancestor of Sulla, who urged the Romans, when voting at the consular elections, to choose a bitter personal enemy who was a good military man—because, he said, "It is better, if you are going to be treated roughly, to be treated roughly by a fellow citizen than by a foreigner."

Polybius thought that the greatness of Rome was derived from its constitution, the balance of three elements. Namely, the One (the executive power of the consuls), the Few (the Senate), and the Many (the people choosing those who will lead them in peace and war). But in effect only a few of the most eminent senators really determined policy; a consul might be almost unrestrained during his year in office, but knowing that the ex-consuls would be waiting for him when the year was up, he tended to conform to their views. There were generally about twenty-five ex-consuls living at any given time—fewer, sometimes, in the late republic when there had been wars and civil wars and the government was weak, especially in the years 78–70 B.C. One must note that the consuls generally came from families that had held consular power before; this was first pointed out by the German scholar Gelzer in 1912. Polybius ignores this reality, partly because he was a Greek. The notion of balance was standard Greek doctrine, and schematizing was the great strength and the great weakness of the Greek intellect. One would have thought that Polybius, meeting consuls and ex-consuls during all those years in Rome, would have employed his searching intellect to find out how the system really worked. The Greeks had the habit of antithesis (notably between name and fact), but he did not adopt that technique in dealing with the Roman constitution.

Although the Roman aristocrats were ambitious and ruthless men, they had a sense of cohesion. They depended on popular election, and although the elections themselves depended on the influence of birth or rank, the opinion of the voters did amount to something. But there were subtle or complicated methods of thwarting what we would call democracy. The secret at Rome was social cohesion between the leaders and the voters, a kind of mutual confidence. Certain Roman historians—Sallust, for instance, writing in disillusionment just after the fall of the republic—seem not at all interested in the Polybian view of balance and of the way in which constitutions change and degenerate. For Sallust, a kind of moral and social degeneration caused the fall of the republic; he looked back at the period between the second and third Punic Wars in the second century B.C. as a good period, a period of stability. He does not invoke the constitution or the organs of government but talks of a period of *concordia*. Modern critics of Sallust have said that his view of Roman history is rather rudimentary because he was influenced by moralistic preoccupations. But what if these were not merely moralistic, but sociological? For various phenomena—empire, wealth, power, ambition, rivalry, new education, and economic progress—had broken down the *concordia* of ancient days.

What is the importance of the Gracchi? What were they trying to do, and what impact did they have?

The year 133 B.C., the tribunate of Tiberius Gracchus, has been chosen as the beginning of the revolutionary era that ended with the fall of the republic, the dictatorship, the civil wars, and the monarchy of Caesar Augustus. The choice may be misleading in certain aspects. Should we put the start of the revolutionary period at 145 B.C., where Polybius ended his own history? Before we start on Tiberius Gracchus we ought to cast backwards a few years: the great irritation at Rome produced by the strain of the Spanish wars, the ill-success of certain generals, and the trouble over recruiting. It became difficult to get the right sort of soldier, for Rome was still a city-state on the ancient Greek model, where the citizen-soldier had some property. And so there was in those years a distinct breakdown in *concordia*.

A second mistake in the concentration on the Gracchi is the biographical fallacy. We have Plutarch's lives of the two brothers, but we should look behind Tiberius Gracchus and examine his supporters. He was a young man in his middle thirties when he became tribune, but we should look in his background for some important politicians—ex-consuls like his father-in-law, Appius Claudius, and others. This point of view is strongly emphasized in a fine and learned work by a German scholar, Münzer, published in 1921. If the policy of the Gracchi was important, then there were people behind Tiberius Gracchus and behind Gaius Gracchus—they were not just isolated idealists. I would add something negative to the investigation: in examining certain noble families who were not very prominent in the next generation and missed the consulship, I would guess that this was so because they had been among the noble supporters of the Gracchi. Of course there are many other reasons why certain families might drop out: deaths in the family, impoverishment, a bad defeat in the field, or a bad political mistake.

On the other hand, we should not regard these two young men merely as the tools of older politicians. We must not forget that they were of the highest aristocracy themselves. Tiberius Gracchus was a grandson of Scipio Africanus; Cornelia, the mother of the Gracchi, was the daughter of Africanus. Furthermore, we can see the actions of Tiberius Gracchus as the results of a split that went back some years in the Scipianic family, faction, and connection. A treaty made in Spain with the people of Numantia was disowned by the Roman government. The Roman government delivered over to the people of Numantia the general who had made the arrangement, but not the man who was with him as his quaestor—namely, Tiberius Gracchus—and there emerged in Tiberius a double feeling of resentment and frustration. However, there was more here than just factional fighting among the nobility, or an individual's pride and anger. There was also a program.

In its essentials, the program of the Gracchi was quite simple. Tiberius Gracchus had seen the rich grow richer and the poor, poorer; his own interest lay with the "good" poor, or the poor farmer. As a result of wars in the east and the west, Italy had become highly prosperous in certain regions, where subsistence agriculture had been replaced by grazing for profit, and by the vine and the olive. Many people had lost their lands or had been tempted into selling them to profiteers. The crisis was not economic, nor was it a crisis of unemployment. In Greek history, the decline of the old peasant soldier had produced conflicts and civil wars between oligarchs and extreme democrats. To maintain the stability of the Roman state, which was then governing Italy and responsible for much of the world (though it tried to evade as many responsibilities as possible), internal stability was essential. One had to build up the middle class and the peasant farmers —the class which had provided soldiers in the past. To accomplish this, state land which had been occupied by individuals was taken back by the state and leased out in inalienable lots to the rural proletariat in order to turn them into a middle class. This transformation is surely the great secret of some modern states which call themselves democracies: in the United States, nearly everyone is middle-class by income and by way of thought. In the jargon of modern England, this is called "property-owning democracy."

Naturally, Tiberius Gracchus' opponents thwarted him. They put up another tribune to veto him. Tiberius appealed to the people, arguing that if a tribune defied the manifest will of the people then he was no true tribune and ought to be deposed. Thus one starts down the path of arrogance and illegality. My view of Tiberius is mixed, for I see him also as a man of great quality and ability, a conservative reformer who wanted to build up the old-fashioned citizen army.

The Gracchi were responsible for a great deal. Tiberius' proposal raised the question of the basis of property in the state; furthermore, because some noncitizens had occupied Roman state lands with the connivance of the government, the question of the position of the independent allies of Rome came up, and the notion arose of giving citizenship to the Italian allies. A concatenation of proposals, disappointment, and resentment ensued—and then the allies of Rome seceded at the end of the year 91. Internally, the question of sovereignty—what was the tribunate, after all?—and that of the army came to the fore. Tiberius and Gaius Gracchus also brought a certain discord to the possessing classes by excluding senators from the jury courts for certain very important matters, such as prosecutions for extortion. Nonetheless, I think that the third war with Carthage, or the year 145, might be a better choice for the beginning of the revolutionary era; one could see the crisis building up, and that date would not leave out Scipio Aemilianus, the leading man in Rome in the 130's.

The first century B.C., *after Rome had defeated Carthage and built up its empire, began with certain definite social and political problems. As the century went on, the issues became more clouded, and they seem to disappear in a power struggle between various groups. Is that true?*

In the Jugurthine war which brought Marius to prominence, one can see the role of irritation and anger. Then came the great German wars—the invasions of the Cimbri and the Teutones. The civil wars arose out of the Italian war in which the allies seceded from Rome (91 B.C.). Sulla came back from the East to re-establish the old system, but that system tended to break down under the claims of empire in the 70's. There were not enough ex-consuls about to act as senior statesmen and to direct the government. Some of the new consuls of the 70's (the old aristocratic families brought back by Sulla) were not very good; moreover, there were enormous military tasks in Spain, the Balkans, and the East which made it necessary to give people extended commands. For example, a man appointed to deal with southern Asia Minor and its coastal pirates served as proconsul for four years; he was succeeded by Marcus Antonius (whose son became much more famous later on), who exercised a wide command to deal with the pirates of the Mediterranean coasts. A few years later, a special command was made for Pompey the Great to deal with the pirates and the war with Mithridates. These emergencies of foreign policy contributed to the breakdown of the post-Sullan oligarchy. As a parenthesis, one should notice that Julius Caesar did not *have* to conquer Gaul, although he probably did have to deal with trouble with the Helvetians (from modern Switzerland), who were migrating to the southwest of France and came into contact with the northern boundary of the Roman province in the south of France. His was a design of ambition in the first instance.

In Italy itself there were large, unsolved social questions, particularly that of the rural poor. A large number of them served in the Roman legions, for proletarian armies existed by that time. The men served for adventure, subsistence, or loot, and their first loyalty was to their general, who would make provision for them (in money or land) at the end of their service. This produced a dangerous nexus between the proletarian army and its commander. Furthermore, there were a large number of broken and desperate men in various parts of the back country of Italy, as was revealed by the Catilinarian affair in 63 B.C.

How do you explain the conspiracy of Catiline?

This is very difficult, because so much was written and said about him. When a lot of historical evidence exists, difficulties begin. In the history of these years, so much is known from different historians and from the speeches and letters of Cicero that specific chronology becomes very important. Cicero's accounts try to make Catiline out a desperate revolutionary. Sallust, who wrote later (in the period of the Revolution), similarly did not like revolution, being a good landowner in the Sabine country. But how revolutionary was Catiline really? And when did he start?

As long as one had a chance of being elected to the consulship in Rome, why be revolutionary? And who wanted to destroy the Roman constitution or seriously intervene in the distribution of property? Catiline was blocked for his candidature for the consulship in 66 for 65; he stood again in 64 but was defeated because the leading politicians supported a safe man indeed—Cicero, an eloquent and successful man, but one who normally would not get their support for the consulship. Catiline was defeated again in the next year, 63, when he was outmaneuvered in various ways and was induced—perhaps foolishly—to leave Rome and put himself at the head of a minor insurrection started by an old soldier in the neighborhood of Florence. It is clear that he would not have had recourse to revolution or have entered into a local rising until in some way or other he had been discredited in Rome.

What are your views on Caesar?

Considering the swift success and the genius of Caesar, it is difficult not to fall under his spell. For the modern world his story has become obscure and distorted because its end is known: ambitious youth to consul, to proconsul of Gaul, to civil war, dictatorship, and assassination. Consequently, it all seems to move in a design. But we must allow for chance, as did the ancient historians—particularly Thucydides. One must use reason, but events sometimes will not listen to reason. Caesar believed in Fortune, "which holds dominion over the nations": that phrase occurs in a speech made up by the historian Sallust.

Caesar certainly was a great man, but we must look at him in the light of his time and his career. His first ambition was not to rule the world but to secure for himself and his family the first magistracy of Rome, the consulship. One should see him not as a would-be despot but as an ambitious member of an old family which had not been consistently prominent in the last three or four hundred years. The Julii, Caesar's family, belonged to the oldest aristocracy of all—the patriciate—but the patriciate tended to be squeezed out, to fall back under pressure from newer families which became an old aristocracy in turn, like the great Metellan house. Caesar's acts of ambition and recalcitrance become comprehensible in this light.

In more political systems than one, it has been true that the man who wants to end at or near the top as a comfortable and respected conservative does well to begin as a radical (although not an extreme radical). Though he came out against the prominent group in the Senate (one might call it the "government" although it was not a cohesive body), Caesar was careful not to antagonize people too much. For example, before he entered the Senate he was co-opted into a priesthood at Rome. He became *pontifex* in about 72 B.C. These colleges of priests tended to be controlled by the politically successful or the socially eminent, and it is an interesting sign if an allegedly dangerous young man gets taken up by the influential and respectable.

Caesar managed to move in a fairly straight line in his magistracies. In the year 63 he was elected to the praetorship for the next year; he naturally wanted the consulship as soon as possible, and got it in 59. In the meantime, two interesting things happened in the year 63. The office of *pontifex maximus* was vacant, the head of the state religion. He was required to know a lot about ritual, and by virtue of his position he exercised a lot of political patronage. This post, normally held by senior ex-consuls, was then vacant and open to direct election. Though not yet a senator of consular rank, Caesar put up his candidature against certain senior rivals and was elected. That had happened before, in the year 103, and it was a strong indication that a certain individual was going to be an important politician.

A Roman politician needed two things that would be highly detrimental to a politician today. It was a good thing for him to make enemies, because it showed that he was a man of consequence who might be able to make a deal later on; it was also a good thing to contract debts, because he could then blackmail his creditors into supporting his political career. Caesar did both these things. Further, it was desirable not to appear afraid in an emergency. Of course, one other way of making a good political career was to be a safe man—not to take risks.

Toward the end of the year 63 there was a crisis: the conspiracy of Catiline had been detected, certain of his adherents had been arrested by the consul Cicero, and there was a debate in the Senate about what was to be done with them. In the debate a young man (younger even than Caesar) carried the day. This was Cato, who argued, "These men have conspired against the state; they are public enemies; they should be put to death." But Cato spoke after Caesar, and anyone of consequence was bound to support Caesar's notion, which was "Don't do anything rash. Don't set an evil precedent. Somebody else may draw the sword later on, and you do not know where this thing will end." Caesar proposed to hold the guilty men in custody until the end of the emergency and then to proceed against them by law. Here is a delightful paradox, is it not? Cato normally was regarded as a defender of the republic, hence a champion of the law, but he was prepared to override the law because the state was in danger. Caesar generally was regarded as not terribly keen on tradition or legality, but he took a firm stand for legality here. What was he up to?

Some people suppose that Caesar had been involved in the background of the Catilinarian conspiracy and was doing his best to save some of the old friends whom he had lately ditched. But perhaps not. Caesar wanted to bring himself into prominence and to take a stand—deliberately to run a risk. He knew that this would pay off eventually, because he was not afraid of anybody. The Caesar that I see was the last of the Roman nobles rather than the first of the emperors. His actions led to command of the war in Gaul (which was what he wanted), to the defeat of Pompey, to the civil war, and to dictatorship. But did he want these things? Does anyone really want civil war and dictatorship? When he got the dictatorship he did not know what to do with it. He was in a very awkward position, and his remedy was to leave Rome, to go to war again, to get out of a difficult position and a poisonous atmosphere. He could not very well resign; he had to hold supreme authority for the sake of stability. But in the end (we are told fairly credibly) Caesar did not seem to care whether he lived or died. He did not bother to keep a bodyguard, for the presence of a bodyguard showed that one was a tyrant. Some of his friends said that he was in bad health and did not care very much. Which may be the case.

Are you suggesting that Caesar had no very clear remedies for the social and political problems which he faced?

Yes: he tied up the situation as best he could and then left it. He had not wanted to destroy the existing system but to rise to the top of it. His tragedy was that in the end he had no rivals left, and the game was ruined. Among the Roman nobility politics was the great game, and to play it, rivals were needed. After the civil war, the rival who seemed worthy of Caesar (Pompey) existed no more, and a large number of the ex-consuls were dead. I see Caesar as baffled and melancholy: as one Roman emperor is supposed to have said of himself, "I have tried everything, and it is no good." Caesar really was a tragic character. We have a misleading piece of dramatic literature—Shakespeare's *Julius Caesar*—a very peculiar piece of work that does not bring out Caesar's tragedy at all but deals with the dilemma of Marcus Brutus. If one were to write the drama of Caesar, disillusionment would be the theme, and it could be done in a drama of the old-fashioned French type of the three unities. It could be compressed into twenty-four hours, beginning on the fourteenth of March at a dinner party at the house of Lepidus. It is on record that the talk at the party turned to death, and Caesar asked which death was best.

What is your opinion of Mark Antony?

Mark Antony was likewise wrecked by his subsequent history—involvement with the queen of Egypt and defeat at Actium. The world went to his rival. He was defeated in another sense—by the Ciceronian documentation. The oratory of Cicero, especially the *Philippics,* has been much admired throughout the centuries. To me, the best of these were the fighting speeches toward the end, when Cicero advocated the hazardous policy of declaring Antony a public enemy and of legalizing the private army raised by Octavian. These were real political speeches—wonderful, to my mind. (Parenthetically, the historian Tacitus said that Cicero's best speeches were his last.) The immortal *Second Philippic,* a denunciation of Antony—a masterpiece of defamation, insinuation, and mendacity—has always been admired, but it was never delivered. It is a literary product. Thanks to Cicero, Mark Antony is in a weak position in the estimation of historians. And naturally, the defects of his character have been emphasized: drink, the foreign woman, and so on.

It has been assumed without question that Antony wished to step into Caesar's place after his assassination, but I think it more likely that Antony was trying to hold things together, to keep his head above water in the midst of widespread disorder. His remarks at Caesar's funeral (as recorded in certain sources) do not compel us to believe that he was trying to raise the mob. One must remember that he was consul, with large discretionary powers and the responsibility of holding the government together. I think that he wished to assert himself—not as the heir of Caesar the dictator, but rather as the leader of the Caesarian party.

There ensued the maneuvers of 44 and 43, civil war again, and the pact of the three Caesarian leaders—Lepidus, Antony, and Octavian (the Triumvirate). We must hold that Antony was the senior partner, although subsequent history tends to assume Octavian the more important. The credit for the victory at Philippi went to Antony, and when they divided the world among themselves, Antony took the richest part—the eastern lands. This, of course, led to his involvement with Cleopatra. How much more did he do for her than he would for any other eastern vassal? Certainly he rebuilt Egypt (which did not threaten Rome), but he took over certain imperial responsibilities. In Asia Minor, from the Black Sea down to Syria and Palestine, Antony built up a series of vassal principalities which he awarded to new men, not to members of old dynasties—to able people like a certain Herod in Palestine, and Amyntas in Galatia.

One reason for the breakdown of the republican system had been the existence of an empire, which placed powerful strains and stresses on the government at Rome. One way of holding an empire is to govern it as little as possible—hence devolution. Antony's method in the East was to use vassal princes and city governments as far as possible. Augustus and his successors continued to use vassal princes in the East and devolution of authority to towns or muncipalities in the Roman west: hardly any government was exercised directly. Antony knew this secret, but by his efforts on behalf of Cleopatra and his personal attachment to a very able and seductive woman, he exposed himself to propaganda—to charges of "giving away territories of the Roman people to foreigners." From this arose the allegation that he wanted to set himself up as a monarch in Alexandria, or to make war on Rome and the West and install Cleopatra in the capital. As the split developed between Antony and Octavian, the latter was able to mobilize the West. Italy and certain western provinces swore an oath of allegiance to Octavian and demanded that he lead them in the war which he eventually won at Actium. After a decade of civil war, however, one wonders whether these supporters of Octavian were really eager to save the country from despotism, to protect Rome from this (very distant) menace of a foreign queen. Ought we not to assume that the thing was very well managed?

Do you see Octavian as fundamentally different from the other leaders?

No: he became different in the course of events, through various accidents and opportunities. Towards the end of Caesar's life there had been nobody left equal to him, and he no longer needed the advice of anybody older. At Caesar's death, Antony was in the prime of life—about thirty-eight—but he lacked the opportunity that presented itself to Octavian. He lacked a cause, while Octavian could claim the task of avenging the assassinated adoptive parent. At the same time, Octavian could gather to him and take advice from older people. By the course of events and by his success he came to tower over them; also, he was *divi filius* as well as the victor in the civil wars.

In the period after Actium—when Octavian became Augustus, with a name greater than that of an ordinary mortal—it was easy for him to get agents and advisers. And he had the time to build up a system. Caesar spent very few weeks or months in Rome between the outbreak of civil war and the Ides of March. The effective period of his predominance was very short indeed. He put out vast plans, many of which came to nothing, and he was subject to disillusionment—ultimately, he did not care. After Actium, Octavian had a clear task in front of him. Caesar was the last of the nobles, but Octavian was the first of the emperors, and a real monarch. Much of his effectiveness was the result of chance. If he had been assassinated in 27 B.C. or had died in 23, he would have been remembered from the period of the Triumvirate —a time which ever afterward he wanted to live down. When he died in A.D. 14, the Triumvirate had receded into the distant past.

What were Augustus' relations with the old aristocratic families?

First of all, young men emerged through the wars, and he needed to use some of them as consuls, provincial governors, and army commanders. But no Roman wished or planned to destroy the republic. The rivalry of great men like Caesar and Pompey ended by destroying it, but they had wanted not its destruction but primacy within the system. One can define the republic as the constitution, or as the institutions of the state, but from a Roman point of view one might define it in terms of the old families. Romans could not think of the republic without them. To the aristocrat, the republic *was* its aristocracy. It is recorded that in about 92 B.C. an aristocrat asked a tribune of the plebs: "What business have you meddling with our *res publica?*" To gain support, and from his own predilections, the victor in a civil war did his best to conciliate the aristocrats. (One should remember that next to Antony in the campaign of Actium was a republican admiral called Domitius Ahenobarbus, nephew of Cato.)

In the course of the years, through various alliances with relatives of his own, Augustus won the support of ancient houses like the Fabius family or the Valerius Messalla family, who were conspicuous in the restored republic. The reign of Augustus did nothing to diminish class distinction of this kind. In fact, members of the most ancient families became consul more easily under Augustus than they had in the last thirty years of the republic. Patronage had been canalized; men of birth did not have to struggle and spend their money because the great *patronus* (one might almost say "the boss") Caesar Augustus was there to subsidize impoverished aristocratic families so that they could come back into Roman life.

The renovated Caesarian party thus had—in a crude definition—two types of supporters: old families who were reconciled, and new men who were winning the consulship through merit and the patronage of Augustus. He helped new men just as Caesar and Pompey had. And like Caesar and Pompey, he was eager for alliances (political or social) with the old families. It was no accident that the new monarchy was an aristocratic monarchy. Plebeian blood came into it through Marcus Agrippa, a friend and ally of Augustus (of no known ancestry) who married Augustus' daughter Julia. Some of the Julian and Claudian Caesars (such as Caligula) were ashamed of that plebeian component. The heir of Augustus' power, however, was Tiberius, of the ancient patrician Claudian house. Further, as a result of Augustus' policy of bringing in everyone that mattered, Mark Antony and his admiral Domitius Ahenobarbus were the ancestors of emperors. Claudius had in him the blood of Mark Antony, and Nero was the last male of the Domitius family.

The aristocratic resurgence was impermanent. While some of the oldest families were attached to the dynasty, most of them perished. Many members of these families were accused of conspiracy or put to death in later years. Similarly, descendants of other noble families which did not intermarry with the dynasty—the descendants of Pompey, Crassus, and various members of the Piso family—came to an end either because they conspired or because they were alleged to be involved in intrigues. After Nero, hardly any of the great old families were left.

Did they really conspire? Did they not totally accept the new order?

Certainly there were genuine conspiracies, but very often these were invented. Aristocrats were prosecuted for high treason, for magic, or for astrology (investigating the length of the emperor's reign). They refused to accept the new order for a number of reasons. First, it had arisen out of civil war; Augustus was a usurper (a mere Octavian taken into the family of the Julii). The descendants of Pompey and Crassus regarded themselves as the social equals of the dynasty even though they had fallen behind in the political race and power was monopolized by Augustus and Tiberius. Julius Caesar was deified after his death, and Augustus was *divi filius,* but these people recognized the deification for what it was—a social and political device to impress the lower classes. Since the monarchy had emerged out of civil war, the great aristocrats were prepared to believe that some accident—the extinction of the dynasty by violence, disease, or poison—would leave any one of them qualified to rule. A similar phenomenon occurred after the death of Nero, when the emperor Vespasian was socially inferior to the great noble families. (And the same sort of thing happened in England when the great families looked down on the early Hanoverians.)

Was Tacitus a spokesman for the aristocracy?

Certainly he reflected this atmosphere, although he was not an aristocrat himself. He was writing the annals of Rome from A.D. 14 to 68, and he could not help reliving it and getting some of the feeling of the period. This was the period of Tiberius, who was himself the head of a great ancient family—the Claudian house—and in various ways did not approve of the monarchy. He was a republican of sorts, though emperor. There was still much of the republic left, continuity being provided by the old families or what Tacitus calls the "great names" (*magna nomina*). In Tacitus' time these great names were replaced by a new aristocracy, people who had risen in the service of the government or under the patronage of the Caesars from the towns of Italy or the Roman west.

Were the people in charge of the Roman government at the end of the third century descendants of this new aristocracy?

No, the thing renewed itself all the time. Various aristocracies, once they had got what they wanted (in the first instance, the consulship), could survive for generations or fade out for one reason or another, like dynasties of emperors. Once the process of social change in the aristocracy began, it was continually enhanced as the monarchy brought in its own servants. New families rose to the consulship and thus belonged to the new aristocracy. In the time of Augustus, some of the families of the men who came up in the civil wars were not so fertile as those of the old aristocracy. The gradual rise of families in the service of the Caesars was accelerated from time to time by civil war: a development of thirty to fifty years might be telescoped into five or ten years, as happened after the fall of Nero. He was followed by three emperors in quick succession, and then the power went to Vespasian, who was proclaimed by the armies of the east. Subsequently, Vespasian brought into the Roman Senate officers from the eastern legions and prominent men from the cities of western Asia Minor.

Would you say that the history of the government of the empire in the first two centuries A.D. *was the history of successive aristocracies?*

Yes, if we regard it as the history of the governing class. Of course the personalities and tastes of emperors counted for a great deal from time to time, but they were by no means omnipotent. Often they were in the hands of their servants and had to do things for various people or groups to avoid antagonizing them. They had to give away consulships as rewards or for encouragement. The personality of an emperor, or a crisis, could speed up promotion on occasion. This occurred after the assassination of Domitian, when the weak emperor Nerva had to adopt as his son and successor the army commander on the upper Rhine—the man we know as the emperor Trajan—who happened to come from Spain. The assassination, the end of the Flavian dynasty, and the accession of Trajan (Nerva died conveniently) meant a clear acceleration of change, although there was continuity, of course, through the people who served the commonwealth, whatever its government. The new emperor promoted a number of his friends, Romans from Spain and the south of France. Later on, in the year 113, he went to fight the Parthians, and this resulted in even more promotions, especially for people from the cities of the Greek east. As a young man Trajan had been with the legions in Syria; his father was a provincial governor and he knew the eastern city aristocracies very well. Perhaps even more from Trajan than his successor Hadrian (the notorious philhellene), Greeks in the Senate received advancement.

Would you compare the ideals and attitudes of the new aristocracies of the first two centuries of the empire with the old aristocracy?

The old notion of aristocracy in the republic was based on personal excellence and competitiveness. But with the new system and with centralized government, with Augustus and his successors in control of patronage, the requisite qualities became slightly different. Good education and training, an absence of too much idealism or fanaticism: these qualities made a man good enough for his job, but not too good. Tacitus mentions a man who held a provincial governorship for twenty-four years as "equal to his job but not superior" (*par negotiis neque supra*). Even in the reign of Tiberius, this described the good civil servant. It was basically a middle-class ideal—not quite a business ideal—and was embodied not only in the new administrative class but in the emperors themselves, who were servants of the state and tried to be unobtrusive and to do good. The emperor Antoninus Pius (138–161), for instance, seems to have had no discoverable personality, and surely this was the secret of a happy epoch.

Some of the rulers of the first century of the empire had too much personality. Tiberius, for example, felt himself an old aristocrat and was disappointed and resentful against Augustus. He hated the system but had to do his duty. Claudius, who became emperor by accident, was very peculiar. Nero, whose education was perhaps of the wrong sort, broke out of control after a time. On the other hand, the emperors of the second century had a certain inner control. How far was this due to Stoic philosophy (and what was peculiar about Stoic philosophy?), and how far was it just the normal behavior of the upper order of a Greco-Roman civilization?

Certainly a Greco-Roman civilization existed by the second century. The emperors were members of the educated class, and they had begun to prefer to write in Greek instead of Latin. Hadrian was a friend of everything Greek; Marcus Aurelius wrote his memoirs in Greek. Fifty years before, Trajan had written military memoirs or *commentarii* like an old Roman. The Antonine emperors wrote in Greek, beginning with Hadrian (an esthete), and continuing with the dutiful and self-obliterating Pius and Marcus Aurelius, who was worried about the condition of the empire and the state of his soul. Men from the Greek east entered the Senate and rose as far as the consulship before the end of Domitian's reign. Trajan also encouraged them. In the second century, with provincials from the Roman west, these people formed an amalgam representing the educated classes east and west, which was also the urban class of city magnates and the landowning class. The apparently national Roman and Italian movement, with the defeat of Antony by Augustus, had temporarily disguised the reality that the world was Greco-Roman.

The emperors and higher social classes of the second century can be described as a kind of Greco-Roman consensus of the wealthy and civilized. Some had been wealthy for a long time; others had risen in the imperial service; others had risen out of commerce after three or four generations to buy land and enter the government and the Senate. About the year 150, the Roman Senate—getting on for a thousand members—represented all sorts of people of different backgrounds and from different areas, particularly wealthier areas such as southern France and Bactria. The Antonine dynasty was partly Spanish, partly from southern France.

When trouble came, Romans looked back to the Antonine dynasty as the great dynasty of their history. Beginning in 96, after the assassination of Domitian, with the brief reign of Nerva, or with Trajan (the good emperor) or Hadrian (good, but slightly sinister), the second century led up to the real climax of excellent government under the two Antonines, Antoninus Pius and Marcus Aurelius (138–180). That, of course, was the age Gibbon had in mind when he set the beginning of his work at the year 180, the death of Marcus Aurelius. Some people thought that the government was excellent because sons did not succeed fathers but emperors were chosen by merit; in reality, however, the emperors did not have sons (Nerva, Trajan, Pius), and there was no theoretical basis for their exclusion. When the emperor did have a son, he succeeded.

The ancient notion of the Antonine prime was most clearly and powerfully expressed by the historian Cassius Dio, who was not only an historian of the empire writing in Greek, but also a senator from the Greek east and the son of a senator from the province of Bithynia. He represented the educated classes of the world. He became senator and consul, and—as was appropriate—an ex-consul who wrote history. His description of the period after 180 was of an age turned to "rust and iron"; everything went bad, went downhill.

This notion has been enormously important, as recognized and perpetuated by Gibbon. But it is not certain that the age was quite so robust and resilient as it ought to have been. In the reign of Marcus Aurelius there was war in the East, then the plague, then wars against the Germans in the Danubian countries. One would have expected the empire to make a better showing, and one wonders whether some of the powerful Illyrians who emerged in the third century might not have been more effective than Marcus Aurelius—highly educated, conscientious, devoted to the truth, and torn in mind. At that stage it would have been impossible for a common soldier to rise to be emperor, as happened in the third century.

Turning away from the aristocratic classes, what did the empire mean in the lives of the common people?

A native non-Roman could be recruited into the auxiliary troops (not the legions, which were composed of Roman citizens) and rise from there. The auxiliary soldier, serving twenty-five years, received Roman citizenship on discharge and might have a family. In certain areas, Roman citizens could get government employ. Ex-legionaries could become centurions and rise from there to the officer class. In short, it was possible to rise quite high in one generation, and this does not happen in all civilizations. For example, at the end of the first century A.D., there was a man who began as a common soldier or centurion in the legions, held various military employments, became financial officer in a province, and ended by governing a region as large as the modern Bavaria. The army, in a sense, was the equivalent of public service. To be sure, the army was not always fighting, and to be an officer one needed civilian qualities. These avenues of advancement were, in the main, for the literate—the city population.

Literacy was fairly widespread in the Greco-Roman world. But in the empire of the first and second centuries A.D. there were large backward areas—Brittany, the northwest of Spain, the Alpine regions, and the back country of the Balkans—which were not much changed by the imposition of Roman rule. The Romans exercised as little government as possible, and they were very glad if people desired to learn Latin, show a bit of economic enterprise, and go into the army. They made no effort to impose the Latin language in the East; but it spread fairly naturally in the West because it was the language of civilization. In parts of the distant West, however, Latin did not spread: Albanian (a pre-Latin language) survived in the Balkans, and Basque in northern Spain. Certain areas of the empire must always have been backward, simply because they were not favorable to city civilization. Cities in the empire had to depend on their *territorium,* and they often developed at the expense of the surrounding territory. From the language phenomenon and other indications, one can assume that there were large areas which did not change much after the Romans took over. Similarly in the Turkish empire, the central government did not control certain parts of Asia Minor closely. Some of these regions were so poor that the government could not be bothered with them, and it limited its efforts to the towns and main roads.

One ought to emphasize the stability of the empire over centuries, but existence in the empire was not always ideal. We lack evidence for this, but it seems likely that the rural poor must have been very close to serfdom. The lot of the city proletariat was probably lighter; for reasons of climate their existence was reasonably comfortable, and the bourgeoisie felt a kind of duty toward their city which included the provision of buildings and games, and free distribution of food and oil. However, we cannot be sure what the life of the urban poor was actually like.

Would you discuss Roman slavery as an economic and social system?

I have not studied this question much, whereas other people (particularly Communists) have done so in the last thirty years. One has always known that ancient civilizations depended largely on slavery. Judged by ancient literature, the house slave was treated very much as one of the family. Industrial slavery was a different matter. I personally am not without interest in economics or the study of society, but so many scholars have taken up the question of slavery that I have found myself slightly bored with it.

Very often, when investigating the political and administrative class, one cannot discover where their estates were, how they or their grandparents made their money—out of oil in Spain or metalwork in Campania? Then I assume that because people had a certain status they had enough of a financial basis, an agricultural basis, or a basis of slavery. Seneca (a great man of letters and a tutor of Nero) came from the south of Spain, where his family had lived for a hundred and fifty years. I assume that they had vineyards and olive groves, but there is no evidence. In fact, there is no instance of the name in the inscriptions of Cordova, but I assume that theirs was a comfortable family. Some literary men came from humble backgrounds, but they were not impoverished and did not always need patrons in order to survive. They were not members of the old aristocracy: Roman nobles had no interest in writing as such. Warfare, the law, possibly military commentaries like those of Caesar—these were acceptable occupations for an aristocrat. Such people as the Latin poets—Lucretius, Vergil, and so on—were reasonably prosperous people from the cities of Italy.

Obviously, Roman cultural life had a very strong economic basis, but one cannot get enough evidence to write the history of the educated class and the governing class with strict attention to incomes and property, though towns of origin and significant relationships can often be discovered. There was continuity between the late republic and the empire (the political system changed, but not the social), and the recruitment of the Roman upper class widened all the time to include people from all over the Roman world. Finally it included the splendid people of the third century A.D., who held the thing together although they were not very polished characters. The emperors who came from very low social backgrounds, from the Danubian and Balkan regions, were not much liked by the culture snobs, but they saved the empire.

7

The Later Roman Empire and the Beginnings of Medieval Society

A. H. M. JONES

THE HISTORIOGRAPHICAL CONTEXT

The causes of the decline and fall of the Roman Empire in the West have been called the greatest problem in history because it is part of the problem of why any great political system deteriorates and fails and why any civilization disintegrates and gives way to another social and cultural system. Since Gibbon's *Decline and Fall* (1776), a host of master historians have investigated these monumental themes and a host of solutions have been propounded: the devastating impact of the Christian ethos (Gibbon); the excessive size of the empire in relation to its political institutions (Gibbon, Ferdinand Lot); the economic disintegration of the Mediterranean world (H. Pirenne, F. Oertel); the limitations of the classical mind (C. N. Cochrane); the consequences of class struggle (M. Rostovtzeff); the racial mongrelization of the Roman elite (T. Frank); and not least, the impact of the German invasions (R. Latouche).

By the 1960's the problem of the later Roman Empire needed not further theorizing but a new, thorough, comprehensive analysis of the actual operation of the political, economic, and social institutions of the fourth- and fifth-century Mediterranean world. And this was provided in the vast, monumental study published by the Cambridge scholar A. H. M. Jones. No aspect of Roman imperial life escaped his intensive investigation, and the result falls within the best traditions of empirical British scholarship, where theorizing follows from mastery of the material and is always conditioned by shrewd common sense.

Born in 1904, Jones in his long academic career established his reputation as an authority on both ancient Greece and the later Roman Empire. Working steadily and quietly in his study in his imposing seventeenth-century manor house just outside of Cambridge, this deceptively frail-looking man represents a generation of scholars devoted to detailed research and patient extrapolation of wide-ranging conclusions—a generation of great historians we may never see duplicated.

Chronological Outline

31 B.C.–A.D. 200: The era of the Pax Romana, the period of two centuries of relative peace under the empire inaugurated by Augustus.

212: The Edict of Caracalla extends Roman citizenship to virtually all free inhabitants of the empire.

270–275: After a series of incapable rulers, the emperor Aurelian, titled the "restorer of the world," repulses the invading barbarians.

284–305: Reign of Diocletian. The reorganization of the empire into eastern and western spheres under the dual administration of two coequal *Augusti*.

303: Diocletian declares a general persecution of the Christians which lasts until 306 in the West and 313 in the East.

312: Constantine wins the battle of Milvian Bridge and converts to Christianity soon afterward. The Edict of Milan (313) proclaims equal rights for all religions and returns confiscated property to the Christians.

324–337: Constantine reunites the empire under his sole rule.

325: Constantine summons the first ecumenical council of the Church to meet at Nicaea to deal with the Arian controversy.

330: Constantine dedicates Constantinople as his capital. Death of Constantine in 337.

370–430: Era of the Great Church Fathers—Saint Ambrose (339?–397), Saint Jerome (347–419?), and Saint Augustine (354–430).

379–395: Reign of Theodosius the Great, who is forced to allow the Visigoths to settle within the empire (retaining their own political institutions) and uses them as his soldiers. After his death, the division of the empire between his sons proves to be permanent.

410: Alaric sacks Rome and dies soon afterward. In the next ten years the Visigoths establish independent kingdoms in southern France and Spain.

429–442: The Vandals gain control of Africa.

452: Attila invades Italy but stops short of attacking Rome. After his death in 453, the Huns no longer threaten the empire.

455: Gaiseric and the Vandals sack Rome, destroying a large part of the city.

476: With the support of Zeno, the emperor in the East, Odovacar (chief of the Herculi, a small German tribe) deposes Romulus Augustulus, the last emperor in the West. This marks the traditional end of the Roman Empire in the West.

489–526: Theodoric defeats Odovacar and reunites Italy as the kingdom of the Ostrogoths.

527–565: Reign of Justinian in the East. Africa is recovered from the Vandals and Italy from the Ostrogoths.

529: Saint Benedict founds the first truly Benedictine monastery at Monte Cassino, near Naples.

Norman F. Cantor

There is considerable discussion among historians as to whether the population of the later Roman Empire declined, and what factors were responsible.

A. H. M. Jones

We have almost no figures for population. All our evidence is indirect, but I think that one can deduce that the population was below the optimum, at any rate. The most important evidence for this is the series of laws which tied various classes of people, particularly agricultural workers, to their jobs. It is fairly apparent from these that there was a shortage of agricultural labor, and probably of other essential workers such as miners. We know about certain classes only, because it was those that the government was interested in. They were anxious to keep up the army, the miners, and above all the agricultural workers on whom the feeding of the empire (and its tax returns) depended.

A shortage of labor does not necessarily mean a shrinkage of population; it may mean, as in the last war in England, a greater demand for manpower for the army. The Roman army was greatly increased by Diocletian—perhaps doubled—and the recruits were drawn exclusively from the peasantry. This then might partly account for the shortage of agricultural labor. But there is one piece of evidence which proves an absolute decline in population. There was a substantial and progressive shrinkage in the cultivated area. This means that less food was produced, and since the Roman Empire never had an exportable surplus and never imported food, fewer people can have been fed.

We can deduce that from the third century A.D. there was a perennial shortage of manpower, and one can find certain reasons for it. There was a serious outbreak of plague at the end of the second century, and it recurred from time to time in the following century. This may have started off the decline, but it is not so easy to understand why the population never recovered. The Roman Empire was of the primitive agricultural population pattern, and in modern societies of such a pattern the birth rate is high and population growth is checked only by lack of food. It tends to recover very quickly from any natural disaster such as plague or famine, and to reach the highest total which the area can sustain at subsistence level. Why didn't this happen in the later empire? My theory, which does not command general assent, is that the level of taxation reached so high a figure that the peasants were chronically undernourished and could not afford to raise many children. We know, for instance, that the rate of taxation in Egypt under Justinian was three sevenths of the average gross crop, and that is very high compared to the tithe, which was a common form of taxation under the Roman republic. There is evidence of widespread infanticide in the early fourth century; it was perhaps checked by the spread of Christianity. There are several records of famines, in which the peasants flocked to the towns for bread and despite the grant of relief died in large numbers. We also have some detailed information about nine peasant families—a very inadequate sample—and they were nearly all extremely small; to be precise, one with four children, three with two, and five with only one child.

Did the population decline have an effect upon economic conditions, industry, and trade? Presumably it did affect army recruitment.

Primarily, of course, it affected agriculture. There wasn't enough manpower for efficient cultivation, and this was one cause of the great increase in deserted lands in the later empire—up to a fifth of its total lands were abandoned, partly because there were not enough people to cultivate them. One must remember that the principal industry of the empire was agriculture: it accounted for something like 95 percent of the national income. However, I don't believe that the decline would have had much effect on industry and trade. There is some evidence of a falling-off in certain industries, perhaps because industrial workers preferred to go into the country and become farmers. The same applies to ordinary urban craftsmen, at least in the West.

It is difficult to tell how much the population decline affected army recruitment—the evidence is curious. Diocletian instituted regular conscription, and apparently he called up men for the army almost every year. Justinian, however, was able to raise quite substantial bodies of volunteers without using conscription at all, which rather contradicts the previous evidence. His recruits, however, nearly all came from certain mountainous areas, Isaurians and Armenians from eastern Asia Minor, Thracians and Illyrians from the Balkans. It may be that these poor highlanders did not pay much tax and did breed, exceeding the limits of their food supply. Some of them, notably the Isaurians, had before Justinian's time supplemented the resources of their own country by widespread brigandage, and when this was suppressed were driven to take service in the imperial army, and also as laborers in the building industry.

The history of industry and trade in the later Roman Empire has been much debated. Do you think that the forms and the quantity of industry and commerce in the Mediterranean world underwent any marked change between the beginning of the third century and the end of the fifth?

I should be inclined to say No. Throughout the history of the Roman Empire, there was some trade in essential foodstuffs and cheap clothing for the very large towns, but most of the trade was in luxury articles—objects bought by the upper classes, such as high-grade clothing, silk, slaves, silver, jewelry, spices, and perfumes. There is no sign that the luxury trade diminished; there always was a wealthy class, and it always spent its money on luxury goods. As time went on this class tended to become more concentrated, and trade may have diminished somewhat with increasing differentiation in wealth. There was a sharpening cleavage between the wealthy upper class and the great mass of the population—the peasants and the workers—who tended to become poorer. However, even in the most prosperous days of the empire I don't think that the peasants bought anything except local products. There were potters, carpenters, smiths, and weavers in most villages, and the products of different villages were exchanged at country fairs. The only large-scale commerce in cheap manufactured goods seems to have been in clothing. We happen to know that cheap woolen clothing known as *Antiochenes,* which is woven in Syria, was exported in the early fifth century in Rome—it was only large towns with a big working class population that provided a sufficient market to attract this type of goods.

Many historians have said that one of the most significant changes in the later Roman Empire was the elimination of the urban middle class or bourgeoisie. Would you agree with this, and did it have any economic effects?

The urban middle classes were subjected to heavy financial burdens as decurions or *curiales*—that is, members of the city council. They were expected to finance the local civic services to a large extent out of their own pockets. They provided the tax collectors for the imperial government, and tax collectors were liable for any deficits in taxation. If the collector could not pay, the burden was shared around the whole *curia*—the city council. However, this economic burden could be reduced. The civic services could be cut and made less expensive. The collection of taxes was not entirely efficient; arrears were allowed to accumulate, and these were written off periodically and the collector was relieved of his burden.

The curial class did diminish in numbers and in wealth, but it is fairly clear that the main reason for this was not that the *curiales* became impoverished, but that they disliked their status, and made strenuous and often successful efforts to get out of it. A good many curial families rose to the senatorial class. Others went into the civil service or the law or the Church or into other professions where they could legally or illegally gain immunity. I would hesitate to say that the middle class diminished very much. Rather it changed its name; its members were no longer called *curiales* but lawyers, civil servants, doctors, priests, and so on. The senatorial order became much larger and came to include persons of middle-class origin and middle-class wealth and status.

These changes in the middle class did not mean that fewer people were involved in commercial activities, however. One must remember that in antiquity the average merchant was a very humble man, below the rank of a *curialis*—technically, a plebeian. Most merchants worked on a very small scale; the only important ones were in a few of the really big commercial towns. At Alexandria, for instance, we do hear of a merchant whose capital amounted to something like fifty pounds of gold. He was a fairly wealthy man, but he could not compare with landowners whose estates brought in thousands of pounds of gold annually.

Was there a change in land ownership, in the way the land was worked and the peasantry exploited, in the centuries beginning at the end of the second century? Were there significant differences between the eastern and western parts of the empire in forms of land ownership and exploitation?

In land ownership, the general tendency was toward the continual building-up of large estates. That process is difficult to verify in detail, but in general the number of peasant freeholders diminished because they could not stand up to taxation and other difficulties. They had to borrow (and thereby mortgage their plots and ultimately have them seized by creditors) or to put themselves under the protection of a big landlord. Patronage took a variety of forms, but most often it meant that the peasant was protected against the imperial tax-gatherer in return for monetary payments to a great landowner or for surrendering his land to him.

There was a difference between the East and the West, but I think it went back to a much earlier period. One gets the strong impression that the large estate was much more dominant in certain western provinces such as Italy, Africa, Gaul, and Spain. In some eastern provinces, on the other hand—in the Balkans, for instance, and in Syria, and above all in Egypt—quite large numbers of peasant proprietors survived down to the sixth century. The reason, I think, is that the Roman nobles began to build up their estates at a much earlier date in the West. From 200 B.C. they had money to spend, and they spent a good deal of it investing in land. While land was being absorbed into big estates in the West, things remained more or less unchanged in the East; and not until the fourth century, with the foundation of Constantinople and the formation of a wealthy, land-hungry aristocracy there, did big estates begin to build up in the East.

As for the status of the agricultural worker, the main legal change was the rise of the colonate. In the third century the tenant, or *colonus,* had been a free man. He paid rent (and if he didn't pay he was turned out), and he could leave at the end of his lease if he was discontented. But by the beginning of the fourth century, *coloni* were not allowed to leave their farms, and legally they could be put in chains if they tried to escape. My theory is that the colonate arose initially from a fiscal measure of Diocletian, who based his tax system on a poll tax and a levy in kind assessed on the agricultural population. These taxes were based on a series of censuses, in which the land was assessed according to area, use, and quality, and the agricultural population counted. Probably in order to make it easier to collect the poll tax, an edict was issued that the peasants must stay in the place in which they were registered on the census. This law was highly acceptable to landlords, whose tenants were constantly throwing up their leases, and it continued to be enforced even when the poll tax was abolished. In evidence for my thesis, there are a couple of laws which abolished the agricultural poll tax in Thrace and Illyricum, but declared that the peasants remained bound to the land. A third law, issued by Theodosius I, introduces the tied colonate into Palestine, where for some reason it had not hitherto been applied, for the express benefit of landlords. As a result, descendants of peasants originally registered in the census were tied to the place where their ancestors were registered.

Gradually, further restrictions were placed on the peasants. They were not allowed to bring civil suits against their landlords except for excessive rent. They were not allowed to sell their own property without their landlord's consent. Ultimately they were not allowed to join the army, and they could not be ordained as priests without the landlord's consent. They came to have very much the status of serfs and became assimilated with the agricultural slaves, who went through the same kind of process in reverse. By this period, agricultural slaves were almost always hereditary. They were allowed de facto to marry like free men; they were allowed to own property de facto; they could not be sold away from the land which they cultivated. They had become very much like the free *coloni* who were tied to the land; they had improved their social position while the free peasants descended into the colonate.

Of course, the *coloni* were not the only agricultural workers in the later empire, although many books on the topic seem to imply that they were. There were considerable numbers of free peasant proprietors throughout the period. There were also a variety of tenants who were not *coloni adscripticii*—not tied to the soil. By the sixth century, if not earlier, this class had become quite considerable. On some farms, the *coloni adscripticii* had died out and been replaced by newcomers, who (because they were not descended from the original peasants registered in the census) were not tied. In the East, however, the emperor Anastasius ruled that free peasants who stayed thirty years or more on the same farm were obliged to stay there (and their descendants also), but without the other disabilities of *coloni adscripticii*—they could join the army or take holy orders, they had full control over their own property, and could even give up their leases if they acquired land of their own sufficient to support them.

Did the emergence of the colonate system have general social or political significance? Did it strengthen the power of the nobles, or weaken the state? Did it have any effect on taxation or on the military system, or was it just a natural economic change?

I think that the formation of the big estates and the growth of the colonate had a bad effect fiscally. Many free peasants put themselves under the protection of a great landlord precisely in order to avoid taxation. It is one of the features of the later empire that great men were able to evade taxation, not so much by brute force as by influence and social pressure on the authorities. They could gain official immunities or rebates, or they could postpone payments long enough for them to lapse under a general remission. The humble man paid his taxes on the nail while the rich man paid late, if at all. In that way, I think that the growth of large estates was detrimental to the government. There may be no strict connection, but in the eastern half of the empire, where there were fewer large estates, the fiscal system was much more efficient. Militarily, too, the colonate weakened the empire, since the army was recruited from the peasantry, and *coloni adscripticii* were from the early fifth century debarred from military service. It is hard to believe that the government could have made a concession so deleterious to the defense of the empire to the big landowners, but it certainly did. The effect must have been worse in the West, where *coloni adscripticii* were commonest, than in the East, which had more free peasants.

It is often said that the later Roman Empire saw the beginnings of feudalism. It is true that there was a growth of great estates, but landlords drew money rents from tenants. They had no jurisdiction over them, though some of them illegally maintained private prisons. They derived no military power from their estates; some illegally maintained bands of barbarian slaves or hired Isaurians, but they never mustered their tenants to defend them. The power of landlords lay in their money wealth, which enabled them to bribe the agents of the government.

Historians have talked about apathy and the corruption of public spirit in the later empire. Would you analyze what this meant, and the reason for it?

The reaction of the population to the barbarian invasions was certainly apathetic. In only three or four cases did the local population or the local gentry make any spontaneous move to resist the barbarians. They did not welcome the invasions, but apparently they had no idea that they could do anything about them. There are two circumstances which explain this phenomenon.

In the first place, the population of the empire had for centuries—since the reign of Augustus—become accustomed to being defended by a standing professional army. The civilian population, particularly in the interior provinces of the empire, had lost all military spirit and did not know how to set about organizing a resistance movement.

In the second place, the unit that excited patriotism and devotion in antiquity had always been the city, and perhaps only a unit of that scale could excite such feeling. In the earlier empire, when the cities had become mere local government authorities, there was nevertheless an extraordinary fund of civic patriotism, and even in the later empire something of that spirit survived. But the empire was too remote, and too impersonal to rouse that kind of emotional response.

It is symbolic of the attitude of the ordinary subject of the empire that he worshiped the emperor as a god. Even when the emperor became a Christian, he revered him as the representative of God. The emperor was regarded as a benign, distant, superior power. A man might pray to the emperor to help him, but it would not occur to him that he could help the emperor in return—any more than he could help God.

Was the empire overcentralized in the later period, and too heavy a burden on the population? Were the landowners less well educated or less devoted to the traditions of Rome and of classical culture than they had been in the second century?

The empire was fantastically centralized. By a law of Zeno no recruit might be enrolled in a frontier regiment except by a document drawn up in the central secretariats at Constantinople. Army commanders had to send up returns of strength to the capital each year, and on the basis of these the praetorian prefects allocated rations and instructed provincial governors to supply and deliver them, and finally the amount of rations delivered was checked against the returns of regimental strengths. This centralization caused all the more delay and frustration because communications were so slow. In 356 an imperial messenger managed to get from Milan to Constantinople in twenty-nine days—a record performance—but in 360 another imperial messenger took eighty days to get from Constantinople to Rome.

The economic burden of the empire was also very heavy. As I said just now, the tax rate by Justinian's reign had reached nearly one third of the gross crop. There are continuous complaints of the ruinous burden of taxation, but such complaints must be taken with a grain of salt—in what age have people, and particularly rich people, not grumbled about taxation? Much marginal land was, it is true, abandoned, because the taxes absorbed all the profits, but it must be remembered that a large number of senators, after paying tax, drew vast incomes from their estates.

The landowning aristocracy remained a remarkably learned group through the sixth century. Many of our classical texts were revised by members of the great senatorial families of Rome. The Roman aristocracy remained pagan remarkably late—down into the fifth century—essentially for literary and cultural reasons. They could not bear to give up their devotion to the old classical culture. But even after they became Christians they retained their strong literary culture. In the East, too, there survived a certain amount of literary, philosophical paganism, and the older aristocratic families were learned in classical culture.

Is there any evidence in the later empire of what we might call nationalism?

In my view, there was nothing you could really call nationalism. There was a certain amount of regional sentiment. The common view is that certain of the heresies, such as the Monophysite heresy which was particularly strong in Egypt and Syria, were concealed expressions of nationalism. One of my objections to that theory is that it is based on distorted evidence: for a considerable period (as far as I know, until the Arab conquest) Monophysitism was not restricted to Egypt and Syria; there were centers of Monophysitism in Asia Minor and even in Europe. Furthermore, Syria was not by any means unanimously Monophysite, and of course is not so, to this day. The one country which always was solidly Monophysite was Egypt, and I think one can infer that this did express regional loyalty to their own patriarch.

Many authors have connected the Monophysite heresy with nationalism on the grounds that the church of Alexandria used Coptic and the church of Antioch, Syriac. This again is based on false historical premises. It is true that when Greek died out in those countries after the Arab conquest, Coptic and Syriac became the only languages of the Monophysite churches there, but before that—under the Roman Empire—both the Orthodox (Chalcedonian) Church and the Monophysite used Greek and Syriac, or Greek and Coptic. The great leaders of the Monophysite movement spoke and wrote in Greek, and this notion of linguistic nationalism is false, I think.

This leads to the question of the effect of Christianity and the Church on the empire. Let me suggest several propositions: first, that Christianity put forward a new scheme of values which distracted men from secular considerations; second, that the Church persuaded men to serve it, who otherwise would have served the empire; third, that the Church itself became an economic burden.

On this last point, it is not true that the Church did not pay taxes. It paid the ordinary standard land tax and was immune only from certain extra, irregular dues, and in that sense it was not an economic burden. On the other hand, it did tend to acquire large estates, contributing to the general tendency toward the accumulation of land in a few hands. Many of its estates were large before they belonged to the Church, because most of the Church lands were given to it by wealthy men. But it is also true that many quite humble men left small bits of land to the Church, which gradually built up enormous estates from them.

Economically speaking, the Church was a dead loss—it was unproductive. It did, of course, do something by providing for orphans, widows, the aged, and the sick, but most of its revenues went toward the salaries of bishops and other clergy, on buildings, and on their maintenance. It was one of the nonproductive elements of the empire, weighing on the economy like the civil service and the army. It was a big element, too. People often speak of the multitudes of civil servants in the later empire, but the clergy were infinitely more numerous and paid on a considerably higher scale.

As for its effect on public service, the Church taught that it was very perilous for the soul, if not sinful, to go into the civil service or take higher administrative posts. In that way it discouraged serious Christians from serving the state. Some men were even attracted from the imperial service into that of the Church. A case in point is Ambrose, a provincial governor, consecrated bishop of Milan.

Will you talk in general terms about what happened in the expanding bureaucracy of the later empire? Who were the people who became civil servants? Would you describe their recruitment and training, their attitudes and their efficiency?

I will describe the civil service proper—that is, the men who made a career of serving as officials, not the head men (ministers, provincial governors, and so forth) who changed every few years and were not professional. It would appear that most of the civil servants of the empire possessed the characteristics associated with the "perfect" civil servant: extreme conservatism, devotion to red tape, departmental jealousy, and so on. Imperial civil servants did not receive any training, but they were naturally expected to have had a normal literary education. They served for a number of years varying according to different ministries from twenty to thirty years or more. Promotion was strictly automatic, by seniority; they moved up a place every year or every two years. They learned their various rituals through practice. Much of the work was mechanical, but a number of able men did emerge from the civil service.

There always was a tendency for the bureaucracy to grow, especially in the higher and more profitable offices—those nearest the emperor. There is no sign of any excess of civil servants in the offices of provincial governors, but in the palatine ministries (those directly attached to the palace) the government held periodic purges, declaring that the numbers in a certain ministry must be reduced to a certain total. Twenty or thirty years later there would be another purge. In the meantime there piled up a waiting list of men who were doing the work of the ministry but receiving no salary, thereby establishing a claim to get into the next staff vacancy. The higher the ministry, the greater the profits—not so much in salaries, but in fees. A civil servant lived on fees received from the public, and since higher ministries had higher fees, there was strong pressure to get into the top ministries. At the lowest level, the offices of provincial governors, the civil service was hereditary—son was legally obliged to follow father. But in all other offices recruitment was voluntary. The entrants seem to have been mostly middle class, and there was some tendency for fathers to claim a preference for their sons. In the very highest ministries places were so valuable that they were sold by the senior clerks on retirement to the applicant highest on the waiting list.

Was there a great increase in the number of courtiers, of the people who hung around the emperor? Did they play an important role in politics?

The emperor lived a curiously secluded life. It was part of the tradition established by Diocletian that he appeared in public only on more or less ceremonial or state occasions, when there was a solemn meeting of the privy council or the Senate or when he went to church on Sundays and festivals. Most of the time he lived in what was called the "sacred bedchamber," where he was attended mainly by eunuchs. Any outsider who wished for an interview with the emperor had to get past the eunuch barrier, and the eunuchs could thus become very important and influential. They often became extremely wealthy by collecting large tips from those who wished to see the emperor. From time to time they became dominant figures in the government, but only when there was an exceptionally weak-minded emperor.

Our information about other courtiers is sparse. Evidently a considerable number of senators and office seekers did hang about the court, trying to obtain jobs for themselves or their friends. Appointment went to those who were in immediate contact with the emperor or had friends in contact with him; those who were far away were unlikely to get what they wanted. Courtiers of this type could make great fortunes in two ways. They could petition for grants of crown lands, particularly lands which had just accrued to the crown as estates of condemned felons, or by escheat. Secondly, they could exploit their influence with the emperor by recommending to him aspirants for lesser official appointments such as provincial governments—and receiving for their services a very substantial consideration.

To what extent was the emperor in charge of his own government? Did he have a sense of what was happening in the empire?

This varied from emperor to emperor. The ordinary conscientious ruler did a great deal of work himself. In some cases—Constantine, for example, or Justinian—I think that you can trace a personal style in the laws which they dictated. All emperors were expected to do a good deal of personal jurisdiction. In a number of laws emperors give the full details of cases they have heard, because these cases led to a revision of the law. It is true that a good many of the detailed, technical, administrative changes were drafted by the responsible minister, but I think that one can say broadly that any vigorous emperor carried out his own policies.

It is clear from Procopius' detailed narrative that Justinian decided on the expedition to Africa, which opened his conquest of the West, on his own initiative. He first decided on the expedition himself and sent instructions to the relevant ministers. They were horrified, for all previous expeditions to Africa had been disastrous failures. Finally John the praetorian prefect sought an audience with the emperor and succeeded by powerful arguments in inducing him to cancel the project. But soon after, an exiled African bishop convinced Justinian that God was on his side, and he ordered the preparations for the invasion to go forward.

What was the effect of the partition of the imperial authority?

The division was designed by Diocletian because the task of administering and defending the whole empire was too much for one man. He held that four men were needed for the task. As far as one can see, this had no deleterious effects until the death of Theodosius in 395, which was followed by a bitter quarrel between the governments of East and West.

There were certain inherent difficulties in the division of the empire into eastern and western parts: the resources and the burdens of the two halves were ill-balanced. The eastern half was certainly much richer; it produced far more in taxation and probably was also more populous. Also, it had a considerably shorter frontier to defend. The western half of the empire had a very long frontier; it was sparsely populated and on the whole rather underdeveloped. If the two halves were to be absolutely self-contained, this placed a very heavy burden on the weaker section. The eastern emperors did make a series of attempts (mostly unsuccessful) to help the western emperors out of their difficulties, but they never committed more than a small fraction of their resources to the defense of the West. The result was that the western empire collapsed in face of mounting barbarian pressure, and the eastern empire managed to contain the barbarians.

At the end of the fourth century, where did the ranks of the army come from? How were they paid and organized, and who were their generals?

The army was raised partly by conscription in the Roman provinces, partly from the sons of soldiers, who were legally obliged to serve, and partly by volunteers, some from the provinces, but most from the barbarians beyond the frontier. It is difficult to estimate the proportion of barbarians; Germans were highly valued as fine troops, and there was a very high proportion of Germans in the best regiments, such as the imperial guard. This was not so in the ordinary frontier regiments.

Boys joined the army at the age of eighteen. They received practically no pay; they were issued rations, and these were on a very generous scale, far superior to the standard of living of the ordinary peasant. They received a pound of meat, four pounds of bread, and a pint of wine a day. They also received their uniforms, arms and armor; and if cavalry, their horses and fodder for them. The only actual cash they received was five gold *solidi* every five years. The men were almost all peasants, and for them the army offered an extremely good standard of living.

Officers sometimes rose from the ranks of ordinary soldiers, but it was more usual for a man of middle class background to join at the rank of what was called *protector*—an officer cadet. After a year or two he was commissioned as a regimental commander. The nationality of the officers varied very much from reign to reign, but there were a considerable number of Germans and other foreigners such as Persians; but the bulk of the officers were Roman citizens, mostly from warlike areas like the Balkans. As far as we know, the German officers in the Roman army were completely Romanized in their sentiments.

Was the number of German soldiers along the Rhine-Danube frontier close to the number the Romans could put into the field? How did the two armies compare as to their state of military technology?

The Germans certainly were inferior in technology; their weapons were crude and of poor materials. We know almost nothing about numbers—no one ever counted a German army; it would have been impossible. The impressions given by contemporary authors are impressions only. The only possibly genuine figure we have is from Victor Vitensis, who, writing sixty years later, says that Gaiseric counted the Vandals when they crossed the straits from Spain into Africa. We are told that the whole tribe, including old men and children and slaves—and presumably women—numbered 80,000. This figure might include 20,000 or perhaps 25,000 fighting men. It looks as if the Romans had an enormous numerical superiority. We are told by Agathias that the number of the Roman army in the fourth century was 645,000. That sounds like a great many, but one must remember the area that the army had to cover. There was a very long frontier covered by static garrison troops, who account for nearly two thirds of the total number, leaving mobile armies of about 100,000 in the eastern part of the empire and 110,000 in the West.

Of these only about 35,000 could be spared for Gaul—the Rhine frontier—and about 50,000 for Illyricum and Thrace—the Danube frontier. The rest were required for Spain, Africa, the eastern front, and the central reserves.

Was the weakness of the Roman army that it lacked a mobile force, a large group of soldiers that could be put into the field at any one place? How did the Roman cavalry compare with the German?

Gallienus created a small mobile army in the 260's, and Constantine greatly strengthened it. But this army could not move very fast. That is just a matter of technological development; before the days of the motorized army, no fighting force could be very mobile.

And so we very soon find—already in the time of Constantine's sons—that large sections of the mobile army are more or less permanently stationed in the main areas of danger—behind the Rhine, the Danube, and the Euphrates—and only a small proportion are uncommitted and available for service on any front. Since armies moved so slowly, it would have been dangerous to leave any danger spot denuded of troops. The Romans used more cavalry than they had in the early days of the empire. The Germans had very little cavalry. The great cavalries were those of the Huns and other tribes of the South Russian steppes, and of the Persians and other Oriental peoples. The Romans learned from them the technique of the mounted archer, which they used with great effect against German infantry.

At what point do you think the German invasions became irreversible? Some authors have put the great turning point at the Vandal conquest of Africa.

It seems to me that the real turning point came earlier, when Theodosius I gave the Visigoths lands within the empire. This was the beginning of the federates in a new sense. Hitherto the Romans had made use of contingents from allied tribes outside the frontier, but these contingents had gone back home when the war was over. Now the whole institution was transformed, and for the first time a coherent group of Germans under their own chieftain was settled inside the empire, controlled only by a treaty—which soon proved a scrap of paper.

It was very difficult for the Roman government to control the Visigoths, partly because Theodosius had fought a long and exhausting war and had been unable to destroy or drive out the tribe. So when Alaric, king of the Visigoths, after Theodosius' death, began to blackmail first the eastern emperor and then the western for better lands and huge money subsidies, both governments generally preferred to yield to his demands rather than fight. But the basic cause of the collapse, I am quite certain, was the westward movement of the Huns. There was a very bad period for the empire in the third century when the Germans were breaking in everywhere, but Diocletian and his colleagues had held the line. Then there was a period when the empire was fairly secure, and that was followed by the arrival of the Huns. The Huns struck terror into the hearts of the German tribes. It was the panic inspired by the Huns that impelled the Goths to seek refuge within the empire in A.D. 376, and it was probably the same fear that thirty years later drove on the Germanic hordes that invaded Italy under Radagaesus in 405, and impelled the Burgundians, Vandals, Sueves and Alans to burst across the Rhine into Gaul in 407.

What steps were taken by the fifth-century emperors in Constantinople to strengthen their position? Were substantial changes made in the government which contributed to the survival of the eastern empire, or was its survival due to its greater wealth and natural protection? Did the emperors of the East exhibit greater skill in government than those of the West?

It is true that the eastern empire had built-in advantages: it was more populous, wealthier, and less vulnerable militarily. But certainly a number of the eastern emperors in the fifth century did improve the efficiency of their government, particularly on the financial side. We don't know much in detail about his reforms, but the emperor Anastasius undoubtedly cut out a great deal of waste, improved the machinery of tax collection, abolished certain oppressive taxes, and left a large cash surplus when he died.

In the west the emperors set up a centralized high command, with a commander in chief in Italy and subordinate generals in the frontier areas. This had a disastrous political result; the commander in chief became all-powerful and set up and deposed puppet emperors. The eastern emperors maintained a divided command, with five coordinate generals—three in Illyricum, Thrace, and the East, and two commanding the reserve armies. This worked well militarily, and prevented any general from becoming overpowerful.

One reason for the successful financial administration of the eastern empire was the new type of men whom the emperors employed as praetorian prefects. In the west, the government had largely got into the hands of the old senatorial aristocracy—wealthy men without great administrative experience or ability, who tended to favor the great landowners. As a result, far too much immunity was granted to the big estates, and the collection of taxes was slack and inefficient. In the east, however, the emperors employed new men—often lawyers, or financial officials from the praetorian prefecture. Men like that knew the ropes and were able to crack down on abuses and correct them. There were also some obscure but important changes in the handling of barbarian troops. The eastern empire managed to get rid of its federate tribes by persuading Theodoric and his Ostrogoths to go and conquer Italy. Henceforth its federate regiments apparently were properly controlled and well-organized foreign legions of Germans.

It has been said that Justinian tried to do what could not be done—to reconquer the West; that he overextended the resources of the empire and left it exhausted; furthermore, that the invasion of Italy devastated and depopulated the country. Would you comment on Justinian's role in the breakup of the empire?

I don't think that Justinian's design for reconquering parts, at any rate, of the West was misguided in itself. He did, after all, reconquer Africa in one campaign, and Africa was a very valuable country which remained in Roman hands until Carthage was taken by the Arabs around A.D. 700. It is true that Africa proved more troublesome than he had anticipated, but that was not his fault. The Vandals had been extremely inefficient and had allowed the Moors to get out of hand, so that a series of campaigns was needed to bring them under control again. However, this success made Justinian too optimistic, and when Belisarius reconquered Italy and received the submission of the Ostrogoths, he assumed that the thing was finished. When the Ostrogoths renewed the struggle, he too readily assumed that the reconquered provinces would begin immediately to pay their own way. He allowed the war to drag on in Italy, putting in small numbers of reinforcements, until Italy was utterly ravaged, whereas in the first conquest it hardly suffered at all. Moreover he did not supply adequate money; the troops were not paid and deserted in large numbers or just refused to fight. Was that necessary? It seems to me that it was not. When at last Narses was appointed to complete the conquest of Italy, he demanded large bodies of troops and sufficient money to pay all arrears. His demands were granted, and within a year or two he satisfactorily completed the reconquest. It is clear that Justinian's wars had not exhausted either the manpower or the finances of the empire. But by the time that its reconquest was completed, Italy was in a ruinous condition.

Justinian did reconquer two important areas of the old empire, and I wonder if he can justifiably be blamed because just a few years after his death the Lombards decided to invade Italy. That, of course, was the trouble which continually beset the later empire; as soon as one tribe was defeated, another came in to fill the gap. It was an unending task.

On the religious side, it is difficult to see whether Justinian could have done any better. There is no doubt that Justinian himself was an Orthodox Christian, a Chalcedonian, but he did make persistent attempts to find some compromise between the Chalcedonians and the Monophysites. It would be difficult to blame him because none of these compromises satisfied the opposing sides. Quite near the beginning of his reign, he tried out the Theopaschite formula, which should have been acceptable to both but actually caused distrust on both sides. It was then suggested to him that the Monophysites could be reconciled by the condemnation of the Three Chapters, but this condemnation provoked violent (and quite irrational) hostility in the West. The real trouble was not so much that the two sides differed on doctrine as that they were committed to a position. Justinian probably would have done better to leave them alone, but as a Christian emperor he felt it was his duty to God to try and reconcile the two sides.

I understood you to say earlier that you think the period from Diocletian to Justinian was really the last stage of ancient history. Why do you feel this is so?

Contemporaries certainly thought so. They believed that they were the spiritual descendants of the earlier empire, and they made no break in their minds between Augustus and Justinian. In some ways, surely, this was true. For instance, the standards of literary culture were precisely the same, and there was always a conscious harking back to the classical past. There was complete continuity in Roman law. The law under Justinian was basically the same as classical law; in fact, it was largely based upon the old texts of the classical lawyers. There was, of course, a great change in religion—the changeover from paganism to Christianity—but again one wonders how complete that was. The developing theology of the Church absorbed Platonism and Aristotelianism; the study of the classical philosophers continued right down to Justinian. I think I would also say that the later Roman Empire remained essentially a city civilization. There has been a lot of talk about the decay of the cities, but people still thought of themselves primarily as citizens of their native town; an emotional tie of loyalty to the city is strongly evident even in sixth-century writings.

This, of course, was more true in the East than in areas where the barbarians had broken through, where the ancient culture did begin to break down. It is striking, however, that the Vandal occupation of Africa seems to have produced very little effect on African civilization. With the reconquest, Latin literature in Africa sprang into life, and a number of distinguished African littérateurs migrated to Constantinople and became professors and ministers of state.

To what extent did the emperors benefit from their relation with the Church? What impact did they have on its development?

This question takes us back to the much-debated problem of why Constantine became a Christian. Constantine has left a good many statements of his views about the Church, and I think that it emerges quite clearly from these that his motives were in a crude sense religious —not that he knew anything about the moral or religious content of Christianity. He had, however, become convinced that the god of the Christians was a powerful god who gave victory in war to his worshipers. He constantly emphasizes this point, and he quotes his own victorious career as an example. Constantine naturally felt that it was his interest and duty to win the favor of the Christian god, and he did this in the obvious ways by giving money and immunities to the churches.

Constantine learned very soon from his ecclesiastical adviser that God was deeply displeased by any schism or heresy in His Church. He felt that it was his imperial duty to resolve schisms and repress heresies, and he endeavored to do so in the case of the Donatists and once again with Arian controversy. He summoned councils of bishops to decide the technical points, and when a decision had been made he enforced it by exiling the recalcitrant bishops and clergy, by seizing the schismatics' places of worship, and so forth. It was, as Constantine said, part of the duty of a Christian emperor to suppress heresy and schism in order to maintain the favor of God upon the empire. If God were pleased with the emperor, He would give him victory over the barbarians and maintain the prosperity of the empire; if displeased, He would send plagues and famines and allow the barbarians to conquer.

This attitude was maintained, in general, by subsequent emperors. They all felt it was their duty to resolve disputes in the Church and to use the force of the state to suppress dissidents. On the whole, the bishops favored and agreed with this position. They too expected the emperor to use his power to suppress heresy and schism, and only members of the defeated party protested that the Church should be free or that the emperor should not interfere in ecclesiastical affairs. The later emperors also maintained Constantine's techniques; from his time it was established that only an emperor could summon a general ecumenical council for final settlement of a dispute. As time went on, the emperors tended to become more autocratic in their methods, largely because they found it so difficult to achieve unity by persuasion. Instead of summoning councils to settle disputes, some emperors issued imperial edicts.

Why did there develop in the Latin Church an opposition to imperial interference, or at least an attempt to place limitations upon imperial control of the Church?

One can quote Ambrose on this subject in support of either position. Ambrose refused to accept the imperial law which gave toleration to the Arians. On the other hand, he later cooperated with the emperor in the suppression of various heretical sects. At the order of the emperor, he held a council to judge certain bishops, and he asked the emperor for constitutions directed against various heretical bodies. The bishops' attitude was strictly pragmatic. When they found an emperor who would do what they wanted, they welcomed his powers; when they did not agree with an emperor they took the opposite view. I would emphasize, however, that in the general run of affairs the Church and the emperor got along very well side by side.

It is doubtful whether the Eastern church was more submissive to the imperial government than the Western. Some Chalcedonian bishops, including two patriarchs of Constantinople, put up a strong resistance to Anastasius' Monophysite policy, and were deposed and exiled. Many Monophysite bishops resolutely opposed the Chalcedonian policy of Justin and Justinian. If the popes took a very independent line towards the Eastern emperors in the late fifth and early sixth centuries, they were after all quite safe in doing so under the protection of the barbarian kings of Italy. After the reconquest, Popes Vigilius and Pelagius II accepted Justinian's theological rulings.

8

Byzantium

DENO GEANAKOPLOS

THE HISTORIOGRAPHICAL CONTEXT

A main trend in the historical scholarship of the past quarter century has been away from a Western European parochialism—an historical view that was the heritage of nineteenth-century nationalism and imperialism—towards a cosmopolitan perspective that gives full value to, and acknowledges Western debts to other civilizations. Historians of medieval Europe were among the first to depart from parochialism—even early in the twentieth century they acknowledged the cultural achievements of Byzantium and the very important influence of the thinkers, religious leaders, and artists of Constantinople on their western counterparts, from the fifth century right down into the late fifteenth century.

Yet, although the general value of Byzantine civilization has long been known (Byzantine scholarship in the West dates at least as early as Louis XIV's France), it has been only in recent decades that the voluminous sources for Byzantine history have begun to be thoroughly explored. In this work a splendid array of scholars in many European countries, from Russia to Britain, have participated. But since the 1940's, there has been a flourishing school of Byzantine studies in the United States, and nowadays this American group is second to none by virtue of the breadth of its interests and the substantial quality of its contributions. American Byzantine studies has received a special fillip from the Dumbarton Oaks research center, affiliated with Harvard, which has lavished patronage that no other branch of medieval scholarship in the United States has received.

Deno Geanakoplos (born in Minneapolis in 1916) of Yale University stands in the front rank of American Byzantinists. A jovial, highly cultured man (he is also an excellent musician), Geanakoplos in his prolific scholarship has examined many facets of the Byzantine impact on the West and convincingly demonstrated the central place of the eastern Roman Empire in medieval civilization.

Chronological Outline

527–565: Justinian I revives imperial power. From 529 to 535 the Justinian Code is issued, which clarifies the laws of the previous thousand years and adds new ones to create a comprehensive, rational legal system. The Church of St. Sophia is constructed between 532 and 537. North Africa and Italy are regained. The emperor intervenes in religious affairs to support Christian orthodoxy.

568–571: Northern Italy is lost to the Lombards.

570?–632: Life of Mohammed, who founds the Islamic religion.

610–641: Heraclius founds a new dynasty and defeats the Persians. But the weakened Byzantine Empire is unable to prevent the Arabs from overrunning Syria, Mesopotamia, and Egypt. In the next century the Arabs gain control of northern Africa and Spain.

673–678: The Arabs fail to take Constantinople. A second siege fails in 717.

717–740: Reign of the Isaurian Leo III, who initiates the policy of iconoclasm.

869–870: Photius, the Greek patriarch, is excommunicated by the Fourth Council of Constantinople. The final schism with the Western Church occurs in 1054.

989: Conversion of Prince Vladimir of Kiev. The beginnings of the conversion of the Russians to Eastern Christianity and the close connection between Kiev and Constantinople.

1071: Byzantine forces are defeated at the battle of Manzikert, and the Turks move into Asia Minor.

1095: Pope Urban II calls for the first Crusade.

1202–1204: The fourth Crusade under the leadership of the Venetians sacks Constantinople. A Latin Kingdom of Constantinople is set up.

1261: Michael Palaeologus regains Constantinople for the empire.

1325–1345: Rise of the Ottoman Turks in northwestern Asia Minor.

1453: Constantinople is besieged by and falls to the Turks. The Roman Empire in the East is at an end.

Norman F. Cantor
Would you discuss the development and status of Byzantine studies in the West?

Deno Geanakoplos

As regards the status of Byzantine studies, a good majority of the general public of the West, and especially of America, probably would still not even know what is meant by the term *Byzantine studies*. For this lack of understanding, one (often overlooked) reason is simply that today there no longer exists a Byzantine state as such. If one were to mention Russian, French, or even Turkish history, a certain frame of reference would at once come to mind. But the Byzantine state, which at various times covered huge areas in the West as well as the East, was completely destroyed. To be sure, its cultural influence lived on in more ways than many scholars realize—among the Slavs, in the West, even among the Turks and Arabs, and particularly in modern Greece, which regards itself as the continuation or revivification of medieval Byzantium. Yet though linguistic, religious, and probably ethnic continuity can be demonstrated for Greece, the Byzantine state with its imperial ideology and political authority has left no universally recognized successor.

Byzantine studies in America are still relatively new. Indeed, despite the valuable research that is now being carried on in about a dozen American universities, there still too often lingers the feeling, when a professor gives a survey course on Byzantine history, that he must commence with an apologia for its study, something which for almost all other historical fields—even of Southeast Asia or Mongolia—is unnecessary. This apology is necessitated, I think, in large part by the centuries-old prejudice of the Western world against Byzantium, a prejudice which reflects the medieval division of East and West into virtually two different worlds. This cleavage, already apparent by the ninth and tenth centuries, became glaringly obvious by 1204, with the sack of Constantinople by the adventurers of the fourth Crusade. And it was guaranteed permanence in the period before 1453 when the Greeks, recalling the horrors of 1204, came increasingly to fear Western military "aid" and its corollary religious union as much as they feared the potential Turkish yoke. The almost inevitable result of this hostile Greek attitude was that large segments of the Western mind came to look upon the Byzantines as out-and-out heretics and even to lump them with the Turks. Despite all the admirable recent efforts to bring about greater understanding between the Roman and Orthodox churches, the Catholic West has never completely been able to shake off its prejudices against the East, prejudices inherited also by the Protestants.

These are a few reasons, but by no means all (and I have stressed them because they are perhaps less obvious), for the neglect until recently of the study of Byzantine history in the West—a neglect which is all the more remarkable in view of the fact that some important Western medievalists have for some time realized that, from say about A.D. 500 to about 1050, the only European civilization truly worthy of the name was that of Byzantium.

The interest of Western scholars in Byzantium first appeared in the period of the Renaissance, whose scholars were attracted to Byzantium as the repository for ancient Greek learning. Nonetheless, it was not until as late as the seventeenth century that westerners finally became interested in the study of Byzantium and its culture per se. This shift in attitude seems to have begun about the time of Louis XIII of France, who himself apparently translated a book of imperial precepts written for the emperor Justinian by the Byzantine deacon of St. Sophia, Agapetus. The court of his successor, Louis XIV, contained a number of remarkable scholars drawn to the study of Byzantium. Most important was DuCange, who composed stupendous dictionaries of both Byzantine and medieval Latin terms, a genealogy of the Eastern emperors and of aristocratic families, and a history of the Latin empire of Constantinople after 1204. His work was accompanied by valuable contributions of paleographers and philologists such as Mabillon, and at the same time, a number of Byzantine texts, especially histories, were for the first time published. Up to this time there had been no such comparable Western studies; DuCange and his group may therefore be considered the distant founders of modern Byzantine studies, at least from the historical and linguistic points of view.

After DuCange's breakthrough, however, there ensued during the Enlightenment a period of neglect of Byzantium, even of retrogression of interest. Writers like Voltaire, Gibbon, Montesquieu, who idealized ancient Greece and Rome, denigrated Byzantine history, considering it merely an effete continuation of these great ancient civilizations. Nevertheless Gibbon, almost in spite of himself, was an important writer of Byzantine history, and most curiously, in the field of ecclesiastical history. For while he certainly could not appreciate the spiritual, especially the mystical, side of Byzantium's religion, he possessed a true grasp of the questions of ecclesiastical polity and dogma. And because he wove his researches into a most readable narrative, he might well be considered one of the first genuine historians of Byzantine ecclesiastical history.

The study of Byzantium picked up momentum again in the nineteenth century in Russia and other areas of Europe, especially in Germany. By the early twentieth century it had become an accepted field of study in many of the great European universities. The pioneer European school in this period was certainly that founded in Munich, Germany, by Karl Krumbacher. Krumbacher wrote an epochal work in the then difficult and still largely virgin field of Byzantine literature (too few manuscripts had as yet been published), and his scholarly tradition was continued at Munich by Heisenberg, then Dölger and Beck. Today a prominent school of Byzantine studies exists at the Sorbonne under the direction of Paul Lemerle, and one cannot of course omit mention of the famous Belgian school founded by Henri Grégoire. There are also several centers in Italy—in Milan, Rome, and Palermo, among others. In England there have been two important schools, especially under the scholars Bury and Baynes. There has recently been founded a chair of Byzantine studies in Vienna. In Russia, the revolution almost put an end to the impressive activities there of the late nineteenth century in Byzantine studies, but in the last decade or two there has been a genuine revival under Každan, Udalcova, Lazarev, and others. There is, of course, the famous center in Belgrade, Yugoslavia, under the direction of George Ostrogorsky. And in Greece, as noted, where Byzantine history is considered an integral part of its national heritage, all the Greek universities have chairs in Byzantine history as well as in philology, literature, art, and other fields.

It is not surprising that in America, granted its insularity up to fairly recent times, there has not been a corresponding interest, except in a relatively few leading schools. The pioneer scholar was the Russian Alexander Vasiliev, who came to Wisconsin after the First World War. Byzantine studies, however, especially after the Second World War and the emergence to significance of the Slavic east, especially Russia, have steadily been increasing in America, with full-time Byzantine historians now teaching at Harvard (which also has an Institute of Byzantine Studies at Dumbarton Oaks,

Washington), Berkeley, UCLA, Rutgers, Wisconsin, Indiana, Chicago, and Yale. On the other hand, it must be pointed out that the curriculum of practically every college or university now includes at least a few lectures devoted to Byzantine civilization in every general medieval course.

As much earlier in Europe, Byzantine history in America was for long considered rather exotic, something quite outside the mainstream of Western history. But scholars are increasingly realizing that Byzantium had a much greater influence on the development of Western civilization than was previously thought. Art historians agree, for instance, that Western painting was the handmaiden of Byzantine art until the thirteenth century at least. The famous disparaging statement of Vasari—that Giotto freed Western art from "la maniera greca" (meaning the strictures of Byzantine art) itself points up the long Western tutelage to Byzantium. And even with respect to Giotto's innovations in realism and his expression of a greater humanism, it now appears to some that he may have been influenced or at least preceded in this by Eastern artists of the Palaeologan Renaissance. In ecclesiastical literature it has been shown that some Byzantine writings after the famous fourth-fifth century patristic period, were well known and utilized in the West. Aquinas had a copy of John of Damascus' work before him when he wrote his celebrated books. We know that Basil's *Rules* were in almost all the libraries of the important Western monasteries. The writings of later Byzantine scholars, like that of the theologian Maximus the Confessor, were also known in the West. One modern Western church historian has in fact pronounced the writings of Pseudo-Dionysius the most important single influence on Western medieval theological development, aside from those of Saint Paul and Augustine.

A desideratum is not only the study of Byzantine history for its own sake, then, but also to integrate its history with that of Western civilization. Hopefully, more courses can be taught in which a historical synthesis or overview of not only these two but of *all* three major medieval civilizations—Western, Byzantine, and Arabic—can be achieved. The three areas should be considered insofar as possible as one integrated whole. And yet this does not mean that one should neglect the study of internal Byzantine history and study it only insofar as it impinges on other civilizations, especially the Western. Too often, especially in the smaller American colleges and universities, students fail to get a proper appreciation of the continuity and especially the important changes in what is still too often viewed as a static and unchanging culture. In many smaller schools Byzantium, if studied at all, is brought into the curriculum piece by piece and only in connection with some aspect of Western or possibly Islamic history. The student learns about several of the more important early Byzantine emperors (Constantine and Justinian), something about the schism of 1054 "and all that," and about the crusaders that "passed" through Constantinople. But he never learns enough in depth about the institutions of Byzantium so as to appreciate the unusual ethos of this Eastern civilization which, though sibling to Western Christendom, was in many ways so different from it.

One could perhaps argue that this piecemeal method of teaching would provide much information on cultural contacts. But unfortunately this method usually results rather in Byzantium's being treated merely as an appendage of the West and not as a viable cultural organism of its own, which, contrary to Gibbon's view, it definitely was.

Certainly an inhibiting factor in the development of Byzantine studies in America has been the lack of persons with adequate linguistic equipment to do research. Ideally a Byzantine historian should be able to read not only medieval (Byzantine) Greek (which in some periods is markedly different from ancient Greek), but also Latin, French, German, Italian, Russian, and possibly even Arabic or modern Greek. In addition to these languages the ideal researcher should also have some knowledge of palaeography and numismatics, and at least a rudimentary knowledge of diplomatics and art history. But how many Byzantinists today can boast such preparation or qualifications? It should be apparent, then, that one person can hardly do justice to the field of Byzantine studies as a whole, and that ideally a great university should have experts in the various fields of Byzantine studies: art, literature, possibly music, and so on. The number of facets of Byzantine studies (the empire, after all, existed for over a thousand years and at various times contained much of Europe and parts of Asia) is thus almost a defeating factor if one seeks to do complete justice to the field. But there is no American university (except for the specialized Institute of Dumbarton Oaks) where all or even most of these areas of study are represented.

The usual practice, then, is for a university to have one Byzantine historian of considerable breadth, along with a specialist in Byzantine art history. Thus the Byzantine historian will teach a general survey course in Byzantine history, plus several seminars in special areas—relations with the Slavs or the West, or he may, at the same time, perhaps teach courses also in Western medieval, Renaissance, or Islamic history.

The increasing American interest in Byzantine history, on the ecclesiastical side, has undoubtedly been helped by the current ecumenical movement. It is now clear that one cannot understand the origins of the church and the development of patristic and even some later Western theology, without at least some knowledge of the history of the Byzantine church. As for philosophy, it suffices merely to quote the leading Western scholar of medieval philosophy, E. Gilson, who has affirmed that in almost every case of creative advance in Western medieval philosophy, there may be found in the background a Westerner who suddenly comes into contact with an ancient Greek or Byzantine work. A great impetus to Byzantine studies in America undoubtedly has been the rise of Russia to world power. Interest in Russian history has led in turn to study of Byzantium, Russia's spiritual parent. The impact of Byzantium upon Russia can, of course, be exaggerated, but it is undeniable that in religion, political ideology, culture, and to some degree economics, Byzantium was a fundamental force in medieval Russian history.

Another reason for the greater interest in Byzantium is to be found in its literature. Though not so creative as its art or hymnody, it nonetheless produced some works of value which may well have had some influence on those of other contemporary cultures. Thus we find parallels between the epics of Byzantium (Digenes Akritas is one) and the Western Chanson de Roland, the Russian Prince Igor Tale, and even Arabic epic. It seems to me that, paradoxically, despite the growing cleavage of East and West, especially during and after the Crusades, the very close contact produced between the two peoples could not help but increase the mutual influences. Thus I believe that the extent of cultural contact between East and West is still underestimated by modern historians, except by a few specialists in the field. For example an entire circle of Thomists was established in the heart of the Byzantine court in the fourteenth century. All sorts of Western commercial terms filtered through to Byzantium through the ports of Venice and Genoa, via their colonies in Constantinople.

Earlier, to be sure, Byzantine nautical terms had been much used in the West, but as time went on the reverse increasingly became true.

One could easily cite many other influences of West upon East and vice versa. The main point that I wish to make, in answer to your question—and I am afraid I have strayed somewhat from it—is that one of the best ways to develop an appreciation in the student for Byzantine history is to integrate it with the history of other medieval cultural blocs such as the West. Even textbooks should be written with this kind of synthetic treatment in mind rather than with the arbitrary division into Byzantine, Western, Arabic, and Slavic developments presented in separate chapters in the manner to which we have too long become accustomed. Then, when the student's appetite has been whetted, he will, hopefully, want to take more specialized courses in various aspects of Byzantine history and civilization. Maintaining a balance between these two approaches, the horizontal and the vertical, is of course difficult to do, though some attempts have already been made. But I think that if we finally achieve this synoptic view in our teaching of medieval history, while at the same time preserving the organic unity of each culture, we will have made a great deal of progress. In the last analysis, the most accurate evaluation of Byzantium's contribution to world civilization will come when we have studied Byzantine culture not only as an organic unity of its own, but at the same time as both influencing and being influenced by its neighboring cultures.

In your opinion, when was the most formative period of Byzantine civilization? Should we look to Constantine, Justinian, or some other person and time?

I suppose this question hinges upon what is meant by the term Byzantine civilization, and what are the qualities that one usually associates with the Eastern half of Christendom. Byzantium became the depository of the ancient Greek and Hellenistic works at the same time as it fell heir politically to the governmental tradition of the Romans. (As is well known the Byzantines, virtually to the end, referred to themselves as Romans.) Moreover, it developed a type of Christianity which, while certainly derived from the same sources as the Western, became unique. Finally, certain eastern "Oriental" influences that were prevalent in Byzantium but largely absent in the West (where instead the German element was important) flavored the tone of Byzantine civilization and helped to produce different configurations of culture.

But when were all these characteristics and trends synthesized so as to form that distinct culture that we call Byzantine? If historical processes operate in a sculptural fashion, when was the chief molding of Byzantine culture finished? Scholars have differed on this point, one body of opinion pointing to the seventh century, the period of Heraclius and his successors, as the watershed. In that period the eastern, Semitic provinces of Byzantium, Syria, Egypt, Palestine, were stripped away by the Arabic invasions, and Asia Minor (the heartland of empire), southern Italy and Sicily, a part of the Balkans, and certain areas in the Black Sea—that is the essentially "Greek" areas—remained. Moreover, the Slavs penetrated deeply into the Balkans and by cutting off much of Illyricum created a wedge between the Latin world and the Greek east.

Other historians have pinpointed the era of Justinian as particularly formative because of the brilliance of his reign. Actually, current opinion, though admirous of his legal and artistic legacy, tends to view Justinian's celebrated reconquest of the West as rather an anachronism, the result of an outdated imperial ideology. He may thus be considered more correctly as "the last truly Roman emperor." As for Constantine the Great, his importance is certainly tremendous. He not only transferred the capital to the East, continued Diocletian's reorganization of empire, but, most of all, displaced paganism as the favored religion of the state with Christianity, a truly epochal step. Nevertheless, though the first emperor to rule in Constantinople, he too remained primarily Latin and Latin-speaking, one who rather governed an empire whose limits had not changed unduly since the days of the Julian house.

At this point I might indicate that the use of the term *Greek* to apply to Byzantine civilization I use here in a broad, not a narrow, sense. Some scholars object to its use, but it seems to me appropriate if it be used in the same sense that the term *Latin* is applied to the various peoples and general culture of the medieval West. For the culture of the Byzantine empire after the seventh century *was* largely Greek, and the religion was what we would today call Greek Orthodox. Even the last truly "Roman emperor" (Justinian) had issued most of his own laws, the *Novellae,* not in Latin but in Greek. While the many different peoples living in the Byzantine state certainly preclude our labeling it a unitary "national" state in our sense of the term, it is nonetheless true that all or most members of the Byzantine community felt a strong allegiance towards one emperor—the Vicar of God—one Orthodox Church, and one law.

What was the importance of the iconoclastic controversy?

Iconoclasm has been interpreted in various ways, each analysis tending to vary with the age in which the scholar lived. Originally, the iconoclastic conflict had been considered as a strictly religious conflict between Orthodoxy and heresy. Then later it was the fashion to view it essentially as a kind of Protestant revolt against relics, images, and so on. More recently scholars have taken to emphasizing the social and economic aspects of the revolt, especially against the power of the monks and their huge monastic properties. Still other commentators have interpreted the whole struggle simply as an all-out attempt of the emperor to control the Church and clergy.

It seems to me, however, that the pendulum is now beginning to swing back to basically a theological interpretation—partly because modern scholars realize (or are more willing to accept) the extent to which religious concerns actuated the activities of everyday Byzantine life. Although we still cannot affirm with certainty the reasons for Leo III's initial edict against the images (726), it is now increasingly accepted that he had a primarily theological motivation.

It has been theorized that Leo III may have been inspired by the views of the Caliph of Baghdad to issue his famous edict that all images in the Church be destroyed. But since the Caliph was the arch foe of Byzantium and of Christianity, it is difficult to imagine Leo following his lead. Other recent historians tend rather to stress a longstanding Christian opposition to the icons (meaning any image or likeness), which dates as far back as the period of Origen, Eusebius of Caesarea, and Epiphanius. Another modern scholar emphasizes (for a somewhat later period) the influence of such fringe groups as the Armenian sectarians. In any event, the iconoclastic conflict, lasting almost two centuries, certainly was many-faceted and almost succeeded in destroying the empire.

One result of the conflict was the alienation of Italy, as the papacy began sharply to move away from Byzantium. The emperor Leo III, in retaliation, removed southern Italy, Sicily, and Illyricum (including Greece) from papal ecclesiastical control and put them under the authority of the patriarch at Constantinople. In the artistic sphere, the disruption of the production of images produced a marked change of style. The various images of Christ, the Virgin, and the saints were, for a time, largely done away with, sparking a return to the Alexandrian Hellenistic style best noted for the realistic representation of birds and flowers. After the iconoclastic struggle, there was virtually no more sculpture in the round, perhaps because such three-dimensional art too readily reminded the observer of pagan statues. The style that did evolve after the conflict's solution was a much less "realistic" style which aimed at conveying eternal realities rather than physical impressions. And this was to remain in general the standard hieratic style until the end (with a few exceptions to be noted).

The central theological point resulting from the long conflict was the distinction between actual worship due only to God, and veneration of the icons. It is perhaps unreasonable to assume that the common people had the capacity to think with such sophistication. Yet subtle theological distinctions *were* made along these lines. Neoplatonic thought was woven into the discussion—the idea that the icon is in itself a channel of grace worthy of veneration. The pros and cons of the iconoclastic controversy became widely known and were of some consequence in the Western court of Charlemagne, though they were not really understood by him. Finally, an important recent development in iconoclastic studies is the realization that the struggle did not end completely in 843. Dvornik, for instance, has shown that over a half century later, the great patriarch Photius was still writing treatises against the surviving proponents of iconoclasm.

What was the effect of the iconoclastic controversy on the position of the emperor?

The iconoclastic emperors, it is true, during their regimes, succeeded in imposing their will on the Church and actually for a time altering the doctrine of the ecumenical councils. But in the long run they were to prove unsuccessful, demonstrating that indeed there did exist in the Byzantine state checks on what has wrongfully been called the emperor's Caesaropapistic power. And the successful opposition to iconoclasm in general produced a diminution of imperial authority with respect to the monastic community. It also gave encouragement to religious reformers such as Theodore of Studius, who at times went so far as to claim that the emperor should have little or no power over the Church. His view did not prevail, however.

Would you discuss the striking aspects of Byzantine piety that may have contributed to the fervor of the iconoclastic struggle?

Some historians have concluded that the emperor in this conflict was striking particularly at the power of the monks. If this is true, it ran contrary to one of the distinguishing features of Byzantine piety—deep respect on the part of the people for monasticism. In the empire most persons in high places founded a monastery or would enter one just before death to insure the salvation of their soul. Yet everyone, even those who did not found monasteries or actively champion the position of the monks, was deeply attached to the magnificent ceremonies of the Church as well as to what has been called by Bréhier "the imperial liturgy" of the palace court. Both of these complexes of ceremony, the religious and the civil, depended to a large degree on material objects such as rich vestments, incense, and (in the palace) on the mechanical objects of the throne room. In a society so moved by what may be termed the visible word, it is not surprising that the program of the iconoclastic emperors with its destruction of the icons—perhaps the most important of these visible expressions of eternal verities—would be met by tremendous opposition. Both the mutilation of monks and the destruction of icons (among which the holiest were considered those believed to be "not made by human hands") thus posed a threat to the whole world view of Byzantium.

Some scholars, it should be noted, have viewed the iconoclastic struggle as basically a conflict between Greek "intellectualism" and Christian religiosity, and to them the triumph of the icons meant the triumph of Christian incarnational thought over Greek intellectualism. But there are other views too, which we have no time to mention here.

Was there a tension in Byzantine history between the monastic and the secular clergy?

On the local level, though here our sources are woefully scanty, good relations and close cooperation seem usually to have existed between the monastic and secular clergy. However, monastic relations with higher, secular ecclesiastics, were often strained, at least through the period of the iconoclastic struggle. Though the monks technically fell under the jurisdiction of the local bishop, they often, because of their exalted position in the mind of society, attained considerable freedom of action and expression. Some monks criticized the ecclesiastical hierarchy as worldly and as overly subservient to emperors whom they considered heretical. (Recall the case of Theodore of Studius against patriarch Nicephorus in the Moechian conflict, or, earlier, of Maximos the Confessor who refused to commune with a whole group of prelates who supported the Monothelete emperors.)

In the eighth century and increasingly in the ninth, however, it became the practice to select bishops from among the monastic clergy, a factor which understandably served to reduce tension between the two groups. In the Palaeologan period tension still existed, to be sure. However, it no longer represented a distinct conflict between secular and regular clergy because over the main religious issue of the time—religious union with Rome—opponents of union could be found not only in the monastic clergy but also among the secular, especially on the parish level. The few proponents of union (aside from high civil officials of the emperor) were almost invariably to be found among the high prelates who were often more "politique" minded.

As regards East and West I think we may affirm, in general, that there was considerably less tension in the East between monastic and secular clergy than in the West. One point to be stressed is that unlike the East, Western bishops were *not* chosen from among the monastic clergy.

Western monasticism became concerned with the reform of the whole church and of society in the eleventh century. Is there any parallel to this in the East?

This, I do not think, occurred to the same extent in the East as in the West. In Byzantium there were individual monks who fought against the sins of individual emperors. For example, the thirteenth-century patriarch Arsenios (a former monk) inveighed against the usurper Michael Palaeologus throughout his life. And Polyeuctes spoke out against the murderer of Phocas, John Tzimisces. I do not believe, however, that one can properly compare the activities of these few monks with the comprehensive reform movement in the West. It may be exaggerated to say that tenth- and eleventh-century Byzantine church and society did not need some reform. Yet I think it can be shown that in that period the Eastern church never sank to the depths of its Western counterpart. Gibbon compares the flaws of secular and monastic clergy in East and West and concludes that the Eastern church (he did not really care for either, it must be noted), was morally superior. For instance, he points out that examples of Western clergy riding into battle at the head of troops (a not rare phenomenon in tenth- to eleventh-century Western history) is apparently absent in the East. Moreover, the moral scandals of the papacy were alien to the Eastern patriarchs as a whole.

Patriarch Michael Cerularius of the mid-eleventh century has been termed an Eastern Hildebrand. Yet Michael, unlike Gregory VII, can hardly be termed a product of monastic reform. Rather his patriarchate seems to reflect more the ambitions of a man motivated by sheer political considerations. He was after all related to the imperial house and as a young man had been made a monk against his will.

But the chief reason, it seems to me, why there is no similar monastic movement in the East for reform of society as a whole is that the concern of the Eastern monk was primarily for individual salvation, rather than for service to the community. In the East, eremitical forms of monasticism were more common than in the West, where monasteries also became involved in social welfare. The Eastern monks (with the possible exemption of the Studites) were less rigidly organized than the Western with their multiplicity of orders. Byzantine monasticism, to be sure, experienced serveral revivals because it too had need of them. (We note especially the reforms of Theodore of Studius and Simeon the New Theologian.) But the goals of these two monks were different from those of Western reformers; their programs were still largely in the mold of Saint Basil's ancient "rule."

What was the role of the Byzantine Church in education and scholarship? Was Byzantine learning entirely ecclesiastical?

It is sometimes said that in the West the first important lay scholar was Dante. Obviously if one looks hard enough he can find earlier examples. But the point is that, in general, there was no literate lay class in the West until relatively late. In Byzantium the reverse was true. Many, if not most, of the laymen of the great cities of the empire could read and write, and a considerable number went on to higher studies in the university, where they received training in law or medicine or philosophy, all of which were useful to those desirous of rising in the civil service. (Important in connection with the middle class is, of course, the survival of Byzantine cities throughout the entire Middle Ages in contrast to the West.) This more widespread Byzantine literacy should be kept in mind when one compares the role of the Eastern and Western churches in education.

In the West, educational standards up to about the fourteenth century were preserved almost exclusively by the clergy. In the East a comprehensive system of lay education existed alongside religious schools. The first medieval university of Europe was founded in Constantinople in the fifth century by Theodosius II (though in another sense it may be considered simply as a continuation of ancient pedagogical ideals). There was also a patriarchal academy in Constantinople (founded in the ninth century) for the clergy, although when the university did not function (as under Basil II), laymen seemed also to have attended classes there. We do not unfortunately know very much about the patriarchal academy, but it seems that it emphasized the study of letters as well as theology.

An interesting aspect of all this is the interaction of Greek classical learning with the Christian tradition in Constantinople. The Byzantines who had inherited the classical Greek, or rather Hellenistic, culture, managed to synthesize it with the Christian ethos in a highly successful and generally uncontroversial manner. There continued, of course, some conflict between the pagan and Christian heritage. Platonism, for example, was not always accepted, in ecclesiastical circles at least, and unlike Aristotle (who was so necessary in constructing an argument), Plato's philosophy, because of its content, seemed dangerously close to being a rival religion. In the eleventh century, for example, when a monk in Bithynia saw Psellus reading Plato, he crossed himself so as not to be contaminated. Nonetheless, the existence of a tradition of lay education meant the continued circulation and reading of Plato's works. And even in monastic circles, dislike of the classics was far from universal. Saint Basil himself, the virtual founder of Byzantine monasticism, had exhorted his followers to read the literary works of the ancient Greeks in order to train their minds and better to understand the writings of Christianity itself.

Would you discuss the contributions that the Byzantines made in science and philosophy?

It has been said that the Byzantines made no truly original contributions in science, and I suppose that in general this is correct. However, we may qualify this somewhat. Scholars have really not studied Byzantine science thoroughly enough to be able to write it off so easily. The Byzantines, like the Arabs, knew and continued much of ancient Greek and Hellenistic science, occasionally effecting a few improvements. For example, the Byzantines developed "Greek fire," which one modern writer believes led to the development of gunpowder in the later period. Anthemius of Tralles not only wrote on parabolic mirrors, but as a joke harnessed steam to simulate a kind of minor "earthquake." In the same period, John Philoponos rejected Aristotle's notion of the impossibility of producing a vacuum. In engineering and architecture, the Byzantines figured out how to place a dome over a square on a colossal scale as at St. Sophia. But it must be noted that most of their scientific advances remained on the level of "toys" (like the hydraulic automata of the imperial palace) and without any real practical application.

In medicine, also, the Byzantines carried on the ancient Greek tradition. They produced several excellent doctors. Paul of Aegina, for example, wrote a treatise on surgery in the seventh century which had influence on the medical science of the West as well as the Arabs. The first Western medical school was at Salerno, near Naples, and it is said that Arab, Jewish, as well as Byzantine influences played a part, the Byzantine least of all. But scholarship has now indicated that perhaps the Byzantines played a larger role there than had previously been allotted to them.

Moving to Byzantine philosophy, there exists as yet no comprehensive history of it, perhaps because it was so closely integrated with theology. Among those who mingled philosophy with their theology, Neoplatonism was central in the third to fourth centuries. Aristotle was perhaps less important then, but when we move to John of Damascus in the eighth century, we find that he constructed a synthesis of Aristotelianism with Greek Christianity. (There seems to be a paradox here, as the spirit of the Greek Church seems far more in tune with Neoplatonism.) Aristotle then remained important in the Greek Church for several centuries, while Platonism, because of certain of its pagan beliefs, was actually frowned upon up to the eleventh century.

Under Michael Psellus of that century, Platonism gained ground rapidly, however, and he is sometimes credited almost single-handedly with reviving its study. One scholar has gone so far as to say that the whole Platonic revival which later spread to the West during the Italian Renaissance can be traced back to Psellus. Thus no one school of philosophy, whether Aristotelian or Platonic, was dominant through the entire Byzantine period. One cannot, with some scholars, term the histoy of Byzantine philosophy really "static." To be sure, there seems not much development or progress in "pure philosophy" as apart from theology. Yet, as we have noted, there were frequent changes of "fashion."

It is sometimes said that the greatest cultural achievement of Byzantium was in the visual arts. Do you agree with this?

Byzantine art has become quite popular in recent years, perhaps because, aside from its sheer technical perfection, it was semi-representational. That is, it was not photographic. It attempted to represent something of the other world. For this purpose, Byzantine artists developed techniques which, from the point of view of color, line, and stylization in general, were remarkable.

We will not here go into the controversial question of the origins of Byzantine art, though we do know that the other-worldly character of this new aesthetic was firmly entrenched by the sixth century. The Byzantines did not apparently use perspective. But the point is that they really had no use for it in their other-worldly depictions. Though the observer can easily identify the subject portrayed, realism was often sacrificed to achieve the a-spatial world of eternity. The ethos, the piety of the Byzantines, helped to structure their art as it structured so many other aspects of their lives.

Byzantine art, then, cannot be studied apart from the entire ethos which produced it. And it is the artistic means Byzantium developed to express this ethos, with its subtlety of line and richness of color, that marks the originality of its contribution to culture. One has only to look at the magnificent mosaics of Ravenna, those at St. Sophia, in Palermo, and elsewhere to understand this. To secure a true appreciation of the place of this religious art, one must envision it in a Byzantine church with its great arching dome representing heaven, with the magnificent decorations on the walls, and the hymnody which was being chanted during the service while thousands of candles were casting their illumination.

The influence of this Byzantine art was of course great. Until the thirteenth century, Byzantine art was in fact the model for the grouping of the figures, the liturgical sequence, and the symbolism of Western art. Contrary to the nonspecialist's view Byzantine art was not static, though it may have appeared to be so in each single epoch. For example, some of the art of the so-called Palaeologan period, 1261–1453, reflected important changes. In certain areas, in Constantinople and Thessalonika especially, more emotion began to be expressed in the art produced. Some scholars even assert that the realism of Giotto had its seeds in Byzantium in this period. I don't know if we have enough evidence to settle this question positively, but there certainly seems to have been a good deal of artistic dialogue between East and West in these last two centuries which, when completely disentangled, should prove very enlightening for the art historian.

It is perhaps possible that El Greco may be considered the last (and greatest) of the Byzantine painters, though actually he is a post-Byzantine. A recently discovered notarial document shows that he was still living in Crete at the age of twenty-six and was presumably therefore under the influence of Byzantine (and

Venetian) artists of that island for a much longer time than previously supposed. If we compare certain of his works with paintings of the Palaeologan period, one may find some striking similarities, especially in the elongated figures, the remarkable contrasts in color, and the emaciated look of the subjects.

How were Byzantine artists supported?

Many artists were, of course, monks and were supported by their monasteries. In the iconoclastic struggle, for instance, the name of the monk Lazarus appears: his hands were cut off because of his continued production of icons. The monk Panselinus was a great painter of (probably) the fourteenth century, a figure in the so-called Macedonian Renaissance of the Palaeologan period who decorated the Protaton on Mt. Athos with remarkable paintings. Patrons also supported ecclesiastical as well as secular art; for example, the statesman Theodore Metochites of the fourteenth century financed the remarkable paintings which decorate the Church of Our Saviour in the Chora in Constantinople. A great deal of art of course was commissioned by the emperors (as well as by the patriarchs). Unfortunately, except for a few examples like the traces of the Great Palace in Constantinople, almost no secular Byzantine art survives, though Byzantine historians tell us about emperors (like Michael Palaeologus) who had hunting scenes and pictures of their "triumphs" painted or depicted in mosaic in their palaces.

It is sometimes said that romantic trends in Byzantine literature influenced the West. Can you comment upon this?

The word *romantic,* of course, conjures upon the image of eighteenth-century literature in the West. In twelfth-century Western medieval literature, there were the stirrings of a new kind of emotionalism, a new concern with individual personality and motivation; it was addressed to the growing audience of literate laymen as something to be enjoyed. It is indeed difficult to draw a connection between these literary developments in the West and those going on in the East. We may, however, point out that in the fourteenth and fifteenth centuries, there were popular in both East and West the so-called Franco-Greek romances, epic poems about love and adventure. It is possible that their genesis may be traced to the East, but it is equally possible that during the Crusades such influences came rather eastward. A few scholars consider the prototype to be the novel of Hellenistic times. In any case, fourteenth- and fifteenth-century Byzantine poets translated Western romantic narratives into Greek, and some twelfth-century French romances had their settings in the Greek East and appear influenced by Greek elements. Probably the most we can say positively about these phenomena is that there was a mutual give-and-take of influences at work here.

In what field was Byzantine literature strongest?

Byzantine literature has often been criticized as being one of the weakest or least original facets of the Eastern aesthetic contribution because it too slavishly imitated classical Greek models. To some degree this is quite true. But I wonder if it may not be somewhat exaggerated. The Byzantines spoke one type of Greek and often, the scholars that is, wrote in a different, more archaic idiom. It is this circumstance that is supposed to have stymied their originality. It seems to me that it could have been possible (though far from easy) to talk in one medium and write in another and still be original (witness the Latinists of the Italian Renaissance). Perhaps we should look elsewhere also for reasons for this lack of originality in Byzantine literature. Perhaps to the nature of their "corporate" society, where state and church exerted certain strictures toward uniformity in modes of thought. Or perhaps we may look rather to the Byzantine lack of our modern "idea of progress." In certain classical literary forms (history, epigrams, lyric poetic forms) the Greeks had achieved perfection in the past; why then, the Byzantines may well have thought, try to surpass them in these areas (except of course in the new, purely Christian forms such as hymnody). In any case, not all Byzantines wrote the archaic form of Greek. Examples of writing in the spoken vernacular exist and, with further research, there probably will be more found.

Satire was a favored literary form in the court. One popular account called the Timarion was a satirical story of a descent into Hell, distantly reminiscent of Dante. In the writing of history, the Byzantines, unlike the West, had a continuing tradition from the very beginning to the end. But the true historians of course, except for the chronographers, almost entirely modeled themselves on the ancient Greek works such as those of Thucydides and Herodotus. Their contribution here was of generally high quality but not always original.

Byzantine hymnody has recently been termed by several musicologists and literary critics perhaps the single most important cultural contribution of Byzantium. This is from the perspective of an examination of Byzantine culture itself, without gauging its contribution on the scale of its influence on the West. Unfortunately, the exceptional quality of Byzantine hymnody is scarcely known in the West except to a few specialists. (By hymnody I refer to hymns written to be sung, though they were not always, in the liturgy, and virtually thousands were composed by both monks and laymen.) The greatest hymn writer was Romanos the Melodist of the sixth century; another was John of Damascus.

The modern Western mind finds it difficult to appreciate these hymns because they are so mystical, so transcendental. There is little hint of human emotion in them, but analysis reveals them to be masterpieces. The greatest of all, the Akathistos, was a paean of thanks to the Virgin for saving her city of Constantinople from the invaders. The symbolism, meter, and language are majestic; they strongly echo the strains of religious mysticism and a certain patriotism. Even though it is more difficult for us secular-minded moderns to empathize with these other-worldly hymns than with the more "humanized" Western ones ("Stabat Mater" for example), it is impossible not to recognize and feel something of their power. But one must study the peculiar form of piety that we have been discussing in order fully to appreciate them. Here again in hymnody there is a field for more research but through study of the originals, not through translations, which, here in particular, sometimes sound almost trite.

Is there a substantial amount of unpublished manuscript material for Byzantine history?

I do not mean to imply that every area we have discussed is a virgin field. Even in hymnody there are several competent American scholars who work directly in the Byzantine materials. Relatively speaking, however, these various areas have not yet been integrated into the general field of Byzantine and European history.

One of the basic problems in doing research in Byzantine studies is to track down the sources. After the Latin occupation of Constantinople after 1204, hundreds of manuscripts were taken westward. And later, during the Renaissance, not only Westerners but, more often,

Byzantine refugees and exiles themselves brought manuscripts to sell in Italy or elsewhere. The source material, in other words, was scattered all over Europe. The Bibliothèque Nationale, the British Museum, Soviet libraries, those in Venice and the Vatican, besides several collections in Greece (at Patmos, Athos, and so on) are among the important treasure-houses for such manuscripts. Indeed, almost every great European library contains Byzantine manuscripts in its collections, many of which have not yet been carefully read and some of which are not even catalogued. Thus, it is often difficult even to locate the manuscripts needed for a particular bit of research in a certain discipline. Very often it is necessary to peruse the catalogues of the libraries for a long period of time before moving on to the manuscripts themselves. Luck is not a negligible factor here and neither is frustration. The archaeological finds in Constantinople are far more valuable than the manuscripts that have remained in the fortress city.

What was the evolution of Byzantine law after the Justinian Corpus?

Again here in Byzantine law, a great deal has been done by specialists. But the material has not been fully integrated into the main corpus of Byzantine historical studies. In contrast, in the West there has been a greater synthesis between the area of constitutional history and social movements.

Byzantine law was not so static as one may think. Indeed it did not stop developing after Justinian's reforms, although the Justinian Corpus remained in the background of all subsequent legal developments throughout Byzantine history. The Justinian Corpus had to be revised, however. Three of its four parts were written in Latin, and Justinian had forbidden their translation into Greek or any other language. After Justinian's death the character of the empire became increasingly Greek, and, more important, Byzantium went through many profound social and economic changes which ultimately had to be reflected in the law. The *Ecloga* of the Isaurian emperors, which had as its goal a "more humanitarian" reform of the Justinian codes, represents a large-scale introduction of ecclesiastical and popular law and custom into the empire's official legal system. But the Isaurian legal reform, like its iconoclastic religious program, was, officially at least, discarded by the Macedonians who, under Basil I and Leo VI, attempted a return to a more purely Justiniac system, through reshaping all the laws into what is known as the great code, the *Basilica.* This code, with the addition of subsequent imperial edicts, remained officially in force until the end of the empire. It was therefore the longest-lived code of all. Nevertheless, legal practices as revealed, for example, in Harmenopoulos' *Hexabiblos* of the fourteenth century, continued to change and develop.

More attention should be paid by Westerners to the field of Byzantine canon law. Very few of the Byzantine commentators on the canons have been translated, and it is not necessary to point out that a more complete understanding of the Church on the part of specialist and nonspecialist alike hinges on this kind of research.

How do you view the development of the Byzantine state—the imperial offices, the bureaucracy, and church-state relationships?

Much research has been already done on the Byzantine court, and contemporary sources give us a good picture of the extremely complicated hierarchy of offices for certain periods at least. Up to the eleventh or twelfth century, the court was the richest in Europe. The complexity of the civil service probably served as a model for some of the Western courts, Norman Sicily being a case in point. (Diehl even asserts that Byzantine practices influenced protocol at the court of Louis XIV of France.) There is no doubt that the Byzantine civil service was highly developed, and this was a key factor in the strongly centralized administration of the government. By contrast, regional governors in the contemporary Abassid Arab empire were somewhat more independent than local governors of the Byzantine administration. Byzantine lines of communication were more direct between emperor and his agents in the provinces. This meant that with greater centralization, in periods of stress the emperor could mobilize his forces very rapidly.

The relationship of church and state is one of the questions that has attracted great attention. But all too often scholars have regarded the problem from a Western point of view. Quite erroneously, not a few have reached the conclusion that the emperor had complete control over the Church as well as the state. The major flaw in this "Caesaropapistic" view is its lack of understanding of the Byzantine church-state structure and its fallacious equation with the parallel situation in the West. The Byzantine empire was supposed to represent the Kingdom of God on earth, the emperor being God's Vicar. In a sense, then, there could be no real split between church and state. While it was true that the two were organized differently, together they formed one organic whole.

One way of judging the emperor's powers over church and state would be to examine his powers over the various aspects or spheres of this complex. What we now call the secular aspect of the state was certainly completely controlled by the emperor. In the last analysis, everyone seemed to accept that he was absolute in the empire—the very fountainhead of law. As for Church government or polity the emperor could appoint and even (when he forced the issue) depose the patriarchs. But though legal precedents empowered him to appoint the patriarch, there was no legal justification for his power to depose the spiritual head. Nevertheless, this lack of legality never kept the emperor, in practice, from carrying out his will in this area. In some periods of crisis, the emperor even took over ecclesiastical property, although he first tried to persuade the Church to sanction his actions.

In another vital area of ecclesiastical activity, however, the emperor could never exert full control. This was the innermost heart of the Church—the machinery of dogma and the administration of the sacraments. On a number of occasions, the emperor, it is true, tried to impose his dogmatic interpretations upon the Church, the temporary success of the iconoclastic emperors being one example. But it cannot be said that in the long run he was able to impose his will upon the dogma of the Church. The question of Caesaropapism is complicated by the fact that the emperor had certain traditional sacerdotal or rather liturgical powers, some of which today seem remarkable. He could preach to and cense the congregation; he could even administer communion to himself, though it first had to be consecrated by a priest. The Western observer is apt to misread these circumstances and extrapolate the faulty conclusion that the Eastern emperor had full Caesaropapistic powers. But he had no power to change dogma or administer the sacraments, the core of sacerdotal power. Hence the term *Caesaropapist* is misleading.

Would you assess the development of the Byzantine aristocracy and its relationship with the emperor?

One cannot, I think, affirm that Byzantium's class structure was as stratified and crystallized as that of the West. In the tenth or eleventh century in the West, it was virtually impossible for a peasant to rise up into the ranks of the nobility. In Byzantium, however, the name of Emperor Basil I readily comes to mind, who before founding the Macedonian dynasty, was a lowly stable boy. And earlier, Emperor Justin, who had been a peasant.

The civil aristocracy of Constantinople, composed generally of variously ranged bureaucrats, possessed a similar flexibility. Advancement depended on ability coupled with imperial favor. (Michael Psellus, who rose to be president of the Senate in the eleventh century, was a parvenu of humble origin.) The other major aristocratic group, on the other hand, the great landed magnates of Asia Minor, lacked this kind of flexibility. They tended more to constitute a caste system, intermarrying and preserving their properties wherever possible. But increasingly they tended to advance their own powers at the expense of the central administration or the poorer landholders, especially the peasants of the region.

Both of these groups, the civil bureaucrats and the landed magnates, were members of the Senate, but as time went on the Senate became a more and more negligible factor in the apparatus of the state. By the last few centuries it was simply an honorary body. The heyday of the civil aristocracy was the mid-eleventh century. Until the death of Basil II in 1025, the emperors, with the aid of the civil bureaucracy, had managed with some degree of success, to control the ambitions of the great magnates. After that date, in the absence of strong emperors, a power struggle broke out between the civil bureaucracy and the landed magnates of Anatolia. This was one of the underlying reasons for the near-collapse of the Byzantine state in the mid-eleventh century. The civil aristocracy and the emperors they put forward continued to work against the ambitions of the landed magnates but, unfortunately, to the detriment of the army.

The magnates, on the other hand, and the emperors drawn from their ranks, were generally effective military leaders, but their personal territorial aggrandizement in Asia Minor ultimately weakened one of the traditional military strengths of the empire—the independent peasant-soldier with his small landholdings. With the passing of time, the ruling families of Asia Minor expropriated more and more power. From the late eleventh through the fourteenth centuries, the emperors even granted virtual local autonomy to these lords for services rendered, which were usually military in nature. In addition the magnates began to assume certain judicial functions. There was thus a kind of incipient feudalism beginning to develop in Byzantium (stimulated also by contacts with the West, especially after 1204, the Latin conquest of Constantinople). And it was this factor which proved to be the termite in the house of centralized government during the last four centuries.

Feudalism is of course a complex term, with different meanings in East and West. In Byzantium there was, to be sure, always a centralized state, though its control over various territories became looser in later centuries. In the West, feudalism primarily took the form of contracts between individuals, and an entire hierarchy of feudal nobility developed. In the East no such feudal nexus (with its characteristic subinfeudation) existed, and for a long time, the land grants given to local lords in exchange for services were not hereditary, that is not until the reign of Michael Palaeologus. Thus in the East, political fragmentation was never complete, and a chain of feudal hierarchy with its accompanying subinfeudation never developed.

But the most obvious reason for the

Byzantine state's weakness in the mid-eleventh century was the appearance of formidable enemies on its frontiers. The empire was ringed on all sides, by Normans on the West, Patzinaks in the North, Seljuks from the East, not to speak of other more minor enemies. The emperor still had his traditional army and navy; but because of their growing weakness he was forced to hire mercenaries to bolster his military capacity, which was debilitated still further by the internal strife in the government and threatening might of his rivals for power.

According to Oman, the Byzantine army was the best in the medieval world up to the crucial Battle of Manzikert in 1071. But its deterioration had actually begun earlier. The Byzantine army organization, which was based originally on the Roman model, was developed even further by the Byzantines. Their main weapon was the heavy-armed cavalry, and their generals, in their battle plans, worked out careful strategies to meet every anticipated situation and every conceivable opponent. For example, if they were to battle Frankish knights (who were noted for meeting their enemy head-on), they would use one tactic, and against the Seljuks or nomadic peoples, they utilized different tactics. The effectiveness of Byzantine strategy is known to us from several detailed military manuals that remain.

The Byzantine army had special corps; there was one doctor for so many men and a large number of logistics experts who were responsible for maintaining the supply lines. A basic reason for the collapse of the army after the mid-eleventh century, as we have emphasized, was the gradual disappearance of the free peasantry. Most of the recruits had come from Asia Minor, and when large sections of that area began to fall to the Seljuk Turks, the Byzantines lost a major source of military strength. Meantime, the mercenaries that the emperor was increasingly forced to rely upon were not always dependable, especially when he could not pay them adequately. Many of these hired soldiers came from the West and at various times even included Turks.

Before the eleventh century, was there obligatory military service?

I have already alluded to the independent farmer-peasant who, before the eleventh century, had to serve in the army, supplying his own horse in exchange for a small piece of land, with both land and military obligation tending to become hereditary. But the number of free peasants in Asia Minor was considerably reduced when the landlords, as noted, began to buy up or expropriate their lands. With the decline of the peasant holdings, there was the corresponding decline already referred to in the number of men who could be called upon to render military service.

From early times there were military quotas for the various villages which had to outfit and supply so many fighting men for the armies of the state. We are not sure exactly how each local area worked out its obligation, especially under the stress of the new landlords.

A subsidiary and very important military arm was the so-called Akritai, who usually guarded the Anatolian borders against invaders, especially the Arabs and then Turks. Usually they were rewarded with grants of land, and this gave them that vested interest which encouraged them to perform vigorously as defenders of the area. Unfortunately, this system declined with advances of the nomadic tribes (especially Turks) into Asia Minor, and the Akritai's efficacy was almost completely destroyed in the reign of Michael Palaeologus as a result of his absorption with the threat of Western invasion.

What was the emperor's source of income?

It was primarily a system of public taxation which was very carefully worked out. The system was initiated with the reform of Diocletian and Constantine in the fourth century, and was more or less completed by Anastasius and Nicephorus. The work of these emperors in fiscal reform was so effective that the Byzantine gold coin was accepted at full value as a medium of exchange not only in Byzantine areas, but throughout the West and even in areas of the Far East. It was "the dollar of the Middle Ages." Without exaggeration it may be said that it resisted inflation longer than any other currency the world has known. From the end of the sixth century until the mid-eleventh this coin remained completely undepreciated, though of course in later centuries of the empire, and especially in the last two, it lost the greater part of its value.

The taxation system was very efficient, despite its apparent cumbersomeness. Every fifteen years a census was to be taken in the empire, and taxation lists were scrutinized and restructured if necessary. Taxes were levied on land, commerce, and even on certain monasteries. The empire had customs agents at all the important ports. In addition, the emperor of course could draw upon the usually large resources of his own estates. The expenses of the empire, with its hugh bureaucracy, outlying provinces, and perpetual enemies, were enormous. In later centuries when the empire had lost many of its provinces, the emperor had to cut back on his civil expenses and the bureaucracy became financially unwieldy. More and more, the emperor was forced to grant concessions for freedom from taxation to the magnates for the empire's immediate needs, which were usually military. All this further emaciated the economic state of the empire. To make matters worse, in 1081 the emperor had to grant the Venetians complete exemption from the payment of commercial duties in return for military aid against the invading Normans. And soon enough the Venetians, followed by Genoese and Pisans, had taken over almost the entire Byzantine carrying trade. In the final century or so these cities could have starved the Byzantines into submission had they wished to do so. After the early eleventh century, the number of problems facing the empire grew constantly in number and magnitude. It was an increasing spiral of deterioration. Byzantium's most fundamental problem, I suppose, was that she was constantly surrounded by dangerous enemies. All too often, the empire had to deal with foes on three or even four fronts at one time. Not many states have ever had to face comparable situations. A contribution of Byzantium that is always noted is that it stood as the bulwark of Western Christian civilization against the teeming hordes of Huns, Arabs, Bulgars, Avars, Russians, Cumans, Turks, and so on. In the Dark Ages Byzantium bought time for the West so that the latter could restore its own political, social, and economic equilibrium and then take advantage of the cultural influences flowing in from Byzantium. Had Byzantium fallen much earlier than 1453, a good part of the Greek cultural tradition might have been lost forever or been severely altered.

What was the role of the merchant in Byzantium? Was there a bourgeois class?

In the West, by the seventh century, the merchant class as such had virtually disappeared, not to reappear until about the late tenth century. In Byzantium, it never disappeared; neither did urban civilization. Many middle-class merchants lived in the Byzantine cities and engaged in the carrying trade. At least until the eleventh century, Constantinople was the great commercial nexus of the empire. Through the port of the capital filtered much of the trade of the East. It was the greatest entrepôt, in fact, of all Europe. Byzantine merchants imported goods from widespread areas: slaves from the Balkans, furs, timber, wax, and honey from Russia and the Black Sea area, silks, spices, and other luxury items from the Far East. For a long time indeed, Byzantium was the commercial middleman for much of Western Europe as well. But, as I have noted, the Byzantines gradually relinquished to the Venetians, Pisans, and Genoese their hold over the carrying trade, and these Italian cities eventually came to dominate the entire economic life of the empire.

The Byzantine state played a major role in the development of industry (at least in the early and middle periods), whereas in the West the initiative (when merchants reappeared) was usually taken by private citizens. One reason for this was that eastern merchants did not usually have the great funds of liquid capital that western merchants possessed, say by the fourteenth and fifteenth centuries. Secondly, there was a Byzantine tradition of state control over vital industries; the silk and munitions industries are cases in point. The central government sent out gifts of silk and rich brocades to foreign potentates, thus making this prized commodity (like others) an instrument of imperial diplomacy. Byzantine merchants never seem to have developed the credit system (at least in the Western sense), a phenomenon about which much more research has to be done. Possibly, one reason is that wealth continued to be measured and investments were made primarily in terms of land and not so much in commerce. I might point out that the influence of Western merchant practices upon the East is also a fruitful area for investigation. In the later period Westerners introduced some of their commercial and merchandising methods into the East, especially via Galata and other Latin-held areas. But, in the last analysis, Byzantium by then lacked adequate capital for making any extensive use of such techniques.

Was the merchant class in Constantinople literate, and may we associate any particular political or social ideals with them?

The merchant class as a group was generally literate, I would say. They could read and write in order to carry on their affairs, but whether this means they went on to the university is something else. Many of them had surely gone through elementary and secondary schools, and so in the early stage their education was the same as that received by the future bureaucrats and ecclesiastics. The university concentrated on the training of civil officials. From the evidence of the manual of the Byzantine guild system, the *Book of the Prefect,* there is good reason to believe that the merchants attached importance to being able to read and interpret certain legal texts in order to carry out the rather strict rules of the guild and not to fall afoul of governmental trading regulations.

As for the ideals of the merchants, it is difficult to generalize, except to say the obvious—that though imbued, like all others, with the idea of salvation in the other world, examples of money-grabbing merchants can be found in the Byzantine sources. It does seem, however, that there was some sort of connection, in the earlier period, between the various demes of the city, the circus parties, and the guilds (merchant or otherwise) of Constantinople. But this is a difficult question to analyze here with any accuracy and in any detail. Indeed the sources themselves are not always clear in this connection.

What was the Byzantine role in the Crusades and the impact of the Crusades upon Byzantium?

From early days there had been some commercial and intellectual contact between East and West, but the Crusades marked the first real confrontation of the two societies as such. The Crusades, in some senses, had a more direct impact upon the East than even the West. For in the fourth Crusade of 1204, for example, the hostility growing between East and West during the earlier crusading expeditions reached a shattering climax with the sack of Constantinople itself. The looting of the capital and the ensuing occupation by the Latins created a real emotional trauma among the Greek population which was never to be healed.

The immediate political result of the fourth Crusade of course was the destruction of the Byzantine empire. Runciman asserts that the disruption in 1204 so weakened the Byzantines that later they were never able effectively to restore their power, and thus could not stave off complete collapse two and a half centuries later. The year 1204 was thus an underlying cause of 1453. Social interaction between East and West nevertheless increased steadily after 1204. Thousands of Western merchants established themselves along the coastline of Greece, in the Black Sea area, in the Aegean isles, and in Constantinople itself. They brought their ideas and their capital with them and sometimes (as in Crete) some of them were gradually even assimilated into the Greek population. Even after the Greek reconquest of Constantinople in 1261, a large residue of Latins remained in the eastern empire as well as in other Latin-held areas, and their influence came more and more to be felt by the Byzantines, who at the same time disliked them all the more.

Cultural contacts had already been increasing steadily from the eleventh century, and paradoxically enough, increased yet more rapidly after 1204. After that date the West was more advanced culturally than in earlier times, and it now itself had more to offer to the East.

But this cultural interchange had significant repercussions, intellectually, for the Western world. Soon after 1204, a number of Greek texts were brought to the West, one of the most famous being Aristotle's *Politics*. These works were translated into Latin by such people as William of Moerbeke, Latin Bishop of Corinth, who also translated works of Archimedes. (We have recently learned that Aristotle's *Poetics* was at this time first translated rather than during the Renaissance.) Many of Aristotle's works of course had already been brought into the West from Moorish Spain and Sicily earlier in the twelfth and thirteenth centuries. But these were not the original texts, and they had been considerably worked over by the Arabs. Another important period for the development of philosophy began in 1438–39, when the Byzantine delegation to the Council of Florence brought with them the original Greek manuscripts of Plato. The effect of these and other literary treasures that were brought westward was almost incalculable for the development of the Renaissance. These works included, besides the Platonic corpus, the rhetoric of Hermogenes, the ancient tragedies, such historians as Thucydides, and so on.

Western historians usually study the crusading movement until 1270, the expedition of St. Louis, and often neglect the movements that followed. But crusades continued to be launched from the West, often under papal leadership. The Byzantine historians constantly mention such later Western expeditions, often noting bitterly that though they were ostensibly supposed to be going to Jerusalem, they too frequently ended up wreaking havoc in Byzantine or former Byzantine territories. The Byzantines in fact regarded these expeditions not as holy crusades but simply as predatory expeditions against themselves. And after 1204 and the Latin occupation of Greek areas, one may understand that their apprehensions were not unfounded. From the fourteenth century up through 1453, some popes, realizing the value of Constantinople as a bastion against the Turks and also as a steppingstone to Jerusalem, occasionally even launched crusades in the explicit aim of saving Byzantium itself. Scholars have of course commented on this shift in the crusading ideal, but few have taken the pains to study the Byzantine reaction (I shall publish two chapters on this problem shortly). The conflict between the two churches of East and West, which permeated so much of both people's mentality, repeatedly hindered military cooperation between East and West. For the Easterners, religious beliefs tended to be identified with their ethnic feelings, and they found it difficult to accept the proffered aid of the pope or other Western leaders when the question of union was involved. For the Greeks' compromise in religious belief was tantamount to the sacrifice of "national" integrity.

The period of the Crusades also saw the influx of some Western writings into the East. The works of Thomas Aquinas, for example, under the "Prime Minister" Demetrius Cydones, became popular in the Byzantine court itself in the fourteenth century. Cydones and others sought to demonstrate that the Greek and Latin viewpoints were not antithetical, and they tried to erect intellectual and religious compromises, especially over the celebrated question of the *filioque*. A Latinophile party now arose in Byzantium, which struggled until the very end with the more zealot tradition-minded group over the problem of saving Constantinople from the Turkish threat. Should the Greeks accept Latin aid against the Turks (along with religious union) or, as the more zealous Orthodox preferred, cooperate with the Slavic world? A certain group at the very end even advocated giving in to the Turks in the hope that the latter might ultimately become Hellenized.

Even after 1453, certain popes, usually humanists and under the influence of the famous Greek Cardinal Bessarion, sought to launch crusades to recover Byzantium. But despite the interest of such individuals, the West as a whole was too involved in its own political squabbles to pay much attention to Constantinople, whose population by now they tended to write off. Nevertheless, Venice with its extensive Greek possessions remained involved in Eastern affairs until as late as the seventeenth or eighteenth century. In such Venetian-held areas, the mixture of population produced many interesting social and cultural amalgams.

While the Crusades produced some positive results for the West, it cannot be overstressed that they also produced an animosity between East and West that was almost impossible to resolve. Thus the two worlds could never act together effectively to repel the Turks. The political and military schism produced by 1204 was far more significant than the religious schism of 1054. For the papal bull of 1054 did not excommunicate the emperor, the Greek people, or even the clergy in general. It was directed only against the patriarch Michael Cerularius and his followers, and almost immediately afterward, up to 1453, repeated attempts (no less than thirty) were made to reunite the two churches. The Greeks could never forget that during the Latin occupation they were forced to accept "Catholicism" with papal supremacy. That the negative results of the fourth Crusade cannot be underestimated is therefore apparent. The Latin conquest of Constantinople was one of the great tragedies of medieval history, as it almost irrevocably, psychologically at least, severed the two Christian heirs of the classical tradition and, by sapping Byzantine strength, led almost inevitably to the fall of Constantinople to the Turks later.

The impact of the Crusades, as scholars have often pointed out, also had noteworthy commercial results. Long-range trade with the East increased greatly. It is sometimes not noted, however, that the Florentines also participated in this commercial expansion when, after 1406, they took over the Pisan colony in Constantinople. While much work has certainly been done on the Crusades from the Western viewpoint, more can be accomplished from the point of view of Byzantium, especially in connection with its role in the later Crusades.

Would you delineate Venetian-Byzantine relationships?

Venice has long been a favorite subject of research for medievalists. And in fact the emergence of Venice as a great power was to a great degree connected with the fourth Crusade. The story of Venice's rise to commercial pre-eminence has been told many times and well; but its role as an intermediary of Greek culture between East and West has, until very recently, largely been overlooked. [See my book, *Greek Scholars in Venice: Studies in the Dissemination of Greek Learning to the West* (Cambridge, 1962).] To be sure, the mentality of the Venetian merchants was not always attuned to cultural matters, though they learned to speak the everyday Greek of the Mediterranean basin. But, except in a few cases, this did not lead them to attempt to read the ancient Greek masterpieces. Venice for centuries had been almost an outpost of the Byzantine empire, and relations had become even closer when she acquired colonies in the Greek east. But despite her long contacts with Byzantium, it was rather owing to the influence of the nearby university of Padua and then more distant Florence, that the Venetians, by the latter part of the fifteenth century, began finally to become interested in humanistic studies. At that time, they began to see the practical benefits that might be gained through a perusal of classical texts on government, for example in Plato's *Laws*.

Just before and after 1453, a host of Greek émigrés, often highly cultured, flocked from Greek areas into Venice, the usual port of entry to the West. Venice then began to serve as a cultural filter in the spread of classical Greek learning for Western, including Northern, Europe. The role of Venice in spreading Greek learning in the Renaissance is highly significant. Until a century or so ago it was thought that the Greek émigrés themselves brought about the movement of the Italian Renaissance. But of course this theory is untenable. The intellectual resurgence of Italy was originally rather of Latin inspiration. It is undeniable, however, that that element which did more to widen the intellectual horizon of the Western Renaissance was the reintroduction of Greek learning. And in this respect a great deal of impetus came through the Greek refugees who arrived in Venice in the fifteenth and early sixteenth centuries. The Western Middle Ages had known much of Aristotle, certain scientific works of the ancients, a little Plato. But they were almost entirely devoid of the literary, dramatic, and historical works of the classical Greek period. These works were introduced for the first time into the West during the Renaissance, as many Byzantines fled westward. An important and often-overlooked stopping-off point for the fleeing Hellenists was the Venetian-held island of Crete. A primary example of the role of Crete is to be seen in the career of Marcus Musurus, a Cretan who in Venice edited for Aldus, first editions of the works of Plato, Aristotle, Euripides, and others. These Greek émigrés also began to lecture for the first time on the *original* Greek texts of Aristotle, especially at the University of Padua, now under Venetian rule. The graduates of Padua disseminated the Greek learning they had acquired throughout Europe, and Erasmus himself came to Padua and studied with Musurus. The Greeks of Venice soon became organized into a legally recognized community with its own church, docks, and school. One scholar has pronounced this colony, because of its preservation of the Greek tradition. "the seedbed of modern Greece."

Of course there was some degree of interaction between the Greek community and the Venetians. One of the products of this cultural admixture was El Greco, himself born in Crete. It is a curious phenomenon that the small island of Crete now sent out cultured men who spread out as far even as Russia. This diaspora of Greeks lasted at least to 1600, to become one of the most remarkable aspects of post-Byzantine history. Byzantine influences did not end in 1453 with the death of Emperor Constantine XI on the ramparts of Constantinople.

The Byzantine contribution to the Renaissance was great. Not only did the Greeks transmit much unknown material of the ancients (such as Plutarch and Plato's treatises on education). Byzantines taught the Westerners how to deal with these technically, because the Latins could not by themselves have disentangled the linguistic nuances. Byzantine methods for the study of the classics were, it seems, therefore transmitted to Renaissance scholars. But their influence in this respect still awaits careful study. We assume too readily that classical Greek learning was passively transmitted by the Byzantines. But it is impossible to suppose that the ancient literature passed through the sieve of Byzantium without change. (Here I think the philologists should take the lead in investigation.) The order in which the Byzantines studied the classical texts (the plays of the tragedians for example), their approach to these works, the textual emendations they made (sometimes unwise), must have colored the ancient works with at least a certain Byzantine tinge. And this in turn, it seems to me, must have affected the Renaissance approach, if not the text itself, to the study of the classics and, by extension, our own attitudes today. Byzantium was not merely a repository of ancient Greek learning; it was also in some ways a modifier.

What was the influence of Byzantium upon Russian culture?

Byzantine influence on the Slavs was more pervasive than even its influence upon the West. Byzantine culture infiltrated into the West; it influenced certain fields more than others, but crept in more or less sporadically, accomodating itself to the social and intellectual climate it found. In the Slavic regions, on the other hand, the Byzantine influence swept over the cold plains of what in some cases was yet an intellectual wasteland. Slavic peoples, the Bulgars, Russians, and Serbs, were converted *en masse* to Orthodoxy. From the viewpoint of religion certainly, and from that of many aspects of culture, the medieval eastern Slavs were intensely Byzantinized.

The Moravians were the first to be converted, in the ninth century. For political reasons the Moravian ruler asked Byzantium for missionaries. He was afraid of the Frankish advance upon his borders. Patriarch Photius thereupon sent two monks, the Greek "Slavic" apostles Cyril and his brother Methodius as missionaries. The two monks did a good deal of work: they translated the sacred Orthodox books into "Slavonic" (marking the beginning of that literature) and laid the groundwork for the expansion of Greek Orthodoxy among the Slavs. The heritage they established in Moravia outlasted the political life of the Moravian state. Bulgaria was another region to feel the impact of Greek missionaries. Besides wanting a counterpoise to Western political pressure, the Bulgar Khan requested Greek missionaries because, in part, he aspired to establish an autocracy over his boyars similar to the central authority of the emperor in Constantinople. Vladimir was prince of Kiev in the late tenth century when the Russians were converted by the Byzantine church. As the old Russian account goes, Russian emissaries, taken to attend a liturgy at St. Sophia, felt "as if they were in Heaven itself." Thus when they returned home, they helped to persuade their prince to convert to the Byzantine religion rather than to any one of several other choices. To be sure, there were political motivations for Vladimir's conversion as well. He wanted commercial concessions from Byzantium and an imperial marriage alliance.

One basic reason for the success of the Byzantine missionary activity among the Slavs is certainly the fact that they permitted the translation of their liturgy and sacred books into the native vernaculars of the prospective converts. This is something the Western church would not permit until the present day.

It is not easy to evaluate the degree of Byzantinization undergone by the various Slavic peoples. Communist scholars have in past decades tended to play down the Byzantine contribution to their culture, and the Greeks have, on the other hand, probably overemphasized it. Perhaps the best evaluation is somewhere in between. Certainly the Russian alphabet is derived from the Greek. The Russian liturgical and ecclesiastical texts, codes of law, canon and in part civil, and some political ideologies, were based on Byzantine examples. Much of the autocratic political theory which surrounded the Russian institution of czardom came from Byzantine antecedents (though one should certainly not overlook the Tatar influence here as well).

It is interesting to note, however, that the Slavic peoples, did not inherit the Byzantine classical traditions to the same degree as the West did. One reason is that the agents of conversion of the Slavs were generally monks, who would naturally be more interested in the works of Christianity than of classical paganism. One opinion has it that Kiev did not accept the pagan Greek classical works because it was not yet sophisticated enough to appreciate them. But this does not really seem valid, because in the eleventh and twelfth centuries the society of Kiev was quite urbanized and in some respects quite equal to that of some Western areas. In one sense, despite the great benefits conferred on the Slavs by their conversion to Byzantine Christianity, because translations were almost invariably made into the vernacular, the native scholars were deprived of the necessity of learning Greek and consequently could not move on to the classical texts.

There was, it seems, Byzantine influence upon Russian epic poetry. The Prince Igor cycle betrays stylistic and other borrowing from Byzantine models. The most famous of the Byzantine epics, Digenes Akritas, was first known to the West through a Slavic version even before the Greek text was discovered. The Byzantine influence on Russian canon and some Russian civil law has been noted. In addition, Russian art of the time of Vladimir and Yaroslav and again in the fourteenth and fifteenth centuries was highly Byzantine-inspired. In connection with Russian painting, I might mention a painter who is only now becoming better known—Theophanes, a Byzantine émigré to Russia who had earlier painted in Constantinople and elsewhere. Theophanes "the Greek" journeyed through the expanses of Russia and left many works. He was possibly even the teacher of the great Rublev. Certainly, he reveals remarkable and in some ways new qualities. He has therefore been ranked as one of the two greatest medieval Russian painters.

If one studies the post-Byzantine period of 1453–1600, he will discover, as emphasized earlier, that the influence of Byzantine culture continued despite the fall of Constantinople to the Turks. Much progress studying the Byzantine impact on the Russians was made by the Russian scholars in the later nineteenth century, but Byzantine studies dwindled after the revolution. There has been recently a revival of this work, and now the Russian Byzantine school is making rapid advances. As is to be expected, a particular area of interest is Byzantine-Russian trade relations. Was communal landholding originated in Byzantium or was it something indigenous to and brought by the Slavs? Moreover, the Russians are now doing more to investigate the cultural aspects of Byzantine influence, in poetry, vocabulary, and structure of language. This Byzantine influence existed in different fields of endeavor in Russia just as in the West. But in the Slavic East, which was less developed and located closer to Constantinople, the Byzantines had more of an open field, culturally and socially speaking, to work their influence. Fifty years after the conversion of Russia, the Russian ecclesiastical hierarchy consisted almost entirely of Greeks appointed by the Constantinople patriarch, who, it can be believed, tutored some Russians in the complex workings of Byzantine administration as well as in more strictly religious matters.

How do you view the relationship between the Byzantine and Islamic worlds?

Social and cultural interaction between the worlds of the mosque and the cathedral existed over a long period. Of course, from the beginning of the eighth century onward, the Arabs repeatedly attacked Byzantium militarily, besieging Constantinople itself on at least three different occasions. But although the Arabs trekked through Asia Minor with their armies, they never seemed to remain there for any long period of time, partly because of the difficult problems of terrain. Water is scarce on the cold tableland of the Asia Minor plain, and provisioning a large army is most difficult there. The Arabs did manage, however, to disrupt the Byzantine communication system and commercial traffic. The demographic changes of Asia Minor also are significant in this period.

There are two phases in Byzantine-Arabic relations. In the first, which stretched from the seventh through the early tenth centuries, Byzantium was on the defensive. The Arabs seized Sicily and in 828, even the island of Crete. Previously they had stripped from Byzantium the rich eastern provinces of Egypt, the Byzantine granary, Syria with its important trading cities, and Palestine. To a considerable extent these losses made the Byzantine empire retrench and therefore become more "Greek." The Arab conquest was rapid and phenomenal, and before the Byzantines were aware of the magnitude of the Arab threat it was too late.

When the Arabs first conquered these areas, Muslim culture was not very advanced. They adopted many of the facets of the civilization of the subject Byzantines. Especially the Arabs adapted the administrative systems they found. Nor did they treat their new subjects badly. Byzantines helped them to construct their first real navy. It should be noted that the provinces of Egypt, Palestine, and Syria, for religious and other reasons, had been disaffected with Byzantium and thus did not always put up determined resistance to the Muslim advance.

The Arabs were fascinated by ancient Greek science and philosophy and they now, especially in Alexandria, had access to more material for translation. The Arabs (especially later in Baghdad) even made a few advances of their own beyond the ancients, in optics and pharmacology, for example.

The second great phase of Byzantine-Arab relations encompassed the later tenth and early eleventh centuries. In this period, Byzantium took the offensive, penetrating into Syria, the edge of Mesopotamia, and parts of Palestine. The relations between the two spheres were close. We know that ambassadors (as before) were exchanged and that each culture respected the other. The Byzantines even had a mosque in Constantinople for the Arab East.

The introduction of Aristotle into the four worlds of revealed religion—Western Christianity, Greek Christianity, Judaism, and Islam—had interesting consequences. Aristotle viewed the world through the lens of reason, not revelation, and this sparked a collision in all four systems. In the West, the crisis was resolved only by Aquinas. Aristotelianism was similarly adapted by the Greek John of Damascus to fit it inside the theological framework of Eastern Orthodoxy. Maimonides walked the same intellectual tightrope in Spain. True to the pattern, when the Muslims moved into Spain they attempted to do the same thing. This created a severe crisis in Arab thought, further complicated by the fact (not generally known), that some of the Muslim scholars were fond of Platonic and Neoplatonic thought.

Arab science was probably in advance of the Byzantine, though it must be noted again that Byzantine science has not yet been thoroughly examined. We know that in the twelfth century there were a number of hospitals in Constantinople, with one medical center having special doctors and wards for certain diseases.

Some Byzantines undoubtedly were also interested in certain aspects of Muslim culture. They were particularly intrigued with occultism and Arab alchemy. The interaction of the worlds of the West, Byzantium, and the Arabs is clearly evidenced in the intercultural exchange of the important astronomical treatise of the ancient Greek Ptolemy, the *Almagest*. I repeat again that medieval intellectual history will have been studied most thoroughly when we have integrated the histories of Islam, the West, and Byzantium and fully documented the cultural interaction.

The Arabs did everything they could to procure ancient scientific and philosophical Greek texts, even from the Byzantines in Constantinople. It is strange that the West, which likewise clamored for ancient Greek works in the twelfth and thirteenth centuries, preferred to borrow them from the Arabs and not directly from the Greeks. This was in large part caused by their animus toward the Byzantines in the medieval period. Eventually, in the Renaissance, Western scholars did realize the significance of the original texts.

Would you discuss the relationship of the churches of East and West?

This relationship is today being investigated with ever-increasing interest. Despite growing estrangement, ultimate schism, and the failure of all medieval attempts at ecclesiastical reunion, it is clear that the impact of the Byzantine church on the Western was considerable. The early ecumenical councils had all taken place in the East, and the formulation of doctrine in the great councils was largely the work of the Eastern fathers. Many stories of the Virgin originated in the East, and Greek liturgical hymns were circulated in the West. The piety of the Byzantines became widely known among the Latins as more and more Westerners traveled to Constantinople, and especially in the ninth to eleventh centuries when Byzantine monks came to the Western areas.

These monks had more of an influence on the Western reform movements of the tenth through the twelfth centuries than is often supposed. Several recent studies demonstrate that during the Western Cluniac reform movement, some of the more important monasteries, particularly in the region of the Lorraine, came under the direct influence of a number of Byzantine monks. The Byzantine monks' interest in the Eastern church fathers, their willingness to do manual labor (in contrast to the Western monks' dependence on serfs), and their relative disassociation from the feudal order impressed the Westerners. The extent of this influence must be further investigated. But undoubtedly there was a good deal of contact between the monastic systems of East and West, and the eruption of significant reform movements in the one makes us glance inquiringly at the other.

On the other hand some Byzantines, in the late thirteenth and fourteenth centuries, became fascinated with Western Scholasticism. But it should be noted that many Greeks began to use the new philosophic methodology of Scholasticism rather to combat the Latin theology, which was becoming more and more disseminated (or rather "propagandized") in the East during the great debate over religious union with Rome in the years before the fall of Constantinople to the Turks.

Other aspects of culture were disseminated in both areas as a result of ecclesiastical relations; for example, there was a kind of dialogue of architectural techniques. Some of the refinements of the Western style were adopted in the East. The ornamentation in the monastery church of Daphni outside Athens is a case in point.

We should not conclude, then, following the belief held until recently, that after 1054 there was little relationship between the Western and Eastern churches. The schism of 1054 has been too often overplayed. A greater understanding of the history of the schism would not only enlighten historians but ultimately might help to engineer a reunification of the two churches. The Greeks have always recognized papal primacy of honor and, among the patriarchs, the pope is accepted as "first among equals." But the Greeks have not been willing to accept his *jurisdictional* authority over the Eastern churches. It is impossible to say if a true theological and especially "ecclesiological" union will ever come about. But a closer rapport is certainly constantly developing, and the increasing interest manifested in Byzantine ecclesiastical studies among both Catholics and Protestants bodes well for Christian unity.

9

Medieval Islam

GUSTAVE E. VON GRUNEBAUM

THE HISTORIOGRAPHICAL CONTEXT

The pretensions of monarchs and the ambitions of statesmen have left a rich legacy for historical scholarship. Just as the arrogance of Louis XIV as the Sun-King inspired Byzantine studies and Napoleon's invasion of Egypt inspired a French school of Egyptology, so the imperial dreams of Kaiser Wilhelm II produced not only the Berlin-to-Baghdad Railway but also the first great centers of Islamic and Arabic scholarship in the German universities at the beginning of the twentieth century. This reawakened a dormant Austrian interest in the Middle East, derived from the old Habsburg struggles against the Turks. It was at the University of Vienna that the leading Islamist of our day, Gustave von Grunebaum (born in 1909) received his Ph.D. in 1931.

Like so many of the best German-speaking scholars of his generation, von Grunebaum found refuge in the United States. From 1943 to 1957 he was associated with the distinguished Oriental Institute of the University of Chicago. Since 1957 he has been Director of the Near East Center at the University of California at Los Angeles.

In relation to available material, the history of the Arabic-speaking world has been among the most underdeveloped fields of historical knowledge. Medieval Islam was a heavily populated, wealthy, intellectually vibrant civilization which profoundly affected both the economic and cultural development of Western Europe from the eighth to the thirteenth centuries. As yet, only certain aspects of medieval Islam are known in convincing detail; many crucial problems remain to be investigated. Von Grunebaum's

Medieval Islam (1946) was a revelation because he integrated literature and religious history with political and social change and made the medieval Arabic world come alive to us as no previous book had done.

Now von Grunebaum, a generous, enthusiastic man, presides over the leading center of medieval Islamic studies in the world. With his industrious colleagues, many of whom he himself has trained, he is revealing the contours of this vibrant and complex civilization, which the reawakening of Arabic societies in our time makes even more significant and relevant to our concern.

Chronological Outline

570?–632: Life of Mohammed. The Hegira (622), or journey to Medina, traditionally marks the beginning of the Muslim era.

632–661: The Arabs move beyond Arabia into Mesopotamia, Syria, and Egypt.

661–749: The Umayyad caliphate. Northern Africa and Spain come under Muslim control, but Constantinople repulses the Arab forces.

c. 700–725: The appearance of Sunnite (orthodox) and Shiite division within the Muslim religious community.

749–1258: The Abbasid caliphate rules an international empire. At its magnificent capital of Baghdad ancient texts are translated into Arabic, and philosophical speculation and poetry flourish.

756: A Umayyad dynasty is set up in Spain. Arabic scholarship flourishes at the great court at Cordoba. Particularly notable are Averroës' (1126–1198) commentaries on Aristotle.

968–c. 1100: The Fatimid dynasty transforms Egypt into a brillian center of Muslim culture.

1071: Byzantine power in Asia Minor is destroyed by the Seljuk Turks in the battle of Manzikert.

1095–1292: The Crusades. In 1187 Saladin unites various Muslim states and regains Jerusalem. After his death in 1193 Muslim unity again evaporates.

1249–1517: Spared the Mongol devastation, Egypt under the Mamluks is the great stronghold of Muslim civilization.

1258: The Mongol hordes overrun Baghdad.

1325–1345: Rise of the Ottoman Turks in northwestern Asia Minor.

1453: The Ottoman Turks sack Constantinople, ending the Byzantine Empire.

1492: After almost four centuries of struggle the Spanish Christians succeed in expelling the Arabs.

1520–1566: In the reign of Suleiman the Magnificent the Ottoman Empire reaches its zenith.

Norman F. Cantor

What were the political, economic and social conditions in the Arabian peninsula during Mohammed's lifetime?

Gustave E. von Grunebaum

It seems to me important to realize that Mohammed began his preaching in a backwater of ancient civilization and outside any other main currents of influence. It is necessary to bear this in mind to understand both Mohammed's achievement and, in terms of the contemporary scene, certain weaknesses. Arabia—apart from the southern section, the Yemen, which has its own fate and history—had never been united before the era of Mohammed. It had been a tribal region with the exception of perhaps three of four sections which were what may be called urban areas. Actually, only Mecca would fit the modern sense of the term *urban*.

Some attempts had been made at the establishment of principalities. There had been two such in the marginal areas under Byzantine and Sassanian sponsorship and one roughly seventy years before Mohammed's birth in the center of Arabia. The latter attempt was made under the aegis of the South Arabian kings and, with the decline of South Arabia, or rather its conquest by the Ethiopians, this principality lost its political and demographic support and collapsed.

The north central area of the Arabian peninsula, which is all we are talking about, could not quite keep out of the political conflict that dominated the Near Eastern area through the fifth, sixth, and seventh centuries—a conflict between the Byzantine empire and the Sassanian in Iran. This is especially true for South Arabia and for Mecca. Mecca, a town located at the crossroads of two important commercial and traveling roads, from the Red Sea into what is now called Iraq, and from the Yemen to Syria and Egypt, had a certain importance for the competing Byzantines and Persians. The sympathies of the Meccans seem to have been with the Persians. We know this fact indirectly, for Mohammed seems to have favored the Byzantines, as one passage in the Koran suggests. In practical terms, this involvement must have been rather minor but nevertheless, it is important to bear in mind that the leading clans in Mecca did know that the world was large, that they did have regular contracts throughout the peninsula and certainly into the Byzantine area and Sassanian Iraq. The areas surrounding Mecca were controlled by alliances of various kinds comprised of the major tribal confederations settled in both the north and the south of Mecca.

The other major settlement, which perhaps was not really urban, is the town that has come to be known as Medina, the town of the prophet. The Yemenites, who had been moving from the south to the north for upwards of a millennium, were very likely responsible for the founding and sustenance of this community. In Medina, the social configuration was quite different from Mecca. There were a number of smaller Arabian tribes, two of them important, and a few Jewish groups, three of them important during the five-year period following Mohammed's move from Mecca to Medina. In this small territorial area, tensions of a very considerable kind must have existed.

It is very difficult for a European to quite figure out how these semi-independent and semi-interconnected tribes could have lived so close to one another in such a very small territory—warring, uniting, and warring again. Apparently, there was such a drain on their manpower in a drawnout civil war that they were willing to invite a foreign arbitrator. In those days, someone who came from a distance roughly four hundred kilometers away from one's home was a foreign person indeed.

The standard of living in the desert seems to have been fairly comparable with the standard of living that we know from travelers' descriptions from the eighteenth and early nineteenth centuries. I do not want to overdo the old cliché of the "unchangeable desert" because it does change: for one thing, the Arabs were converted to Islam with the multiple social consequences which this change engendered. But on the whole, then as later, the Arabs were rather poor and their income was precarious. Their income was largely pastoral, and consequently they were fully dependent on the vagaries of the weather cycle. Their own path to self-enrichment was either raids against the settled populations or more often, inter-tribal raids which may have profited momentarily one tribe over another but which also guaranteed the annihilation of any material progress whatsoever. This view may, of course, be contested in the case of the principalities under Byzantine and Persian sponsorship because they obviously received subsidies and their armies were organized. They were sufficiently developed politically, especially in the case of the wards of Byzantium, to be able to make major plans. It seems, for example, that the real reason why the Byzantines and the Arabs came into conflict, which ended with the abolition of this buffer state, was the plan of a more enterprising Arab leader to unite somehow all the Monophysite dissenters from Upper Mesopotamia up to the Egyptian border. I suppose making large-scale political plans presupposes a certain measure of financial independence and political maturity and much greater operational alertness than could possibly have been found among the other tribes of Arabia.

Mecca itself was rather a structured town. It was controlled by a number of clans that were connected by their common descent from one tribal group, whose fame is rather retroactive, since this was the tribe that Mohammed was born into. It would have been impossible for Mecca to present even the semblance of unity if there had not been some kind of coordination among the tribes, at least in matters of commercial and what we might call foreign policy. Mecca was also demographically structured, as the upper crust occupied a certain part of Mecca, and those who were removed from power lived away from the center of the town.

Mecca was a pilgrimage center. The town originated as a settlement when a well was found in an otherwise barren valley, and with this as its one source of water, Mecca developed. Its economic raison d'être was marketing and, indirectly, religion. In the Arabian setting it was a very important place. The "truce territories" of Mecca was a center where at regular intervals the tribes of northwest Arabia and also southwest Arabia gathered. The occasions of these gatherings were commercial, military, and cultural. There was recitation of poetry, and legend has it that the poets were crowned or given prizes.

Intellectually speaking, Mecca was a passive center. It is striking how few of the recognized poets were city people. The really great poets, great in the eyes of contemporary and subsequent observers, were without exception tribal people. The urban poets were considered second-rate even though their political importance, as satirists and propagandists, was all the greater because of the urban setting. Later, owing to the development of Islam, the situation changed; branches of knowledge were cultivated which would normally not lend themselves to study without a regular urban school tradition.

In light of recent scholarship, what do we know about Mohammed's life and teaching, and how do these teachings compare with the doctrines of Judaism and Christianity?

As with every major historical figure, Mohammed became ever more important as time moved on and his community gained in influence and in emotional attachment to his personality. Mohammed, according to the Muslim tradition, was born in 570. It is more likely that he was born about 580, however, but in this context it makes little difference. He lived in a time in which both the Byzantines and Sassanians, the two dominant powers in the world known to him, were locked in a merciless struggle; consequently, he lived in a period of crisis and, as it turned out, of decline.

Stories have it that Mohammed used to accompany caravans into the Syrian fruitland. Again this is difficult to verify. If the stories are told in order to show that he first had acquaintance with various Christian sects, he did not profit very much by these visits from what we see of his knowledge as expressed in the Koran or his authentic sayings. But all this is in the realm of hypothesis since there was no need for him to travel outside Arabia in order to get information. For it is certain that there were groups of Jewish people within reach, and it is more than likely that there were fairly large numbers of stray Christians in the Meccan area. Mecca had a sizable floating population, as would exist in any commercial center.

These transient populations were representative of a number of religions, but they did not contain any theologians. In addition, it does not seem that the orthodoxy was as well represented as some splintered and extreme sects. Again, when you consider the language barrier between a Greek- or Syriac-formulated Christian theology, a Persian-formulated Zoroastrian theology, and the Arabic of that time, misunderstandings are not to be marveled at. The long and short of it is that we can accept it as probable but not certain that Mohammed had some kind of contact with Judaic and Christian circles. The less one defines the specificity of these circles, the more one remains on solid ground.

As far as the Christian circles are concerned, they cannot possibly have been Orthodox ones because the Koran, while displaying a great deal of respect for Jesus, also included many apocryphal legends not accepted by the Church. There was a refusal of the Trinity and a refusal of the reality of Jesus' death. This would not be worth mentioning had it not had some important consequences. It was impossible then (and has remained so since) to effect a real dialogue between Christianity and Islam because of these incompatible concepts of basic Christian doctrine. As regards the Jews, the differences of opinion turned on one point: was or was not Mohammed pre-announced in Jewish Scriptures? The language curtain protected Mohammed and his adherents from any investigation of this matter.

It is quite clear that in the beginning, Mohammed was convinced that his message was identical with that of Christians and Jews and in fact with every major book containing revelation then in existence; obviously God had not contradicted himself. While God may have adjusted himself to local conditions, in essence His message must necessarily have been the same. When Mohammed came to Medina and saw that the Jews did not recognize him as a figure foretold in their Scriptures, there was no other way for him and his adherents to react but to feel that the Jews were either in error or engaging in willful distortion.

Mohammed, then, was regarded as God's instrument for rectifying the entangled interpretations of Scripture. The very generic tone of his religious teachings lent an air of authenticity to Mohammed. His sayings were simple, straightforward, and did not betray the flavoring of Persian and Greek influence; in fact he did not know Greek, Hebrew, Syriac, or Persian. I might add that Mohammed was very concerned with keeping his own message free from any such distortions to which in his view the earlier revelations had fallen victim. He took great pains to put his teachings into texts that were carefully noted down and preserved. The feeling that he had come as a confirmer and validator he shared, probably without knowing it, with Mani who had grown up in the Zoroastrian milieu. A good many striking similarities exist between the prophetic consciousness of Mani, who died in the 270's, and Mohammed. Both evinced a universalism, both viewed minor deviations from fundamentals as local variations of no particular importance, and both sought to establish a synthesis of several truths into one system.

In contradistinction to the adherents of Mani, who does not occur in the Koran at all, and in contrast certainly with the Christians, the Muslim community was from the very beginning at one and the same time a religious and a political community. In terms of the Arabian tradition, they became simultaneously a religious community and a new tribe. It is not that somebody who adhered to Islam had to leave his own tribe, for you cannot leave something that you are born into. But there was a transference of loyalty from the physical tribe to this new grouping. This was effected by profession of the faith, a shared ritual, emigration, marriage, common victories and defeats in wars, and shared political and administrative action. One "lived into" Islam.

A Muslim's faith united a spiritual with a political factor. Without political integrity, one cannot choose or implement one's own religious convictions, and this realization was ingrained in the Muslim community at a very early stage. The fact that the Muslims had worldly success seemed to indicate that history was indeed on their side and reinforced their political and religious convictions. The unity between the political and religious goals and views stood unchallenged until much later times.

Here is, I suppose, basically the greatest difference in attitudes, outlook, and fate between the Christian and Muslim communities. The Christians had the good or bad luck, depending on how you look at it, to have to wait three hundred years to gain power in the Roman state. Consequently, a certain disassociation between spiritual and worldly success was built into the Christian tradition. The Christians were for this reason somewhat less vulnerable to political defeat because they knew that their true triumph was intended to be achieved on another level. Islam, on the other hand, was successful almost immediately. There was a period of troubles of some five or ten years, and then Mohammed and his followers moved to Medina. For hundreds of years following this, the Muslims dominated over an enormous expanse. The Christians did not need to Christianize Roman law right away; they worked out very slowly and haltingly a church organization and a church law. The Muslims immediately had to make their theological decisions with an eye to practical problems. There were provinces to be governed, there were people outside of direct religious communities and not speaking Arabic, there was for many a generation a vast majority of non-Muslims. They had somehow to come to terms with these facts—they had to evolve a theology and a written law that took these factors into account. The responsibility was theirs, and what kept the empire together was ultimately just Islam. Here lies the existentially decisive difference between Islam and Christianity.

To Mohammed, authority or precedent in religious doctrine was possessed only by the Jews and Christians. What then are other major similarities and dissimilarities between Islam and the other two religions? Islam does not recognize a borderline between the secular and religious aspects of life. Religious injunctions are supposed to govern a person's life from conception to resurrection.

There is absolutely nothing for which there is not some religiously approved way of either doing it or not doing it. This by and large is also the stand of so-called classical Judaism. The Talmudic Law tries to take care of everything. As in Islam, secular problems are to be solved on the basis of purely religious insights. In practice, naturally, this will not be so; but were the Muslim or the Talmudic community to examine itself, it would find no facet that it could declare outside the all-encompassing set of laws. This is the principal similarity between Talmudic Judaism and Islam.

The religious tenets of Islam are closer to Christianity than one might think from examination of the more obvious and virulent differences. The fabric of both religious systems is woven around the assumption that there is only one God, that there is an unfathomable gap between Creator and created, and that there will be a resurrection. The ritual aspects and forms of community worship of Islam have come out of the same Judaic atmosphere as Christianity. In the theological structure, in the debate between reason and faith, between intellectual and inspirational perception, there is a nice repetition of that which the philosophy of late pagan antiquity left to the Christian Fathers. There are similar basic positions to be elaborated, defended, and abandoned in a similar milieu. In addition, since both the Christians and the Muslims used after a while the same intellectual tooling, the Aristotelian method, they tended to come out with kindred systems even though the point of the arrow goes in different directions.

Medieval Jewish philosophy, too, was profoundly akin to this development —a successful assimilation of the Greek philosophical method and an adjustment of problems that are implied in the Jewish theological system. However, from the point of view of world history, the Christian-Muslim dialogue was more important than the Jewish-Muslim dialogue. The differences with the Jews had no political implications as the Jews lived under the Muslims throughout the High Middle Ages. I suppose there really was no possibility for the Jews to revolt even if there were the inclination. The Christians, however, had the whole West, with possible support from the Byzantine East, and their views had to be taken a little more gravely.

How do you account for the emergence of religious groups and sects in Islam?

The theologians in Islam were a minority just as they were in the West. The intellectual slogans, however, which animated the populace with attenuated and at times somewhat misunderstood versions of the faith came from this relatively small group which at least for a period processed for the masses whatever knowledge was deemed necessary for them. The precise content would naturally vary from region to region.

The intellectual traditions of the conquered continued with some Muslim varnish on it, just as a converted Roman had previously endured the superimposition of the Christian attitude upon his inherited pagan orientation, with much of Christianity not seeming in need of modification. In like manner Islam took in different types of intellectuality which, at least to those who held them, seemed quite compatible with Islam. To take another example, monotheism proved quite compatible with Persian ideas of social structure and the Persian ideal of the heroic figure and social ethics. You accept the fact of monotheism, the fact of revelation, the fact of prophecy, and the fact that Mohammed is the last prophet. Having done so, you continue living the way you were. You do pay the poor tax, you do pray and fast, but with this, you remain a Persian. The identity remains essentially stable, or so it seems to the convert, while the content of the identity is profoundly altered.

The conclusion has forced itself on me that in the Middle East from at least the time of Alexander the Great down to Mohammed's time, all religious and philosophical movements that had any popular appeal whatsoever can be structurally outlined around a very limited number of recurrent religious motifs. There is, for example, the motif of the communication between God and man through the medium of revelation. There is the corresponding motif of the prophet. These motifs have consequences with which you have to contend. For example, if it is God's way to communicate with man through a prophet, is this a permanent or occasional state of affairs? Can mankind live with only occasional visitations or does there have to be a guide in presence at all times? You can reduce the major and perhaps also the minor sectarian differences to the giving of different answers to the identical questions. For example, for hundreds of years, people have been beset with the question, Whence evil? Usually only two answers offer themselves. Either God created both the good and the evil and, with more or less guidance, we have to separate the two principles for ourselves, or there are, very conveniently, two gods. Many of the sects or deviations in Islam (but not only in Islam) during the Middle Ages are due to the resurgence of this dualistic hypothesis.

Here is another example of religious schism along these lines. We know that God has been in the habit of rousing prophets at intervals, and Mohammed claimed that he was the last of all such heavenly messengers. But is it possible for mankind to go on without direct guidance? "Yes," said the orthodox (Sunnite) view, as Mohammed has left expressly or by implication a sufficient number of directives. But others disagreed and insisted that a permanent leader was a prerequisite in man's permanent crisis. This is the religious motif around which Shiism, or rather the several Shiite sects, grew. I do not mean to suggest that these splinterings happened because of any formal council decision ruling such-and-such a theological dogma to be deviant. But rather that every rebellious group quickly adopted religious views that had been discredited by the rival establishment.

Without much difficulty a table of the major religious motifs operative in the formative period of Islam could easily be drawn—no more than eight or ten would have to be listed. You would be satisfied that the concept of a book revelation had been universally accepted. Everyone agrees that there have been prophets, but the nuance of whether or not these prophets were human or divine (or both, and in what proportion) provides a convenient point of division. If the prophet is a human being, does he have an heir? How is this heir to be recognized? The fractionalizing questions continue. And thus out of less than a dozen fundamental motifs which recur constantly and which have a tremendous emotional appeal, the splintered kaleidoscope of many sects arises quite easily. Although their teachings will in some cases come out far removed from Mohammed's teaching, all the interpretations taught by the sects, though, can be readily analyzed back into the molds of the basic religious forms.

On the other hand, it would be misleading to try to play down the political and social implications of these schisms which were the basis for so many uprisings. All too often, dogmatic differences merely serviced political objectives.

What were the roles of Aristotelianism and mysticism in Muslim culture?

Aristotelianism was first nothing but a method. It introduced the syllogism as against reasoning by analogy. It gave the categories and certain concepts with which spiritual and intellectual data could be organized. The Greek apparatus was taken over. This apparatus, of course, had been developed on certain types of thought, and it is not a simple matter to separate content from method; but as much as possible, it was the apparatus that was accepted and the thoughts discarded. There are certain basic positions of Aristotelianism which, for a revealed religion such as Christianity and Islam, are inacceptable. The belief in the creation of the world and in the resurrection and Judgment Day was incompatible with Aristotelianism.

Throughout Christianity and Islam, there is a cleavage between the thinkers who accept the philosophical Aristotelian viewpoint and those who do not. The more intellectual theologians in the eleventh and twelfth centuries try to prove the orthodox position with Aristotelian technique to make a rational case for the verities of the faith.

The Muslims had more Greek works in translation at their disposal in 1100 than the Christians. The Muslims, then, initially were in both a better and worse position than the Christian scholars as they had to accommodate more data to tradition but were technically much better able to do so. Around 1200 or a little earlier, the Christians became fully acquainted with Aristotelianism along with Arab commentaries through Spain and through the Byzantines. This new learning sharpened Christian thinking and the techniques of presentation of intellectual problems. It did away to a very large extent with unsystematic and enumerative or metaphoric treatment.

What Aristotelianism did in Europe, and this is most important, is make possible a breakthrough to reality, to the direct observation of nature. Aristotelianism did not have this effect for the Arabs. This seems to show that it is up to the recipient what he will do with any given body of data, since essentially the Christians and the Muslims were exposed to the same body of Aristotelian science and philosophy. As I mentioned before, the Arabs actually had more of the Aristotelian corpus than the Christians, but what they had was read differently: it had in the Christian culture of the thirteenth century the effect of reconnecting man with the reality of nature and thus to stimulate natural science and at the same time prompting a reformulation of the Christian system. In Saint Albert the Great's (d. 1280) work there are a number of striking statements to the effect that while the theological truths are unalterably given, everything else is open to exploration. It seems to me that the taking over of Aristotelianism by the West got man back to a concern for the reality of nature and into the role of an observer intoxicating him at the same time with the dynamics of the newfound intellectual possibilities. Islam, on its part, had become fearful of the Aristotelian system and put on guard against the possible disintegration of its theological positions. Islam tried to use these Greek methods only to firm up theological formulations, and it must be admitted that in the late eleventh century the neatness of Muslim theological argument and presentation was greatly improved—some fifty years before the same process begins in the West.

It is a puzzling question why the Muslims, despite the fact that their basic materials were richer than those accessible to the Christians, did not move toward a "scientific revolution" as the West did. This problem, of course, has intrigued all students of Islam. A full explanation cannot be given, as it is difficult indeed to unravel the multiple motivations and causes behind the historical process. Perhaps our own intellectual shifts will elude historians of the year 2500, abundant documentation notwithstanding. We can, however make certain observations.

I have already referred to the restricted use the Muslim theologians made of Aristotelianism. It is a peculiar coincidence that at this very moment of history, the Muslim community, including the intellectuals, became wary of being original. Original investigation became more closely identified with dissent and alienation in Islam than in Christianity, the latter proving better able, though not, of course, without bitter conflicts, to absorb the new spirit of inquiry within its framework of theology. Muslim scholars concentrated more and more on filling in the gaps left by the classics, Greek and Muslim, and the tone of intellectual work in Islam came to be one of subservience to the ancients. The Muslim scholars and scientists cultivated the heritage of classical learning, while in the West, theologians and scholars alike began to take the attitude that revelation left many areas open to examination and dispute. The means that Aristotelianism provided for a more thorough investigation and a more systematic ordering of nature gave an enthusiastic impetus in the West to creative "branching out" and the general intellectual tone of undaunted reconsideration.

This, then, is one of the at present not fully explainable problems of medieval history. At the very moment that Islam reached its intellectual height, it became fearful of upsetting the intellectual scaffolding, while the West on the basis of practically the same materials spurted forward to a new era of investigation and discovery.

The Muslim community has been accused of overloading some professional endeavors at the expense of others in the Middle Ages. For example, the Muslims developed many legal experts but left the field of medicine largely to Jews and Christians. The study of human anatomy and of the workings of the body in general was regarded as almost useless. There was little investigation for investigation's sake in Islam. Such investigation was not banned; it was just regarded as a waste of time. The Arab scholars came to believe that curiosity is no virtue in itself but is justified only when serving a specific purpose. The peculiar switchover from the overt curiosity of the eighth and ninth centuries and even of the eleventh century to the later pragmatic "don't-rock-the-boat" attitude is not easily explainable. One might ask, Why did people make such a choice against their own better practical interests?

I believe that in the tenth and eleventh centuries the structure of orthodox Islam was greatly endangered by the Shiite extremists. It was in a precarious position both intellectually and politically. We know from various sources that the Shiite philosophies, which were more directly exposed to Hellenistic influence than the orthodox segment of Islam, were highly attractive to many of the best minds of the period, and they were also pushed forward by a keen sense of their importance. There is a poem by an early (Fatimid) Shiite which runs to the effect that the Shiites are "young" and will sweep the orthodox hierarchy and their rulers into the ashcan. This attitude found many adherents at the time, and the movement caught on. The reaction of orthodox Islam was to seek consolidation and to redefine its basic tenets in a conservative reform movement. As I have said before, the perfection of theological discussion increased considerably. The attitude taken was that the community had to continue whether or not science could be cultivated and good government achieved. The period was one of economic and political disruption. But religion, the theological self-consciousness of the community, had to be preserved at any cost. In addition, the community had to be assured a political and social structure within which it could function. Thus, the rival law schools attempted to smooth out the differences among themselves to suppress possible civil strife. Private persons and princes alike labored to solidify the fabric of law, the basis of tradition. The best minds were poured into this project, and the state finances assisted the expensive operation. This heavy investment aimed to firm up the framework of traditional social thought; this endeavor generally precluded the appropriation of talent and money to the natural sciences. The primary objective was to keep the community intact through troubled times; everything else was secondary and outright dangerous.

When the Shiite challenge to orthodoxy thinned out, the Mongols came on the scene, intensely destructive for the first decades of their raids and rule. Muslim intellectuality, then, acquired a tone of apprehensiveness, a pragmatic attitude aimed at preserving the community. The yardstick for relevance in Muslim intellectual endeavor was whether or not a line of thought or a program would serve to maintain the social and political integrity of the community.

The rise of mysticism, later the proliferation of mystical orders in the Muslim world, both expressed and contributed to anti-intellectualism. Not every mystic, of course, was an obscurantist. Generally speaking, however, people whose primary concern is with intuitive insights and with the peculiar sensation of getting beyond this world, are not interested in investigating the world of natural phenomena and developing science. Their concentration is wholly somewhere else.

Islam has always tried to regulate life under God by the law. Inevitably, there is a measure of dryness, pedantry, soullessness in legalism, and many of the truly pious felt that something was missing. The daily forms of Muslim devotion did not in any sense insure the immediate, saving communication with the Divine which they sought. From the ninth century on—and that is not to say that this trend began just at this time—little circles of mystics grew up to which the immediate revelatory experience became more important than the ordered preservation of the orthodox Muslim community. These nuclei of mysticism increased in size and importance with the political turmoil of the period. In the tenth century, there grew up an immense variety of intellectual schools and tensions. It is by far the most interesting era of Muslim intellectual development. The path of the mystics began to be systematized in religious books describing just how to work out this unique mode of access to the transcendental.

In a way, mysticism in this period stood for something egalitarian and democratic. The study of the law was difficult and required a great deal of time and money. It was nothing that could grip the masses. Mysticism, in a somewhat simplified form, can. Certain peak experiences were alleged to be accessible to all—many people in this period thought that with the proper training nearly everyone could reach the ultimate religious goal of contact with the Divinity.

The disintegration of social structure lent momentum to the spread of mysticism. The first brotherhood with some continuity in terms of property ownership and intellectual teachings is traceable in the twelfth century. Before this period, the groupings were somewhat less formalized. The mystical brotherhoods tended to become the real spiritual home of the people, and this went so far that in nineteenth-century Turkey, for example, practically every adult male in the Turkish-speaking areas was a member of a mystical organization. The same would be true of Egypt and the same is true today for the Sudan and, to turn to a different section of the Muslim world, for Senegal.

The individual orders represent different types of mystical experience, different attempts at rationalizing it, different manners in reaching the Divine. Some are more contemplative, others more ecstatic. Some are organized as a formal hierarchy transmitted from generation to generation; others are less structured. But there is no doubt that from the middle of the twelfth century on, in spite of the many reservations uttered by orthodox theologians, the mystical version of Islam becomes more and more the true religion of the people.

One curious side note to all this is the fact that as a mystical order became more established, it was caught up in the day-to-day administration of the properties sustaining a structurally increasingly complex enterprise. This is not true of the formative era of mysticism, but the rebels will often become the establishment, and the mystical brotherhoods once confirmed as ongoing entities found themselves ever more closely involved with the momentary social and political conditions of their community. In reviewing their significance, let me say once again that the mystical attitude is largely antithetical to the scientific attitude.

Is there any continuity of theme or form between the great literary achievements of medieval Islam and the literature subsequently produced in the West?

Practically every trait of later Western and Islamic romanticism is adumbrated in Hellenistic poetry. As with all the heritage reaped by Arabic literature from the Greek, the earliest phase that we know must have occurred has not left any, or only the barest trace of, documentation. We find the thread of romantic love motifs in pre-Islamic poetry, and it is found considerably stronger in the Umayyad period because this dynasty ruled large areas that for centuries had been exposed to Greek culture.

In the early Abbasid age a number of poems seem to anticipate somewhat bewilderingly the major motifs of troubadourial literature. This strain disappears or is submerged in the East fairly soon, but it comes to the surface again in tenth-century Spain with the spread and efflorescence of Islamic culture. The real birth, however, of the troubadourial patterns in Muslim Spain dates from the beginning of the eleventh century.

It is indeed astonishing that precise details of prosody and poetical form (but much less of content) did cross the language barrier between Islam and Christendom. The parallels between the motif patterns and forms of "troubadour" poetry in Spain and in the Christian Provence and northern France do suggest an interchange of cultural elements. It is highly unlikely that systems of poetry of such similarity should have developed in full independent of one another. The bilingual and bicultural Christian population of Muslim Spain must be viewed as the most likely transmitter.

In southern France one has occasion to see how this interchange of poetic forms was effected. In the eleventh century the worship of the Virgin Mary had spread very much in the opulent area of the Provence. This religious fact was accompanied by the social fact of the well-born woman acquiring a considerably greater role than she had been playing during the preceding centuries. Social realities and the Hellenistic tradition transmitted through Ovid as well as less directly through Arabic poetry gave their impetus to the art of the troubadours. I do not wish to underplay the contribution of the Provençal poet, yet the similarities in structure, form, and motifs are too strong to prevent the assumption that the poetic techniques of troubadour song and more particularly of their love poetry were worked out spontaneously in the Provence.

Where, then, is the reality that links these poetic creations on both sides of the Pyrenees? Did the Muslim social setting offer any traits conducive to the revival and sustenance of Hellenistic romantic ideals and the subsequent spread of these ideals to the West? The distinctiveness of Muslim Spain must here be remembered; for as a colonial country it presents a situation different from the rest of the Arab world.

As an intellectually colonial area, Spain took all its cues from the East until the middle of the tenth century. With the disintegration of the East and with its own coming of age, Spain continued its own development of Arab poetry in a very specialized way: Spanish poetry was court poetry, poetry about nature and love. It was in Spain that strophic forms within Arabic poetry were born. This was a departure from the strict metrical traditions of previous Arab poetry. Strophic poetry was exceedingly rare in the East, but it was to become very popular in the West. Innovations in Islamic Spanish poetry can be attributed partly to the curious intellectual and social amalgam that was Muslim Spain which gave rise to several divergent cultural configurations integrating indigenous (alternately classical) Arab traditions.

Would you comment on the qualities and the contributions of Arab historiography?

I suppose that one could say that the highest achievements of Arab historiography are cast in the forms of annals and chronicles. The beginnings of Arab historiography are concerned with the life and deeds of the Prophet. It seems that the first annals were almost exclusively concerned with the campaigns of Mohammed, but obviously other data must have been collected simultaneously. Withing a hundred and fifty years of Mohammed's death, we have the unsurpassed biography of the Prophet, and by 800 there is in existence a massive body of material dealing with the formative era of Muslim expansion.

Much of Arab historiography is concerned with the securing of legal precedents and justifications for present activities and actions. If history tells you that in conquering country *X*, property was handled in such and such a manner—it gives the legislative and executive branches of government a framework from which to work out comparable situations. Precedents are thus established for land distribution, taxation, and methods of administration. The historian's task was, in part, to help erect a comprehensive, consistent, legal system around which an expanding empire could grow. The subjective viewpoints from which historical data were collected varied greatly from area to area and period to period, but the form remained fairly constant.

The biographies of the Prophet were no doubt influenced by Christian hagiography. However, each of these biographies displayed the imprint of the locale in which it was composed. In fact, stories and incidents would at times be manipulated to reflect favorably or to their disadvantage on contemporary personages or groups by showing their ancestors as the sympathizers of the Prophet or as incurring his displeasure.

The possibilities for polemics within this kind of literature were myriad. From our vantage point, it is often difficult to dissociate truth from fiction. I would not like to give the impression, however, of deliberate inaccuracy as a constant in Arab historiography. When a history of the Prophet is written, the temptations to partisanship are many; in plain history, the author's outlook will still show but the manipulation is considerably less—caliphs come and go but history as the collective memory remains.

The greatest and certainly the longest and most comprehensive history of the classical days is Ṭabarī's (d. 923) *Annals of Prophets and Kings*. Unfortunately very little of his work has been translated into Western languages. His technique of presentation was perhaps defective as historiography but extremely useful for our own studies. When Ṭabarī was faced with two different reports on an identical event, he just put them side by side and left it to the reader to decide. Thanks to this method, we are often able to separate the several political viewpoints, regional prejudices, and also various schools of historiography, and in many cases to understand the rationale of their distinctiveness. More often than not we are also assisted in getting to the heart of the facts by a careful analysis of the conflicting reports.

The horizon of most Muslim historiography is strictly Muslim history—Europe is hardly ever discussed. In addition, the local historians who wrote about their own province or town also largely excluded from their narrative the non-Muslim groups. What we do know about the minority communities is garnered from surviving documents, tax rolls, and the like. Or we may read historical accounts written within the minority groups themselves in almost the same exclusive manner. But in the aggregate this literature does afford a remarkably accurate perspective on the events of each period.

A little later, perhaps beginning in the eleventh century, we meet historians of considerable stylistic power. Ṭabarī retains the style of his source. He was very conscientious, a good collector, and he left the material as he found it. But a Miskawaih (d. 1030) in addition knew how to write. His sources were largely documents, and many of the events that he examines in his works he had in fact participated in. He belonged to that class of professional officials which had controlled the administration since early Abbasid times—so he knew how to evaluate the documents he was using. He, too, like most Arab historians, keeps to the annalistic mode of reporting, but he transcends it by narrative skill and enriches his tale by portraits of the actors matchlessly drawn.

One further observation—the great literary-historical science of the Muslims was biography (rather than history proper). The numerous surviving works of this genre portray nearly all social categories within Muslim culture: rulers, theologians, soldiers, and intellectuals. We have thousands of sketches of a biographical nature which vary greatly in style and in quality but which taken together represent a passkey into Muslim culture. The biography is no doubt the supreme cultural contribution of the Muslim Middle Ages.

We can assume in general that the bureaucracy and administration of the Islamic state was derived from Roman and Byzantine antecedents and that much of their political thought is under the influence of Persian ideas. Would you explain how this system worked, emphasizing the unique contributions and developments of the Islamic period.

Well, for one thing, I would like to omit the word *Roman*. It is true that much of the Roman tradition has come through Byzantium, but it is surprising how little in general survived from the Latin tradition as such; this may not be entirely true for Muslim Spain, but it does hold for the Muslim world as a whole.

As for continuity and distinctiveness, one should first of all not underrate what it means to change the language of administration from Persian or Greek to Arabic and to adjust foreign ideas to different situations and needs. Besides, to some extent, internal administrative continuity was established in most sections of the Muslim world as locally rulers tended to come from the same section of society.

Many of the social conflicts in Islam were worked out within or by means of the administration. It is very likely that there were vicious political fights over the control of administration between the people of Christian or ex-Christian ancestry and the people of Persian ancestry or affiliation in the period from 870 to 950. The true nature of this social conflict was submerged in the processes of political maneuvering. Yet one can see that each faction had resonance from a wider stratum of the populace. While the feuding coteries or parties were generally loyal to the central administration, they provided one way in which the Persian and other non-Arab or non-Muslim influences could assert (or reassert) themselves politically on the local level as well as in the capital.

Secondly, Islamic law has evolved a peculiar tax system whose theoretical structure tends to disguise its connection with the Byzantine, although it shares its discriminatory taxation of religious dissenters and the basic concept of its land tax. Its inability to cope adequately with commercial and industrial and altogether with urban income was, however, its own. A more obvious difference was in the fundamental principle of Muslim administration. The Muslim state separated, whenever possible, civil administration and military administration. There were a few governors who had full military and civil power (including the right to collect taxes) within their provinces, but on the whole, the central government tried to secure the allegiance of the provinces by dividing military and civil power. Byzantium, for security reasons, gave the local governors total power over provinces, which were small, compact political units. In the Muslim world, however, the administrative units were very large and not significantly broken up.

The Muslim law, in its original conception of a tax system, did not take into account an urban economy. Lawful taxes, or more exactly the taxes whose justification is anchored in scripture or in early tradition, bear on land, certain customs duties, and on the taxation of the protected unbeliever. The early traditions give no workable clue to the appropriate taxing of trade profits, urban real estate, industrial production, nor do they provide an income tax. In practice, the demands of the state were in the beginning and through the "good" period of the caliphs not overly oppressive; but from the tenth century on, shrinking resources clashed with growing needs. The customs duties affected few people and certainly did not impede trade, and the taxation imposed in return for religious protection was compensated by exemption from military service, a safety measure rather than a reward; it is true, though, that the exact purchasing value of the imposts is hard to assess. Nevertheless, as long as this tax system worked as intended, it seems to have been strict but, disregarding occasional excesses, not harsh.

In this connection, I might reiterate that there was a tax not on income but on property. This was a charge of approximately 2½ percent; if you owned 40 camels, you would be asked to "donate" one. In theory, the government may use the income from this impost only for purposes of social assistance such as the relief of Muslim persons, the construction of public works, a pension system, and so on.

From the time of the caliph Omar (634–644), that is to say, a few years after Mohammed's death (632), there was established a list of all Arab Muslims according to their position in society, date of conversion, kinship to the Prophet and his tribe, and so on. Upon examination of each Muslim's credentials, he was awarded a pension. Where applicable the pension entailed military duty. Gradually, with the decrease of the relative importance of Arab fighters in the army in favor first of northeast Persians, later of Turks, the recipients of these pensions diminished in number until in 831 pensions were abolished altogether except for payments to descendants of the Prophet. This pension system has no equivalent within Byzantine administration.

The Muslim government was not always a successful householder. The loopholes in the system of taxation, the looseness of control over the outlying provinces, and the increasingly stiff demands of the mercenary armies put the government in the uncomfortable position of having rising costs and falling income. The government was forced to levy new taxes for which scriptural justification could not be found; time and again a new government would come in and abolish the "illegal" taxes only to have to reinstate them a short while after. It must be remembered that both "lawful" and "unlawful" taxes were largely modeled on the observer practices of the neighboring countries. In Byzantium, too, the land tax was the mainstay of state finance. As already suggested, the Byzantines also imposed a tax upon unbelievers. As in Islam, this tax was collected from the individual through the community. The customs rates were discriminatory: the rates for Muslims, for nonbelieving subjects of Islam, and for alien unbelievers were in a proportion of 1 : 2 : 3. For example, a Muslim merchant coming back from an export-import expedition might pay 5 percent of value, a merchant who was a non-Muslim subject paid 10 percent, and a foreign non-Muslim, 15 percent. Practice did not always insist on carrying out the stipulations; in any case, the rates collected did not appear to have been prohibitive.

It seems to me that the manner in which the caliphate of Baghdad was ruled in the ninth and tenth centuries was rather original. Theoretically the remains of the central government of the eastern Muslim Empire were to be ruled by a number of boards and ministries. Each province had an administrative representative in the capital. The bureaucratic divisions were made both by subject matter, such as taxation, accounting, or affairs of court, and by region. This crisscross concept of administration, had it worked, would have indeed been a masterly system. However, because of breakdowns in the capital and disloyalties in the provinces, the system failed. The fact remains, though, that the concept of provincial administrative representation in central government was a remarkable innovation.

Islamic law allows no exemptive privilege. In the Christian West, the medieval towns were products of exemptive privilege; the territory of the town was exempted from the jurisdiction of the lord of the surrounding region. No such concept existed in Islam, and without it the corresponding concept that the (exempted) city territory had to set up its own autonomous administrative machinery could not arise. The city authorities were just as much direct appointees of the central government as any other.

The cities were no doubt the nuclei of Muslim life—the economic, political, and cultural centers of gravity—but they were, in theory, and as much as possible in practice, not treated differently from any other part of the Muslim community. Naturally, there were no guilds or urban militias in the countryside, so reality and theory conflicted to a certain extent. But the city was not exempted from the jurisdiction of whatever representative of the central government, civilian or military, had charge in its area. Beyond the recognition of a specifically urban crafts and market control and a jurisdiction to enforce it, Muslim law did not deal explicitly with urban problems; as a consequence, perhaps, one notes not infrequently a certain clumsiness in dealing with urban matters.

Islam began as a ruling minority; pluralism of religious affiliation was natural and unquestioned. There were, of course, attempts at forceful conversion but these were rather rare and always confined to restricted areas. The eschatological hope that before the Last Day would dawn all would have been converted was strong, but this expectation did not make conversion of mankind a direct concern of the government.

In the period we have been discussing, Islam did not undergo the transition from personal to territorial jurisdiction that was so characteristic of certain parts of Europe. Muslim law was strictly personal in nature: this meant not that one did not have to obey the local representative of the central government, but that you were born into a set of laws that in regulating the status of your religious community also regulated your immediate personal status, and that if you did not change your community affiliation, you stayed within these rules. The law of the Christian communities excluded polygamy, but a Muslim having several wives would stay within his. Local custom and kinship arrangements would tend to supersede and prevail over any central, all-encompassing set of laws, although it must have been difficult to adhere to "personal" law in certain circumstances. A merchant from Fes in trouble in Medina could not expect to be judged by the rules of his far-removed, native community.

The non-Muslim communities living in Arab territory tried to block out a similar system of local autonomy—that is to say, their religious or traditional law prevailed internally wherever it did not come into conflict with Muslim law. In external controversies, Muslim authorities did intervene. It was possible, however, to appeal a local decision to higher Muslim authorities and thus cross from the laws of one section within Islam to another.

If you were a non-Muslim, your property, the exercise of your religion within certain limits, your safety and personal freedom, unless you were a slave, were guaranteed in return for your acceptance of a kind of second-class citizenship. Non-Muslims were not allowed to rise to the high executive office on the level of governmental policy making, and it was generally forbidden for non-Muslims to carry arms. The government had the right to appoint the head of a non-Muslim community, usually on presentation; these positions must have been very influential, as a good deal of bribing occurred. Owing to surviving documents, we have a good picture of how this system worked in Egypt from 1150 to 1250, during part of which time Maimonides and his son were at the head of the Jewish community. Incidentally Maimonides wrote a number of private letters, and we cannot help but be struck by the curious ambivalence he maintained toward the Muslem regime. He is obviously pleased with his high position at court, but, at the same time, he is depressed by his precarious position in the Muslim community. He actually says in one of his letters that the Jews are better off under the Christians than under the Muslims. Maimonides' statement may well have been in error, but it shows that a great deal of irritation on both sides must have been the rule under the Muslim system.

The Jews, of course, were a conspicuous and fortunate minority. They were highly respected in court and firmly established in the professions and the intellectual life. In addition, they had international trade connections extending from Spain and Tunis to Egypt and on across the Indian Ocean. This succesful coexistence of the Jews with the Muslim majority could not, however, allay a constant sense of uncertainty. Still, one can say that the acceptance of pluralism assured the survival of the minorities in the Muslim world.

How would you characterize the lifestyles and patterns of culture of the Muslim administrative classes?

High officials certainly were quite well off. In contemporary consciousness their standard of living rated rather high. On the whole, the standard of living seems to have been satisfactory for great segments of the urban population. The difference between urban and rural conditions was as glaring as it has continued to be till today.

We do have records of none-too-rare incidents of social unrest, and it would not be rash to assume that economic difficulties helped to bring these about. One reads frequently about the uncertainties of governmental policy, the uncertainties of trade routes and harvests, but apparently there were no universal economic crises to shake the Arab world. Baghdad in the ninth and into the tenth century must have been very prosperous, and Cairo from perhaps the eleventh into the fourteenth century was amazingly so. Between 1300 and 1340, Cairo underwent a huge physical expansion. Following this period, however, Cairo shrank, as had begun to happen in Baghdad as early as the end of the tenth century, with the city less and less able to fill out its walled spaces.

In the great days of the empire, there were two different kinds of intelligentsia, two different kinds of education. There were also a few educational "systems" outside the mainstream. These were cultivated by the small segments of society that acquired a Greek-inspired, philosophical education usually coupled with some professionalism. The public able and willing to listen to philosophical disquisition must have been quite substantial in tenth-century Baghdad and in comparable centers as well.

The more prevalent educational system was curiously centered in religious studies—the law and theology were and could not be strictly separated. One was trained in the data of the Muslim religion and in the auxiliary sciences needed to understand and develop the workings of theology. Grammar is a prime example of the importance of the auxiliary sciences; without grammar and lexicography, it is impossible to understand the Koran and the prophetic tradition. And, without the understanding of these traditions, understanding the law would be impossible. Thus, a whole cluster of the so-called Arab sciences developed that were designed to facilitate the understanding of the religious materials and which grew themselves to be independent and worthwhile studies.

This educational system, then, turned around the theological nucleus. One would need to become versed in ancient poetry, for example, in order to learn lexicography (among other things), and poetry would in turn lead the student to the Arabs' pre-Islamic past and to genealogy. History or political geography fits into the category of Arab science as well. Without the detailed knowledge of the imperial provinces, or the delineations of the imperial roads, the Arab administration would not have been able to function.

In this form of education, the law was the skeleton of the faith. An orientation toward the developing and the administering of the faith was both motivation and purpose and necessarily drew in the supplementary examination of certain other areas of learning. On the other hand, there were foreign sciences inherited from classical antiquity which were not really needed in religious fulfillment. These include the natural sciences and philosophical studies. Incidentally, there was debate as to where medicine, history, and political theory belonged and to what extent the study of logic was legitimate.

The other major form of education was considerably more humanistic in outlook and tone. In this system the concentration was upon literary studies and the development of style in the widest sense of the word—style of thinking, writing, speaking, and behaving. At every turn it betrays Persian influence, which is not to suggest that Persians had no share in forming the religious sciences. This system was in fact to a point an alternative to a religious education, although it included a good measure of specifically Muslim materials. Its proponents viewed it as a body of intellectual and behavioral patterns which made life in court more refined, less boorish, and less boring.

This educational system was socially important. It established a connecting link between the rulers and those of their educated subjects who were not of the religious class. But in shaping the ways of the court and of polite society altogether, it provided a style of life and manners that could form a link between the more devout and the more worldly. *Adab* is a culture of form rather than a culture of subject matter, an education wide open to history, to legends, to traditional folklore and narrative of all sorts. For man, his idiosyncracies and foibles are intensely interesting to it, and so are wit and elegance in debate. This humanistic trend did not take as firm a hold nor did it have the depth or intensity of the later European Renaissance, but it was far superior to anything the Arabs had earlier produced along these lines.

These two types of education, almost of culture, were separate and recognized as such even though there was a great deal of contact and crossing between them. The contemporaries clearly distinguished between the *'Ālim,* the person of religious and legal training, and the *Adīb,* the person who lived by belles-lettres, political theory, and Persian manners. As long as this dual educational system existed, the cultural stability and cohesiveness of the Muslim world was assured. Later, with the ascendancy of ruling groups that were neither Arab nor Persian, and that were not wholly assimilated into the ethos of Islam and the possibilities of its civilization, this cultural link between the masters and the educated was severed. A constructive connection between ruler and ruled thus disappeared, and this loss of connection is one key factor in the decline and sterilization of Muslim culture in the later Middle Ages. (You may view *Adab* as similar in its connective functions to French Classicism in the era of Louis XIV when it linked the court and the *grande bourgeosie.* In France, however, the connective proved more durable.) With the dissolution of this cultural link, the only tie between the later military rulers of the Arab countries and their subjects was religion. There were a number of remarkable cultural figures in Mamluk Egypt but the type of society that we have been discussing in the caliph's court of the tenth century was already dissolving. The decline of Muslim culture in the late Middle Ages is due largely to the barbarization of the ruling classes.

The Mamluks holding power in Egypt and Syria from the middle of the thirteenth century were people who had as children been imported into the Muslim domain as slaves from the steppes of Europe and Asia. Upon the fulfillment of their apprenticeship and their subsequent manumission, they entered the ruling class. The Mamluks sought to guarantee their descendants a measure of social preeminence. They established foundations to assure them the power of an inheritance. Very early the Mamluks struck out as sponsors and founders of mosques and colleges in the area of religious studies until they gained if not intellectual, at any rate administrative, control of this segment of education.

When after the middle of the fourteenth century the Mamluks became impoverished, they attempted to ease the financial straits of the state by confiscating the foundations supporting the schools of religious studies. This toppled the fabric of the religious sciences, and prospective students channeled themselves instead into commercial activities. The economic shrinkage of Egypt from about 1340 on had a direct and traceable influence on the decline of learning.

How did economic life in tenth- and eleventh-century Islam function; what were the economic bases of society?

Again, I must preface anything I might say by pointing out that the enormous area and diversity, not to mention the time span, of the Muslim empire precludes any sweeping generalizations. The economic ups and downs are for the most part local phenomena and rarely reflect widespread and consistent trends.

If one must generalize, however, it may be said that the cities were governmental and military bases—making them in a sense the economic centers of Islam. The equipping of the armies, the principal expenditure of the government and military, was the task of the city. In addition, the major cities such as Baghdad, Damascus, and Cairo, were seats of lavish, wasteful courts where conspicuous consumption was the dominant style. Hence, again, a good deal of work for artisans and manufacturers. In areas that bestrode major trade routes, there was much local and international commerce. Cairo had an important share in this exchange of goods and credit as did Baghdad and Alexandria.

The economic vibrancy of the cities was often contingent upon rural holdings. A good proportion of the land surrounding a city was generally owned by the urban residents. People tended to spend the money they earned from the land in and on the towns. The city dwellers often gave of their time to oversee their rural investments—if they did not prefer the role of the "absentee landlord"—to make sure of their tenants. The city thus often came close to a parasitic exploitation of the land. Besides, as already suggested, the city had the income from commerce, governmental contracts, and other activities not transferable to a rural setting, such as the manufacture of textile, the principal industry of the age. It was also the natural center of education and learning.

There was a general but uneven decline in prosperity in the Islamic heartlands in the later Middle Ages. In Baghdad and the fruitland of Iraq, this decline had started with the neglect of the irrigation systems, beginning late in the tenth century with the constant civil warfare in this area.

The decline of economic and intellectual endeavor should not be overemphasized, however. It would have been impossible for the later Middle Ages to have been at least as productive in the quantity of its religious, scientific, and literary writings as the earlier period of Muslim culture without the continued support of a leisure class that was concerned with these cultural achievements. As so frequently, but by no means always, intellectual and economic upsurge tended to be closely linked in the Muslim domain.

One more important point must be made. Islam's peculiar system of army remuneration was ruinous to the state. When in the ninth and tenth century the caliphs remunerated their mercenary generals with grants of land, they did not insist that these men become resident lords. The generals soaked the land immediately for all it was worth and ruined it. They then demanded other land. The European lord, at least, protected his holdings and his peasants out of self-interest. He could not move on to ever-virgin plots of land, so he was bound to make the best of what he had. At most, he would establish a sub fief, but he was never totally removed from his domain and the responsibility of tilling it conscientiously. The Muslim soldier barons, on the other hand, were absentee landlords of the worst sort; land was part of their payment and they had the power to compel replacement. (Here you have the essential reason for the ruin of Iraq.)

Would you discuss the reasons for political instability in large segments of the Muslim empire?

Political instability was certainly a problem, especially as religious law had no precepts to offer on this count. The new ruler could be chosen by a committee or commission again appointed by the departing ruler. There was one final possibility—force. He to whom God gives the power holds it as of right: the community could not do without that legitimacy of which the ruler is the guarantor. Curiously it was impossible for custom to solidify one set of succession rules such as primogeniture without division of territories to settle once and for all the ever-present threat of civil war on a prince's death.

Contributory to this heritage of governmental instability was the fractionalism caused by the manner in which the ruler dealt with his lands. Since protection from without and order within was all that was expected of him, little heed was paid to integrating the often heterogeneous and accidentally acquired areas under one hand. Localism was rife. Loyalty went to religion and culture; political allegiance rarely went beyond casual obedience. The Muslim masses and the Muslim elites had less hesitation about changing things by means of force than most of their contemporaries and certainly much less than stated religious and political principles would lead one to expect. The West at this time was very unruly, too, but it would seem with less unconcern and more deeply devoted to ideas of hierarchical stability.

Muslim communities in the late Middle Ages became increasingly less interested in the turmoil caused by rulers as long as they provided security from foreign invaders and preserved the people from the encroachments of the unbelievers. This kind of indifference is a legitimation of revolt; civil uprisings and military usurpations in the towns were bewilderingly frequent. In the Syrian cities of the tenth and eleventh centuries, the rise of citizen militias that shared the power with the appointed governors gave for a brief period the hope of self-rule. But the professional armies of the territorial dynasts won out. The habit of violence continued, though, making a stable administration a rare occurrence and establishing that habituation to crisis which is still so characteristic of the Fertile Crescent.

10

Medieval Culture

R. W. SOUTHERN

THE HISTORIOGRAPHICAL CONTEXT

The revelation of the facets of medieval Western European cultural and intellectual history was initially, and still largely, an achievement of German scholarship. In the first four decades of this century, German medievalists—some of whom had to seek refuge in the United States in the Nazi era—brought their vast learning and passionate industry to bear on the complex interaction of medieval political-social institutions and the heritage of Christianity and classicism. They exhibited for the first time what were the actual ingredients of the ecclesiastical-centered "spirit" of the Latin Christian world.

The weakness of medieval German scholarship was a tendency to elitism and abstraction. In the Hegelian mode, they concentrated too exclusively on higher thought, on pure ideas, and on the political and intellectual elite. In the 1940's and 1950's these limitations were, at least in part, corrected by the work of two brilliant English historians—David Knowles and R. W. Southern—who focused on popular piety and individual personalities as well as on higher thought and the categories of elitist culture. Southern's *The Making of the Middle Ages* (1953) may plausibly be claimed as the single best book ever written on medieval church and culture. A series of extremely perceptive and sensitive pictures of the actual meaning of Christian culture in the functioning of medieval government and society was presented in highly sympathetic and compelling fashion to the lay reader and undergraduate student.

Richard Southern typifies all that is best in twentieth-century British scholarship. Born in 1912, and graduating from Oxford in 1932, Southern was a student of F. M. Powicke, who in the latter part of his long academic career turned from rather pedestrian institutional analysis to a more rewarding, if not quite successful study of the life-style and world view of the thirteenth-century nobility. Southern belongs to the last generation of English scholars who did no formal graduate work. Research fellowships sustained his inquiries into medieval culture until in 1937 he became Fellow and Tutor of Balliol College, Oxford. In this capacity, until he was given a distinguished chair in 1961, he introduced Oxford undergraduates to medieval history and was famed as a brilliant teacher. Southern is now President of St. John's College, Oxford. He is a beautiful Englishman—tall, handsome, delicate in health, mellifluous in voice—reminiscent of the Romantic poets of the nineteenth century. He is almost entirely self-taught and completely independent in judgment. He really loves the Middle Ages; he is perfectly competent in contemporary society, but obviously has no liking for it. Only in the late 1950's, after repeated invitations, could he bring himself to visit that bastion of modern materialism, the United States. Southern's delicate eyes can ignite with fury at the foibles and defects of other scholars. He is extremely generous and warm to his students, but sets standards for them that none can meet. To the best of the German scholars, history was a science and a profession, to be organized and advanced; to the best of the English scholars (at least before the 1960's), history was the highest kind of art, a calling for a chosen few of genius. Southern is perhaps the last of this kind of English poetic historian.

Chronological Outline

768–814: Reign of Charlemagne. Centralization of the Frankish monarchy, theocratic rule over the Frankish Church and the revival of learning under the direction of Alcuin.

787–925: The ninth-century invasions. Bands of Norsemen push far into France, and the Muslims gain control of all northern Africa and the Mediterranean basin.

814–887: Disintegration of the Carolingian empire upon the death of Charlemagne. In 843 the Treaty of Verdun divides the empire into three parts.

867: Decline of the papacy beginning after the pontificate of Nicholas and lasting until the second half of the eleventh century.

910: The founding of Cluny.

936–973: Reign of Otto the Great in Germany. Otto consolidates the feudal duchies, invades Italy, and is crowned king of the "Roman Empire" by the pope in 962.

987: Election of Hugh Capet as king of France initiates the Capetian dynasty.

1002: Henry II succeeds to the German throne and rules until 1024. The Salian and Hohenstaufen emperors rule until 1268.

1066: The Battle of Hastings. The Norman, William the Conquerer, invades Britain and establishes the most effective feudal monarchy of his time. The great Domesday survey is made in 1086.

1075–1122: The age of the Gregorian Reform—the extension of the reforming Cluniac impetus marked by the struggle over lay investiture between Henry IV of Germany and Pope Gregory. The excommunication and the penance of Henry in the snow at Canossa in 1077.

1090–1133: Life of Saint Bernard of Clairvaux, the most famous member of the Cistercian Order.

1100–1135: Reign of Henry I in Britain. Great expansion of royal administrative power.

1142: Death of Peter Abelard, a prime figure in the medieval controversy over universals, whose *Sic et Non* presented without solution the conflicting theological arguments on 158 important problems.

1152–1190: Reign of Frederick Barbarossa in Germany. Conflict with the papacy eventually forestalls German unification until the nineteenth century.

1154–1189: Henry II Plantagenet rules in Britain. Consolidation of the empire by inheritance, and his marriage with Eleanor of Aquitaine in 1152.

1198–1216: The zenith of the medieval papacy—the pontificate of Innocent III, a brilliant and effective administrator who works to restore the political power of the papacy. The Albigensian Crusade against the heretics of southern France.

1200–1225: The birth of the Mendicant Orders—the town-dwelling Franciscans and Dominicans meet the challenge of the growing anticlericalism of the new urban centers.

1214: The Battle of Bouvines. Philip II of France defeats the anti-Capetian alliance and catapults France to the first rank of feudal monarchies.

1215: The Magna Carta is sealed at Runnymede. The English barons enforce their rights under feudal contract with King John.

1226–1270: Reign of Louis IX (Saint Louis) in France.

1266–1308: Duns Scotus begins the advance of the Oxford Franciscans towards nominalism. William of Occam (d. c. 1349) extends this to a statement of extreme nominalism that effects a revolution in scholastic philosophy.

1274: Death of Thomas Aquinas, one of the greatest medieval theologians, whose *Summa Theologica* was an attempt to integrate classical learning and Christian theology.

1292: Death of Roger Bacon, the greatest medieval exponent of observation and experiment.

Norman F. Cantor
Was the Carolingian empire just another ineffective barbarian kingdom, or can it be credited with real accomplishments in church organization, learning, the development of kingship and of effective political institutions? What was its legacy to the tenth and eleventh centuries?

R. W. Southern

In practical affairs, the Carolingian structure was not nearly so effective as people used to think. It was a blueprint that could be given practical effect only imperfectly in that disorganized society. Nevertheless, in certain areas the Carolingian contribution was fundamental to the future development of Europe.

First of all, Carolingian scholars gathered together the material on which the later scholastic and intellectual development of Europe depended. They assembled the texts, began the process of organizing the classical inheritance, and made widely available manuscripts which had previously been confined to a few centers. Although it was not a period of original thought, the Carolingian era provided the material and some of the methods which later were used so successfully in the schools and universities.

Secondly, although the secular organization of the Carolingian empire did not stand up very well, the ecclesiastical organization established during this period was much more successful, particularly the organization of dioceses and parishes. By legislation about tithes, parochial organization, and ecclesiastical discipline, the Christian way of life was made obligatory, and certain standards of discipline were enforced. The papal administration was not very highly developed during this period, but in the infrastructure of the Church the Carolingian contribution was very effective.

Thirdly, the Carolingian contribution to the development of kingship was interesting even if it was not of lasting importance. Byzantine symbols and ways of thinking about government were transferred to the West, and although these did not survive in the long run, they did provide a certain temporary respectability to Western political life. And certain ideas proved suggestive in the future: the divine sanction of secular rule, the right of the secular ruler to control the Church, and the claim of the emperor to exercise a large voice in the direction of the papacy and the election of the pope.

There has been a tendency to exaggerate the importance of the Carolingian contribution to royal government. Historians who have concentrated on symbols and formulae as guides to the political thought of the Middle Ages have emphasized the continuance and importance of these symbols and formulae long after they ceased to be living realities. The mere continuance of forms did not mean that the ideas behind them stayed alive in western Europe. After the twelfth century, if not before, there was a rapid decline in the significance of these rituals and formulae in secular government. Nevertheless they provided a fund of symbols and ideas on which opponents of papal power could draw, and continued to draw, till the sixteenth century.

Two things were happening in the political and social world of the tenth and eleventh centuries: the intensification of the feudal framework and the growth of urban communities. What was the impact of these developments on church and empire?

To answer this question I must first say something about the relations of church and empire and the ways in which these relations changed.

The idea of imperial oversight over the papacy was appropriate enough in the underdeveloped Europe of the ninth century, especially when that control was slight and intermittent. In the eleventh century, however, the situation was quite different. The power of the emperor was recognized as flimsy in comparison with the growing power of local rulers and of the increasingly powerful papacy itself. Instead of a source of order in a chaotic political situation, the imperial authority came to be regarded as an intrusion into a new and growing political order.

Until the eleventh century, papal claims to primacy had been satisfied in the West by a very general and intermittent superiority admitted by all people and deeply cherished by local churches so long as it did not interfere with their traditional status. Emotionally and imaginatively, Rome's position was immensely strong: it was a center of pilgrimage and sentimental attachment, where people could go for advice and could feel they were in contact with the ancient world and with the earliest days of the Christian Church. However, this strength was not translated into administrative activity until the middle of the eleventh century, when there appeared in Rome a group of men who believed that the general papal supervisory power could be converted into a detailed power of governing and directing local churches. The "reform" of the Church was really a confrontation of two ages of government—a ritualistic age and an administrative age. I do not believe that the papal reformers of the eleventh century expressed any new ideas. Rather they gave their ideas a new look in practice and brought together systematically ideas which had been held together loosely and in a general way in previous centuries. The old idea of the primacy of Saint Peter was spelled out in detail and drawn up as a code of law and as a series of governmental claims, and this had an effect on all ecclesiastics and (to some extent) on every ruler in Europe.

I do not believe that this development was associated with feudalism, although feudalism was another aspect of the large-scale social change taking place in western Europe. This change partly consisted in the replacement of an ideal of government expressed in terms of ritual and ceremony by one expressed in terms of law and administration. But it also included the development of local powers based on military force and on the economic control of the services of the peasantry. These local powers had comparatively little to fear from the growth of papal power—unlike the emperors they were not competing in the same field of government, and they could watch the decline of imperial power, and even the confrontations between popes and kings, with equanimity and satisfaction. The growth of papal universal power, therefore, was made possible in the first place by the collapse of imperial pretensions and by the localization of all other secular powers, which had neither the will nor the power to resist to claims of the papacy.

What was the influence of urban life on ecclesiastical institutions and ideas at this time? I do not think that this influence was felt until much later, somewhere around the end of the thirteenth century. Nevertheless, the towns were important: they were both the expression and the cause of a growing ease of life in western Europe. The growth of wealth made possible the expansion of the scholastic institutions of the twelfth century, and these in turn were fundamental to the growth of the theoretical structure of the Western church.

What was the role of Cluny in church life and in reform? What was the relationship between Cluny and the papal reform of the eleventh century?

Cluny was probably the most successful and powerful monastic revival in medieval Europe. Its success depended on its clear idea of its own goals (its definite ideas about what a monastic order should be) and on the lay support which it received. To its lay benefactors, Cluny offered some hope of permanence in maintaining a high level of religious observance within the structure of monastic life. They could be sure of the prayers of the monks, of a place of burial for themselves and their families, and of a respectable place for any relatives who wished to join a monastic order.

No ecclesiastical reformer of any kind could doubt the value and aims of Cluny, which explains the appreciation and support of such Hildebrandine popes as Gregory VII and Urban II. Nevertheless, the aims of Cluny were not specifically those of the revived papacy, and in some respects the methods of Cluny were inimical to the methods of the papal reformers. The papacy aimed at the revival of papal authority and the systematic exercise of papal control over the Western church, and ultimately over the Church Universal. This did not contradict monastic reform, but the two were very different. Cluny made its great mark in the world when papal authority was at a very low ebb, and the reforming monks did not need papal power to achieve their successes; similarly, the revived papacy did not need Cluny. Cluny achieved its success with the cooperation of lay benefactors throughout Europe; the reformed papacy, on the other hand, achieved its ends despite the opposition of lay powers. The papal doctrine that the pope had the right to supervise the actions of lay rulers (if necessary, to depose them) made the friends of Cluny in some degree the enemies of the reformed papacy.

Another great aim of the reformed papacy was to supervise and to exercise control over every branch of the ecclesiastical life, including the monastic. Again, there was an area of concurrence: Cluny had been from the beginning a monastic order under the direct protection of the pope without intermediate episcopal interference. Protection, however, is not the same as control, and with the growth of papal claims friction developed between Cluny and Rome. This emerges very clearly from the letters of Peter the Venerable, in which the abbot rehearsed the great benefits brought to the papacy by the Cluniac order and the privileges which the popes had given to Cluny in return. Peter the Venerable promised the pope that Cluny's support would continue so long as the papacy continued to respect its privileges and immunities. He wrote to the pope almost as one sovereign authority to another. The incompatibility of temper between the pretensions of Cluny and those of the reformed papacy is very evident in these letters, but by this time Cluny had reached the end of its development so there was no opportunity for the conflict to develop.

To sum up, the Cluniac and Hildebrandine movements were different in their aims and to some extent conflicting in temper and associations. Cluny had no more conspicuous friends than the Tusculan popes of the first half of the eleventh century, who were anathema to Gregory VII and his friends. And by the first quarter of the twelfth century, when the reformed papacy was just coming into its stride, Cluny was a spent force. Essentially it neither helped nor hindered the growth of papal power.

It would seem that the more important members of the College of Cardinals in the second half of the eleventh century came from northern Italy or from Lorraine. What was there in the Church or in the intellectual or social situation in northern Italy or Lorraine to inspire the movement of reform?

I think that the really decisive influence here was the initiative of Leo IX in choosing men. It is almost impossible to overrate his achievement in bringing together a concentration of men dedicated to the development of papal claims and papal authority. I cannot see that the local situation had much to do with it. The two great men of the movement were Humbert, who came from Lorraine, and Gregory VII, from Rome. We do not know Humbert's scholastic background (his theoretical thinking reveals no particular finesse); his power lay not in his education but in his ferocious personal dedication to papal authority and in the truculence with which he was willing and able to express papal claims. Likewise, Gregory's schooling had little bearing on his ideas; he was a man of outstanding personal force and initiative and courage who was prepared to go to any length to forward the cause of papal authority. His association with the commercial aristocracy of Rome was important, but only because it provided him with the funds to raise the Romans in support of the pope.

To what extent was the twelfth-century papacy—its policy and its institutions and attitudes—a fulfillment of the ideals of the Hildebrandine period? To what extent was there change in the policy of the papacy?

There must always be change when grandiose plans drawn up in large (and perhaps sometimes too exuberant) terms are applied in detail. The men of the late twelfth century who developed the papal position, such as Alexander III, were men of quite different temperament from Gregory VII. They worked out details with which he would have had no sympathy, but they worked them out along the lines implicit in his *Dictatus Papae*.

Gregory's position was theoretically unformed in certain respects. He proclaimed the overriding authority of the papacy over the ecclesiastical and the secular hierarchy alike, but he left unclear the ways in which this was to be brought about. He sent out legates in all directions to hear cases; he urged them to refer cases to Rome; he attempted (unsuccessfully) to force bishops and archbishops to attend councils in Rome. In his attempts to extend control over the secular world, there were elements which scarcely added up to a coherent policy: his claim to feudal overlordship over England, similar claims to Corsica and Sardinia, his interest in the tribute paid by Poland and other countries on the edge of Europe, his concern to build up a body of *milites Santi Petri,* his vision of himself as the leader of some kind of expedition to the East, and his rather ambivalent dealings with the emperor (sometimes fairly friendly, at other times violent to an exaggerated extent). The variety of papal activity reflected a strong desire to press papal claims on every possible front without regard to theoretical coherence.

By contrast, Alexander III concentrated his energies on developing a legal system to cover a very wide area of secular and ecclesiastical life. In favorable circumstances it was a system capable of indefinite expansion. Alexander III certainly thought that secular rulers exercised their offices under papal supervision; but he was content to go as far as circumstances permitted and leave the full practical implementation of this theory to the future. He dealt with emergencies as they arose, but with a good deal more moderation and finesse than Gregory VII. Unlike Gregory he controlled a very formidable governmental machine, and his theories did not outrun his means of implementing them: their expression was perfectly adapted to the practical situation in which he found himself. The difference between him and Gregory VII was largely one of method and temperament, for after all they both believed that all power had been put into their hands by Christ for the government of the world as His deputies on earth.

What aspects of medieval culture, government, and scientific knowledge were affected by the Crusades? Do you see them as central or peripheral to the culture and society of the thirteenth century?

In every system there comes a point at which the system is tested and breaks down, and I see the Crusades in that light. In some ways the Crusades were a logical development of the theory of a united Christendom under papal authority: had it not been for the popes' initiative and constant preoccupation with the Crusades, they would probably have petered out after the fall of Jerusalem in 1187. The organization of the Crusade was the last great objective of a papally controlled Europe: their aim was nothing less than the total integration of the outside world into the Christian scheme.

Practically speaking, however, the Crusades were little more than interesting, tragic episodes in medieval history. They created a Latin kingdom in the Muslim world; they brought about interesting relations between eastern and western Christendom and between the Muslim world and the Christian world, but they remained quite peripheral to the development of Europe. I consider the Crusades significant chiefly as the testing point at which a great theory came up against the ineluctable resistance of facts.

In the late eleventh and early twelfth centuries there was a new kind of emotional attitude in Christian life, a new piety, a less formal religion, and a greater concern for the individual in literature. Why did this upheaval in religious feeling take place at that time? What was there in learning, in the Church, or in society that contributed to this phenomenon?

In its broadest sense, the movement you describe represented an increased interest in the natural world—an attempt to look scientifically on the natural world, to discover its construction, its laws, and its main features. The natural world necessarily, included man.

The movement existed and gained momentum in western Europe from the early years of the twelfth century onward. In a broad sense it was a continuing movement in Western history down to the present day. The first phase came to an end, however, in the late thirteenth century with the creation of great theoretical structures like the *Summa Theologica* of Aquinas, which combined the scientific interests of the previous centuries with the great structure of revealed religion. This structure contrasted very strongly with the way of life and the intellectual temper of the period from the seventh to the eleventh century when supernatural channels of causation and authority were the only channels that were thoroughly understood and valued.

Why did this change occur in the early twelfth century? First of all, the new society that was rapidly growing in numbers and in complexity required a new type of government by men trained to think about practical problems and their solution. Hitherto, government had worked by appealing to supernatural authority, to supernatural modes of proof in legal cases, and so on. But now what was needed was an elaboration of systematic law and practical expedients for enforcing it. This could only be carried out by men with some kind of academic training. Hence there was a growing demand for trained men, and this led to the rapid growth of schools and universities which were the center of all scientific progress.

The source of this natural understanding of men and the world was ancient thought and literature. By the end of the eleventh century that body of ancient learning had become thoroughly assimilated and could be purveyed to fairly large numbers of students in the schools. I look on various works of the early twelfth century, such as William of Conches's *Philosophia Mundi,* as expressions of the mastery of the Latin past. For the first time in five or six hundred years, people in western Europe could go on to develop in new ways the ancient methods of investigation and contemplation of the world as a natural organization. This tendency was given a tremendous impetus by the discovery of the texts of Greek science in the twelfth century. The translation of the scientific works of Aristotle, Galen, and Ptolemy introduced to the West a great and complex scientific view of the world. This was absorbed into the university curriculum and became part of the ordinary teaching of the schools in the thirteenth century.

The same kind of thing happened in the monastic life, where a similar spirit of scientific enquiry encouraged a new interest in man and his will. By the end of the eleventh century, monks felt oppressed by the weight of liturgical and formal religious observances. Why this occurred is not clear—I suppose that something which seems exciting when it is new and developing seems burdensome when it becomes an old routine. Perhaps it was nothing more complicated than this that caused monks in the late eleventh century to rebel against the weight of observances and to seek a new kind of personal freedom in the monastic life. The monastic movements of the late eleventh and twelfth centuries represented (at least in one of their aspects) a search for greater personal freedom within a monastic routine. When formalities and accretions are stripped away, man begins to investigate his own nature. In the eleventh and twelfth centuries this shift in emphasis from routine to the inner self was occurring throughout the monastic world. It is hard to say why it happened, but it is clearly connected with the general growth of scientific enquiry—the switch from ritual to reason—that I have described already.

You have talked about the improvement in government, about protomodern techniques in administration, about the new learning, and the new search for self. Was all this part of the same movement, or were there points of tension between bureaucracy and rationalism and the new feeling?

I have already indicated that the developments you mention were in some way part of this same movement. But of course they led men in different directions. I do not think that the divergence was deeply felt for quite a long time. Twelfth-century literature, for instance, includes a great deal of complaint and satire about the ways of governments, the habits and morals and avarice of administrators. But I think that this is largely superficial criticism by people who would themselves liked to have been in the positions of those whom they criticized. Although the search for order within and the search for order without are not the same thing and are in danger of clashing (social order may inhibit expression of the self), I see no development of a sense of basic hostility between the two until the fourteenth century. By then it was fairly clear that the great apparatus of law and government was getting nowhere; disorder was increasing more rapidly than the machine intended to repress it, and this produced a great disillusionment with government and with the processes of systematic thought. As a result, the great figures of the fourteenth century (Petrarch, for instance) who were taking further steps in the search for self-expression were in complete despair about the external search for order in government. This breakdown occurred quite late in the Middle Ages and was not conspicuous until the last years of the thirteenth century.

What exactly was the issue between Saint Bernard and Abelard? Were they in dispute about values and what should be done in the Church and culture, or was this largely a personality difference?

I think that it was primarily a personality difference, which needs scarcely any elaboration. Bernard suspected the right of a man of Abelard's character to engage in debate about the deepest issues of the Christian faith. By "Abelard's character," I am discussing not his relations with Heloise but his brashness, his assurance. Bernard does not seem to have been opposed to the scholastic approach to theology—he was, after all, a patron of Peter Lombard. On the other hand, he must have thought it much less important than the old kind of theology based on the authority of the Fathers and consolidated by Christian life in a monastic setting. From this point of view Abelard seemed a dangerous sort of man, and Bernard was easily (too easily) persuaded that he was full of poison.

Abelard always reminds me of Bertrand Russell, a man of wonderfully keen and lucid intellect but with compulsive failures of judgment, especially in personal affairs. Abelard's life was punctuated by a series of extraordinary errors in his practical decisions: his becoming a monk at St. Denis was ludicrous; his sending Heloise into a nunnery was hard to understand except as a hysterical reaction to his emasculation; his becoming Abbot of St. Gildas was an absurd step; his collapse before Saint Bernard at the Council of Sens was a personal failure which seems to have no explanation in the intellectual situation. As a man he was somehow fragile and vulnerable, and this must have made him very attractive to pupils but quite inadequate in the face of great personal difficulty.

Many people consider themselves conservative while they are actually producing something quite new—Anselm, Gregory VII, and certainly Bernard can be taken as examples. One can talk of Bernard as a conservative as opposed to Abelard, but I do not think that is a fair description of his total work or his total effect on the world.

What was the new ground that Bernard was breaking? Bernard's real permanent contribution to medieval Christianity —leaving aside the great political splash he made and his role as an inspirer of religious foundations—was his passionate desire for an intimate understanding of Christian truths, for the incorporation of Christian truths in individual personal experience. In his own way this was what Abelard also wanted. He too wanted a fuller and more personal understanding of the Christian faith—but in intellectual terms, and not (or at least not conspicuously) as a result of prayer and personal dedication. Bernard wanted to understand while keeping the mystery intact: Abelard wanted understanding without mystery. That is a very great difference, but whether it arises from a difference in personality or from some other source I don't know.

How was the heretical movement of the twelfth century related to the movement of introspection? How was it related to political, social, and economic factors? Did the spread of popular heresy indicate a failure on the part of the organized Church administration to adjust to social and economic change?

I see little connection between the movement toward introspection and the growth of heresies. There were two kinds of heresies in the twelfth and thirteenth centuries. The academic heresies—those condemned in Abelard, Gilbert de la Porrée, and others: they created no popular movement and had no future. The second kind, popular heresies, arose out of widespread hatred of the ecclesiastical machine rather than academic or theological enquiry. They grew up among people who had reached a certain degree of material and intellectual independence but felt themselves to be outsiders from the hierarchical structure of the Church. These people saw the immorality of the clergy and the extortions of the representatives of the hierarchy and they sought religious experience in the esoteric doctrines that were endemic in various parts of Europe—doctrines with a distant Manichean origin, or doctrines centered on the search for purity and absolute standards of behavior which were beyond the reach of human beings yet always desirable.

These heresies were closely related to social and economic conditions. In their most threatening form, they arose mainly in towns. Whereas in the countryside a man who thought differently from his neighbors was both isolated and vulnerable to persecution and therefore kept quiet about his beliefs, in the towns malcontents of this kind were able to join in small groups, encourage each other, and form a movement. They had a certain independence of life, without enough regular education to tie them to the doctrinal system which this education fostered and supported.

So far as we can judge, the communication between the upper hierarchy of the Church and its lower strata was pretty flimsy in the twelfth century. The Church laid down disciplines to be observed; but to ordinary people it said little about the experiences and thoughts which were the fruits of life in monasteries and universities. In the thirteenth century this was recognized as one of the great weaknesses of Christendom, and the remedy took the form of trying to communicate these thoughts and experiences in popular manuals of instruction for the use of the parochial clergy. Yet I do not think that this remedy was effective in limiting the growth of popular heresy. People who were fed with information from above did not become participators in the experiences and thoughts that made the official system of Christianity acceptable. The proof of the failure of this remedy is the continued growth of popular heresy throughout the Middle Ages.

The heresies of the twelfth and thirteenth centuries were not highly intellectual, but they developed more intellectual content as time went on. For instance, Joachim of Fiore's doctrines about the end of the world and the age of the Holy Spirit helped to give intellectual content to a great deal of religious and social discontent, and this continued in the fourteenth and fifteenth centuries. The spiritual teachings of Eckhart had a similar effect; while not themselves heretical, they were open to heretical development. They provided intellectual and religious justification for those who asserted the primacy of individual experience and desired an immediate contact between the individual and the divine love without the intermediary assistance of the Church and its sacraments and disciplines.

Why was the Church so unsuccessful in dealing with urban societies?

For the same reasons that it is unsuccessful in such societies today. The parochial system was devised to deal with small populations, more or less isolated from each other, and satisfied with a fairly routine kind of religious observance. I don't believe that the ordinary medieval village was highly religious or deeply impregnated with Christian doctrine, but Christian doctrine was accepted, and it was the only source of comfort or appeal for the people in emergencies. With a larger population, life was more precarious, the opportunities for gaining wealth were greater, and the parish was no longer a viable unit. No doubt the thirteenth-century friars did something to mitigate the lack of contact between the parish clergy and the people, but the success of their efforts was limited. Friars easily became complacent like other people, and medieval towns were violent and disorganized places which encouraged resistance to the teachings of an official hierarchy among those who had no share in its rewards and inducements.

Why did the Thomists of the thirteenth and fourteenth centuries attempt a kind of synthesis of the whole of supernatural theology and natural knowledge? Why was it accepted to some degree, then attacked so fiercely in the intellectual world?

One must remember that while to us Thomas Aquinas stands for medieval thought, and for a kind of finality, this is largely because he is more accessible, more readable, more publicized than others. To his contemporaries, he was one of many. Like Einstein, he was one of the most successful and influential operators in the areas of general scientific thought. Aquinas was one of the most criticized writers of the day simply because he said more things that were controversial. In the thirteenth century no one criticized him for combining natural thinking with revelation in a systematic way—that was the general trend. They criticized him for his details. The general criticism came later.

Why was there a growth in pessimism about the Thomist, or any other synthesis? I think that this is the rhythm of any great intellectual movement: for a time it carries all before it, and every generation seems to be getting nearer to the proposed ideal. Then comes a point where further work takes one no nearer the goal. At this point there arises a suspicion that the system itself is ill-founded and liable to break down. This is what happened in the fourteenth century. But why did this change occur? Perhaps because there is always a limit to the pursuit of an intellectual ideal. The buoyancy of systematic thought in the twelfth and thirteenth centuries was sustained by the continuous flow of new material to be mastered and integrated into the system. New Arabic and Greek material started coming in about the 1120's, and the flow continued until about 1250. After that date there was no new material to be integrated, and there was nothing to do but chew over again some of the more indigestible parts of the old material. This produced a sense of frustration and ill temper. One should not exaggerate, however—many academic philosophers and theologians continued to work on the old problems quite happily and with no sense of impending doom. Only we can see that they were getting nowhere.

It is traditional to speak of the improvement in government administration and bureaucracy in the twelfth century. But what exactly did medieval government achieve? What role did it play in people's lives?

Medieval administration was not effective in a way that modern government would recognize. Government continued to grow because its officials made a profit out of it, but its effectiveness did not increase directly with its size. It would not be fair, however, to say that it was totally ineffective. The English legal system settled thousands of cases of land ownership that would otherwise have been settled by violence. Many solutions were achieved, particularly in small matters, but medieval government fell down in big things, because in these, men were not prepared in the last resort to accept a legal decision without putting it to the test of force. Medieval government was ineffective at the point where its force was not sufficient to ensure observance of its decisions.

This is particularly true in papal administration, which worked pretty well in small matters: questions of tithes, privileges, rights of churches and monasteries, and so forth. It worked less well when some political element was involved in an ecclesiastical case. In the end it generally prevailed, but only after a tussle. It acted least effectively where the element of politics was dominant, where the interests of rulers were really engaged, and where only a small element of ecclesiastical discipline was involved. One may say that the same principle applied in papal and royal administration: they were successful over the large areas where it was not worthwhile for their opponents to take up arms in serious resistance. With all its failings, however, medieval governments provided a great deal of peace and security for ordinary people.

Did medieval government ever establish a genuine bureaucratic situation in which it could operate without the strong personal leadership of the king?

No, I cannot think of any case where the administrative machinery continued to work effectively under a weak or incapable king. Politics were never far from the surface in medieval government: when a king lacked martial ability or did not have a reliable standard of behavior or a respected personal force (in the eyes of the aristocracy), warring factions would arise and the administrative machine would begin to break down under the stress of disorder at the top. Even today, you cannot keep a government going unless you keep happy the people who matter. The trade unionists of today have replaced the magnates of the Middle Ages, but the same principle applies.

Looking at the period from mid-eleventh to late thirteenth centuries, how had the teachings and values of the Church and the exercise of royal law and administration altered the way of life and the ideals and attitudes of the feudal aristocracy?

I am reminded of some lines of Dr. Johnson:

> How small of all that human hearts endure,
> That part which laws of kings can cause or cure.

I think it would be wrong to believe that government, whether ecclesiastical or royal, did much to change the life or thought of large numbers of people. Government could only try to keep up with the growing complexity of society and provide solutions to new problems as they arose. The only area where government did have an effect on thought was in the area of law. The growth of government was based on the growth of law. This in turn helped to limit and define the types of action that were generally acceptable in society. This didn't mean that people in the later Middle Ages were less cruel, self-interested, or violent than their predecessors, though in some ways they were more civilized. They appreciated comfort, art, and the refinements of life more than people of an earlier generation. But this came about through economic and intellectual developments which law and government only followed and responded to.

What was chivalry? Was chivalry a social fact or an ethereal, literary creation?

Chivalry was a code of martial behavior based on an elaborate respect for feminine whims. Outwardly it called for extravagant pomp and display, inwardly for intense loyalty and self-abasement. As for its practical influence, life always imitates literature to some extent. The literature which we admire provides norms of behavior which we try to follow in our daily lives. I think this is true of chivalric literature, as of any other popular literature. It set up ideals of conduct which never thoroughly permeated society but did affect it in many ways, particularly in the more showy and superficial forms of pageantry. It really is impossible to say whether or not literature caused any great internal changes in the way of feeling of aristocratic people. So far as one can judge, they treated their wives just as badly as before. The show of chivalry was often merely a cover for more practical and brutal unavowed designs, just as an outward show of religion often in all ages has been. The growth of family estates and the protection of rights, real or supposed, were more important practically than any chivalric code of behavior, but chivalry satisfied a need for color and pageantry, without which life would have been very drab.

Clearly, the aristocratic attitude and way of life did change. Even the growth in convenience and comfort in life must have made some changes. Men became less brutal, less rough and ready, more articulate, more open to subtle ideas. Although they moved to protect their families and their estates when these were threatened, a greater part of their lives was devoted to elegance, display, and even literature than to meeting daily emergencies. Habits changed, but policy remained unaltered.

Would you comment on the writing of history in the twelfth and thirteenth centuries? Did historical writing undergo any marked changes? Was there deeper social understanding and perception of personality and personal motivation?

There was much more comment on personalities in the fourteenth century than at any earlier period of historiography (e.g., Walsingham and the fourteenth-century *St. Albans'* chronicle). There was a prejudice and misinformation, of course, but efforts were made to describe people. A century earlier, Matthew Paris was very anecdotal but gave no clear picture of the characters of the people he was describing. There are a few exceptions—he seems to have understood the king quite well—but generally he is very flat on personalities. This is true, too, of the French writers of the thirteenth century. There is little in the *Grandes Chroniques* that shows a widespread interest in human character. Joinville's picture of Louis IX is an exception but it is all somehow too sweet—a copybook character. From an earlier generation, the panegyrics on Philip Augustus are interesting, but more for the attitude to monarchy which they express than for their character drawing.

Earlier still, it is extraordinarily difficult to find any striking character sketches in the historical writings of the twelfth century. The English historians were pre-eminent in Europe, but their attempts at character sketches were very formal and were drawn not from life but from idealized pictures. One exception is John of Salisbury's *Historia Pontificalis.* This brings its characters to life. But for the most part, the best writers, when they came to describing men or women, were dominated by rhetorical models which provided ready-made characters. There was a deep interest in human beings, but it took a long time for this to show itself in accurate observations of character. One must remember that the renewed interest in man in the twelfth century took the form of a renewed interest in the science of man as developed in the ancient world. For their descriptions of men historians looked to books which told them what men were like: they were not very quick to describe men from their own experience.

Even the great increase in autobiographies in the eleventh and twelfth centuries was provoked by something other than an impulse to describe life from within. Abelard's *Historia Calamitatum,* the most interesting of all, was written to console a friend in trouble, and it is primarily an account of those events in Abelard's career which will serve this purpose. Similarly, Gerald of Wales was leaving a record of the claims of St. Davids as an archbishopric, and his own autobiography was woven into the record. If he struts absurdly on the stage, this is largely because he wants to be remembered for his work for the archbishopric of St. Davids, work which he hoped his successors would continue. Autobiography had a long way to go before it became an intimate account of human experience.

Can modern scholars write biographies of medieval men? Can their personalities be reconstructed, or are they fundamentally elusive?

I think that there are severe limitations on the biographer of any man who lived before the end of the thirteenth century. I came across them in trying to write about Anselm, a man who revealed a great deal of his inner self in his prayers and letters and theological works. One can get a clear picture of his talents and limitations and one can understand something of his psychological makeup, his unique mixture of emotional sensibility and yet inflexibly logical mind. One can give an account of his systematic thoughts, his friendships, his attitude to political life and to ecclesiastical affairs, his impact on the people he met. Yet the whole falls far short of Peter Brown's biography of Saint Augustine. Here one can follow the changes of Augustine's mind and the dynamics of his development from year to year; and his personal history can be fitted into a detailed picture of a turbulent world of uncertainty and violence and fear. For Anselm, this kind of thing is impossible. The material doesn't run to it. One could of course make guesses about his psychological development, but they would be no more than guesses. As for his larger environment, we know it only in a very general or very particular way—a few friends, a few incidents, a handful of letters. The decisive things in his life were his relations with his parents and later with his friends, his acute experiences of sin and his intellectual and emotional experiences of God—but the external details are very thinly documented. And then his contemporary biographer—though he was an intimate friend and a devoted and observant companion—wrote in a literary convention which required him to suppress much that he would instinctively have included and to emphasize what he might well have omitted. It is a wonderful experience to live with these documents, but they do not provide the material for a full biography. One comes to know these people very well—but rather as one knows a friend whom one never meets—it is not easy to say much about them.

All this applies to other figures as well as Anselm: one could not write a biography of Bernard which would explain and make vivid his impressions and intentions at many different moments in his life. What is true of these highly articulate and formed characters must be even more true of contemporary lay characters, whose thoughts can be known only from their actions. Actions are a very dubious index to motives and thought. I doubt if there will ever be a satisfactory biographer of any twelfth or thirteenth-century lay statesmen. Frederick II comes closest to providing the mass of material, the diversity of activity, and the range of mental equipment necessary for any solid biography. But no one has yet produced a plausible human being from all this material. Similarly, in England there is a great deal of material about Frederick's contemporary, Henry III, but even Powicke's book on Henry III is much more a study of the society of the time than of the man. Henry III is a very unsubstantial figure in that book, as is Simon of Montfort—its other major character. The same may be said of Louis IX of France: he remains a figure in a stained-glass window.

I think that Dante is the first European of the Middle Ages of whom a biography might be written like that about Augustine. After all, Dante left a mass of material about his mind and his reactions to the world. But that material is so compressed, so shaped and formed into a didactical or poetic form, that it would be very hard to get out of it all that there is. Dante put more of himself into his poetry than any other medieval writer, but his poetry is after all so much more important than its author (or at least than anything we can know about its author) that to dig in his poetry to discover the man behind it would be like digging up a rose bed to look at the roots. Descration.

Are the limitations on biographies of twelfth- and thirteenth-century personalities due to the dearth of material or to an intellectual problem—that these people did not see themselves as distinct personalities?

I think that the problem is largely one of material—and of something else as well. The limitation of material is decisive, but there is also a certain lack of drama about twelfth-century characters, a lack of importance in their activity, which makes biography fall a bit flat. Biography needs a situation of large, general importance—great political or military events with grand and momentous consequences—and this inspiration of important events and issues is lacking in all the great twelfth-century figures that I can think of. Their importance lies in their approach to cosmic questions: man's soul, destiny, religious truth, and so on. But for biography one needs a more colorful and dramatic setting, with the main character at the center of events, possessing an intellectual power and articulation that gives some clue to motives and character. I should opt for Frederick II, on the whole, if I were forced to choose a subject for a biography in the twelfth or thirteenth century.

In older scholarship it was said that the Anglo-Saxon government and Church were backward and primitive; that the Normans brought rationalization, modernization, and enlightenment to England. Many recent writers disagree, portraying the Normans as barbarians who learned from the Anglo-Saxons. Would you comment on this?

The older writers were writing mainly about government and the structure of society, and in this area I believe that they were right and that the modern reaction has gone too far. With the Norman Conquest, a new aristocracy was imposed on the country, and a new military and social organization came in at the top. This is incontrovertible. The modern school of historians has emphasized the elaboration of administration under the Anglo-Saxons and the permanence of Anglo-Saxon institutions throughout the period of the conquest. But they sometimes confuse the existence of a *mechanism* of government with the *operation* of government, and if you look at the last stage of Anglo-Saxon administration you are struck by the great paucity of documents. Anglo-Saxon government may have had a system of taxation and formulae for drawing up documents that were very advanced, but in the operations of government there was a marked lack of vigor and control and a striking relaxation of effort. We do not know what was actually produced in the royal treasury as a result of Danegeld, and we are too apt to take the theory for the deed. The absence of documents enables us to think what we like, to interpret the evidence as we wish.

The Norman contribution, on the other hand, is comparatively well documented. The Normans took over the forms of Anglo-Saxon government, but they introduced many changes. Feudal military service is one, and I agree more than most recent historians with the views of J. H. Round that it was quite different from the Anglo-Saxon system. Certainly Anglo-Norman England was a much more active, productive place than Anglo-Saxon England. It was not necessarily a more agreeable place. On the whole, the Norman Conquest was deplorable: it concentrated wealth and power in the hands of a military aristocracy and probably impoverished a wide range of the people in that middle stratum of society which later became known as the gentry (and we all have a great inclination to prefer the gentry to the military aristocracy). The military aristocracy did serve some purposes, however. With wealth concentrated in fewer hands, a greater surplus was left for works of building, scholarship, art, and for a vigorous governmental machine than there had been before the conquest. On the whole I am inclined to be favorably disposed towards the old school of historians, always admitting that their area of historical inquiry was limited. No doubt for 90 percent of the population, and over large parts of the agrarian scene, the way of life went on unchanged. The things that did not change, however, were the least significant or the least knowable; dramatic and violent changes occurred in the things of most importance and with a substantial influence on the future of the country.

Germany came out of the Middle Ages with an ineffective central government. What was wrong with the German political situation?

It was not necessarily something wrong in Germany that produced this result—one must not take the French and English pattern as the norm. But you are right that whereas the English and French kings managed to consolidate and increase their power *pari passu* with the growth of aristocratic power or perhaps even faster, in Germany the opposite was the case. Why?

In Germany, royal authority needed drastic modernization in order to survive in the more competitive political world of the twelfth and thirteenth centuries. A widely ranging jurisdiction was required, a system of law courts, and a financial system with local officers. The German kings failed to produce this. This is one of those cases in which it is a disadvantage to have developed too soon. The German kings were saddled with an old-fashioned model of kingship—very impressive, too impressive to scrap, and too rigid to modernize. Their claims were too great to be abandoned, and much too great to be realized. It was partly a question of geographical area. Germany was too large an area for the exercise of effective governmental control. The area of Germany must have been four or five times that of the English kingdom and two or three times that ruled by the French kings. Medieval Germany was very unevenly developed, with a wide range of different types of cultivation and settlement. Perhaps the best chance for the development of an effective kingship would have been a divided, localized Germany of the kind that existed with Frederick Barbarossa and Henry the Lion, but even that was not a very rational division.

Barbarossa failed in his effort to base royal power in the family lands and surrounding area of Franconia and Swabia because he, like every German king, was thinking of Italy. The medieval German kings spent a disproportionate amount of their energy on establishing claims in Italy which could only be maintained by very great military effort and expense. Medieval rulers in general were always thinking of the rights which they ought to have, and this was their great weakness. The re-establishment of a lost position was the first objective of every ruler. They thought first of all of handing on to their successors intact the kingdom which they had inherited, and they tended to concentrate, therefore, on marginal areas where they were in danger of losing territory. Consequently, a disproportionate amount of political and military activity was centered on disputed areas where the returns to be expected were minimal.

The medieval German kings, after all, were not trying to develop a system like that of the English and French rulers. From their own point of view they were not on the losing side. And if one looks to the Hapsburgs as their successors, one cannot say that they represented a losing cause.

By the end of the thirteenth century there were certain significant differences in the organization of the English and French governments: differences in the legal system, in the bureaucracy, in the position of their parliaments. How do we account for the different developments in two countries whose dynasties and aristocracies belonged to the same culture?

As you point out, there were significant differences—but there were also similarities between the two countries in government and society. The differences were superimposed upon a large area of common organization, and they can be explained in two ways. First, under the Anglo-Norman and Angevin kings the main function of England was to provide money and men for the defense and reconquest of their French possessions. It was an immense task because the French had a strategic advantage, and so the English kingdom was organized to raise huge sums for this purpose. The structure of the royal government was evolved partly for financial reasons and partly to exhibit and preserve royal rights in England with the least possible exertion. A centralized, effective military-financial-legal system therefore grew up in England a good deal sooner than in France.

Second, the Anglo-Norman and Angevin kings somehow lost much of the royal demesne in England by the end of the twelfth century. I myself think that the bidding for support in Stephen's reign was the major cause of this, but there were other causes too. The rewarding of faithful servants, the rewarding of foreign allies, and the bidding for support for comparatively unpopular governments meant that the English kings had always to be ready to sacrifice their future interests for their present needs. As a result, by the end of the twelfth century the English kings derived only one third as much income from land as they had derived at the beginning of the century. In France, on the other hand, the kings could live on the revenues of their demesne and needed a less elaborate administrative system. Since the English kings were denuded of their natural revenues from the land, they had to turn to taxation. This could be enforced only with the consent of the taxpayers, and consequently, Parliament developed as a very important institution. In France there was no necessity for the growth of a similar body, and the parliament of France tended to become increasingly legal while the English Parliament became increasingly financial and political in orientation.

Further, the Normans came to a country where the land was divided between a great many minor landlords. To make sufficiently large fiefs for his more important followers, William the Conqueror had to give them lands belonging to five, six, or more Anglo-Saxon tenants scattered throughout the country. In order to maintain the complicated system of land tenure that emerged from this redistribution, a royal legal system was necessary; no feudal courts could exercise the kind of jurisdiction necessary to settle the many disputes about land. And since men had interests scattered throughout the country, the English king could never deal with each province separately as the French kings did; they had always to deal with an assembly representing the whole of the country. In the Parliament of England, therefore, magnates and representatives of the whole country came together, whereas in France there was a much more localized organization of estates. These are the three features of the difference between England and France that I should be most inclined to emphasize.

In the United States the two books which are most widely read on medieval history are your book The Making of the Middle Ages *and Marc Bloch's* Feudal Society. *What do you think of his picture of feudalism as a network of political, social, intellectual aspects?*

I think that Bloch's is a very interesting book, but it does not seem to hang together very well. Clearly, everything that happens is connected in some way with other things happening at the same time, but not so closely that the historian is able to give a clear account of the connections unless he limits himself in some way. Alternatively (or at the same time), one can give a sense of unity to a large theme by building the work round the experiences of recognizable people. I think Bloch's book suffers from an insufficient limitation of subject matter and an insufficient realization of substantial personalities. It seems to me to lack warmth. I suppose he had no great sympathy for medieval people, especially not in their religious or ecclesiastical aspects. And his book, though it was a wonderful pioneer effort, has a certain lack of center. Looked on as a systematic account of a community, it is too empirical (though I approve of this) to be quite satisfactory. It is a system without a systematic foundation. Maitland (who I think was Bloch's chief model) could do this kind of thing because he took the law as his foundation and he looked at society only insofar as it could be subsumed under the law. The law provided the system, and society the illustrations. There are no real people in Maitland either—only litigants and mouthpieces for ideas—but despite this, his legal foundation made it possible for him to write a great and satisfying work of history. Bloch aimed at a greater comprehension of society in all its manifestations. He put society in the foreground. The result (as it seems to me) is that the book is all surface—a brilliant one, but it leaves my intellectual and human sympathies unsatisfied.

I ought to add, however, since you have mentioned my book in the same breath as Bloch's, that I would speak much more critically of my own work if I had to, which luckily I don't.

Friedrich Heer sees in the twelfth century an open society with freedom for radical thinking, for new forms of ideas, for controversy. But in the thirteenth century, he claims, church and government clamped down on freedom of thought, and in this closed society the creativity of medieval culture slowly but surely stultified. Is there anything in this?

I think not. People have often made similar distinctions between the twelfth and thirteenth centuries, but to me the most important feature of these centuries is their single continuous development. This is chiefly to be seen in the ordering and systematizing of knowledge, the ordering of government and society, the attempt to bring everything under some kind of rule of law and to impose unity on society, essentially under the leadership of the pope. There were different views of papal leadership, but by and large the idea of a single leader is the most characteristic feature of the whole system, and the pope was the only real candidate. I see the whole development as a steady process of ordering and systematizing, of bringing all the elements of human experience into a general framework of thought and practice.

The real break in medieval society

took place where most people have always imagined it—somewhere around the year 1300. This is the break that needs to be explained: it is far more profound than any supposed break between the twelfth and thirteenth centuries.

The Inquisition is suggested as a symptom of the difference between centuries. Well, the Inquisition simply organized a lot of very disorderly and violent operations against heresy that had been going on throughout the eleventh and twelfth centuries. It was more oppressive simply because heresy was more widespread, and heresy was more widespread because the social conditions in which it thrived were themselves more widespread. I doubt whether the oppressiveness of the Inquisition had any great bearing on the development of thirteenth-century society. I see no sign that any big ideas or big initiatives were snuffed out by inquisitorial processes. Nor do I believe that there was any diminution in the originality of thought or of artistic, political, or any other sort of activity in the thirteenth century. On the contrary, I should have thought that the systems of the thirteenth century were not only intellectually more powerful than those of the twelfth, but also more original. You cannot say that there is more original thought in the systematic treatises of the early twelfth century—those of Hugh of St. Victor, William of Conches, Anselm of Laon, Peter Lombard—than there is in those of Bonaventura, Aquinas, or the great figures of thirteenth-century scholasticism.

It is quite clear, though, that the works of the early twelfth century are more readable than those of the thirteenth. Abelard certainly was a more readable author than most scholastic writers of the thirteenth century, and I believe that there were two reasons for this. First of all, early twelfth-century Latin was still (in the main) the Latin of the ancient world, and it was on the whole a finer instrument than thirteenth-century Latin. Second, the thirteenth-century writers were more scientific, they had more complicated programs, and they wrote a Latin which had been formed for the purposes of academic discussion, with a new vocabulary and a great deal of grammatical change to fit in with the needs of the time. I think this is rather a sign of inventiveness and originality than the opposite, but it does not make for pleasant reading. People have too often been misled by appearances; they found what they were looking for in the early twelfth century—some kind of classical elegance. They could not find much of it, but they did find a little, and they made too much of what they found. But I don't think that that difference justifies the kind of distinction Heer has made between the two centuries.

11

Medieval and Renaissance Economy and Society

ROBERT. S. LOPEZ

THE HISTORIOGRAPHICAL CONTEXT

It is on its economic and social side that Western Europe between the fall of the Roman Empire and the fifteenth century experienced its most radical changes. The greater part of what is today Western Europe was in A.D. 500 a pitifully underdeveloped, thinly populated frontier of the Mediterranean world. By 1000, intensive colonization was under way, and heavy inroads were made in the vast forests and swampy regions. By 1200, international commerce, booming population, and urban growth were widespread. By the fifteenth century, in spite of a debilitating economic depression, urban life, particularly in northern Italy, had been richly developed.

In spite of the paucity and complex character of the source material, historians have been very successful in charting the course of these dramatic and critically important economic and social changes. This field has attracted scholars of the highest caliber—Henri Pirenne and Marc Bloch were pre-eminent in the 1920's and 1930's, and several historians of great insight and learning have worked on these subjects in the past three decades, among whom M. Postan in England and Robert S. Lopez in the United States stand in the front rank.

Lopez was born in Italy in 1910 and received a D.Litt. degree from the University of Milan in 1932. Leaving Mussolini's Italy, he received a Ph.D. in history from the University of Wisconsin in 1942. Since 1946 Lopez has been at Yale University; currently he is Durfee Professor of History and Chairman of the Medieval Studies Program. Few Italians of Lopez' generation achieved distinction as historians: they were too much given to easy philosophizing and the proclamation of political and moral bromides. Lopez seems much more German than Italian in temperament, or let us say he belongs to that generation of American scholars who subscribed to the zeal, discipline, and industry that marked German *Wissenschaft*. He is a careful student of source texts, a brilliant analyst of institutions, a firm and highly successful trainer of graduate students, a highly effective academic administrator. But what makes Lopez' scholarship of such great value is his aptitude for generalization: his ability to see broad patterns of change and impart a sense of what institutions meant in daily life. Nor is he at all one-sided—he commands a vast knowledge of medieval culture and politics and can define the complex relationship between economic change and other aspects of medieval civilization.

Chronological Outline

Fifth and sixth centuries: German invasions of western Europe accelerate economic disintegration of the Mediterranean world.

Seventh and eight centuries: Muslim expansion an additional blow to the Western economy, turning the Europeans away from the Mediterranean.

Ninth and tenth centuries: entrenchment of feudal and seignorial institutions.

Late tenth and eleventh centuries: revival of commercial and naval power of the Italian cities; internal colonization in northern Europe; European penetration into the Mediterranean.

Twelfth and thirteenth centuries: population growth and urban expansion.

Fourteenth and early fifteenth centuries: war, plague, and economic depression.

Norman F. Cantor

Would you begin by describing the impact of the German invasions and the Muslim expansion on the economy and society of Western Europe, and then describe the development of seignorial and feudal institutions?

Robert S. Lopez

In my opinion, neither feudalism nor seignorialism (or manorialism) can be regarded as direct consequences of the German invasions or the Muslim expansion. Certain symptoms of seignorial economy appeared in the Roman territory before the German invasions; a development in this direction was quickened where the Germans came, but was slowed down where the Muslims ruled. Feudalism developed much later, as an attempt to reconstruct a workable system of government after the last remnants of the Roman organization had dissolved.

At first, both the Germans and the Arabs were responsible more for giving the finishing stroke to the decadent institutions of Rome than for building anything new. The Arabs, however, conquered a larger and richer part of the world than that occupied by the Germans, came in touch with less depressed civilizations—those of Byzantium and of Sasanian Persia—and displayed a greater ability to assimilate the cultures to which they fell heirs while preserving a more original and fruitful native tradition. Therefore, after the first shock was passed, they could open new intellectual and economic horizons.

On the other hand, the greater originality and richness of the Arab (or, indeed, Islamic) culture made it harder for it to communicate with the barbarian and Christian West. As Pirenne has pointed out, the Muslim expansion tended to detach politically and morally a great proportion of the old Mediterranean community from its western and northern rump, and to create a new, autonomous community whose center was first in Damascus and then, still farther, in Baghdad. The hostility between the Muslim and the Christian worlds has been overstressed; it was not impossible for Baghdad to build bridges towards Constantinople, which was more of an equal, and there was no consistent effort to build a wall against the intellectually and economically inferior West. It is nevertheless undeniable that a dialogue between Muslims and Christians became harder because religion, language, and institutions were now radically different, and also because the Muslims were not overly interested in what the West had to say or to sell. What dialogue there was was certainly interesting, but there was altogether too little of it.

To go back to the Germanic invasions: no doubt they were technically the military cause for the fall of Rome, but Rome was already collapsing when they occurred, and it was Rome's weakness rather than the strength of the barbarians that determined the collapse of the old order. In my opinion, the first if not necessarily the decisive cause of the collapse was the decline of the population. In turn the causes of the population decline are not too difficult to find. To begin with, the margin of human surplus had always been small. Life expectancy was short, there were many diseases, and it took very little to disturb the balance and produce a deficit instead of an increase. In the third, fourth, and fifth centuries there were recurrences of some great epidemic diseases that had been quiescent, as far as we know, in antiquity. We give them the general name *plague,* which covers various strains of diseases that usually moved west from a center in the Far East or Central Asia. We know that malaria, too, increased in these centuries. Malaria is connected with mosquito-breeding stagnant water, which is connected in turn with deforestation and with overexploitation of the soil. But the incidence of plagues cannot be pinned down to easily identifiable causes, except to some ill-known and ill-knowable "pulsation" of the climate. It does seem that there was climatic change during these centuries.

A remedy would have required a lot of planning and intelligence which was not available to the invaders. Time had to solve the problem, and in time there was regermination. The forests grew again when there were fewer people to cut them, and the flow of water came back to some extent. When the population grew again, there was a new blossoming of civilization. Once the plagues and epidemics had thinned down the population, there probably was collective immunization; also, men were living too far apart by then for plagues to spread as easily as they had in an earlier age of comparatively easy communication and thickly settled population.

For almost five hundred years—for the first half of the Middle Ages—the population of Europe was inadequate to solve much more than the problem of bare subsistence. It was inadequate physically and materially; also—and this is harder for an historian to explain—it seems to have been inadequate morally. Inventiveness and technical ability seem to have declined with physical ability. We do not know why—there may be a link between nutrition and intellect—but certainly this was a rather barren period, at least in fields requiring sophisticated reasoning.

In conditions such as these it was particularly difficult for the poor man to fend for himself, whether he was a serf, a slave, or a small farmer. In the late Roman Empire, increased demands for taxes and military service were placed on the diminishing population, which grew less and less able to carry the burden. The German invasions diminished tax revenues, more through inefficiency than good will. They did not give much in return for taxes, either: public services gradually collapsed.

Some of the old Roman institutions continued to work for a while, more or less, but eventually even the roads fell to pieces. By the tenth century the old roads in most places were no longer usable. It should have been easier by sea, because there is no need for upkeep on the sea, but ships do not last forever, and there was less naval construction and less organization to keep it going. Much of the communication of the early Middle Ages was by river, where small barges were used, indicating the diminution of trade and the simplicity of the appetites and desires of the population. The upper class changed from a refined elite which had studied and seen the world into a new elite whose simple tastes are revealed in the *chansons de geste*. They liked to eat and drink; they liked women, gold, and luxuries, but quantity was more important than quality.

Probably the most significant phenomenon of the early Middle Ages was the almost complete collapse of town life. The pillar of Greco-Roman society, and to a large extent of earlier societies, was the city-state, which was not just a city but an agricultural district with a capital. The capital had a specific function which was not purely economic, although it did serve as a center of exchange for artifacts made in the town and agricultural surpluses made in the country. The Greco-Roman city was mainly a residence of landowners and political, religious, and military cadres. By bringing people together, it provided intellectual and economic stimulation which is not available in the country. A city is not divided into families who live practically the same kind of life and produce practically all the food they use. It is made up of interdependent families; it differs from the country, I'd say, as a cellular organism differs from an amoeba. This complex organism did not survive the catastrophe of the late Empire, not so much because people fled the town for the country—some also fled the country for the town—but because the sophistication of tastes diminished and communications broke down. If the towns survived at all, they had to produce their own food and could spare little time or leisure to produce artifacts, for which there was in any case little demand. In the early Middle Ages, the center of life gradually shifted from the town to the country, from an intellectually sophisticated elite to a tough society of country barons.

This did not mean that the lower strata of the population necessarily became much more wretched. The difference between a Greek or Roman slave or proletarian and a patrician was probably greater and more poignant than the difference between the humblest serf in a manor and the richest lord, or even the emperor. Charlemagne ate more than his peasants, and had something to eat even when they died of starvation, but he did not eat really differently. In a compassionate view of history, the inumerable shortcomings of the early Middle Ages must be weighed against this limited leveling off and the gradual disappearance of slavery.

Serfdom replaced the slavery of Roman times, and it was quite different. In Roman law a slave was a piece of property like a cow; the neuter pronoun was used when referring to a slave. No doubt a good farmer milks his cows instead of killing them, but still, a cow is a cow. A slave had one advantage over a cow; he could be made into a man, he could be freed. Then he became by law the equal of all other men. But only a portion of the Roman slave class was freed.

In late Roman times, slaves diminished in number with the rest of the population, but probably more rapidly because their standard of living was lower. Because they were diminishing they had to be spared, and their lords began to treat them a little better. Families of slaves were kept together (to encourage reproduction) and very often were given a house and a piece of land. This land was not absolutely the slave's, but it was practically his as long as he worked on it. As the manpower shortage became more serious, it was in the lord's interest to keep his slaves on the land, and most of the slaves were gradually transformed into serfs. A serf was not mere cattle, even in relation to his lord, because in theory, at least, he could not be killed. The neuter gender was never used for him. He had limited legal rights and was bound to serve his lord or whomever his lord would sell him to, but the services were limited by law or custom.

The question arises whether and to what extent this change was due to Christianity. In my opinion, Christianity had practically no connection with it: Christianity concentrated on the kingdom of Heaven. Although council after council and pope after pope agreed that a man might free his slaves as an act of great charity, they worried lest slaves would be freed too fast for stability. Slavery was one of the imperfect institutions which were inevitable in an imperfect world; there is no reason to be shocked at that, it is perfectly natural.

Another part of the Roman population merged with the former slaves to form the big class of serfs: poor freemen. As the Roman Empire declined, their responsibilities became very hard to bear. In the late Roman period and the early Middle Ages, more and more freemen gave up their free status, and usually not because they were forced to do so. That is, they were forced, but by the economic conditions of the times rather than any act of violence. They simply could not live independently. The serf of a powerful man was better off than a freeman who could not pay his taxes nor raise his crops —serfdom was a form of insurance. Often, but not always, serfs were better off under an ecclesiastic institution than under a lay lord; this helps to account for the growth of ecclesiastical properties.

The gradual amalgamation of the Roman and barbarian communities and ways of life also affected the patterns of settlement and the exploitation of the soil. There were several types of medieval villages, but we shall consider here the two basic varieties: the Mediterranean and the manorial. In Mediterranean agricultural lands there is not much water, the soil is rocky, and the layer of earth is not very deep. Every peasant has to do a lot of work—mostly with his hands—to get a crop from land which cannot be plowed too deeply. Although the climate is favorable, his land will not produce too much. He generally does not have much usable land to spare for cattle. He lives very simply, with a great deal of independence, and generally encloses his field. He works it (and I'm speaking here of extreme "typical" cases to accentuate the difference between the two types) almost like a garden.

Ties between people in this Mediterranean village are social. They live close together, because the arable land is very thickly settled. Intensive agriculture is possible under this system because little wasteland is set aside for cattle, and so the inhabitants live close together and know one another well. They are tied together by certain farming operations (wine, for instance) and by the necessities of irrigation. They have to agree on the upkeep and distribution of the irrigation system, without which the land would probably relapse into desert. In many cases they also have to agree on terraces and other arrangements used to prevent erosion of the thin soil.

This type of village was the beginning of Greco-Roman civilization, of the city-state, and so forth, and the Romans exported it with good success wherever they went. It did not disappear in the early Middle Ages, but it tended to decline because it required too much manpower. Moreover, land is eroded no matter how much care it gets if deforestation has gone too far, and in the early Middle Ages it *had* gone too far. The Mediterranean village was dwindling, contracting, throughout the period.

The other type of village is a village of abundance, and if we oversimplify we may call it the northern village or manor. It is characterized by thin settlement; people do not exploit the land fully or tame it totally; there is a great deal of water and a scarcity of sun. The land is plowed less frequently but more deeply. It cannot possibly be fully exploited because the population is not very thick, so there is a good deal of wasteland or forest, some of which can be used for cattle. There is a possibility of dependence upon cattle and a tendency to exploit the land without refertilizing the soil—to move from one piece of land to another. This type of agriculture is close to the nomadic system. It was characteristic of the non-Greco-Roman lands of the ancient world—of practically all the lands beyond the Roman frontier in which there was agriculture at all. (Some of these ancient lands did not have agriculture at all; they had nomadism.)

The semi-nomadic type of agriculture melded to some extent with the Mediterranean form in the late Roman Empire and early Middle Ages. In Gaul, and even northern Italy, the land lent itself to the northern system, which was easily adapted to an underpopulated civilization where agricultural techniques were not sophisticated. Thus manorial agriculture and settlement, in a modified form, spread from northern Europe to large parts of the former Greco-Roman territory. It was simpler than Mediterranean agriculture, and in its early form it did not need or permit the growth of a large population.

The garden type of agriculture had permitted great concentrations of population in the early civilizations; it is still the dominant type of agriculture in heavily populated parts of east and southeast Asia. However, the manorial type has potentialities for growth which the Mediterranean does not. Mediterranean agriculture saturates the land and eventually creates a closed circle. You cannot exploit more land or mechanize farming because you would not know what to do with the surplus people. The northern type, on the other hand, allows for a more elastic agriculture; growth can be absorbed by spilling over into the wasteland.

Again, the inefficiency of German political structures led to states where every village tended to be isolated, left to itself without any possibility of help or probability of tyranny from a central power. Political decentralization created villages with a dominant lord and a large number of serfs who did not revolt because they needed the lord and he needed them. Combined with northern-type agriculture, this system produced what we call the classic manorial village. There were all kinds of variations, of course, of a manorial-style village administered by a community of peasants. The latter was commoner in more primitive societies because they were still less politically organized—among the Slavs and in some parts of northern Germany, for instance. Also, the Mediterranean type of village existed in other parts of Europe—in Wales, for instance, where the soil resembled that of Italy.

Were there significant differences between the economic development of Italy and France between about 500 and 900?

First of all, there were two Italies and two Frances. There was Lombard Italy, mostly in the north, and Byzantine Italy mostly in the south; Mediterranean France, which came close to the development of Italy, and northern France, which developed in a very different way. On the whole, the town did not decline as much in Italy as in other parts of Europe. Civilization remained centered in towns; the Goths, the Lombards, and the Franks kept their administrative centers in towns, not in the baronial castle. There was a denser ecclesiastical organization, and bishops, prelates, and monasteries tended to keep the center of life in towns. There were closer connections with the Byzantine and Muslim worlds, which were at that time more advanced and more complex. There were free men in the Italian towns at all times, and there were traces (though only traces) of self-governing institutions in towns throughout the early Middle Ages. French towns, especially in the north, had few freemen and hardly any autonomous life.

On the other hand French agriculture, especially in the north, was generally more successful than in Italy, especially in the south. The land was richer and more forested, and probably the rural population was better off (and not as thick) as that of Italy. Moreover, Italy had been devastated more throughly by a series of wars, especially by the war between the Goths and the Byzantines. Once France was occupied by the Franks it did not have very serious invasions; in fact, it had four or five hundred years of comparative peace—a very long spell. Nevertheless, harvests were generally poor and famines frequent in early medieval France as well.

Altogether, France had fewer communications than Italy, and a more agrarian life—a more typical early medieval way of life, as we imagine it. It was not perhaps poorer but more primitive. Italy was more complex; in some areas it was Byzantine, or at least close to Byzantium. The Lombard areas, on the other hand, were less unlike northern France than those of Aquitaine or Provence.

What was the impact of the Viking invasion on economic development?

I do not think the Viking invasions were very significant in the development of Europe, even though they quickened the growth of certain institutions. Like other invaders of Europe in the ninth and tenth centuries—the Magyars, the Saracens, or the Slavs—they provoked a reaction; Europe had to organize itself to check their attacks. Their positive contribution was strongest, of course, in the countries where they settled, but Normandy, for instance, was solidly French a hundred years after the Viking conquest. Nobody would call the Norman Conquest a Viking invasion of England.

The Vikings were Germanic, and they strengthened the early Germanic strain so far as they went. Recent studies have rehabilitated the Vikings to some degree. They were not only plunderers; they were willing to cultivate, to trade, and so forth, when they could not get things by stealing them. And their expansion westward as far as Newfoundland was certainly admirable, as was the literature of early Scandinavia.

How do you account for the growth of population and the internal colonization of the tenth century, and would you relate this to the beginning of urban growth in the tenth and eleventh centuries?

The tendency of every species is to grow and fill the earth as long as there are no obstacles to its expansion, and there was no reason why the population should *not* have started to grow again in the tenth century, or possibly somewhat earlier. There was no great plague from the eighth to the fourteenth century, and probably malaria had diminished through reforestation. We don't know much about climate, but it appears that this was a time of greater warmth in most of Europe.

I do not think that political or military factors were responsible for the rise in population. If the population take-off could have been started by political forces, one would have expected it in the Carolingian period, but in spite of the efforts of Charlemagne and his successors, Europe was not then quite ready to start again. Europe started to grow in the period of greatest localism, of complete collapse of the central power. The central power was pulverized by the Vikings and other invaders, and the later development of power was on a local basis, as was the growth of population itself. Innumerable small centers recovered their energies. The smallest and handiest kernel of recovery was the center of an agricultural district, or a city.

Everywhere, population growth both called for and permitted greater crop production, and this in turn permitted concentrations of people who did not have their own food. It also gave more purchasing power to the agricultural population, creating potential customers for urban products. Agricultural colonization and urbanization were two facets of the same phenomenon of expansion.

"Internal" colonization is a relative term: to an isolated manor, a nearby forest is external. If it is possible to colonize your backyard, that's the first thing you do. The farther you go, the more initiative, more capital, and more risk it takes; but the rewards may be greater if the faraway lands are less thickly settled and do not require fertilization. There was room for internal colonization almost everywhere in Europe; but external colonization began almost simultaneously. Colonization was a patchy, haphazard kind of thing. By and large we can say that the most successful internal colonization took place in France and England—especially France, which had a lot of fertile, flat land that had been inadequately exploited in the loose, elastic system of the manor.

Progress in agricultural techniques accompanied internal colonization. The breeding and utilization of animals improved. In the north, where there were some of the best breeds of cattle, you find the greater changes in cereal culture. In the south there is increasing utilization of the mule in transport and a greater diversification of garden vegetables. There is the well-known revolution—but a very *slow* revolution—from the two-field to the three-field system. I think the importance and novelty of this has been exaggerated, but so far as it went it did bring about a substantial increase of food supply. Yet yields normally remained low. At most we can postulate an average yield of four times the seed for the leading cereals. In all probability the single greatest factor of increased food production was the expansion of cultivated areas, both at home and abroad.

England and France had such extensive possibilities for internal development that there was little external colonization. The foremost proponents of it were the Germans and the Iberian peoples. The Germans, on the whole, were more successful because they went to fertile, thinly-settled land. Gradually they expanded into the Baltic region, where they clashed with the westward expansion of the Slavs.

The Iberian peoples expanded into less fertile land. Moreover, they were the only important nation in this period whose expansion was not adequately supported by population growth, largely because a good proportion of the former inhabitants—Moors, Jews, or whatever—ran away or were ousted as the expansion proceeded. A deficiency of manpower is also visible in Scandinavia. Curiously, the Scandinavians went the farthest—a truly admirable expansion—but they left behind an underpopulated and relatively backward homeland.

On the other hand there were peoples for whom urbanization was a more significant outlet than agricultural expansion. Urbanization was a general phenomenon, but it was most intense in northern and central Italy and in what we might call Greater Belgium—that is, the region which has as its center modern Belgium and includes the Low Countries and northern France. They colonized internally at first, then spilled over (Flemish peasants helped the Germans to colonize faraway land; Italians went to the Mediterranean ilsands, Dalmatia, and so on). After a while, both groups turned to trade as their form of colonization; in other terms, commerce rather than agriculture was their expanding frontier.

Was there any important relationship between the Crusades and economic change?

Yes, but I think that the Crusades were an effect as much as a cause of expansion. For two centuries before they started, the population had grown, and Mediterranean trade had created naval equipment and knowledge of the Muslim world.

No doubt the Crusades acted as a catalyzer in quickening the awareness of opportunities and civilization in the Levant, especially among those Europeans who had not been previously involved in Mediterranean trade. Still it is always doubtful whether war is the best agent of penetration. In the short run the military cost of the Crusades may have exceeded the economic and intellectual returns, and in the long run, greater returns might have been acquired through peace.

This is especially true for the Italians, who are often depicted as the sordid profiteers of the enterprise, though they also spent their blood and their money. They had already penetrated the Levant, and the countries with which they had the best business dealings were not near the Holy Land. Too often, the wars limited their relations with the Black Sea countries, with the Mongols, and with North Africa. It is true that they built ships for northerners, and it was helpful to them to have a larger fleet. So in a way the Crusades were helpful to the economic development of Europe, but I don't think they were a major factor.

Were there significant improvements in agricultural technology and crop yield in the twelfth and thirteenth centuries?

There were, but precise dates and localization are hard to determine, especially because the diffusion was slow and spotty. They can be followed only through random archaeological findings, occasional drawings, scattered accounts of estates, and a few manuals of agricultural techniques. By the fourteenth century the average yield of cereals seems to have exceeded four times the seed, but local variations are very great, and some of the increase may be due to the abandonment of marginal land. Up to that time, the main factors of improvement seem to be the very slow spread of rational rotations of crops (not necessarily the three-course system), irrigation, some use of green manuring, some terracing of the steeper slopes, and, above all, better tools and animal husbandry. On heavy soil the diffusion of the wheeled plough was highly beneficial; so were the increased use of iron in agricultural implements, and more efficient types of harnessing and shoeing for draught animals. It is more debatable whether the replacement of oxen by horses was as widespread or as useful as some writers have assumed.

How do you view the development of trade in relation to the growth of cities?

The growth of trade in the later Middle Ages is a much more dramatic, though quantitatively smaller phenomenon than the growth of agriculture. It produced a qualitative difference, a new way of life. But we must distinguish types of trade. As I have stated on other occasions, the general tendency of commercial expansion is to transform yesterday's luxury into today's treat and tomorrow's necessity; but progress in the medieval commercial revolution was far from spectacular, for it started in a milieu where the luxury demand of a few wealthy people weighed more than the ordinary consumption of the masses. Actually the gap between rich and poor widened during that period, but the poor of the thirteenth century would have looked rich in the tenth. If you compare the food given to beggars by monasteries in the same regions from the tenth to the fourteenth centuries, you see a tremendous change in diet. By the fourteenth century, the indigents in Florence protested and rioted because they were doled black bread instead of white.

The largest and most expensive group of items in west-to-east trade was clothing—above all, wool, but also linen. The other very important item of trade was spices, which originally traveled from east to west, but by the thirteenth century traveled just as much from Italy to the east. "Spices" included a lot of things which we would not consider spices today—copper, for instance, and flax. Manuals of merchandise describe "heavy" spice, which included cans of dyestuffs, medicinals, condiments, and a good many raw materials. These were very often the mainstay of long-distance trade. Ships that were filled with clothing going east came back loaded with spices (mainly), or with raw silk and cotton. Nevertheless, the overseas west-east trade also included rather cheap and heavy commodities which were carried somewhat shorter distances. Fine spices and first-quality cloth could even bear the expense of land transportation as far as China. As standards of living and expectations rose, everybody became entitled to have cloth, and cheaper cloth became more widespread and important. The relative importance of Flemish first-quality cloth diminished because there was more cloth on the market.

Staples also traveled over substantial distances, especially where there were regional deficiencies. Some parts of Italy had to import grain, and certain regions became regular suppliers and still grow grain today—regions around the Black Sea, for instance. Many kinds of wine were exported, including the great wines of Gascony and Burgundy, as well as sweet wines of the eastern Mediterranean which are less popular today. Salt, of course, was exported everywhere from the sea plains and the mountains. Works of art, jewels, furniture, and weapons traveled everywhere.

Even the increasing rarity of famines in Europe is to be credited not only to the success of agriculture, but also to trade. By the thirteenth century they were very few and mostly in underdeveloped regions, because in a year of bad harvests towns could import grain. The famine of the fourteenth century was an exception, which we'll mention later on.

In most of Europe, the most important, regular consumers of trade goods still were the lay and ecclesiastical nobility, but in Italy and Belgium the demand of bourgeois purchasers soon became paramount. As shops were established in the towns, local periodical markets lost their exclusive position. International markets had a more important function (and some survive today) in bringing people together. Here, as time went on, more and more buying was done from samples; goods were shipped later, paid for later, and so on. By the thirteenth century, trade had grown so that even international fairs were not needed—in the larger towns like Florence, Venice, Milan, Genoa, and Bruges, goods from everywhere were always available, and samples could be inspected at any time.

The growth of self-governing institutions in the communes is connected with the growth of trade in much the same way that feudalism is connected with manorialism; it is a matter of congeniality rather than necessity. It became *easier* and more valuable for towns to become autonomous when trade increased. At first the towns did not differ from the villages in the sense that both wanted autonomy during the period of localism in the tenth and eleventh centuries; their motives were similar to those of the French lords who defied their king. In fact, the first leaders of the movement for urban self-government were small nobles rather than merchants. The merchants soon got into the act, however, and before long every town that was worth its salt established a government of merchants, by merchants, and for merchants.

It is not always easy to distinguish between a merchant and an aristocrat, and in fact one characteristic of the early period is that in the more progressive towns noblemen became merchants and merchants, noblemen. The distinctions between nobleman and merchant and between trade and manual labor, which I believe crippled the development of the Roman city-state, did not exist in the Middle Ages. As for the distinction between merchants and craftsmen, it hinged mostly on the fact that a man could make a fortune in trade if things went well, even without much capital, but he could not do so in a craft because his productivity was limited by the dearth of available mechanical help.

There was mechanical improvement in this period, of course; the technical revolution went much farther in craftsmanship than in agriculture. The water mill, for instance, was gradually adapted for a whole series of industrial uses from grinding grain or dyestuffs to triphammers and bellows. In the textile industry, the pedal loom replaced the hand loom, and the spinning wheel appeared. Still, these were limited inventions; they sped up the craftsman's work, but not very much. It was hard for the craftsman to buy these machines, and very often he had to rent them or to pawn what he did own in a bad year.

However, a craftsman did not necessarily remain a craftsman. Normally he sold at least his own products and was thus in a way a merchant, and if he sold the products of others, too, he might gradually rise in economic, social, and political status. In towns where the greatest development of industry occurred, it was not merchants but merchant-craftsmen who emerged at the head of the commune. In some places they were buyers and sellers of raw wool, or in some cases later on, they were weavers. However, the weavers who were only weavers remained in the proletariat.

As for the interplay of the development of trade with that of communal institutions, it varied from region to region and from city to city. The only acceptable generalization is that so long as economic growth continued, that is, normally until the early or mid-fourteenth century, every generation of successful merchants saw its political and social dominance challenged by fresh layers of newcomers to affluence; the result was a most agitated public life, but also a continuous broadening of the ruling class. Eventually this included not only merchants but also the more prosperous craftsmen. The merchants, even where they conquered power through some form of union or guild, soon split into factions and sometimes tried their fortune single-handedly; craftsmen usually made their bid through their guilds. These had irreplaceable value in a world without effective mechanization; it helped craftsmen to hold their own against excessive exploitation by the richer merchants. But even these generalizations ought to be qualified as soon as we quit the larger cities of Italy and Flanders and move to the less thriving, less autonomous ones of other parts of Europe.

The medieval Church had a very powerful impart on any aspect of life; its size, prestige, and wealth were enormous. But in economic matters it is often hard to decide whether its influence differed from that of powerful lay institutions, and if so, in what directions.

In agriculture, it is generally believed that ecclesiastic administrators were better educated and often more devoted to their institution than the stewards of a lay landlord. The Church did not die out as a lay family might; but the absence of hereditary succession created intervals during which its property was especially threatened, and the new abbot or bishop might have completely different ideas from his predecessor.

Until the twelfth century at least, the Church remained primarily a land-based institution, even though bishops lived in cities and many monasteries were just outside city walls. Certain monastic orders, especially the Cistercians, have been credited with an important role in land reclamation; recently Georges Duby has called attention to the role of anchorites in the same field. But it is hard to assess the importance of the Church, whose documents as a rule are well preserved, as compared to that of laymen, whose documents are more scattered.

As to trade, apart from pilgrimages, whose importance as promoters of commerce has generally been exaggerated, the Church contributed an economic theory that was largely in contradiction with its own economic practice. Almost throughout the Middle Ages canon law, in agreement with the Bible and with Greek philosophers, regarded interest-bearing loans as sinful usury, no matter whether they were extended to the needy poor, the profligate rich, or the merchant. Yet the pope and a large proportion of the clergy needed the help of bankers and money lenders very badly, and gave help to them in return. This was not a direct process: though Italian bankers acted as collectors for the papacy and carried out all sorts of financial operations, they received little or no payment for their services. However, they had the pope's protection, they handled Church goods, and they were part of the ecclesiastic system of long-distance communications. The Italian merchants could rely on their galleys and their superior force at sea, but it would have been hard for them to accomplish what they did on land without the pope and the Church.

However, we cannot say that the Church participated directly in trade; in that sense it was the prisoner of its own doctrine. On the other hand, one cannot imagine its expansion or the policies of Innocent III or Gregory VII without the assistance of the bankers.

The Church always distinguished between licit and illicit trade, but there was a certain suspicion of commercial gain per se which was not a factor in its view of agricultural earnings. Agriculture seemed more natural. This bias was not entirely original with the Church; it went back to antiquity—to Aristotle and to Jewish theory.

I think that the attitude of the Church had a very slight effect on those who were not part of it. Like an island in the middle of a river, the Church attitude forced the stream of trade and commercial development to go around it, but the river still ran to its goal.

What was the relationship between the growth of royal bureaucracy and economic change in the twelfth, thirteenth, and early fourteenth centuries?

This varied in different countries, but the most essential change was the replacement of vassals by paid employees. Personal loyalty was still required, but a salary does not imply loyalty, at least beyond the hours of employment. On the other hand, a man who does not work for his salary can be fired. The growth of a money economy with direct revenue from taxation allowed the sovereign to hire employees. How much this alternative was used depends first on how much the king was willing and able to tax; taxation depends in turn on the power of the sovereign; the power of the sovereign depends partly on his ability to tax. This would look like a closed circle, but favorable circumstances and the ability of the king made it possible to break the circle.

The circle was broken best and earliest in England, where the influence of a money economy can be traced back at least to the first kings of the Norman dynasty, and even earlier. Even though England was by no means the most developed country in Europe from an economic viewpoint, the king was strong enough to exploit the available riches of the country. It took longer in France because the royal power did not grow very fast. For a long time the French king was a small sovereign of a small region, and for the twelfth century one should speak rather of the relationship between economic change and the growth of local bureaucracy: the bureaucracies of Normandy and Flanders grew faster than that of royal France. The royal bureaucracy began to grow under Philip Augustus, and it grew very fast from then until the reign of Philip the Fair.

The only significant monarchy in Italy, the kingdom of Sicily, was founded upon the bureaucratic traditions of the Byzantine Empire and the Islamic rulers, and it was bureaucratic from the start. It has been said that Frederick II founded the first modern state. This is true only if you consider his wishes rather than his achievements, but still the mentality was bureaucratic.

The Spanish monarchies were too much involved in warfare to become truly bureaucratic. The Visigoths had been better organized than most barbarian kingdoms, but with the *Reconquista*—which is in many ways the key to the entire story of medieval Spain—the monarchy became more and more military, and bureaucracy tended to disintegrate rather than advance. This is just one more aspect of the tragic incompleteness of developments in Spain.

In Germany one cannot speak of royal bureaucracy, but of bureaucracy in the different feudal states. Germany remained feudal too long ever to mature as a bureaucratic monarchy. The German kings did try to build a bureaucracy upon paid serfs, but this arrangement had no great success.

I would say that the most successful bureaucratic growth occurred in the papacy and the city-states. The papacy could rely upon clergymen, who were literate and were accustomed to sit down, and were not so inclined toward military adventure. Writing and accounting are the lifeblood of towns, where the atmosphere is conducive to the growth of bureaucracy.

Let us consider the European economy in the middle of the thirteenth century. What major differences of development had taken place in the various states?

We must distinguish between states in which agriculture was still overwhelmingly predominant and those in which it was to some extent balanced by trade or industry. England and France (if we do not include in France the Low Countries or Provence, which was not under the French Crown in the thirteenth century) were still predominantly agricultural. This does not mean that they did not have towns or trade, but with a few exceptions their towns were mainly centers of local exchange, where the people at the surrounding countryside exchanged farm produce against fairly ordinary town products and imports. The welfare of the average French or English peasant was probably greater than that of the average peasant in any other country, although peasants in the older parts of Germany may have been approaching this status by the late thirteenth century. Contemporary literature mentions the progress, even "insolent progress," of the peasants of southern Germany, and in some parts of Germany the peasants had never been serfs. However, there were important differences between the old parts of Germany and the lands of colonization, where the land was primitive and the regime almost colonial. The Teutonic Knights, for instance, have been compared to plantation owners of more modern times.

My impression is that France had more of a middle class than England, but a good proportion of it was bureaucratic rather than commercial. This tendency has continued in France until our own time. The English middle class was numerically smaller, but I believe it was more commercial and independent. There was good craftsmanship, and the towns were smaller but perhaps more enterprising than the French towns.

Italian cities were immensely richer than cities in other places, sometimes richer than entire countries. The estimated value of incoming wares in the port of Genoa in 1297 (I think) was nearly four times as large as the revenue of the kingdom of France in the same year. On the other hand, Italy had far less farming land than France or England, and much of it was overpopulated. The Po Valley was fertile and its peasants were relatively well off, but in the Apennines they were quite poor.

Spain had a lean economy; towns were not very large, and they were mainly agrarian, much like those of France. Spain had a very large number of small noblemen, who abstained from manual labor and thus did not contribute very much to general productivity. What protected Spain from slipping far below the level of other countries in this period was its comparatively small population. Moreover, some parts of Catalonia and the Basque provinces were prosperous, and even Andalusia had not yet entirely lost the prosperity it had at the time of the Muslim occupation.

Taking whatever definition of capitalism you wish to present, to what extent can we call the European economy at the end of the thirteenth century capitalist or precapitalist?

One must first, of course, define capital, and I don't think there is any easy definition. Obviously there was capital in the Middle Ages and indeed in antiquity. Agricultural capital was composed mostly of land, much less of tools; in factories and workshops it was composed mostly of inventory, much less of machines. But capital is not the same as capitalism.

If one defines capitalism in terms of the so-called profit motive, then I think the European economy (especially in the towns) was definitely capitalistic in the thirteenth century. In this sense there was a sharp change from antiquity. The ideal of the ancient Roman was not so much growth as stability in a golden mean—to live happily with what he had. In the medieval towns, expectations were rising. There was continuous turmoil as people tried to rise higher; there was less respect for birth, and the main basis of distinction was wealth. Of course old wealth was better than new, and old citizenship better than new, but this feeling still survives in our own society. There was interest in invention and innovation and a desire to open and develop new markets, at least on the part of the progressive elements of the population. On the other hand, Europe was as diversified in the thirteenth century as the world today; if you fix your attention on Nepal or Paraguay, rather than the United States or Belgium, the world is not capitalistic today. In the Italian cities that were the New Yorks of that period you find a distinct drive to increase the possibilities of selling things to other people. Certain elements of today's capitalism, of course, did not exist—advertising, for instance. But what was the guild if not another form of the modern cartel? Just as industries merge to eliminate competition, so did medieval guilds, and they had no more need to advertise competing goods than do different branches of the same cartel.

Absolute quantities, of course, were infinitesimal compared with those of today, and if a quantitative definition is given for capitalism, then the thirteenth century undoubtedly would not fit its terms. There was a certain tendency to try to sell expensive goods to a few rather than cheap goods to many. Also, although they looked for new markets, they knew that their opportunities to enlarge the existing market were comparatively small. However, I think these differences are of emphasis only, and that the capitalist principles have not changed.

Do you agree with the view that the European economy went through a long depression in the fourteenth and early fifteenth centuries? If there is something in this view, what contributed to the situation, and to what extent did Italy participate in it?

As you certainly know, this is a debated question. The majority of scholars (the depressionists) think that there was a definite depression in the period you have mentioned. However, there is a large minority who minimize depression, or argue that it was fully overcome after a while. With certain qualifications, I am with the depressionists. Let me say, though, that this dispute cannot be completely solved without quantitative data that we simply do not have. In agriculture we have very few statistics; in certain aspects of trade and industry, a few more. We have a few in population and taxation. The documentation is fragmentary, but what exists is all on the side of the depressionists, and that is what convinces me that we are right.

At the root of the depression we find the same problem that occurred at the end of the ancient period, but in a less dramatic form. There was a decline in population, apparently for the same reasons, and this time we have more information. The population declined almost everywhere, more in the towns than in the country, but in the country, too. There is no doubt that the decline was connected with a sudden return of the plague and other epidemics. There had been no major outbursts of epidemics from the eighth century to the fourteenth, when one was followed by many others. These epidemics followed on some other circumstances that may have paved the way for them; there had been a succession of bad harvests and famines a little while before. These may have been connected again with climatic changes, and these in turn with deforestation and overpopulation.

Optimum population depends at all times on whether the available soil under current technology is sufficient to feed the people. Toward the end of the thirteenth century there were signs that the population was too dense, but in earlier periods, changes in techniques had been adopted to allow the soil to maintain more people. When there were too many people in the twelfth century, some of them emigrated to the east; when there were too many in the thirteenth century, the three-field system was adopted; at all times people moved from country to town, or there was progress in irrigation, and so forth. In the beginning of the fourteenth century, however, technology did not respond to the need for more food. We are forced back to imponderables for an explanation of why technology did not improve enough. There was a certain slacking of inventiveness, but that may be a consequence as well as a cause. Invention is not useful if society is not receptive to it, and it may be that a society becomes less receptive as it grows old—that it adapts to an equilibrium that seems good enough.

There were traumatic causes, too, just as there were at the end of the Roman Empire—again, war. However, the fourteenth-century wars were less serious than the German invasions or Muslim expansion, because Europe had a cushion. Instead of reaching into the heart of Europe, the invaders stopped at the Byzantine Empire. The Mongols invaded most of Asia, but they penetrated Europe only in southern Russia; the Turks invaded a good deal of the Balkan peninsula but they did not conquer the West. There were wars inside Europe, of course; the Hundred Years' War had bad consequences for France, but not all of France was devastated. It did cost a great deal of money, and it reduced the opportunities for trade. There were frequent wars among the little Italian states. They were not very bloody, but they scorched the earth, and the loss of trade was a great blow for states which lived by trade.

The possible impact of diminishing political liberty is harder to assess. It has been claimed that despotism diminished the economic resiliency of the cities. By the end of the thirteenth century, the first dictators had appeared in Italy. At the same time the selfish ruling oligarchies of the French towns had given up their liberties and come entirely under royal control. The English towns did not lose many liberties because they had always been less free, but the English guilds became very inelastic. Everywhere in Europe the guild was no longer a door to new commerce; it accepter fewer apprentices because there was less opportunity.

There is a dynamic of depression just as there is a dynamic of expansion. Both are chain reactions, and if the first explosion is missed, the others are apt to miss too. Still I am ready to admit that the depression of the fourteenth century was much less profound than the depression of the late Roman Empire. It slowed down development but produced no Dark Ages. Also, it did not affect every aspect of life. Accumulated capital and skill were not destroyed. Advances were still being made in some fields, including science and mathematics.

In any depression one must distinguish between more- and less-developed countries. Italy was the most highly developed country in this period, and therefore in an absolute sense probably lost more than any other country; but it had a great deal of resiliency. The Italians had skill and energy and know-how, and they managed to open up new markets. When they could no longer grow sugar in Cyprus, they started to grow it in Madeira, and later in Brazil.

Some countries and regions had not yet begun to develop at all, and so the depression hardly affected them. There was no overpopulation in Poland or Serbia, and with plenty of room to grow, Poland had not real depression. In Serbia there was a depression, but it was mainly due to the Turkish occupation and not to economic conditions. There were some cities—new ones, for the most part—which did well even in depressed countries; Antwerp, for example, grew while Bruges declined.

It was the average countries which suffered the most, I think. They were sufficiently developed to feel the economic depression, but they did not have enough to spare to weather bad times. France was very hard hit (partly due to the Hundred Years' War); England not quite so badly, and in fact there is a continuing debate over whether the English peasants may not actually have improved their status during this period.

What was the condition of the European economy by 1500? To what extent had it recovered from the depression, and what regional or national differences can be identified?

Although there were marked differences in the rate of recovery, there is little doubt that there was a general improvement from the second half of the fifteenth century on. The population stabilized, and people had the impression of recovery even though there were no important changes in the direction of the economy in this period. The fifteenth century was not a time of great changes (like that of the shirt) nor an age when serfs became free. No new liberation movement occurred except in some parts of Spain. The sixteenth century suffered from many wars, but on the whole continued to improve. By 1500 some new crops appeared. Among former luxuries that became relatively commonplace were oranges and fruits of that kind. Nobody knew about vitamins, of course, but they were helpful anyway. There also was the beginning of a tendency to produce and sell cheaper wares to a wider market. The rate of change of fashion accelerated, and people bought a larger amount of less expensive things, making a little more work for more people.

The search for new markets to replace the old continued, and it eventually had great importance. The late fifteenth century was the period of the great Portuguese advances around the African coast, and the first colonization of Atlantic islands—Madeira, the Canaries, and so forth. With a return of interest in northern exploration, some parts of Russia which had been cut off by the Mongols came again into view. Most of east central Europe from Poland to the Balkans got into closer communication with western Europe. Then came the great discoveries in America, but these are beyond our period.

France had recovered from the Hundred Years' War by 1490 at least enough to start on expansive conquests of other lands, even though its towns had not come back to predepression level. England had suffered rather less from war—I don't think the Wars of the Roses were very destructive. I am struck by the increase of sheepruns in England during this period, when there could not have been an increase in demand for wool. In the late fifteenth century sheepruns spread almost everywhere, but most particularly, of course, in England and Spain. By the end of the century there was a sheep for every two Spaniards, and the number grew and grew. Even regions in Italy which were not well suited to sheep had them, and some of the consequences were serious. In Spain and Italy, moreover, the sheep ate vegetation which could not be spared.

My impression is that Germany was fairly well off in this period—if I may make a sweeping generalization, Germany seems to be better off when it is politically low. There is a certain safety in being divided and thus prevented from overambitious enterprises. The towns of Germany especially were in a good position, and it may be that by 1500 the towns of southern Germany actually had greater production and population than in the thirteenth century. Marginal land was abandoned when the population diminished, which helped to improve agricultural yield.

Italy still led Europe in skill and enterprise and investment. Italians had if anything increased their share of the foreign market, and Italian bankers, merchants, and financiers were prominent everywhere. There was also a definite improvement in agricultural technology. Greater care was given to conservation of soil, and new crops were introduced—rice, for instance, which was important because it produced more calories per acre than other products. Northern and central Italy had a full and mature economy; it was about to become overmature, but it was still fighting. Southern Italy, however, presented a picture of decadence like that of Spain. The countryside had been devastated—overgrazed, deforested—it was already very like what it is today, a depressed area far below the standard of the rest of the country. There were a few patches of prosperity, and Sicily still exported grain, but whether this was because of a surplus or because the peasants ate too little, I do not know—I suspect the latter.

One question that has always bothered me is that of the political failure of the late medieval bourgeoisie. The bourgeoisie of northern Europe never really played a significant role in political life, and the Italian bourgeoisie of the fourteenth and fifteenth centuries gave up their republican institutions and subjected themselves to dictators, or to the rule of the prince. How do you account for this political impotence?

The entire history of the Italian city-states was marked by struggle and turmoil. There was a continuous pressure of newcomers to wealth trying to rise to the political top, and in a world of rising expectations you cannot expect anything but strife. Even the triumph of a dictator at first did not necessarily mean the permanent downfall of democracy, but only a temporary solution to a political crisis.

Protest, danger, and dissatisfaction are congenital to democracy; they are not pathological so long as there is hope of remedying existing evils—if the dictator can be kicked out, if the corruption can be cleaned up, if better democratic leadership can be found. When people give up hope of improving the system by political participation, then there is trouble. I think the basic reason for loss of hope after the mid-fourteenth century is the end of the continuous economic progress that had led to social and political strife. When the real depression began, in the late thirteenth or early fourteenth century, it became difficult to rely on democratic change. The rich were sitting pretty and the poor were doomed.

Not all democracies failed the same way or at the same time. The Florentines had a dictator for a short while in the fourteenth century but they threw him out and continued as a progressive (if unruly) democracy right through the fifteenth century. Their democracy broadened as time went on, but as early as the thirteenth century, noblemen were excluded from government. The lower classes got more and more representation in the commune, and taxation became fairer. Corruption and tax evasion were common, of course, but still Florentine democracy blundered without falling.

In Venice, on the other hand, there was a strange political freezing. The higher aristocrats, instead of bickering and thus allowing the lower classes to rise, formed a sort of union—the Great Council—and continued to rule Venice for centuries. However, they paid enough attention to the principle of *noblesse oblige* to avoid serious opposition. They were as careful to govern well as if they had been popularly elected officials, and Venice was the first town to care for the old and the unemployed by social legislation. Also, the Venetian aristocrat paid for his powers with his person; they were always fighting and never idle, and if their government cannot be called a democracy, still it was not even a collective tyranny.

Milan is a sad example—it succumbed. Milan had been an independent commune in the eleventh century, and had long been in the forefront of democratic evolution. But it also was among the first cities to accept dictatorship, and I do not think any satisfactory explanation has been found for its failure.

In Genoa, anarchy had always been the rule. It never became a stabilized oligarchy or dictatorship—in fact it never became anything for more than a few months.

I think that one can draw certain conclusions from all these various examples. The depression put a stop to the economic progress that had permitted strife and corruption to exist without harming anyone too much. Moreover, the citizen armies which had fought the communes' wars of independence gradually disappeared. The president of the most important bank in Siena had fought against the Florentines at the battle of Montaperti in 1260; in fact, almost every able-bodied citizen was drafted. But as wars became almost continuous, it became more convenient to hire mercenaries. Gradually it was no longer true that every citizen could defend his liberty, and that made it possible for dictators to take over.

As for France, it is my impression that the continuous rising of the lower classes never really operated there. The French cities had never been much involved in trade; even that part of their ruling class that was made up of enriched merchants and craftsmen imitated the landed aristocracy instead of concentrating on town government. They became more and more selfish and idle; they were bureaucrats, and in any case the French king limited the liberties of the towns. The local leaders became no more than royal tax assessors and collectors, and there was none of that healthy strife and turmoil *within* the cities that marked the Italian communes.

The Spanish city, I believe, was an archaism. It was still very much like a Roman city ruled mostly by landowners. The towns were very proud, and they were fully represented in the Cortes, but the mentality of the town leaders was that of the nobleman and not of the merchant bourgeois.

Is there a relationship between economic decline in Italy and what we call the Italian Renaissance? Isn't it unusual in history to have great intellectual and artistic development in a time of economic difficulties? Doesn't it usually happen the other way?

I do not believe that a direct, quantitative correlation can be established between the wealth of a country and its intellectual or artistic development. To quote only two instances, Victorian England was richer than Elizabethan England, but Kipling was not as great as Shakespeare; Bach, Beethoven, and Goethe appeared at a time when Germany was far below her political and economic peak. But it is legitimate to look for a congeniality of a particular type of literature or art with the economic and political circumstances of its time.

No doubt the statement of Giovanni Rucellai, a rich merchant of Renaissance Florence who started the first large art collection of his time, is significant: spending money, he said, is more amusing than earning it. A man like him, or a Medici banker, did not need to increase his wealth but he could win prestige by embellishing his city and looking like an intelligent, cultured man. The traditional basis of distinction (noble birth) had not been important in Italy for a long time, and investment in culture was a more profitable means to power.

Yet in terms of actual monetary value, not as much was spent on art in the Renaissance as during the Middle Ages. The cost of a medieval cathedral was far greater than that of a Renaissance mansion or painting. On the other hand, the cathedral was built to the glory of God and only indirectly to the glory of the builder; the mansion and the paintings were much more clearly to the glory of the owner.

In Italy the great age of economic growth ended by the time of Boccaccio and Petrarch, both of whom were sons of successful merchants. They did not have to spend as much time in trade as their grandfathers, and they could invest their leisure in the arts. By the fifteenth century, too, the Italian urban class had ceased to be swollen by immigration. In the twelfth and thirteenth centuries, very few citizens of the Italian towns had been native-born—in 1200 almost three quarters of the population of Florence was made up of people born in the district, not in the city. In the Renaissance, however, the upper class in the cities was mostly descended from a long line of city dwellers.

Again, there had been practically no illiteracy in the Italian towns by the thirteenth century; but culture tended to be polarized toward economic and political gains, and literature and arts were more of a hobby. In the Renaissance, the "amateurs" in culture became eager to spend all their time in nonprofit cultural pursuits.

In general, in the Middle Ages expensive constructions for religious purposes were made by a society rather than an individual; and they often swallowed up whatever surplus might be available for economic growth. Italian towns, however, used their surplus in trade while the going was good, and turned to cultural pursuits when they had sufficient reserves.

What areas or problems in medieval economic and social history could most helpfully be explored, and what methodology should be applied?

First of all I should like to say that although my specialization may be economic and social history, I believe that historical compartments are artificial and that we must combine all possible approaches in one; true history is total, no more and no less economic than intellectual, political, military, or artistic. But if I must confine myself to economic and social aspects, I would say that the main achievement of my generation has been to shift emphasis from prominent individuals to ordinary people, and from a small number to entire collectivities. The next logical step would be to turn from qualitative to quantitative interpretations, and this in fact seems to be the tendency of economic and social historians younger than I.

For the medieval period, however, the extant documents will never yield sufficient evidence for a sustained quantitative interpretation; and I am not sure that this is really a serious disadvantage. History is a Muse and a work of art, even if it requires scientific exactitude in dealing with authentic raw materials. We can use economic models and statistical measurements as tools, but we cannot make a skeleton alive if we do not cover it with a body, and quality is to quantity what the body is to the skelton.

Again, my generation has studied economic history for its own sake or in a search for the economic motivations that underlie the historical process. Some younger economic historians are more concerned with providing economists with data and political planners with lessons; it is good to be useful to others, but history does not have to be useful so long as it fulfills its own goal.

Agricultural history is probably the

most promising field for the younger economic historians; it has long been neglected because documents are few and rather unglamorous, but it employed by far the largest part of the medieval population. My generation inherited from the preceding ones a preference for trade and industry; I cannot help sharing that preference, if only because the greatest motor of change and progress in the Middle Ages was commerce, even if it was the occupation of a minority. And it is in commerce, rather than in agriculture, that we can find a minimum of quantitative data, barely enough to guess at general trends and fluctuations.

Probably the most interesting debate today concerns the depression of the late Middle Ages. We disagree in the first place on what is the test of depression. What matters most, total production or per capita production? Quantitative data on production, at any rate, are hard to gather. Data on distribution and consumption are even rarer. The discussion probably never will end, but the hardest problems are those which engross historians most.

Of course there are many areas in social history which are totally unknown. I wish we knew more about the silent parts of the population. Women, for instance, were more than half of the population in the Middle Ages as today, and we know almost nothing about them. Peasants, proletarians, and small artisans are nearly unknown too, and it is easy to misinterpret whatever information we have. Protests may indicate an intolerable situation or, on the contrary, rising expectations. We cannot assess them quantitatively; it requires flair, and flair very often leads in the wrong direction. Expression of satisfaction also can be interpreted ambivalently. Peasants are normally silent even today. It a peasant learns to write and writes about peasants, then he is no longer a peasant but a writer, and his reaction is not typical of his class.

One of the things that interest me is domestic architecture. I would like to know more about medieval houses, bridges, docks, and utilitarian objects like clocks. I also would like historians to study languages as documents of social history. The linguists, who are becoming more and more theoretical and mathematical, give us little help. We should train many young people to become linguistic historians. Law also is an important source of social history; we might profit from going more deeply into private law and its changes. Then there is literature, including folk tales; their transformation from one period to another may be very significant. Palaeobotanics, medieval archaeology, aerial photography, are other promising fields; and of course, there remain enormous numbers of ordinary written documents to be studied and analyzed.

I would conclude that the real problem today is finding the time to read all that is being written. When I was a young man I could read most of what was published in my field, partly because my field was narrower (as one grows older, one's field necessarily grows broader). Now the quantity of written material is increasing so fast that we are getting close to the predicament of the scientists, who must read abstracts instead of books. In history, however, abstracts are not enough, because details are often the most interesting and important part of a book.

12

Government and Society in Renaissance and Reformation Europe

G. R. ELTON

THE HISTORIOGRAPHICAL CONTEXT

The political history of the period from the late fifteenth to the mid-seventeenth century is both highly complex and critically important for the development of European civilization. In this period an intermediary stage between medieval and modern political systems developed; this early modern state was marked by the ideal of the divine right of kings, a new consciousness of the sovereign power of the state, and the establishment of bureaucracies to strengthen royal power and control society. But this process of centralization and political rationalization was complicated, and often diverted, by religious struggles, by boom-and-bust cyclic economic trends, by the need of royal government to placate ambitious and restless aristocracies, by long periods of international and civil war, and by varied consequences of political experimentation.

To establish a coherent pattern out of these diverse developments requires an historical mind of unusual toughness and clarity, and these qualities distinguish the work of G. R. Elton, who now holds the chair of Constitutional History at Cambridge University. Born in 1910, Elton came to England from Prague as a child; he is the son of an eminent émigré classical scholar. He brings to the study of the early modern state not only a love of archival research—which must be intensively pursued if the realities of the diurnal functioning of sixteenth-century governments are to be revealed—but also a cool, commonsense temperament freed from traditional illusions and sentimental sophistries about the problems of power and social control. His first book, *The Tudor Revolution in Government,* fundamentally altered the accepted view of the political history of Henry VIII's reign. His *Star Chamber Stories* brilliantly revealed the functioning of a sixteenth-century judicial system. In other works, Elton has exhibited extraordinary powers of synthesis, surveying the whole course of Tudor history in a magisterial volume and the interaction of religion, politics, and economic change in early sixteenth-century Western Europe. Extremely generous and gracious toward younger scholars, a superb supervisor of graduate students, Elton has not sought but has not flinched from controversy and scholarly debate. Prolific, absolutely dedicated to the academic life, immensely learned, self-confident and bold, Elton has become one of the most influential British historians of his generation.

Chronological Outline

1328–1498: The House of Valois fights "the Hundred Years' War" with England, expels the English from French soil, and establishes a powerful national monarchy.

1399–1461: The House of Lancaster rules in England.

1415: Henry V wins a great victory over superior French forces at Agincourt and reconquers Normandy.

1431: Joan of Arc is burned by the English at Rouen.

1455–1485: The War of the Roses, a dreary civil war between the rival English houses of Lancaster and York. Henry, Earl of Richmond, defeats Richard III at Bosworth Field in August 1485 and becomes King Henry VII, the first Tudor.

1516: Sir Thomas More publishes his *Utopia* in Latin.

1527: Henry VIII of England breaks with the Church of Rome when the pope refuses to sanction his divorce from Catherine of Aragon and his marriage to Anne Boleyn.

1527: Italy becomes the battleground for the Habsburg-Valois wars. Rome's preeminence in the Renaissance is ended when Spanish and German mercenaries sack the Holy City and capture the pope. Florence and Milan decline rapidly in economic and political importance during the sixteenth century.

1534: Passage of the Act of Supremacy, the decisive beginning of the English Reformation, which appoints the king the supreme head of the Church of England.

1562–1598: The religious wars in France culminating in the Edict of Nantes, which ends the persecution of the Huguenots.

1563: Completion of the establishment of the Anglican Church, the Church of England.

1564: The death of Michelangelo and the birth of Shakespeare.

1588: The defeat of the Spanish Armada marks the beginning of the general decline of the Spanish monarchy.

1589–1792: The House of Bourbon rules in France.

1603: Personal union of England and Scotland under the House of Stuart.

1641–1649: The Puritan Revolution and civil war in England.

Norman F. Cantor

We will be discussing the political and legal institutions of early modern Europe, and social change as it affected these institutions. Would you begin by taking a look at the recent literature on the subject?

G. R. Elton

I will comment on the recent work in English history, because that is what I know best. Since the war, administrative and legal history have been emphasized above all else, and new sources have been opened up. Until recently, students of the sixteenth century relied extensively—almost exclusively—on traditional sources, mainly chronicle material and letters. Only in the last twenty years has the record material of this period been reviewed, and this has made a considerable difference. It also has helped to redirect interest toward the study of the actual working of an administration. When I started work (about twenty years ago), most historians of the Tudor period were content with fairly loose generalizations, and they tended to be constitutionalists—politically directed in interest and interpretation. Use of the records has changed all that and produced a swing in the other direction, somewhat to the neglect of traditional approaches. Of course there have been other developments as well, particularly in economic history, and we have exploited a much greater variety of sources than was available in the 1940's.

Two important things have happened to the writing of English history: the proliferation of historians and the proliferation of records used. This thickening of the ground has been profitable, on the whole, in the acquisition of knowledge. Synthesis has not been lacking either; there have been various attempts to gather together the results of all this work, and there have even been major controversies within the field of sixteenth-century history, all of which helps to advance our understanding of the period.

If it is true that at the end of the thirteenth century the governments of England and France were remarkably effective (for medieval governments), how do you explain the decline of leadership and the collapse of administration in the fourteenth century? Was the failure of medieval government at its peak of accomplishment due to certain inherent limitations, or was it caused by external matters such as economic decline, or plague?

Obviously the decline was influenced by such things as plague and overpopulation, which was marked toward the end of the thirteenth century in western Europe and produced its own Malthusian controls. It was affected also by the attacks on Europe from the East. But the fundamental trouble of Western monarchy was built into it, and the strength of the Crown under Edward I in England or Philip IV of France was somewhat illusory because it depended quite excessively on individuals. A monarch's effectiveness depended more on his personality than on permanent machinery, and the system was always liable to collapse. It did have machinery at its disposal, some of which was highly advanced, efficient, and bureaucratic. But without a strong king the machinery did not work, or it produced no results when it did work. According to the records, revenues were collected and cases of justice decided; in fact, however, they were not.

The western European monarchies underwent crises not of kingship, but of royal families. In England, every good, strong king was followed by a bad, weak king. The worst thing that could happen to a medieval monarchy was a minority and/or a disputed succession, and this was very much a feature of the period in both England and France.

The Hundred Years' War operated in both countries to weaken the position of the dynasties in respect to their governments. The war was extremely expensive, and it could not be financed from the personal resources of the Crown. Taxation required the cooperation of taxpayers, and therefore served to strengthen parliamentary and similar institutions, with all the resultant complications. From the dynastic preoccupations of the monarchs (which caused the war) there flowed constitutional, administrative, and antimonarchic consequences which helped to weaken the declining governments. But weakness was natural to medieval monarchy, and it was bound to run into difficulties sooner or later as long as it depended on individual personalities.

When did a fundamental change in the structure of royal government occur? Was it in the last two or three decades of the fifteenth century, or did the apparent changes of that period simply reflect the coming of peace, economic growth, and the accession of strong personalities to the throne?

I don't think that any one line of development applies across the board. In late fifteenth-century France, the revival of monarchy owed a great deal to the Hundred Years' War. In the late stages of the war, the king won the power to tax without consent and thus equipped himself with military power, and eventually with a standing army. Even by the late fifteenth century, France was an absolute monarchy to a degree unknown elsewhere, and French institutional development had undergone a genuine change. By 1480, an administrative reorganization designed to equip the monarchy with bureaucratic institutions in the service of the Crown was under way; the process was not complete, however, until the reign of Louis XIV.

The French situation was not reproduced anywhere else—not even in Burgundy, which led in administrative reform, institutional change, and social transformation. The dukes of Burgundy set the style for the courts of Europe, particularly in the one element that held together the bodies politic—the visibly glorious monarchy of the sixteenth century. The stress on kingship and the splendor of monarchs, and the elaborate and elevated courts with extremely refined ceremonial, originated in Burgundy and were widely copied, especially in early sixteenth-century France and in England from about the reign of Henry VIII.

In late fifteenth-century England, however, there was no major institutional transformation but rather a recovery of the methods and achievements of an earlier monarchy. Edward IV and Henry VII found and revived a machinery which had once been capable of effective government. They used the institutions of their own households, in which machinery for administration had always been available, and they used them efficiently. The growth of the resources of the monarchy required the administration to keep pace in efficiency and complexity.

The economic revival is relevant here. The difficulties of the early fifteenth century (in England especially) were in part simply a reaction to financial difficulty. Impoverished nobles compensated for their economic problems by such things as the ransom of prisoners, the loot of war, and the struggle over the Crown and its sources of patronage. By the middle of the century, however, the economic structure was improving and there was a general increase in prosperity. This encouraged the monarchy to rely on a wider range of support than could be provided by individual great lords. Edward IV had a deliberate policy of directing a kind of propaganda appeal to the people, and this meant both the gentry class and the layers below. The facts of the economy allowed the king to find ministers, servants, and supporters in a much wider area of society, and the Yorkist and Tudor monarchies were national monarchies in a new sense—monarchies of genuine national appeal supported by a large, landowning, wealthy section of the country.

I do see continuities from Edward I into the late fifteenth century, but I do not see any major transformation (in England) at that time. However, the period from the 1520's onward did lead to genuine and drastic changes in England and France alike. This was most evident in England for two reasons: the coming of the Reformation, which in England was directed from above and called for direct governmental action, and the accident of a personality. Henry VIII's minister Thomas Cromwell was a man of highly bureaucratic tendencies, and under Cromwell there was a deliberate recasting of the administration to meet new needs. I call this a revolution because the recasting was based on the principle that government must not be vested in the person of the king to the degree that was inevitable in the Middle Ages; that it must be vested in a machinery working under the king, but independent in its continuity (and therefore to some degree in its efficiency) from accidents of the king's personality, his death, his minority, or his senility.

What new tasks were undertaken by governments in the sixteenth century? Did they become increasingly involved in the life of society?

The involvement of government in society was most marked in England, which had the advantage of an ancient centralized tradition and a relatively small territory—an advantage augmented by the loss of the French possessions in the fifteenth century. The country concentrated upon itself in the sixteenth century, and the state took over tasks that subordinate or coordinate authorities had previously carried out. This is most noticeable in religion: the things done by the state in the later sixteenth century for the salvation of souls were not tasks of monarchy before the reign of Henry VIII. Certainly the monarchy gained strength from the Reformation, and not only in its doctrinal position and its claim to authority. The Crown gained a lot of money from the Church, even though it had to spend a good deal in order to administer its new responsibilities. The state had to replace the old Church courts, to unify the judicial system; it had to create machinery to administer its financial gains from the Church; it had to devise means of persuasion and enforcement every time a new line of religious truth was promulgated. Problems of control, created by the spread of knowledge, were enormously increased by the Reformation, and without the administrative reforms of the 1530's, these tasks would probably have been impossible.

In the early sixteenth century, new force and direction was given to the traditional English concept that it is the king's duty to look after the bodies of his subjects—that the social organization of the nation should be the charge of its head. He must look after the poor, protect the innocent, and so on. In the 1530's and 1540's a powerful group of pamphleteers and thinkers made a specific policy (called the Commonwealth Policy) out of this general principle. They produced quantities of reform suggestions, of which some were sensible and some were put into action, and thus made that period the first period of modern legislative action. The pamphleteers of the 1530's—in a sense, perhaps, a liberated generation—suddenly realized that man can make his own improvements in *this* world, that we don't have to wait for God to put things right in the next. They were not always so naïve as to suppose that the making of a law was equal to the remedy of a grievance, but they did believe that society—embodied in the legislative organ of the king-in-Parliament—could remake itself, and they were optimistic about the possibility of reform. Cromwell believed this himself, and reforming activity was continuous from the 1530's.

The monarchs generally left these reforms to pamphleteers, humanists, and ministers. Elizabeth, for example, felt that such matters could safely be left to Parliament, which must be kept out of everything that really touched the affairs of state—that is, dynastic war and foreign policy leading to or from war. In the sixteenth century, war grew bigger and more expensive, and at the same time it was modified by more regular (and more expensive) diplomatic procedures. The growth of foreign services, embassies, and so forth, was a marked feature of the period. By the end of the century most of the European powers had representatives resident in the major capitals. All this cost money and required extensive organization.

War itself was very expensive by this time, and it required a regular army, which in the first instance meant mercenary forces. Kings could no longer rely on lords with their retainers, though the armies of Henry VIII were still recruited that way. Expensive artillery was needed, and standing armies (preferably paid, although very few armies were ever paid on time). None of this was completely new, but it was so increased that it would have been impossible without reform of the machinery of government.

Was humanism a political ideology? Did the humanist education of most men in the government in the sixteenth and seventeenth centuries make a difference in the way they acted?

Their education certainly made a difference, but whether they had a consistent political theory is another matter. Humanist education was directed toward three ends: to produce scholars (education has always done that, and in the present context it is not important); to produce an educated upper class; to provide trained servants for the state. The education of the gentleman was a preoccupation of humanist theorists throughout the sixteenth century; it was expressed in an outburst of general textbooks for the education of the gentry, which replaced the earlier concentration on the education of princes. Princes were not entirely neglected, but they seemed less important to the theorists than those who would advise the princes and do their work for them. In England this finally led to the ideal of the Christian gentleman and knight, the Sir-Philip-Sidney figure. It was a plaster-saint image, but very influential—the first public school man, the all-rounder.

Humanists who were trained as scholars or teachers came up against the basic question of whether they should take their training into court. The problem of the giving of counsel, of doing socially useful work, exercised many of the humanists—notably Thomas More, who finally decided that it was his duty to take service under the Crown, to become an administrator and ruler himself. Erasmus, on the other hand, stuck to pure scholarship: he was a privy counselor to Charles V but never advised him on anything. Erasmus took the line that it is the duty of the scholar to remain undefiled, but most of the humanists—and especially the generation after Erasmus—saw it as their proper task to take their intellectual skill into the service of the reforming monarchies.

The political theories of the humanists varied according to the state or society they served. English humanists, on the whole, were constitutionalists. They believed in the supremacy of the law and did not, by and large, support the more extravagant claims of the Crown. Those who supported absolutism tended to be ecclesiastics—church lawyers, at first, and later on High Church bishops who found absolutism preferable to constitutional arrangements which gave a voice to the laity of the Church. On the other hand, among the many humanist servants of German princes in the first half of the century there was little insistence on the limitations of princedom. They seemed to accept the supremacy of princes and work along from there. In France, the political views of the humanists ranged from old-fashioned constitutionalism to descriptions of the French monarchy as it was, which was much more absolutist than most people realize.

One must remember that humanist training in the fifteenth and sixteenth centuries was linguistic, philological, and rhetorical. It did not look for truth in some new discovery or in the dispassionate inquiry of the scientist, but in the authority of the past. It went back farther than those it attacked, back to the authority of Cicero and Seneca and Tacitus rather than Saint Thomas or Anselm or Augustine. It was an extremely bookish training, and not many of the humanists escaped into a genuine understanding of their own social system. This gravely limited their influence, of course. Occasionally, when they were able to look at contemporary society, analyze it, and prescribe for it (like Thomas Starkey in England or Jean Bodin in France), they were very effective. But most of them, like any intellectuals in politics, overestimated their importance.

Is there any evidence that the works of Marsiglio of Padua or Machiavelli influenced the men who conducted government in northern Europe in the sixteenth century?

It is always difficult to identify the influence of any writings on men of action. Even when correlation has been established between what a man did and what he might have learned from a book, that is not to say that correlation actually existed. Given certain eternal tasks of government (like maintaining order, preventing disaffection, and keeping itself in power), Machiavellianism is inescapable. All governments are bound to practice that touch of realism that Machiavelli introduced into the discussion of politics. Turning it the other way around, Machiavelli looked at the situation with a clear head and described what he saw.

Marsiglio is in a slightly different category. He was trying to provide a philosophic basis for the state, which Machiavelli never attempted, and therefore his analysis could be helpful to people who faced certain major issues—conflicts of rights, for instance. I think that this happened during the early English Reformation, to this extent: that Marsiglio's attack on the powers of the Church and the pope inside any given state met a ready response among those who had to fight their way out of the dilemma caused by Henry VIII's desire for a divorce. These people wanted to provide a philosophic basis for the reorganization of England into a unitary body politic, which was Marsiglio's type of body politic.

The first printed edition of Marsiglio's book appeared in English in 1535, about two hundred years after it was written, and the translation was slightly doctored to suit English circumstances. This is not to say that Cromwell and others used Marsiglio's work as a blueprint, but those who thought along the lines of destroying the power of the papacy found the argument set out better than they could put it themselves. It was a clarification of their own minds as well as a useful instrument of propaganda. However, it was not a great influence—there were very few copies of the book. Also, as in any country in any century, the kind of mind that was applied to the problems of government in sixteenth-century England was not fundamentally philosophical. Cromwell may be an exception to this rule; he seems to have had a genuine interest in political thought of an academic variety.

What were the significant differences between English and French landed society? How did the governments in both countries control landed society and draw upon its resources, and how did landed society react to the reforming power of the Crown?

I must stress again that I am too ignorant of the French situation to speak with any confidence. However, asked to define the main distinction between England and France—and this is a symptom rather than a cause—I would say that whereas the English Crown involved landed society in the activities of government, making it part of the system, the French monarchy built up a system of government and administration by the side of the existing social structure and hierarchy, creating a juxtaposition or even a situation of enmity. For instance, the total common involvement of Crown and society in England after 1530 is exemplified in the sovereign authority of Parliament, which included the king. The king, the Lords, and Commons jointly formed a sovereign body which could do anything within the realm. There was no such authority in France, where sovereignty belonged to the king alone.

Because the English nobility and gentry were part of the governmental system, it was proper and possible to tax them. In France (and Spain, too), the Crown bought its freedom from wealthy, landed men by letting them retain or augment their wealth. Even in the reign of Elizabeth, the Chancellor of the Exchequer, reflecting on taxation, took it for granted (in a casual aside) that of course one would tax accordingly to ability—the wealthiest would pay most. In sixteenth-century Europe this was an exceptional, even an extravagant, notion.

The Tudor system could work only when the Crown's actions met with sufficient approval from those who held social and political and economic power in the localities, for only then would they execute orders from above. The coherence of the state, the preservation of order, the suppression of opposition, the maintenance of the true religion—all these depended on the total cooperation of the nobility, the gentry, the justices of the peace, and the mayors and aldermen of the towns. Central government was ineffective unless it knew what was going on locally and could expect its orders to be obeyed. I have always thought that the real difference between Tudor and Stuart government was that Stuart counselors—and especially Stuart monarchs—had no idea. When Charles I summoned an army to fight the Scots in 1639, he assumed that the nation was at his back; in fact, he had almost no support at all. The effective governors of the Tudor system, men like Cromwell and Burghley, had to spend every day of the year writing and receiving letters, maintaining a network of information and knowledge and understanding.

The common involvement of the king and landed classes meant, of course, that the landed classes retained a great measure of potential power. The system could produce a government which was effective and well served as long as interests agreed, but it would cease to be effective if any conflict of interests grew too large. The maintenance of cooperation was a political problem solved by political means—by persuasion, by propaganda, by grants and gifts and concessions.

The French kings, for reasons which are in part historic and in part geographic, attempted to create an effective royal administration independent of the local powers of landed society. The ancient divisions of the realm still existed in the sixteenth century, but they existed without real meaning. The reality of administration was handled by representatives from the center; a royal system was created by the side of the traditional structure of power and society. This is exemplified in the officeholding nobility, rival to the ancient nobility and the ancient social structure.

Would it be true to say that the great difference between English and French politics in the sixteenth century was that the English aristocracy had become feeble, diminished in number, and relatively quiescent politically?

I'm not sure I see it quite that way, but it certainly is true that the English aristocracy was quite different from the French. For one thing, there was not that top layer of the aristocracy—princes of the blood and inheritors of the separatist sectors of the realm—in England in the sixteenth century. Also, even though there were men of ancient lineage who resented upstarts, the Crown was strong enough to secure at least the recognition of men promoted by the king to high office and high status. Pride of blood was much less serious in England, and the English aristocracy was continually freshly recruited from those the king ennobled. This gave the nobility a different cast of mind from that of France, where the ancient nobility continued to resent the officeholding nobility and to consider themselves in a separate class.

Primogeniture made a difference, too. The English noble class effectively amounted to the peers of Parliament, always a small number whose families had more in common with the landowning gentry than with each other. The French noble class was much larger, and the nobles were equipped wih privileges that the English nobility never had, especially the relief from heavy taxation. An English nobleman could avoid heavy taxes only by falsifying his returns—a very limited method, by comparison. One of the big differences, I suggest again, is that it was taken for granted in Tudor England that a nobleman served the Crown. His standing in the realm depended on the Crown as well as on his inheritance, and this committed him to social duties. Many of them did carry out burdensome tasks if the Crown called them, and I don't think that the French Crown could demand service of this kind from the nobility.

The English noble class was bound to remain rather small because every creation created only one nobleman in that family forever after; in France, it created a noble family. When the Tudors did create peers, they made it the lowest rank—barons, by and large—and only in the reign of Elizabeth was the baron linked fully with the noble class rather than the gentry. The distinction between a knight and a baron was imprecise at least as late as the reign of Henry VIII, and knights commonly were not addressed as Sir but Master. We speak of Sir Thomas More, but his contemporaries spoke of Master More.

The small size of the English noble class, then, was not so much a consequence of the destruction of noblemen in the wars of the fifteenth century—that has been exaggerated, although there certainly was a great loss of blood and some loss of lives. Much of that nobility, too, was of recent creation; in fact most of the English nobility has been of recent creation since the twelfth century. The really ancient families of England have always been found in the lower ranks of society.

In the light of the scholarship of the last twenty years, how would you evaluate the changes in agrarian society in England in the sixteenth century, and how does Tawney's interpretation of the agrarian problem stand up today?

On this point it is not the scholarship of the last twenty years but of the last few months which really matters, because no one has seriously gone over Tawney's book again until quite recently—indeed, in a new book by Eric Kerridge. Tawney recognized the inadequacies of his own book, but no one else analyzed agrarian society and so his conclusions were accepted. His chief point was that a capitalist revolution took place in agrarian society in the sixteenth century, that land got into the hands of those who wanted to make a direct financial profit out of it instead of using it as a means and criterion of social standing and a cement of social relationships. This revolution was expressed in two ways: in massive enclosure for exploitation by animal husbandry and intensive corn growing, and in the consolidation of estates and the driving out of small landholders by the extensive raising of entry fines and exploitation of the weaknesses of tenants' rights.

Of this analysis, very little still stands; I think no one would now suppose with Tawney and his generation that land had ever been anything but a source of wealth. What else was it? Medieval society derived virtually all of its wealth from the land, mostly very directly, and the power structure and social structure rested on relative levels of land-based wealth. To suppose that thirteenth- and fourteenth-century landlords were not interested in profits is to make them into idiots. The idea of sudden capitalist exploitation is nonsense, and even the idea that the new owners of the sixteenth century were less committed to ancient ties of loyalty to their tenants has been refuted. The most intensive exploiters of land in the later Middle Ages tended to be institutions like monasteries, for the excellent reason that they were stewards rather than owners. They tended also to be conservative and to use most intensively the ancient methods of control over tenants. The actual methods used for raising wealth from land did change in the sixteenth century, but the principle was not new.

Enclosure contributed very little to the agrarian distress of the period. A great deal of the enclosure that took place before 1600 actually had been accomplished before 1500, and most of it involved the enclosing of scattered lands into single farm units. Some kinds of enclosure *were* socially dangerous, especially the imparking of land, which took it altogether out of production. There was some depopulation from enclosure; in the Midlands, certain arable fields became enclosed sheep runs, destroying husbandry and houses and affecting agrarian employment here and there. But the best opinion now puts little weight on enclosures and their alleged effect on agrarian problems.

Tawney's view that sixteenth-century landlords aggravated the problems of the peasantry by exploiting the weaknesses of tenants' rights has stood up until now, but I do not think it will survive the criticism that Tawney misunderstood the law touching these matters and therefore mistook the rights of tenants altogether. The bulk of the English peasantry, particularly the substantial peasantry, were well protected in law against exploitation by their landlords. That most unfortunate group, the small holders and tenants-at-will, were not protected and were hard hit by agrarian change—as they have been hit by similar changes in any century.

One has to generalize ahead of the data here, but I think the important factor in the sixteenth century (as in the thirteenth and again in the eighteenth) was an increase in population. Our figures are not very adequate so far, but work is going forward on this subject. If one supposes, as a rough estimate, that the population of England and Wales approximately doubled between 1500 and 1600, I doubt that estimate is far wrong. That range of increase is not large by modern standards, but it was very marked by the standards of the sixteenth century. It is similar to the increase in population between 1180 and 1280, which led to an agrarian boom. In the thirteenth century and in the sixteenth, land was used much more extensively in an attempt to meet larger needs. The effect of the increase was to provide opportunities for intensive exploitation—opportunities for the progressive user of land.

At the same time there was the notorious price rise of the sixteenth century, on which a great deal of work has been done in the last twenty years. The traditional explanation for this inflation—that it was the consequence of the great increase in Spanish silver from the New World—was first offered by Bodin in the sixteenth century and will not quite do today. Neither the geographical nor the temporal facts fit the thesis. In England, for instance, there was massive inflation long before any Spanish silver could have had an effect. War may have had something to do with it: war tends to be inflationary because of government borrowing and spending. But whatever the causes of the inflation, its effects on the individual landowner were varied. If he could sell on the rising market, well and good, but if his income remained fixed he was in a bad way.

Most fifteenth-century landlords had been content to live off fixed rents. Their period was one of stable prices and static population, and not much could be gained by intensive cultivation, especially on a grand scale which required heavy investment and administrative overhead. Inflation forced landlords to switch to direct exploitation. Some went in for farming or other uses of land like the discovery of minerals; others took advantage of the increased profits of the peasants and small farmers by raising their revenue from these men. Usually this was not done by raising rents (which often were difficult to raise in the law) but by increasing entry fines—that is, the money payable on entry on a particular holding.

All this produced a very lively agrarian situation. Add to it the great market in land, which was much stimulated by the confiscation of ecclesiastical property and its redistribution among the gentry. It was a disturbed and potentially revolutionary situation, and many landowners of all classes went to the wall for personal reasons—a family died out or was extravagant or (on the peasant level) their rights in law were not as good as their neighbors'. This often was a matter of historic and legal accident, but at any rate it was clearly definable for each man in terms of law. Landowners were bound in all they could do by the state of the law. The law guaranteed existing rights, and if the rights existed, the man was safe. Resistance to the occasional attempts to override the law was immediate and always effective. It was a very complicated situation, and its terms were set by the law and not by what we would call economic considerations.

On the whole, this was a cohesive society right down to the peasant level, but of course at the bottom there was a class of the true poor which increased throughout the century. This class existed through the lack of tenants' rights at certain low levels of society, and through the pressure of population increase with subsequent unemployment and drain on resources. The problem of the poor grew larger but remained, in the main, a problem of unemployment, which was not solved by the ineffective measures of the sixteenth-century state.

How do you view the so-called rise of the gentry during this period?

I have always thought this was a very odd term—I have imagined a group of rather portly gentlemen floating upward upon rose-colored clouds, wafted upward by Tawney and pushed down by Trevor-Roper. The controversy over the "rise of the gentry" started with Tawney's analysis of James Harrington, the seventeenth-century philosopher, where he found the statement that in the sixteenth and early seventeenth centuries there was a rise to economic predominance of what he called the gentry, but what he might have defined as middle-sized estates rising at the expense of really great estates *and* of peasants' holdings. Tawney tied this to a class analysis by distinguishing between the nobility and the gentry, claimed that the gentry was getting the upper hand of the nobility, and supposed that the gentry rose as a whole class. He conceived this as one of the fundamental social transformations behind the political troubles of the seventeenth century.

Against this, Trevor-Roper explained that there were in the gentry class those who did well and those who did poorly. Tawney himself would not have denied this obvious truth, but Tawney did misconceive the unity of the gentry. The Civil War was a war inside the governing order—gentry versus gentry—and to assume a solid gentry class is to mistake the nature of the war. Trevor-Roper drew attention to the division within the gentry between those who fought for the Parliament and those who fought for the king, and he looked for a socio-economic explanation. He identified those who rose or fell in wealth and power after about 1540, and he committed himself to the view that those who rose were those who could rely upon resources outside their estates—in the main, Crown officers and Crown patronage; those who fell were those he called "mere gentry," with no income beyond what their estate yielded. Tawney argued that the exploitation of landed resources was the basis of gentry wealth in the sixteenth century, but Trevor-Roper argued that landed estates were only a source of loss and decline without the fructifying flood of royal favor. This thesis, too, is easily disputed. The circumstances surrounding individual fortunes are so multiple that no one has yet reduced them to any kind of scheme. Trevor-Roper tried to amend his original idea by suggesting that the opposition was one of court versus country, that attitudes were determined by officeholding, and that attitudes distinguished the rising and the falling gentry. In other words, he tried to transfer his original emphasis from the economic to the ideological. However, almost all the leaders of the Parliamentary position under James I and Charles I, and the leaders of the Long Parliament, were officeholders. Once again the parties don't match the facts.

Stone's recent interpretation of the economic problems of the gentry adheres to the old Tawney distinction between nobility and gentry, stating that whereas the gentry (allowing for variations within this group) rose in power and wealth and influence, the nobility declined. The figures here are capable of great tolerances: some people read them as decline and poverty, and some as a slight improvement in standing. Beyond this, the big difficulty remains, as always, in the distinction between gentry and nobility. Stone defined nobility in effect as those who held peerage titles; their younger brothers or collaterals do not come into his analysis at all. The people outside the compass of the analysis have the same habits, ambitions, sources of income, means of livelihood, and ways of life as those inside, and I consider this an inadequate definition of a social class.

It is true (and this is where Tawney really began) that in the years between 1500 and 1600, or 1500 and 1650, the number of middle-sized estates increased and the number of very large estates declined. An important reason for this was the disappearance of the monastic estates and the very serious inroads into episcopal estates. In other words, it was the Church that went down the drain. My impression is that the share of land held by the Crown and the nobility remained about the same, while the number of estates held by individuals, to be described as gentlemen and middling landowners, grew considerably. When the big estates of the Church were distributed among a large number of laymen, what really happened was not a rise of the gentry but a great increase in the numbers of individual landowners. Many of these were younger sons of landowners who would not have been able to acquire land without a redistribution of Church property.

The significance of this, of course, is the diffusion of landed wealth to a larger group. There were many more landowners in 1640 than in 1540, and thus a place in society—an absolute requisite for political influence—was open to a larger number of people. It is here that I see a tie-up with politics, in the increased strength of the House of Commons and the pressure for seats in the House, which was much greater in the reign of Elizabeth than ever before. When we speak of population increase we think of the peasantry, but the upper classes were also increasing; the only people who did not increase were the Tudors themselves.

To what extent did ideas of law and legislation change in the sixteenth century? Was there an advance from the medieval idea of law as custom and tradition to the idea of law as a social mechanism which one can consciously create or reform?

In the later Middle Ages the doctrine of law as custom and tradition—the Thomist doctrine of law as something laid down for eternity—had already been challenged by the voluntarist doctrine of Occam and the nominalists. Their influence was quite strong in sixteenth-century England, and the transformation in that period was one of degree, but it was a marked change nonetheless. The medieval states had legislated, of course (every society makes laws for itself), but in the sixteenth century lawmaking was recognized not only as a proper but perhaps *the* proper activity of the state. Legislation became a means of reform and alteration.

If you look at lawmaking under Edward I, whose reign brought perhaps the first period of massive activity in the defining of law, the legislative authority belonged to the king, and this was true at least until the middle of the fifteenth century. In form at least, the king was the only lawmaker. He might take advice; he might require consent; he might need to issue his laws on the occasions of Parliaments; but he was the only one who made the laws. Only after about 1450 did the phrase "by the authority of Parliament" become customary in the making of statutes, and only in the 1530's was the authority of Parliament conceived as the king-in-Parliament—the single, sovereign lawmaker. The king, the Lords, and Commons acted conjointly, and their authority was that of the curious constitutional trinity which has remained the formula (and to some extent the reality) ever since.

The clarification of legislative authority in the 1530's quickly became a commonplace of the political thinking of the time, and it both underlay and contributed to (and, in a sense, arose from) the intensive legislative program of that decade. Behind it lay a somewhat inchoate recognition of the power of human beings to order their society by making law, replacing the old idea of the obligation of human beings to adhere to a law that was immutable, eternal, and entirely customary. This is not to say that law as custom ceased to be recognized. It was very much there right through the century, and it still is: the common law of the realm is the custom of the realm. The sixteenth century was one of the periods when the common law was enormously altered, almost transformed, and a great deal of work remains to be done in this field. There are massive materials on the law and the law courts which have been little exploited so far because of technical difficulties.

I would like you to discuss the significance of the Court of Star Chamber. Was it an improvement in the operation of the common law, or was it something that could operate outside of the common law?

There are one or two things that we would be wise to remember about sixteenth-century law, about the new prerogative courts and their contribution to the law of England. The supremacy and primacy of the common law were never in the slightest doubt. The common law was the law of England, and no one seriously supposed that it could be replaced. The law of England was the law of custom and judicial decision, augmented by various legislative processes recognized by the state, of which statute is the dominant form. The orders of certain courts could also take a legislative form, particularly in Chancery. Judges, in a sense, were legislators too.

At the beginning of this period, there were two real problems of the common law. One was that the needs of society, its relationships and its economic and political problems, changed constantly and the law could not always keep up. The other problem was that of effectiveness, of making the law work to enforce order and individual rights. This was a procedural problem, but there were substantive problems too. The law needed changing in many respects (especially the land law), and most of the attempts to change it came to nothing. Further, the common law was very dilatory; its processes depended on the activity of the sheriff enforcing writs, and its decisions in virtually all cases (especially civil cases) depended on a jury. It was not easy to get the jury together and to make it render a true verdict. The processes of the law in all civil disputes—land title, debt, contract, fraud, and so on—were very slow indeed, but its final decision was effective.

Conciliar courts such as Star Chamber provided, on the whole, a much swifter administration of justice. They enabled men to bring more and diverse matters to court; they allowed matters to be considered on grounds of equity as well as customary law, and therefore they could modify or even transmute the law. But their final decisions were rarely very effective. Ultimately, the only decisions recognized by litigants, by lawyers, and by the courts were those rendered by the common-law courts. In every conciliar case the defendant reserved his rights at common law, and this meant that when the case went against him he could, and often did, take the matter farther at common law. The conciliar courts had the advantages of speed, of breadth of approach, and of relative informality concerning procedure as well as what was heard. They had the disadvantage that the chances of making their decisions stick were far less than at law.

The procedural advantages introduced by the new courts were picked up to some extent by some of the common-law courts and thus influenced later developments. In particular, whereas medieval law knew a great variety of writs to start action and so forth, there was only one writ from the nineteenth century onward—the conciliar writ of subpoena, which is now the only writ of summons. Witnesses were used in common law, certainly by the fifteenth century, but the conciliar courts developed the use of witnesses—the manner in which they were interrogated and their evidence assessed—and this development survived. The main contributions of conciliar courts touched matters in which the common law had been deficient, particularly in criminal law. Medieval criminal law never really got beyond obvious offense against the person. Such matters as slander and libel, and the problems of enforcement involved in perjury and contempt, were developed by the conciliar courts.

Star Chamber was and remained the privy council in session as a formal court, obeying all the rules of publicity and regular procedure. It was a popular court; indeed, it was largely developed by popularity. Litigants pressed upon the council with pleas and bills of petition, and the council responded by organizing itself into regular sessions as a court. It rendered relatively swift justice and had the weight of the council behind it. It had advantages from the point of view of the Crown in that it could be used to enforce social and political policy. However, it was not a political tribunal. In particular it could not touch those matters with which it has been associated in the popular mind—it couldn't touch life or freehold, the ultimate rights of the individual. In consequence, it could not hear pleas in which a man's life was at stake such as felony or treason, and no treason trial was ever held in Star Chamber.

Was sixteenth-century England becoming a more peaceful, less violent world? Was there an improvement in social order and police power?

We really don't know the answer to that. Of necessity, it is the cases of disturbance that survive as evidence. The man who never hit anybody over the head didn't get into the records of the criminal law, and yet he must have existed. However, the police and law court evidence is bulky and the population was not very large, and my general impression is that it was a century of considerable disorder and violence. However, it had a better hold on police problems than the fifteenth, if only because those in whose hands the final action lay—justices of the peace, local gentry or nobility, even village constables and the like—were more willing to cooperate with the central government than they had been in the faction-ridden fifteenth century.

As late as the eighteenth century, after all, England was recognized in Europe as a particularly disturbed and violent country. Its modern reputation for law-abidingness, even apathy in the face of disturbance, appeared in the nineteenth century when a regular and effective police force was instituted at last.

It is clear that the sixteenth-century state had enough power to suppress any serious attack on its authority. The so-called Tudor peace includes several major uprisings and a large number of riots. In enclosure riots, outbursts of religious disaffection, and big political uprisings, the authority of the state was challenged by great and small citizens. Some of these were forestalled by the detective powers of the government, and various serious challenges were overcome by the superior organization and power of the state and its claim to the allegiance of the greater part of the nation. In that sense public order could be and was maintained, but the private disturbance, local quarrel, robbery, rape, and murder continued.

The split with Rome and the establishment of a national church were effected with almost no opposition within Parliament. Yet religion later became a critical issue within the House of Commons, and religious divisions seem to deepen during the century. Can you explain this phenomenon?

From 1529 (the meeting of the Reformation Parliament) to 1559 (the Elizabethan settlement), it would be essentially true to say that the Crown led in the settlement of the structure of the Church and the nature of religious truth. Certainly there was opposition to the king's proceedings against the pope, especially when these began to tend toward the introduction of new and heretical opinions, but this was unlikely to show itself within Parliament. (There was some opposition within Parliament, organized by the friends of Catherine of Aragon and supported by people like Thomas More.) However, because the settlement was devised and led from above, there was little opportunity for active, well-led opposition to develop within Parliament or elsewhere—the country was being led or driven in one direction.

There was much more division on religion later in the century, and it expressed itself in Parliament after about 1560. After that date the leaders of the nation (particularly the queen herself) supposed that further change was neither necessary nor desirable. She hoped to hold the line, but after thirty years of upheaval over religion nobody could suppose that matters of faith and of the Church were not of primary concern. Elizabeth succeeded remarkably well in holding the line of 1559, at least officially, but underneath the apparent maintenance of a uniform system, transformation was widespread and some of it went a long way. There were parts of the realm in which the official parish organization ceased to operate and was replaced by the sort of semirevolutionary or potentially revolutionary cell that marked the beginning of the Huguenot movement in France.

At the same time that the Crown decided to slow down or stop the processes of change, the processes of history produced a sizable, powerful group to whom the settlement of religion required something much more drastic than the line of 1559. Their example was Calvin's Geneva, and up to a point, Knox's Scotland. We know now that the so-called Presbyterian movement of the reign of Elizabeth was not entirely revolutionary or utterly hostile to the existing order, but it certainly was very reformative. It wished to go much farther than the settlement in many directions—in the ordering of the Church, in services, definition of the faith, the powers of the bishop, and the powers of the Crown in ecclesiastical matters. For various reasons (one of the chief of which is that the settlement had been achieved within Parliament), Parliament was the proper arena for this opposition action.

Perhaps, too, religion meant more to people at this period. Conventionally, we suppose that it did. The second half of the sixteenth century was marked by active Calvinism in Europe and by the active phase of the Counter-Reformation. The early sixteenth century was not an irreligious or a faithless age, but its faith was relatively cool and formal. The late sixteenth century, after fifty years of quarreling over religion, was stirred up and passionate.

There were social aspects to this question. The truly sectarian or separatist movements of the reign of Elizabeth —movements of people who thought themselves the only saved men, the only saints, and wished to set up separated churches—were movements of the underprivileged. They tied up very little with either the Church of England or the Church of Rome. They were not part of the Puritan or evangelical, activist wing of the Church of England. They were more closely linked with the small, sometimes millenarian groups of the later Middle Ages, or with Anabaptism. They were not direct ancestors of the sects of the middle seventeenth century, either; they were much more a survival of Lollardy, transmuted by acquaintance with the new religions.

The mainstreams of Puritan reform, whether they were specifically Presbyterian (wishing to change the government of the Church) or more generally reformist (wishing to produce a better clergy and a more moral nation inside the existing framework), were essentially upper-class movements. Often they were carried by the bishops themselves, by the gentry (the Puritan gentry was a new phenomenon of the age of Elizabeth), and to some extent by the universities. Many of the people who exercised political power, people on whom the Crown depended, were turning toward a more earnest involvement in religion and toward what is loosely called Puritanism. This was partly because of their education and because they came under the influence of active preachers. It was also, perhaps, a reaction against the previous generation, which had been marked by time-serving attitudes that idealistic young people did not like.

The Puritans were bound to appeal to anybody of sensibility with an interest in religion. They had answers to all the questions; they seemed sincere and concerned. They often were men of holy lives who were deeply concerned about the salvation of souls. Much of the official church seemed to be based on politics and time serving, and it was inadequately served by men the Puritans called dumb dogs—non-preaching clergy, and so on. One of the immediate consequences of the Reformation had been a great decline in the production of new clergy, and between the 1530's and the 1550's many parishes were left empty or filled by inadequate men. When the new generation of university-trained clergymen, who had come under the influence of Puritan thinking and Calvinism at Oxford and Cambridge, went out into the country they showed up by contrast as men of training, ability, and zeal, and the older generation looked shabby by contrast.

To what extent was the reforming attitude that dominated the 1530's perpetuated in the late sixteenth century?

The impetus of the 1530's was not dead by the late sixteenth century, and things still needed doing. There was continued preoccupation with reform, but many of those most anxious for reform were sidetracked into religion. Also, the upheavals of the earlier period required a period of consolidation, and so the reign of Elizabeth reflected less concern for reform and more concern to prevent disturbance.

Elizabeth did not show that marked self-confidence that gave Henry VIII his attitude of effortless superiority, perhaps because she led a very different life in her youth. Also, the international situation had changed, and the religious settlement was under constant attack from both sides. The government of Elizabeth, even more than that of her father, had to rely on the active cooperation of the propertied classes, and it was apprehensive that it might lose that support. When Thomas Cromwell or the privy council of Henry VIII wrote to the localities, they were quite straightforward and severe; the Elizabethan council could be severe but was much more likely to be careful of feelings. Burghley was certain that a solution that disturbed nothing was preferable to a solution that disturbed something—fundamentally a highly conservative attitude, whereas the 1530's and 1540's had been radical decades.

By the 1530's, a great many problems in society and the state had accumulated, producing a large radical potential. Thanks to Henry's quarrel with Rome and Thomas Cromwell's particular equipment, that potential was expressed in reform. However, after thirty years of radicalism it is not surprising to find conservatism and a preoccupation with order. The prevalent conservatism of the government had social effects, of course. It was very slow to cope with problems of poverty and unemployment. It did not like to tackle deficiencies in administration, and even slipped backward in some places where reforms had been undertaken. Vested interests that had been suppressed fought back in the reign of Elizabeth. However, I don't want to exaggerate this conservatism, because at no time was it total. There was always some reform mixed in, but this was quite a different age from the 1530's.

What were the economic problems of the late sixteenth century? Apparently there was a slowing down of economic growth in all of Europe, but why does Elizabeth's government seem to have been particularly hard up?

I can't say very much on the general economic situation, which is a highly specialized and expert subject. In England a number of rather obvious and important phenomena had occurred since mid-century. In particular there was the destruction of the trade in unfinished cloth, which had maintained the rather high level of expansion in the first half of the century. Here a variety of circumstances combined to cause trouble: the most important was probably an overproduction crisis in mid-century from which the cloth trade never recovered. Also, the general European economy was much disturbed by civil war in France and religious war generally. Markets were less secure than they had been. The English economy depended ultimately on the export of its one manufactured product—cloth—and disturbances could and did affect the economy.

On top of that, England was at war from the late 1580's on, and other misfortunes occurred at about the same period. Elizabeth's reign was a happy one down to about 1585 because (for reasons which no one understands) it was free of plague and major epidemics. But in the 1590's there was plague again, and some very bad harvests—a sequence of three disastrous years which led to the usual problems of famine and inflation. Together with war, this made the 1590's a period of economic decline which was felt all over Europe—a by-product of war, the collapse of order, and the destruction of trade routes.

We may have overestimated the economic difficulties of the Elizabethan government. It is now held by some good opinion that it was never in danger of bankruptcy—that at no time were the ordinary needs of the Crown not covered by its ordinary resources, nor the extraordinary needs (largely defense and war) so excessive that the situation got out of hand. The Crown was certainly not lavishly endowed, but it was just about adequately endowed. Of course, with the war taxation of the 1590's there was discontent and evasion, and the Crown did not get what it should have.

It is worth remembering that the Crown of England was the only major power of Europe that never actually went bankrupt in this period, and that was largely because of its financial structure. The government itself and public opinion in general still recognized a division between ordinary and extraordinary expenses. Ordinary expenses (those incurred in the normal conduct of affairs) were supposed to be covered by ordinary revenue, mainly revenue from lands, from the profits of justice, from various rather out-of-date feudal rights, and from customs duties. Extraordinary expenditure (mainly war and the preparation for war) entitled the government to ask for money, which had to be voted by Parliament.

However, the ordinary expenses of the Crown were growing faster than its resources, and the Crown too often realized its capital assets by selling off Crown lands. Expenditures increased largely because of inflation and the growing complication of government, not really because of extravagance and corruption. The court was always extravagant, partly because all of the Tudors had extravagant tastes and partly because they rightly believed that a king must not appear mean or ragged. The glory of the Tudor court was a political instrument. Second, much of what was regarded as extraordinary expenditure ought, in the conditions of an early modern state, to have been regarded as ordinary—the building of fortresses, the maintenance of a standing force, and so on. These were no longer occasional or extraordinary phenomena. There were also problems of collection, of securing a proper return from the taxpayer. It is said that tax assessments were much nearer correct valuation in the first half of the century than the second, and this probably reflects the unwillingness of the Elizabethan government to offend powerful interests. They maintained the principle that taxation applied to all and was graduated by ability to pay, but they avoided any serious attempt to extract their due from the wealthy: that would have been too disturbing to the social order.

There were qualifications to these financial problems. For example, the Crown extracted a good deal of ecclesiastical revenue by forcing bishops to exchange valuable assets for valueless assets. It continued to benefit from the system by which civil servants were paid directly by fees from those who used their services, so that there was almost no increase in official salaries throughout Elizabeth's reign. But on balance, increasing costs were insufficiently covered by regular revenue, and it was very difficult to collect extraordinary revenues.

It seems to me that the French government, which was highly successful in the early sixteenth century, was particularly unsuccessful in dealing with doctrinal differences later in the century. Would you discuss why this was so?

In the first place, an unsubdued regionalism with noble leadership survived in France. Secondly, France was Calvin's own immediate target; he always hoped to turn his native country toward his own way of thinking. On top of that there was a collapse of central authority after the premature death of Henry II, with a revival of the medieval problem of what to do when the king is inadequate. The central government was effective only when it used its powers properly, but Henry's successors were not the right people. Historians have speculated that this might have happened in England with Edward VI's succession; that it did not, I think, shows the difference between the English system of government (re-formed to take into account the natural structure of hierarchic authority) and the French (with a purely royal system of administration). This left a deep social division between those with local power, or claims to power, who were not given authority when the kings were strong.

This division was perpetuated even when the monarchy recovered from civil war under Henry IV and Richelieu, at least sufficiently to produce a *Fronde* in the middle of the seventeenth century. It was really only after the defeat of that last outburst of old-fashioned aristocratic disaffection that the kings finally got the better of it—at the cost of destroying the social basis of monarchy altogether. When it came to the crisis, one hundred and forty years later, the *ancien régime* had very little to rest upon.

In the sixteenth century the Habsburg rulers of Spain were greatly feared, but in the seventeenth the Spanish monarchy was feeble. Did the Spanish institutions of government somehow fail to keep pace with social and economic change, or was the superiority of Spain an artificial phenomenon that derived from its control of vast resources?

The decline of Spain is now not thought to be so rapid as we had believed, and perhaps the Spanish hegemony was not so marvelous as it has been painted. The great age of Spain is supposed to have been the age of Philip II, but that may be because of the elimination of France for thirty years. The restoration of the French monarchy affected the standing of Spain right away, and this quite independently of the personal decline of the Spanish monarchs.

It is true that the Spanish activities of the sixteenth century overextended the nation's resources without investing in the future. No attempt was made to create a stable foundation of economic prosperity. One must remember, however, that the decline of Spain went together with a marked expansion and consolidation of Spanish power in the New World in the seventeenth and eighteenth centuries.

Spain was not a unified kingdom in the full sense until the early eighteenth century. There were separate administrations and institutions for Castile and Aragon (itself divided into three parts). Aragon's representative institutions were allowed to survive because the country was too poor to be taxed, but in Castile, the alliance of the Crown and the nobility against all other interests meant that there was no broad base to monarchy. There was a great interlocking of councils and courts, which in theory covered all contingencies and provided the Crown with a means of administration and government, but in practice they cut across and canceled each other until they were in mutual deadlock. The overelaboration of administrative machinery often meant that there was a total absence of administration in the Spanish dominions.

The essential weakness of these absolute monarchies was their refusal to utilize the natural (and therefore cheap) means of running things. If a monarchy could accomplish its ends by means of the natural hierarchy of society, it cost nothing but a few favors, a kind word, and continuous pressure. Failing that, it was necessary to create central and local bureaucratic organizations, properly financed, interlocking, and activated. The disadvantages were fiscal weaknesses and the problems of distance and communication. The ambition of the Spanish monarchs was to dominate a bureaucratic monarchy, and they were moving in that direction.

Was there a common factor in the rebellions of the first half of the seventeenth century—the Fronde, the Catalonian, and Portuguese rebellions—and the Great Rebellion in England?

Historians have looked for common elements in these rebellions, but their theories do not apply to the English situation, where the division between the bureaucracy and the natural hierarchy did not exist. None of these rebellions had a single cause, but the dominant causes of the Fronde, I would say, arose from this division. I don't think the theory works out anywhere else. It certainly was not the problem in Catalonia, where the situation was a straightforward reaction to certain maladministrations and local, personal, and political rivalries. It was not the problem in Portugal, which seems to me a straightforward nationalist revolt.

What one can perceive in these rebellions is the degree to which state power was not yet absolute and monopolistic—the degree to which rebellion can succeed. In the Spanish rebellions, Portugal won and Catalonia effectively lost, indicating that the state power was sufficient to deal with an uprising but could not defeat a separatist, nationalist movement. In France, the state won. The English Civil War is in a different category altogether. It was not a conflict of a region against the center but a general breakup of the nation. However, everything came back to normal in the end, and the Restoration must be remembered when we look for deep reasons for the disruption in the mid-seventeenth century. I do not think there was any one cause for the rebellions; they seem to me to have been specific and particular events.

In the last two decades there has been a sizable literature on the causes of the English Civil War. To what extent do we now understand what it was all about?

I would say that it remains entirely puzzling unless you believe, as I do, that we have been proceeding along the wrong lines. In general it has been assumed that upheavals of this kind don't happen by accident, that there must be causative circumstances so fundamental that they provoke an irreconcilable conflict. Historians, starting thus with an end-product, have had to find really profound sources of disturbance. They have said that divisions over constitutional matters, or law, or religion, became so severe that the two sides were forced to war. However, there is little difficulty in showing that the outbreak of the war had nothing to do with Puritanism or anything like it. In the first session of the Long Parliament, Pym (the leader of the opposition) came in with a fully prepared political program and no program for the Church. He avoided discussion of the Church because he knew it would disrupt the unity of his party, and the outbreak of the war cannot be said to be a result of differences over the Church.

As for the constitution, too, people really agreed on fundamentals even when they differed on particulars. Most people accepted the idea of a monarchic government with the cooperation of Parliament, and differed only over how Parliament should work and what should happen in it. It is not true that the common lawyers were against the king: most of them were in the king's employ.

Old-fashioned, rather crude Marxism interprets the war as the revolt of an urban and bourgeois-directed civilization whose ideology was Puritan-Calvinist against a feudally supported court whose ideology was High Anglican, or Catholic. This is easy to disprove, because the parties were not constructed this way. One can respond—as Christopher Hill has done—by elaborating the bourgeoisie into gentry, or what he calls the "industrious sort," but the more you do so, the farther you get from the actual conflicts that led to war. This particular line is pointless to pursue.

Then there is the Trevor-Roper thesis that identifiable divisions existed within the government itself. Obviously there were divisions, and when the war finally broke out, men of the same class and type were on opposite sides. The "court versus country" thesis doesn't get one far, and in general, interpretation based on social analysis does not explain very much.

I suggest that the work along these lines has been carried forward on the mistaken assumption that the conflict was profoundly irreconcilable, so much so that it can be explained only by enormous (and preferably sociological) causes. These assumptions have never been proved, and if you trace what actually happened, step by step, through the years before the war, you come to very different conclusions. If the conflict was so profound, why was the whole system back in being only eleven years after the king was executed and the republic established? I am inclined to accept the war as, in a sense, an accident—an unwanted, unforeseen outcome of a conflict which was largely produced by incompetence and the gradual accumulation of distrust.

Parliament was a working institution with an important part in the normal government of the day. Its cooperation was required in making laws, levying taxes, and the consideration of big political problems. Political debate and political conflict were neither improper nor unlikely. However, this institution worked properly only when the government saw to it, and in the sixteenth century this task was effectively performed.

From the beginning of James' reign, the maneuvered cooperation of the Tudors was not efficiently (and sometimes not at all) carried out. The king showed a genius for picking the wrong men as his servants. Most members of the parliamentary opposition knew they could do the job better, and knew too that under Queen Elizabeth they would have been Chancellors of the Exchequer and Treasurers of the Household. It was a normal parliamentary situation: people of ambition, ideas, and interests brought their affairs to the House. I am not saying that the Parliaments of James I were as easy to manage as those of Henry VIII, but the difference is one of degree only.

Down to 1628, anyway, there was nothing in the parliamentary situation which was past remedy. Nor was there in the Church situation; down to the death of James it looked as though the so-called Puritans, the active part of the church, would get the better of everybody else. It looked that way until the accession of Charles I, which promoted the other side. Until the 1630's there was nothing remotely revolutionary about the situation; James I had not many more problems than any other monarch. Political strife arose out of disagreement and incompetence in problems that agitated everybody, especially in foreign policy. The Thirty Years' War and the failure of England to stand up for Protestantism were a great element of distrust between the king and the Puritan gentry.

None of this was the cause or even the precondition of the war. If it was the precondition of anything, it was of the collapse of trust which in 1640 produced a king without a party and a united political nation in command of Parliament. We must look for causes of the division into Civil War parties between late 1640 and early 1642, not any sooner. It was in those years that some people were driven to drastic measures and others stood back, preferring even King Charles to the revolutionary Parliamentarians.

Certain aspects of the prewar situation can best be understood in the context of the second stage of the war and the very serious social and political situation that emerged. One must make a careful distinction between 1642 and 1649 and post-1649. The republic, the Levellers, the millenarian and genuinely revolutionary dreams of many of the Puritan clergy and some of the laity—these were elements of true revolution and they had roots in the prewar situation. But they are a very small part of the whole story. The English Revolution has never been digested by standard revolutionary doctrine, perhaps because its leader was a conservative! Because of Oliver Cromwell, the revolution never worked itself to its logical end. The one man who could control the army was the one man who did not want a social revolution. He was capable of revolutionary actions (like cutting off the king's head), but he was quite incapable of planning a transformation of the body politic. Cromwell was no statesman, but he was capable of keeping the revolution (such as it was) alive. After his death it ended, because the events of 1649 showed those who had dominated society before the war that they had made a mistake in breaking with the king.

The English Revolution was not much of a revolution, and the Restoration was very easy. The year 1660 was not a new start but a restoration of the earlier system, modified only in small ways. If the progressive changes of the Tudor period had been continued, I believe that 1660 would have been very much the same without the revolution or the war. The realm of England had been established as a single body politic, governed by the sovereign legislative authority of the king and Parliament, in 1534; it still was that in 1689 and in 1714. Not even the memory of the rebellion and the Civil War lasted very long.

Why did the House of Commons turn against the prerogative courts?

This did not happen until the end of 1640, and I see two reasons for it. The use which Archbishop Laud made of the courts made them suddenly appear to be dangerous instruments of autocracy—and of bishops' autocracy, which was particularly resented. He had turned to the Star Chamber to enforce ecclesiastical policy, and penalties were inflicted on gentlemen who were not supposed to be subject to that kind of thing. Besides that, the men who dominated the Long Parliament were common lawyers who happened to be opposed to the Crown and its courts. Many common lawyers were not opposed to the prerogative courts, but these men did not predominate in the Long Parliament.

Pym and Hampden and some others seem to have been angry men. What was the reason for their bitterness, and exactly what did they want?

They certainly wanted better government, which to some extent meant less interfering government. They wanted protection for the reformist wing of the Church. However, like all Puritans of their persuasion, they had no specific idea of what they wanted to do with the Church when they got it. They resented illegal taxation; they wished to protect property. Also, the opposition to the Crown after the 1570's never saw the situation in purely English terms. When they saw King Charles, they thought of the king of France and of Philip II and of Continental despotisms in which a failure to call parliaments or estates had resulted in oppression and the downfall of property rights. Men like Pym and Hampden thought they were protecting rights, and the king was equally certain that he was justified in protecting his prerogative. Charles I failed at his most important job. He made every sort of claim for his kingship and achieved none of them, and that is an indictment in political terms.

I think that the eleven years of non-parliamentary government were in themselves a frustration. Year after year, these men saw things get worse and could do nothing about it. When they did get their Parliament, they quickly found that it was impossible to trust King Charles. The anger so obviously expressed in the first and second sessions of the Long Parliament was a reaction against the government as embodied in Strafford and Laud—hence the violent, personal attacks. Charles made it plain that his duty to God overrode everything else, that the promises he made to rebellious subjects were made for momentary advantage only. That is what lost him his head in the end. These men, like all men of Puritan nature, were self-righteous men who knew what should be done and were enraged when others failed to do it.

Puritanism evidently lost its hold on the gentry sometime during the 1650's. Is that because it was discredited politically?

Not very much work has been done on that subject, and we know more about the spread of Puritanism among the upper classes than about its decline. One possible answer is the shift in generations; the men of 1660 were not those of 1620. Certainly one important explanation is that Puritanism had achieved power and revealed itself, and the bulk of the gentry was not pleased with what they saw. With that went a decline in the deep, serious zeal which had attracted many young men to the Puritan cause. Puritanism was revealed as an overwrought, overzealous, and censorious religion which the self-confident, propertied gentry class was not likely to tolerate for very long.

13

The Reformation

A. G. DICKENS

THE HISTORIOGRAPHICAL CONTEXT

During the period 1910–40 it was fashionable among historians to interpret the Reformation in terms of social, economic, and political change and to view the upheaval in the Christian church in relation to—sometimes as a mere reflection of—the ambitions of capitalists and princes. The past three decades have seen a salutary reversal of this trend. Historians have sought to understand the religious experience of the sixteenth century in and for itself, and while not neglecting the secular implications and involvements of the Reformation, to analyze the complex spiritual and intellectual movement of Christian faith that begins in the late fifteenth century and did not much diminish in intensity until the middle decades of the seventeenth century. When all qualifications have been made, it has become clear that the Reformation was essentially an effort by the best European minds for almost two centuries to find God and define the nature of the Christian faith. This passionate religious quest immensely complicated the course of political, social, and economic change, and the secular situation probably inhibited the realization of the heavenly city on earth that the reformers sought. But the religious quest must be the central focus for understanding the explosive historical phenomenon known as the Reformation.

In the English-speaking world, A. G. Dickens, now the Director of the Institute of Historical Research at the University of London, has played a crucial role in the restoration of a proper perspective to the interpretation of the Reformation. Born in 1910, Dickens for many years quietly devoted himself to detailed (and highly valuable) research on the ecclesiastical developments in northern England in the early sixteenth century.

In the past few years, however, Dickens' many years of reflection and wide reading have borne fruit in magnificent works of synthesis—*The English Reformation, Reformation and Society in Sixteenth-Century Europe,* and *The Counter-Reformation.* This reserved, industrious scholar, with a Neville Chamberlain mustache and modest mien that might seem to promise little in the way of originality and brilliance, has proved himself to be one of the most forceful and far-ranging historical minds of his generation.

Chronological Outline

1483: Martin Luther, the son of a miner, is born in Eisleben, Germany.

1517: Partly in protest against the sale of indulgences by the Dominican monk Tetzel, Luther publishes the *95 Theses* at Wittenberg. Traditionally, this marks the beginning of the Reformation.

1520: Luther burns the papal bull and the canon law and is excommunicated.

1521: The Edict of Worms. Charles V, the German emperor, declares Luther a heretic.

1524–1525: The Peasants' War against the social and economic oppression of the German feudal system is savagely suppressed. Luther repudiates the peasants and their revolutionary credo, *The Twelve Articles.*

1529–1534: Papal power is limited in England, with the result that Henry VIII becomes the supreme head of the Church in England.

1531: Formation of the Schmalkaldic League of Protestant princes and imperial cities.

1534: Ignatius de Loyola founds the Jesuit Order.

1536: John Calvin publishes his *Institutes of the Christian Religion* and introduces the Reformation into Geneva in 1541.

1545–1563: The Council of Trent, called by Pope Paul III, effects some genuine reforms in the Roman Catholic Church without altering, however, any essential dogmatic bases.

1546: Death of Luther.

1546–1547: The Schmalkaldic War. Urged by the pope, Charles V attempts to subdue the Protestant city-states of Germany and restore the unity of the Roman church.

1553–1558: Queen Mary attempts to re-establish Roman Catholicism in England.

1555: The Religious Peace of Augsburg allows each German prince to choose between Lutheranism and Roman Catholicism. The Calvinist religions remain banned.

1556: Charles V retires to a monastery. His younger brother Ferdinand I succeeds him as emperor, while his son Philip succeeds to the Spanish throne.

1559: Pope Paul IV publishes *The Index of Prohibited Books,* which lists the works of the outstanding heretics to be destroyed by the machinery of the Counter-Reformation.

1598: The Edict of Nantes. Henry IV, the first Bourbon king of France, establishes religious freedom for the Huguenots.

Norman F. Cantor
What was the relationship between the Protestant Reformation and late medieval heresy?

A. G. Dickens
For a Reformation historian it is an interesting exercise to take up Dr. Gordon Leff's admirable book, *Heresy in the Later Middle Ages,* and work through it with the Protestant Reformation in mind. In surveying the spectrum of heresy we may perhaps make a rough-and-ready distinction between two types of phenomena: first, heretical traditions widely diffused in European society but creating, at most, hole-and-corner sectarian groups unable to exercise significant influence upon the Reformation; and second, what might be called territorial heresies, more or less firmly established and organized in particular areas of Europe. These latter were compelled to come to terms with Protestantism, but at the same time they were too big for Protestantism to ignore or reject.

The diffused heretical traditions could doubtless be broken down into a number of classes. The antipapal, anticlerical, Erastianism of Marsiglio of Padua influenced many later thinkers and was revived to great effect in Reformation Europe, notably in the England of Henry VIII. It was little concerned with the basic doctrines of Christianity, but it undoubtedly contained (by Catholic standards) a heretical doctrine of the Church —which explains why Thomas Cromwell could finance the translation and publication of Marsiglio's works. A very different heterodox tradition had sprung originally from the Calabrian Abbot Joachim of Flora, who died about 1202 and had prophesied a "third age of the church" in which a new order of leaders would replace the existing hierarchy. This notion had been taken over by the Spiritual Franciscans, who believed themselves destined for leadership. Such pretensions, coupled with their denunciation of property holding, set them upon a collision course with the papacy, which drove them into heresy under John XXII. But similar prophetic ideas continued to circulate on the eve of the Reformation. They reappeared, for example, in Thomas Münzer, one of Luther's most important rivals and a major founder of the new sectarian and spiritualist movements of the sixteenth century. We have an excellent general account of various millenarian movements in Norman Cohn's *The Pursuit of the Millennium,* which merits careful study by historians of the Reformation.

Another surviving heretical tradition was represented by the movement known as the Free Spirit, ostensibly a perversion of Rhenish mysticism and perhaps of Neoplatonism. It seems to have been influenced in the fourteenth century by the famous mystic Meister Eckhart. In its more extreme forms it could be crudely pantheistic and antinomian, even to the point of organizing sexual irregularities under the guise of purification rites. To its advanced exponents, the spirit of man was divine and entirely free. The Church had no legitimate authority; the priesthood and sacraments were of no avail. The "Free Spirit" remained active in various parts of Germany and Switzerland during the early years of the sixteenth century. We should like to establish major links between these late medieval sects and the sectarian and spiritualist movements which sprang up so rapidly in the 1520's. Thomas Münzer was such a link, yet one would like to find additional evidence of contacts at the grass roots between medieval radicalism and Reformation radicalism.

I now turn to what I called the territorial heresies—those established major phenomena which could not avoid becoming entangled with the Protestant Reformation. The most important and recent in origin was that of the Hussites of Bohemia and Moravia. It was less impressive for the novelty or originality of its teachings than for its secular achievements: it had helped to create a nation which had defied both foreign enemies and Catholic crusaders for more than a century. By 1520, however, the Czech movement was ambivalent as a model for reformers, since Catholic controversialists were able to make much of the bitter divisions within the movement and to infer from them that heresy meant the downfall of earthly kingdoms.

The most interesting faction to emerge from the early internal struggles was that of the Bohemian Brethren (often known as the Moravian Brethren), headed from 1494 to 1528 by Luke of Prague. These men ultimately found themselves able to accept Luther's justificatory and eucharistic teachings, and in 1522 they made overtures to Luther. In 1542 they achieved a loose union with the Lutheran Church, retaining their own disciplinary system of public and private confession. Many of them migrated to Poland and there united with the Calvinists in 1555. Meanwhile, Luther had welcomed not only the Brethren but the conservative right wing of the Hussites as evangelical Christians. Despite these rapprochements, Bohemian and Moravian Protestants never became thoroughly assimilated to Lutheranism; they retained a vigorous individuality at least until these lands were forcibly restored to Catholicism after the Battle of the White Mountain in 1621.

In the days of Luke of Prague, radical Puritan groups called Amosites appeared in some rural areas of Bohemia. They opposed and excluded townsmen and members of the nobility, desiring to build a simple society of saints upon the principles of the Sermon on the Mount. They were in effect forerunners of the Anabaptists, and were naturally absorbed by the latter when Anabaptism spread to Bohemia in the 1520's.

The second of the major heresies was that of the Waldensians. The merchant Peter Waldo died in Bohemia in 1217 after his movement expanded into many parts of Europe, and its early connection with Bohemia survived at the beginning of the sixteenth century, when uneducated Waldensians repeated prophecies that a great Messiah-king would come out of Bohemia to reform the church. In Italy a considerable missionary organization and the professional clergy held together far-ranging Waldensian groups who believed in a simplified Gospel-oriented Christianity; many of them upheld a symbolic interpretation of the Eucharist which foreshadowed that of Zwingli. For this reason, and because of the facts of geography, their natural affinities were with Reformed, not Lutheran, Protestantism. Eventually they decided to link with the Zwinglians, but the Piedmontese Waldensians preserved a great measure of independence within the Reformed tradition. Subjected to repeated and bloody persecutions, they have survived as a largely autonomous church even to our own day.

The third major heresy flourishing on the eve of the Reformation was the English Lollard heresy deriving from Wycliffe and surviving in the early fifteenth century as a popular, largely underground movement strongest in Kent, Essex, East Anglia, Buckinghamshire, and the Thames Valley. Along with others, I have written at considerable length on the survival of this heresy and its innumerable recorded connections with Lutheran publicists and booksellers active in England during the 1520's. Intermittently persecuted by several bishops between 1500 and 1530, Lollardy seems nevertheless to have been gaining rather than losing in strength when it encountered Lutheranism. Scriptural, antisacramental, and anticlerical, it consisted (like Waldensianism) of working-class congregations held together by a few wandering missionaries. Certainly its proletarian spirit continued to color popular Protestantism in England up to the reign of Elizabeth.

In surveying the whole field we should not exaggerate the role of the three major heresies. Certainly they provided regional springboards for the new Protestantism, and the Reformation would not have progressed so swiftly or had the same proletarian backing without the heresies. On the other hand, the major religious leaders of the Reformation did not derive their doctrines or social ideals from predecessors. Luther developed his system from the Bible and from the Augustinian tradition before he ever studied Huss. Further, had Protestantism not arisen under Luther's leadership it seems most unlikely that the older heresies would have broken through on their own. Their progress was slow. They had no great leaders, publicists, or theologians, and they lacked new ideas for the new age. With some exceptions in Bohemia, they had little or no control over printing and small command of the literary techniques which contributed so much to the victories of Protestantism. Looking at the whole story from the fourteenth century, one can say that the Catholic Church had held the older heresies to a position of stalemate. Something more massive and forceful was needed to break through and win over much larger areas of Europe.

To what extent did the Reformation perpetuate ideas and attitudes propounded by the Renaissance humanists? To what extent was the Reformation antihumanistic?

The whole of the Protestant, biblical Reformation, and in particular the careers of its intellectual leaders like Luther, Zwingli, and Calvin, was based upon a principle which was first elaborated and illustrated by the humanists. This is the belief that the individual scholar, armed with the resources of modern philological knowledge and textual criticism, can arrive under God's guidance at important truths (perhaps hitherto concealed) about the meanings of ancient literature. Before Luther arrived, Colet and Erasmus had applied this principle to the text of the Bible itself. To all men of learning with a spark of independence, one aspect of the Renaissance could be expressed in certain questions expecting an affirmative answer. When it comes to interpreting the sense of a passage of Saint Paul, should we not prefer Erasmus to an unlearned pope, or to a scholastic theologian who lacked humanist historical and critical techniques and who cannot possibly compensate by mere intellectual ratiocination? Indeed, might we not prefer to follow modern scholarship rather than the consensus of a General Council? On the subject of indulgences, must we not prefer the biblical specialist Dr. Luther to Tetzel, a Dominican fund raiser with transparently vested interests and not much pretense to any sort of learning?

The Reformation was essentially an attempt to rediscover the Christianity of the first Christian generations. It came when it did not solely because of the sub-Christianity of the Renaissance church, but also because—thanks to the classical humanists—scholars had the techniques necessary to re-explore this precious bit of the ancient world. This seems to me to be the most important link between Renaissance and Reformation, between humanism and Protestantism.

During the crucial years between 1517 and 1521, Luther and the German humanists were linked in opposition to common enemies: the Renaissance papacy and its fiscalism; the reactionary Dominicans with their esprit de corps and their hatred for the humanist tradition. Luther inherited this situation as well as the patriotic sentiments which marked German humanism.

As the Reformation developed, humanism completed its domination of the educational scene from the grammar school to the university, from the secular treatise to the language used even by Catholic theologians and fathers of the Church in council. From the early years of the sixteenth century, every man who wanted to exercise influence among educated Europeans had to be at least on friendly terms with humanist style and language. Whatever his opinions or values, a man who could not put on a fair humanist act was apt to become a figure of fun. For Luther and the reformers, the need for Greek and Latin literacy expanded into a need for vernacular literacy. It was essential to the Protestant outlook that even men of humble status —more strikingly still, even women—should be able to read the Bible for themselves. Luther himself asserted the need for better and wider popular education, but it is fair to add that his motives were social and practical as well as religious.

In the struggle between Protestantism and reformed Catholicism, modern education was the chosen weapon of both sides. Ignatius Loyola, the retired soldier, went back to school with boys; and in later years schools and colleges formed the very basis of his apostolic action. On the Protestant side, a humanist education was equally important. It was of the utmost significance that alongside the volcanic prophet of Wittenberg there stood his orderly, academic little lieutenant Philip Melanchthon, the greatest German humanist of his day—a Professor of Greek whose reputation (quite as much as Luther's) brought thousands of students to the shabby little town on the Elbe. Virtually all the other major reformers, both Catholic and Protestant, were accomplished humanists, though their responses to the various elements within humanism no doubt varied a great deal. Zwingli was a deep-dyed Erasmian before he had ever heard the name of Luther, and he wrote nobly of his hopes that God would find some way of saving the souls of the great saints, sages, and heroes of the ancient pagan world. Calvin was technically, though not theologically, among the greatest of all the sixteenth-century humanists—one whose classical feeling enabled him to write exquisite French and thus to influence not only men of learning but society at large.

I turn now to the second question: to what extent was the Reformation anti-humanist? The main points here are obvious and familiar. It is true that Renaissance humanism was only in rare cases pagan, agnostic, atheistic, or openly anti-Christian. On the other hand, the devout and biblical humanism, the fusion so perfectly accomplished in a man like Lefèvre d'Étaples, did not typify the whole situation. The historical, philological, archaeological, and artistic pursuits of the humanist represent an overflow of interest into nontheological, non-Christian fields. Humanist history, whatever the Christian professions of its writers, did not make the Cross central to all human history. When Machiavelli, in enforced retirement, came home from his sordid day of gambling at the village inn, he put on his best clothes, entered his study, and began hours of deep and unwearied delight in vital contact with the great minds of the past. But these minds were not the fathers of the Church: they were those of the sages, the orators and poets of pagan antiquity. The Renaissance made non-Christian interests more possible, more licit, more pleasurable. From the time of Petrarch, or earlier, the humanists stressed the dignity of man, claiming that in some measure he could take control of his own destiny.

Humanism was then primarily a technique of learning and teaching, based upon a more intimate relationship with the Ancient World, yet it could have philosophical and moral implications not wholly remote from those which characterize the so-called humanism of our own day. If it harmonized with any theological tendency, it harmonized with Occamism, because Occamism was Pelagian to the extent of claiming that a man could contribute something toward his own salvation from his own resources. It was no accident that Occamism grew along with humanism in the fourteenth century or that Erasmus, insofar as he held a systematic theology, maintained the fashionable Occamism of his day. It was over this issue that he finally came to grips with Luther.

The major Protestant churches embraced theocentric and Christocentric principles, rejecting decisively the anthropocentric tendencies which humanism had developed. For Luther, man's free will, though effective in worldly relationships, was utterly ineffective in regard to his own salvation. Man did not even cooperate in a small way in the cleansing of his soul by Christ; indeed, his soul was never truly cleansed in this life. Saint Paul's famous texts on justification did not mean that man was made inwardly good, but that Christ hung a cloak about him to hide his sinfulness. If a moral improvement did occur (Saint Paul's "sanctification"), this constituted no title to salvation, no claim on the grace of an infinitely pure and mighty God. If Luther's view was non-Occamist, it was even more nonhumanist. The dignity of man did not exist because man was a marvelous piece of work, but because Christ died for him. It was not easy for Luther, filled with this overwhelming conviction, to live in harmony even with a controlled Christian humanist like Melanchthon, whose Christianity was tidy, moralistic, and anxious to stress the responsibility of man without detracting too much from God's sovereignty and Christ's sacrifice.

The short answer to our question is that biblical humanism and (much less important) patriotic German humanism were both closely linked with the Reformation. Philosophic humanism, however, contained an anthropological tendency quite at variance with the Christocentric teaching of Luther and Calvin. Needless to add, behind the war of ideas one may also observe temperamental and experiential contrasts in the clash between Luther and Erasmus and in the subtler differences between Luther and Melanchthon. Here lies the antithesis between the once-born and the twice-born, between the tranquil faith of the civilized Christian humanist and the evangelical faith of a man who has been pulled from the abyss by the strong hand of the Redeemer.

It has sometimes been claimed that the generation that came to maturity around the year 1500 was inclined to radical solutions in politics and religion alike. If you agree with this view, how do you account for this development?

There seems to be some truth within this generalization, but it calls for some careful distinctions. Radicalism was hardly the keynote of European politics around the year 1500. Throughout most of the Continent, especially France, Spain, England, and much of central Europe, men were declaring decisively in favor of strong monarchies and administrative machines which offered protection against internal anarchy and foreign foes. The trading class had most of all to gain here, for the major princes held together large areas wherein people could trade peaceably with the aid of viable currencies. Life was in any case short and insecure; civil peace appeared a major blessing and an obtainable one. When a Frenchman looked back at the Hundred Years' War or an Englishman at the Wars of the Roses, even the heavier taxation demanded by a Louis XI or a Henry VII became tolerable. Certainly, royal propaganda made the most of these ugly memories of anarchy.

Nevertheless, on the lower levels of society it was far easier to entertain radical notions. Landlords and their lawyers were at work in many parts of Europe to extend and intensify serfdom, and it was hard for a peasant or small tenant to see that the landlord contributed much to his security or well-being. Peasant unrest around 1500 belonged to the Middle Ages. It was related to the Peasant Revolt of 1381 in England, to the savage *Jacquerie* in France and the continuing *Bundschuh* movement in Germany. But it is doubtful whether this unrest became any more radical around 1500 or throughout the sixteenth century. By far the greatest peasant rising was that in central and southwestern Germany in 1524–25—a rising put down by the princes and lords at a cost of perhaps a hundred thousand lives. But the demands of these German peasants were hardly revolutionary. They wanted to be relieved of certain specific dues and burdens, but they continued to accept the stratified class structure of the age together with the broad legal and economic patterns which had characterized society over the last five centuries.

We should not forget that even in the closer-knit urban societies, strong tensions often existed between the unprivileged workers and the rich merchants who dominated the city councils. But such restiveness seldom worked toward radical changes in the urban constitution, and it did not significantly amalgamate with the deeper discontents of the peasantry. Even so, to some extent the broad spirit of discontent could be captured and canalized by educated leaders into religious or political channels—perhaps on occasion even conservative channels. As in modern protest movements, there were a lot of muddled sheep with volatile emotions instead of clear-cut purposes. Certainly many of the malcontent German peasants transmuted Luther's religious message into a plea for liberation from economic and social servitude, and they were savagely disillusioned by his notorious pamphlet *Against the Thieving and Murderous Gangs of Peasants.*

An ideological shift in the reverse direction can be observed in the largest rebellion of Tudor England—the Pilgrimage of Grace in 1536–37—where there is an enormous weight of evidence for social and economic motivation. The north of England had as yet been little touched by Protestantism, though anticlericalism and Lollard opinions were far from unknown. Under these circumstances the pious Catholic leader Robert Aske and some clerical leaders were able to include in the program a condemnation of the king's semi-Protestant advisers and to express their sympathy, both economic and religious in origin, with the monasteries scheduled for dissolution. This was canalization toward the right, not the left.

Altogether, when we look for discontent on the lower levels of European society on the eve of the Reformation, we find plenty of it. It nevertheless represents nothing new, and it does not enable us to ascribe the Reformation to social and economic grievances. It was not very clear or determined in its objectives, and as protest movements go, it was not very radical. Sixteenth-century men in general accepted a good deal of restraint and inequality. Except for a few radical clerics, the Church assured them that these things were ordained by God.

I have already spoken of religious radicalism and have shown its very real limits in Europe as a whole, at least before 1520. If we outline the conditions that prepared the ground for the Reformation, we ought surely to stress anticlericalism: the critical spirit applied by hardheaded laymen (and even by a number of the clergy) to the Catholic Church. Along with the portentous development of self-governing cities—the very root of the Renaissance—we observe the notable growth of lay education. In princely courts and in the increasingly numerous schools and universities, a vastly increasing number of laymen were acquiring intellectual independence. Long before Luther's Reformation, the lay people who ran his future strongholds—Nuremberg, Strassburg, and Augsburg—administered their own schools, chantries, and almshouses; many could even write Latin documents without the aid of clergymen. Everywhere there was a growth of lay competence and claims to management.

One could produce numerous examples of anti-clericalism throughout the Middle Ages, but it seems to have become more common, more bitter, more articulate, and also perhaps more potentially constructive around 1500. Not only in the writings of the northern humanists, but in the popular literature of the day (especially in Germany and France) appear many attacks on the papacy and on the hypocrisy, avarice, and simony of ordinary monks and priests. These writers were not Protestants, nor were they making the old *Decameron*-style jokes about lecherous confessors. Their attacks were serious, and bitter in tone; they castigated pope and clergy; they did so as moralists and as Germans or Frenchmen.

Yet while anticlericalism doubtless formed a background and a springboard for Protestantism, it was emphatically not the same thing. These Germans and Frenchmen had nothing positive to oppose to the official theology. Without a new theology that could be defended on the basis of the Bible, nothing comparable with Luther's or Zwingli's Reformation could have emerged. As a footnote, one might add that a number of writers and artists around 1500 feared religious and social radicalism and had dark forebodings concerning revolutionary change. In my *Reformation and Society in Sixteenth-Century Europe,* you will see an illustration showing the Church as a great Noah's Ark being swamped by the seas. The date is 1497, the picture comes from Johann Lichtenberger's *Prenostication.* If the age had an especially poignant sense of insecurity, may this not have been because life in cities had begun to offer so many people a little more than in the medieval past?

Is there any value in a psychological interpretation of Luther?

Not long ago I read an article in one of our British illustrated magazines which purported to reduce many great historical figures to psychologists' types. Under a postage-stamp portrait of Luther, the reformer was encapsulated as follows: cyclothymic [milder form of manic-depressive], sense of guilt, self-reproach, anxiety, moods, depressive phases, melancholia, emotional, impressionable, combative, inclined to drink heavily. Certainly, if the last-mentioned characteristic forms a vital clue, there must have been a high proportion of cyclothymics in the German population of Luther's day! This pretentious nonsense apart, I feel that historians must resist the temptation to bristle whenever a psychologist invades their territory. If we try to keep the psychologist in order, it should be on their use of historical evidence, not within the expertise of their own subject. Historians should not regret that psychologists discuss historical figures, but rather that they so seldom attempt the task.

So far as I have read the psychologists on Luther, their analysis seems to fall into two theories: one, that he was some sort of manic-depressive; two, that the young Luther's revolt was connected with an identity crisis—that is, the effort of a young man to win independence from his parental domination and become a person in his own right. I find it difficult to accept that Luther's mental history conformed very closely to the usual manic-depressive patterns. For one thing, his famous attacks of depression never really hampered work demanding the most extreme concentration. While suffering these attacks as a friar, he was learning

Greek and Hebrew very successfully with little or no guidance apart from the poor textbooks then available. Later on, so far from finding the depressions debilitating, he emerged from every attack to conquer tasks of superhuman magnitude. He tells us that it was in the very depths that he found faith and healing. How many manic-depressives have composed three hundred and fifty separate works, effectively interviewed thousands of people, written countless thousands of letters as a spiritual counselor, and fulfilled a multitude of other public and private tasks?

Turning to the identity crises, we encounter the book *Young Man Luther,* a rather verbose but distinctly interesting work by the experienced psychiatrist Dr. E. H. Erikson. Here the adolescent Luther creates a terrible, vengeful God in the image of his own severe and angry father. He shifts his obedience to this deity and ultimately lets fly the venom of his defiance against the pope. Parallel with this, the schoolboy Luther is thrashed for speaking German instead of Latin during school hours and becomes fanatically attached to the German language. Once again, his mother beats him for some trivial offense and in his resentment he dethrones the Virgin Mary.

Luther may indeed have passed through such an identity crisis, but these and a very few other clues to that effect have all been selected from hundreds of anecdotes mainly in the late (and rather unreliable) *Table-Talk.* True, the psychologist must select what is significant from a mass of detail. Yet if there are pieces of evidence in apparent contradiction, they should at least be acknowledged. Luther himself tells us that a picture of Christ judging the world, together with a host of other impressions, engraved upon his young mind the terrible images of God and of Christ the judge. That these images sometimes obsessed and terrified him can be understood without introducing the supposedly oppressive figure of Hans Luther. Moreover, Luther did not in fact react fanatically against Latin in favor of German: he remained bilingual, writing pamphlets in both languages, and he continued to transact his personal devotions in Latin as he had been taught. Certainly he did not savagely dethrone the Virgin Mary, but wrote beautifully and reverently about her in his *Treatise on the Magnificat.* His strictures against the old type of saint-worship were backed, like every aspect of his theology, by exhaustive and intellectual investigations into biblical Christianity. In general, one might plead that all "child-versus-parent" hypothesis, like all religious experience, should be reviewed in the light of contemporary uses and expectations. Despite his two or three grumbles about acts of parental severity, Luther's relationship with both his parents remained quite exceptionally cordial until the end of their long lives. By contemporary standards Hans and Margarete Luther seem to have been far from severe parents.

How far can psychiatric investigation explain the major results of Luther's life and work, his extraordinary place in history? The identity crisis contributes nothing here. Why did all the millions of young men who suffered from heavy-handed fathers fail to produce a sensational impact upon history? Why had it to be Luther alone? Was it not because of his exceptional powers both subliminal and intellectual, most of all through an exceptional literary genius exercising itself in rational argument about biblical Christianity as opposed to medieval and Renaissance Christianity? In my submission, psychiatry has so far done little or nothing to explain Luther the writer, the preacher, the agent of history; and this Luther is the one who interests me. I believe that it was not the neurotic elements of his mind which forged a great machine of theology, tore a whole civilization asunder, and altered the course of Western history. Was he not too big, too creative, too effective—too eccentric, if you like—to fit into these neat psychological molds?

Would it be correct to regard Luther as a German nationalist?

This would be correct, but only in certain senses of the term *nationalist.* Luther's earlier years were spent in a period when Germans, led by their literary men, were asserting their nation's claims to a high place in history and an important role in European culture. These humanists displayed a wide spectrum of religious and secular attitudes. Interested in ancient times, they wanted to give their own people a history comparable with that of the Romans. But one cannot see that this movement bore any close relation to the practical politics of the German princes and cities. It was an academic assertion, a sort of cultural touchiness characteristic of emergent nations, not a popular political nationalism centering upon the aggressive assertions of an actual state. Moreover, it had one particular target. In the minds of the German humanists, German nationalism was a counterblow against the arrogant claims of Italian humanists and politicians, who dismissed other nations as barbarians.

The German tradition at the point when it was inherited by Luther can be seen, for example, in a work on universal history by Johannes Nauclerus published in 1516. Here the German race appears as the aboriginal people—the *Urvolk*—of Europe, whose blood and vigor were injected into the Italian, French, and British population during the early Christian centuries. This process, claims Nauclerus, culminated in the crowning of Charlemagne: the sign of a divinely ordained superiority in the German people. To the literal minds of these very medieval men, the world authority of Rome was really and truly handed over on Christmas Day in A.D. 800. Thus German patriotic feeling had no real parallels in Italian-style humanism. In the minds of some German scholars at least, it had a supernatural sanction—a religious and teleological character—in its assertion of a divine destiny for the Germanic race.

Insofar as these ideas had any practical implications, they exalted the Holy Roman Empire. Humanist academics worried little about the creaking judicial, fiscal, and military machinery of the empire, but today we know that the Habsburgs after 1500 were an international family increasingly centered upon Spain and the Netherlands; we know that in Germany, effective power was in fact passing to the territorial princes. German literary and academic patriotism was stillborn in terms of real politics, but in 1520 the empire was still regarded as necessary and viable. In fact, the most vital elements in German culture and religion were the imperial cities, independent states which wanted desperately to believe in the imperial structure as a guarantee of their independence.

Under the pressure of events and of his own conscience, Luther marched forward from this point to form an outlook of his own. His reactions cannot be understood, save on the supposition that he was a man of religion from first to last. His primary attitude to the German people was that of a prophet concerned to recall them to what he regarded as true Christianity, the Christianity of Jesus and Saint Paul. To accomplish this, and not to glorify the German people, he translated the Bible, using the German of the Saxon Chancellery which could be understood by High and Low Germans alike. He knew that he had to stand close to the people for whom he was working, and he tells us that he deliberately sought to capture the idioms of popular speech. He says that "[his] teachers were the housewife in her home, the children at their games, the merchants in the city squares." He wanted above all to make Christianity nonscholastic and meaningful to ordinary men and women.

Luther's closeness to the nation did not mean that he glorified alleged national virtues. Repeatedly he castigated the drunkenness, extravagance, and other sins of the Germans. He realized that there was a great amount of backwardness and barbarity in many areas of his country, and he did not see the Germans as world conquerors. His Reformation had a Teutonic flavor, but he did not think that God was a German god or that the Germans were fit to rule the other nations. Luther shared some of the attitudes of the humanist patriots, but only within the context of his religious motivation. On his early visit to Italy, he detected a great deal of profanity, superstition and poor Latin amongst the clergy and people in Rome, and he transmuted the anti-Italian views of the German humanists into antipapal views. In the indulgence controversy and its sequels, Luther and his backers did reveal a species of nationalism, but in his mind it was religious rather than secular. Luther truly hated the papacy, but this emotion is hardly to be comprehended in the term *nationalism.*

Like the humanists, Luther respected and wanted to retain the Holy Roman Empire. Until 1530 or later, he opposed those who wanted the Lutheran princes to form an armed allegiance against the hostile emperor Charles V. Indeed, to the end of his life he wrote and spoke in terms of affection for "our dear Emperor." He hoped against hope that Charles would come around to something like his viewpoint, that reconciliation could be won within the empire. To us he looks something of a political simpleton. He could not fully understand the complex international inheritance which prevented the Habsburgs from becoming German rulers concerned with the interests of the German people. In regard to worldly affairs, Luther's mind presents a certain mixture of shrewdness and naïveté. Even so, we modern observers enjoy the privilege of hindsight, and there were few among Luther's contemporaries who enjoyed a much clearer political vision.

I hope it is at least clear that Luther's nationalism did not resemble that of Frederick the Great, let alone that of Hitler! His greatest contribution to the national history of Germany was probably his development and standardization of the German language.

To what extent did Luther's German contemporaries understand his religious message?

For social historians of the Reformation, here is a most significant question—even though it cannot be answered with much certainty or exactitude. The question concerns several million people in very varied social settings. Even among working-class men and women, there were great differences. Let us envisage two imaginary people. One is a literate craftsman in sophisticated Nuremberg who can absorb a stimulating cultural atmosphere; as the Reformation took root he is exposed to the eloquence of some of Germany's more advanced preachers. Our second workingman is a serf living a hard, almost cultureless and brutish life on a remote manor in Pomerania: if he gained any real impression of Luther, it must have been by much more gradual processes. True, Luther said simple things and complex things. Certainly the masses understood his resonant protest against the obvious and crass abuse of indulgences. But what about his Real Presence doctrine of the Eucharist (miscalled consubstantiation), or his key doctrine of justification by faith alone? A great deal depends, too, on whether we are discussing the confused early days of the 1520's or the 1540's and 1550's, by which time a settled and educated Lutheran pastorate was teaching the people doctrine on the basis of Melanchthon's *Loci Communes* and Luther's catechisms.

I take it that what interests us most is the degree of understanding of Luther's message which developed between 1518, when he became famous, until the late 1530's, when the Lutheran reform had become firmly established throughout much of Germany. Looking at these two crucial decades, we might profitably try to discover how much ordinary people knew about his doctrine of justification by faith alone. This was the hub of Luther's teaching, from which the rest of his doctrine radiated, but it probably was little understood even among educated Germans during the early years. Some of the most widely read of Luther's tracts, for instance the *Address to the Christian Nobility,* either do not mention his justificatory teaching or bury it in a mass of less important topics. The scores of popular tracts by unknown or obscure writers yield a handful of brief passages on this theme, but in general they here reveal an imperfect understanding. In general, they concentrate on the attack on indulgences, on anti-Roman propaganda, and on the priesthood of all believers. Not even the famous Confession of Augsburg taught much about Luther's key doctrine. Ecumenists like Philip Melanchthon naturally were anxious to conceal novelties in wads of theological cotton wool—to look safe, traditional, and "Catholic." As for the Romanist theologians, far from highlighting Luther's novel views on justification they cast his teachings in terms of ancient heresies which they understood better. Many of the humanist scholars tended to see Luther's battle as a facet of the struggle between their own kind and the reactionary Dominicans.

At the other end of the social scale, the peasantry notoriously distorted Luther's appeal for spiritual freedom into a demand for secular liberation. Countless thousands of working people all over central Europe joined the Anabaptists or other sectarian movements during the later twenties and thirties. So many of the little people of Europe wanted to grasp at an easy millennium, or to detheologize religion rather than (with Luther) to retheologize it.

However, I sense still another side to the social history of the Lutheran Reformation. It was no mere political, economic, or social movement. Evangelical religion was not a creed imposed by self-seeking princes on dutiful subjects but a popular mass movement in many of the German imperial cities and in countless smaller towns. Like the earlier Renaissance, the German Reformation was very much a function of the free townsman and of his instinct for urban solidarity, and this mass movement was set going not by lay magistrates but by Lutheran preachers. There exists no better introduction to the social realities of the Reformation than the urban studies summarized in Bernd Moeller's *Villes d'Empire et Réformation* and more recently extended by Gerald Strauss on Nuremberg and Mrs. Chrisman on Strassburg.

Luther wrote especially to help those who had been through the spiritual slough of despond, but such harrowing experiences can have applied only to a small minority. Communication between the tormented prophet and the ordinary man had obvious limits. This familiar distinction between the once-born and the twice-born has existed in the Lutheran Church since its beginning. Nevertheless, Luther worked with superhuman energy to bridge the abysses between himself and his contemporaries. He was a great communicator, a popular writer who put across a religious message more directly, more effectively than any man of his generation, and the practical implications of his theology were clear and widely accepted. From 1518 until about 1524 there existed a marvelous union on the practical level between the reformer of the German church and a very large part of the nation. Then came the aftermath of the honeymoon, when the exact implications of the marriage contract had to be defined. Yet though the period of maximum accord between prophet and people was brief, it produced results deeper and more widespread than the foundation of territorial churches. Through his writings, most of all through his German Bible, Luther attained a permanent and a major place in a popular culture ever increasingly literary in character.

In the light of recent scholarship, what is the merit of the interpretations propounded by Weber and Tawney on the social significance of the Reformation?

For many years this question has provided an academic exercise beloved of college professors; it is the subject of countless essays and at least two books of readings compiled for those concerned with the theme. This situation seems intelligible in relation to history at the undergraduate level—it is good clean fun and sharpens the wits of the young—but one may doubt whether many senior historians are still seriously interested in the theories of Weber and Tawney.

The story began in 1904–05 with Max Weber's essay *The Protestant Ethic and the Spirit of Capitalism.* Weber admitted, of course, that capitalist practices had existed before the Reformation. Yet he claimed that the spirit and ethic of that worldly ascetic, the modern businessman, stemmed from Calvinist theology, especially from the doctrine that a man must serve God strenuously even in his worldly vocation. The elect stood in God's favor in this world as in the next, and the Calvinist or Puritan businessman regarded worldly opportunity as a trust or stewardship assigned to him by God. In business, calculation replaced traditionalism, and the Reformed businessman gave up the intensive and unorganized acts of charity (so characteristic of Catholicism) in favor of a life of systematic, rationalized activity. Weber thus inverted Marx's materialism and allowed ideological factors arising from religion to shape the economic world.

In 1926, R. H. Tawney published his *Religion and the Rise of Capitalism;* and this book fast became an orthodoxy. Throughout the English-speaking world, and to no small extent outside it, Weber is known chiefly through Tawney's book; yet the two names are much too closely linked. In fact Tawney, a rather doctrinaire socialist and a distinguished (though perhaps overrated) historian, brought Marxism back into the picture. He largely accepted Weber's ideological process but added a converse economic process whereby business motives influenced religious life and organization. Tawney described a two-way interaction between the religious and the economic world.

Why is our present attitude toward Weber and Tawney less than devout? First, large-scale capitalism, together with much of its characteristic methodology and techniques—such as double-entry bookkeeping—flourished in the later Middle Ages. The proponents of Weber's theory retort that it is the spirit of capitalism, not its practices, to which Weber refers, but that involves us in subjective considerations and disallows both proof and disproof. As Tawney himself conceded, the great centers of sixteenth-century banking and high finance were in Catholic countries—Antwerp, Lyons, Genoa, Venice. Augsburg is not a real exception, because all the great Augsburg banking families remained Catholic.

The historical basis of Weber's thesis is scarcely any stronger in relation to the seventeenth century. After 1600 there were indeed several big banking houses headed by Protestants in the Netherlands, Switzerland, France, and elsewhere. Richelieu himself found it safest to bank with Huguenots! However, H. R. Trevor-Roper has remarked that most of the leaders of these businesses were nominal rather than devout Calvinists. Their ways of life were sumptuous, completely uninhibited by the ascetic spirit ascribed to such men by Weber. Certainly their alleged Protestantism did not stop them from financing the Habsburgs and other anti-Protestant rulers. In some Protestant countries, notably in the Dutch Republic, political conditions favored the businessman, but this is not a part of Weber's thesis.

Second, let me glance hastily at Calvinist and Puritan economic theorists. Did they supply modern big business with an ideology, an ethic, a spirit of capitalism? For Calvin and his leading disciples, the answer seems unequivocally negative. It has been urged that they actually opposed selfish capitalism much more energetically than the leaders of any other Christian church of that day; Calvin demanded that even bankers be governed by the Sermon on the Mount. He questioned whether a Christian could legitimately take interest, though he finally sanctioned moderate interest when it represented a fair share of the profit which had been made possible by a loan. But Eck of Ingolstadt, Luther's famous Catholic opponent, had allowed this many years earlier—and so did many other Catholic writers both before and after Calvin's time. Calvin's own ideas were conservative and moralistic. He forbids the taking of interest from the poor, or from borrowers who have lost their money through no fault of their own.

What about English Puritanism and its mighty offshoots in the New World? Most of the available evidence reveals that the Puritans were unworldly, unmercenary, beneficent, and almost morbidly scrupulous over mundane affairs. Michael Walzer, by no means a hostile critic of Weber, specifically discusses in his *The Revolution of the Saints* the connections between Calvinist "saints" and capitalism. He does not believe that the moral discipline of the saints favored systematic acquisition; on the contrary, they held narrow and conservative economic views. The saints urged men to seek no more wealth than they needed for a modest life and to use any surplus in charitable giving. They advocated economic restriction and political control as against entrepreneurial activity, and the Puritan businessmen of the seventeenth century were in fact generous givers.

Weber provided no historical examples in his famous essay, except to cite the case of Benjamin Franklin, a strange Puritan indeed! Tawney does better as an historian, yet even Tawney's evidence is unimpressive in bulk and weak in pertinence and quality. He produces a number of late seventeenth- and eighteenth-century economic writers who talk his way, then optimistically takes them to represent "later Puritanism." He does not wholly ignore the embarrassing fact that every Puritan writer, at least during the period before 1660 when Calvinism and Puritanism mattered, argued for the traditional restraints upon the profit motive. He simply believes that Calvinism had a suppressed or latent urge towards the capitalist spirit, and that this emerged later on. Weber and Tawney failed, then, not only because they found too little supporting evidence, but because there remained so much evidence in actual contradiction.

Are we to conclude that no vestige of evidence exists to connect the Reformed religion with the religion of the balance sheet? Perhaps Tawney's late evidence does mean something to this effect: that after the decline of Calvinist Puritanism, men who inherited some of its secondary characteristics were prominent in the business life of some Western countries. Benjamin Franklin and his like in colonial America could, I suppose, be resurrected in this residuary role. Certainly in eighteenth-century England many successful businessmen were also Protestant Dissenters, though this is in large part explained by far simpler phenomena. By this stage, the separate traditions of dissent and profit were blending harmoniously into a duet that is still being sung, but even this alliance was not specifically neo-Calvinist. Excluded from so many branches of political and public life, English Nonconformists as a whole were free to transfer all their energies to the one public sphere open to them. Like the other great-great-grandchildren of Reformation men, they had thrown off most of the ideology of Luther and Calvin, and for the most part they were moralistic believers in self-help, affected not a little by the new rationalism. No one could be more different from Luther and Calvin than a moralistic Pelagian with rationalist overtones, but this development could perhaps be viewed as a minute residuum of truth in the theories of Weber and Tawney. I suppose they saw the pattern in their own nineteenth- and early twentieth-century worlds, and wanted to imprint it upon an earlier and very different age.

Why did Calvinism become the dominant form of Protestantism in the late sixteenth century?

To answer this question adequately, we must first take a glance at Calvinism's competitors. By 1550, the radical sects (including the Anabaptists) had failed to coalesce over large areas, to take over states, or to capture much of a following in the middle and upper classes. They could not be rooted out, but their capacity for overall expansion had vanished. Lutheranism retained control over nearly all the vast areas it had conquered between 1520 and 1550, but it, too, had lost its enterprising qualities and was falling into chronic internal quarrels. Patching up the latter, the Lutheran churches entered into an age of orthodoxy, when intellectual theology failed to disguise a spiritual torpor lasting until the rise of pietism after the middle of the seventeenth century. Meanwhile, the political world of the Lutherans in Germany and Scandinavia was passing through a stable and unexciting period. After the Peace of Augsburg (1555), the Lutherans hoped that they would be left alone by the Habsburgs and other Catholic powers. To have overthrown the Habsburgs in Vienna would merely have left the Lutherans themselves to face the menace of the Ottoman Turks. Altogether, the Lutheran solution involved stability and conservatism. They had won liberty of worship with the Augsburg formula *cuius regio eius religio,* and they had no intention of endangering this fragile peace.

What a contrast between this cautious, immobile, unchallenging world and the world of Calvinist enterprise throughout the second half of the sixteenth century! Not only was Huguenotism advancing in France, but militant Calvinist leaders, even though they represented a small minority, came to the fore with the great revolt which created the Dutch Republic. Calvinism became the main doctrinal force behind the rise of dissenting English Puritanism, and it was equally the theology of the Anglican Establishment. Its headquarters at Cambridge provided innumerable Anglican parishes with Calvinist clergy. In Scotland, Calvinism overcame Catholicism and created in that small kingdom a mighty fortress from which Presbyterian Calvinism was to make formidable incursions into world history. Between 1550 and 1600, Calvinists were still putting up a fight in Poland against both the Jesuits and the Unitarians; in Hungary, Calvinist missionaries created tenacious minority churches against the somber background of Turkish occupation. Even in Germany, Calvinism achieved minor conquests in the Rhineland and Westphalia, while in 1563 the Elector Palatine took his state into the

Reformed camp, and Heidelberg became a main Calvinist center within the empire. By a strange alchemy, a religion which stressed man's weakness and his need for strong external discipline became involved with a range of political causes which on balance contributed much to civic and national freedoms in Europe—and its involvement was most highly visible in the wastes of New England and the Civil War battlefields of old England.

Calvin's *Institutes of the Christian Religion* and the functioning theocracy of Geneva might be designated as exhibits *A* and *B* of the Reformed religion. In the *Institutes,* the strong points of Luther's teaching were molded into an architectural structure. The one important change—Calvin's doctrine of the Eucharist—was more credible and more easily intelligible than the Lutheran equivalent, yet without falling into the bare rationalism of Zwingli. From beginning to end, this is a book about the Bible. It appealed with enormous efficiency and resource to the one tribunal which in sixteenth-century Europe could be set up alongside or above the Catholic Church. Especially in later editions, the *Institutes* were both systematic and comprehensive, but they remained innocent of scholastic subtleties and abstractions.

Geneva became internationally famous during Calvin's later years. It seemed to provide what Lutheran moralists complained that their own churches failed to provide—an example of a Christian policy which could put into action the highest standards of religious observance and morality. We know now that Genevan society was far less perfect than its admirers imagined, but it was the public impression which made history. About a quarter of British Protestant exiles from the Marian persecution of 1554–58 went to Geneva, and many of them recorded precisely the impressions that Calvin wanted to disseminate throughout Europe. The most famous of all these pronouncements was that of John Knox, who thought Geneva "the most perfect school of Christ that ever was on earth since the days of the Apostles." To us, the Genevan experiment seems to be based on punitive legislation, but in that age such sanctions did not shock ordinary law-abiding townsmen. A close secular and religious discipline based upon harsh punishments was the hallmark of city life even during the late Middle Ages. Moreover, the Genevan pastorate, like the Society of Jesus, preferred to persuade, to educate, to produce willing obedience and apostolic activism. Geneva was an exceptionally clean, charitable, and in many spheres, cultured community. By the 1550's, it was also a highly organized training school for missionaries, most of whom issued forth to convert Calvin's own native country of France, where their successes proved real but limited.

Geneva was directed by men who combined rigidity on basic doctrine with broad and flexible views concerning ecclesiastical methods and structures—men who believed more than most in the brotherhood of the human race, men who shared something of the wide horizons of the Jesuits. An important influence upon the young Calvin had been that of Martin Bucer, one of the few genuinely ecumenical figures of the age. Nevertheless, in the defense of what it deemed the essentials of belief, Calvinism produced uncompromising and dedicated agents, men prepared to pick up the available political weapons and to afford a steely opposition toward the Church of Rome and all its champions. If we call the later sixteenth century the age of Counter-Reformation, then Calvinism provided the prime opposition to the trend of that age.

Concerning the regional factors behind the success of Calvinism, I can only provide a few examples. Luther's presentation of the Gospel had claims upon the German spirit with which no rival presentation could compete on level terms, and Germans were by no means confined to Germany. There were great communities of them in the trading cities from Scandinavia down the East Baltic through Poland to Transylvania. All these communities went over to Luther and formed centers for later conversions to Lutheranism. But where there were few Germans, a religion crisply presented in Latin and French without Teutonic overtones could compete successfully. We know that the Polish and Hungarian nobles who went West for their education, and received it in Latin, often remained unimpressed by Luther. A great number of them turned Calvinist and won their less-traveled compatriots to the cause. In Poland as in France, Calvinism allowed great landowners to be elders of the church and otherwise to control their local congregations: it was not a religion for townsmen only. On the lower levels, German traders and colonizers had never been loved by Slavonic and Magyar populations, and these readily followed the lead of the nobility. As for France, it could only be won (if won at all) in French, and Calvin thought and wrote in French as elegantly as in Latin.

In each of these countries, one can cite other social pressures which helped to further or hamper the extension of Calvinism. In the Netherlands, the great revolt which began in the 1560's gave an admirable opportunity for Calvinism—though very much a minority creed—to prove itself a trainer of leaders. Here the revolutionary movement transcended social class, but fighters for liberation are not always liberals, even after the fighting stops. The old regent-oligarchy, consisting of liberal Erasmians rather than dedicated Calvinists, exploited democratic and Calvinist enthusiasm, yet recovered its leadership at the end of the religious wars. In the Netherlands at least, this restoration seems no bad thing. An essay in H. R. Trevor-Roper's book *Religion, the Reformation, and Social Change* demonstrates that we cannot claim Calvinism proper as the pioneer for the liberal Enlightenment of the late seventeenth and eighteenth centuries. Former Calvinist countries like Holland, Switzerland, and Scotland took leading roles in the Enlightenment not because of their Calvinist backgrounds but because rigid Calvinism had meanwhile been succeeded by liberal skepticism. This is especially true of the Dutch Republic, where the regent class never abandoned the cool and tolerant spirit inherited from Erasmus.

Finally, I shall mention the case of English Puritanism, in which Calvinism was not the sole ingredient but surely the most substantial. In *The Revolution of the Saints,* Michael Walzer describes Calvinist Puritanism as a reply to the spiritual confusion resulting from the Renaissance and the Reformation, from the breakup of a feudal and traditional society, from the widespread rejection of patriarchal rule at local and national levels. Out of this confusion there emerged at first political exiles, vagabonds, and heretics; then groups of free men came together and shaped society on a basis of religious ideology. They sought to establish a new order through rigid self-discipline and group discipline. Enemies of the old order, yet fearful of spiritual and social anarchy, they found in Puritan belief and organization an answer to selfhood as well as to the turbulent forces of the age. In the end, however, the need for vigilance and rigor became less pressing; and in the world of Restoration England, the Puritan saint was no longer needed. In late years most of us have become suspicious of general theories which seek to assess a complex age in a single, relatively simple, formula, yet I do not doubt that Dr. Walzer here achieves at least one valid insight upon the historical function of Calvinist Puritanism.

To what extent was the English Reformation in the reign of Henry VIII an act of state and to what extent a religious movement?

In a recent essay, John T. McNeill has forcefully protested against the tendency to minimize religious motivation in a period obviously replete with plain examples of that phenomenon. Such a criticism I have long made concerning the English Reformation. In this field, the underemphasis on religion has not in general been occasioned by any Marxist stress upon material motives. The strong constitutional and parliamentary inclinations of the British have registered upon their historians, some of whom have been happy to reduce religious and ecclesiastical history to the semblance of a constitutional textbook. Again, many of the most scholarly historians of the English Reformation have been members of that vocal Anglican minority which started with the Oxford Movement and turned a hostile face not merely toward Puritanism but toward the Reformation origins of the Church of England.

Let us nevertheless control our natural reactions. A state Reformation did take place in England, and in its own right it exercised great influence upon the religious and social history of the English people. It was of immense significance that Henry VIII cut off papal authority from the realm, abolished monasticism, diminished the wealth of the Church, and took control of doctrine and church organization. It was equally important that Elizabeth took a politic hand after the Marian reaction, that she made a tacit compact with the returning exiles to set up a state church, decisively Protestant in belief while it retained the conservative liturgy of Thomas Cranmer—a liturgy wholly different from those of the Reformed churches. Moreover, all these constitutional processes left so great a deposit of documents as to distract historians from the history of religion in England. If we concentrate to the point of hypnosis on the records of the state Reformation, it is easy to conclude that no other Reformation of consequence occurred! The constitutional documents have a fallacious self-sufficiency. Yet if we look a little further, we find the religious Reformation also quite heavily documented. We are under no compulsion to rest content with parliamentary statutes and royal injunctions.

Any attempt to understand the English Reformation might begin with two simple and incontrovertible propositions: first, that there must have been a religious Reformation because in 1520 the English people were predominantly Catholic while by 1580 they were predominantly Protestant; second, that a religious Reformation began and made some progress in English society well before Henry VIII's divorce and the acts of the Reformation Parliament. Protestant belief came to England in several ways. The first was the native tradition of Lollardy, which grew stronger (not weaker) from the last years of the fifteenth century, provided reception areas for Lutheranism, and imbued many districts with a tenacious popular radicalism. Then after about 1520, the Lutheran group headed by Robert Barnes flourished at Cambridge and extended in the later twenties to Oxford. Meanwhile, a monied and resourceful association of merchants centering upon London and Antwerp financed the biblical translation and pamphleteering of William Tyndale and his associates. Tyndale, a bitter critic of Henry VIII, was forced to remain in Antwerp but became the hero of the English Reformation. Long before the Reformation Parliament, thousands of copies of his New Testament were flooding in, the prefaces highlighting Luther's interpretation of St. Paul. They were avidly bought by middle- and even working-class people, though a copy cost a craftsman two or three weeks' pay. Copies appear even in the records of otherwise conservative country squires. But this religious Reformation was neither doctrinally static nor wholly Lutheran; by the early thirties it was influenced by Zwinglian and more radical trends. It has been maintained by some historians that there occurred among the English leaders a proto-Puritan stress upon law as opposed to gospel—a covenant theology moving away from the evangelical emphases of Luther.

The two English reformations, political and religious, converged for the first time in the mid-thirties. The king's minister, Thomas Cromwell—the man who drafted the famous statutes of the Reformation Parliament, the main architect of the state reformation, the popularizer of Marsiglio of Padua, and the backer of an Erastian propaganda campaign—showed himself to be also a supporter of the religious Reformation. In Cromwell's case, the two Reformations became linked in one unfervent man to whom reform bulked large, yet without very deep spiritual connotations. For many years Cromwell had been interested in biblical translation, and with great assiduity and determination he set forth the "Great Bible" as an act of state. This was a crucial action, because public knowledge of the Bible became the factor which made the Reformation irreversible. The conservative king, apparently caught winking, allowed this momentous step without foreseeing its ultimate effects. It seems likely enough that Cromwell foresaw them reasonably well, but his opportunity was brief. In 1540, Henry listened to Cromwell's enemies and the minister was overthrown on a variety of charges, amid which heresy played a prominent part.

Cromwell's policy of the open Bible was soon disapproved by the king, who tried to limit Bible reading to the educated classes but seems to have failed completely. Henry attempted a doctrinal reaction on Cromwell's fall, but there is every sign that Protestantism kept advancing in English society despite the king's reactionary attitude throughout the last years of his reign. After Henry's death in 1547, the Duke of Somerset was made Protector—and became the first English ruler to pursue a distinctly Protestant policy. This policy could be described as a second and more advanced stage of the state Reformation, but was it not in fact the climax, the acknowledgment, of the socioreligious history of Henry's reign? In other words, the state Reformation was taken over by a gradually developing religious Reformation. For the first time, Protestantism had won over the ruling classes, a fact amply demonstrated when Somerset was overthrown in 1549 by his rival John Dudley, Earl of Warwick, and later Duke of Northumberland. Instead of using the Catholic party, Northumberland—himself no religious zealot—judged it politically adroit to avoid reversing Somerset's Protestant policy, and indeed to promote it in more radical forms. The decision of Somerset in 1547 and the decision of Northumberland in 1549 both arose from the advances made by the religious Reformation throughout English society during the reign of Henry VIII. They are also tributes to the work of Thomas Cromwell, and they found an auxiliary force in the liturgical projects quietly but skillfully pursued by Cranmer between Cromwell's fall and the death of Henry.

Had there been no state Reformation in England, the religious Reformation which preceded it would doubtless have developed apace. After all, the Protestant Reformation was initiated by neither king nor Parliament. For three important periods—in the twenties, in the years 1540–47, and throughout the Marian persecution—it actually made headway against the persecuting policy of the state. In all three cases it won success through its strong appeal to intellectuals, to many members of the middle orders including the gentry, and most of all to the merchants and populace of London and the southeast. All things considered, the Reformation flourished because it was a religious movement armed with a vernacular Bible and attracting a considerable measure of bourgeois and popular support. At some stages it was opposed by the state; at other stages it captured the state; and state policy in some degree affected its timing and progress. Certainly in the person of Queen Elizabeth, the state modified the church settlement proposed by the more continentally minded reformers, leaving many issues still to be fought out.

The terms Counter-Reformation and Catholic Reformation have been used to designate the development of sixteenth-century Catholicism. Which term is the more accurate, or should these terms refer to quite distinct developments?

As early as 1834 Leopold von Ranke began working his way toward the concept of Counter-Reformation as a large-scale movement forming one of the dominant features of a whole period of history. Admittedly, Ranke still wrote of "Counter-Reformations" in the plural, envisaging a series of parallel movements throughout Europe. Again, he was far more interested in the political rather than in the religious aspects of both Reformation and Counter-Reformation; we should not go to him for an analysis of the spirituality of either movement. Even so, in Book II of his *History of the Popes* he likens the Protestant Reformation and regenerated Catholicism to two streams that rise together on the summit of the same mountain and then, after some hesitant movements, seek their paths to the valleys in opposite directions and become forever separated. We must give Ranke credit for the concept of Counter-Reformation which sees it arising from the same reforming impulses as those which produced the Protestant Reformation.

Before the end of the nineteenth century, it was widely recognized that the Counter-Reformation was more than an anti-Protestant movement, that it had roots in medieval Europe. The expression "Catholic Reformation" (used by Maurenbrecher in 1880) has been taken up by historians anxious to show that the movement was no mere reflex against Protestant pressure, that it began before Luther and would have developed even without his threat to Catholicism. Quite clearly, both processes did happen: the one arising from pre-Reformation reform and spontaneous piety, the other a riposte to Protestantism. Today the dispute Counter-Reformation versus Catholic Reformation seems little more than semantic. For my own recent survey I have retained the traditional title, but so far as possible I have sought to say "Catholic Reformation" when referring to spontaneous recovery and "Counter-Reformation" when referring to specifically anti-Protestant effort. But in practice one can hardly achieve precision or consistency, since at many points the two are firmly welded together. Both titles should be taken as conventional rather than precisely meaningful, and neither can be declared illegitimate.

What does modern scholarship reveal about the actual movement? To develop Ranke's aquatic metaphor, many of the little streams of Catholic Reformation were running long before the name of Luther resounded throughout Europe. Without doubt, much sixteenth-century Catholic spirituality was linked with the Netherlandish *devotio moderna* of the previous century. Among the devotional books most commonly republished and in the hands of pious sixteenth-century Catholics was the famous *Imitation of*

Christ, which had been circulating since about 1418. Even after the struggle with Luther had been joined, the greatest Catholic figures were those less concerned to beat Luther than to lead people to Christ through Catholic teachings. The two nations which dominated the Catholic Reformation looked at religion with Mediterranean eyes: they saw Moors and Turks out of their windows rather than heretical Saxons. And when Francis Xavier waded knee-deep through the snow on his lonely two-hundred-mile walk to Kyoto, it may be assumed that he was not devoting much thought to the specters of Luther and Calvin. Of the dozen towering religious figures of the Counter-Reformation (excluding the popes), perhaps only one, Peter Canisius, was primarily and directly engaged in the struggle against Protestantism.

The Catholic Reformation should surely be envisaged as operative before Luther, yet it was a slow starter, and during the 1520's few of the activities and institutions which we associate with the term had passed their infancy. Some, like the Society of Jesus, were yet unborn. Above all, the papacy and the Roman curia were untouched: the spirit of reform made little mark upon Rome itself until around 1540. We may agree that a Catholic Reformation had started and would surely have developed even without the terrible challenge presented by Luther, but we cannot very profitably conjecture what forms this development would have taken. The actual Catholic Reformation was in fact faced by Protestantism before it had matured, and it was impelled to generate spiritual and material resources in order to meet this challenge. The missionary effort of Loyola and Canisius occurred within a Europe vibrating with the impact of Luther and Calvin—a world in which Catholicism was faced by one of the two greatest schisms in the history of the Christian Church.

After the last session of the Council of Trent in 1563, a great Europe-wide movement compounded of revived Catholic spirituality and politicoreligious reaction came into being. The many streams had now joined to form a great river, yet the currents still flowed unevenly and contained a great deal of earthy sediment. The greatest mystics and the most rigorous policemen both tended increasingly to come from Spain—that brilliant and forceful eccentric of the European family. Militant and muscular Counter-Reformation certainly continued here and there throughout most of the seventeenth century. We observe this aspect at its least attractive in the treatment of Bohemia by Ferdinand II, or in the dragonnading of the Huguenots and the Protestants of Orange by Louis XIV. At the other extreme, we see a glorious efflorescence of spirituality in Saint François de Sales and Saint Vincent de Paul. The movement remained ambivalent to the last, and it is no wonder that it has acquired two names.

One can no longer think of the dichotomy "Catholic versus Counter" as the major problem of the Counter-Reformation. The movement presents far more interesting questions. What are the precise connections between the policemen like Paul IV and Pius V, and the true saints like Philip Neri and Saint John of the Cross? Were the Spanish mystics, so harassed by the Inquisition, creators or victims of the movement? Did the reviving Church or papacy really cramp the intellectual development of the West? If it did so, was this because of the revival of Thomism which marked the Counter-Reformation? Should the Counter-Reformation be regarded as dividing Europe into two rival cultures? What were its effects upon art and music? For example, was the baroque style really created out of Counter-Reformation religion? Assuming the latter declined after 1660 with the rise of rationalism, did its models ultimately inspire the revived Catholicism of the nineteenth century? Again, we can see the Catholic Reformation as a golden age for religious orders, for the regeneration of old ones, and the foundation of new orders (like the Society of Jesus) with some original ideas. But did this siphoning-off of talent tend to slow down that still more urgent and long-awaited feat—the rehabilitation of the parish clergy? I tried to suggest brief answers to some of these questions in my recent book, but I fear that in most cases authoritative verdicts must await fuller investigations than those we can at the present undertake.

One tends nowadays to see the movement rather less as a fight against heretical movements and rather more as an internal shift *within* Catholicism. Late medieval Catholicism was capacious, many-sided, still flexible or even vague on some important issues, very much subject to conflicting religious and cultural tensions. On the other hand, Tridentine Catholicism arose from a process of pruning, clarifying, and decision-taking which had its culmination in the last session of the great Council in 1562–63. These processes are superbly summarized in the canons and decrees of Trent. But alongside the triumph of Tridentine orthodoxy may be seen a second victor—the papacy, which in truth many of the Trent fathers did not want to see so totally victorious. Nevertheless, the Council, seemingly overcome by a death wish, ended by abolishing conciliarism and handing the Church over to a papal monarchy which called no further General Council until 1870. Despite a certain strengthening of the bishops within their dioceses by the Counter-Reformation, the papacy has managed to avoid any real sharing of central authority until our own day.

Among the losing causes at Trent were conciliarism, Pauline theology, biblical humanism, and the conciliatory attitudes toward Protestantism which these causes had tended to foster. Perhaps the most interesting emphasis to be driven underground, or half underground, was the Pauline-Augustinian concept of salvation by faith. This had appealed to Catholic reformers like Contarini, yet in Jesuit and Dominican eyes it bore a suspicious resemblance to the teaching of Martin Luther. Repressed by Rome after 1540, this emphasis survived in the theology of Michael Baius and ultimately revived in force with the Jansenists, so creating new perils for seventeenth-century Catholicism. Here was a traditional component of Christianity which one could expel with a fork, yet with little hope of preventing its return.

14

Russia to 1700

MICHAEL CHERNIAVSKY

THE HISTORIOGRAPHICAL CONTEXT

There are several reasons why the early period of Russian history down to and including the reign of Peter the Great at the end of the seventeenth century is a subject of the highest importance and the greatest historical interest. The first derives from the crucial role that Russia has come to play in the modern world, particularly since 1945. To what extent can the characteristics of Russian culture and Soviet policy be said to lie in the early era of Russian history? A second aspect of the importance of early Russian history lies in the cultural mix from which Russian civilization arose. Early Russian history offers the spectacle of the interaction of Slavic, Mongolian, Byzantine, and Scandinavian ingredients. The cultural historian is faced with the fascinating task of trying to discriminate among the contributions of these various cultures to what became Russian civilization. A third significant aspect of early Russian history—indeed of all Russian history—is the autocratic nature of Russian government. Russia presents an example of a continuity of autocracy in its political form, and it is the historian's task and also his ambition to try to establish the foundations of Russian autocracy and its functional development. Additional themes of crucial importance in early Russian history are the development of the Church and the central role that the Church and ecclesiastical culture played in Russian life, and on the nature of Russian rural society, the history of the peasantry, and its descent into serfdom.

Russian history down to Peter the Great is among the most difficult undertakings for the professional historian. The sources, particularly until the fifteenth century, are extremely fragmentary and hard to interpret, and the linguistic problem is a very formidable one. It is not surprising that most of the important scholars in the field have been native Russians. Michael Cherniavsky was born to a Russian émigré family in China in 1922. His family came to the United States, and he received his Ph.D. from the University of California at Berkeley in 1951. He has taught at Wesleyan, the University of Chicago, Rochester University, and now is a professor of Russian history at the State University of New York at Albany. Cherniavsky has published several important studies in early Russian history: his *Tsar and People* is celebrated as a monumental contribution to the understanding of the development of early Russian kingship. With his cosmopolitan background and with an unusual linguistic capacity for an American historian, he has achieved an international reputation as one of the most important scholars in the field. Cherniavsky is a disciple of the great German medieval historian Ernst Kantorowicz, but he has broadened out from Kantorowicz's somewhat schematic history of ideas approach to place intellectual history within the context of functional social change. Cherniavsky is not only a great scholar, a man of enormous learning and tremendous technical capacity, but also an historical thinker of the first order. He is an unusually attractive human being, bubbling with vitality, humor, and warmth. Cherniavsky is interested in all facets of contemporary culture, extremely generous to students and colleagues, and has a wide range of friends on two continents. In many ways he is reminiscent of the cosmopolitan European intellectual of the early twentieth century.

Chronological Outline

400–700: The East Slavs settle on the territory of present-day European Russia.

c. 880–912: Prince Oleg unites both Novgorod and Kiev under his control. Beginning of Kievan primacy.

978–1015: Reign of Vladimir the Saint, who brings Byzantine priests to Kiev to convert the Russian populace to Eastern Christianity.

1019–1054: Reign of Yaroslav the Wise, the greatest ruler of the Kievan period. Construction of the Cathedral of St. Sophia and the revision of the Russian law codes.

1237–1240: The Mongol conquest establishes the Khanate of the Golden Horde which rules Russia with a light hand for two centuries, leaving most local administration to the native princes.

1462–1505: Ivan III, the first national sovereign of Russia. His predecessors had already shepherded Moscow to prominence, and when he defeats Novgorod in 1478, its last rival is vanquished.

1533–1584: Ivan IV (the Terrible), the first Russian ruler to be formally crowned Czar, savagely suppresses the Council of Boyars and institutes a personal reign of terror.

c. 1600: The Time of Troubles—chaos besets the Russian state.

1613–1645: The reign of Michael Romanov, the first of the Romanov dynasty which rules until 1917. Serfdom is firmly established.

1689–1725: Reign of Peter the Great (b. 1672).

1697–1698: Peter becomes the first Russian sovereign to travel abroad and determines to westernize Russian customs and society. Russia becomes a military power, and education, trade, and industry are encouraged with varying degrees of success.

1703: The capital of Russia is moved to the newly founded St. Petersburg.

Norman F. Cantor

Let's begin with the historiography of medieval Russia. What has been the contribution of pre- and post-revolutionary Russian historians, and what are the main differences in interest and approach between Soviet historians and Western scholars?

Michael Cherniavsky

Before the revolution, scholars tried to handle the whole of medieval Russian history right down to the time of Peter the Great and to establish a conceptual framework by periodization. They were struggling with the basic premise that the history of medieval Russia ran a different course from that of the West. Russian historians were trained in Western history: their model was Western medieval historiography, and they applied its criteria (rather blindly) to Russian history.

Russian history was profoundly influenced, if not dominated, by the problem of how to interpret the apparent beginning of history *ex nihilo*. There was no Russian history, and suddenly it began. The explanation that emerged focused on the birth of the political nation; its major argument (in volume of writing and violence of debate) concerned the origin of the Russian state. Out of this argument developed the general positions of Normanist and anti-Normanist.

On the Normanist side there was the premise that Russia was nothing but a prehistoric tribal society until the Vikings imposed order on chaos. Viking conquests profoundly affected the development of political institutions in Russia, they actually heralded the birth of a state. The obvious difficulty here is: what are the necessary preconditions for the emergence of a state, even with the help of such effective organizers as the Vikings? That question led to the next stage of Russian historiography, the conception of Kliuchevsky (one of the greatest of nineteenth-century Russian historians) that the Russian state owed its existence to the Vikings in another sense: that the Scandinavians organized a commercial economy in Russia, providing a surplus, a special geopolitical orientation, and a raison d'être for the state. This was expressed in the Primary Chronicle in the classic description of the Russian state as "The way from the Greeks to the Varangians."

The anti-Normanist position was first expressed in the context of ideological struggles within nineteenth-century Russia. Its adherents opposed what they saw as a theory of outside influences, of borrowed practices that determined Russian history. According to the Slavophiles, the Slavs had an independent existence regardless of the Scandinavian dynasty, and the origins of Russian identity could be discovered within pre-Norman Russia. The anti-Normanists had the worst of that argument, partly because the level of archaeological work was so low, but also because their premise was not based altogether upon history but on logic, and even on theology. They emphasized the rapid Slavicization of the dynasty and of the ruling class of invaders, who adopted Slavic names, customs, and behavior.

Basically, prerevolutionary (Normanist) Russian historiography was dominated by this problem: if the early Russian state was founded in the "Western" context (things must be twisted a little to interpret the pagan Scandinavians as Westerners in the ninth century; they had not themselves reached the level of political statehood), one must determine points of similarity with the West. In other words, how long and in what ways was Russia in the proper path: how long and in what ways did the Russians behave like the French and the English, and when did things go wrong? The periodization of Russian history was determined by decisions made on this issue.

First there was the Kievan state, which was viewed favorably—it had close relations with the West. Historians boasted of the dynastic involvement with the family of Harold of England, who sought refuge in Kiev after 1066, and pointed out that Harold's soldiers fled from England and served the Byzantine emperor or the Russian Grand Prince. But what happened to the Kievan state? The majority of historians argued for the Mongol invasion as another *deus ex machina*. Things were going well in early medieval Russia, but then the catastrophe of the Mongol invasion brought physical destruction to the country. However, there is a curious problem here, because if all the prerevolutionary historians were asked "What were the effects of the Mongol invasion?," their answers would differ wildly. Some believed that the invasion had no effect except a sort of general impoverishment; others, that although the invasion had no cultural impact in a specific sense, it did lead to a coarsening of morals, to the introduction of Asiatic despotism and brutality at a time when Russia was isolated from Western influences. As for the next period (the early Muscovite era), it was believed that by interfering in political struggles and impoverishing the country the Mongols made this stage of feudal disintegration more serious in Russia than elsewhere. The unification of Russia under a particular dynasty was regarded as a process of liberation from the disorder and devastation of the Mongol period.

The extent to which this prerevolutionary historiography was ideologically determined is apparent if we consider the quality of the historians. Men such as Soloviev and Kliuchevsky were major historians by any criterion; I would put them in the class of Ranke or Mommsen. How much intellectual bankruptcy did they display? I believe that their thesis of the creation of a centralized medieval monarchy around Moscow was bankrupt because it focused on the unreal problem of why this unification happened around Moscow instead of some other town. It is obvious from the map that the distances between the various possible centers is in the neighborhood of a hundred miles, and therefore that the suggested geopolitical explanations are irrelevant. It has been suggested, too, that there was a special inherent genetic quality in the Moscow dynasty that they were greedy, sly proto-Machiavellians who bought up property, patiently increased their patrimony, and did not take chances in battle. One could add that their long reigns did provide stability; most of them began to reign at an early age and ruled for many years.

Let me pause here to summarize prerevolutionary historiography. Basically, the historiography of the Kievan period is based on the *deus ex machina* of the Varangians, and on a state which began from nothing but was characterized by vitality and by the prosperity derived from its enormously successful (nonmedieval) commercial economy. Economic success was expressed in the physical, material achievements of the state: the construction of cathedrals and palaces and the great walls of Kiev. Prerevolutionary historians did *not* deal (to my knowledge) with the apparent disproportion between the material success of Kiev and its cultural expression. Normally we would expect the creation of surplus capital to result in a cultural flowering, but the paucity of cultural material in Kievan Russia is well established and is best symbolized by the existence of only one historical account for the first two centuries of Russian history.

At this point in prerevolutionary historiography there is an arbitrary, nonsequitur transition from the Kievan period to the next *deus ex machina,* the Mongol invasion—ignoring the period between the mid-twelfth and the mid-thirteenth century, when the center shifted from Kiev to the northeast, to the area of Vladimir. No explanation is given for this, although there is a vague suggestion that it occurred because the trade routes shifted from the Baltic-Black Sea axis to the Baltic-Caspian axis along the Volga River.

After the Mongol period, with its enormous cost in devastation, we come to the growth of the centralized Russian state. Here one gets into a mass of detailed material, and the chief historiographical problem (it seems to me) is a lack of awareness that Russian centralization coincided—chronologically at least—with similar processes in the West. For some reason, prerevolutionary historians abandoned the comparative method at this point, and interpretation of the early Muscovite period was dominated by the ideological struggle between liberal Westerners and more reactionary Slavophiles. They focused on the sixteenth century, which has been regarded as a period of extreme, unequaled autocracy whose symbol is Ivan the Terrible. The terror exercised by Ivan has been interpreted as an indication that as a consequence of alienation from the West (in this context, from the Renaissance and the process of secularization), Russian centralization resulted not in the introduction of humanist criteria but only in the growth of state power. Northeastern Russia was successfully unified by the Moscow dynasty, which then played a disproportionate role in the state. It has been argued that no real social classes emerged during the period of centralization, or that all of them, to some degree or other, were enserfed by the state. Kliuchevsky suggested that the enserfment of Russian society began at the top, that the aristocrats were the first to be made a subservient to the state. The argument goes on to suggest that in Russia, centralized monarchy was not a normal and healthy development, but was unbalanced by the domination of the state. For this reason it is possible to explain Russian history in terms not of social forces but of the personal characteristics of particular rulers.

If we trace the whole historiography from Karamzin, the Russian Ranke, who published his great history in 1819, on down into the Soviet period, we find that the reign of Ivan the Terrible is usually explained in terms of personal madness. Madness is used to account for the contrast between the end of his reign and its first seventeen years, with its successful conquests, the destruction of the Mongol state that had blocked Russian expansion to the east, the conquest of the Volga basin, and the spontaneous frontier expansion through Siberia towards the Pacific. However, his war against Poland to gain outlets to the Baltic was a failure, and in his madness the czar hit out—not against the aristocratic class (which was not blocking him), but at individuals. Heavy penalties were paid for the czar's madness, including the depopulation of the Russian center and the end of a seven-hundred-year-old dynasty—the oldest dynasty in Europe. No constitutional conception was available to handle the problem of the end of a dynasty, and the policies of Ivan the Terrible (characterized in this context as "non-policy" based on paranoia, with the usual modern analogies to Stalin) ended in civil war.

The civil war was characterized by the explosion of the Cossack social group, representing the more active peasants, while the aristocracy revealed the enormous tensions within itself by its willingness to accept pretenders to the throne. The struggle was finally resolved by the healthy elements in society, including the service gentry (created since the late fifteenth century to fill the need of a centralized monarchy for a bigger administrative apparatus), the free peasant communes of the north, and such town populations as did exist. The political crisis was overcome in the early seventeenth century by the establishment of the Romanov dynasty (vaguely related by marriage to the old Riurikid house), but Russia still suffered from isolation from the West. Despite its success in reunifying the country, the Romanov dynasty expressed and encouraged Russian backwardness.

It seems to me that the prerevolutionary historiography of medieval Russia reached its peak in the interpretation of the seventeenth century. The country was pulled together at the expense of the peasants, and the process culminated in the famous law code of 1648. Peasants were not allowed to move, and the statute of limitations on the recovery of runaways was extended indefinitely. Russian isolation utimately resulted in the creation of a xenophobic society set apart by Orthodoxy and by a theocratic monarchy which was ritualized and ceremonialized to a point of virtual insanity. There was cultural and psychological stagnation, too. At that period the West was explosive in power and influence, in economic progress, and in the development of a strong bourgeoisie and a secular culture. Russia faced the challenge by developing the notion that everything from the outside, from the non-Orthodox world, was corrupt. All foreign elements had to be isolated, even physically (foreign doctors and architects were not allowed to leave their own quarter in Moscow). In theory, then, the medieval period was prolonged until the appearance of another arbitrary change, another *deus ex machina.* In Kliuchevsky's biography of Peter the Great is stressed again the importance of accident in the upbringing of the child Peter, who became a man of enormous will and power and used the autocracy to drag Russia by the hair into the modern world.

The most interesting aspect of the relationship between pre- and post-revolutionary historiography concerns continuities and discontinuities. Under the impact of Stalinism, many Soviet historians took anti-Normanist positions out of pure chauvinism, and these were often carried to the extreme of neo-Slavophile arguments. They simply assumed that Russians had the qualities and abilities to develop a political state. One important result of this assumption has been the extraordinary achievement of Soviet archaeology, and the increasing use of archaeology by historians who are becoming aware that this is the only way to crack the problem. They use archaeological discoveries to show that political society, or civilization (in the primitive, original sense of *civitas* or "city life"), did not arise overnight with the arrival of the Vikings. It is impossible to conceive of a reversion to agriculture by a medieval society which was first based on trade and commerce; one must posit an original agricultural basis, and in fact the archaeological evidence supports that assumption. According to the more sophisticated Soviet historians, early Russian society was agricultural and feudal (in Soviet historiography, a political state inevitably involves the development of social classes). The *comitatus* of the ruler—the men who administered his possessions and fought his battles—could only have been rewarded with land, and this we can assume even without sources. Landholding is meaningless without manpower, and so one must extrapolate the economic and political bonds that must have existed between landholder and peasant. According to this argument, by the twelfth century Russia had full-blown feudalism on the Western model, with a chivalric code and a system of personal vassalage. This is based on the conception that feudalism is defined primarily by economic relationships (agricultural means of production) and accompanied—as in the West—with a social organization based on a formal, institutionalized, personal bond between ruler and vassal, with personal and political obligations on both sides.

Soviet as well as prerevolutionary historians tend to ignore the twelfth-century period of the decline of Kiev and the shift to the northeast. All one can do is read the Chronicles and try to form some sort of hypothesis; very little work has been done on this period. The Soviets also avoid the question of the comparative cultural level of Kievan Russia and western medieval Europe. Their interpretation of the Mongol conquest, too, is similar to that of the prerevolutionary historians. They believe that its impact was negative, that the Mongols did not influence Russian society culturally or change its direction but impoverished the society without making any contribution.

What changes, then, came in with Soviet historiography? Their major achievements concern the problem of the centralized state, first in using archaeology to show the continuity between Slavic prehistory and the emergence of a political state. This permits a valid comparison with western Europe in the development of town life before the political state, in the focus of towns around what was essentially a feudal castle, a protected place. Soviet historians argue that centralized monarchy was possible only because the resources of society increased—that the government at Moscow could unify northeast Russia simply because resources were available for the task. Thus one must posit improvements in agriculture, the successful development of town life, and the existence of a vital and prosperous ruling class.

I would argue, then, that Soviet historiography is especially useful for this particular period, beginning in the fifteenth century. Like their predecessors, the Soviets have largely bypassed the so-called appanage period of endless strife among the princes. I think they are quite correct to point out that centralization under Moscow did not succeed because of any genetic qualities of the dynasty but because of the Russian aristocracy, whose interests (because their possessions were scattered over the northeast) favored unification. The dynasty was supported by another major institution of medieval society—the Church—whose economic and social interests and ideology emphasized centralization and homogeneity of law. It was a powerful, priestly, and secular aristocracy that provided the motive power for centralization.

Most of the Soviet historians were pupils of a generation of outstanding scholars who were primarily philologists. Right now the best Soviet historiography is in the textological stage which was represented in the West by the German medievalists of two generations ago. The Soviet scholars' work on texts has allowed them to do a great deal of useful work in political theory, where clichés have until recently dominated interpretations of Russian autocracy, of the Russian Church, of Moscow as the third Rome, and so on. Much of this material has been placed in proper perspective simply by a careful examination of texts.

With all their skill at textology, I would argue that the Soviet historians have not sufficient breadth of comparative education to realize that the madness of Ivan the Terrible was not unique in sixteenth-century Europe. It seems to have been a period of insane or peculiar rulers. And yet the latest Soviet work (published in 1968) still resorts to the czar's insanity as a historical cause. There is now some physiological evidence, at least. Ivan did suffer from a horrifying form of arthritis for the last thirty years of his life. We now have material explanations instead of mystical or arbitrary statements, but no one has discerned any real policy in his Reign of Terror and we are left to conclude that the centralized monarchy declared its bankruptcy at the height of its success.

In the 1930's there was an attempt to argue for the development of a genuine city economy and an all-Russian market in the seventeenth century, but today, historians are forced to admit that there was actually a decline in commercial activity and a decline of towns. At the moment, in fact, the best Soviet historians are faced with a peculiar conclusion: that the consolidation after the Time of Troubles must be interpreted within the context of the decline of city life and economic activity. Soviet historians dispose of the seventeenth century as the selfish triumph of feudal society, of the gentry at the expense of all other classes. They see the imbalance in Russian society not as the result of overwhelming autocratic power outside and above that society but as a function of the power of the ruling class, which absorbed all privileges and thus distorted Russian development—foreclosing all possibilities of raising an economic surplus. At the beginning of the modern period, then, Russia was frustrated in the development of a modern army and of modern industry by the absolute monopoly of the ruling class over the economic resources of the country. This leaves the Soviet historians dependent on a "cult of personality" interpretation of Peter the Great, who managed somehow to break through this unworkable system. It is not clear, however, just how this was done.

I do not mean to bypass the question about the contribution of Western historians. Unfortunately, however, most of the teachers of American historians were émigré scholars, and thus American scholarship remains within the framework built by Kliuchevsky. Great as he was, his ideas are a hundred years old, and it is time to move on. Americans are not much influenced by Soviet historiography, partly because of the ideological confrontation and partly because it would be difficult to educate American textologists (for lack of texts) or American archaeologists (because they are not on the spot). Americans can adopt most Soviet historiography only at second hand, and that is why the conceptual framework established by the bourgeois, liberal historians of the 1880's survives to this day.

Is the Normanist, anti-Normanist question resolvable?

Yes, and it is ironical that a question like this should continue for a hundred and sixty years! Part of the problem is cultural, I think: it seems to me that Russians, Americans, and Spaniards all ask, "Who are we?" "What is it to be a Russian, an American, or a Spaniard?" All these people are on the periphery in some way, perhaps because we have at some time accepted the premise that one must be a Frenchman to be a European. These "peripheral" nations are bothered by questions as to where the boundaries of Europe run: in the eyes of any particular historian they run along the lines of "include me and exclude the others." The Normanist controversy has exceeded its legitimate historical existence, I believe, because of the cultural set of Russian society.

The question can be set aside, if you like, simply because it is based on semantic confusion. After all, it is impossible to argue that there were *no* Vikings in Russia or that the dynasty was *not* Scandinavian. It does not follow, however, that the presence of Scandinavians implies any particular talent for political organization, in the sense of creating a state out of nothing. Part of the trouble arises from the fallacy of thinking in terms of a modern, rational state (where the introduction of foreign rule is evidence of weakness) and failing to recognize that "foreigner" had a different meaning in the ninth century, if the word existed at all. One part of the problem centers around the word *ros* (Russian), which appears in the Primary Chronicle (now shown to be a compilation, with many layers). It is possible to argue that *ros* means Scandinavian: that it is an institutional term referring to the *comitatus,* the band around the prince; or that *ros* is a Slavic word, because toponymically it is encountered often in South Russia.

One could dispose of the controversy by pointing out that although the military aristocracy and the dynasty included a significant number of Scandinavians, it probably included an even greater number of Turkic peoples. We neglect one of the more fascinating historical problems—the proper characterization of the so-called age of barbarian migrations and, more important, of the enormous and complex role that the Asiatic steppe—the Turkic peoples and civilizations—played in the formation, culture, and history of Russia and the whole east of Europe. A considerable amount has been written about the period, but we tend to underestimate its duration (at least in eastern Europe) and cultural consequences. There was an extraordinary fluidity of thought and institutions as well as people.

I would like to suggest that the Normanist problem is irrelevant. If we study the archaeological evidence (primarily of burial customs), we find that Scandinavian and Slavic burials alike were overwhelmed by what obviously was the dominant cultural mode—the steppe burial. We can still identify Slavic burial mounds because they used mass graves and cremations, but we have difficulty identifying Viking graves because the Scandinavians adopted the model of the steppes. Strict archaeologists might infer from this that there were no Scandinavians—which would be nonsensical, considering the sources. The argument is meaningless, because what really existed were Slavic tribes in prehistoric state which evolved into political entities—at first, perhaps, local princely entities, and then a general Russian state. This state evolved not under the impact and model of the North (which was barbaric itself), but out of steppe culture and steppe economy. The trade with Constantinople came from the Asian steppe, whose peoples were also engaged in political relations with Constantinople. On that level, at least, one can bypass the controversy.

I would like to turn to some historical problems which have been avoided, but for which we have now enough evidence to permit hypothesis. For the first two centuries of Russian history we must depend upon one document, with about half a dozen non-Russian references that are too slight to mean very much. However, we do know that Kiev was materially impressive: eleventh-century Kiev was physically unmatched in Europe and second only to Constantinople. Thus we know that resources were available for walls, churches, and palaces, but we don't know very much about these resources.

One can hypothesize that the basis of Kievan society was agricultural, and probably still a "collecting" agriculture rather than a "producing" agriculture. The Byzantine sources (treaties with the Greeks) indicate that one major resource of the Russian state was the slave trade, and we may posit that the slaves were taken from the Finno-Ugrian tribes in the area into which Russia was then expanding. I think that part of the process of conquest and assimilation was the collection of slaves from the Finno-Ugrian peoples. I think, too, that the economic history of medieval Russia can perhaps be explained best by its possession—in fact, monopoly—of an extraordinarily valuable natural resource: furs. Sable, ermine, fox, even squirrel, were evidently as valuable as gold and silver mines.

Given these resources and the investment in Kiev, then, how can we explain the absence of scholastic culture, of incipient universities in monastic schools? Further, how can we explain the existence of only *one* chronicle to describe the entire period, of which the earliest known copy was made in the fourteenth century? There was an enormous disproportion between material prosperity and cultural accomplishment, and the great philologist Roman Jacobson suggests that it might be explained in part by the nonmissionary tradition of the Greek Orthodox Church, with its liturgy in the native language. Christianization forced the West into classical civilization by the sheer necessity to learn Latin, but the impulse to learn Greek in Russia was purely intellectual. Of course the early Russian hierarchy was Greek; there were no Russian bishops at that time, and some educational training was needed. But it does help to explain why the main expression of Russian culture was translation, which evidently resulted in very narrow intellectual interests. The number of things that were translated and became part of the Russian intellectual tradition was pitifully small: they were not even the works of the fathers of the Church, but compilations of didactic writings of a rather primitive kind.

I would like to suggest that something else might have been involved beyond the lack of incentive to learn a universal culture. I would not accept an explanation based on national character, with the Russians as anti-intellectuals, but one could offer a hypothesis that the material success of Kiev reflected an enormous emphasis on material needs—that is, of the need for defense against the steppe. Kiev was an impressive city, and among its most impressive features were its gigantic walls, huge structures that were built around all the southern cities because of the threat from the steppe. A basic function of a great city is self-defense, and this may have caused a distortion (by Western standards) in the allocation of resources. For whatever reason, the disproportion between the material and cultural achievements of Kiev leaves plenty of scope for hypothesis.

How do you account for the apparent economic decline of Kiev in the twelfth century?

The traditional explanation (which I do not find very convincing) is that Kiev was simply unable to withstand the pressures of the steppe, of the endless nomadic empires which kept cutting the trade routes. I believe that we may have underestimated another factor—the relation of the decline of Kiev to the decline of Constantinople, which was badly hurt by the Crusades and by the rise of the Italian republics. Venice and Genoa were beginning to take over the East-West trade, and their interests were focused more on the east than on the north. Their colonies in the Black Sea region were intended to intercept the silk route from the Far East through Persia.

A third explanation (my own),

which may seem arrogant and revisionist, requires us to look at one of the perpetual problems of Kievan history in a slightly different light. No constitutional system of succession of power (as we understand it, no rational system of primogeniture) had been established in Byzantine or Russian society. Elaborate theories have been cooked up to explain this, but basically they amount to the argument that the tribal principle was preserved as a guide in questions of succession. Power descended to the senior member of a tribe or clan, and given the many possibilities within the tribe, this resulted in struggles between uncles and nephews which were exacerbated by the artificiality of the whole tribal conception in this instance. The tribe was the tribe of Rurik, and if Rurik was a legendary figure, then nobody really knew who was related to whom, or how. However, it is possible to discover a certain periodicity in the political life of Kiev. There were consolidations of power which lasted through two generations, and these may represent attempts by a central authority (which we symbolize with the title Grand Prince) to create a patrimonial base like those of Western rulers. These attempts occurred whenever a strong prince ruled, and thus the problem of succession and family seniority is really irrelevant.

I suggest that the Grand Princes, like Western medieval monarchs, were trying to build a base in which their control would not depend on personal contract with a free aristocracy (i.e., the feudal contract) but would be exercised in terms of patrimonial ownership. The ruler needed a base in which he was accepted as the natural ruler, and there were regular attempts on the part of various branches of the family to *use* the Grand Principality to increase the patrimonial base. They did this in a manner reminiscent of the West, by accusing vassal princes of breaking their feudal obligations and thus losing their rights over a particular territory—in a sense, by foreclosing the feudal mortgage. However, the rulers of Kiev had little success in building up a patrimonial base sufficient to maintain their ideological pretensions. The patrimonial base of the dynasty as a whole was insufficient to hold together the enormous political society of Kievan Russia and to mobilize its resources against pressure from the steppe. I believe that the decline occurred through internal weakness rather than external pressure, that there was a decline in population and a decline in artisanship analogous to the situation in early medieval Rome.

Supposedly there was an important shift of population during the period from the mid-twelfth century to the mid-thirteenth. This has been explained by Kliuchevsky in his famous statement that Russian history is the history of colonization—the Russian Turner thesis, which posits that the colonization was spontaneous, that peasants simply went off to clear the land and were followed by princes. Without a strong, entrenched aristocracy or a strong Church, the princes of the new northeastern area were able to pull things together into a new center.

I would like to modify this conception of the twelfth century. The primary sources are increasing but are still very few, and secondary work just doesn't exist (even when one speaks of Soviet medievalists, one normally means people who work in the fifteenth century and later). However, the archaeological evidence does show that the northeast was *not* a new area. On the contrary, the northeastern cities seem to be within the same chronology as Kiev. I would agree that the shift to the northeast took place in the context of the political breakdown of Kiev. But what takes place in the twelfth century is not so much a movement of population from the south to the safety of the forest as a demographic explosion in the northeast—probably caused by the successful assimilation of the

Finno-Ugrian peoples of the area by the Slavs. The Kievan dynasty was unable to create a sufficient patrimonial base, and with the decline of Kiev came the rise of at least two other centers, one in the northeast and one in the extreme west—Carpathian Russia (which we can ignore here, arbitrarily, because it was incorporated into the Lithuanian state by the fourteenth century and more or less dropped out of Russian history).

The decline of the Byzantine trade did not signify the triumph of barbaric steppe nomads who broke up all lines of communication. On the contrary, these Turkic empires were more than eager to promote the trade which was the source of their revenue. With the decline of Byzantium, the trade route from the Black Sea shifted to the Caspian—a perfectly rational attempt to get ahead of the Genoese and Venetian colonists by acquiring a direct route to the center of economic power—the steppe empires and Persia.

It may be that the princes of the northeast were able to succeed in a context of very slight political change. They were still playing, on the face of it, the endless game of the *rota* system of seniority, yet there was a different proportion in the northeast between the patrimonial base and the claims of the sovereign. Northeastern Russia emerged as the political center in 1156, when the man who held the title of Grand Prince of Russia and Kiev moved his capital, permitting a looting of Kiev that shocked his contemporaries. He settled in the northeast, where the Grand Prince held an overwhelming proportion of the political state in direct, patrimonial (not feudal) terms. That is, he owned the territory, and while a degree of fragmentation occurred (he had to take care of his sons), there was some clearing away of claims. Merely by leaving Kiev he removed from contention a number of princely families. The move was rationally based on economic considerations—Suzdalian Russia had as its neighbor the great and prosperous Bulgarian empire on the Volga—but it also served to take the whole area of the declining south out of competition, and it allowed one particular dynasty a fresh start. The rulers faced the same old problem in the next two centuries, because primogeniture did not exist as a principle of entail, but the impetus of the twelfth century was sufficient to maintain the concentration of power.

As a peripheral society—which it was, at least in its early stages—Kievan Russia picked up the prejudices of the mother society of Constantinople and took them more seriously and (to be blunt) more stupidly. For instance, the east-west Church split was taken very seriously in Russia, and it is surprising how soon after 1054 the Russians picked up the lesson that Latins were heretics, worse than Slavic infidels. To eat at the same table with a Latin, even to speak to one, was to endanger one's immortal soul. However, there seems to have been a decline in this kind of superstition in the northeast in the twelfth century. There was more contact with the West, not only in relations by marriage, as in Kievan Russia, but in the importation of German metalworkers and architects without chauvinism or fear.

In my view, a cultural explosion occurred in the twelfth century, particularly in public investment—churches, public buildings, and so on. There was no single city to equal Kiev, partly because there was a complex of cities (the triangle of Rostov, Suzdal, and Vladimir). Each was smaller than Kiev, but each represented an astonishing investment in architecture and art, primarily ecclesiastical. The influence of the Caspian trade route is evident in the onion domes of the beautiful white stone cathedrals built in profusion between 1150 and 1220; even more significant, the cathedrals are smaller, with fewer mosaics (indicating that the cities were poorer than Kiev at its height) and more sculptures and bas-relief. Santa Sophia in Kiev is an imitation of the cathedral in Constantinople, but in the twelfth-century cathedrals of the northeast we find themes that are new in Russia: Alexander the Great in his chariot, Hercules killing the lion—pagan themes with mythological references. Evidently there was an infusion of nonecclesiastical Byzantine or classical culture, supported by the presence of masters and works of art from western Europe.

I believe that there existed in the West at this time a general cultural style which we call Romanesque, of which ecclesiastical architecture was only one expression, and I would characterize northeastern Russia as Romanesque at this period. One of the great Soviet medievalists in literature, D. S. Likhachev, has done a statistical study to show that most writing was done by laymen, not clerics, by the twelfth century. We do not find monastic schools transforming themselves into universities, but one *can* find a minor secularization of culture (a feature of Romanesque Europe) expressed artistically by an infusion of nonecclesiastical themes.

All of this seems to me to add up to a definite and separate period of Russian history: the Suzdalian period, which lasted only a century. If *The Tale of Igor* is authentic, we can point to a great secular poem written at that time and registering secular elements of this culture. I would like to enrich this conception of the Russian Romanesque, but I am unable to do so because there is not enough evidence.

Another element in all this is the relationship between Russia and Constantinople, currently a touchy subject because the historians have done nothing with it. Obviously Constantinople was the cultural center, with only the steppe Turkic world as a competitor. At the same time, a certain ambivalence was manifested by various Slavic societies in different degrees. In the societies closest to Constantinople (the Serbs and the Bulgarians), the weight of the Byzantine *auctoritas* was such that they denied it by claiming it for themselves, establishing their own patriarchs and emperors. The Russians were farther removed, but their ambivalence was revealed in political theory during the Kievan period, with the prince deriving all of his power from God. The Kievan princes made no real challenge to the Byzantine emperor, and I think it is not accidental that the challenge finally came in the twelfth century. The founder of Suzdalian Russia, Andrew Bogolyubsky, made a genuine issue over the role of the emperor in the Church. He claimed ecclesiastical autonomy, saying that the Russian Grand Prince had the right to nominate his own bishops and rule his church. Eventually he lost the struggle, but it could not be accidental that at a time when there was greater tolerance toward Latin thought and culture, with an overall style which we associate with the West, the Russian Grand Prince made a claim to juridical independence.

How would you view the impact of the Mongol invasions in the light of recent scholarship?

The problem can be summarized very briefly at least in the context of the work of M. Roublev, a young medievalist presently working in America but trained in France. He was the first to phrase in hard, economic-social terms the problem: "What did the Mongol conquest and yoke really cost?" and therefore "What did it mean?"

Until now, historians have argued either that it meant nothing—because the Mongols did not live in Russia and thus did not interfere in Russian development—or that they were a bunch of barbarians who looted and destroyed and thus ruined the country. (This is the prerevolutionary argument of the liberals, which has been picked up by the Soviets—particularly since the clash with China!) I should mention, though, that the great Russian orientalist, V. V. Bartold, did at least suggest in the 1920's that the Mongol conquest might have encouraged and promoted Russian trade, because Russia was included in the greatest commercial empire in the world. The western traveler Friar William Rubruque said that the Mongol empire was so well organized that a virgin with a sack of gold could travel safely from the Danube to Peking with both her treasures intact.

Roublev has required medievalists to reconsider all of Russian medieval history, but I find his argument more convincing in its broad premise than its details. Simply by compiling Mongol raids during the two centuries of Mongol sovereignty, he has demonstrated that the devastation in some places was such that Russian society simply gave up. Cities were abandoned, then rebuilt, rebuilt again, and finally given up. The cost of destruction is virtually incalculable. The other aspect of the cost is the tribute paid to the Mongols, and there Roublev establishes the amount of the tribute and makes a hypothesis as to its frequency. The amount of silver (in a society without silver mines) indicates that we have underestimated the resource of thirteenth- and fourteenth-century Russia. It could only have been a surplus, which means that they were doing damn well! I don't yet buy Roublev's argument that the tribute was paid yearly; that would require a rewriting of the economic history of Russia, and indeed of all of Europe. If we allow that the tax was periodic (every two, three, or five years), and that sometimes the Mongols were not able to collect it but add it to the destruction of the raids, we can understand why building in stone virtually ceased during this period, and why the Russian principalities were unable to mint any money. (Coinage picked up only in the 1380's.)

In the context of political theory, the Mongol ruler was acknowledged as a sovereign from the very beginning; his legitimacy was not questioned. In the Chronicles there is no support for the belief of various historians in a concept of national liberation. Pejoratives were never used against the Mongol Khan and the legitimacy, probably even the glory, of this ruler was recognized within his Russian *ulus*. The Khan was of the Imperial blood, and Russian princes were exhorted to obey him, to protect their principalities against his exactions and punishment by placating him.

Roublev has raised a point which I would like to take a little farther, as it may be an important consequence of the Mongol conquest. First, sovereign power rested with the Khan: a prince struggling for the Russian throne needed his confirmation, and Khans and their advisers were bribed and persuaded to grant the charters that confirmed a ruler. Also, Russian rulers bore the enormous responsibility of collecting the Mongol tribute. I have collaborated with Roublev on the statistics of the tribute, and I think he has found good reason to claim that the right to collect the tribute may have accounted for the success of Moscow. Not only did it give the Grand Prince of Russia (who happened to be of the Muscovite house after 1328) opportunities for malfeasance of funds, but Moscow itself paid nothing. Thus we can discern a built-in advantage for the Muscovite house, and this is much more convincing than any inherited tendency of Muscovite princes to save money and buy up principalities.

Tribute is a tricky proposition because it tends to be traditional. One principality might increase its wealth but still pay very little because its predecessors paid little; another might be penalized because its wealth declined under an intolerable burden of tribute. With the evidence that Moscow paid nothing, it appears that the success of the Moscow house in gaining the Grand Principality was not just theoretical but highly tangible, worth about a thousand rubles in silver (a year, if the tribute was annual).

This does not undercut Roublev's additional contribution, which is to point out that the Mongol burden on Russian society lasted far beyond the period of centralized Mongol power. In the earlier period the Mongol state was strong and centralized, and we can assume that tax collection was regular. Later, when the Mongol state entered into its "feudal period" of decentralization and internecine strife, the Russian princes could get away with paying less but the physical cost to Russia increased because each Mongol princedom began to raid and loot. In the fifteenth century, Moscow became stronger than the Horde, but the physical cost of the invasion continued or even increased. The raids continued because there was no one to control them, and the Russian frontier zones were really devastated. This may help to explain Moscow's success in the sixteenth century: a number of competitors were knocked out by the monstrous burden of an open and chaotic frontier.

The most obvious contribution of the Mongols to Russian history was in the realm of political theory. Medieval Russia (and all medieval societies) acknowledged sovereignty in regular and symbolic terms on its coinage. In the West, coins bore the name and image of the sovereign: in Russia, with an Islamic sovereign (as a Mohammedan, the Khan could not have his portrait on the coin), the name of the Russian Grand Prince appeared on one side of the coin and the name of the Khan on the other, with the Arabic inscription "May he live forever." The coins of Ivan III, Grand Prince of Russia, reflect the formal liberation of Russia in 1480. On one side of the coin is the image of the Grand Prince; on the other, in Arabic letters: "Ivan, may he live forever." I am suggesting that exactly *because* the Mongol rulers were seen as sovereigns, the Grand Princes were their successors; they were replacements rather than liberators. The Khan was legitimate, and after 1480 the Russian ruler was equally legitimate. He laid claim, in effect, to the patrimony of the Khan.

Finally, what was the cultural contribution of the Mongols? Was Kliuchevsky right when he said that the whip and torture were Mongol contributions? To those who have lived through the Hitler age, the idea of "Asiatic" barbarism is a little indecent. We lack material on this subject; there are a few remnants of Mongol customs, but not much that we can identify. We are left, always with speculation, with a strong intimation that for northeast Russia, to put it symbolically, Sarai on the Volga or Kazan represented civilization just as much—more—than did Riga or Cracow—and properly so.

Could we turn now to the Muscovite state during the fifteenth and early sixteenth centuries? What were the roles of the Church, the aristocracy, and the czars?

The Russian Church followed a pattern which was very much, but not entirely, like the Byzantine. In the Caesaropapist system of Constantinople, there was no question of the emperor's nonlayman status. He held certain privileges within the Church: he summoned councils and made Church laws, and these features were repeated in Russia. The first great council in Russia under Ivan the Terrible was summoned by the czar, who posed the problems (the hundred questions that gave it the name of Hundred Chapter Council) and issued its answers as imperial laws.

There are other aspects of the Russian Church which place it (in Western terms) in the tradition of Gallicanism.

Obviously its organizational and ideological tradition emphasized centralization from the beginning. The Church was organized as the metropolitanate of Russia, and in some of the more confused periods (such as the thirteenth century) it was the only identifiable Russian institution. However, we should note that the Church led the way in acknowledging the legitimacy of the Mongol Khan, and the Mongol charters confirmed the immunities and privileges of the Church in exchange for its prayers for the Khan. As late as the sixteenth century, in the face of temptations to confiscate by the Russian Grand Prince, the Church justified its property by reference to the Khan's charters.

Until the fifteenth century at least, the metropolitan of Russia, and probably many of the bishops, were determined by Constantinpole, and most of them were Greek. In spite of this, they were unable or unwilling to maintain the image of Russia as a province of Byzantium. Once they got to Russia they evidently participated in the creation of a new political theory in which the Russian ruler was an imitation of the emperor, on a smaller scale, and thus of Christ. As in the West, the seat of what might be called monarchic theory was the monasteries. Russian monasteries were in some ways also royal monasteries; they were established by laymen, had lay patrons, and the various princely houses supported particular monasteries. The Trinity monastery, some forty miles outside of Moscow, provided everything from money to ideologists for the Muscovite house.

The question of the Church becomes particularly interesting in the second half of the fifteenth and in the sixteenth century, for which period we can make use of Soviet scholarship. The traditional historiography is that the Church stuck with the Prince of Moscow, but the situation in the sixteenth century was much more complex than has been supposed. One must take into account the fall of Constantinople, which did produce a crisis in Russia. There was the possibility of genuine autonomy; but on the other hand, there was the need to reformulate one's philosophy in a world where an "eternal" institution had vanished. The Russians moved with extreme caution on this golden opportunity, and when the Prince of Moscow appointed a Russian metropolitan in the 1440's, he did so with apologies.

I see a close analogy with the West here, first in the full-blown "Gallicanism" of the Russian Church, which preferred to regard itself as autonomous. After 1450 there were no more Greek metropolitans, only Russians who should have represented protonational identity as uniquely Russian symbols. However, it was during this period that the first clashes occurred between the monarchy and the Church—which again is reminiscent of what happened in the West. In the reign of Ivan III during the second half of the fifteenth century (which marks the end of the successful centralization of northeast Russia), there were arguments between the Grand Prince and the metropolitan over ritual and dogma. These arguments seem trivial to us, but they were serious enough so that on one occasion at least, Ivan forced the resignation of a metropolitan.

By the end of Ivan's reign the metropolitan had become the chief respondent to the apocalyptic mood of Russian society, and I emphasize this because I think that it can help us to understand the sixteenth century. In Russia and in the West at that time there was a widespread belief that an age was ending. There was talk of the end of the world in 1492, not because of Columbus but because it was the end of the seventh millennium since the Creation. The metropolitan reacted by publishing a castigation of this apocalyptic mood, arguing that what was coming was a new age, with a new Constantinople

(Moscow) and a new Constantine (Ivan III).

The fifteenth century marked the beginning of various heresies, of which the most important was the so-called "Judaizer" heresy. It was misnamed—after all, Christian heresies tend to be fundamentalist to some degree: they return to sources, to the Old Testament, and therefore have monotheistic, Arian, Judaic qualities. Among those accused of this heresy were members of the administrative elite of the Russian state, including the metropolitan and the Grand Prince himself. The Judaizer heresy reflected the fundamentalism which was so important in European thought at the time, and it also took up the question of Church property. The Orthodox part of the Church tried to fight the heresy, led by the archbishop of Novgorod, whose adviser was a surprising choice (given Russian intolerance toward Latins), a Dominican by the name of Benjamin. The archbishop wrote to the Grand Prince that they knew how to handle heretics in Spain. His advice was not followed in the 1490's, but heresy was condemned at a council. The government hesitated for a number of years (mainly over the issue of property), and the crisis lasted until a deal was made at a second council in 1503. Heretics were condemned and burned (the metropolitan had died before that time), and the issue of property was dropped.

The Russian Church committed itself to the glorification of autocracy during this period, and various churchmen attempted to emphasize the distinction between a just and an unjust prince. Their solutions were no more satisfactory than that of Aquinas, but they tried—and the man who tried hardest was Abbot Joseph Sanin of Volokolamsk who became the chief ideologue of imperial autocratic power after 1503. In that context, the doctrine of the Third Rome was only the frosting on the cake. The traditional argument has been that there was a strong antiproperty movement within the Church, but this was not the case. The Third Rome doctrine was formulated by the monk Philotheus in two letters to the Grand Prince in which he stated that the first two Romes failed through heresy, that a fourth Rome there shall not be. Moscow was the seat of Orthodoxy and its ruler the emperor of all Christians; if he let go, men would lose their chance of salvation. This doctrine is often misunderstood as disguised imperialism, as a physical claim to Constantinople, but it was the exact opposite. Who would want the corrupt Constantinople if he had the pure one? At no time was the doctrine taken up by the government, but it *was* picked up at the end of the Russian "medieval" period by the Old Believers in an attempt to appeal to the ruler.

The first clash between the prince and the aristocracy came at the end of the fifteenth century, as did the first clash between prince and Church. During the fourteenth and fifteenth centuries the aristocracy was regarded as the social base of the monarchy; its members were the natural advisers of the prince. With successful centralization in the mid-fifteenth century, the aristocracy increased in numbers; and once sovereign, unemployed princes had to be fitted into the aristocratic hierarchy. There was little sense to the first clash: Ivan III reacted violently against a small group of *boyars,* indulging in execution, exile, cutting out of tongues, and so on. The testimony of their trial reveals that these men were accused of complaining that the Grand Prince did not rule with the aristocracy but with a small group of his friends, that he was removing himself physically from the people, that the court was being corrupted through the influence of Ivan's Greek wife.

There are two questions here: the specific question of Russian political theory and the more general problem of what is called the Great Crisis of the sixteenth century—that is, the role of a ruling class within a centralized monarchy. If one argues that the Russians had a standard conception of an autocrat in the form of a monarchic cult of a different variety than the Western ones (e.g., the French cult of the sacred blood of the dynasty), one must recognize that there were fewer theoretical limitations on the Russian ruler than on Western monarchs. I would argue that there was some difference in the exercise of power, though less than one might expect, and considerable difference in theory.

On a theoretical level one must take seriously the Western legal tradition, which allowed for a constitutional distinction between officeholder and office. It was the *idea* of an office that made possible all the substitutions and fluidity and flexibility of Western political thought. The Crown is perfect, immortal, and ubiquitous, but one can debate over who best represents its interests at a particular moment. The Russian theory was different, and here we confront a mystery. No distinction between person and office evolved in Russia, and the Russian form of the ruler cult (based on the assumption that the prince is a saint in his person) did not encourage questioning of the principle that the prince's will was law. The prince's will was law in the West, too, but by definition it had to be a good will, making it possible to raise the question, Suppose it is not a good will? In Russia, the prince and his office were equally exalted, destroying the distinction between person and office as well as the distinction between human and natural law. The prince spoke as a saint, and it was not possible to formulate a theoretical limitation to his power.

The next question concerns the mysterious conflict between the prince and the aristocracy, which began in the late fifteenth century and culminated in the blood baths of Ivan the Terrible. As I mentioned before, this has traditionally been explained in terms of Ivan's madness. As Kliuchevsky pointed out, there was no real reason for a clash: the aristocrats admitted that the Prince was all-powerful, and they obeyed him. I believe that the conflict began long before Ivan the Terrible and that his madness, therefore, is not relevant. What *is* relevant, and makes the situation in Russia both similar to and different from the West, is that the power of the Grand Prince was unlimited yet restricted by the absence of a middle class.

I would like to argue that the rise of centralized monarchy in Russia was marked by an economic and social development—the rise of cities. But Russia did not have a long or steady enough development to produce a self-conscious social group to act as an identifiable political force with a corporate identity. There were guilds of merchants, and Ivan the Terrible used them, but they do not compare to the French *noblesse de la robe*. The expansion of the ruling class and the creation of a service gentry dependent on the prince took place at the end of the fifteenth century as a natural consequence of centralization, resulting, as it did elsewhere in Europe, in a shortage of manpower to run the state and the army. Even though nothing limited the prince in terms of real political entities, he fell into bloody conflict with the aristocrats because there was no social group to play off against them. The only group with any corporate identity was the ruling elite upon which the prince depended, and all he could do in any disagreement was to hit out against individuals who dared to oppose him.

Ivan the Terrible was enormously successful in his early years in expanding the state to the east, and this in spite of the tension between the manpower requirements of the army and frontier and the need for men to till the land and provide an economic base for expansion. The government was also aware of the need for a maritime trade. This was the Age of Discovery, when the English explored the northern Arctic route to Murmansk and Archangel and made contact with Russia. Ivan also committed himself to a war with Poland and Livonia over the Baltic. Here we find the first hint of disagreement within the elite; individual aristocrats advised against the war because it was expensive and Russia already had immense possibilities in the east.

Ivan responded to the disagreement by creating the infamous *oprichnina*. He retired from the capital, agreeing to return only when the panicked populace agreed to allow him to rid the country of treason. He divided the nation into two, with parallel institutions. His men dressed dramatically in black, rode black horses, and carried dogs' heads and brooms to symbolize that they were dogs of the czar who would sweep treason from the country. In reality, however, they were from the same social group as the aristocrats. Ivan never challenged the hierarchy itself, and after the blood bath of 1564–72, the *oprichnina* was abolished and its members hunted down and executed.

My hypothesis is complex, but I believe that the social-political imbalance in Russia forced the government to strike against individuals because it could not play the political game of balancing one group against another. Ivan and his predecessors did not deny the rights and privileges of the aristocracy, but one aspect of centralization is rejection of autonomous social entities. Ivan may have been insane, but I do not think that his insanity explains the blood bath. I believe that the czar was insisting that the ruling class must give up its pretension to autonomy even while he confirmed its privileges; that individual *boyars* must accept the decisions of the ruling elite as a whole. He did not accept the aristocrats' independent responsibility toward the state. He hit out at individuals who overstepped the line of the czar's authority in some undefined way, but he never hit out at the *boyar* council itself.

Ivan's behavior was irrational partly because Russian political theory was not clearly formulated and failed to distinguish between person and office. The concept of treason is possible only within a certain conception of the state, and in a famous correspondence with a former friend and member of the *boyar* council (Prince Kurbsky, who not only turned against the czar but deserted to Poland) Ivan claimed that by opposing the ruler, who is the image of God, a man injured his own immortal soul and the souls of his ancestors. If the czar is a saint, and Christ-like, then a claim to partake of his authority is blasphemous and heretical. His arguments were heavily theological, and indeed the lack of distinction between person and office fits into the concept that the purpose of the state is to provide salvation. Interference with the ruler is interference with the divine purpose.

Another intellectual strand in Russia at this time was, I think, the Renaissance conception of the autonomy of political activity in human life. With all the changes in criteria, the ruler was no longer measured in terms of piety but effectiveness, and this may shed some light on the clash between the monarch and the aristocracy. The concept of human autonomy penetrated downward from the prince, exacerbating the difficulties between Ivan and the *boyars*. Ivan was responsible for the salvation of men; and when the aristocrats disagreed with him they were committing blasphemy as well as treason. At the same time they had not learned to appreciate the new dimension of monarchy within the secular theology in which to disagree with the czar about a war was to endanger the state.

The conception of human political autonomy emerged in a world where rulers possessed the enormously increased power of centralized monarchy. This placed a huge burden upon them, and Ivan the Terrible was not the only mad ruler of his period. Dracula of Wallachia, for one (of the late fifteenth century), was presented in legend as a monster of cruelty and *justice*. The men of the Renaissance, unlike those of the Middle Ages, did not put much faith in divine grace: they could accept that a prince must be feared but might not be loved because men are evil, pitiful, and cowardly. The impact on a man like Ivan the Terrible was powerful, because unlike the Machiavellian Italian prince who accepted it all rather calmly, Ivan was tortured by the realization of evil. He belonged to the northern Renaissance, which still concerned itself with questions of sin rather than those of human nature. In the realm of political morality, however, he had to act, and he claimed that the aristocrats did not understand that in politics, morality is the success of the state. He was willing to grant them privileges in sharing the administration, but he denied them any understanding of the function of the state. This difficulty, I believe (even more than the czar's arthritis), was responsible for the bloody and apparently meaningless clash.

A centralized monarchy needs service gentry, and Russia needed them so desperately that they were recruited among runaway serfs, peasants, and bondsmen. Thus for Russia, the cost of successful centralization was greater than for most European countries; the country's lack of resources, economic and human, became critical with successful unification and empire building. The service class differed from the aristocracy in that the latter was an elite by birth, while the service gentry had no identity independent of the ruler. It owed its economic existence and political power to the ruler, to the government. Its members were given estates for service—but only for service; they were not hereditary. During the sixteenth century the government made a successful attempt to assimilate the elite into a wider ruling class. The aristocrats were allowed to hold the top of the pyramid, but from Ivan III through the sixteenth century, the czars tried to deny them an autonomous corporate identity. One confirming piece of evidence here is the government's attempt to fuse patrimonial possessions with fief possessions. The legal distinction remained until the time of Peter the Great; in practice, however, Ivan III argued that service was owed to the state for any estate. A great nobleman who owned his estate owed personal service to the czar, and no economic or hereditary status allowed a man to say, "I am I, and need not have any relationship to the state, to the Crown, to the ruler." There was a process of fusion, of the creation of a service class in which the aristocracy was simply the elite and not an autonomous group. In Russia, as in the West, the aristocrats resisted the process.

Something very curious took place in Russian society at the time of Ivan the Terrible. Russia had a Renaissance society in the legitimate sense that it was city-oriented and a part of Europe (it presented no xenophobic features). It is anachronistic to argue about "Westernization" in the sixteenth century; Russian princes hired Italian architects, German doctors, and so on. We find little distinction in clothes or manners between Russians and western Europeans, and Russians even shared in the Renaissance trademarks of syphilis and homosexuality.

Ivan called together a new institution for Russia, the equivalent of the estates-general in the French pattern. The estates were called to perform a function, and they were not assembled (as in France) after the middle of the seventeenth century when that function was accomplished. In the majority of the estates, the gentry and the merchants were the significant elements. They were asked to approve policy and to supply money, and in that sense there was vitality to city life. However, by the time of Ivan's death everyone was conscious that society was in a crisis. It is estimated that 40 percent of the lands around Moscow—the center of the Muscovite state—were abandoned because of depopulation. These lands represented the main economic resources of the state, and 40 percent was a serious loss. Thirty percent of ecclesiastical lands were abandoned. In the last years of Ivan's reign there were constant attempts to limit church property and to mobilize more resources, but it seems to me that this policy not only failed but overstrained the state.

When you were talking about historiography you stressed that the interpretation of Peter the Great has always been based on personality, on the assumption that a big change had occurred in a personal, almost miraculous way. I understood you to imply that you had doubts about this. What is the background of Peter the Great? How do you place him in a political, social, and institutional context?

You touch on what is, I think, the most interesting and central problem in Russian history. I believe that the key to it is that marvelous abstraction—possibly the most misused of all abstractions, at least until recently—the word *Westernization*. Obviously there was cultural borrowing in medieval Russia, but we do not call it *Byzantinization*. Our assumption that culture flows downhill like water is dangerous, because if culture always flows downhill, then Greek culture should have swamped Turkic when the Turks conquered Constantinople. In terms of etymology, at least, the reverse is the case: there are more Turkish words in Greek than Greek ones in Turkish. Let us put this in the specific context of Peter the Great.

Obviously, Russia borrowed military technology from the East before the fifteenth century, because that was the center of a higher technology. However, there was a significant change with the critical sixteenth century and the shift to firearms. After all, why *did* Ivan the Terrible shift to firearms? Not in order to imitate the superior technology of the West—a bow was superior to a musket until after the Napoleonic Wars—but because of the social implication of firearms: as in the West, firearms allowed the mobilization of larger numbers of the "dregs" of society, while the bow required practice and a population free enough to devote the time to that practice. If we look at the kind of borrowing Russia did, at the Russian life-style in the sixteenth century, we find aspects of a Renaissance society. If we then jump to Peter, we are forced to say that what we mean by "Westernization" seems to be the reverse—a violent expression of xenophobia and antiwesternism.

How can we account for this? It would be nice (and one of my projects is to check this in detail) to argue that something happened between the second half of the sixteenth century and the reign of Peter the Great which reversed the cultural perception of Russian society and made it xenophobic. We tend to think of the Petrine aristocracy as heavy and bearded, in dirty clothes, as against the dandies of Ivan the Terrible, but I have not been able to identify any specific moment of change. The Time of Troubles and accompanying foreign intervention produced some reaction to outsiders, but it also got the Russian ruling class into Polish clothes. The epitome of medieval Russia (at least in the context of political theology) seems to lie in the seventeenth century with the gentle czar Alexis, under whom the imperial theocratic ritualization of life was overpowering—so much so that the visiting patriarch of Antioch wondered how one could go on, day after day, spending eighteen hours out of twenty-four on the cold stone floor of a church in the Russian winter. And yet under Alexis (Peter's father) there was secular theater in Russia, and from Ivan the Terrible through Peter, the flood of foreign doctors, architects, artists, and merchants from the West continued—except for a brief kick on Oriental medicine under Ivan. There was Westernization in Muscovite art from the beginning without anybody making a fuss, for instance.

I connect Westernization (or anti-Westernization) with the schism which tore apart Russian society in the mid-seventeenth century. This was a religious expression of what I believe was the reaction of the lower classes of Russian society to the modern secular state. In the seventeenth century, when the government found itself torn between the needs of an administrative and military apparatus (represented by the gentry) and the economic resources of the country (represented by the peasants), it inevitably chose to go along with the ruling class, and serfdom was, in effect, confirmed in 1648.

Periodically, too, in the course of centralization there was a need to regularize local rules and customs which had diverged over the centuries. In 1551 Ivan the Terrible held a church council in order to establish some common rules of liturgy among all the principalities he had added to Russia. At this council, for instance, it was established that the sign of the Cross be made with two fingers. In the mid-seventeenth century, exactly the same process took place. It was conducted in a rational manner by examining Greek texts to discover the correct versions; quite rightly, the Old Believers said that there was no one text to use—all held errors. The purpose was to impose regularity and similarity, or order and uniformity—the values most prized by the secular state. The reaction amounted to a major social rebellion, particularly on the part of the most active peasants—those who were not enserfed. The rebellion was strongest in areas where no private estates were handed out—in the north, on the frontier, and in Siberia.

I think it is significant that Peter proclaimed and believed in religious tolerance. Personally he was not only tolerant but utterly blasphemous in his amusements—and yet no one persecuted the Old Believers with such violence. I believe, however, that they were not persecuted for their religious beliefs as such, but for their rejection of state authority and their conception that Alexis, his son Peter, and all the Russian rulers in their corporate dynastic authority were anti-Christ. This revealed their view of the secular state, which in effect promises salvation in this world and thus offered nothing to the lower classes of Russian society. If salvation is here, then there is no pay-off for the enserfed classes. The increasingly extreme groups of schismatics rejected the existing order in its entirety.

The schismatics' manuscripts graphically portray their vision of the kingdom of Anti-Christ and its clergy. They show a church, an altar, the new kind of cross—and in the place of the priest, serving mass, an officer of Peter's regiment of guards. The clergy of the new state was the professional army—and indeed, it is difficult to imagine a portrait of any eastern or central European ruler out of military uniform between the seventeenth century and 1917!

Reform, after all, had been a recurrent and perpetual theme from the time of Ivan the Terrible, and Peter's policy of breaking out to the Baltic certainly was not new. Ivan failed at it; Peter succeeded, after twenty-one years of war. In that context, Kliuchevsky's idea that Peter's reforms were consequences of war makes perfect sense. Armies became professional at this time simply because the feudal, semiprofessional army was no longer effective. An army needs money, and this need alone produced some significant reforms. Taxation shifted its base from the medieval one of land to that of the individual, and this quadrupled the resources of the state by providing an inducement to peasants to repopulate and till the lands. The more a peasant tilled, the more he had left for himself, because the tax was on himself rather than on the amount of land he cultivated.

For Peter's administrative reforms, however, I have yet to find a convincing cause. No one has shown me how the Senate and colleges differed in essence from the *boyar* council and *prikazy* of earlier times except through a certain rationalization of function. I think that this aspect is not as significant as the legal and cultural elements in the Petrine reforms.

The Old Believers reacted correctly (in a very primitive sense) to the secular, modern state, which has much more power to intervene in the life of the individual than had the medieval state. The Petrine laws reflected the power of the state, whose administrative apparatus had reached a point where it could intervene on a new level. These laws prescribed behavior—for instance, they proscribed the writing of letters behind closed doors, indicating that thought was the concern of the state as it had been the concern of the medieval Church. Peter knew that his reforms were being rejected as a new religion, and hence his strictness on beards, and even on the wearing of Russian boots. (The law prescribed that a man found making nails for the heels of Russian boots had his nostrils torn out, was whipped, and sent to Siberia for seven years.) In other words, Peter was very serious about the possibilities of the secular modern state, and he was extremely severe toward those who committed the unforgivable crime—that of failing to acknowledge its legitimacy.

Peter has traditionally been credited with Westernization in the sense of dragging Russian society into the modern Western world. If we accept the conception of the new religion, this formulation becomes suspect. One does not drag a ruling class into anything, unless one is looking for a social revolution, and the fact is that many members of the ruling class joined Peter enthusiastically. Obviously there were individuals who resented the emperor's personally shaving off their beards—but then, one difference between Peter and Ivan the Terrible is that Ivan, though insane, was enormously talented and easily the best-educated man in Russia, while Peter was a genuine boor as well as a maniac. The crudeness of his manners passed belief: Peter would have embarrassed Ivan the Terrible.

My case on Peter hinges on his being joined by the elite. To sum up: by Westernization we mean the provision of new forms for the new religion of the secular modern state. The state recognized, at least subconsciously, that it was a new religion, and it looked for new forms from those societies (in the West) which had achieved modernization—just as it borrowed religious forms from the East during Christianization a few centuries earlier. The West provided officers from the huge pool of unemployed soldiers who were thrown out of work by the end of the Thirty Years' War. The military uniform and its associated clothes became the vestments of the new religion, and the levée, the court ceremonials, and so forth, were its ecclesiastical practices.

There is another aspect of Westernization—xenophobia, reflecting the alienation of the masses. They were cut out; there was no salvation for them in the new religion. Old Believers and other schismatics formed over 20 percent of the Russian peasant population right up to 1917. One would have expected them to die out with the emancipation of the serfs in 1861, yet actually there was an enormous increase in their numbers. The secular state offered them very little, and they rejected it in return.

If the secular state was as I have described it, then the traditional interpretation of Peter's achievement is based on a myth—that Peter created modern Russia by genuine reform, by bringing new men into the ruling class. I would argue that the old elite actually benefited from the new religion. My findings (partly my own and partly from a dissertation by some of my students) are that the pre-Petrine and post-Petrine aristocracy was made up of the same families. (There is much more continuity between the fifteenth- and eighteenth-century aristocracy in Russia than in England.) Indeed, the post-Petrine aristocracy was more tightly closed, more thoroughly intermarried—more aristocratic, in fact—than the sixteenth-century aristocracy. I am suggesting that there was no influx of *uomini novi* at all. There was an increase in the size of the class because the apparatus of the state needed more men; there was passive mobility, as at any period, but no real change of personnel.

The aristocrats accepted the new religion (of which they were the main beneficiaries); they obeyed the emperor and adopted Western customs mainly because these allowed them to separate themselves more and more decisively from ordinary people. This is not to argue that a sixteenth-century *boyar* could be confused with a peasant, but only that the gap grew wider all the time. The ruling group was socially and politically the same as that which had ruled Russia in earlier times, but its members took on a new life-style as acolytes of a new religion. The "new men" who defeated Charles XII of Sweden belonged to the great Russian *boyar* families dating from the fourteenth century, and thus you cannot speak of a social revolution.

I believe, therefore, that Peter's significance was limited to the institutionalization of the new religion of the secular state. He appreciated it so vividly that he conducted a careful re-symbolization; he even adopted a new title. (Ironically, he abandoned a title which was indisputable—Czar—and was willing to fight a war to have Austria acknowledge him as *imperator.*) He translated into Russian the title *pater patriae,* which was then presented to him by the Senate. Peter did all the things associated with new secular orientation of society. The point I am making, however, is that this process dated back to the time of Ivan the Terrible. Peter institutionalized the change, and did so at a time when social tension over the new orientation—over the coalescence of a large ruling class with a virtual monopoly of power—had increased until the forms of a new religion were demanded by the threat of genuine social revolution. Peter was stubbornly resisted; some men burned themselves when they heard that the czar's men were coming to take a census. I would argue that this violent rejection was a consequence of the ritualization of the new religion of the secular state.

15

The Expansion of Europe

J. H. PARRY

THE HISTORIOGRAPHICAL CONTEXT

The increasing recognition of the need to view European history in a world perspective and to examine the mutual interaction of Western and other civilizations has made the expansion of Europe from the late fifteenth to the seventeenth century one of the most crucial moments in the European past. The problems that present themselves to the student of this subject are many: the changes in attitude and naval technology that made overseas voyages possible; the motivation and organization of exploration, trade, conquest, and colonization; the European impact on overseas societies; the effect of overseas venture and colonization on European society, economy, and government and the penetration of the significance of expansion and contact with overseas societies into the European consciousness; the various forms that empire building took and the reasons for this variety—these are only some of the themes that remain to be fully explored by scholars.

Until recently the historiography of the early modern expansion of Europe has been more distinguished by colorful narrative and nationalist myth making than by fruitful analysis of the complex problems arising from the subject. In recent years a more detached and reflective body of historical literature on the expansion of Europe has appeared, and all the assumptions and dogmatisms of the earlier writings on the subject have been re-examined. J. H. Parry, an Englishman born in 1914, who holds the unusual chair of Oceanic History at Harvard, has been in the forefront of the new historiography on the expansion of Europe. A vivacious stylist who commands an expert knowledge of the naval technology of the sixteenth century, Parry gives due recognition to the romance of exploration and discovery. But he also sees the overseas movement in its worldwide perspective, as in his *The Age of Reconnaissance* (1963), and examines the complex social, cultural, and political phenomena involved in the expansion. A tall, handsome man, who expresses readily his love of both the challenge of the sea and of the pleasures of country living, Parry is temperamentally well suited to understand those intrepid soldiers, sea captains, and gentlemen who inaugurated Europe's climb to world hegemony.

Chronological Outline

1420–1460: Prince Henry the Navigator's interest sparks Portuguese exploration of the west coast of Africa.

1492: Sailing for the Spanish crown, Christopher Columbus reaches the Bahamas and Cuba.

1493: The Line of Demarcation. The pope divides the non-Christian world between Spain (which receives a monopoly over the western hemisphere) and Portugal (Brazil, Africa, India).

1497: John Cabot and an English fleet sail around Greenland and Newfoundland and down the New England coast.

1501: Second voyage of Amerigo Vespucci down the Brazilian coast in the service of Portugal. Vespucci becomes convinced that he has discovered not Asia but a New World.

1510: The Portuguese conquer Goa.

1513: Balboa (a Spaniard) crosses the Isthmus of Panama and discovers the Pacific Ocean.

1519–1522: Ferdinand Magellan heads a Portuguese expedition that circumnavigates the world.

1524: Sailing for France, Giovanni de Verrazzano explores the North American coast from Cape Fear to Newfoundland.

1535–1536: Jacques Cartier navigates the St. Lawrence up to the present site of Montreal.

1572–1580: Francis Drake becomes the first Englishman to circumnavigate the globe.

1607: Founding of Jamestown Colony, the first permanent English settlement in America.

1608: The French explorer Samuel de Champlain follows the New England coast down to Cape Cod, founds the French settlement of Quebec, and discovers the lake that bears his name.

1609–1611: Sailing for the Dutch and subsequently the English, Henry Hudson explores New York and the Hudson Bay region while looking for a northwest passage to the Orient.

1612: The British East India Company establishes its first trading station in India, at Surat. By the end of the seventeenth century, the English are the predominant trading power there, while the Dutch have established their predominance in the East Indies.

1620: The Pilgrims arrive at Plymouth.

1624–1626: The Dutch establish settlements in New York.

1625–1664: French settlement in the West Indies. Richelieu organizes the Company of the Hundred Associates to colonize New France.

1664: Surrender of New Amsterdam to the English, who rename the colony New York.

1673: Fathers Marquette and Joliet explore the Mississippi.

1682: La Salle reaches the mouth of the Mississippi and takes possession of the river valley (Louisiana) for the French Crown.

Norman F. Cantor

In your view, when did the expansion of Europe begin? Were the expansions of the fifteenth century something new, or were they simply extensions of earlier movements such as the Crusades?

J. H. Parry

Historical periods are often artificial and arbitrary, serving only to break down the study of history into a number of smaller categories. The so-called Age of Expansion is generally acknowledged to have begun in the middle of the fifteenth century with the extension of Portuguese fishing and trading voyages down the coast of West Africa and with the founding of Portuguese and Castilian settlements in the Atlantic Islands. These movements certainly differed from medieval crusading adventures outside Europe, in the sense that they were permanent. The results have endured to the present day.

I think it may also be said that the fifteenth century marked the discovery by westerners that their techniques in several important fields were markedly superior to those of any other people. I do not mean to imply Western cultural superiority, but rather certain specific technological advantages.

In the middle of the fifteenth century, the area of Western European power and culture was contracting. Islam was the expanding civilization of that time, and the Europeans felt pushed to the wall—or more literally, to the sea. Islam was advancing in the Balkans, across the North African deserts, and in many other places. Constantinople fell in 1453, and in the 1480's the Ottoman emperor invaded Italy to set up a slave market. Muslim merchant princes pushed into the islands of the Malay archipelago, and Muslim conquerors invaded India many times. The huge, predatory empire of the Ottoman Turks threatened the smaller principalities of Europe, and the Europeans were well aware of the danger.

I think we can date the turn of the tide between the middle and the end of the fifteenth century. This does not mean that the Europeans had reversed the Muslim advance, for that did not happen until the middle of the seventeenth century. They were, however, beginning to find ways to bypass Islam, exploiting contemporary developments in shipbuilding and gunnery.

Among the antecedents of the Age of Expansion, the Crusades are perhaps the most difficult to analyze and classify. Except as an illusion in men's minds (particularly in the case of Spain), it is difficult to find any line of continuity between the attacks against infidels in the Holy City and the later stages of expansion overseas. The age of the general Crusades was over by the end of the thirteenth century. The fourth Crusade was in effect a Venetian effort to secure economic privileges in Constantinople. Its main result was to weaken Byzantium, the chief bastion of Europe against the Muslims. Thereafter, the pattern of the crusader changed or faded out of the mind of Christendom. Crusades became local, limited, subject to government as parts of deliberate policy, and frankly associated with other objectives than the recapture of the holy places. The successful crusades of the eleventh and twelfth centuries had not been led by governments at all, but by loose associations of feudal magnates. The crusaders followed as vassals of a local lord, not as servants of any government. With success it became apparent that the organization of these expeditions precluded full exploitation of victory. The states they established were personal and temporary—primitive indeed in comparison to the surrounding Muslim states. A relatively small military effort on the part of the Arabs was sufficient to overthrow the crusading kingdoms.

The idea of the crusade lingered on in parts of Europe where Muslims and Christians lived side by side—chiefly in Spain and Portugal. Spain was not divided neatly by the two faiths. The country was a patchwork of Muslim and Christian principalities whose alliances with and against each other were subject to change at any moment. There was no continuous drive of one faction against another, but there were commanding personalities who from time to time upset the unsteady equilibrium. Isabella the Catholic is an obvious example, for she crystallized Christian feeling against the Muslim states.

I cannot believe that all the Castilian knights concentrated on bashing the infidel at home and abroad. The belief that every Christian gentleman should take time out to slaughter infidels was used as propaganda, or as a means of recruitment for all kinds of other purposes. No doubt Prince Henry of Portugal, that rather primitive and atavistic leader, really believed that it was the duty of Christian gentlemen to kill Muslims. At the same time, however, he knew that a prerequisite of infidel bashing was the endowment of expensive knightly orders. The necessary capital was amassed, at least partly, by fishing, slaving, and the production of wine, corn, and timber in the lucrative island settlements. Economic considerations were thus placed high on Prince Henry's list of priorities, right next to the crusading impulse.

There is little evidence in the writings of those who financed, organized, or commanded the early voyages of overseas exploration that these pioneers thought they were carrying on the Crusades. Men with schemes for voyages often appealed to the crusading ideal, however, in order to win royal and ecclesiastical support. There were those in Europe—including Prince Henry and his brother, Prince Pedro—who looked at the world as a whole and considered the strategic importance of contacting various far-flung Christian communities. Many of these outposts existed on the eastern flank of Islam; they included the Copts in Abyssinia and the so-called St. Thomas Christians in India. A few Christians were left even in Peking, from the remains of the missionary embassies of the thirteenth century. Europeans generally overestimated the size and importance of these communities.

Spiritually minded Europeans felt

also that even though Western Europe possessed the Christian revelation, its interpretation and application of the faith left much to be desired. There were a great many Christians in Europe, but few of them were what Henry's religious contemporaries would have called "good" Christians. When one examines the conduct of public life in the first half of the fifteenth century, one can understand this feeling. It was a black time for Europe in many respects. Plague, demographic contraction, and incessant internal war darkened the century between the period of the Black Death in the middle of the fourteenth century and the beginning of the era of exploration. Schism in the Church encouraged the belief that the contemporary religious community was not living up to the Christian ideal. The central doctrines of the Church were not as a rule openly challenged, but European society clearly was not what Christ had preached, not the City of God which Augustine had proclaimed. It was possible that one or another of the Christian societies beyond the Muslim curtain might have been more successful. Perhaps the church that Saint Thomas was said to have founded in India could serve as a corrective example for the European Christian community.

These yearnings were not paramount in the mind of the merchant who wanted to finance a trip or the explorer who wanted to make his reputation by commanding a voyage. But spiritual dissatisfaction gave to those with secular motivations suitable arguments with which to beg support from monarchs and from the pious in general.

How might we account for the intense interest in overseas exploration and maritime enterprise which marked the end of the fifteenth century?

A tradition of cultural and commercial contact with Asia had existed in the West since ancient times. East Asia was a principal source of silk at a time when silk culture was hardly known in Europe. Vast quantities of Chinese and Persian silk traveled to the Muslim and European worlds alike.

Throughout most of the thirteenth century, eastern travel was possible for anyone willing to ride a camel or donkey for five thousand miles. During that century the Mongol Khans dominated central Asia, and they were fully capable of maintaining order along the caravan routes. Their immense empire extended to the extremities of the Turkish steppe; secured by the Mongol cavalry and powers of organization, it guaranteed the link between East and West. Some Europeans took advantage of this relative safety to travel as far as Peking, where political and missionary embassies from the West were courteously received. We have thirteenth-century accounts of more than a dozen of such visits, and there must have been more than surviving records indicate. A handbook existed which listed with reasonable accuracy all the routes to Asia, the commodities that might be obtained there, the political arrangements of the area, and the tolls and duties that a traveler had to pay. The mere existence of such a book demonstrates the frequency of travel between the two cultures in this period.

In the middle of the fourteenth century, contact between West and East was interrupted by the Black Death and by the breakdown of Mongol power, which made travel in Asia considerably more dangerous. The rise of the Ottoman Turks in the Near East and the Levant did not in itself inhibit East-West travel, but it made it more expensive. The more powerful the princes encountered along a route, the more tolls the traveler had to pay. In addition, the Turks became more hostile after they were converted to Islam, and they were apt to handle Christian travelers roughly. For many reasons, land travel became difficult and the silk routes dried up.

The re-establishment of a native dynasty in China after the collapse of the Mongol empire brought back the traditional Chinese contempt for western "barbarians" and made China a sealed kingdom once again. The break between Europe and the East was so complete that Europeans were not even aware of the extent of the change. When Columbus sailed, he did not know that there was no longer a great Khan in central and eastern Asia, and still proposed to address himself to such a prince.

The problem for ambitious Westerners in politics, religion, or commerce was to establish contact with places which they knew or thought existed, and to re-establish it in areas with which they had lost touch. Their desire to knit up the hundred-and-fifty-year-old rupture with the East provided motive enough for exploration. The problem was to find the practical means to implement their ambitions.

The fifteenth century was a period of rapid and dramatic development of transport, particularly in travel by sea. The steady improvement in the reliability, maneuverability, and speed of European ships was not, however, a consequence of the desire to rediscover the East. Remarkably, almost all of the early overseas expansion was conducted in ordinary ships designed for fishing, carrying, and coasting. The improvement in ship construction arose rather from a hybridization of various technical traditions, as a result of the greatly increased contact between the North European Atlantic coast and the Mediterranean area. In the late fourteenth and early fifteenth centuries, northern Europe was beginning to recover from the long attrition of plague and war. As prosperity returned and North Europeans started to search for markets, they looked first to their Mediterranean neighbors.

The Mediterranean region did not share fully in the economic resurgence of the fifteenth century. The demographic recovery which accompanied the increased productivity of land was not equally felt throughout Europe. There was a great deal of virgin land in comparatively thinly populated northern Europe, where the rainfall is always well distributed throughout the year, and the fifteenth century brought a marked increase in yield per acre. One can only guess at the reasons why the Mediterranean yield did not increase as well. The shores of the Mediterranean had been scratched and nibbled by peasants and their goats for millennia, and it is likely that by the fifteenth century this process of erosion and gradual attrition of natural resources had begun to take its toll. During the fifteenth century, the productivity of the Mediterranean area decreased while its population increased, with damaging results.

All of this encouraged northern shipowners and merchants to try to market their goods in Italy. The peoples of the Mediterranean began to import grain in the sixteenth century. They even learned to eat rye, a northern grain usually unpopular with southern Europeans. Hitherto all North-South shipping had been in southern hands. The ships that had moved between the harbors of Italy and the ports of France, the Low Countries, and England were designed to carry light luxury cargoes—the silks and spices of the luxury trade. It was not until trade began to move the other way, fairly late in the fifteenth century, that the cargoes changed in character. Even the Mediterranean fisheries were beginning to fail, and northern Europe began to send salt fish and meat, grains, and the like to the South. Two very different traditions of ship design met for the first time.

The Mediterranean peoples—particularly the Venetians—possessed the oldest and most sophisticated shipping tradition of Europe. Different ships were designed and used for different purposes. They built surprisingly large, heavy-timbered, multi-masted ships to carry certain bulky commodities within the Mediterranean area. A steady annual movement of about 15,000 tons of grain traveled about the Mediterranean, and ships to carry it were built in considerable numbers in Adriatic ports. They were built on a preconstructed frame and had strong, flush-fitted planking, more than one mast, and lateen sails. For maneuverability and speed in trade or naval fighting, the Mediterranean people used galleys. In the relatively calm seas and predictable weather of the Mediterranean, these galleys with their independence of the wind were very valuable.

Neither the grain ships nor the galleys were really suited for the ocean. The grain ships of Venice were too big, heavy, and too slow; they were designed for carrying capacity rather than maneuverability and coastal trading. The galleys, of course, were simply unsafe for the Atlantic conditions except in a good summer. They also were economically unsound for Atlantic trade; they had to carry too many rowers (and too many provisions) to carry much cargo. Galleys did cross the Atlantic in the sixteenth century, but these were military ships without cargo.

In northern Europe there was a completely different maritime tradition based on fishing and coasting. The northern ships were not meant to carry bulky commodities, except for salt—essential for the preservation of meat and fish, and therefore perhaps the most important single raw material carried by sea in the Atlantic Europe of the Middle Ages. Northern shipping was based on Scandinavian and German design. The ships were simpler in construction than those of the Mediterranean, and they usually did not have preconstructed frames. Their primitive planking was called *clinker-planking,* meaning that the planks overlapped and were fastened to each other instead of to a frame. In stormy seas, this flexible construction contributed to safety, but it imposed limits on size.

Despite their favorable design for rough weather, the northern ships were comparatively primitive. Because there was no framework but rather a shell constructed out of the planks themselves, the ships were necessarily comparatively small. In building them, it was necessary to use whole planks. In addition, the rigging was fairly primitive until the middle of the fifteenth century. The simplest kind of sail—the square rig—was used exclusively for centuries. Very few of the northern ships had more than one mast, and the lateen rig was unknown. It is true that a square-rigged ship has possibilities of development because such sails may be mounted one above the other on the same mast. Also, square rig provides the most efficient method for sailing with the wind abaft the beam. On the other hand, the primitive type of baggy square-rig known in the Middle Ages was virtually useless with the wind before the beam.

The lateen rig performs much better on a wind and has a long, oblique yard which gives a long leading edge—the key to efficient sailing with the wind before the beam. However, it is less efficient with the wind astern, and the long and heavy yard is awkward to handle. A big lateen-rigged ship had to have several masts, because it was generally possible to have only one lateen sail on each mast. Second, a large crew was needed to handle the yards, so that beyond a certain point—two hundred tons, perhaps—lateen-rigged ships were uneconomic in competition with square-rigged.

When the sailing methods of North and South began to mix, hybrids resulted. These hybrids developed on the "street corner of Europe"—southwestern Portugal and southern Spain. Some time during the middle of the fifteenth century, it occurred to some unknown genius to combine the best of the two traditions in one ship: to join the bold (sheer) and the simple lines of the northern hull with the preconstructed frame and stout planking of the Mediterranean. As for rigging, a combination of lateen and square sails was put together. The square sails were divided for ease of handling, improving their pulling power with winds astern, and lateen sails allowed a much better performance on a wind.

A capable and versatile ship was born from this marriage of the maritime traditions of North and South. It is very difficult to tell when the birth took place, for there are very few reliable contemporary pictures of ships. The sketches that appear on maps are helpful, but it is difficult to form clear pictures of what these ships were like and when the innovations actually took place. Nevertheless, there is little doubt that by the second half of the fifteenth century, the best qualities of both traditions had been combined to produce ships capable of making long voyages without oars and of heading fairly close into the wind. For the first time, ships could follow the intricacies of an indented coast.

In the middle of the fifteenth century, then, there existed powerful economic and religious motives for expanding once again to the East, and innovations in ship design made such voyages possible. This coincidence of motive and method explains, I think, why large numbers of voyages took place in the second half of the fifteenth century. The Europeans' knowledge of the East was hopelessly out of date, but they sailed confidently to establish contact once again.

Would you say that a change in intellectual attitude—a boldness or curiosity—sparked the expansion? Did the intellectual forces of the movement we call the Renaissance play any part?

There certainly was a change in attitude, but I am inclined to think that it was a result and not a cause of overseas expansion. Most of the explorers were practical men, good ship handlers but not learned scholars. The men who financed the voyages relied for advice upon scholars, who relied in turn upon classical authorities. One of the great events in the intellectual history of Europe was the recovery of most of Ptolemy's *Geography* at the beginning of the fifteenth century. It is difficult for us to imagine the reverence with which this compendious and self-confident authority was received. It took great courage to suggest that Ptolemy had never been to India—that he might be seriously wrong. Of course there was no evidence for that view, either, but with the first voyages a cumulative process of questioning began.

It is difficult to define intellectual curiosity, and one cannot find much evidence of it in the exploratory voyages. The explorers thought they knew where they were going—usually toward the East, directly or indirectly—and they knew what they wanted—the commodities that Europe had gone without for a hundred and fifty years. They thought they understood the political situation in the East from reading Marco Polo. There is little reason to believe that the voyagers were interested in new lands; they wanted new routes to old lands.

After the big discoveries had been made and their descriptions circulated through the new medium of printed books, it became known that the classical authorities were wide of the mark and that the world was much larger than anyone had realized. Two huge continents had been found as well as an ocean, wider than the Atlantic, that no one had heard of before. Perhaps, then, there might be new intellectual worlds to discover as well, with horizons beyond anticipation. Throughout the Middle Ages and the fifteenth century, any educated European would have sided with classical authority in any conflict of views. In the sixteenth and seventeenth centuries this deference was diminished, very largely because of the geographical discoveries of the period. Without any such intention, the explorers had invalidated classical sources and opened the door to widespread skepticism about classical "givens." This change in attitude was more an effect than a cause of the voyages of discovery.

What motivations were involved in the Spanish expansion?

In the second half of the fifteenth century, Spain was still a geographical expression, a collection of kingdoms fortuitously united by a royal marriage. In the course of the century, there had been a variety of possibilities for dynastic matchmaking on the Iberian Peninsula. There was no compelling reason for Isabella of Castile to marry Ferdinand of Aragon; she might as easily have chosen the prince of Portugal, or another. Thus by a chance of royal marriage, much of Spain was loosely united, in circumstances that made Castile the dominant partner of the union.

Castilian predominance was significant because Castile, the most powerful and aggressive kingdom on the peninsula, was nevertheless economically and socially backward. Most of its land is rocky and arid, and Castile had the only predominantly pastoral economy in Europe. It resembled parts of the Near and Middle East more than western Europe. Rainfall was sparse there, and arable farming of the North European type relatively unproductive. Castile's problems were exacerbated by its warlike history. Throughout the Middle Ages the kingdom was disturbed by constant fighting between Christians and Muslims. In these circumstances, mobile wealth—herds of animals, for instance—was preferable to fixed wealth, producing a society in which even feudalism was of a primitive nature. The system was tied less to land tenure than to personal loyalty among fighting men.

Castile also fostered a religious primitiveness that was maintained until fairly modern times. The crusading ideal was still widespread in the fifteenth century; it still was the duty of a gentleman to kill his share of infidels. Until the conquest of Granada in 1492, this could be accomplished at home in Spain. Granada was not really a menace to the other Spanish kingdoms during most of the later Middle Ages; it was too small and torn by internal intrigue. Contemporary accounts give the impression that Christian Spaniards found it a convenient means of keeping alive the martial spirit. As a sort of internal scapegoat or tournament partner the relatively harmless Granada served a purpose, though it certainly was never formulated in those terms.

In the reign of Isabella, the queen's own religious dynamism sparked a revival of religious feeling which expressed itself in anti-Muslim and anti-Jewish prejudices quite alien to the Spanish tradition. In medieval times the Spanish had been reasonably tolerant of different religions, once the dissidents submitted; the hardening of feeling under Isabella was something new. The trend coincided with events in the Levant which were making Granada a military menace for the first time—not because of any perceptible change in Granada itself, but because of the possibility that the Granadans could appeal to the growing power of the Turks. If the Turks were to expand in North Africa (as eventually they did), and if Granada were to provide a bridgehead in Spain, Spain might be catapulted back into the eighth century. Fear of the Muslim advance haunted the Christian kingdoms of Spain. It accounts for the rising hostility against the Moorish kingdoms in the late fifteenth and sixteenth centuries, and it gave Spain an especially powerful reason to try to outflank the Muslims outside of Europe.

I think that it was most natural for the Castilians, of all the Iberian peoples, to take to the sea, once the technical means of oceanic travel were at hand. The Castilians, with their religious feeling, their relatively primitive and loose social organization, and their tradition of mobility and conquest, adapted to the rising realities of Atlantic travel more readily than any other kingdom. The hybridization of marine technology occurred primarily in Portugal and in Castile, after a period of steady trade with northern Europe and the expansion of the Castilian fishing fleet. The Mediterranean met the Atlantic on the Iberian Peninsula, not only in a technical sense, but in a spiritual sense as well. The confluence of spiritual and economic motives, enlivened by the rise of technical capacity, met in Lisbon, Seville, and smaller harbors up and down the coast.

What was the background of the expansion of the northern peoples?

The Northerners displayed a good deal less enthusiasm than the Spaniards in the early days of long-distance voyaging, and such excitement as they did feel was largely imported. The Cabots, for example, were Italians who for various reasons—not all of them creditable—had chosen to settle in England. One must remember the primitiveness of the northern maritime tradition. Their ships, while fairly efficient, were mostly very small and not designed for long voyages. There was no space for the provisions required on a transatlantic trip.

In addition, northern navigation was less advanced than Mediterranean; charts were unknown in northern waters into the fifteenth century! Many of the northern ships did not even carry compasses, which, though known earlier in China, were not used even in the Mediterranean until the thirteenth century. The activities of northern seamen until the middle of the fifteenth century were confined to the Continental Shelf; they groped around with one foot on the bottom. They had an intimate familiarity with tides and soundings, but they were much less sophisticated than Mediterranean sailors in the use of charts and compasses.

One can speculate that the North—satisfied with life as it was—was not driven to exploration by the tension of the Mediterranean principalities. Northerners did not feel the religious pressure of the South; they were not face to face with the Turk and the Arab. Furthermore, the North had little capital to invest, still less the financial machinery needed in mobilizing capital. The early Spanish and Portuguese voyages were financed to a striking extent by Italian and South German investors.

Successful exploration required ships large enough to carry the necessary provisions as well as complicated equipment and trade goods. All this required a larger initial investment than northern kingdoms—where it was difficult enough to raise money even for the major purposes of government—could muster. Despite these difficulties, there was considerable interest in oceanic exploration in England in the later years of Henry VII and the early reign of Henry VIII, arising probably from the close commercial contact with Spain. By contrast, there was virtually none in the Low Countries or in Germany in the same period, presumably because the seamen and shipowners there were fully occupied in exploiting the lucrative trade and fishery of the Baltic and North seas.

What, then, accounts for the involvement of the North in expansion during the sixteenth and seventeenth centuries?

There were several reasons for the growing involvement of northern Europe in overseas exploration, including its growing prosperity and the spur of competition. By the middle of the sixteenth century, a large amount of silver was coming into Europe from the Americas, and this financial transfusion encouraged building and expansion.

A half century earlier the Portuguese had opened up regular commercial contact with India and points farther east, but they had not fully exploited their advantage. For a time at the very beginning of the sixteenth century, they had established a partial monopoly over the spice trade by preying on Arab shipping and by constricting the supply via the Levant to the Mediterranean, but they could not govern the fluctuating market for very long. The old spice route up the Persian Gulf or the Red Sea reasserted itself, and there was ding-dong competition throughout the sixteenth century. If war interrupted one of the routes, the other prospered for a while; the Portuguese route by the Cape of Good Hope did not assert clear primacy for a long time. One reason (not yet sufficiently investigated) for its eventual success may have been a change of climate in northern Europe. The onset of a period of colder, wetter weather in the middle of the sixteenth century may have made transport over the Alps more difficult. Perhaps the increased difficulty of overland transport encouraged the northern Europeans to turn to the sea in an effort to outdo the Portuguese. Northerners were heavy consumers of spice; they liked to eat meat, which was preserved in spices and salt, while the southerners ate more fish, which was preserved only in salt. Throughout the Middle Ages the bulk of the spice trade was directed to northern countries.

It is important to remember, too, that while the initial breakthroughs of maritime science were southern achievements, the continuation of these innovations and their constant adaptations were centered in the North. Northerners had their natural resources, particularly an abundance of timber, to implement the accomplishments of the South. Mediterranean timber was vanishing like its grain supply. In Spain, Portugal, throughout the Mediterranean region, it became increasingly difficult to build ships as timber became more and more expensive. Further, the South lacked any natural system of internal waterways to transport timber from forest to shipyard.

All these factors played parts in the gradual achievement of northern dominance in shipbuilding toward the end of the sixteenth century. Before long, northerners attempted to eliminate the southern middleman and deal directly with the East, just as the Portuguese had sought to do in the late fifteenth century. In particular, if alternate routes, North–East or North–West, could be found—as the shape of the world indeed suggested—they might avoid perennial battles along the traditional routes.

Northern shipping exploited the Spanish and Portuguese developments of the fifteenth century; it did not strike out radically on its own. Surviving pictures of northern ships indicate that the bold (sheer) so well suited to Atlantic voyages was retained, but that the combined lateen-square rig of the South was imported whole. It is fairly clear, however, that the Dutch took the lead in another important development: the principle of breaking up the area of square sail, for ease of handling.

With the benefits of southern technological advances, it was to be expected that the North would finally assert its natural superiority in maritime affairs. Not only did the northern sailors have timber, they had the rough, unpredictable Atlantic waters for practice. Sometime between 1590 and 1600, the total number of ships owned in the Netherlands first exceeded the total number of ships owned in Spain and Portugal. Increasing construction in the North, together with greater willingness to innovate and experiment, widened this gap.

Would you consider the effect of overseas expansion upon the economy of Europe, with special reference to the rise of what historians call commercial capitalism?

Obviously, contact with the Americas and the Far East greatly increased the variety and number of commodities handled in Europe. The diversification introduced by these products revolutionized European trade. The luxury market boomed, revealing the passion of sixteenth-century European society for clothes. Silk was used more and more in the manufacture of expensive clothing. Food plants introduced from abroad were propagated in Europe and found a large market in the late sixteenth and seventeenth centuries. The introduction of the Peruvian potato, for example, was a prime factor in the demographic explosion of the eighteenth century. Cacao, which was first brought to Spain during the sixteenth century, became an important article of trade in the seventeenth. Cochineal, the only natural red dye, which can be used in food, livened up the salted meat which formed the chief winter diet of the North. Edible food dyes were for a time in the sixteenth century the second most important commodity imported from the Americas. Silver, of course, was the most important.

Any increase in commodities handled increases the number of people involved in trade and the amount of money that is moving around. Eventually, commercial activity provides its own momentum and generates larger markets. The most important factor in this commercial explosion was the great influx of precious metal from the New World. From the 1560's onward, silver (not gold) stimulated a considerable range of financial activities in Europe; it helped to make possible European investment in Eastern trade. Very few European products were of any interest to the East in the sixteenth century; but there was a serious shortage of silver in China, and throughout the East, and the relative abundance in the West evened out the balance of trade.

What was the impact of Europeans as merchants, colonialists, and empire builders abroad? Were there any revealing differences between the policies of the various European countries?

I believe that differences among the European colonial empires can be attributed most accurately to differences among the peoples and situations encountered by the Westerners. There were sharp contrasts, for instance, between the behavior of the Spanish and the English in colonial America. The Spaniards married and mingled freely with the Indians, while the English did not—presumably because the natives of Spanish America were more civilized, numerous, and attractive than the peoples of North America.

The Spanish government did its best to preserve the total number of workers in the Americas as well as certain elements of native culture, subject, of course, to religious conformity. This policy arose, no doubt, from a mixture of economic and cultural motives. On the other hand, neither the government in London nor the English settlers felt much responsibility for the Indians they encountered. Here again, it may be argued that policy varied with the native cultures. A large number of the Spanish Indians decided, willingly or not, to throw in their lot with the Europeans. Within a generation or two of the conquest, large numbers of Indian craftsmen put on trousers and moved into the Spanish-dominated towns, particularly in Mexico and in some densely populated areas of South America. In North America, however, the people were few and primitive. They had all the land they could use, and they were not anchored even by agriculture to any one spot. Most of their sustenance came from trading, hunting, and fishing. They were not forced to deal with the white men, and their only reason for doing so was to obtain rum and firearms. There was no cultural contact, and no fusing analogous to that of Central America.

As for New France, its only commodity in the early years was fur—an Indian product. Colonists had to trade with the red men or compete with them, and as the settlers expanded they attempted to eliminate the Indian middlemen and hunt for furs independently. This involved a kind of Indianization, a pushing out past the settlements into rough forest, and self-indoctrination into the Indian means of frontier survival. Frenchmen generally were more willing to do this than their English counterparts.

If France had allowed its Huguenots (and similar urban groups) to emigrate, the story of New France might have been very different and its resemblance to the Massachusetts colony more striking. As it was, the French colonists were not town- and village-bred "respectable" citizens concentrating on small-scale cultivation and craftsmanship, like the English. This kind of analysis cannot be proved, but the differences in socioeconomic background seem more important than any inherent psychological differences between Frenchmen and Englishmen.

There were important physical differences among the colonies, too. Virginia (and even Massachusetts) was much more attractive than much of the bleak forest land held by the French. Like it or not, the French apparently could not support themselves by agriculture and had to move out into the forest, where they mixed with the Indians.

As far as we know, New Amsterdam was a trading post only, with no cultivation worth mentioning. Less than two thousand Dutchmen lived there when the English took the place in 1664. They were nearly all concentrated in the port of New Amsterdam itself, although there was a smaller trading post—a way station for the fur trade—up the river in Albany. The Dutch did not produce colonies of the French and English kind, partly because they were not sufficiently numerous. The Dutch traders came from a very tiny and industrious country, close to fine timber resources and boasting a highly developed fishing tradition. Their explorers—often the best in Europe—possessed the combined skills of ocean and coastline.

The Dutch, a hardheaded and realistic people, recognized the vulnerability of their geographic position and the difficulty of raising enough food on their tiny stretch of territory. They turned to the sea quite deliberately for its harvest of fish and for trade. They looked for the proverbial fast buck wherever it could be made without investing large numbers of human beings, a resource they did not have. This is particularly obvious in the East, where they established a careful network of trading factories around areas of planned production. They made no bones about it; they were parasites upon the people who had got there earlier, and not themselves producers. The only important exception occurred in Brazil, where as conquerors the Dutch took over the Portuguese system of sugar production and became planters themselves.

How did European colonial policies in Asia compare with those in the Americas?

First of all, even though the East was practically a synonym for wealth in the popular imagination, and although potential investors in overseas trade were most attracted to Eastern ventures, the total volume of eastern trade was considerably smaller than the volume of trade with the New World. The absolute volume of tonnage to both areas grew larger all the time, but the predominance of American trade increased throughout the eighteenth century. Eastern trading companies were prominent in the European capitals, but there is evidence that governments were well aware that more money was to be made in the West—particularly in the Caribbean, the most important commercial center of the New World. The protective fleets sent to the Americas were much larger than those sent to the East. The glamor of eastern trade was gradually overshadowed by the plodding but steady stream of commerce from the colonial West.

Nearly everywhere in the East—and by East I mean everything east of the western part of the Indian Ocean, excluding Africa—Europeans had to deal with states and empires as powerful and well administered as any European nation. For geographical and climatic reasons, economic necessity had encouraged the formation of very large political communities in many areas of Asia. A maximum of centralized control over masses of unskilled labor was required to deal with the demands of large populations, often in harsh environments. Flood control, irrigation, and defense were centralized systems, often dictated by social and religious considerations.

Until at least the middle of the eighteenth century, such states as the Ottoman and Persian empires, the Mughal empire in India, and above all the Ming and Manchu dynasties in China, commanded European respect. Westerners did not sail into Chinese harbors with guns, but with humble petitions for trading rights. The granting of commercial privileges depended less upon intimidation than upon the particular mood of an Eastern government at a given moment. Permission to trade implied restrained conduct, because any of these empires was powerful enough to enforce its decisions. There were many episodes in which Westerners were punished for fighting (even with each other) in eastern ports. At the end of the seventeenth century, for instance, the English East India Company was severely castigated in Bengal.

Eastern governments exerted varying degrees of control over trade within their territories. Generally they were well disposed toward Western commerce, particularly when it brought them munitions of war. Further, European ships were sometimes useful to the landed Eastern empires. Western fleets often carried pilgrims to the Red Sea region. They also policed the seas and provided some measure of protection against pirates. In fact, some Eastern kingdoms allowed trading privileges specifically on the condition of European naval support being made available when required. Europeans were thus employed as naval mercenaries.

The Chinese, however, were reluctant to allow any contact at all with the West. The first Manchu monarchs of the seventeenth century were more lenient, but generally Europeans were allowed to trade only under very limited conditions in stipulated places, usually Canton. The prices they paid and the commodities they handled were fixed by government and enforced by small groups of local merchants. In the eighteenth century, the Chinese imposed upon the West restrictions analogous with those that the Westerners imposed upon the colonial territories of their own empires.

There was one important exception to the Eastern domination of the visiting Europeans—the Malay archipelago, where the later Middle Ages had been a period of disintegration. With the spread of Islam and the defeat of the Hindu kingdoms, a large number of small merchant princes had established themselves in the islands. The Dutch were faced not with a centralized power but with a network of petty states weakened by incessant internal intrigues. The frequency of succession disputes in the Malayan kingdoms made possible the Dutch financial stranglehold on the islands, for ambitious princes invited the visitors to aid them in their quarrels. Certainly the traders did not bring anything that the Indonesian princes wanted; they did not even have enough silver for trade. They earned high profits only by winning exclusive rights to a commodity that was in demand in Europe or elsewhere in Asia. Japanese copper, for example, could be sold in India at advantageous prices. China was an excellent market for Indonesian pepper. A great network of local trade existed within the East itself, and the Dutch managed to do what every European power would have liked to do: control the trading rights and markets of an entire area in certain favored commodities.

Once the local princes were bound to the company by debt, mortgage, or military protection, the next stage was control of the amount and nature of production. The Dutch had only to inform the head man just how many balls of yarn or pounds of pepper they desired yearly, and production over the quoted figure could be destroyed. They directed what spices could be grown, in order to guarantee that the islands they controlled most directly maintained an exclusive supply. By the beginning of the eighteenth century, most of Java was ruled by treaties of this kind, and in many other islands production was controlled by the Dutch and their local collaborators. Needless to say, the system required the constant use or threat of force. It was costly to maintain. Ultimately it impoverished the area and hurt the Dutch themselves.

During the seventeenth century, these consequences were not foreseen, and Dutch prosperity seemed assured and permanent. The immediate financial benefits were obvious: circumstances were ideal for profit taking, since commodities obtained at nominal cost could be sold in Europe at very high prices. No one recognized the long-range devastation of the islands or the long-range cost of maintaining an imperialist position in the islands. The forts, ships, and armies added up to a formidable overhead. From the beginning of the eighteenth century the Dutch began to lose money, though for a long time their losses were concealed by primitive accounting. By 1780, their company was bankrupt.

All this was possible only in Indonesia. As always, differences in policy among European colonial powers depended more on the situations they found than on inherently different philosophies. I have no doubt that the English or French would have exploited the islands in the same way if they had been able to do so. All the European powers were potentially parasitic, but in the East such opportunities were relatively rare. The English eventually became revenue collectors and controllers of production in Bengal; but conversely, the Dutch behaved with great restraint in India. Each took what he could get, depending upon the circumstances he encountered in any particular place.

How do you account for the French and English takeover of India in the eighteenth century?

To begin with, the Europeans did not take complete control of India in the eighteenth century. Conditions certainly changed, throughout the century, to the advantage of the Europeans, because of the political disintegration of some of the major Indian states. With the continuing exception of China, the large empires of Asia failed to establish any firm principle of governmental succession. It is not completely clear why most Eastern kingdoms lagged behind Western Europe in this respect. It may be that polygamy was responsible, for it laid open Eastern courts to frequent harem intrigues and squabbles over succession. By contrast, the fixed succession rules common to European kingdoms gave them the strength and stability to outweigh the populousness and size of the Asian kingdoms.

Above and beyond rules governing succession to the throne, most of Western Europe had a general heritage of rule under law, both written and commonly acknowledged, which enabled the machinery of government to go on functioning under weak rulers. In most Indian states government was more personal, less defined by law, more authoritarian under strong rulers, more chaotic under weak ones. Easterners tolerated a good deal more authoritarian dictation from strong rulers, and expected a more paternal protection from them, than Old Europeans; conversely, they were more ready to abandon weak or defeated rulers. In the West, government was a concept in itself, separate from the person of the monarch; Eastern rulers, unrestrained by any such concept, could behave more capriciously when in power, but were more easily unseated by military defeat. When the Mughal empire in India began to disintegrate in the eighteenth century, the machinery of succession and of governmental conduct in its vassal states was not sufficiently institutionalized. No framework of convention existed to withstand the stresses of the Mughal collapse or to survive as a stabilizing force in itself. A blow at the center of government struck at the very fabric of a polity, which lacked traditions or precedents with which to heal itself. The Europeans moved into the vacuum created by the Mughal collapse.

Would you say that the overseas expansion of the Europeans benefited the Asians in any way?

I can think of no way in which it did them any good whatever until the end of the eighteenth century. On the whole, it had very much the contrary effect. In the early period the West had little to offer even in technology.

In the eighteenth century, however, many eastern countries with native maritime traditions began to adopt western innovations in shipbuilding. The Europeans introduced a real technical improvement in the shipping of the Indian Ocean, where hulls had usually been sewn rather than spiked. This afforded great flexibility (especially for surf landing), but it had obvious disadvantages for ocean travel. With western-style shipbuilding, inactive shipyards began to service and construct the vessels of the traders; the most famous of these were in Bombay, where Parsee firms built fine big ships of western type.

European ships were much more powerful in battle than those of the East, because the Westerners had superior armament. Asian potentates began to imitate the western armament system to some extent, but no Asian kingdom owned or built a battle fleet that could stand up to a European naval force.

The discovery of the New World pumped a good deal of silver and new crops into China, and the population explosion of the eighteenth century could not have taken place without maize. Whether this (or the example of European naval armament) was a boon to the Asians is a matter of opinion.

The East Indian companies, hoping to eliminate the necessity of exporting European silver, cast around Asia for products which could be bartered for Chinese tea. The companies thus served as middlemen for internal eastern trade, and one of their prime commodities was opium. The European attitude toward this trade resembled that of the slavers: "Who are we to say what is good for our customers?" Raw cotton as well as opium was produced in India and sold in China. The cotton yarn imported into China by European traders served to clothe the expanding population of the huge country.

As for cultural contacts, it is difficult

to discern any major European influence upon Asian literature or other art forms. Some missionary enterprises had a powerful effect upon Asian ideas. Some of the Christian communities, especially those on the Malabar coast of India, had a constant cultural dialogue with the surrounding towns. On the whole, however, Western religion—like Western culture—had had a very small impact on Asian life by the end of the eighteenth century.

I am sure that in the last hundred and fifty years the West has made significant contributions toward efficient administration and just government in the East. Europe has been a benefactor of the East on this score, but not before the end of the eighteenth century. During the period of expansion, the government introduced by the West to Asia was inefficient, corrupt, and grasping.

Would you discuss the parallel developments of naval armament and the voyages of expansion?

The development of naval armament was a key factor in the success of European expansion, but the reasons for this are not completely obvious. Europeans did not invent explosives or gunnery. The Turkish capture of Constantinople in 1453 was greatly assisted by artillery. On that occasion the Turks used bigger guns than had ever been manufactured in Europe. The Europeans, however, were the first to mount naval guns successfully. This occurred around the beginning of the fourteenth century in the Venetian ships used in small local wars.

Nearly all medieval ships' guns were made of iron by a process that involved forging. The gunsmith bound a number of iron rods and hammered them together; then iron hoops clamped the whole barrel together. The gun threw a small, polished stone ball weighed in ounces rather than pounds. The forged gun was never a decisive weapon on land, where much larger guns cast in one piece around a clay core were more commonly used. These were too heavy to hoist to the upper decks of a ship; they could only be moved about by teams of mules or oxen. They were used for battering fortifications (as in Constantinople) rather than armies in the field, and a few survive today.

Until about 1510, all guns mounted in ships were carried in the castle structures at the ends of the vessels. As supplements to the crossbows and small arms of the sailors, they were used against the enemy's men rather than against the hull of the enemy ship. The *Regent,* the famous combined merchantman and man-of-war commissioned by Henry VII, carried two hundred small guns. Many of them pointed inboard through small ports in the castle structure to fire into the ship's waist in the event of forced boarding. Once barricaded in the castle, the ship's company could make the waist a death-trap for boarders.

At some time early in the sixteenth century, an alloy of copper was used for the first time in gun founding. It was very difficult to melt enough iron ore at one time to cast a gun of large size, and fifteenth-century iron guns tended to be brittle because the iron was not cast at a high enough temperature. Therefore the guns had to be very thick and heavy, precluding effective use on ships. If the bore were narrowed and lightened, the gun would not withstand the successive shocks of many explosions; it was not much safer than the forged gun of the period, which tended to split along the seams. The man in front of the muzzle was often in no more danger than the man firing the gun.

The new alloys of copper, tin, and zinc brought a genuine breakthrough in shipborne gunnery. All of these metals were easily available in Europe, but not in many other parts of the world, at least not all together. Almost all the best sixteenth-century guns were made of the new bronze and brass alloys, and these almost exclusively in Europe. Guns of tapered thickness could be made, and powerful weapons could be lightened. The alloys made possible the development of guns of higher caliber; that is, greater proportion of the length of the barrel to the bore, improving range and accuracy. By the end of the sixteenth century the guns mounted on ships had a "random" range of a mile or so, and a "point-blank" range of perhaps four hundred yards.

Ship design was modified to accommodate more and more guns. As heavy cast guns began to replace the light forged ones in the early sixteenth century, they were moved out of the castles and into the main hull. Embrasures were cut in the gunwales of the upper deck, and as ships grew larger, more guns were mounted between decks. Holes were cut in the sides of the ship. By the middle of the sixteenth century these small round holes had become large square ports that could be hinged and secured against the sea. Guns could do more than fire point-blank, and gunnery had reached a stage of efficiency that was not fundamentally improved until the nineteenth century.

The ports in the side of the ship had important implications for marine design. The walls of the vessel obviously had to be strengthened to withstand the recoil of many guns. From early in the sixteenth century until the end of wooden ships, fighting vessels were almost always much bigger than any other kind. Hitherto, merchant ships had always been larger than warships. When the warship became a floating battery it was no longer suitable for cargo, and after the middle of the sixteenth century there was increasing differentiation in design between ships meant to fight and ships meant to carry.

Another effect of the specialization of the fighting ship was the elimination of the distinction between soldier and sailor on shipboard. It was no longer necessary or desirable to grapple and board an enemy ship; it was preferable to maneuver so that a whole broadside could be delivered into the enemy hull. By the end of the sixteenth century, the soldiers carried even in a big warship had dwindled to a very small number. Sailing skills in conjunction with gunnery decided sea battles. Soldiers became mainly a landing force, although they also served as a bodyguard for the officers in case of mutiny.

The social effect of the introduction of guns to seagoing people was of the greatest importance. Soldiering was the most highly respected profession in most European countries until the sixteenth century, but with the introduction of maritime gunnery on a large scale the sailor was recognized as a fighter in his own right. The sailing master was no longer a mere technician under the command of a soldier; the fighting officer had to be a good sailor in order to utilize his fire power to best advantage. One key to the relative success of various European powers at sea was the extent to which they learned this lesson. The Spanish and Portuguese were relatively conservative, for they retained the notion of two separate bodies of men on shipboard: sailors and fighters. It may be that the Iberian governments were backward in this respect because their military traditions were more deeply ingrained and their social hierarchies more rigid. The English and the Dutch were pioneers in the development of the ship as a fighting unit. This development in martial efficiency at sea had important long-range effects on the social structure of several European countries and on the history of maritime conflict.

How did the slave trade develop during the Age of Expansion?

From the very beginning of the era of expansion, even in the first half of the fifteenth century when the Portuguese vessels were making their initial explorations down the West African coast, one of the commodities most in demand and supply was slaves. The financial success of Prince Henry's voyages was largely due to the opening of the slave trade about 1440.

The Moorish invaders of the Iberian peninsula had slaves, and the African slave was a familiar figure in Christian and Muslim Spain throughout the Middle Ages. There was no prejudice against slavery, no sense of social conscience about it. I have come across little evidence that anyone in the sixteenth century had any serious doubts about the morality of purchasing African slaves. If the Spanish and Portuguese thought about it at all, they reassured themselves that the Africans had been slaves in the kingdoms of the African rulers who enslaved and sold them. Some Spanish writers even argued that by removing the slaves from their infidel masters and transferring them to the Christians, a service was done to them.

A steady flow of slaves from upper and lower Guinea began to enter Portugal in the 1440's. In the middle decades of the sixteenth century, when the Indies trade became paramount in the Iberian peninsula, the population of Seville probably was about 10 percent African slaves. Slaves were introduced into the West Indies by the Spaniards from about 1520, encouraged by the government because of the attrition of the native labor supply from smallpox and other causes. Forced labor of some sort was essential, for the Indians would neither work willingly for wage nor, as subjects of the Spanish Crown, could they be lawfully enslaved. Imported slaves worked in the gold washings and the plantations, and throughout the three centuries of Spanish empire in the Americas they were in vigorous demand as stevedores, miners, and plantation hands.

The slave trade itself was never of central economic importance to Spain, because the Spaniards never had direct access to the slave supply on the Guinea coast; they usually depended on the Portuguese, who had their own competing market in Brazil. When the English, French, and Dutch entered the Americas, they too sought to profit from the traffic in slaves, supplying their own settlements, and replacing the Portuguese as suppliers to the Spanish colonies. The eighteenth-century slave trade was a formidable operation employing a great number of ships. The agreements under which the English and the French sold slaves to Spanish America had the force of international treaties. The slave and sugar trades dovetailed, and between them gave so much employment to auxiliary trades that they comprised the most important complex of business between Europe and the Americas.

The revulsion of feeling against the trade at the end of the eighteenth century is something of a mystery. I think that emotional indignation had not been aroused earlier because the slave trade seemed so distant from those who enjoyed its profits in London and Paris. They never saw it. Indignation grew because a small group of people in European cities began to make manifest the horrors of slavery by showing manacles, whips, and the like in public places.

The trade changed in the eighteenth century, not from humanitarian pressure but economic motives. Slave labor on the plantations became less profitable as sugar prices declined. In addition, the power of the West Indian interest was diminishing as trade with North America grew more profitable than trade with the Indies. It is difficult to sort out economic and moral motivations, but each had its effect, and the success of the abolitionists was largely due to their ability to demonstrate the horrors of the trade in graphic style. Once the agitation began, it gained ground very rapidly indeed; before 1780 few people had called attention to the moral objections to the trade, but after that date there seemed to be no justification for its continued existence, except an economic necessity which grew less pressing year by year.

Would you discuss the development of piracy in this period?

The maritime rivalries of European powers throughout the world encouraged the parallel growth in numbers and sophistication both of privateers and pirates. The favorite ground of European predators was, for several centuries, the West Indies, where valuable commodities such as sugar and silver were regularly carried by merchant ships. Some of the privateers were respectable members of French, Dutch, or English society who commissioned vessels to attack Spanish shipping. By "judiciously managing" a ship, as the phrase went, English squires could counter the inflationary spiral that cut into their fixed incomes at home. The majority were not very successful, and except for unusual strokes of luck the life of a privateer was precarious and hard. Spaniard-baiting in the West Indies was dangerous and generally unprofitable, and only an exceptional man like Francis Drake could steer through its hazards to command a fortune. Many privateers in time of war turned common pirate in time of peace.

Piracy continued for such a long time in the West Indies that a tradition of violence arose in the area. It was sustained by the constant fighting among rival European powers, whose wars in the area were often fought by mercenary buccaneer ships. In the last forty years of the seventeenth century any band of cutthroats could get letters of marque from one or other colonial governor. It was not economically or logistically possible for the European governments to maintain formal fighting fleets in the West Indies; they had to resort to mercenaries. Toward the end of the century, however, first the English and then the French concluded that buccaneers were unreliable and that they tended to become a plague to all commerce. They entered into agreements to suppress the buccaneers, a move which had the effect of turning these part-cattlehunters, part-settlers, and part-pirates or privateers into full-time pirates. When they were gradually suppressed in the West Indies they sailed farther afield, and Madagascar became one of the main pirate bases of the world.

The first two decades of the eighteenth century were perhaps the most famous age of piracy as a profession, partly because the War of the Spanish Succession kept the English and French warships too busy fighting each other to fight the pirates as well; partly because still more privateers were commissioned, only to turn pirate at the peace. Later in the century the activities of the Spanish Coast Guard, who operated indiscriminately against pirates, smugglers and fair traders, and who were often no better than pirates themselves, became a *casus belli* between England and Spain in 1739.

The pirates were closely connected with the expansion of imperial activities by the European powers. None of the European nations objected if pirates plundered a commercial rival. In addition, when pirates captured a merchant vessel they sought to find the best market for its cargo, thus becoming middlemen in clandestine trade and contributing to the prosperity of many New England harbors. It was often possible for a lucky and successful pirate to buy his way back into respectable life at the end of his career—perhaps to join the Coast Guard or the Navy, or to become governor of a West Indian colony with instructions to suppress piracy.

Piracy, then, was not just a predatory activity on the fringe of ocean commerce. It was woven into the fabric of oceanic trade, and the borderline between the privateer, the pirate, and the genuine merchant captain was not at all clear.

What were the effects of the Age of Expansion upon the prosperity of the European nations?

It is never possible to work out the precise balance sheet of any colonial venture. We know that the Dutch East India Company spent a great deal more than it took in. From about the middle of the 1690's it began to build up a deficit. This, of course, was, at least ostensibly, a trading company; it is much more difficult to strike a balance for a colonial enterprise. Would Spain have been less prosperous if its economy had not depended upon imported silver from the West Indies? Even if we had all the information which was available to contemporaries, an answer would be only an informed guess.

There were some obvious success stories. The prosperity of the Brazilian sugar plantations certainly boosted the Portuguese economy in the seventeenth century, and Portugal could not have maintained the purity of its famous gold currency without Brazil. It is also true that taxation and duties from the sugar and slave trades of the West Indies contributed considerably to the financial prosperity of the English economy throughout most of the eighteenth century. I think that this ceased to be true at about the time of American independence, but the decline was not immediately recognized. Generally speaking, public opinion exaggerated the importance of colonial trade because its manifestations were socially obvious, even obtrusive. In England, the contrast between the money-baron sugar traders or the Bengal nabobs and the more conservative English landowners probably caused the public to overestimate the relative importance of colonial trades, and trades nearer home.

In fact, European trade employed more than half of English shipping in the middle of the eighteenth century. The American trades, including the West Indies, were next in total volume; third came the East Indies, followed by the Mediterranean and the Levant. Volume in all these categories was increasing in absolute terms. The eastern trade, of course, involved relatively small quantities of very expensive items (of which tea was vastly the most important), and this too gave it an exaggerated glamor and prestige.

In what ways did the expansion impinge upon the political and social thinking of the day?

Even in the late fifteenth century, Europeans were beginning to realize how small their part of the world really was. The few world travelers of this period, with their admiring descriptions of foreign countries, must even then have given Europeans something to think about. Romantic literary allusions to the outside world were frequent quite early in the Age of Expansion; Shakespeare himself was remarkably accurate in his use of sea terms, as in his account of the storm in *The Tempest*. There is a tone of wonder and fascination in the depiction of foreign islands in both *The Tempest* and *Don Quixote*. Isles of fantasy were patterned more and more upon accounts of real but equally wondrous voyages of exploration.

I do not think, however, that one can demonstrate any impact of the discoveries upon serious thought until much later. It is characteristic of a highly sophisticated and rather narrow, privileged, educated group to develop a cult of the primitive. In the second half of the eighteenth century, such a cult of the noble savage arose among the elite classes of Europe. Its influence upon political thought has, on the whole, been exaggerated. Many of the earlier Utopians—Thomas More, for example—certainly used the image of the noble, simple savage as a contrast to the sophisticated corruption of European man; but it was a literary device and not a literal attempt to describe reality.

I think that the whole complex of settlement, trade, colonization, and conquest was marginal to the life of Europe—economically, intellectually, and in every other way. While Europe had a tremendous impact upon the rest of the world, the reverse impact is much less apparent. The habit of command and the habit of empire affect ways of thought, and the introduction of large numbers of exotic commodities affects ways of life. However, I doubt whether the development of European thought was very powerfully influenced by the expansion. As late as 1817, a distinguished and well-informed historian of India could still speak of "these polished barbarians."

Were there any great contemporary historians of the Age of Expansion?

As one might expect, most of the sixteenth- and seventeenth-century historians were Spanish and—to a lesser extent—Portuguese. Many of their writings took the form of annals or eye-witness descriptions. Some writers produced prose epics to amuse, to glorify their country, and to serve as historical accounts, thoroughly mixing fact and fiction.

From the late sixteenth century through the eighteenth, massive Spanish histories were written, and many of them were of high quality. The *Decades* of Herrera is an excellent history of the Indies, commissioned by the government and based upon large volumes of official reports. Under Philip II particularly, the Spanish government demanded information about the economic, social, and administrative state of the Indies, and the reports accumulated to become the bases of massive histories. These are not for the most part reflective or interpretive; historical scholarship was still in its infancy. They are something more than annals and something less than critical histories, reflecting pride in great deeds and interest in exotic description. They also offered cautionary warnings of mistakes that ought not to be repeated. Nothing of comparable quality was written outside the Iberian peninsula at this early date; though one should not forget the work of the great editors and compilers of eyewitness accounts: Fracanzano da Montalboddo Ramusio, Hakluyt, and De Vry.

Have there been important recent changes in interpretation of the Age of Expansion?

In the last twenty or thirty years historians have learned a great deal about the details of trade and settlement, and they have become increasingly willing and able to look at the story from the non-European point of view. As more information emerges it becomes apparent, for instance, that inherent differences among European colonial powers were less significant than differences among the social, political, and economic situations that they encountered around the world. This view, expressed before, represents one recent change in historical interpretation of the Age of Expansion.

Countries that had been under European rule for a considerable time—India, for example—have become historically articulate in the last few decades, and their views have begun to affect the European view of expansion. Some Africans, too, are writing excellent analyses of the impact of Europe upon their continent. There has been a worldwide reaction against the alleged injustices and inhibitions of European colonial rule. The old notion of the complementary relationship between the capital of a highly industrialized European country and the labor force of an unindustrialized country has been challenged. The influence of European educational systems has worked as a reverse Trojan horse, since dependent peoples, or the educated among them, have learned to desire the economic and political freedom that they study. Contemporary experiences, then, have modified the historical evaluation of the colony by Europeans, and vice versa, and modern attitudes towards national independence, self-determination, democracy, and so forth, are often read back into the colonial period. This can mislead; the formulae of 1776 are not always applicable to the circumstances of twentieth-century Africa or Asia.

Has the withdrawal of European control given us a new perspective on the effects of European expansion?

Yes, I think it inevitably has affected our understanding of the entire process of colonization. Curiously, the granting of independence to former territories aroused great excitement and enthusiasm in some imperialist countries. Many people regarded the shift to native control as a challenge to European ingenuity and good will. For example, a great deal of work and money went to the territories in an attempt to create universities. Now, however, there is considerable disillusion; independence was not as simple or as rewarding as people hoped it would be. I believe the dissatisfaction is unreasonable; even the richest and most stable states in Latin America were slow to reach any political or financial equilibrium; why should Africa, for example, be expected to do better?

It is not surprising that the African ex-colonies should have to endure teething troubles. Hardly any of the newly independent countries are natural unities; they were thrown together by the accidental cricumstances of European discovery and colonization. This is not to say that the work of the colonizers should be undone, for that would be impossible. In any event, nearly all the "natural" African unities are too small to evolve as sovereign states of the Western variety. No African that I have met wishes to return to the middle of the eighteenth century; nor is there any reason why he should. The effects of European expansion—good or bad—are permanent. To achieve the Western-style states they want, Africans must transcend the linguistic and regional barriers that inhibit the growth of financial and political integrity on a national level. This is bound to be difficult and sometimes artificial. As European withdrawal and the emergence of new states continue, these processes will undoubtedly continue to enlighten historians about the significance of the Age of Expansion.

16

Iberian Civilization in the Old and New World

LEWIS HANKE

THE HISTORIOGRAPHICAL CONTEXT

The role of the Spanish and Portuguese peoples in overseas exploration, settlement, and empire building during the sixteenth century is one of the great achievements of European history, and one that has not been given its due in traditional historiography, particularly in the English-speaking world. Liberal Protestant historiography was more concerned to denigrate the Iberian achievement, when it did not ignore it, than to appreciate the magnitude of the task that the Spanish-speaking Catholics undertook and to examine dispassionately the qualities of the first important overseas European societies. Recent historiography, while not blind to moral failings of the Spanish-American empire, particularly its treatment of the native peoples and cultures, has taken a very different perspective on Iberian civilization in the Old and New World. We now recognize the political skill and military power of Spain and Portugal under Habsburg rule, and we are coming to appreciate both the governmental and cultural attainments of the Iberians in the New World. Furthermore, the disappearance of the European overseas empire in our own day has allowed historians to examine in a less partisan spirit the institutions and social structures of the Spanish- and Portuguese-American empires. In addition, twentieth-century experience with multi-racial societies and with the problems of the government and modernization of pre-industrial societies allows us to consider the history of Latin America from a fresh and highly relevant standpoint.

No scholar has done more to illuminate the history of the Spanish empire than Lewis Hanke. Born in 1905, he was Director of the Hispanic Foundation of the Library of Congress from 1939 to 1951 and Director of the Institute of Latin American Studies at the University of Texas in the following decade; since then he has been successively Professor of Latin American history at Columbia, the University of California at Irvine, and the University of Massachusetts at Amherst. Hanke's *The Spanish Struggle for Justice in America* was a pioneering, classic work on the moral and ideological aspects of the sixteenth-century Spanish empire. He has made important contributions to modern as well as earlier Latin American history. A brilliant teacher, a generous helper of younger scholars, and a warm and outgoing person, Hanke exhibits all the qualities of the best kind of academic scholar.

Chronological Outline

1492: Granada falls to the forces of Ferdinand of Aragon and Isabella of Castile, and the Moors are expelled from the Iberian Peninsula.

1495–1521: Reign of Manuel the Great in Portugal. Wealth flows in from the East Indies, and Portugal is the leading commercial nation in the West.

1516–1556: Reign of Charles I of Spain, founder of the Habsburg dynasty.

1519–1524: The Spanish conquistador Hernando Cortez subdues the Aztecs and conquers Mexico.

1532–1533: Pizarro conquers Incan Peru.

1547: Birth of Miguel de Cervantes Saavedra, author of *Don Quixote.*

1556–1598: Reign of Philip II, a fanatical Roman Catholic. The revolt of the Moriscos is severely repressed in 1571.

1567: Beginning of the prolonged struggle for independence in the Calvinist Netherlands.

c. 1575: El Greco, Greek by birth, arrives in Toledo and paints there until his death in 1614.

1580: Philip II initiates Spanish rule in Portugal. During the next sixty years Portugal is neglected, and its commerce and empire dwindle.

1588: Defeat of the Great Armada by England.

1599: Birth of Velasquez, the greatest painter of the Spanish school.

1618: Habsburg Spain becomes embroiled in the political and religious issues of the Thirty Years' War.

1640: Portugal regains its independence but is no longer a major power.

1721–1806: The era of the first serious insurrectionary movements and wars of independence in the Spanish colonies in Latin America.

1811–1825: Spanish power in Latin America is broken. Paraguay and Venezuela (1811), Chile (1818), Peru (1821), Mexico (1821), and Bolivia (1825) proclaim their independence.

Norman F. Cantor

What do you consider to be the most fruitful approach to the relationship between Iberian history and the history of Latin America?

Lewis Hanke

The best approach for an American is to stand in the New World and look at the history of the Iberian nations in Latin America. In the past, most historians have stood in Europe and studied the ideas, institutions, practices, and influences given by Europe to the New World. However, the manuscripts and publications upon which the story rests are to be found in the great centers of the New World as well as the European archives. The Archivo General de la Nación in Mexico City, the great archive in Buenos Aires, the national archive in Rio de Janeiro, and even archives in little-known towns are overflowing with material. In the sleepy little town of Sucre, in Bolivia, there is a remarkable collection of manuscript material and rare printed items on practically every aspect of the history of Spain in America. The material has been collected and organized by a Bolivian scholar with little material support from outside; he is one of the archival heroes encountered occasionally in that part of the world.

To understand Latin American history, one must go beyond the archives to appreciate what might be called the *mestizo*—the mixed race—complexion of New World history. I don't mean here the physical mixing of races, but rather that mixture of institutions and ideas which characterizes Latin American history. For example, in order to avoid manual labor in the silver mines, the Spaniards adopted an old Inca institution by which one seventh of the men in any village had to serve in the mines for a stated period of years. Thus they adapted for their own purposes an ancient local method of exploitation. The Spaniards also patterned much of their legal code in the New World after the code of the Incas. Francisco de Toledo, the greatest viceroy Spain ever sent to Peru, based his ordinances and much of his whole style of government on ancient Inca law. The mixture of men, of blood, of ideas and institutions, gives Latin American history its special flavor and meaning.

Does the history of Latin America exist as an entity—as a distinct subject?

It does in the United States and in certain other parts of the world. In Latin America they are inclined to consider all the countries together during the colonial centuries, but they see a rupture in this unity after about 1810, with the emergence of strong nationalistic feelings. After 1810 and the wars for independence, Argentine historians study Argentine history, Brazilian historians study Brazilian history, and so forth. However, a number of Latin American thinkers have recently been giving increasing attention to the problems of common background and common interest among their nations.

A certain unity is imposed upon Latin American history by the European heritage. The unifying effects of the European tongues—Portuguese in Brazil, Spanish throughout most of the rest of Latin America—can hardly be overestimated. Although the accents of the New World differ from those of the Old, the literature and history of the two worlds are parts of a total civilization which seems cohesive to me. Another important factor is the common religion. Although the number of Protestants in Latin America is increasing, and Jews have played an important part there since the sixteenth century, still the cast of civilization—the structure of society, the way people think and feel—is strongly colored by the Catholic faith. Then there is a vaguer set of circumstances concerning ways of life, how people look at things, what political theories appeal to them, and how they organize their families; all these things, I believe, were very much influenced by the European background.

The theme of revolt lends continuity to Latin American history: through the centuries, the Indians, the Negroes, and the *mestizos* have risen up against oppression. The revolutionary movements of the nineteenth century were not isolated instances; revolution seems to be endemic in Latin American history. Today there is a new kind of revolution throughout the area—a revolt against tradition. There is enormous popular sentiment against the traditional, hierarchical Spanish-Portuguese way of life. Latin Americans blame this tradition—in which the many were exploited by the few—for their difficulties in entering the modern world.

Geographically, of course, there is unity in the great area of Latin America, which stretches from the Rio Grande to the southernmost tip of South America—an area so vast that all of Europe between Madrid and Moscow could lie in Spanish America and be lost. But what gives Latin American history its special charm is the variety of responses of its separate parts to the European heritage, and this variety may derive partly from geographical considerations. Geography, of course, is not just facts about rainfall and the length of rivers. We must seek to understand what the French call human geography—the study of the total influence of environment upon man. I think it was Schopenhauer or Nietzsche who said that Latin America would never be able to struggle to its feet because nature was so overpowering there. Latin American history offers historians an excellent opportunity to compare what two similar (but slightly different) nations achieved in an enormous area under similar (but slightly different) geographical conditions.

What special problems are involved in research in Latin American history?

To begin with archives: the amount of material left in Latin America by the Spaniards (who were bureaucrats *par excellence*) is staggering. Despite the popular image of the lazy Spanish-American, I don't believe that any other empire in history was as carefully constructed as the Spanish empire. When I look through the documentary records of this great work I am both exhilarated and depressed. I am exhilarated because I can go to the archives and find out the kind of instruments—the kind of shovel, the kind of seeds—taken by a colonizing expedition to America in 1519. I can find out when the ship sailed, how many mariners were on board, what was the captain's name. But I am a little depressed by the bulk and diffusion of the material.

The Spaniards were among the most historically minded people in the world. Columbus began the tradition of writing about the New World, and everybody followed him. The Spanish Crown stimulated the writing of history. I think until the Scottish Royal Historiographer was established in the eighteenth century there was no other European nation with official chroniclers; a system of historians for Spanish America was established by Philip II in 1572. Not only that, but the Spaniards seem to have invented the questionnaire about 1569 to expedite the administration of their empire. Questionnaires were filled out by every governor in the New World and returned to the Crown. The questionnaire of 1569 included about fifty questions: the kinds of Indians in the town, their language, the prevailing winds, crops, local history, and so on. By 1601, this questionnaire had become a printed volume of three hundred pages. The royal government also commissioned ecclesiastical histories of the New World.

One can think of the historical

documentation of the empire as in two parts: the records of the central government, and the local records, which are scattered all over America in local archives. Even Paraguay (today one of the poorest and most backward nations in Latin America) has a magnificent archive. In its capital city of Asunción, founded in about 1540, there is a splendid archive with manuscripts concerning territory now in Uruguay, Brazil, Argentina, Chile, Peru, and Bolivia. One of the tendencies of historians (and I'm glad to say we are now getting away from it) has been to emphasize the work of the central government—what the Council of the Indies disposed, or what the viceroy decided. If we are going to understand the social and economic history of Latin America, we must consult local archives, including municipal records and parish registers. In the colonial period, the parish registers recorded the ethnic origins of man and wife, which is helpful in tracing the slow emergence of the *mestizo* race. When you combine the large and imposing central governmental records in Spain with the local records in America, you have a highly impressive body of historical documentation.

In dealing with all this material one must reckon with a set of prejudices. The Spanish and Portuguese tended to overemphasize and even distort what they accomplished in the New World; later on, when the Spanish-Americans and Brazilians became independent, they tended to underplay the achievements of the mother countries. Written history has been affected by these fundamental prejudices, which we describe as the *peninsular* and the *creole* attitude: the attitude of the Spaniard or Portuguese with wealth and an important office versus that of the colonial—born in the New World—for whom opportunity and riches were not so readily accessible.

In the nineteenth century, and more particularly in the twentieth, there has been an attempt to bring the Indian into Latin American history. History is usually written by conquerors—one does not find much documentation by the conquered. It is difficult to find out just what the Indian people thought of their conquerors, although anthropologists and others have made significant contributions to this question in recent years. Social scientists have made it clear that the mass of people in Latin America have not shared in Iberian civilization; indeed, one sociologist has said that at least half of the people in Latin America today make their living from the land, and that the majority of them are using instruments and methods which are no more advanced than those used by the Egyptians at the dawn of history. This may be one of those grandiloquent phrases enunciated by sociologists, but it certainly is true that life is crude in the rural provinces of Latin America. Historians have learned from social scientists to question the traditional elitist approach to Latin American history, which emphasized the dominance of Spanish institutions in the New World.

One of the major problems of historians of Latin America is economic, of course, and Latin American historians have had to struggle against their environment. In both Brazil and Spanish America the collection, decipherment, and publication of any material requires an heroic effort. There has been little government help for historians in most parts of Latin America, and historians from outside Latin America simply do not have the instruments—bibliographies, for instance—which historians of Europe or the United States take for granted. Thus we have documentary problems, problems of diverse interpretation, and a very unequal development of the apparatus of scholarship. If you are looking for problems, we have them.

What is the condition of the archives in Spain itself today?

In terms of protection and organization, they are in excellent condition. There is a great deal of material, and there are archival guides to important collections. I am thinking not only of the great archives of Seville but also of the colonial archives in Lisbon and the great national library of Madrid as well as the great collection that was formerly the king's private library. France V. Scholes and I were apparently among the first historians to go through this library fairly systematically—that was under the Republic, in 1933, when any historian could use the library. We discovered then that it held a tremendous wealth of material.

In Spain the archives are generally accessible, but in Portugal the ancient, exclusivist attitude still exists. Even back in the fifteenth century, when the Portuguese were making their great explorations and discoveries, they did not publish their materials but kept everything to themselves—and to some extent they still do. It is possible to get into the public archives if you are an historian, but to get into the private collections is very difficult.

Another aspect of the European archives is that just as Peruvian silver traveled all over the world, so the manuscripts concerning Latin America have strayed far afield. For instance, the first volume or so of the municipal records of La Paz, Bolivia, are in the British Museum! These manuscripts traveled because certain ambassadors had acquisitive instincts, or visitors saw manuscripts neglected and brought them home to be preserved, or archival material was captured by conquering armies. Nobody really knows all the reasons why manuscripts move, but they do, and Spanish manuscripts have moved a great deal.

Who are the most important historians of Spain, Portugal, and Latin America—those who have shaped our understanding of the development of Latin American civilization—and of the main historical trends and interpretations?

If I confine myself to the twentieth century, I would begin with Rafael Altamira—the man who first acquainted Spain with the need to study the history of Spanish America. After the Spanish-American War of 1898–1900, a famous generation of philosophers and thinkers speculated about what had gone wrong: Why had Spain lost the war? One explanation was the Spanish indifference to their true historical experience. Altamira established the first chair of Spanish-American history in Spain in about 1906 or 1907—rather late, considering how long Spain had been in the New World and the magnitude of the Spanish achievement there. Altamira worked hard and got his students interested, and they produced imaginative and broad-ranging studies and research projects, elevating the level of the doctoral dissertation in Spain and assuring the continuation of Altamira's work through successive generations of historians.

Altamira understood law as an integral part of the structure of Spanish life—not as a rigid external structure, but as the core of social life. He emphasized the administrative decentralization of Spain in the New World. To study the laws of the Indies and the ordinances devised by Spain to govern American political affairs, ecclesiastical affairs, mining regulations, and maritime activity was not enough: Altamira believed that one must find out how the Spanish laws were applied in the different provinces of the New World, how the different ways of life in the various provinces influenced the Spanish laws. The *encomienda,* for example—the system through which the Spanish government (from shortly after Columbus until the early eighteenth century) rewarded *conquistadores* by allowing them to exact services and tribute (not land) from a certain group of Indians—was not a uniform system throughout Spanish America. The *encomienda* in Chile was quite different from the *encomienda* in Venezuela. Only recently, during the last ten or fifteen years, have scholars in the various countries been studying local records to apply this basic concept of administrative decentralization.

Another man I admire greatly is Jaime Vicens Vives in Barcelona, who died in 1960. He was not primarily concerned with Latin America (his field was the place of his native Catalonia in the general history of Spain), but his high standard of bibliography influenced Spanish historiography. His *Index of Spanish History* was established in 1955 and has continued since his death to be the best available annotated bibliography of Spanish-American history.

It is difficult to mention any one Portuguese scholar as the leader in the study of Brazilian history. Portuguese scholars tend to look upon Brazil as only one part of their larger empire—Cabral, after all, was going to India when he happened to discover Brazil. Perhaps the name of Karl von Martius—a scientist and a foreigner—should be mentioned here. Von Martius was in Rio in 1838 when the first historical society was established in South America, and he won a prize in 1839 for his essay on how the history of Brazil should be written. Von Martius was a German—not a Portuguese or a Brazilian—but his essay seems to me the starting point of Brazilian historiography. Von Martius believed that the distinguishing characteristic of Brazilian history is the way in which the Portuguese, the Indians, and the Negroes have mixed and developed. He also emphasized the geographical dimensions and variety of Brazil, from the Amazon in the north—that river which is really a moving lake on which oceangoing vessels can travel for two thousand miles—to the southern plains, which resemble the plains near the Rio Grande.

The work of the Brazilian historian Gilberto Freyre was brought to the attention of English-speaking readers by Alfred A. Knopf in New York long before there was any boom in Latin American studies. Freyre's *The Masters and the Slaves* is perhaps the most widely read book on Brazilian history in the United States and in Europe. Freyre, I believe, gave substance to Von Martius' idea of the history of the Portuguese in Brazil as the history of the mixing of races, especially as this mixing took place on the *fazendas*—the great plantations.

We might emphasize here the importance of the *fazendas* in Brazil, especially in the northeast where sugar was raised. Like the English gentry, the Portuguese lived on the land. They controlled the people on their land in a feudal, despotic way, according to Freyre. Even the Church was subject to the master, since the priest usually was a younger son or a nephew. In this, Brazil was quite unlike Spanish America, in which the old Spanish urban tradition thrived. Spaniards were town people who established towns all over their new world, but the Brazilian gentry lived on their land.

Freyre's work gave a special character to our thinking and writing about Brazilian history. His was a broad-brush treatment (only recently has the archival and monographic history to which we are accustomed been established in Brazil) which emphasized the way in which the owners of these great *fazendas* raised large numbers of children—some legitimate and some not—and established a racial basis for Brazilian society. It should be said that Freyre developed some of his ideas on racial aspects of history while he was a graduate student at Columbia University in the early 1920's, where he studied with Giddings, the sociologist, Franz Boas, the anthropologist, and the historian James Harvey Robinson.

A third historian I should mention is Ricardo Levene of Argentina, who was both an historian and an entrepreneur of history. He taught for many years, published documents and popular histories, and it is said that even Juan Perón was one of his students. He was devoted to the care and support of the documentary archives and was able to find funds for their support, with the result that Argentina has a remarkable collection of guides to municipal and provincial archives. Another Argentinian—a contemporary of Levene's—was Emilio Ravignani, who directed the best historical review in Latin America. He also sent representatives to Spain to copy documents on every aspect of Argentine history. There is no one in Argentina today—or indeed in South America—who can compare with these men; we are still suffering from the effect of Perón and later dictatorships on the university tradition.

Mexico is another great center for history, and here I would mention particularly Silvio Zavala and Edmundo O'Gorman of the University of Mexico. These men are at opposite poles in historical interpretation, but each one has made an important contribution toward focusing ideas and publishing documents in Mexican history.

The Chilean José Toribio Medina, who almost never left Santiago, published between two and three hundred volumes of documents and bibliography. His outstanding work was bibliographical: for instance, he published eight volumes listing all the books published in Mexico in the colonial period. This was more than a mere catalogue: he made a study of each author (often based on Spanish manuscripts) and an analysis of the contents of each book. He noted where copies of each book could be found and added other useful information. Medina set up and printed his own books, with the help of his wife, and they worked day and night. I don't know of any historian or bibliographer who comes near him in accomplishment.

Today, as never before, professional historians are at work in Latin America, and they are more open to the currents of the world, more conscious of the standards of scholarship, and more determined to achieve standards which will be recognized in other parts of the world. There is even a rather interesting group of Marxist historians in Latin America. Some are mere party liners, but others are something more. I should mention Germán Carrera Damas of Caracas, the author of the monograph *The Cult of Bolívar.* This is worthy of special notice because the Spanish-Americans rejected Spain and everything to do with Spain after they won political independence, and they sought what historians call a usable past. In the nineteenth century there grew up a special emphasis on the revolutionary period and the revolutionary heroes—Simón Bolívar, José San Martín of Argentina, Morelos and Hidalgo of Mexico. This "usable past" got out of hand, to the point where supporters of San Martín as a hero didn't like Bolívar, and vice versa. When the Spaniard Salvador de Madariaga, now of Oxford, wrote about Bolívar in a patronizing, peninsular fashion, the Venezuelans rose up in wrath and even passed formal resolutions in the Academy of History in Caracas against de Madariaga and his nefarious interpretation of Bolívar. The shadow of Bolívar still hangs over every historian in Bolivarian countries—in Venezuela, you have to write first about Bolívar or you are not an historian. Carrera Damas has published some chapters from his monograph in reviews and has received angry, insulting letters, but he is going to publish his volume of Bolívar anyway, and that takes courage. Perhaps we will see the shadow of Bolívar lifted from Latin American history.

Have there been English and American historians who have made significant contributions to Iberian or Latin American history?

We must certainly mention William H. Prescott, who decided back in Boston in the early 1840's that he was going to devote his life to the story of the conquest of Mexico and the conquest of Peru. It was fortunate for the United States that there were two great historians of that era: Francis Parkman, who turned the attention of his readers to the north—to the Jesuits, to the French in Canada—and Prescott, who described the glorious exploits of the *conquistadores*. Americans were very chauvinistic in the 1850's; they were not really interested in anything except the expansion of their own continent. These men helped to mitigate the parochialism of Americans, and they were great popular writers—best sellers.

After Prescott I think of Hubert Howe Bancroft, a California businessman who produced thirty-nine volumes on the Pacific basin and collected a great library which is still the nucleus of the Bancroft Library at the University of California at Berkeley. Bancroft invented oral history back in the 1880's (long before Allan Nevins developed it), and he had people go out to interview elderly citizens who remembered the old Spanish Empire in Mexico. His work is still a valuable, connected story of the great West Coast from Alaska to Panama.

In 1895 Bernard Moses gave the first course on Spanish-American history at Berkeley, and if you believe as I do that the history of Latin American civilization should be taught—not because of the Good Neighbor Policy or because of Latin American Communism but because it is an important part of the history of mankind—then you must go back to the man who established the first course. Just before the Spanish-American War in 1898 Moses told a meeting of teachers that we must cultivate the neglected half of American history—by which he meant the part which had to do with Spain and Portugal. He pointed out that we could learn something from our enemy (this was on the eve of war), that a knowledge of Spanish culture would help us to discover that there are other civilizations than our own. In this attitude, Moses was a pioneer in this country.

Among more recent historians of Latin America I should mention Henry C. Lea of Philadelphia, who devoted much of his life to a monumental history of the Inquisition—a landmark in ecclesiastical history. Roger Merriman of Harvard wrote a four-volume work, *The Rise of the Spanish Empire in the Old World and the New,* which is still a standard work. Its first two volumes (particularly Volume I on the medieval period) are not up to the standard of the last two, particularly Volume IV, which presents a masterful synthesis of the intricacies of European diplomacy in the time of Philip II. John Elliott, the young man who has recently gone from Cambridge to the chairmanship of the history department of King's College in London, is more than just a promising member of the new generation of historians. His is the most solid work we have on the revolt of 1640 in Catalonia. We should also mention John Parry of Harvard, and Pierre Chaunu, the young French scholar who with his wife Huguette has published a nine- or ten-volume work on the economic history of Spain and Spanish America in the sixteenth and seventeenth centuries. John Lynch of the University of London has contributed to our knowledge of both Spain and Spanish America.

Can we view the history of the Iberian Peninsula and of Latin America as part of the general history of Spanish and Portuguese civilization?

I think we must. The medieval Iberian background is a vital and indispensable element of the history of Latin America. As Charles A. Bishko has emphasized in his work on the history of Spain and Portugal, the influence of these countries is a continuing influence in the modern world; for example, the greatest intellectual migration to Latin America came about as a result of the Spanish Civil War, at which time a number of important scholars, historians, and artists left Spain for the New World. I have mentioned Rafael Altamira: he was one of this group. Through the years, with or without political connections, Spaniards read the poetry and prose produced in Spanish America, Brazilians were in touch with what Portuguese were doing, and vice versa. Spain and Spanish America, Portugal and Brazil, form a cultural whole, and many Spanish-Americans and Brazilians studied in Europe and published their works in Europe.

There are changes in influence, of course. In Brazil today you will not find much sympathy for Portugal. As a matter of fact, the school headed by the historian José Honório Rodrigues believes that Brazil must develop a wholly independent foreign policy, independent of the United States and of Portugal. Increasingly, the younger scholars in Brazil are unwilling to support Portuguese policy in Africa. Thus far—or until recently—Brazil has not opposed outright any Portuguese policy, but there is a growing number of scholars who want to cut the umbilical cord. In spite of them, however, Portuguese and Spanish connections have been maintained with Brazilians and Spanish-Americans since the sixteenth century, and they are still important.

Did medieval Iberian history play a role in the history of Latin America, and what was its legacy?

Roger Bigelow Merriman made the striking statement that the history of Spain in America began in a cave in Covadonga. He meant, of course, that it began at that moment in 716 when the Spaniards first began to push back the Muslims. The famous *Reconquista* began in the cave of Covadonga in northern Spain and culminated at Granada in 1492 with the final expulsion of the Muslims. During this period Spain developed a head of missionary steam—a warlike attitude, a depreciation of Muslim culture, and an insistence on a unified, integrated culture of its own—which accounts for its warlike attitudes after 1492 and for the insistence that Moors and Jews and converts should not go to the New World. I've often wondered whether the Muslim theory of a just war with missionary connotations was absorbed by the Spaniards during the medieval period.

Medieval Iberian institutions had an important influence on the development of Latin America. We think particularly of the *encomienda,* the institution by which Indians were required to give service and tribute to certain Spaniards. The *encomienda* was developed in medieval Spain to reward those who supported the war back of the battle lines. Knights and others were given grants of land, sometimes grants of people, and (what they never got in the New World) jurisdictional power over groups of people as the battle line advanced. In America the institution was modified by American conditions and attitudes. The *encomenderos* never got jurisdictional rights because the Crown was always fearful that they would rebel so far away from royal authority and then there would be a new group of nobles to put down, just as Ferdinand and Isabella had to put down the Spanish nobles. Another medieval institution was the *residencia,* that system by which Spaniards always had a final judgment on royal officials. The viceroy had to stay at his post, and anybody who wanted to complain about him or his activities could do so. These *residencia* records became an important part of the documentation of the Spanish work in America.

In Portugal, things were not so closely organized as in Spain. The Portuguese never developed any council for Brazil comparable to the Spanish Council of the Indies. Portugal never had official historians for Brazil; they kept their activities quiet. But we are told by Gilberto Freyre that during the medieval period Portugal developed a certain kind of toleration which gave a special note to Brazilian history. There was a favorable attitude toward mixing with people of different color because for a while Muslims of different color had been the lords in Portugal, and during the medieval period dark-colored women came to be preferred over others. Freyre says that the racial democracy of Brazil had its origins in the mixing of peoples in Portugal under special conditions in the Middle Ages. Today anthropologists and others insist that the "racial democracy" of Brazil must be closely examined, and some of our anthropologists do not share Freyre's rhapsodic view of the situation in Brazil. However, it is obvious to anyone who has visited Brazil that there is a special kind of relationship between the races there, and Freyre and others say that this goes back to the medieval period.

What was the structure of government and society in the Iberian peninsula at the end of the fifteenth century?

Ferdinand and Isabella were firmly in control at the end of the fifteenth century, and Spain was ready for empire. The king and queen had put down the rebellious nobles; Spain had developed legal institutions under lawyer-type officers loyal to the Crown; it had a unified, hierarchical social structure. In August 1492, Columbus set forth from Palos in southwestern Spain, and in April of that year Granada fell to Spain, liberating the military and ecclesiastical forces for use in the New World. A third important event of 1492 was the publication of Antonio de Nebrija's *Grammática Española,* the first organized grammar of any European language. When it was presented to Queen Isabella, she said, "What's this book good for?" and one of her courtiers is supposed to have replied: "Sire, language is the instrument of empire." At the very moment, then, when Spain had a unified monarchy, its nobles in order, and its Church under the domination of the Crown, the Spanish language was developed as an instrument of colonization. The Spanish empire exists still wherever Spanish is spoken—wherever people are influenced by the art and philosophy which come to them through the Spanish language.

Sixteenth-century Spaniards also made an unprecedented attempt to study other languages and other cultures. When Nebrija's pupils got to the New World they threw themselves into studying its languages because they realized they could not convert Indians unless they could reach them in their own tongues. The vocabularies and grammars of the Indian languages prepared by Spanish priests—mostly in the sixteenth century—comprise a great corpus of philological material. Bear in mind the great variety of Indians in the New World: a modern anthropologist has said that even today, more separate languages are spoken by the Indians in an area of fifty square miles around the Isthmus of Tehuantepec in Mexico than in all of Africa south of the Sahara.

Not as much is known about Portugal in 1500; the heroic figure of Prince

Henry the Navigator has overshadowed the study of the late medieval period. However, the situation is similar to that of Spain in that Portugal was an expanding nation, ready to take on new activities. In Portugal as well as Spain there had been a reform movement in the Church and the monasteries in the latter part of the fifteenth century, and the young friars who went out to the New World were influenced by reforming zeal as well as Nebrija's linguistic rules.

I would like to ask one question here: Why was there such a desperate effort to Christianize the Indians and not the Negroes? Missionary work went on among the Indians during the 1520's and 1530's, and the forties and fifties, when Luther had split Europe asunder. Contemporary writers pointed out that Cortez and Luther were supposed to have been born in the same year—one, they said, to split Christendom apart, and the other to make possible the development of a New Jerusalem with no troublesome Protestants. All this would come about if they could speak to the Indians and make them Christians. There was a passionate and very well organized ecclesiastical movement to win over the Indians so that the seamless web of Christendom could be woven again in the New World.

The missionaries did not only learn languages in the New World; they also studied Indian cultures. The first modern anthropologists were Spanish friars. The greatest of them was Bernardino de Sahagún, whose impressive work was written in the Aztec language in the sixteenth century and is just now being made known to the English-speaking public. Sahagún decided that in order to Christianize the Indians he needed to know everything about them—their feasts, their educational methods, their gods, everything—and he spent two years in one Indian village and then went on to another, questioning everything. This was the greatest concerted, organized effort up to that time to learn about the culture of another people.

What are the differences between Spanish and Portuguese colonies with respect to the pattern of settlement and government?

We must remember, first of all, that Brazil was never the center of the Portuguese empire as Spanish America was the center of Spain's; it was always, to some extent, a marginal land—even after sugar was developed in the seventeenth century and gold was discovered in the late seventeenth and eighteenth. Second, Portugal was never as administrative-minded as Spain. Portugal did not establish a Council to the Indies until the period between 1580 (when Philip II took over Portugal and its dominions) and 1640 (when the Portuguese were "liberated" from Spain). For those sixty years Portugal and Brazil were dominated by Spain, and there was an attempt by the bureaucratic Spaniards to organize Portuguese imperial institutions. They got them to organize a Council to India (which included Brazil) but there was never the same kind of corpus of laws and ordinances for Brazil that there was for Spanish America.

Patterns of settlement were dissimilar, too. In the early years the Portuguese gave great quantities of land to important Portuguese, but this was done only very rarely by the Spaniards. True to their administrative genius, Spain had from the very earliest days a carefully devised set of ordinances for every town. Shortly after Cortez conquered Mexico City, while the ruins of the ancient Indian capital were still smoking, a geometer walked in the ruins and laid out the avenues of Mexico City. The great law of 1573 provided a very careful plan for the settlement of towns in the New World. The land had to be high enough to avoid disease; the streets to be laid out in such a way that the winds would blow through properly; the plaza to be big enough to hold a bullfight or a procession. The church was to be on a certain side of the plaza, the town council on another. Everything was regulated in Spanish America; in Brazil, not at all. The streets go every which way, like those of medieval towns. The Portuguese stayed out on their *fazendas* with their slaves and their large, loosely organized families; they visited the towns only occasionally and took little pride or interest in them.

Moreover, no books were printed in Brazil during the whole of the colonial period. Think of the hundreds, the thousands, of Spanish publications which José Toribio Medina located and recorded in his great bibliographies. There was nothing like that in Brazil, nor was any university founded there, although the University of Mexico and the University of San Marcos in Lima were established by royal order in 1551. The Portuguese were not even much interested in keeping their new land free of heresy. They did not extend the Inquisition to Brazil, and many Jews and others went to the New World. When you compare the Spanish work in Spanish America to the Portuguese work in Brazil, you see that despite the common heritage—in religion, in institutions, and in medieval background—there were enormous differences in the organization of the empires.

What was the impact of America on the Iberian states and societies in the sixteenth and seventeenth centuries?

Ever since the publication of Earl J. Hamilton's classic work of thirty years ago on the rise of prices, we have known that inflation was an important effect of the influx of silver and gold into Spain and other parts of Europe. Although Hamilton's work has been criticized in recent years, I tend to believe that no one as yet has shaken Hamilton's basic thesis. The new wealth also gave to the kings of Spain a remarkable degree of independence from their parliament. In this period parliaments in certain countries were becoming more restrictive of the Crown, but not in Spain or Portugal. The money from the New World may not have been as important in percentage as people once believed, but still it was free money. The Crown got one fifth (the royal *quinto*) of all the silver and gold from America, and the king could dispose of this as he saw fit. The outstanding economic historian of Spain, Ramón Carande, whose fundamental work on Charles V and his bankers is one of the notable economic works of this century, has said that the king actually got more money from parliament and from the Church than from the New World. Even so, he did not have to ask for the new money, and he could spend it as he liked—against the Protestants, the Turks, the French—which gave the Spanish Crown a special dimension of independence or irresponsibility.

The influence of America on Europe is a difficult subject; it has not been sufficiently studied to draw any far-reaching conclusions. The newly rich Americans who came home and built imposing houses or churches in small villages (these are still visible today) must have had an effect on Iberian *mores,* but we have no documentation. New World themes were not much used in art, surprisingly; one would expect that the dramatic nature of the conquest and the new wealth would have been expressed in artistic motifs. On the whole, this is a subject on which we need more investigation.

Looking at the sixteenth and seventeenth centuries as a whole, how did the Iberian peoples deal with the problems arising from multiracial societies?

Very few women accompanied the *conquistadores* in the first years of the sixteenth century; the conditions of life were too hard. Thus there was mixing from the beginning between Spaniards and Indian women—we have good records on this. We know also that there was a Spanish policy in the early years of marriage to the daughters of Indian *caciques* (chieftains) so that the Spaniards would win property and position through marriage. In Peru we find the same thing—some of the Spaniards married Inca princesses. Some of them lived with Indian women and did not marry them; back in the early part of the sixteenth century we find an ambivalent attitude toward marriage. As the years went by, many children were born of mixed marriages and many more were born illegitimate, and there grew up a group of *mestizos* who were looked down upon for their illegitimacy. Often their fathers left and the Indian mother had to bring up the child alone. Some attempts were made to help them—the Crown established a special school for *mestizo* orphans—but there was growing prejudice, too, to the point where *mestizos* were not able to get important government positions and generally were not allowed to enter the religious orders. Salvador de Madariaga believes that part of the turbulence of the New World is derived from the resentment of the *mestizos* toward their white fathers. Mixing went on through the whole colonial period, and the *mestizo* society grew proportionately larger as many Indians died of disease and overwork. In the eighteenth century, despite some liberal regulations and a few changes, it was increasingly difficult for an Indian or a Negro to get a position or to go to a university.

The Spanish-American Indians had notable defenders, beginning with Bartolomé de Las Casas, the Dominican friar who attempted to protect their lives and property from the Spaniards. In Portuguese Brazil there was no great struggle on behalf of the Indians except when António Vieira, a Jesuit and one of the great figures of the seventeenth century, worked on their behalf. He was a great preacher and a diplomat of considerable power in Europe, and he had ideas on developing the Portuguese economy by incorporating *conversos* (new Christians) into Portuguese life. He opposed the Inquisition and defended the Indians, but not the Negroes.

One of the great mysteries of history is why the conscience of the Spaniards and Portuguese twinged more easily on behalf of the Indians than that of the Negroes. One explanation is that the Iberians had been accustomed to Negro slaves in Europe, and their consciences had thus been blunted. Also there was the tremendous desire of the priests to win the Indians for Christianity in order to build a new Jerusalem without Protestants.

In the seventeenth century there were two or three interesting Jesuit defenders of the Negroes, but they were not battlers like Las Casas. One was Alonso de Sandoval, who pointed out that some of the Negro slaves were Muslims who could read and write Arabic and were intellectually superior to their masters. He pointed out that they came from different cultures, different tribes, different parts of Africa, and he advocated the establishment of a school to study African culture. Sandoval was the first Africanist, but neither he nor any other Jesuit defender of the Negroes intended that they should be freed. They believed that the Spaniards should treat the slaves justly and kindly, that they should be Christianized, but that was all. This was not at all the idea expressed by Las Casas in 1550 when he said at Valladolid that all the people of the world are men, and opposed the Aristotelian doctrine of natural slavery. Valladolid was one of the great moments of Western history, but a new atmosphere took over in the seventeenth century. The sixteenth century was a great period of expansion, when all kinds of ideas were expressed and all kinds of hope appeared. The seventeenth century settled down to what some historians call the colonial siesta, but all through these centuries the quiet revolution of blood relationship continued, making Latin America the social and economically turbulent part of the world it is today.

What is the general significance of the year 1550 for the history of Iberian civilization?

The disputation in 1550 and 1551 between the Spanish Dominican Bartolomé de Las Casas and the Spanish Renaissance scholar Juan Ginés de Sepúlveda was one of the great moments in the history of mankind. It illustrates the influence of events in America upon the course of affairs in Europe and in the world. The dissertation was held because the king and his council had received various letters charging that the Spaniards were cruel and unjust in their conquest, and the council decreed in 1549 that conquest must cease until the king and his advisors could determine whether or not this was true. Some of the greatest theologians and legal experts of the time sat on the commission. Unfortunately we do not have the exact voting record of the members, but we do have the basic documentation: the statements by Las Casas and Sepúlveda—both very long-winded. Sepúlveda, trained in Renaissance studies, had studied at Bologna with the great Aristotelian scholar Pomponazzi. He maintained that the Indians were natural slaves—that they should be treated well but that they could not escape from their status—and he used all the authority of Aristotle to support his views. Las Casas, who had at that time about half a century of experience in the New World, said there was no reason why a Christian nation should adopt such a doctrine. He argued that just conquest could be carried on only by Christian principles. No formal vote was taken—apparently it was a close and very touchy decision—but after a while the conquests were resumed. However, the famous law of 1573—the ordinance which governed Spanish conquest for the rest of the colonial period—expressed Las Casas' principles: namely, that peaceful means should be employed and force used only as a last resort. Embedded in the ordinance is a kind of apology or justification: the Spanish were ordered to explain to the Indians all the benefits of Spanish rule and to tell them what Spain had accomplished in bringing seeds, animals, plants, and—above all—Christianity and civilization to the Indians. These ideas have been ringing down through history ever since.

In one marvelous passage Las Casas said that all the people of the world are men, that no one is born enlightened, that all of us must learn from those who have gone before. Everyone could become a civilized, Christian being, and he emphasized education and religion as methods of bringing all the people of the world into civilized life. Here I think there is a similarity between the mid-sixteenth century and the mid-twentieth, when the revolution in transportation and communication produced another era when large numbers of people were suddenly confronted with others of very different religion, background, color, and *mores*. In our own day this brought about another dispute about the essential nature of man, and Las Casas' arguments cropped up again in the discussion over the United Nations' Declaration of the Rights of Man. The debate of 1550 appears to have a special relevance for us today.

What was the role of the Church in sixteenth- and seventeenth-century Spanish culture and society; particularly, what was the place of the friars and of the Inquisition?

The Church was one of the fundamental institutions of Spain and Spanish-America, Portugal and Brazil. I would like to distinguish between two periods: the early, expansive period up to about 1570, when the orders were given carte blanche to go to the New World and bring the Indians into the fold. At the same time the Crown acquired through various royal patronage bulls enormous power over the Church—over appointments, the collection of revenues, and so on. The peculiar relationship between the church and the state in Spain and Portugal is illustrated by the famous bull *Sublimis Deus,* issued by Paul III in 1537 because there had been complaints from friars in America of cruelty to Indians. Paul said in this bull Indians were rational beings with souls, that their property and lives must be respected, and they must be Christianized. The bull, of course, embodies standard Christian doctrine, but it was not sent immediately to the New World. Every bull that went to America from Rome had to go through Spain and to be approved by Charles V, and in order to show his authority he held up the bull —even though he subscribed to its essential doctrine—because he had not himself initiated or approved of it.

There was a great change in about 1570. The Crown turned the screws of royal control a little tighter; the Spanish government insisted that the Indians were largely Christianized (although in fact they were not); and the great period of ecclesiastical expansion was over. The king put the friars under the authority of the bishops, curtailing their independence and submitting them thus to royal authority also. Before 1570, the friars were the ecclesiastical *conquistadores* who went into the New World and accomplished marvels—we're told that two Franciscans baptized fourteen thousand Indians in one day in 1530. After 1570, the bishops were in charge and the friars were curbed.

The Church still had an important role in nonecclesiastical activities and institutions—hospitals, for example, and universities. Many of the outstanding professors were priests. The Jesuits were famous, too, for their pharmaceutical work; they prepared drugs for the missionaries and introduced European drugs to America and American drugs to Europe. Here again there was profitable interaction between the two worlds. Ferdinand and Isabella found that churchmen were among their most loyal administrative officers, and they occupied many important positions even up to that of viceroy.

As the years went on, the ecclesiastical, missionary zeal of the churchmen diminished and they became important landowners and slaveholders—they became the capitalists of the new society, the people who had money to lend. The Church became a powerful economic institution, but it remained still a powerful ecclesiastical institution which performed many services for society. The churchmen were the historians of the New World; they had no family responsibilities and could devote long periods of time to research and writing. They carried on the literary traditions of Spain and Portugal, producing poems, novels, and histories as well as useful chronicles of colonial life. The Church was a multifaceted institution, and although it is possible to criticize it very severely for its conservatism and economic position, one must recognize that churchmen were also the preservers and carriers of civilization, just as they had been in Europe in the Middle Ages.

As for the Inquisition, that had an interesting and separate history in the New World. As I've mentioned, the Portuguese did not extend the Inquisition to Brazil, so there was a more open situation there than in Spanish America, where from the beginning there was one big problem: were Indians subject to the Inquisition? One of the early inquisitors hauled an Indian to the Inquisition about 1531 and—I believe—burned him. This was attacked by the authorities, and finally it was decided that Indians, being new Christians, should not be subject to the Inquisition. This was a great victory for toleration, in a way, and after 1570 no Indians were brought before the Inquisition.

The victims of the Inquisition, for the most part (and here we depend on the documentation provided by Medina), were the usual kind of heretics—poor Christians—or they were foreigners, or the so-called Portuguese Jews who arrived in the New World during the period of Spanish rule over Portugal between 1580 and 1640. Throughout the whole colonial period, the Inquisition in the New World was not at all the powerful institution that it was in Spain. In the eighteenth century it became more than ever a political instrument to keep out the works of the philosophers (Rousseau and others) who were deemed to be dangerous or critical of monarchy—but as in the case of many other laws in the New World, these rules were not always enforced. The Inquisition was another European institution with a special development in America because of the special conditions and circumstances there.

Would you attempt a general assessment of the favorable and unfavorable characteristics of Spanish rule in America? It has been portrayed as one of the greatest achievements of human government, and also as one of the darkest periods of history.

This is a subject on which volumes have been written. It can be summarized briefly as the white legend versus the black legend, and the conflict between those who defend Spain and Portugal in America and those who denounce them is a permanent part of our historiography. It is difficult to make any meaningful remarks in such a brief compass, but we must distinguish among the centuries and between Spain and Portugal. There was no monolithic "Spanish (or Portuguese) rule" in America; there was administrative decentralization, and no common denominator can be applied to all parts of the vast territory of empire.

Moreover, although the Spanish laws may have been very strict and very detailed, they were not always enforced. One of the phrases quoted by people who denounce Spain is *obedézcase pero no se cumpla*—"let this law be obeyed but not enforced." The true meaning of this concept has been distorted, and it has medieval precedents which are not always recognized. In the Middle Ages it was used to prevent a law devised for one situation from being applied automatically to another. Spanish-American viceroys used it not to challenge the royal authority but to delay in enforcing an unacceptable law until they had an opportunity to appeal to the authority and present their arguments. Every modern judicial system acknowledges the right of appeal through certain processes.

The conflicting interpretations of the famous New Laws of 1542 exemplify this concept as well as the controversy between those who support Spanish rule and those who decry it. In 1542, as a result of a powerful propaganda effort by Las Casas and other friars, Charles V and the Council of the Indies were prevailed upon to pass a series of laws known as the New Laws. Their essential elements were (1) that no new *encomiendas* were to be granted; and when the Spaniards who held the Indians died, those Indians were to be put under the protection of the Crown; (2) that Indians were to be taken away from those who mistreated them; (3) that royal officials could not legally own Indians. A tremendous controversy resulted, and in 1545, after another propaganda campaign by those who wanted to keep the *encomienda,* some of these basic laws were abolished—an important reversal. The viceroy of Mexico and New Spain believed that these were unwise laws

—certainly those Spaniards to whom they applied found them unacceptable. Fearing that the laws would lead to revolution, the viceroy suspended them; he obeyed them, yes, but he did not enforce them until he had a chance to report back to Spain and point out their disadvantages. The viceroy of Peru, on the other hand, enforced the law and took Indians away from their owners. Peru was much less civilized than Mexico; it was a turbulent land with a civil war raging, and the viceroy was captured and executed. One of the famous old rebel captains, Francisco Carbajal, put the viceroy's head on a string and carried it up and down the Andes as a symbol of disdain for royal authority. Faced with threatened revolution in Mexico and actual war in Peru, the Crown and the Council of the Indies took another look at the New Laws and abolished some of the least popular.

The actions of Spain have been the subject of a tremendous propaganda campaign since the early sixteenth century. Las Casas himself, toward the end of his life, wrote several treatises designed to persuade the king and the Council of his point of view. These were seized at once by political enemies of Spain and translated into Flemish, English, Italian, Latin, German, and Dutch. The editions illustrated by Theodore De Bry are worth far more than a thousand words: they show Indian women killing their children because they did not want to have a Spanish child; they show Spaniards killing Indians, setting dogs upon them; they show Indians committing suicide in preference to living in a Spanish civilization. These pictures carried all over Europe the idea that the cruel Spaniards were killing, indiscriminately and in the most unchristian way, the mild savages of the New World. They were the single most powerful element in the creation of the widespread idea that Spaniards are essentially a cruel people, and we still find this idea embedded in the emotional consciousness of English-speaking peoples.

No one who studies the actions of Spain and Portugal in America will defend all of them; there is no need for such a defense. We try to understand them in order to describe them honestly, and we must think first what Spain and Portugal were like themselves during the colonial period. The European nations have been criticized for failing to introduce the Enlightenment to Latin America or to develop science there, but they could not introduce what they did not have. I regard the struggle for justice in Spanish America, even though it frequently failed, as the first confrontation between European people and a large mass of people of a different color and different religion. If Spain produced a Sepúlveda—a scholar who used his learning to apply the Aristotelian doctrine of natural slavery to the Indians—it also produced a Las Casas, who was bold enough to say, "This is unchristian. This is not what Spaniards should do. You should not use force." Spain produced both these men, and if you examine the history of Spain in America you must look at both sides of the coin: the cruel *conquistador* and the Christian priest. Both represent authentic reflections of the Spanish spirit and character. This question cannot be conclusively answered, but I believe that if you study the history of Spain and Portugal in America you will find that their problems were much like those we are facing today. In questions of racial tension and social justice, it is hard to say that we have done very much better in this century.

May we consider the supposed decline of Spain in the seventeenth century? Was this just a political and military decline, or did it involve fundamental economic, social, and cultural matters? Did the burden of ruling an empire contribute to the decline of Spanish power, and how was America affected by it?

The decline of Spain is one of the great historical problems, and we must distinguish first of all between real and apparent decline. Modern historians see a decline in the seventeenth century, but contemporaries did not perceive it at all—for them, Spain remained a powerful (and widely hated) nation. One basic element of the decline was made clear to us in Earl J. Hamilton's detailed, statistical studies of the price revolution following the great influx of New World silver. Another element was the slow decline of Spain's administrative capacity. The outstanding rulers of sixteenth-century Spain—Charles V and Philip II—were great administrators by any standard, and they rode the waves of European history as none of their successors were able to do. Perhaps another element was the lack of a challenge after the sixteenth century, that great period when Spain was at the center of the European world for the first time in history. It was the home of the greatest empire of its time, developing new institutions and adapting medieval institutions to the needs of the New World. This may have been related to the cultural coming-of-age of Spain; printing was introduced in the late fifteenth century, and the debates of the sixteenth century were conducted in print.

In the seventeenth century Spain was suffering from the long, corrosive effect of the rise in prices and the resulting social and economic disequilibrium, and the rulers of Spain could no longer meet the problems of Spain. Too, the rising monarchies of Europe gave increasing competition just when Spain had fewer resources with which to meet its challengers. In the eighteenth century the Bourbon monarchs brought some of the French administrative ability to Spain, and much was done to tighten the imperial administration. French institutions such as the intendant system were adapted to the needs of the New World. They strengthened the defenses of the northern frontier of Mexico against the English, improved the colonial administration, and arranged for scientific experts or technical advisers to visit American mines. However, this period was not comparable to the sixteenth century because the Crown itself was weak (except for Charles III), and the empire lacked a central core of strong administrative authority.

In this period, problems became so complicated and the administrative apparatus so involved that continual confusion and red tape produced a kind of paralysis, a slowdown in all the operations of the empire. For example, production at the great silver mining center at Potosí in Peru went down steadily in the eighteenth century, partly because no one in authority had sufficient energy to confront the problem. Thus the great influx of silver which influenced prices in the sixteenth century diminished, the foreign experts were unable to halt the decline, and the imperial bureaucracy was too vast and complicated to work decisively or effectively.

I tend to agree with Hamilton that the emphasis on the role of the Inquisition and of censorship has been exaggerated. Hamilton said that there were certain economic attitudes, institutions, and prejudices which helped to undermine Spain over the long pull of the seventeenth and eighteenth centuries, and that these might help to explain her decline. As we look back now we can see that no empire can exist through a long period of time without undergoing tremendous changes, and of course great changes did take place in the eighteenth century, including the opening up of the intellectual life, the quickening of trade, and the appearance of the United States to the north. Remember that at the very end of the Spanish empire—after 1800—Yankee merchants and Yankee skippers were in

Buenos Aires, off Chile, in Peru, and in Mexico. A combination of European and North American influences combined with the basic situation in Spain to bring about the Spanish decline.

What was the impact of the Enlightenment on Spain and Latin America?

Here's another interesting example of the way in which a European movement affected the New World. Intellectual currents did travel across the Atlantic: some of the writings of Rousseau and other French philosophers and English philosophers came into Latin America, so far as we can tell from lists of books from libraries and from the records of the Inquisition. However, the improvement of agriculture was an important part of the Enlightenment in Spain, but this was not carried across the ocean. The cultivation of tobacco and sugar and wheat went along just as it had for generations.

In mining, some of the new chemical and physical methods of developing silver and gold were applied in the New World. In New Spain and Mexico there was established a school called by Alexander von Humboldt (perhaps the most alert and knowledgeable European traveler ever to come to the New World) declared to be the equal of anything in Europe. He also praised the school of fine arts, but not the state of agriculture. Again, a European movement had a different development when it reached the New World.

To what extent is 1810 a dividing line in the history of Latin America? What is the relationship between the colonial period and the modern period?

Despite the arbitrariness of choosing any one date as a dividing line, I think 1810 is still significant in the political history of Latin America. It was a watershed: the time at which Spanish-Americans became conscious of themselves as different from the Old World. Because of the Napoleonic invasion of Spain and Portugal, the mother countries were in such a tumultuous situation that it was possible then for the New World to hope for real change.

How much actual change took place in the period of revolution and independence between 1810 and 1830? We must recognize that no tremendous series of social and economic changes took place as was the case in the English colonies. On the other hand, slavery was abolished in many countries—Indian slavery at least, and sometimes Negro slavery. There was a desire to throw off the racial distinctions and laws relating to racial matters which had become increasingly important in the eighteenth century.

Economically, there was great destruction, first of all. In Venezuela, we're told, about half of the male population between eighteen and fifty years of age was lost between 1810 and 1830, and in other parts of Latin America there was considerable loss of lives and property. All the ports were opened to foreign influences. British merchants and American sailors came; American ships and American goods came; there was foreign investment. The British, in particular, had naïve ideas about the money they were going to make from these newly opened nations, and there was a fever of speculation. British capital was available for almost every kind of enterprise. Some of their projects were conceived without knowledge of the realities of Latin America, and many British investors lost their shirts.

The opening of Latin America to economic influence produced an intellectual opening. Groups of scientists and artists visited Brazil, Mexico, Chile—some of our best representations of Latin America in the 1830's and 1840's came from European scholars. I mentioned before that the German Karl von Martius developed the basic interpretation of Brazilian history.

At this point perhaps I should say that we are now very conscious of the special place of Brazilian history in the whole range of Latin American studies. In times past, most of us learned Spanish rather than Portuguese and studied Spanish America rather than Brazil, but today Brazilian history is considered an integral part of Latin American history and its subtle and interesting differences are recognized. For example, the Brazilians are proud that they are not men of force and action; they consider themselves to be men of peace, who have achieved social and political ends by persuasion. The Brazilian revolution was a primarily peaceful transfer of power from one group to another, in contrast to the bloody wars of Spanish America.

The period 1810–30 was one of great change in some respects—economically, politically, culturally—but historians now realize that many of the institutions, ideas, and practices of the colonial period endured. Even with the abrogation of the oppressive Spanish laws, the Indians were no better off under the new regimes. In some respects they were worse off without the protective laws of Spain. The wealthy, powerful Creoles who supplanted the wealthy, powerful peninsular Spaniards oppressed the Indians even more than the Spanish colonials.

Even with new ideas from Europe, there were no great intellectual changes. During the revolutionary period there was a feeling that the Church had been an oppressive part of the old colonial regime, that it was too powerful economically and should be reformed. In Peru there were some forward-looking priests—their lives and activities are just now being studied—who proposed a modern Church: a poor Church, with married clergy and a concern for the poor. Their proposals were struck down by Rome and were not raised again until Vatican II. The new ideas were forgotten, and the Latin American Church kept the position it had held in the colonial period. It was a political-economic power, a wealthy institution allied to the interests of those in power, with no concern for the people. One of the first things the Mexican revolutionaries of 1910 did was to strike at the Church.

Thus although there were changes after 1810 there were also continuities, such as the exploitation of the Indians and the power of the Church as a bulwark of conservatism. The period between 1810 and 1830 is being re-evaluated by historians.

What is the importance of the study of Latin American history today in the light of the contemporary world and contemporary problems?

I think we are beginning to see Latin America as a kind of microcosm of the problems of development everywhere. Today, when problems of development and underdevelopment are so much in our minds with respect to the new nations of Asia and Africa and the Near East, we look on Latin American history after 1810 as a long story of the struggle for development. Various nations which never before manifested any special interest in Latin America are now studying Latin American history and affairs; these are no longer regarded as marginal matters cultivated by a few dedicated individuals.

We see now that the problems which Latin America has faced since the sixteenth century are the fundamental problems: how do you educate a great mass of illiterate people; how do you develop the agricultural potentialities of an area where there has been no real progress for centuries? The problems faced by Spain and Portugal as expanding nations of the sixteenth century are world problems, best expressed in the 1550 dissertation between Las Casas and Sepúlveda. Their arguments are now fundamental parts of such works as the contemporary civilization course at Columbia University, where the great problems of the world are presented to our students.

Latin America is no longer on the periphery of the world. It is a large, varied kind of laboratory, in which over a great expanse of territory and throughout four centuries of history men have faced many of the problems and circumstances now being faced by other nations in their struggles to enter the modern world. The study of Latin American affairs has challenged the interest of scholars in many lands, and it seems to me that this wide interest cannot help but enrich our studies.

17

The Scientific Revolution

A. R. HALL

THE HISTORIOGRAPHICAL CONTEXT

The past quarter century has seen the full emergence of a whole new historical field—the history of science. This development accords with the general historiographical tendency of modes of historical thinking to respond to contemporary concerns. It has become increasingly clear that it was modern science, making its initial breakthrough in the New Physics of the seventeenth century, and the later application of science to industrial and military technology, that separated Western culture so sharply from other civilizations and gave Europe the power and wealth to achieve its hegemony over East Asia and Africa in the nineteenth century. Consequently, no subject in European history appears from the present standpoint to have been more significant than the Scientific Revolution.

Inevitably, two approaches to the history of science have appeared. One is a strictly intellectual history of science, which examines the work of the great scientists and the development of scientific ideas in and for themselves. The other approach follows a social interpretation that tries to relate scientific ideas to other aspects of contemporary culture and to changes in economy, class structure, and politics. The latter approach, in the long run the most fruitful and necessary, as yet has received only minimal consideration and has not yet been pursued by a master scholar. The first approach has been intensively followed by several historians of the first rank, and the literature in this field is an impressive one.

Among the leading scholars in the intellectual history of early modern science is A. Rupert Hall, Professor of the History of Science and Technology at the Imperial College of Science and Technology, University of London. An Englishman born in 1920, Hall is married to Mary Boas, a leading American scholar in the same field; together they make a formidable research team, and have separately and together published several important studies of facets of the scientific revolution. In his more recent work, Hall has exhibited an increasing interest in the social history of science and in the personality of seventeenth-century scientists, particularly Sir Isaac Newton. Hall is typical of the postwar generation of English historians—very industrious, highly professional, generous to students and colleagues, open-minded and free from establishmentarian snobbery, outspoken and clear-headed.

Chronological Outline

1452–1519: Leonardo da Vinci, inventor and artist.

1473–1543: Copernicus speculates that the earth and all the planets revolve around the sun and stands the Christian Ptolemaic universe on its head.

1543: Vesalius, the father of modern anatomy, publishes his *On the Structure of the Human Body.*

1564–1642: Galileo invents the telescope and discovers the moons of Jupiter in 1610.

1571–1630: Kepler, a Copernican, shows that the paths of the planets are elliptical rather than circular and theorizes about other natural mathematic relations of the universe.

1596–1650: René Descartes develops analytic geometry.

1600: William Gilbert, an early English Copernican, publishes his *De Magnete* and founds magnetism as field of physics.

1614: John Napier, a Scotsman, invents logarithms.

1616–1642: The persecution of Galileo by the Inquisition, which keeps all of the works of the Copernican astronomers on the prohibited *Index* until 1835, marks the clerical reaction to scientific discoveries which is part of the prevalent religious fanaticism.

1620: Francis Bacon, English statesman and philosopher, publishes his *New Organon,* which outlines the principles of the new inductive method of scientific investigation and documents the flaws of the Aristotelian system of scholastic logic.

1628: William Harvey, heir to Vesalius' advances in anatomy, publishes his *On the Motion of the Heart and Blood in Animals.*

1632–1723: The Dutch inventor of the microscope, Antony van Leeuwenhoek.

1657–1666: The founding of the first scientific academies—the Florentine Academy of Experiment (1657), the Royal Society (1662), and the Académie des Sciences (1666).

c. 1661: Robert Boyle, the father of chemistry, formulates a law (Boyle's Law) governing the behavior of gases.

c. 1675: Isaac Newton and Gottfried Leibnitz, working independently of each other, discover infinitesimal calculus.

1687: Newton's *Mathematical Principles of Natural Philosophy* explains and vindicates Kepler's laws and Galileo's observations in an overall theory of gravitation and a mathematical universe.

Norman F. Cantor

Fourteen years ago, you published what has been regarded as a definitive study of the scientific revolution. We might begin by discussing whether recent scholarship has suggested new approaches, and what you think of your study now.

A. R. Hall

A great deal changes in fourteen years. One learns from other people, directly and indirectly: what others write about the nineteenth century can influence one's own ideas about the seventeenth. Certainly what others write about the Middle Ages (as you know, a very active field during the last fourteen years) can influence one's ideas on the origin of modern science. If I were to write a new book called *The Scientific Revolution from 1500 to 1800,* I don't think I would end up with the same volume at all—I'm sure that its plan and structure would be quite different. I am not rejecting my own book: I still ask my students to read it, and I am pleased when other students find it useful. But one does not want to go over the same ground twice, and if I were doing the book now it would be very different. Some parts of it, I think, are exceptionally good; other parts I did not know enough about, and there was not adequate material at that time. The situation has improved a great deal in the last fourteen years, and I hope my insight as a historian has matured. I still think it's a good book, but I would not want to defend it line by line, paragraph by paragraph, as though it were some kind of bible.

My attitude toward my older book has perhaps been affected because I have written another book on the seventeenth century in which I attempted quite a different approach for a rather different audience. It is a slightly less formal, less didactic book—a little broader and more speculative. I gave myself a bit of freedom because I had written the other first. My impression is that people have not liked this new book as well as *The Scientific Revolution,* but I think it is a better book as far as it goes, even though I can see that it has less general utility as a course book. Some of its chapters are very good, among the best things I have ever written—particularly the chapter on Galileo, which is much more modern and deeper than what I wrote in *The Scientific Revolution.*

Perhaps I should make one thing clear: I do hold to the view that there *was* a scientific revolution, a series of events occurring in a fairly brief period of time which may definitely be described as embracing the origins of modern science. There is, in other words, a genuine historiographical problem concerned with the identification and description of this revolution. I don't look at this problem exactly as I did fifteen years ago; I have been influenced by (among others) Thomas Kuhn's discussion of the structure of scientific revolutions, although I disagree with him on quite a lot of points. I would like to treat the development of the mathematical sciences (the core of mathematical physics with various fringes attached) from the late sixteenth through the seventeenth century—from Copernicus up to the time of Laplace—as the mainstream of scientific development. This is in no sense a new idea: it has always been perfectly obvious that this was the mainstream, but I feel inclined now to equate it with what you might call the scientific revolution, whereas earlier I was inclined to make the scientific revolution a totally inclusive concept.

When I say a "totally inclusive concept" I mean, to use Kuhn's favorite term, that I was inclined in my first book to treat the scientific revolution in the mathematical sciences as creating a paradigm which was adopted later in other branches of science. That there is a limited truth in this is, I think, evident enough from such studies as I. Bernard Cohen's *Franklin and Newton* and the work Arnold Thackray of the University of Pennsylvania has done on eighteenth-century chemistry. But the whole story is more complicated, as I hope my later book, *From Galileo to Newton,* begins to make plain. The development of modern science with the medical and biological areas of knowledge is a different and independent story. Of course, I still can't agree with my old mentor Canon Charles Raven that that is a prior and superior story!

The core of the scientific revolution —the development of mathematical physics—runs (conveniently) from Copernicus through Kepler and Galileo up through Newton and his successors to Laplace. This development includes, obviously, all of what one might call the metaphysical aspect—the idea of nature, the idea that there is a correspondence between mathematical theorems and reality. One must include the mechanical philosophy also, because it is decidedly connected with the development of the mathematical sciences although it is not mathematical itself. The mechanical philosophy, along with astronomy, is an important connection between mathematics and physics; the whole business of dynamics and the explanation of physical phenomena, the various aspects of chemistry and physics and so forth, obviously were fundamental to the whole development. This is not just a question of the application of algebra and geometry to scientific matters, as in optics or astronomy. It is a question also of a fundamentally different outlook on nature and on scientific explanation itself. This provides one important key to the connection between one extreme form of mathematics and its other extreme (the inner, metaphysical notion of what the universe is like).

The scientific revolution was more than the introduction of mathematical physics, and more than the rejection of authority and tradition. In another aspect (stated very clearly by Bacon), it involved the beginning of a new philosophical tradition, or at any rate the combination of the sense of innovation with the revival of a much older philosophical notion—Pythagorean, or even pre-Pythagorean. One other important general idea is that of the uniformity of nature, of the abandonment of Aristotelian hierarchies. A great many revolutionary ideas or concepts were involved in the scientific revolution, and some of them had results that were not measurable in terms of mathematization. Mathematics played a very large part in the story, but the core is more than simply the introduction of more mathematics into science, or the prevalence of mathematical argument and mathematical forms of reasoning and demonstration. The basic changes and attitudes of mechanical philosophy were important too. Through the work of Newton, these developments had achieved great success by the end of the seventeenth century, and they represented what most people regarded as a great advance in science.

In what ways, if any, were Baconian empiricism and Cartesian rationalism conducive to the scientific revolution?

Alongside the scientific revolution proper there was a somewhat different movement which might be described as Baconian, and this we have begun to perceive more clearly in the last few years. It might be summarized rather tritely under the words "Let's find out more about the world," or "Let's make our knowledge of the world more useful to us." This concept is based on the assumption that there is a huge mass of phenomena and processes in nature, in the surrounding world, of which we know very little. Our bits of knowledge are accidental, from travelers' tales and so on, and we ought to investigate our environment more widely and deeply than we ever have done in the past. Certainly we cannot (or should not) rely on the accounts of discursive ancient authors like Pliny, or even on the encyclopedists of the sixteenth century. But neither can we rely on "experts" like the botanists who study plants from the pharmaceutical point of view, because their point of view is so limited: they are concerned with the uses of plants in medicine and not with more general questions. People understood this concept very clearly; it is one of the more obvious aspects of Baconian empiricism. One should open one's eyes wider: one should look farther and a great deal more carefully. This attitude leads (as it led Bacon himself) in two different directions.

One direction is the drive to explore, to collect, to observe, to experiment; this led in turn to the organized, empirical parts of modern science. The observational aspect of empiricism is at least as important as the typical laboratory approach, and it is more typical of the seventeenth century than the more exact type of experimentation. The other direction is, on the whole, deplored by the commentators of modern science; it is the outburst of interest in all sorts of queer things—natural curiosities, monsters, anatomical abnormalities, and so on. These things were tremendously interesting to people in the second half of the seventeenth century, and Bacon himself did not by any means regard this "teratology" as trivial or totally insignificant. The urge to go out and look at things, then, could lead in two directions: toward what we regard as a serious scientific path, or toward trivialities—a collector's curiosity. Of course it led, too, toward other straightforward scientific activities such as collection, taxonomy, anatomy, and so forth.

We must recognize that although this drive toward observation was a step toward largeness of vision and breadth of activity, it certainly was not a scientific revolution. It was a separate movement, associated with the scientific revolution; it represented an urge to explore and to know more about the world, but this is quite different from the urge to have better thoughts about the world which was typical of the scientific revolution proper. All this accumulation of knowledge through observation eventually produced some new ideas, and if any revolution arose out of these discursive, empirical, less mathematical areas of knowledge, it was at that later point when increased material produced new ideas.

Over the last few years we have become more inclined to emphasize the significance of this acquisitive, information-collecting enterprise. It had nothing to do with the scientific revolution as such, but it laid an important basis of information and activity for the future and was itself a new (but not intellectually revolutionary) scientific movement. Baconian empiricism had a great deal to do with the development of modern science as a whole, which includes these more discursive, slow-developing, descriptive, and classificatory activities. Empiricism is directly and indirectly relevant to that aspect of modern science; it gave people a key or method to use in the enormous, shapeless task of reducing to order the multivarious world around them.

It is harder to identify the place of Cartesian rationalism. Obviously rationalism (whatever epithet is applied to it) must be important in the development of modern science. However, I am inclined to think that from a historian's point of view, the abstract discussion of method (particularly the more metaphysical consideration of the correct manner of reasoning found in Descartes) has been, in a sense, overestimated. There is a tendency in the history of science and philosophy to go from the particular to the general, and Descartes exemplifies this in the *Discourse on Method* when he says in effect, "I did things this way, and this is the way in which things should be done." I don't know of anyone else who claims to have said *cogito ergo sum*—to have felt the impact of these three words as they obviously affected Descartes. How *could* anyone else have retrodden Descartes' unique human path? I may be sticking my neck out, but I cannot think of anyone in the latter part of the seventeenth century (after 1637) whose work or writings reveal that his general ideas about scientific procedure, or his metaphysical conception of nature, was influenced by the ideas expressed in the *Discourse*. I think that the general discussion in the earlier parts of the *Discourse* is enormously interesting, and obviously of great importance in the history of philosophy, but I do not think that it has very much to do with the scientific revolution.

On the other hand, the influence of Descartes clearly was very important in two different directions. First, there was the particular impulse that he gave to the mechanical philosophy and the mechanical view of phenomena, above all in *The Principles of Philosophy*. Secondly, there were the appendices of the *Discourse on Method*—especially the *Dioptric* and the *Meteors*—which gave people new ideas about how to use mathematics and geometry in the study of physics. There can be little doubt that Descartes created the "model" of a new physics—or rather one might better say of two kinds of physics, mathematical and mechanical. The latter, of course, was largely speculative; it created the "hypothesis" that Newton said he was reluctant to feign (a quite readily identifiable type of hypothesis, by the way, such as Newton did indeed only discuss in private), while the former, mathematical physics, passed through Huygens, Wallis, Newton, and others into the fabric of science.

Perhaps I should make one other, rather obvious, point. When we use the word *rationalism* we often imply that it acts in a negative, critical manner; a rationalist (to use a rather old-fashioned example) may be one who denounces religious superstition. Aristotelian rationalism at one time provided many arguments against the scientific innovators of the sixteenth and early seventeenth centuries—it is often appealed to by Galileo's Simplicio in the *Dialogues*. It is very obvious that Cartesian rationalism began to play, within a generation, such an essentially normative, critical role. Not only professed expositors of Cartesian physics, but philosophers like Spinoza and Leibnitz employ it in this way: so does Huygens. And in general it seems obvious that when the attempt is made to give science a strict axiomatic structure, from which any departure appears contrary to reason, there can remain little room within for creative imagination.

It has frequently been pointed out that the new physics was made possible by an increase in mathematical knowledge. Would you outline the development of mathematics in the sixteenth and seventeenth centuries?

This is an intricate, and certainly a very interesting, question. I don't know of any general study of the relation of mathematics to mathematical science, not for this period or any period. In the applied science of astronomy, for instance, it is fairly obvious that the scientist is concerned with spherical geometry. If the problem is that of computing the height of a star above the celestial equator from certain given measurements, this can be done by a straight transfer from an abstract form of mathematics to the celestial sphere. No particular problem arises there. However, it was by no means always true in the history of mathematical physics (particularly in the seventeenth century) that a scientist took his mathematical formula out of the tool kit and simply applied it to physical problems to get results. It certainly was not that simple, but as the question hints, it does seem that new developments in pure mathematics suggested new phases and types of development in applied mathematics—developments that would not have been possible at an earlier stage of pure mathematics.

I do not think, however, that the development of pure mathematical knowledge is very near to the core development of the scientific revolution. It is true that progress in physics was made possible by an increase in mathematical knowledge, particularly after Descartes' geometry was published in 1637. But I think that the fundamental revolutionary change had occurred before that. The application of mathematical methods to physical problems, the attempt to reduce phenomena to their barest essentials and see them in mathematical terms, was done by Galileo in the *Discourses* of 1634 and by Kepler (rather differently) in 1609 and 1619. These men used quite conventional mathematical methods; in fact, the whole development of mathematical science through the seventeenth century was based on conventional geometrical analyses and arguments. I don't want to be too dogmatic about this—as I said, we do not have the kind of study for the seventeenth century that we need. We need a more careful analysis of the different steps in the scientific revolution in order to find out how much was technical, due to mathematics, and how much was conceptual—that is, figuring out how to put a problem in such a way that it became susceptible to mathematical treatment. Newton and Descartes were both supremely gifted in both respects.

My feeling is that there is a special quality of insight into the application of mathematics, into what I would call the mathematization of nature, which is inseparable from creative mathematical ability. In other words, the mathematical physicist must be a mathematician too. In a very real sense (which I don't think we understand very clearly), mathematical physics—a natural science—is an offshoot of mathematics. I believe it is a psychological question in which more is involved than showing how a physical problem can be made mathematical by applying certain formulas taken out of stock. Mathematicians may understand this, but it is not brought out very clearly in historical discussions.

Why did European mathematics make such great strides in the seventeenth century—much more than in the medieval period?

This is not an easy question to answer, but one can get around it by pointing out that a lot of people *attended* to mathematics in the sixteenth and seventeenth centuries. There just were a lot of mathematicians, and with a lot of able men at work they were bound to move along fairly rapidly. There is more to it than that, of course, but I do not know enough about the history of mathematics to deal with every point of this question in detail. I am convinced, however, that the scholarly incentive to recover the finest works of Greek mathematics was very important. This continued right up to the end of the seventeenth century and beyond. It seems to me that in a very real sense, Greek mathematics was part of the living body of the subject right through the early seventeenth century, when Halley was doing yet more editions of Archimedes and Apollonius. It is hard to say precisely when the study of Greek mathematics ceased to be part of the living body of the subject and became antiquarian or historical. It probably happened with the widespread interest in the totally new methods of the calculus in the eighteenth century, and with the new geometry.

There is a marked contrast between the very complex and abstract ideas studied by the sixteenth- and seventeenth-century mathematicians and the pragmatic and simple-minded interests which apparently prevailed in Europe during the Middle Ages. The fourteenth-century philosophers had good knowledge of the Euclidean theory of proportions and indeed used it in physics, but their ignorance of the pure mathematics of Archimedes and the later Greeks suggests that they were not at all concerned with the more abstract and intellectual facets of pure mathematics. I think that the return to these issues was new and extremely significant in the sixteenth century.

The founding of the learned societies in western Europe has been viewed as contributory to the scientific revolution. Would you outline the development of learned societies in the seventeenth century? Why should they have made their appearance at this time?

One cannot understand the intellectual history of Europe in the seventeenth century without recognizing that the character of civilization was changing in a period of increasing prosperity. The great demographic crisis of the fourteenth century evidently progressed gradually into greater prosperity, particularly, of course, in those parts of Europe that were less devastated by the Thirty Years' War. It may be old-fashioned, but is still useful, I think, to recognize (in a loose, general, and non-Marxist sense) some notion of a rise of the middle classes, the gentry, and the aristocracy. Perhaps there was a rise of the working class, too. There certainly was an increase in prosperity—more money for more activities—and the leisured class was numerically larger.

With prosperity and stability came interest in activities that were not immediately central to survival, to rivalry, or to keeping order among one's tenants. There was a Europe-wide movement toward interest in (and patronage of) architects, musicians, writers, philosophers, medical men, and scientists. The learned society was one offshoot of the richness of the period and of the developments of the arts and of learned life. It was connected in a more specialized way, perhaps, with the revolution of court life, which was moving away from what it had been in the medieval period toward something more like Versailles—magnificence, grandiloquence, and the rest. At a more intimate level, at some of the smaller courts, court life itself became something like the learned society. To what extent was this an instance of life copying art? In other words, was the notion of people meeting and talking a literary notion in the beginning, a mere fiction suggested by books like the *Decameron*?

There is no doubt that the development of societies for the discussion of science, philosophy, and theology reflected the extent to which people were passionately interested in problems about nature, about the interpretation of the scientific-philosophical tradition inherited from antiquity, and about contemporary questions such as "Is Copernicus right or wrong?" We assume that this generalized interest preceded the scientific societies.

Just as people were interested in the ideals, and problems, and burning issues of the day, so they were interested in programs and methods. Interest in method was perhaps particularly marked in the Accademia del Cimento in Italy, and slightly later in the Royal Society in London. The former group explored not only the problems but also the methods and instruments associated with the Florentine scientific tradition from Galileo to Torricelli and Viviani. They were strong believers in the significance of method—the fertility and potentiality of methods and instruments; this belief conditioned their work, which was largely factual and concerned with measurements and questions such as "Does this happen?" There was little discussion of theory or general ideas. The Royal Society had a somewhat similar character, but it was not pinned down to the pursuit of any particular method.

There is a division (historically demonstrable as well as logically obvious) between society activity of what one might call today a research-institute type with a definite program of activity, and the kind of society in which people met and talked about science, discussing the things they were interested in or working on at that moment. This second type of society was first exemplified in the oldest scientific society, the Accademia dei Lincei, which was the loosest of all possible organizations. The informal French societies of the middle of the century were very much of that kind, although many of them also possessed a didactic element. One or two of them were dominated at certain periods by a single individual, such as Pierre Gassendi, who lectured on scientific and philosophical issues. The two types of organization are quite clearly differentiated, although—as one might expect—most actual societies participated somewhat in both styles.

In the latter part of the seventeenth century, the societies provided tremendous public stimulus for science—especially the English Royal Society, which had a wide European sphere of influence. They gave a public position to the new philosophy and activities of science, and this served as a means of communication and of enlistment of support. They helped to make the scientific revolution into a total European phenomenon instead of just a movement in the minds of a few isolated intellectuals. This is obvious when the incredibly slow dissemination of Copernicus' ideas in mid-sixteenth century is compared with the European ferment at the end of the seventeenth century, produced largely by the scientific societies and their connection with scientific periodicals—of which there were perhaps six by the end of the century. Quite a few people were brought into the field of science because these societies existed. It is easy to generalize about the importance of communication, publicity, and stimulus, and perhaps we take it for granted. I think these things are really very important.

Or another way of illustrating the same point might be like this. Science developed from, and of course remained, a philosophic concern with understanding the phenomena of nature, which often raised very profound issues. But modern science has not only been contemplative, as science was in antiquity and the Middle Ages; whether we like it or not, science and scientific men have been much involved in the affairs of the world. One should not, certainly, exaggerate the importance of this involvement before recent times. But I think the historian may note that it came about largely through the activities of the scientific societies, and their publications. Already in the seventeenth century some of them insisted that science was a movement of intellectual and perhaps even practical reform, and they demanded public participation, or state support. So science became already a social phenomenon, even though (in my view) it was still too feeble to modify the world greatly.

The scientific revolution occurred during the era of the emerging bureaucratic state, expanding commercial capitalism, and the Protestant Reformation. Is there any relationship between the new science and these other developments?

This is a very controversial issue, one that historians have been worrying about for a long time. Their answers vary all the way from dogmatic certainty that there is a definite dependence of scientific developments on nonscientific factors, to considerable skepticism, and I include my own position in the latter category. There is an inherent, almost logical difficulty about historical issues of this kind; one is obviously seeking to explain one thing by something fundamentally dissimilar, and the difficulty lies in establishing a firm and coherent connection between dissimilar things. The customary assertion of cause and effect arising from contemporaneity is bound to be weak and ineffective.

I have never understood the basic premise of the question dealing with the Protestant Reformation, at least as it has been presented in the past. It is blatantly obvious that the earliest steps toward the new science, right down to the trial and condemnation of Galileo in 1633, were predominantly associated with the Mediterranean area, with that region of western Europe that was least exposed to the forces of the Reformation. It is curious (and totally irrelevant) but amusing that Copernicus was an inhabitant of the only Catholic country in northwestern Europe. No one in his right senses would try to prove anything by such an instance, but the opposite argument has sometimes rested on simple enumerations of the successes of science in Protestant England and Protestant Holland in the latter part of the seventeenth century. I wish to show the fallacy of such enumeration.

There are, of course, certain obvious things that should be stated. No one would deny that some peculiarity in the organization, the theology, the public position, of the Catholic Church produced Galileo's trial and condemnation. Not only was this a peculiarly Catholic event in its implications, but it had rather severe consequences for the development of modern science in Italy during the rest of the century. As far as I can tell, the condemnation of Galileo had no effect in France (equally a Catholic country) or in the Catholic parts of Germany, but it did have a stultifying effect upon contemporary Italy in spite of the distinction of later Italian work. A certain artificiality was imposed on the development of astronomy, particularly. However, there is no reason to believe that the condemnation of Galileo did anything to hamper the later work of people like Giovanni Baptista Borelli, or Marcello Malpighi, or the elder Cassini, or even of minor figures like Geminiano Montanari of Bologna. It is easy to exaggerate the importance of this, but one must concede that it had an effect and that in the later seventeenth century the balance shifted to northern countries such as Holland and England and France. I don't think that the reasons for this can be found in religion, and certainly not entirely in religious differences. It is difficult to explain why phases of activity—not only in science, but in painting or music or sculpture or writing—seem to pass from one national group to another. It is not plausible to attribute the shifting of emphasis from one place to another solely to such an external factor as religion, alone among all possible social, economic, and intellectual factors.

I think that there is a subtler connection between the scientific revolution and the development of capitalism—of commerce, technology, and industry in the seventeenth century. One could argue from one extreme, as Hessen did in that classic yet ludicrous piece of work published in 1931, that in the seventeenth century, people were really concerned only with lucrative, practical problems like finding longitude at sea, learning how to aim artillery, and so forth. Here you can bring in Bacon's utilitarianism as the model for the concept of man's mastery over nature through science, and of course it is easy to connect this with the ambitions of the rising middle and commercial classes. I think that most of the heat has gone out of such extreme examples of this sort of argument. One has instead the far better reasoned and historically argued books of such recent exponents of the connection as Christopher Hill.

I have published various essays on this subject, which I think still represent my own views. It is easy to make either the "internalist" or the "externalist" position look absurd, but the original issue—whether there is an impartial enquiry into nature, or whether such enquiry was always dominated by considerations of religion or commerce—seems to me (as it does, from his side, to Mr. Hill) real enough. I happen, in a perhaps old-fashioned way, to value the rational faculty of man highly. It seems to me true and important that, in circumstances of leisure, men in all societies have found intense interest in debating mathematical, philosophical, and natural questions. To seek to impose a modulation on this ever-continuing debate, really dominating its whole character and caused by quite other factors, seems to me strange and needless. I simply cannot believe that this is the best way to interpret the development of man's thought. However, few would want to go to the opposite extreme and claim that seventeenth-century scientific interest and activities were totally abstract and devoid of concern for contemporary practical problems. Obviously, scientists are citizens too.

It is now fairly well agreed among historians of science that what really made the scientific movement tick was a combination of the intrinsic importance of problems and activities, and the relation between one person working at a problem and the rest of the group to which he belonged. There was social cohesion among the people who took part in the common scientific enterprise.

The idea of a relation between science and outside affairs is a useful one. One should never dismiss it entirely: it is a mistake in any period to put the separate parts of history in isolated intellectual ivory towers. But equally, one must be very rigorous and suspicious of attempts to explain what people were doing, or the direction of interest one way instead of another, as the result of the play of these external factors. Taken too far, this produces dangerous oversimplifications.

Renaissance humanism and Platonism have been viewed as antithetic to scientific thought and also as contributing to the scientific revolution. What is your judgment on this problem?

During the last five years or so, the question of Platonism (particularly Platonism verging on hermeticism) has received a good deal of scholarly attention. The question of humanism has not attracted as much attention, but I think I should say a few words about it before going on to Platonism. I don't doubt that there is a lot of truth in the traditional view that the revived study of the very impressive Greek achievements in certain aspects of mathematics, science, and medicine had an exhilarating effect on people's minds. You may argue that the Renaissance activity led to re-creation and rebirth, and not to originality. And this may be true, but apparently the exposure to the stimulus of ancient thought did more than raise the level of competence so that effective work could be done. It also gave people something to criticize and question—and with nothing to criticize, there is nothing to be original about! Renaissance humanism introduced people to ideas which had been entirely forgotten by late medieval philosophy.

There was a sort of school, slightly frantic and wild (certainly viewed as such by the Aristotelians), which took up Platonic and hermetic ideas. This in itself provided a certain cohesion and formed a new pole about which thought could crystallize. This is important, because before Aristotelianism (the official doctrine of the schools, and the definition and limits of contemporary thought) could be forced to vanish, there had to be an alternative. There had to be some other set or sets of ideas to act as points of focus, as nuclei about which unorthodox, non-Establishment and anti-Aristotelian notions could cluster. Some of these notions entered permanently into the scientific fabric, though often in a somewhat modified form. The obvious instance is the history of the concept of "attraction," which ultimately forced action-at-a-distance into physics. The existence of alternative nuclei was very significant in the disintegration of the official thought-world which descended from the Middle Ages.

It is quite possible for something to have both a positive and a negative effect: one example of this is the *natur-philosophische* movement which came from Kant and Goethe in the eighteenth century and was influential until at least the nineteenth century. We know now that this set of ideas contained a great deal of rubbish and was often mistaken in points of detail. However, it carried something very important for people of the first half of the nineteenth century: it brought them some creative conceptions that had not been prevalent before: it promoted the idea of the unity and symmetry of nature, for example. Thus this movement made a positive contribution to science even though in itself it was a rubbishy kind of doctrine; in itself it was unscientific and yet it was conducive to ideas that ultimately were scientifically creative. The same is true of Platonism and hermeticism in the scientific revolution.

Is there anything in this association: that the most creative periods in the history of science (I think also of art and literature) seem to be periods of political withdrawal, pessimism, and disillusionment?

There may be something to this. If one thinks of politics as part of the extroverted activities of mankind, one can see that it might be in some profound sense opposed to more personal and introverted activities. These also involve one in society, but in a different kind of social arrangement—into small groups of people of very tight common interest rather than large, revolutionary movements. This is a difficult idea to pin down, but there might be something in it.

Would you define the Ptolemaic and Aristotelian universe? How did Copernicus and Galileo depart from these paradigms? Would you discuss Galileo's personality and career?

It is important to realize just how different from anything familiar and acceptable to ourselves was the early notion of the nature of things, which goes back essentially to Aristotle. The core of Aristotelian and also of Ptolemaic thought is the antithesis or dichotomy between the terrestrial regions (the regions of direct physical experience) and the celestial or heavenly regions. In this system, all science—or at least all science of a universal character—had to have two sets of principles: explanations appropriate for the terrestrial region were inappropriate for the celestial region. There could be no general science of the universe, of physics, or of motion, because everything fell into one or the other category, and each had its own analysis and account of things. That is the fundamental point that was transformed by the seventeenth century.

The transformation began with Copernicus, of course. In Book I of *De Revolutionibus* he explained and carefully worked out certain physical corollaries to the system of motion around the sun, extending the idea of uniformity and constancy throughout the whole of the universe. This was only the beginning, however; the fulfillment of the idea was left to Galileo.

Whether you regard Galileo as a great hero or as a man with faults and weaknesses, you cannot fail to recognize his dominant importance in the scientific revolution of the first half of the seventeenth century—the only figure of comparable importance is that of Kepler. The first question that comes up in any discussion of Galileo is usually that of his independence, or originality, and it is a question with shades of meaning. Nobody has suggested that Galileo copied or plagiarized, but the extent to which the development of his thought was shaped by predecessors is somewhat in doubt. It seems absurd in the light of what has been discovered to suppose that Galileo had no precursors or that the questions he studied had not been contemplated before. Some of the details in the *Discourses on Two New Sciences,* for instance, make it clear that Galileo was brought up in a definite scientific tradition, and it seems reasonable to suppose that his important and truly original contribution was made on the basis of a digest of the earlier tradition of commentary upon the Aristotelian theory of motion. He altered these conceptions and their application. Galileo is important because he came at the end of a somewhat decadent, failing tradition of ideas and greatly transcended it.

The other important aspect of the question about Galileo concerns the nature of his scientific activity. Was he a philosophical scientist, above all, or a great founder and pioneer of experimental science? I tend to waver in my opinion on the question, but basically I believe that Galileo's place in the history of science is fundamentally philosophical or theoretical. No one doubts the importance of his observational work in astronomy and of the appeals to direct experience made elsewhere in his writings (mechanics and physics), but despite the emphasis on observation in his early work, his great book of 1632 is largely theoretical discussions of the nature of things. At times, Galileo appeals specifically to pieces of experimental information or reveals that he has done experiments, but the cast of his major writing is obviously in a theoretical vein—a discussion of ideas and principles. He understood very well that his task was to convince people to look at fundamental issues in a different light, and to see that the new way of regarding ordinary experience (and also some new things which he and others had discovered) gave a better and more plausible apprehension of truth than the old, traditional perspective. It seems to me that he approached the writing of his major works in an effort to convince people to change their minds.

Galileo's scientific personality was very complex, although it does not always appear so. His writings (which were addressed, after all, to a rather widespread, semipopular audience) have an appearance of obvious, winning simplicity which may be rather deceptive. There are recent attempts at denigration of Galileo, and these seem to me absurd, almost pointless, although it must be said that he failed to perceive certain things. His conception of inertia was not completely accurate, and he was remarkably blind to the development of technical astronomy that was going on during his lifetime—even though from a modern viewpoint, this seems closely related to some of the things he was doing himself. It seems strange that Galileo had so little comprehension of Kepler's endeavors. It is understandable that he should dislike certain of Kepler's fundamental ideas and principles because his own ideas and attitudes were very different; evidently Galileo did not realize that although he was starting something new in the tradition of physical astronomy, a very important place remained for mathematical astronomy which his own discussions did nothing to fill. He was content to leave an intellectual vacuum, apparently because he found Kepler's efforts unsatisfactory.

From recent studies of Newton's papers, how do you account for his "genius"? What are the distinctive characteristics of his mind and personality? What precisely was Newton's contribution to modern science? What was the relationship, if any, between Newton's theology and his physics?

One of the most continuously successful developments in the scholarship of the last twenty-five years is the study of the work of Newton and the reconstruction of the scientific mentality that produced the written work we can study today. The student of Newton is in an extremely fortunate position because of the large extent and wide range of the materials Newton left behind. I think it is fair to say that no other seventeenth-century scientist, certainly no scientist of great original stature, left behind such an excellent opportunity to understand the working of his mind in great detail and depth.

The work that has been done so far falls roughly into three headings: the publication of the body of Newton's correspondence; the study (which is still proceeding) by Dr. D. T. Whiteside of Newton's mathematical manuscripts; and the study of the printed works in the context of related manuscript materials—in other words, the study of Newton's books in the light of fresh information and insight gained from the manuscripts. There also have been broader and deeper examinations of the general cast of Newton's scientific thinking: he is rapidly becoming the most intensively studied of all scientists.

If I may, I shall alter the question and ask: What was Newton's power? Whiteside argues that the most important contributant to Newton's success was his extraordinary grasp of mathematics. He was an enormously intelligent man, amazingly quick to see the implications of any given proposition and to know whether these implications were confirmed or denied by facts. He was quick to see whether an argument went in the right direction. Of course he made mistakes, but for the most part he was a powerful thinker who could make things fit together neatly—in some cases, too neatly. We know now that some things are not so neat as Newton wanted to believe. However, merely by insisting on neatness, on fitting together, Newton made enormous scientific advances. Some of these advances had to be undone later on when greater complexities were recognized—these things never fit forever, but Newton was extraordinarily successful in seeing how they could be made to fit in the first place. If you put together all Newton's qualities—his hardheadedness, his logical grasp of antecedents and consequences, his power to fit things together, and his extraordinarily conceptual boldness—you can account for his extraordinary power to deal with problems that baffled his contemporaries.

I mentioned the conceptual boldness that enabled Newton to transform the mechanical philosophy of the seventeenth century, as it had come down over twenty or thirty years from Descartes. He did not hesitate to take in hand the new metaphysical tide in science and alter it, to deny certain things and add others. His conception of gravity far transcended the mechanical philosophy of the seventeenth century. He abandoned the idea which had seemed so constructive and promising for fifty years or more—the idea that everything can be reduced in the extreme to the action of matter on matter, or particles banging on particles. Newton was skeptical about what gravity is and how it works, but I think that in the last resort he never seriously meant to say that it was produced by some species of gravitational particles flying about and pushing together lumps of ordinary matter. One cannot prove this, but I don't think Newton ever really thought *that* about gravity. However, he did think all sorts of other things; on one level he thought that gravity did not have to be explicable in seventeenth-century mechanical terms in order for it to be real and to offer a valid explanation of observable facts. His younger friend, the Scottish mathematician James Gregory, recognized this very clearly when he recorded it as Newton's belief that gravity was the direct product of the divine will.

One tends to see Newton as the summation of the scientific revolution, the coming together of Kepler and Galileo, but there is also a profound sense in which Newton radically departed from the simpler forms of seventeenth-century mechanical philosophy. I hesitate to say that Newton perceived this himself, but he did take a step toward the position in which one must accept mathematical equations as the only reality, in which physical pictures of particles banging on particles will not serve as explanations of why things happen.

Perhaps I might add one or two reflections on the tensions created in the late seventeenth century by the general prevalence of the mechanical philosophy. The most obvious and best-known of these tensions was that between the mechanical philosophy and Christian theology. It has been supposed (I think quite reasonably) that the success of the mechanical philosophy helped to push people toward deism in the eighteenth century. It is equally true, however, that the tendency was powerfully resisted by certain philosophers and theologians in Newton's own lifetime. Their argument was that the reduction of phenomena to mechanical causes leads to a conception of God as a Creator only. In such a system, the universe (brought into existence in accordance with the divine design) is reduced to a self-running clock operating purely by mechanical means, with divine intervention occurring only in the form of miracles. This system certainly does not enter into the basic tenets of the mechanical philosophy, but many people thought that it did. Newton, however, was not only a religious man but far too much of a providentialist to believe that the universe had a purely mechanical existence. Newton's universe was very much a part of God, and God is very much a part of Newton's universe. Newton resolved the tension between Christian theology and the mechanical philosophy by weakening the mechanical point of view.

There were other tensions: for instance the tension between mathematics and mechanical philosophy, which I think that Newton himself truly revealed. In general, these had fitted together very well since the time of Galileo and Descartes. Analysis in the abstract terms of mathematics seemed compatible with analysis in the physical terms of corpuscular motions, and it appeared that what remained was only a question of developing the mathematical theory of corpuscular motion to greater sophistication and detail in order to explain a wider and wider range of phenomena. However, Newton showed that this really was not true for either gravity or optics—or at least that it was not true for the range of mathematical equipment available to him at that particular period. He explored both the mathematical and the mechanical aspects of these subjects at once, and a sort of breakdown of the two occurred. In the end, people virtually abandoned any idea of explaining gravity in corpuscular or ethereal terms, and the Newtonian system of forces became a notion of forces acting at a distance. In other words, it is simply postulated that two bodies *A* and *B* attract each other as the product of their masses and inversely as the square of the distance between them; no hypothesis at all is made about the nature of their interaction. All considerations of mechanism or action are abandoned; this is treated simply as action at a distance.

This question came up again in physics in the nineteenth century, and field theory was introduced to resolve the difficulty. This is not, I think, what Newton himself had in mind. He was prepared to reduce the idea of force to a theological notion—the action of the universe, continually exercised by God, the active agent in the universe. At least he did not try an explanation in terms of a mechanical philosophy; he preferred the mathematical analysis to the pictorial explanation in terms of physical things.

The third tension (and this did not affect Newton alone) existed between the undulatory theory of light and the mechanical philosophy. The undulatory theory itself supposes a medium in which wave motions are carried and does not thus necessarily create any tension, but this assumption sacrifices the simple conception of impact physics which was the basis of the mechanical philosophy. Newton went part of the way along this path when he introduced an undulatory component into his theory of light. However, he did not by any means abandon the corpuscular theory of light; he believed it to be quite essential for the explanation of various phenomena, notably the fact that light moves along straight lines.

Of course, one needs hindsight to bring out such points in merely a few lines. But it is important (and interesting) that Newton knew his work was incomplete: the *Principia* opens with a statement of its incompleteness, and the *Optics* closes with a similar declaration. Newton was supremely aware of the magnitude of the problems that his own achievement created, and which he remitted to his successors for solution.